J. A. Llorente

A Critical
History of
The
Inquisition
of
Spain

JUAN ANTONIO LLORENTE

A CRITICAL HISTORY

OF THE

INQUISITION

OF SPAIN.

FROM THE PERIOD OF ITS ESTABLISHMENT BY
FERDINAND V TO THE REIGN OF FERDINAND VII,
COMPOSED FROM THE ORIGINAL DOCUMENTS
OF THE ARCHIVES OF THE SUPREME COUNCIL OF
THE INQUISITION AND FROM THOSE OF
SUBORDINATE TRIBUNALS OF THE HOLY OFFICE

[*The English Edition Published in 1823*]

With an Introduction by GABRIEL H. LOVETT

The John Lilburne Company, *Publishers*
WILLIAMSTOWN, MASSACHUSETTS

INTRODUCTION

THE seventeenth century witnessed in Europe the emer-
gence of Cartesian rationalism, the theories of Grotius,
father of international law, the philosophy of Spinoza, and
especially the doctrines of Locke and the momentous discoveries of Newton. Descartes was a conservative, but his
Discours de la Methode (1637), exalting the power of reason,
was to become a strong weapon in the hands of those who
questioned theological truth. Spinoza's *Tractatus Theologico-
Politicus* (1670) challenged the excellence of Church and
Monarchy, and his *Etica* (1677) relegated God to the cate-
gory of a pantheistic deity. Locke, aside from submitting
that almost all knowledge is acquired through perception
(Essay Concerning Human Understanding) (1691), claimed
in *Two Treatises of Government* (1690) that governments
exist only to protect the lives, liberty, and property of
people, and that if governments do not fulfill this obligation
the people have the right to change their rulers. Newton's
discoveries caused many Europeans to lose interest in theological questions and to turn their attention to science. But
in an age when Monarchy and the Church were still institutions which were considered by and large the cornerstones
of civilization, it was the doctrines of Spinoza and Locke
that were to a certain extent the most revolutionary of all.
All of these great developments in the history of human

thought left a deep imprint on the men who followed these intellectual giants. In the eighteenth century, French *philosophes* such as Montesquieu, Voltaire, Diderot, and Rousseau, carrying on the intellectual revolution of their predecessors, spread throughout the European continent the ideas that were to undermine so decisively the foundations of the old order. Montesquieu suggested that a constitutional monarchy was the ideal government, and Voltaire spoke out strongly against intolerance and the Church, while Diderot and Rousseau emphasized social equality. It was the age of reason and of enlightenment, and also of enlightened despotism. The *philosophes* applauded the efforts of enlightened despots such as Frederic II of Prussia and Catherine II of Russia, for they saw in them and in their ministers the prime movers of reform, which for many of the reform-minded was primarily to be a struggle against the privileges of nobility and clergy. These latter institutions still wielded a powerful influence in every-day European life and constituted obstacles to the establishment of a political and social system based on reason and justice.

European enlightened despotism had in Spain its counterpart in the government of Charles III (1759–1788) and his ministers. The latter supported to the utmost the absolutist, regalistic Weltanschauung of the Spanish monarch and did their best to modernize their nation. But the enlightened despotism of Charles III and of men like Aranda, Floridablanca, and Campomanes, while pushing administrative, economic, and cultural reform, neither greatly weakened the social-economic power of the nobility, nor decisively loosened the stranglehold of the Spanish clergy on numerous aspects of the life of the country in spite of the expulsion of the Jesuits from Spain in 1767. By the end of the eighteenth century, the Spanish nobility and clergy, numbering 403,000 and 170,000 respectively, out of a total population of approximately 11,000,000, were owners of about two-thirds of the land. Their semi-feudal rights and privileges weighed heavily on the mass of the population, made up mostly of hard-working peasants. Less than six percent of the population was literate. Needless to say, the Inquisition continued to function, though relatively speaking it had considerably mellowed. The power it wielded in the field of censorship continued, however, to be great and was a constant reminder to Spaniards that caution had to be used in any writings dealing with controversial subjects.

In spite of governmental and Inquisitional censorship, which were considerably tightened after the French Revolution (1789), there developed during the second half of the eighteenth century among a minority of Spaniards—enlightened aristocrats, members of the small but growing middle class, and some progressive-minded members of the clergy—a thirst for economic, social, and cultural reform, which in a modest way reflected the intellectual revolution that had been sweeping much of Europe since the end of the previous century. These progressive elements, eager to acquaint themselves with the new ideas, avidly read prohibited foreign books and longingly looked forward to the day when censorship would no longer lay its heavy hand on books published in Spain and entering the country from abroad. While in no way as radical as even the more moderate French revolutionaries and while perfectly willing to maintain the institution of monarchy and to pay homage to Catholic dogma, they wanted a change in the social-economic fabric of their nation. They wished to see the blight of aristocratic and ecclesiastic entail lifted from the land and they wanted the introduction of laissez-faire in the economy. A change had to be wrought in the antiquated edifice of social privilege, and the power of the Church had to be curbed. Above all, they desired to see a thinning out of the ranks of monks and friars, and of course uppermost in their minds was the abolition of the Inquisition.

Many of them took part in the activities of the *Sociedades Económicas de Amigos del País* (Economic Societies of Friends of the Country), which were set up in Spain in the latter half of the century with the aim of fostering agriculture, industry, and commerce as well as the arts through the training in various skills of peasants and artisans.

Among the outstanding reform-minded Spaniards in the last decade of the eighteenth century were the statesman, scholar, and writer Gaspar Melchor de Jovellanos; Mariano Luis de Urquijo, who occupied the post of prime minister in 1799–1800, during the brief period when the royal favorite Manuel Godoy remained out of the limelight of the political scene; and Francisco Cabarrús, a Frenchman by birth and the founder of the Bank of San Carlos.

Among the clergy, too, there was an enlightened minority, the so-called "Jansenists," who advocated a curb on the authority of the Pope in the affairs of the Spanish clergy, strengthening the authority of the bishops, and a return of the erstwhile austerity of the Church. In the last decade of the eighteenth century enlightened churchmen could even be found in the Inquisition, and the forty-second Inquisitor-General Manuel Abad y la Sierra, who held office for two years, was denounced as a Jansenist after his dismissal in 1794.

Two years earlier this enlightened Inquisitor-General had commissioned another liberal clergyman, Juan Antonio Llorente, to look into the problem of book censorship and to present a plan for changing the legal proceedings of the Inquisition. This young man, who had been connected with the Holy Office since 1785, was destined to live through some of the most turbulent years Spain has ever known and to play an important role in them. His importance, however, lies not so much in his political activities as in his famous *History of the Inquisition of Spain*, which first appeared in French, in Paris (1817–1818). This monumental work aroused extraordinary and well-deserved interest throughout the world and became the center of a controversy which can be said to be still continuing in our own days.

Juan Antonio Llorente was born in 1756 in Rincón del Soto, a town in northeastern Castile, close to the Ebro River, which, in that part of the country, divides Castile from Navarre. His family was of the lower nobility and was economically comfortable. Juan Antonio's father died shortly after the boy's birth and his mother also succumbed by the time he was ten years old. Thanks to his uncle, a priest in nearby Calahorra, and thanks also to a friend of the family, the future dean of the cathedral of Tarazona (30 miles southeast of Calahorra), young Llorente received a fine education. A brilliant student, Llorente was ordained as priest in 1779, although he had to receive a papal dispensation because of his youth, and three years later he was appointed vicar general of Calahorra. In 1785, the tribunal of the Inquisition of Logroño, 30 miles northwest of Calahorra, chose the young ecclesiastic for its commissioner.

The years from 1785 to 1790 were a crucial period in Llorente's life, for they determined much of his ideological outlook. A man of letters, residing in Calahorra, became his friend and won him over to the new ideas of enlightenment, which were spreading through the ranks of Spain's intellectual elite. These were the years in which in his own words he gave up "forever, ultramontane principles of jurisprudence, scholasticism in the field of theology and the peripathetics in the area of philosophy and the natural sciences." His interest in letters, specifically in poetry and the drama, increased considerably. ". . . I abandoned the books I had admired until then," he further states in his autobiography. "I began to consult different ones, and every day I realized more clearly that I had been studying on the basis of erroneous principles." The advent in 1789 of the French Revolution beyond the Pyrenees reinforced

the reformist tendencies already present in his general outlook, although the subsequent bloodshed of the French upheaval caused him to question the advisability of entrusting
reform to the too radical-oriented.

In 1789, the then Inquisitor-General, Don Agustín Rubín
de Cevallos, impressed by Llorente's ability, appointed him
Secretary-General of the Inquisition of Madrid, a post
which he filled in an active capacity for two years. Subsequently in 1791 he had to share his time between Calahorra
and the capital since King Charles IV had granted him a
prebend in Calahorra, and his connection with the Inquisition acquired a nominal character. As secretary of the Holy
Office he became thoroughly acquainted with that institution's history and procedures, and this acquisition of first-
hand knowledge enabled him to write the treatise *Discurso
sobre el orden de procesar en los tribunales de Inquisición* (Discourse on Trial Proceedings in the Tribunals of the Inquisition). At the time of the conservative reaction in 1801, this
work caused him to lose his position as secretary of the Holy
Office as well as the privileges to which the title had entitled
him. Moreover, he was forced to pay a fine and retire for
one month to a monastery. His disgrace lasted until 1805,
when the Court commissioned him to write a history of the
Basque provinces. The following year, King Charles nomi-
nated him canon of the cathedral of Toledo, and in 1807 he
was granted membership in the Royal Order of Spain, established by Charles III.

A decisive turn in his life occurred when Napoleon invaded Spain in 1808, putting a temporary end to the decrepit
Bourbon monarchy, and placed his brother Joseph on the
Spanish throne. Like many well-meaning, enlightened
Spaniards Llorente saw in the new order the only effective
instrument by which Spain could be pulled out of the political, social, and economic stagnation in which the country
had found itself since the last decade of the previous century.

Aside from his interest in the general state of Spain he was of course particularly concerned with the Spanish Church. His contact with the Inquisition and his unique knowledge of its history and its methods had convinced him that the Spanish Church must undergo drastic changes. In his eyes the reform of the Church could not be brought about by those who resisted Napoleon. The insurgents seemed, at the beginning at least, to fight for the preservation of the status quo, which meant the preservation of the status quo in the Church and strengthening the Inquisition. Besides, the national uprising against the French emperor smacked too much of anarchy as far as Llorente was concerned, and Llorente, though a man of the enlightenment, had no taste for popular revolt. In this he was perhaps influenced by memories of the horrors of some of the episodes of the French Revolution related to him by French refugee priests who had emigrated to Spain in 1792 and whom he had be-friended. At any rate, given Llorente's primary objective, the abolishment of the Inquisition, he took, after consider-able soul-searching, the only path that seemed to him to meet the needs of his country and joined the ranks of those who thought that a Napoleonic regime could regenerate Spain. He took part in the deliberations of the assembly of Spanish representatives at Bayonne, France, convoked by Napoleon in the Spring of 1808, and he was one of the signers of the Constitution of Bayonne, promulgated in July of that year.

After the abolition of the Inquisition by Napoleon's decree of December, 1808, Joseph, the new king, placed Llorente in charge of the archives of the Council of the In-quisition and of the Inquisition of Madrid. Moreover, officials to whom the Inquisitional archives of Valladolid and other important towns had been entrusted were ordered to place at Llorente's disposal any material he might require.

Thus Llorente was able to write the first thoroughly

documented history of the Spanish Inquisition. It appeared in Paris years after the author had been forced by final French defeat in the Peninsula to seek refuge in France. The work came out in four volumes in 1817 and 1818 in Paris and in French with the title *Histoire critique de l'Inquisition d'Espagne depuis l'époque de son établissement par Ferdinand V jusqu'au règne de Ferdinand VII, tirée des pièces originales des archives du Conseil de la Suprême et de celles des tribunaux subalternes du Saint-Office* (*A Critical History of the Inquisition of Spain from the period of its establishment by Ferdinand V to the reign of Ferdinand VII, composed from the original documents of the Archives of the Supreme Council of the Inquisition and from those of subordinate tribunals of the Holy Office*). The book was translated shortly into English, German, and Italian, and was read everywhere with intense interest. The first Spanish edition, *Historia crítica de la Inquisición de España*, was published in 10 volumes in Madrid, in 1822, at a time when Spanish liberals, having undercut the absolutist authority of Ferdinand VII through the revolution of 1820, were still in power in Spain. Llorente went back to Spain in early 1823, thanks to an amnesty granted three years earlier by the Spanish liberal regime to Spanish supporters of the former Napoleonic regime, but died a few days after his return to Madrid.

Despite his single-minded devotion to the cause of church reform, it is impossible for the historian to render Llorente as a consistent opponent of the old order who threw all his energies and talents into the lists on the side of democracy at a decisive moment in Spanish history. Llorente's reformism is limited essentially to his attitude toward the Inquisition. From the field of democratic progressivism he is actually conspicuous by his absence. What he was always ready to support was some form of enlightened despotism. But between enlightened despotism and liberalism there is quite a difference, and this difference emerged clearly during the

A 8

War of Independence, when the true liberals fought for independence and reform and the *afrancesados* joined what they considered to be another enlightened despotism, that of the Napoleonic regime. Llorente, like most of the other *afrancesados*, approved of reform from above, but not by the true democratic process, advocated by the liberals of Cadiz. He looked to an enlightened despot, be he Charles III or Napoleon, or even the corrupt Godoy, to regenerate Spain. But he was definitely not in favor of a true democratic revolution, like the one the Cadiz liberals set in motion in 1810. No doubt the French Revolution of 1789 aroused his sympathies, but when the Revolution took the path of true political and social upheaval Llorente shrank back, like so many other enlightened Spaniards. The most famous example of this switch is found in the attitude of Count Floridablanca, the enlightened prime minister of Charles III and Charles IV, who became ultra-reactionary when he saw which way the French Revolution was headed. Llorente's own aversion to radicalism, as we have noted above, probably stemmed from his friendship with French emigré priests who sought refuge in Spain in 1792. Some concrete proof of his mixture of enlightenment and conservatism is found in his relations with the corrupt Spanish court of Charles IV. He was introduced to the King and received a prebend from the monarch. After his temporary disgrace he again became a favored figure at court and was commissioned to write a book. He also received a high award, the Order of Charles III. All this implied of course a friendly relationship with the corrupt though somewhat enlightened favorite and dictator Manuel Godoy, without whose support he could not have received these courtly favors in the last years before the Napoleonic invasion. Finally, when already in France after the defeat of the Napoleonic armies, he tried to justify his conduct during the war (joining Joseph Bonaparte) in a memorandum to the unspeakable Ferdinand VII, claiming that he had always been a royalist and implying that it was the liberals who had been the real subversive elements in war-torn Spain. One cannot therefore portray Llorente as a champion of democracy without flying in the face of history.

The *History* was published after the Spanish Inquisition had been abolished, first by Napoleon in 1808, then by the liberal Spanish parliament in 1813. Three years after the work appeared in Paris, the Spanish revolution of 1820 abolished the Inquisition again. Though the momentum gained by the movement in favor of abolition, cautiously initiated among the enlightened elite in the second half of the eighteenth century and reinforced during the Spanish War of Independence against Napoleon (1808–1814), was no doubt a decisive factor in the elimination of the Holy Office, the contribution of Llorente's book to this vital house-cleaning must not be overlooked. By 1820, reformers and the liberal section of the Spanish public, pressing for an end to an abhorred institution, were able to arm themselves with the evidence furnished them by the former secretary and historian of the institution they were attacking, and could thus make doubly sure that the hated Inquisition would once more be decreed out of existence.

The Holy Office reappeared in the form of individual juntas after Ferdinand had regained absolute power in 1823, but these tribunals functioned without the official sanction of the king. It was definitely eliminated after the death of this monarch by the decree of July 15, 1834. In 1822, the appearance in Madrid of the first Spanish version of the *History* had unmasked the true face of the Inquisition to a much greater number of Spaniards, and this again was probably one of the causes of the more or less dormant state of the institution during the years 1823–1834 and of its final elimination in 1834.

Aside from its practical contribution to the struggle to

rid Spain of the Inquisition, the great merit of Llorente's *History* lies in the fact that it focussed the attention of Spaniards and of the world, in a form that had never been employed before, on an institution that had been detested by so many for such a long time. The reaction of Spanish conservatives was, as can well be imagined, ferocious. In traditionalist quarters Llorente's book was attacked as misrepresenting and distorting facts and as exaggerating the misdeeds of the Inquisition as well as the number of victims of the Holy Office. In brief, it was viewed as a sinister contribution to the *leyenda negra*, the "black legend," which to many Spaniards covers with calumnies Spain's traditional religious policy and colonial practices. The 19th century literary critic and historian, Menéndez Pelayo violently attacked the *History* in his voluminous *Historia de los heterodoxos españoles*. Asserting that Llorente's book "is so poorly written that it cannot even aspire to the title of libel or novel . . . ," and calling it "odious and disagreeable, poorly thought out, poorly organized and poorly written, hypocritical and base . . . ," he went on to state that the *Historia de los heterodoxos españoles* may be considered to a certain extent a refutation of Llorente's *History*, thus paying an unwitting compliment to the object of his scorn.[1]

The controversy which raged so fiercely over Llorente's book in the past and present century has still not subsided. Many Spanish conservative historians still look upon it as a monstrous ingredient of the *leyenda negra*. In liberal circles in Spain as well as outside of Spain, and in the eyes of soberminded historians on both sides of the Atlantic, Llorente's great merit consists in having been the first to present to the world a history of the Inquisition based on original documents. If there are mistakes in the work, Llorente's essential integrity cannot be questioned. There is nothing which re-

---

1. *Op. cit.*, (Madrid, ed. of 1932), Vol. VII, Chapter I.

veals him as anti-Catholic or motivated in any way beyond ambitions to expose the machinery of the Inquisition and its effect on the Spanish people.

One of the most controversial aspects of the *History* is Llorente's estimate of the number of victims it made through the centuries. Conservatives naturally claim that his figures are highly exaggerated. Some liberal and impartial historians have tended to support this claim. Henry Charles Lea in his monumental *History of the Inquisition of Spain* (4 vols., New York, 1906–1907) states that Llorente vastly exaggerated the number of victims. A similar position is taken by Henry Kamen in his recent *The Spanish Inquisition* (London, 1965). On the other hand Cecil Roth's *The Spanish Inquisition* (London, 1937) points out quite correctly that Llorente's estimate would seem justified by the probable rate of burnings carried out in the first century of the Holy Office's existence—30 heretics a year by each of 10 tribunals. Roth also calls the reader's attention to the fact that the devoutly Catholic scholar José Amador de los Ríos (1818–1878) placed the number of victims actually burned between the years 1484 and 1525 at 28,540, those burned in effigy at 16,520, and those penanced at 303,847—figures which would amply justify Llorente's total calculations. Finally, Richard Herr in his brilliant *The Eighteenth-Century Revolution in Spain* (Princeton, 1958), a work which has come to be recognized as a classic in the field of Spanish history, writes that in the parts of the *History* covered by his study he has found no case of obvious misrepresentation.

One puzzling inconsistency in Llorente's original work should be noted. In the preface the author accuses the Holy Office of "immolating on its flaming shambles more than *three hundred thousand victims!!*"[2] (This is an accurate translation of the French original.) On the other hand his

---

2. Italics in text.

total estimate of victims of the Inquisition, which appears on the last page of this book, places the number of persons who actually perished in the flames at 31,912. He adds the figures of 17,659 effigies burnt and 291,450 persons "condemned to severe penances." We might explain this discrepancy in the following manner: Llorente's original Spanish draft may very well have mentioned over 300,000 victims without indicating that they were all actually burned; or he may have stated that over 30,000 persons had been burned at the stake. In that case the French translator of Llorente's original draft either made a mistake in rendering this particular sentence of the Spanish clergyman in the preface or simply wrote "three hundred thousand" instead of "thirty thousand," and Llorente did not notice the error upon preparing the final French version for the printer. This error was corrected in the first Spanish edition of 1822, which reads (page 13 of the prologue): "sacrificing in three centuries *close to four hundred thousand* persons." This sentence is quite in consonance with the final figures, since "sacrificing" does not necessarily mean killing.

While the value of Llorente's book cannot be questioned, the value of this English version in condensed form is equally clear. Here is a one-volume abridgment of a work which because of its length might cause only the specialist to read through all of it with sustained interest. This ably translated condensation presents the highlights of the historical evolution of the Spanish Inquisition, the procedural mechanism of the Holy Office, as well as those trials which in the words of the translator "serve as examples of the various laws of the Inquisition, and of its state at different epochs, and which include the persecutions of the most eminent men."

A condensation of such a voluminous work as Llorente's *Histoire critique* is a difficult undertaking, but the translator acquitted himself of his task in a highly creditable manner. The discrepancies between the original and the translation are few. Now and then we find an occasional mistake in rendering a date—1528 instead of 1538 (p. 101)—or a figure—1700 instead of 17,000 (p. 575), and in a few cases the translator left out some passages, the presence of which might have made the meaning of the text somewhat clearer. These minor discrepancies do not, however, in any way, detract from the essential import of this translated abridgment. This book should therefore be of intense interest to all those, of whatever persuasion, who wish to understand the Inquisition, an institution which instilled so much fear in so many persons for more than 300 years.

GABRIEL H. LOVETT

Matawan, New Jersey
December, 1966

LLORENTE'S

HISTORY OF THE INQUISITION.

THE HISTORY

OF THE

INQUISITION OF SPAIN,

FROM THE

TIME OF ITS ESTABLISHMENT

TO

THE REIGN OF FERDINAND VII.

COMPOSED FROM THE

ORIGINAL DOCUMENTS OF THE ARCHIVES OF THE SUPREME COUNCIL,
AND FROM THOSE OF SUBORDINATE TRIBUNALS
OF THE HOLY OFFICE.

———————

ABRIDGED AND TRANSLATED FROM THE ORIGINAL WORKS OF

D. JEAN ANTOINE LLORENTE,

FORMERLY SECRETARY OF THE INQUISITION,

CHANCELLOR OF THE UNIVERSITY OF TOLEDO, KNIGHT OF THE ORDER OF CHARLES III.
&c. &c. &c.

———————

LONDON:

PRINTED FOR GEO. B. WHITTAKER,

AVE-MARIA-LANE.

MDCCCXXVI.

LONDON:
PRINTED BY WILLIAM CLOWES,
Stamford-street.

ADVERTISEMENT.

THE Compiler of the following pages has only attempted to give a free and condensed translation of a complex and voluminous history, with the hope that it might prove of more utility in its present form than in the original works. Those portions which are not calculated to interest or instruct the general reader, and afford no illustrations of the subject, have been passed over. Those trials have been selected which serve as examples of the various laws of the Inquisition, and of its state at different epochs, and which include the persecutions of the most eminent men.

The curious will be amply gratified by the perusal of the history of the secret tribunal; the man of leisure cannot fail in finding occupation and amusement in the pages of Llorente; and the philosopher will discover in them ample scope for reflection on the aberrations of human reason, and on the capability of our nature, when under the influence of fanaticism, to inflict, with systematic indifference, death, torture, misery, anxiety, and infamy, on the guilty and the innocent.

All the records of the fantastic cruelties of the heathen world do not afford so appalling a picture of human weakness

and depravity as the authentic and genuine documents of
the laws and proceedings of this Holy Office, which professed to act under the influence of the doctrines of the
Redeemer of the World !

I offer, with humility, this abridgment of the work to
the public, and while I hope that it will be kindly and
favourably received, I believe that it may prove interesting
and useful to every class of readers.

June, 1826.

CONTENTS.

CONTENTS.

PREFACE.

ALTHOUGH a tribunal has existed for more than three hundred years in Spain, invested with the power of prosecuting heretics, no correct history of its origin, establishment, and progress has been written.

Writers of many countries have spoken of Inquisitions established in different parts of the world, where the Roman Catholic faith is the religion of the state, and yet not one is worthy of confidence. The work of M. Lavallée, entitled the "History of the Inquisitions of Italy, Spain, and Portugal," and published in 1809, has only added to the historical errors of the authors who preceded him. The Spanish and Portuguese writers on the same subject deserve no higher credit; and have not detailed, with accuracy, the circumstances which led to the establishment of this dreadful tribunal. These writers even differ in their statements of the period of its origin, and place it between the years 1477 and 1484. One affirms, with confidence, that the latter date is the true one, because in that year the regulations of the tribunal were enacted;

another decides that it originated in 1483, because in that year Thomas Torquemada was appointed inquisitor-general by the Pope.

The inquisition of Spain was not a new tribunal created by Ferdinand V. and Isabella, the queen of Castile, but only a reform and extension of the ancient tribunal, which had existed from the thirteenth century.

No one could write a complete and authentic history of the Inquisition, who was not either an inquisitor or a secretary of the holy office. Persons holding only these situations could be permitted to make memoranda of papal bulls, the ordinances of sovereigns, the decisions of the council of the "*Suprême*," of the originals of the preliminary processes for suspicion of heresy, or extracts of those which had been deposited in the archives. *Being myself the secretary of the Inquisition at Madrid, during the years 1789, 1790, and 1791, I have the firmest confidence in my being able to give to the world a true code of the secret laws by which the interior of the Inquisition was governed, of those laws which were veiled by mystery from all mankind,* excepting those men to whom the knowledge of their political import was exclusively reserved. A firm conviction, from knowing the deep objects of this tribunal, that it was vicious in principle, in its constitution, and in its laws, notwithstanding all that has been said in its support, induced me to avail myself of the advantage my situation afforded me, and to collect every document I could procure relative to its history. My perseverance has been crowned with success far beyond my hopes, for in addition to an abundance of materials, obtained with labour and expense, consisting of unpublished manuscripts and papers, mentioned in the inventories of deceased inquisitors, and other officers of the institution, in 1809, 1810, and 1811, when the Inquisition in Spain was suppressed, *all the archives were placed at my disposal;* and from 1809 to 1812 I collected everything that appeared to me to be of consequence in the registers of the council of the Inquisition, and in the provincial tribunals, for the purpose of compiling this history.

Never has a prisoner of the Inquisition seen either the accusation against himself, or any other. No one was ever permitted to know more of his own cause than he could learn of it by the interrogations and accusations to which he was obliged to reply, and by the extracts from the declarations of the witnesses, which were communicated to him, while not only their names were carefully concealed, and every circumstance relating to time, place, and person, by which he might obtain a clue to discover his denouncers, but even if the depositions contained any thing favourable to the defence of the prisoner. The maxim on which this was founded, is, that the accused ought not to occupy himself but in replying to the chief points of his accusation, and that it was the province of the judge afterwards to compare the answers that he had made with those which had been given favourable to his acquittal. Philip Limborch and many more of veracity have erred in their histories, from their ignorance of the method of conducting an inquisitorial trial. Those authors relied wholly on the accounts of prisoners, who knew nothing of the ground-work of their own case; and the details in Eymerick, Paramo, Pegna, Carena, and some other inquisitors, are too limited to yield the necessary information.

These facts make me hope that I shall not transgress the bounds of propriety when I say, that I only can give a true history of the Inquisition, as I only possess the materials necessary for the undertaking.

I have read the most celebrated trials of the modern Inquisition, and the details given by me differ essentially from those of other historians, not excepting those of Limborch, who is the most exact of them. The trials of Don Carlos of Austria, prince of the Asturias, of Don Bartholomew Carranza, archbishop of Toledo, and of Antony Perez, the first minister and secretary of Philip II., have been greatly illustrated in many important particulars.

I have established the truth of that which concerns the Emperor Charles V.; Jeanne of Albret, queen of Navarre; Henry IV. king of France, her son, and of Margaret of Bourbon the sovereign duchess of Bar, her daughter; of Don James of Navarre, son of Don Carlos, prince of Biana, surnamed the Infant of Tudela; of John Pic de Mirandola; of Don John of Austria, son of Philip IV.; of Alexander Farnèse, duke of Parma, and grandson of Charles V.; Don Philip of Arragon, son of the Emperor of Morocco; of Cæsar Borgia, son of Pope Alexander VI., and relation of the king of Navarre; of Jean Albret,

duke of Valentinois, peer of France; of Don Peter
Louis Borgia, last grand-master of the military order
of Montesa, and of many other princes against whom
the Inquisition exercised its power. The lover of
history will find the details of the trials of seven archbishops, twenty bishops, and a great number of
learned men, among whom are many of the members
of the Council of Trent, who were unfortunately suspected of entertaining or favouring the Lutheran doctrines. To this list I have added the suits instituted
by the *holy office* against many *saints*, and other per-
sonages, held in reverence by the Church of Spain,
and also of many literati persecuted by this tribunal.
These, for the sake of perspicuity, I have divided into
two classes; the first class comprises those learned
theologians who were accused of Lutheranism, for
having, in their zeal, corrected the text of Bibles already published, or Latin translations from the Greek
and Hebrew editions. The second class consists of
those learned men, designated by the holy office
under the title of False Philosophers, and who were
persecuted for having manifested a wish to destroy in
Spain, superstition and fanaticism.

This history will make known numberless attempts
perpetrated by the inquisitors against magistrates
who defended the rights of sovereign authority, in
opposition to the enterprises of the *holy office* and the
court of Rome; and which enables me to state the
trials of many celebrated men and ministers who defended the prerogatives of the crown, and whose only
crimes were having published works on the right of

the crown, according with the true principles of jurisprudence. These trials will display the Counsellors
of the Inquisition carrying their audacity to such a
height, as to deny that their temporal jurisdiction
was derived from the concession of their sovereign,
and actually prosecuting all the members of the
council of Castile, as rash men, suspected of heresy,
for having made known and denounced to the king
this system of usurpation. In addition to these intolerable acts, will be found accounts of their assump-
tion of superiority over viceroys, and other great
officers of state. I have also shewn, that these
ministers of persecution have been the chief causes
of the decline of literature, and almost the annihilators
of nearly all that could enlighten the people, by their
ignorance, their blind submission to the monks
who were qualifiers, and by persecuting the magistrates and the learned who were anxious to dissemi-
nate information. These monks were despicable
scholastic theologians, too ignorant and prejudiced
to be able to ascertain the truth between the doctrines
of Luther and those of Roman Catholicism, and so
condemned, as Lutheran, propositions incontestably
true.

The horrid conduct of this *holy office* weakened
the power and diminished the population of Spain,
by arresting the progress of arts, sciences, industry,
and commerce, and by compelling multitudes of
families to abandon the kingdom; by instigating the
expulsion of the Jews and the Moors; and by immolating on its flaming shambles more than *three hun-*

dred thousand victims!! So replete with duplicity was
the system of the inquisitors-general, and the council
of this *holy office,* that if a papal bull was likely to
circumscribe their power, or check their vengeance,
they refused to obey, on the pretext of its being opposed to the laws of the kingdom, and the orders of
the Spanish government. By a similar proceeding,
they evaded the ordinances of the king, by alleging
that papal bulls prevented them from obeying, under
pain of excommunication.

Secrecy, the foe of truth and justice, was the soul
of the tribunal of the Inquisition; it gave to it new
life and vigour, sustained and strengthened its arbitrary power, and so emboldened it, that it had the
hardihood to arrest the highest and noblest in the
land, and enabled it to deceive, by concealing facts,
popes, kings, viceroys, and all invested with authority
by their sovereign. This *holy office,* veiled by secrecy, unhesitatingly kept back, falsified, concealed,
or forged the reports of trials, when compelled to
open their archives to popes or kings. The Inquisitors
constantly succeeded, by this detestable knavery, in
concealing the truth, and facilitated their object by
being careful not to number the reports. This was
practised to a great extent in the trials of the archbishop of Toledo, of the Prothonotary, and others.

Facts prove beyond a doubt, that the extirpation
of Judaism was not the real cause, but the mere
pretext, for the establishment of the Inquisition by
Ferdinand V. The true motive was to carry on a
vigorous system of confiscation against the Jews, and

so bring their riches into the hands of the government. Sixtus IV. sanctioned the measure, to gain the point dearest to the court of Rome, an extent of domination. Charles V. protected it from motives of policy, being convinced it was the only means of preventing the heresy of Luther from penetrating into Spain. Philip II. was actuated by superstition and tyranny to uphold it; and even extended its jurisdiction to the excise, and made the exporters of horses into France liable to seizure by the officers of the tribunal, as persons suspected of heresy! Philip III., Philip IV., and Charles II., pursued the same course, stimulated by similar fanaticism and imbecility, when the re-union of Portugal to Spain led to the discovery of many Jews. Philip V. maintained the Inquisition from considerations of mistaken policy, inherited from Louis XIV., who made him believe that such rigour would ensure the tranquillity of the king-dom, which was always in danger when many re-ligions were tolerated. Ferdinand VI. and Charles III. befriended this *holy office*, because they would not deviate from the course that their father had traced, and because the latter hated the freemasons. Lastly, Charles IV. supported the tribunal, because the French Revolution seemed to justify a system of sur-veillance, and he found a firm support in the zeal of the inquisitors-general, always attentive to the pre-servation and extension of their power, as if the sovereign authority could find no surer means of strengthening the throne, than the terror inspired by an Inquisition.

During the time I remained in London, I heard some Catholics affirm that the Inquisition was useful in Spain, to preserve the Catholic faith, and that a similar establishment would have been useful in France.

These persons were deceived, by believing that it was sufficient for people to be good Catholics not to have any fear of the *holy office.* They knew not that nine-tenths of the prisoners were deemed guilty, though true to their faith, because the ignorance or malice of the denouncers prosecuted them for points of doctrine, which were not susceptible of heretical interpretation, but in the judgment of an illiterate monk, is considered erudite by the world, because he is said to have studied the theology of the schools. The Inquisition encouraged hypocrisy, and punished those who either did not know how, or would not, assume the mask. This tribunal wrought no conversion. The Jews and Morescoes, who were baptized without being truly converted, merely that they might remain in Spain, are examples which prove the truth of this assertion. The former perished on the pyres of the Inquisition, the latter crossed over into Africa with the Moors, as much Mahometans as their ancestors were before they were baptised.

I conclude with declaring, that the contents of this history are original, and that I have drawn my facts with fidelity, from the most authentic sources, and might have greatly extended them.

HISTORY

OF

THE INQUISITION.

CHAPTER I.

FIRST EPOCH OF THE CHURCH TILL THE CONVERSION OF THE EMPEROR CONSTANTINE.

THE Christian religion was scarcely established before
heresies arose among its disciples. The Apostle St. Paul
instructs Titus, the Bishop of Crete, in his duty towards
heretics, saying, that a man who persists in his heresy, after
the first and second admonition, shall be rejected; but
St. Paul does not say that the life of the heretic shall be
taken: and our Saviour, addressing St. Peter, commands
that a sinner shall be forgiven, not only seven times, but
seventy times seven, which infers that he ought never to be
punished with death by a judgment of the church. Such was
the doctrine of the church during the three first centuries,
until the peace of Constantine. Heretics were never excommunicated until exhortation had been employed in vain. As
this system was adopted, it was natural that some persons
should write against heresy to prevent its increase. This
was done by St. Ignatius, Castor Agrippa, St. Irenæus,
St. Clement of Alexandria, St. Justin, St. Denis of
Corinth, Tertullian, Origen, and many others.

These faithful imitators of the benevolence of their Divine
Master were averse to oppressive measures. Although the
evil produced by the religion of the impious Manès was so

great, that Archelaüs, Bishop of Caschara, in Mesopotamia, judged it necessary to imprison him, yet he renounced that design when Marcellus (to whom Manès had written) proposed another conference with him.   Archelaüs succeeded in converting the heretic, and not only gave up his intention of detaining him, but saved his life when the people would have stoned him to death.

It is possible that the church was in a certain degree compelled to act in this manner, from the impossibility of employing the coercive measures of temporal power against heretics during the reigns of the heathen princes; but this was not the only motive for her tolerance, since it is certain that when no edicts of persecution existed against the Christians, the emperors received the appeals of the bishops in the same manner as those of their other subjects : this is proved by the history of the heretic Paul of Samosata, Bishop of Antioch.

The council of that town, assembled in 272, perceiving that Paul had relapsed into heresy, after the abjuration which he had made before the council of 266, deposed him, and elected Domnus in his place.   The episcopal house being still occupied by the deposed bishop, he was ordered to quit it, that his successor might take possession.   Paul having refused to obey, the bishops applied to the Emperor Aurelian, who had not then begun to persecute the Christians; he received their complaint, and replied, that as he did not know which of the two parties was right, they must conform to the decision of the Bishop of Rome and his church.   The holy see was then occupied by Felix I., who confirmed the decision of the council, and the Emperor Aurelian caused it to be executed.

As toleration was universal in the Christian church, it is not to be supposed that the church of Spain followed different principles.   Basilides and Marcial, Bishops of Astorga and Merida, apostatized; they were reconciled to the church

without any punishment but degradation, to which they submitted before the year 253, when they appealed to Pope
Stephen.

The Council of Elvira in 303 decreed, that if an heretic
demanded to be re-admitted into the bosom of the church,
he should be reconciled without suffering any punishment
but a canonical penance of ten years, which was the more
remarkable, as this council established more severe punishments for many crimes which appear less heinous. This
seems to prove that the Spanish bishops who composed this
council, among whom were the great Osius of Cordova,
Sabinus of Seville, Valerius of Saragossa, and Melantius
of Toledo, were persuaded, like Origen, that leniency was
the means to convert heretics, in order to prevent them from
falling into obstinacy and impenitence.

SECOND EPOCH.—*From the Fourth to the Eighth Century.*

If the primitive system of the church towards heretics
had been faithfully pursued, as it ought to have been, after
the peace of Constantine, the tribunal of the Inquisition
would never have existed, and, perhaps, the number and
duration of heresies would have been less ; but the popes
and bishops of the fourth century, profiting by the circumstance of the emperors having embraced Christianity, began
to imitate, in a certain degree, the conduct which they had
reprehended in the heathen priests.

These pontiffs, though respectable for the holiness of their
lives, sometimes carried their zeal for the triumph of the
Catholic faith, and the extirpation of heresy, to too great a
height ; and to ensure success, engaged Constantine and his
successors to establish civil laws against all heretics.

This first step, which the popes and bishops had taken
contrary to the doctrine of St. Paul, was the principle and

origin of the Inquisition; for when the custom of punishing a heretic by corporeal pain, although he was a good subject, was once established, it became necessary to vary the punishments, to augment their number, to render them more or less severe, according to the character of each sovereign, and to regulate the manner of prosecuting the culprit.

The Emperor Theodosius published, in 382, an edict against the Manicheans, decreeing that they should be punished with death, and their property confiscated for the use of the state, and commissioning the prefect (Préfet du Prétoire) to appoint inquisitors and spies to discover those who should conceal themselves.

It is here that inquisition and accusation are first mentioned in relation to heresy, for until that time only those great crimes which attacked the safety of the empire were permitted to be publicly denounced. The successors of Theodosius modified these edicts, some of which menaced heretics with the prosecutions of the impartial judges, if they did not voluntarily abjure their errors. Notices were given to known heretics who did not abjure after the publication of the edicts, that if they were converted in a certain time, they would be admitted to a reconciliation, and would only suffer a canonical penance.

When these conciliatory measures were unavailing, various punishments were adopted. Those doctors who, in contempt of the laws, promulgated their false opinions, were subjected to considerable fines, banishment from cities, and even transportation. In certain cases, their property was confiscated, in others they were obliged to pay a fine of ten pounds of gold, or they were scourged with leathern thongs, and sent to islands from whence they could not escape. Besides these punishments, they were forbidden to hold assemblies, and the offenders were liable to proscription, banishment, transportation, and even death in some cases. The execution of these decrees was intrusted to the governors of provinces, magistrates charged with the administration of justice, commanders of towns and their principal officers, who were all liable to various punishments in case of negligence.

The establishment of most of these laws had been solicited by popes and bishops of known sanctity, and it must be allowed that it was not their intention to carry those which decreed the punishment of death into execution ; they only desired to intimidate innovators by their publication.

The church of Spain continued faithful to the general discipline, under the authority of the Roman emperors : the Arian heresy was afterwards established among them under the Goths ; but since their princes have embraced the Catholic faith, the laws and councils of Spain inform us of their treatment of heretics.

The fourth Council of Toledo, assembled in 633, at which St. Isidore, Archbishop of Seville, assisted, was occupied with the Judaic heresy : it was decreed, with the consent of King Sésenaud, that they should be at the disposal of the bishops to be punished, and compelled by fear to return to Christianity a second time : they were to be deprived of their children, and their slaves set at liberty.

In 655, the ninth Council of Toledo decreed, that baptized Jews should be obliged to celebrate the Christian festivals with their bishops, and that those who should refuse to conform to this discipline should be condemned either to the punishment of scourging, or abstinence, according to the age of the offender.

We find that greater severity was shown towards those who returned from Christianity to idolatry. King Récarede I. proposed to the third Council of Toledo, in 589, that the priests and civil judges should be commissioned to extirpate that species of heresy, by punishing the culprits in a degree proportioned to the crime, yet without employing capital punishment.

These rigorous measures did not appear sufficient, and the twelfth Council of Toledo, in 681, at which King Erbigius assisted, decided, that if the offender was noble, he should be subject to excommunication and exile ; if he was a slave, he should be scourged and delivered to his master loaded with chains, and if the proprietor could not answer for him, that he should be placed at the disposal of the king.

In 693, the sixteenth Council of Toledo assembled in the presence of King Egica, added to the measures already established, a law, by which all who opposed the efforts of the bishops and judges to destroy idolatry were condemned, if noble, to be excommunicated, and to pay a fine of three pounds of gold; and if of a low condition, to receive a hundred strokes of a whip, and have half his property confiscated.

Recesuinte, who reigned from 663 to 672, established a particular law against heretics : it deprived them indiscriminately of the wealth and dignities they might possess, if they were priests, and added to these punishments, perpetual banishment for laymen, if they persisted in heresy.

THIRD EPOCH.—*From the Eighth Century to the Pontificate of Gregory VII.*

In the fourth, fifth, sixth, and seventh centuries, the ecclesiastics obtained many privileges from the kings and emperors, and the judicial power became, in some cases, a right of the episcopacy. These acquisitions, and the universal ignorance which followed the irruption of the barbarians, were the causes of the influence which the pontiffs of Rome acquired over the Christian people, who were persuaded that the authority of the pope should be without bounds, and that he had supreme power both in ecclesiastical and temporal affairs.

In 726, when the Romans deposed their last duke, Basil,

Pope Gregory II. usurped the civil government of Rome, and had recourse to the protection of Charles Martel, mayor of the palace, against the King of Lombardy, who aspired to the command in that capital. His successor, Gregory III., offered the dignity of patrician to Charles Martel, as if he had the right of disposing of it. Zachary, who was elected pope, in 741, acted as the temporal sovereign of Rome, and permitted Pepin, son of Charles Martel, to take the title of King of France, after having deposed Childeric III., who was the legitimate sovereign. Pepin was crowned in France by Stephen II., who became pope in 752.

At last, Leo III. crowned Charlemagne emperor of the west, on Christmas day, in the year 800. In this ceremony, which took place at Rome, Charlemagne was proclaimed the first emperor of the restoration.

The popes employed the great influence they had gained over general opinion, to extend and preserve their dominion. Pepin and Charlemagne did not foresee how fatal their example would prove to their successors, when they solicited Stephen II. to release the French from their oath of fidelity to Childeric III. When the doctrine, that a pope possessed the power of releasing subjects from their oath of fidelity, was once established, it became necessary that kings should endeavour to conciliate the popes. Succeeding events shew that this doctrine was favourable to the rise of the Inquisition.

The idea that excommunication produced all the effects attached to infamy, not only to the Christian on whom it fell, but to all who held any communion with him, was another cause of the great influence of the popes, and the progress of the Inquisition. The barbarians had preserved the doctrine of the Druids, which forbade a Gaul to assist one whom the priests had declared impious and abhorred of the gods, on pain of being deemed guilty towards the gods, and unworthy of the society of men. The priests, finding this opinion established, did not combat it, because it added force to the anathemas of the church. Fortunately the popes of the middle ages had not yet thought of commissioning men to ascertain if Christians were orthodox, and the ancient discipline of the church was still pursued towards heretics.

Felix, Bishop of Urgel, in Spain, had embraced the erroneous opinion, that Jesus Christ was the Son of God only by adoption. He returned to the faith of the church, but relapsed sometime after into the same error, although he had abjured, before the Council of Ratisbonne, in 792, and before Pope Adrian, at Rome. The conduct of Felix was very reprehensible, yet Leo III. would not excommunicate him in a simple manner, but only pronounced the anathema against him, in case he refused to abjure a second time. Felix afterwards abjured, and suffered no punishment but deprivation of his dignity.

The Emperor Michel, in 811, renewed all the laws which condemned the Manichean heretics to death. The patriarch Nicephorus represented to him that it was better to convert them by gentle means; but the spirit of the church at that time was so far from moderation, that the Abbot Theophanes, celebrated for his piety, does not hesitate to speak of Nicephorus and the other counsellors of the prince, as ignorant and ill advised; and adds, that the maxims of Holy Writ warrant the custom of burning heretics, because they can never be brought to repent.

Theodore Critinus, chief of the Iconoclastes, was called before the seventh council general, assembled at Constantinople in 869. He was convicted of entertaining opinions contrary to the doctrines of the church: he abjured his heresy, with several of his sect, and was reconciled without being subjected to any penance. The Emperor Basil, who assisted at the council, honoured him with a kiss of peace. We may conclude from this, that if the conduct of the church had always been equally lenient, heresy would not have been so frequent among the Christians.

In 1022, certain heretics, who appeared to profess the doctrines of the Manicheans, were discovered in Orleans, and several other towns; among them was Stephen, confessor to Queen Constance, wife of Robert. That prince assembled a council at Orleans: Stephen was summoned to appear before it, and attempts were made, but in vain, to bring him back to the true faith. The bishops resolved to punish these heretics, and those who were ecclesiastics were degraded and excommunicated with the others. The king immediately afterwards condemned them to be burnt. Several, when they felt the flames, exclaimed that they were willing to submit to the church, but it was too late, all hearts were closed against them. These examples shew the difference which was made between the Manichean and other heresies.

It is necessary to mention several maxims which had been introduced into the ecclesiastical government, and which passed at that time for incontestable truths. The first of these opinions was, that it was necessary not only to punish obstinate heretics with excommunication, but to employ it against every species of crime, which abuse was carried to such a height, that Cardinal St. Peter Damian reproached Pope Alexander with it. According to the second maxim, if an excommunicated Christian persisted for more than a year in refusing to submit and demand absolution, after having been subjected to a canonical penance, he was considered as an heretic. The third maxim held that it was a meritorious act to prosecute heretics, and apostolical indulgences were granted as a recompense for this service to the cause of religion.

These maxims, and several others which prevailed during the fourth epoch, prepared the minds of the people for the establishment of the Inquisition, which was destined to persecute heretics and apostates.

FOURTH EPOCH.

The celebrated Hildebrand ascended the pontifical throne in 1073, under the name of Gregory VII., soon after his predecessor, Alexander II., had summoned the emperor Henry III. to Rome, to be judged by a council. This prince had been denounced by the Saxons, who revolted against him, as an heretic. As he did not appear, the pope excommunicated him, released his subjects from their oath of fidelity, and caused them to elect, in his stead, Rodolph, Duke of Suabia.

The authority which this pope acquired over the Christian princes greatly surpassed that of his predecessors, and although it was directly contrary to the spirit of the New Testament, his successors employed every means to preserve it.

The famous French monk Gerbert being elected pope in 999, under the name of Sylvester II., addressed a letter to all Christians, in which he supposes the Church of Jerusalem speaking from its ruins, and calling upon them to take up arms and fight boldly to deliver it from oppression. Gregory VII. also undertook, in 1074, to form a crusade against the Turks, in favour of Michael, emperor of the east, but as he died before he could put his plan into execution, his successor, Urban II., caused it to be proclaimed in the Council of Clermont, in the year 1095. The efforts of the pope had an incredible success; a numerous army left Europe soon after, which first took the city of Antioch, and afterwards Jerusalem in 1099. The injustice of this war, and the other expeditions of the same kind which succeeded it, would have disgusted all Europe, if the people had not been prepossessed with the absurd idea, that it was meritorious to make war for the exaltation and glory of Christianity: the consequences of a system so fatal to temporal power were felt in France at the time of the Patorians, Catharians,

and other sects of Manès. Alexander III., having sent
Peter, Bishop of Meaux, to Count Raymond V. of Toulouse,
that legate made him and all his nobles take an oath that
they would not favour the heretics who had taken up arms
in defence of their party ; and in the Council of Lateran, the
following year, the fathers declared that though the church
did not approve of sanguinary measures, yet she would not
refuse the assistance offered by Christian princes : in consequence, Alexander not only excommunicated the heretics and
their adherents, but promised all those who should die in
the war against them absolution and salvation, and for the
present granted indulgences for two years to all who should
take up arms.

In 1181, Cardinal Henry, Bishop of Alva, was sent into
France to pursue the war against the Albigenses, but this
expedition did not entirely destroy that party, and a new
council was held, in whose decrees Cardinal Fleury supposes
he has discovered the origin of the Inquisition. He was not
mistaken in this opinion, but it was not at that time actually
instituted, since the bishops alone, as they had always been,
were commissioned to preserve the faith. The council recommended that the bishops, or their archdeacons, should
visit the dioceses once or twice a year, and that they should
cause the inhabitants to take an oath that they would
denounce all heretics, or persons who held meetings, to the
bishop or archdeacon. The council also decreed that counts,
barons, and other nobles should take an oath to discover
heretics and punish them, on pain of excommunication and
deprivation of their estates and employments.

In 1194, Cardinal Gregory St. Ange instigated Alphonso II., King of Arragon, to publish an edict banishing
heretics of all sects indiscriminately from his states; and
Peter II., son of Alphonso, published another in 1197, with
nearly the same injunctions, which proves that the former
edict had little effect.

CHAPTER II.

ESTABLISHMENT OF A GENERAL INQUISITION AGAINST
HERETICS IN THE THIRTEENTH CENTURY.

In 1203, Pope Innocent III. commissioned Peter de Castelnau and Ralph, two monks of the order of *Citeaux*, in the monastery of Fontfroide, in Narbonnese Gaul, to preach against the Albigenses. Their exhortations were not in vain, and the success of their mission was a favourable introduction to a plan which Pope Innocent had formed of instituting inquisitors independent of the bishops, with the privilege of prosecuting heretics, as delegates of the holy see.

On the 4th of June, in the seventh year of his pontificate, he named the abbot of the Citeaux, with Peter and Ralph, apostolical legates. He gave them full powers to prosecute all heretics; and to facilitate the execution of the orders of the holy see, they were to engage in the name of the pope, Philip II., King of France, his son, and all his nobles, to pursue the heretics, and to promise them full indulgences as a recompense for their zeal. The pope invested these monks with the necessary powers to enable them to destroy or establish whatever they might judge to be favourable to their design, in the ecclesiastical provinces of Aix, Arles, Narbonne, and other bishoprics where heretics might be found, only recommending that they should apply to the holy see in all difficult cases; at the same time he wrote to Philip, requesting him to assist his commissioners, and even, if it was necessary, to send the presumptive heir to his throne with an army against the heretics.

The legates encountered many difficulties, because their mission was displeasing to the bishops. The King of France took no part in the affair, but the Counts of Toulouse, Foix, Beziers, Cominges, and Carcassone, and the other nobles of these provinces, seeing that the Albigenses had singularly increased, and persuaded that a very small number would be converted, refused to banish them from their states, as it would lessen the population, and, consequently, be against their interests: an additional motive for this refusal was, that these heretics were all peaceful and submissive subjects.

Peter and Ralph commenced preaching against the heretics; they held conferences with these fanatics, but the number of the converted was very small. Arnauld, Abbot of the Citeaux, called upon twelve abbots of his order to assist him, and (during their sojourn at Montpellier) they admitted two Spaniards to share their labours, who were known under the names of Diego Acebes, a bishop of Osma, who was returning to his diocese, and St. Dominic de Guzman, a regular canon of the order of St. Augustine. They both converted several Albigenses, and when the Spanish bishop returned to his diocese, he permitted St. Dominic to remain in France.

The great feudal chiefs of Provence and Narbonne refused to execute the orders of the legates, to pursue the heretics in their states, alleging that they were always at war with each other; but the legates threatened to excommunicate them, and to release their subjects from their oaths of fidelity. These menaces alarmed the nobles, and they consented to sign a peace.

The most powerful of these princes was Raymond VI., Count of Toulouse. His conduct towards Peter de Castelnau, who had threatened him several times for not performing his promises, induced the Albigenses who were his subjects to assassinate the legate, who was beatified in 1208. The pope wrote to all the nobles of the provinces of Narbonne, Arles, Embrun, Aix, and Vienne in Dauphiny, pressing them to unite and march against the heretics, and promising them the same indulgences which had been granted to the crusaders.

The assassination of Peter de Castelnau had excited among the Catholics the greatest indignation against his murderers. Arnauld took advantage of this moment to execute the orders which he had received from the pope. He commissioned the twelve monks, and others whom he had associated, to preach a crusade against the heretics, to grant indulgences, to note those who refused to engage in the war, to inform themselves of their creed, to reconcile the converted, and place all obstinate heretics at the disposal of Simon de Montfort, commander of the crusaders. This was the beginning of the Inquisition in 1208.

Pope Innocent III. died on the 16th of July, 1216, before he had succeded in giving a permanent form to the delegated inquisition : the continuation of the war against the Albigenses, and the opposition which he met with from the bishops in the Council of Lateran, were perhaps the causes of his failure. Honorius III., who succeeded him, prepared to finish his undertaking.

Innocent had sent St. Dominic de Guzman to Toulouse, that he might choose one of the religious orders approved by the church, for the institution which he intended to form. He preferred that of St. Augustine ; and on his return to Rome with his companions, Honorius approved his choice on the 22nd of December, 1216.

St. Dominic also established an order for laymen. This order has been designated as the *Third Order of Penitence*, but most commonly as the *Militia of Christ*, because those who were members of it fought against heretics, and assisted the Inquisitors in the exercise of their functions ; they were considered as part of the inquisitorial family, and on that account bore the name of *Familiars*. This association afterwards gave rise to that which was called the *Congregation of St. Peter Martyr;* it was approved by Honorius, and confirmed by his successor Gregory IX. Another association was formed in Narbonne, which also bore the name of *Militia of Christ;* it was soon after blended with the third order of St. Dominic. Honorius having formed a constitution against heretics, the Emperor Frederic II. gave it the sanction of civil law at his coronation. In 1224 the Inquisition already existed in Italy under the ministry of the Dominican friars, which is proved by an edict of the Emperor Frederick against heretics at Padua. The efforts of the Inquisition in Narbonne had not succeeded according to the expectation of the pope, who imputed its failure to the negligence of Cardinal Conrad, whom he recalled, and sent Cardinal Roman in his place. The importunity of this legate induced Louis VIII., King of France, to place himself at the head of an army to march against the nobles who protected the Albigenses. But Louis died in the same year, and the pope followed him, without having succeeded in giving a permanent form to the new tribunal which had been introduced into France.

Gregory IX., who ascended the pontifical throne in 1227, finally established the Inquisition: he had been the zealous protector of St. Dominic and the intimate friend of St. Francis d'Assiz. Cardinal Roman was more fortunate than the legates who preceded him: the nobles, weary of a war which had lasted twenty years, wished for peace. The Count of Toulouse, Raymond VII., after the death of his father, who had begun the war, reconciled himself to St. Louis and the church in a Council of Narbonne, and promised to drive the heretics from his domains.

In 1229 another council was held at Toulouse. The decrees were nearly the same as those made at the Councils of Lateran and Verona, except that laymen were then first prohibited from reading the Scriptures in the vulgar tongue. In the succeeding year, many other edicts were published, increasing in severity; but it appears that these rigorous measures failed in effect, as the heresy of the Albigenses penetrated even to the capital of Christendom.

CHAPTER III.

OF THE ANCIENT INQUISITION OF SPAIN.

In 1233, when the Inquisition in France had received the established form which was bestowed on it by St. Louis, Spain was divided into four Christian kingdoms, besides the Mahometan states. Castile was under the dominion of St. Ferdinand, who added to it the kingdoms of Seville, Cordova, and Jean. James I. governed Arragon, and conquered the kingdoms of Valencia and Majorca; Navarre was possessed by Sancho VIII., who died in the course of the following year, and left his crown to Theobald I., Count de Champagne and de Brie. Sancho II. reigned in Portugal.

Many convents of Dominicans existed in these kingdoms after the establishment of the order, but there are no authentic records, to prove that the Inquisition was introduced before the year 1232, when Pope Gregory IX. addressed a brief to Don Esparrago, Archbishop of Tarragona, and to his suffragan bishops, in which he most earnestly exhorted them to oppose the progress of heresy by every means in their power.

The archbishop sent the bull to Gil Rodriguez de Valladares, first provincial of the Spanish Dominicans; he also sent it to Don Bertrand, Bishop of Lerida, in whose diocese the first Spanish Inquisition was founded. Pope Innocent VI. conferred many privileges on the Dominican Friars, and in 1254 extended the rights of the Inquisitors, and in the same brief decreed that the depositions of witnesses should be considered valid, although their names were unknown. Urban VI. and Clement VI. also augmented their privileges.

The Kings of Arragon continued to protect the Inquisition, and James II., in 1292, published a decree, commanding the tribunals of justice to assist the Dominicans, to imprison all who might be denounced, to execute the judgments pronounced by the monks, to remove every obstacle which they might meet with, &c. The hatred which the office of an Inquisitor everywhere inspired in the first ages of the Inquisition caused the death of a great number of Dominicans and some Cordeliers : the honours of martyrdom were assigned to them, but St. Peter of Verona was the only one canonized by the pope. Nothing certain is known of the state of Portugal during this period : it appears that in the thirteenth century the Inquisition was established only in the dioceses of Tarragona, Barcelona, Urgel, Lerida, and Girona.

The convents of Dominicans having multiplied in Spain, a chapter-general of the order decreed, in 1301, that it should be divided into two provinces; that the first in rank should be named the province of Spain, and comprise Castile and Portugal; and that the second should have the title of Arragon, and be composed of Valencia, Catalonia, Rousillon, Cerdagne, Majorca, Minorca, and Iviza.

The provincial of the Dominicans of Castile, designated as the provincial of Spain, possessed the right of naming the apostolical inquisitor in the other provinces. In 1302 Father Bernard was Inquisitor of Arragon, and celebrated several *autos-da-fé* in the same year.

In 1308 Pope Clement V. commanded the King of Arragon and the Inquisitors to arrest all the knights templars, who had not been prosecuted, and to confiscate their property for the use of the holy see; the templars in Castile and Portugal were also arrested.

In 1314, other heretics were discovered in the kingdom of Arragon; Bernard Puigarcos the Inquisitor-general condemned several to banishment, the others were burnt. Many who abjured were reconciled.

In 1325, F. Arnauld Burguete, Inquisitor-general of the kingdom, arrested Pierre Durand de Baldhac, who had relapsed into heresy, and he was burnt alive in the presence of King James, his sons, and two bishops.

In 1334, F. William da Costa condemned F. Bonato to the flames, and reconciled many persons who had been perverted by that monk.

In 1350, Father Nicholas Roselli discovered a sect of heretics named *Begards*, whose chief was named Jacques Juste; they were all reconciled, and Jacques was condemned to perpetual imprisonment. The bones of three of these heretics who had died impenitent were disinterred and burnt. Roselli being elected Cardinal in 1356, Nicholas Eymerich succeeded him. Eymerich composed a book entitled "The Guide of Inquisitors," in which the most minute details of his judgments, and those of other Inquisitors of Arragon, are found.

It is not certain whether the provincial of Castile exercised his privilege of naming Inquisitors; perhaps heresy had not penetrated into the states of Castile.

Pope Gregory IX. dying in 1378, the Romans named Urban VI. as his successor; but several cardinals assembled out of Rome, and elected another pope under the name of Clement VII.

The great schism of the West then began, and lasted till the election of Martin V., in the Council General of Constance in 1417, where Don Gil Mugnoz, who had been elected as Clement VIII., renounced the papacy. This revolution influenced the state of the Inquisition as much as the other points of ecclesiastical discipline. Castile followed the party of Clement VII., and Portugal that of Urban VI. The order of Dominicans was equally divided, and elected different vicars-general. Urban VI. died in 1389, and his party elected Boniface IX., who appointed F. Rodrigo de Cintra apostolical Inquisitor-general of Portugal. He afterwards named F. Vincent de Lisbon, Inquisitor-general of Spain. Castile, Navarre, and Arragon were under the dominion of Benedict XIII., who was elected pope after the death of Clement VII. Such was the state of the Inquisition in Spain, towards the end of the fourteeth century.

It is uncertain if the Inquisition existed in Castile in the beginning of the fifteenth century, for though Boniface IX. appointed F. Vincent de Lisbon Inquisitor-general, his authority was not recognised, as that kingdom belonged to the party of Benedict XIII., who, after the Council of Constance, was designated as the anti-pope Peter de Luna. The town of Perpignan was the seat of one of the provincial Inquisitions of Arragon, whose jurisdiction extended over the countships of Rousillon and Cerdagne, and over the islands of Majorca, Minorca, and Iviza. Benedict XIII., who was recognised in this part of Spain, divided this province and appointed two Inquisitors, who celebrated several *autos da fé*, and burnt a considerable number of people.

The election of Martin V. having put an end to the great schism of the West : the Portuguese monks ought to have submitted to the authority of the Provincial of Spain, who was then a monk of their nation, named F. John de St. Juste; but the Dominicans who were at Constance, persuaded the pope that his jurisdiction was too extensive, which induced the pontiff to subdivide the province of Spain into three parts; the first part was named the province of Spain, and comprised Castile, Toledo, Murcia, Estremadura, Andalusia, Biscay, and the Asturias de Santillana ; the second,

Santiago, was composed of the kingdom of Leon, Galicia, and the Asturias of Oviedo ; and the third, that of Portugal, extended over all the dominions of the monarch.

Martin V. established a provincial Inquisition at Valencia, in 1420, at the request of Alphonso V., King of Arragon ; hitherto commissioners had only been sent there.

The inquisitor of Arragon, in 1441, was F. Michael Ferriz, and that of Valencia, F. Martin Trilles, who reconciled in their districts several Wickliffites, and condemned many others to be burnt. Several inquisitors succeeded these till 1474, when Isabella, wife of Ferdinand of Arragon, King of Sicily, ascended the throne of Castile, after the death of Henry IV. her brother. John II., King of Arragon, dying in 1479, his son, Ferdinand, united that kingdom to Sicily ; he soon after conquered the kingdom of Grenada, which belonged to the Moors, and lastly that of Navarre, which was secured to him by the capitulation of the inhabitants.

CHAPTER IV.

OF THE GOVERNMNET OF THE OLD INQUISITION.

ALTHOUGH the Popes, in establishing the Inquisition, had only proposed to punish the crime of heresy, yet the inquisitors were commissioned to pursue those Christians who were only suspected, because it was the only means of discovering those who were really guilty. There were many crimes which came under the jurisdiction of a civil judge, which the Popes considered no one could be guilty of without being tainted with a false doctrine, and although they were pursued by secular tribunals, the inquisitors were enjoined to consider the accused as suspected of heresy, and to proceed against them in order to ascertain, if they commited these crimes from the depravity natural to man, or from the idea that they were not criminal; which opinion caused a suspicion that their doctrine was erroneous. A species of blasphemy, which was called heretical, belonged to this class of crimes; it was committed against God or his saints, and shewed in the offender erroneous opinions of the omniscience or other attributes of the Deity. It rendered the blasphemer liable to be suspected of heresy, as the inquisitor might consider it a proof that his habitual thoughts were contrary to the faith.

The second species of crime which caused a suspicion of heresy, was sorcery and divination. If the offenders only made use of natural and simple means of discovering the future, such as counting the lines in the palm of the hand, they came under the jurisdiction of a civil judge; but all sorcerers were liable to be punished for heresy by the Inquisition, if they baptized a dead person, re-baptized an infant, made use of holy water, the consecrated host, the oil of extreme unction, or other things which proved contempt or abuse of the sacraments and the mysteries of religion.

The same suspicion affected those who addressed themselves to demons in their superstitious practices. A third species of crime was the invocation of demons. Nicholas Eymerick informs us that, in his office of inquisitor, he had procured and burnt, after having read them, two books which treated of that subject; they both contained an account of the power of demons, and of the mode of worshipping them. The same author adds, that in his time a great number of trials for this crime took place in Catalonia, and that many of the accused had gone so far as to worship Satan, with all the signs, ceremonies, and words of the Catholic religion.

A fourth sort of crime which caused suspicion of heresy, was, to remain a year, or longer, excommunicated without seeking absolution, or performing the penance which had been imposed. The Popes affirmed that no Catholic, irreproachable in his faith, could live with so much indifference under the censure of the church.

Schism was the sixth case where heresy was suspected; it may exist either without heresy or with it. To the first class belongs all schismatics, who admit the articles of the faith, but deny the authority of the Pope, as head of the Catholic church, and vicar of Jesus Christ. The second is composed of those who hold the same opinions as the first, and also refuse to believe in some of the articles, such as the Greeks, who hold that the Holy Ghost proceeds only from the Father, and not from the Son.

The Inquisition also proceeded against concealers, favourers, and adherents of heretics, as being suspected of professing the same opinions. The seventh class was composed of all those who opposed the Inquisition, and prevented the inquisitors from exercising their functions.

The eighth class comprehended those nobles who refused to take an oath to drive the heretics from their states. The ninth class consisted of governors of kingdoms, provinces and towns, who did not defend the church against heretics, when they were required by the Inquisition. The tenth class comprised those who refused to repeal the statutes in force in towns and cities, when they were contrary to the measures decreed by the holy office. The eleventh class of suspected persons, were all lawyers, notaries, and other persons belonging to the law, who assisted heretics by their advice, or concealed papers, records, and other writings, which might make their errors, dwellings, or stations known. In the twelfth class of suspected, were those persons who have given ecclesiastical sepulture to known heretics. Those who refused to take an oath in the trials of heretics when they were required to do it, were also liable to suspicion. The fourteenth class, were deceased persons who had been de-

nounced as heretics. The Popes, in order to render heresy
more odious, had decreed that the bodies of dead heretics
should be disinterred and burnt, their property confiscated,
and their memory pronounced infamous. The same suspicion
fell upon writings which contained heretical doctrines, or
which might lead to them. Lastly the Jews and Moors were
considered as subject to the holy office, when they engaged
Catholics to embrace their faith, either by their writings or
discourse.

Although all the persons guilty of the crimes above-
mentioned were under the jurisdiction of the holy office,
yet the Pope, his legatees, his nuncios, his officers, and familiars were exempt, and if any of these were denounced as
heretics, the inquisitor could only take the secret information
and refer it to the Pope. Bishops were also exempt, but
kings had not that privilege.

As the bishops were the ordinary inquisitors by divine
right, it seems just that they should have had the power of
receiving informations and proceeding against the apostolical
inquisitors in matters of faith, but the Pope rendered his
delegates independent, by decreeing that none but an apostolical inquisitor could proceed against another. The inquisitor and the bishop acted together, but each had the right
of pursuing heretics separately : the orders for imprisonment
could only be issued by both together, and if they did not
accord, they referred to the Pope. The inquisitors could require the assistance of secular power in the exercise of their
authority, and it could not be refused without incurring the
punishment of excommunication and suspicion of heresy.
The bishop was obliged to lend his house for the prisoners ;
besides this, the inquisitors had a particular prison to secure
the persons of the accused.

The first inquisitors had no fixed salary: the holy office
was founded on devotion and zeal for the faith ; its members
were almost all monks, who had made a vow of poverty, and

the priests who were associated in their labours, were generally canons, or provided with benefices. But when the
inquisitors began to make journeys accompanied by recorders,
alguazils, and an armed force, the Pope decreed that all their
expenses should be defrayed by the bishops, on the pretence
that the inquisitors laboured for the destruction of heresy in
their dioceses. This measure displeased the bishops, still
more as they were deprived of part of their authority. The
expenses of the Inquisition were afterwards defrayed by the
fines and confiscations of the condemned heretics: these re-
sources were the only funds of the holy office ; it never possessed any fixed revenue.

Of the Manner of Proceeding in the Tribunals of the Old Inquisition.

When a priest was appointed an inquisitor by the Pope,
or by a delegate of the holy see, he wrote to the king, who
issued a royal mandate to all the tribunals of the towns
where the inquisitor would pass to perform his office, commanding them, on pain of the most severe penalties, to arrest
all the persons whom he should mark as heretics, or suspected of heresy, and to execute the judgments passed
upon them. The same order obliged the magistrates to furnish the inquisitor and his attendants with a lodging, and to
protect them from insult and every inconvenience. When
the inquisitor arrived at the town where he intended to enter
upon his office, he officially informed the magistrate, and required his attendance, fixing the time and place.

The commander of the town presented himself before the
delegate, and took an oath to put in force all the laws
against heretics. If the officer or magistrate refused to obey,
the inquisitor excommunicated him ; if he made no difficulty,
the inquisitor appointed a day for the people to meet in the
church, when he preached, and read an edict which com-

manded that all informations should be given within a certain period. The inquisitor afterwards declared that all who should voluntarily confess themselves heretics, should receive absolution, and be subjected to a slight penance, but that those who were denounced should be proceeded against with severity.

If any accusations took place during the interval, they were registered, but did not take effect until it was known that the accused would not come voluntarily before the tribunal. After the expiration of the period allowed, the informer was summoned; he was told that there were three ways of proceeding to discover the truth, accusation, information, and inquisition, and was asked to which he gave the preference; if he chose the first, he was invited to accuse the denounced person, but at the same time to consider that he was subject to the law of retaliation, if he was found to be a calumniator. This manner of proceeding was adopted by very few persons; the greater number declared, that fear of the punishments with which the holy office menaced those who did not inform against heretics was the cause of their appearance, and they desired that their information might be kept secret, on account of the danger they incurred of being assassinated if they were known.

The inquisitor interrogated the witnesses, assisted by the recorder and two priests, who were commissioned to observe if the declarations were faithfully taken down, and to be present when they were read to the witnesses, who were then asked if they acknowledged all that was read to them. If the crime or suspicion of heresy was proved in the information, the criminal was arrested and taken to the ecclesiastical prison. After his arrest, he was examined, and his answers compared with the testimony òf the witnesses. If the accused confessed himself guilty of one heresy, it was in vain for him to assert that he was innocent of the others; he was not permitted to defend himself, because his crime was proved. He

was asked if he would abjure the heresy of which he acknowledged himself guilty.   If he consented, he was reconciled,
and the canonical penance was imposed on him with some
other punishment; if he refused, he was declared an obstinate heretic, and was delivered up to secular justice, with a
copy of his sentence.

If the accused denied the charge, and undertook to defend himself, a copy of the process was given to him, but
without the names of the accuser or the witnesses, and with
every circumstance omitted which might lead to their discovery.

The accused was asked if he had enemies, and if he knew
their motives for hating him.   He was also permitted to declare that he suspected any particular person of wishing to
ruin him.   In either case the proof was admitted, and the
inquisitor considered it in passing judgment.   The inquisitor sometimes asked the accused if he knew certain persons;
these individuals were the accusers and witnesses; if he replied in the negative, he could not afterwards challenge them
as enemies; in the course of time, every one concluded that
these persons were the accuser, and the witnesses and the
custom was abandoned.   The accused person was also permitted to appeal to the Pope, who rejected or admitted his
appeal, according to the rules of justice.   There was no
regular proceeding before the Inquisition, and the judges did
not fix a time to establish the proof of the facts.   After the
replies and defence of the accused, the inquisitor and the
bishop of the diocese, or their delegates, proceeded to pass
sentence without any other formalities.   If the accused denied the charges, although he was convicted or strongly
suspected, he was tortured to force him to confess his
crime; or if it was thought that there was no necessity for it,
the judges proceeded to pass the final sentence.

If the crime imputed to the accused was not proved, he
was acquitted, and a copy of the declaration given to him,

but the name of his accuser was not communicated. If he
had been calumniated, he was obliged to clear himself publicly by the canonical method, in the town where it had
taken place ; he afterwards abjured all heresy, and received
the absolution *ad cautelam* * for all the censures which he
had incurred. In order to proportion the punishment to
the suspicion, it was divided into three degrees, named *slight,
serious,* and *violent.*

The person who was declared to be suspected, though in
the least degree, was called upon to renounce all heresies,
and particularly that of which he was suspected. If he consented, he was reconciled, and was subjected to punishments
and penances ; if he refused, he was excommunicated, and if
he did not demand absolution, or promise to abjure after the
space of one year, he was considered as an obstinate heretic,
and proceeded against as such. If the accused was a *formal*
heretic willing to abjure, and not guilty of having relapsed,
he was reconciled with penances.

A person was considered as relapsed if he had already
been condemned, or *violently* suspected of the same errors.
The abjurations were made in the place where the inquisitor
resided, sometimes in the episcopal palace, in the convent of
Dominicans, or in the house of the inquisitor, but most generally in the churches. The Sunday before this ceremony,
the day on which it was to take place was announced in all
the churches of the town, and the inhabitants were requested
to attend the sermon, which would be preached by the inquisitor against heresy. On the appointed day the clergy
and the people assembled round a scaffold, where the person
slightly suspected stood bare-headed, that he might be seen
by every one. The mass was performed, and the inquisitor
preached against the particular heresy which was the cause
of the ceremony ; he announced that the person on the scaf-

* The *absolution ad cautelam* is that granted by inquisitors to persons
who have been suspected of heresy.

fold was *slightly suspected* of having fallen into it, and read the process to the people; he concluded by saying, that the culprit was ready to abjure. A cross and the Bible was given to the offender, who read his abjuration, and signed it, if he could write; the inquisitor then gave him absolution, and imposed upon him those penances which were thought most useful.

When the suspicion of heresy was *violent*, the *auto-da-fé* took place on a Sunday, or festival-day, and all the other churches were closed, that the concourse of people might be greater in that where the ceremony was to be performed. The offender was warned, not only to be a good Catholic for the future, but to conduct himself in such a manner as not to be accused a second time; as, if he relapsed, he would suffer capital punishment, although he might abjure and be reconciled. If the offender was suspected in the highest degree, he was treated as an heretic, and wore the habit of a penitent during the ceremony; it was composed of brown stuff, with a scapulary which had two yellow crosses fastened on it.

If the suspected person was to clear himself from calumny by the canonical method, the ceremony was also announced before it took place, and he was obliged to take an oath that he was not an heretic, and to produce twelve witnesses who had known him for the last ten years, to swear that they believed his affirmation to be true. He then abjured all heresies.

If the accused was repentant, and demanded to be reconciled after having relapsed, he was to be delivered over to secular justice, and was destined to suffer capital punishment. The inquisitors, after having passed judgment on him, engaged some priests, who were in their confidence, to inform him of his situation, and induce him to demand the sacrament of penance and the communion. When these ministers had passed two or three days with the prisoner, an *auto-*

da-fé was announced ; the sentence was read which delivered the culprit over to secular justice, and recommended the judges to treat him with humanity.

If the accused was an impenitent heretic, he was condemned, but the *auto-da-fé* was never celebrated until every means had been tried to convert him ; if he was obstinate, he was delivered up to the justice of the king, and burnt. If the unfortunate heretic had relapsed, it was in vain for him to return to the true faith ; he could not avoid death, and the only favour shewn him was, that he was first strangled, and afterwards burnt. Those who escaped from the prisons, or fled to avoid being arrested, were burnt in effigy.

The tribunal of the Inquisition being ecclesiastical, had originally only the power of inflicting spiritual punishments; but the laws of the emperors during the fourth and following centuries, and other circumstances, caused the inquisitors of the thirteenth century to assume the right of imposing punishments entirely temporal, except that of death. The sentence of the Inquisition imposed a variety of fines and personal penalties, such as entire or partial confiscation ; perpetual, or a limited period of imprisonment ; exile, or transportation; infamy, and the loss of employments, honours, and dignities. Those persons who abjured as *seriously suspected* of heresy, were condemned to be imprisoned for a certain time proportioned to the degree of suspicion. If the accused was *violently suspected*, he was condemned to perpetual imprisonment, but the inquisitor had the power of mitigating the sentence, if he judged that the prisoner repented sincerely. If the abjurer had been a *formal* heretic, he was imprisoned for life, and the inquisitor had not the power of shortening the duration of the punishment.

Among the punishments to which heretics were condemned, must be enumerated that of wearing the habit of a penitent, known in Spain under the name of *San Benito,* which is a

corruption of *saco bendito.* Its real name in Spanish was
Zamarra. The first became the common name, because the
penitential habit was called *sac* in the Jewish history.

Before the thirteenth century it was the custom to bless
the *sac* which was worn in a public penance, and hence it
derived the epithet of *bendito* (blessed). It was a close
tunic, made like the cassock of a priest, with crosses of a different colour affixed to the breast. St. Dominic and the
other inquisitors caused the *reconciled heretics* to wear these
crosses, as a protection against the Catholics who massacred
all known heretics, although they might be unarmed. The
reconciled heretics wore two crosses to distinguish them from
pure Catholics, who only wore one as crusaders.

CHAPTER V.

ESTABLISHMENT OF THE MODERN INQUISITION IN SPAIN.

THE state of the Inquisition in the kingdom of Arragon, at
the accession of Ferdinand and Isabella, has been shewn in
a preceding chapter. This tribunal was then introduced
into the kingdom of Castile, after having been reformed by
statutes and regulations so severe, that the Arragonese violently resisted the fresh burdens which were imposed on
them

It is the Inquisition which has reigned in Spain since the
year 1481, which was destroyed to the satisfaction of all
Europe, and which has since been re-established to the grief
of all enlightened Spaniards.

The war against the Albigenses was the first cause of the
establishment of the Inquisition, and the pretended necessity of punishing the apostasy of the newly-converted Spa-

nish Jews, was the reason for introducing it in a reformed state. It is important to remark, that the immense trade carried on by the Spanish Jews, had thrown into their hands the greatest part of the wealth of the Peninsula, and that they had acquired great power and influence in Castile under Alphonso IX., Peter I., and Henry II.; and in Arragon under Peter IV. and John I. The Christians, who could not rival them in industry, had almost all become their debtors, and envy soon made them the enemies of their creditors. This disposition was fostered by evil-minded men, and popular commotions were the consequence in almost all the towns of the two kingdoms. In 1391, five thousand Jews were sacrificed to the fury of the people in different towns. Several were known to have escaped death by becoming Christians; many others sought to save themselves in following their example, and in a short time more than a million persons renounced the law of Moses to embrace the faith of Jesus Christ. The number of conversions increased considerably during the ten first years of the fifteenth century, through the zeal of St. Vincent, Ferrier, and several other missionaries; they were seconded by the famous conferences which took place in 1413 between several Rabbis and the converted Jew, Jerome de Santafé. The converted Jews were named *New Christians;* they were also called Marranos, or the cursed race, from an oath which the Jews were in the habit of using among, themselves. As the fear of death was the cause of most of these conversions, many repented, and secretly returned to Judaism, though they outwardly conformed to Christianity. The constraint to which they were obliged to submit was sometimes too painful, and several were discovered. This was the ostensible reason for the establishment of a tribunal which gave Ferdinand an opportunity of confiscating immense riches, and which Sextus IV. could not but approve, as it tended to augment the credit of the maxims of the court of Rome;

it is to these projects, concealed under the appearance of zeal for religion, that the Inquisition of Spain owes its origin.

In 1477, Philip de Barbaris, inquisitor of the kingdom of Sicily, went to Seville to obtain from Ferdinand and Isabella the confirmation of a privilege granted in 1233, by the Emperor Frederic, which gave to the Inquisition of Sicily, the right of seizing a third part of the property of condemned heretics. Barbaris, through zeal for the interests of the Pope, endeavoured to persuade the king that the Christian religion derived the greatest advantages from the fear which the judgments of the Inquisition inspired. He was eagerly seconded by Alphonso de Hojida, prior of the convent of Dominicans at Seville ; and Nicholas Franco, the nuncio of the Pope at the court of Spain. A report was then spread in different parts of the kingdom that the *New Christians*, with the unbaptized Jews, insulted the images of Jesus Christ, and had even crucified Christian children in mockery of his sufferings on the cross. Ferdinand was willing to receive the Inquisition into his states: the only obstacle was the refusal of Isabella; that excellent queen could not approve of measures so contrary to the gentleness of her character, but her consent was obtained by alarming her conscience ; she was told that it became a religious duty to adopt them in the present circumstances.

Isabella suffered herself to be led away by the representations of her council, and commissioned her ambassador at Rome, Don Francis de Santillan, Bishop of Osma, to solicit in her name a bull for the establishment of the Inquisition in Castile, which was granted in 1478. It authorized Ferdinand and Isabella to name the priests who were to be commissioned to discover in their states all heretics, apostates, and favourers of these crimes. As this measure was displeasing to Isabella, her council, by her order, suspended the execution of the bull until less severe remedies had been tried.

The queen commissioned D. Diego Alphonso de Solis, Bishop of Cadiz, Diego de Merlo, and Alphonso de Hojida, prior of a convent of Dominicans, to observe the effects produced by gentle means, and give a faithful account of them. Their reports were such as might be expected from the situation of affairs; and the Dominican fathers, the nuncio, and even the king, desired that the measures preferred by Isabella should be declared insufficient.

The events of this year proved how displeasing the institution was to the Castilians. In the beginning of the year 1480 the Cortes assembled at Toledo. It was occupied in providing means to prevent the evil which the communication of the Jews with Christians might produce : the ancient regulations were renewed ; and among others, those which obliged unbaptized Jews to wear some distinguishing mark, and to inhabit separate quarters, to which they were compelled to retire before night: they were also prohibited from exercising the professions of physicians, surgeons, merchants, barbers, and innkeepers; yet the Cortes had no intention either of approving or demanding that the Inquisition should be established in the kingdom.

The consent of the queen was obtained, and while the two sovereigns were at Medina del Campo on the 17th of November, 1480, they named as the first inquisitors Michael Morillo and John de San Martin, both Dominicans, as adviser and assessor of these two monks, Doctor John Ruiz de Medina, a counsellor of the queen's ; and as (procurator-fiscal) attorney, John Lopez del Barco, the queen's chaplain.

On the 9th of October an order was sent by the king and queen to all the governors of provinces to furnish the inquisitors and their suite with everything they might require in their journey to Seville; an extraordinary circumstance in that time, and which proves the influence which the Dominicans had already acquired. Their privileges were the same as those granted in 1223 by the Emperor

Frederic. The Castilians were so far from being pleased at the introduction of the Inquisition, that the inquisitors, on their arrival at Seville, found it impossible to collect the small number of persons necessary to the performance of their functions, although they shewed their commission ; and the Council of Spain was obliged to issue another order, that the prefect and others authorities of Seville, and the diocese of Cadiz, should assist the inquisitors in their installation ; this order was also interpreted in such a manner that it was only executed in those towns which belonged to the queen. The *New Christians* then immediately emigrated into the states of the Duke de Medina Sidonia, the Marquis of Cadiz, the Count D'Arcos, and other nobles ; and the new tribunal declared that their heresy was proved by their emigration.

The inquisitors established their tribunal in the Dominican convent of St. Paul at Seville, and on the 2nd of January, 1481, they issued their first edict, which commanded the Marquis of Cadiz, the Count D'Arcos, and all grandees of Spain, to seize the persons of the emigrants within fifteen days; and to send them under an escort to Seville, and seques- trate their property, on pain of excommunication, besides the other punishments to which they would be liable as favourers of heresy. The number of prisoners was soon so considerable, that the convent assigned to the inquisitors was not sufficiently large to contain them, and the tribunal was removed to the Castle de Triana, situated near Seville.

The inquisitors soon published a second edict, named the Edict of Grace, to engage those who had apostatized to sur- render themselves voluntarily : it promised that if they came with true repentance, their property should not be confis- cated, and they should receive absolution; but if, on the contrary, they suffered the time of *grace* to elapse, or were denounced by others, they would be prosecuted with all the severity of the tribunal.   Several suffered themselves to be persuaded, but the inquisitors only granted them absolution when they had declared upon oath the names, condition, and place of dwelling, of all the apostates whom they knew or had heard spoken of.   They were also obliged to keep these revelations secret, and by these means a great number of *New Christians* fell into the hands of the inquisitors.   When the period of grace was passed, a new edict was published, which commanded all persons to denounce those who had embraced the Judaic heresy, on pain of mortal sin and excommunication.   The consequence of this edict was, that an heretic was only informed that he was accused, at the moment when he was arrested and dragged to the dungeons of the Inquisition.

The same fate awaited the *converted* Jew, who might have acquired certain habits in his infancy, which, though not contrary to Christianity, might be represented as certain signs of apostasy.   The inquisitors mentioned in their edict several cases where accusation was commanded.   The following cases are so equivocal, that altogether they would scarcely form a simple presumption in the present time.   A convert was considered as relapsed into heresy, if he kept the sabbath out of respect to the law which he had abandoned; this was sufficiently proved if he wore better linen and garments on that day than those which he commonly used, or had not a fire in his house from the preceding evening; if he took the suet and fat from the animals which were intended for his food, and washed the blood from it; if he examined the blade of the knife before he killed the animals, and covered the blood with earth; if he blessed the table after the manner of the Jews; if he has drunk of the wine named caser, (a word derived from caxer, which means *lawful*,) and which is prepared by Jews; if he pronounces the bahara or benediction when he takes the vessel of wine into his hands, and pronounces certain words before he gives it to another person; if he eats of an animal killed by Jews; if he has recited the

Psalms of David without repeating the Gloria Patri at the
end; if he gives his son a Hebrew name chosen among those
used by the Jews; if he plunges him seven days after his
birth into a basin containing water, gold, silver, seed-pearl,
wheat, barley, and other substances, pronouncing at the
same time certain words, according to the custom of the
Jews; if he draws the horoscope of his children at their
birth; if he performs the ruaya, a ceremony which consists
in inviting his relations and friends to a repast the day before
he undertakes a journey; if he turned his face to the wall
at the time of his death, or has been placed in that posture
before he expired; if he has washed, or caused to be washed,
in hot water the body of a dead person, and interred him in
a new shroud, with hose, shirt, and a mantle, and placed
a piece of money in his mouth; if he has uttered a discourse
in praise of the dead, or recited melancholy verses; if he has
emptied the pitchers and other vessels of water in the house
of the dead person, or in those of his neighbours, according to
the custom of the Jews; if he sits behind the door of the deceased as a sign of grief, or eats fish and olives instead of
meat, to honour his memory; if he remains in his house one
year after the death of any one, to prove his grief. All these
articles shew the artifice used by the inquisitors in order to
prove to Isabella that a great number of Judaic heretics existed in the dioceses of Cadiz and Seville. These measures,
so well adapted to multiply victims, could not fail in their
effect, and the tribunal soon began its cruel executions. On
the 6th of January, 1481, six persons were burnt, seventeen
on the 26th of March following, and a still greater number
a month after; on the 4th of November, the same year,
two hundred and ninety-eight *New Christians* had suffered
the punishment of burning, and seventy-nine were condemned to the horrors of perpetual imprisonment in the
town of Seville alone. In other parts of the province and
in the diocese of Cadiz, two thousand of these unfortunate

creatures were burnt; according to Mariana, a still greater number were burnt in effigy, and one thousand seven hundred suffered different canonical punishments.

The great number of persons condemned to be burnt, obliged the prefect of Seville to construct a scaffold of stone in a field near the town, name Tablada; it was called Quemadero, and still exists. Four statues, of plaster, were erected on it, and bore the name of the *Four Prophets;* the condemned persons were enclosed alive in these figures, and perished by a slow and horrible death*.

The dread which these executions inspired in the *New Christians* caused a great number to emigrate to France, Portugal, and even to Africa. Many of those who had been condemned for contumacy had fled to Rome, and demanded justice of the Pope against their judges. The sovereign pontiff wrote on the 29th of January to Ferdinand and Isabella, and complained that the inquisitors did not follow the rule of right in declaring those to be heretics who were not guilty. His Holiness added that he would have pronounced their deprivation, but from respect to the royal decree which had instituted them in their office, but he revoked the authorization which he had given. On the 11th of the following month the Pope despatched a new brief, in which, without mentioning the first, he says, the general of the Dominicans, Alphonso de St. Cebriant, having proved to him the necessity of increasing the number of inquisitors, he had appointed to that office Alphonso de St. Cebriant, and seven monks of his order. It was at this time that Queen Isabella requested the Pope to give the Inquisition a permanent form which should be satisfactory to all parties; she required that the

---

* Since the publication of this work, the Author has been informed that the convicts were only fastened to the statues of the *Four Prophets,* and not enclosed in them. Andrew Bernaldez, a contemporary writer, and eye-witness of the executions, from whom this fact was taken, is not sufficiently explicit to remove all doubt.

judgments passed in Spain should be definitive and without appeal to Rome, and complained at the same time that many persons accused her of being influenced in all that she did for the tribunal by a desire to seize the wealth of the condemned.

When Sixtus IV. received this letter, he had just learnt that his bulls had met with some resistance in Sicily from the viceroy and other magistrates, and artfully took advantage of Isabella's request, to confirm his authority in that kingdom.   He replied to the queen, and praised her zeal for the Inquisition, appeased her scruples of conscience in regard to the confiscations, and assured her that he would have complied with all her demands, if the cardinals, and those charged with the administration of affairs, had not found insurmountable difficulties in so doing.   He exhorted her to maintain the Inquisition in her states, and above all to take proper measures that the apostolical bulls should be received and executed in Sicily.

The councillors, to whom the Pope had submitted the demands of Isabella, approved of the creation of an apostolical judge of appeal in Spain; and proposed at the same time that no person descended from the Jews, either by the male or female side, should be admitted among the inquisitorial judges.   Don Inigo Manriquez was named sole judge of appeals in all matters of faith.

CHAPTER VI.

CREATION OF A GRAND INQUISITOR-GENERAL ; OF A ROYAL
COUNCIL OF THE INQUISITION ; OF SUBALTERN TRIBU
NALS AND ORGANIC LAWS : ESTABLISHMENT OF THE HOLY
OFFICE IN ARRAGON.

IN 1483, Father Thomas de Torquemada was appointed
inquisitor-general of Arragon, and the immense powers of
his office were confirmed in 1486, by Innocent VIII. and by
the two successors of that pontiff. It would have been impossible to find a man more proper to fulfil the intentions of
Ferdinand in multiplying the number of confiscations than
Torquemada ; he first created four inferior tribunals at
Seville, Cordova, Jaen, and Villa-Real, (now Ciudad-Real,)
the latter was soon after transferred to Toledo ; he then
permitted the Dominican fathers to exercise their functions
in the kingdom of Castile: these monks, who held their commission from the holy see, did not submit to the authority
of Torquemada without some resistance ; they declared that
they were not his delegates. Torquemada did not pronounce
their deposition, as he feared it would injure the execution
of the enterprise which he was commencing, but prepared
to form laws which he found very necessary. He chose as
assistants and councillors, two Civilians, named John Guiterrez de Chables, and Tristan de Medina. At this time Ferdinand, perceiving how important it was to the interest of
the revenue to organize the tribunal, created a royal council
of the Inquisition, and appointed Torquemada president, and
as councillors, Don Alphonso Carillo, Bishop of Mazara in
Sicily, Sancho Velasquez de Cuellar and Bonce de Valencia,
both doctors of law. Torquemada commissioned his two
assistants to arrange the laws for the new council, and convoked a junta, which was composed of the inquisitors of the
four tribunals which he had established, the two assistants,

and the members of the royal council. This assembly was held at Seville, and published the first laws of the Spanish tribunal under the name of instructions in 1484. These instructions were divided into twenty-eight articles.

The 1st article regulated the manner in which the establishment of the Inquisition should be announced in the country where it was to be introduced.

The 2nd article commanded, that an edict should be published, accompanied with censures against those who did not accuse themselves voluntarily during the term of grace.

By the 3rd a delay of thirty days was appointed for heretics to declare themselves.

The 4th regulated that all voluntary confessions should be written in the presence of the inquisitors and a recorder.

The 5th, that absolution should not be given secretly to any individual voluntarily confessing, unless no person was acquainted with his crime.

The 6th ordained, that part of the penance of a *reconciled heretic* should consist in being deprived of all honourable employments, and of the use of gold, silver, pearls, silk, and fine wool.

By the 7th article, pecuniary penalties were imposed on all who made a voluntary confession.

By the 8th, the person who accused himself after the term of grace could not be exempted from the punishment of confiscation.

The 9th article decreed, that if persons under twenty years of age accuse themselves after the term of grace, and it is proved that they were drawn into error by their parents, a slight punishment shall be inflicted.

The 10th obliged the inquisitors to declare, in their act of reconciliation, the exact time when the offender fell into heresy, that the portion of property to be confiscated might be ascertained.

The 11th article decreed, that if a heretic, detained in

the prisons of the holy office, demanded absolution, and appeared to feel true repentance, that it might be granted to him, imposing, at the same time, perpetual imprisonment.

By the 12th, if the inquisitors thought the repentance of the prisoner was pretended, in the case indicated by the former article, they were permitted to refuse the absolution, to declare him a false penitent, and as such condemn him to be burnt.

By the 13th, if a man, absolved after his confession, should boast of having concealed several crimes, or if information should be obtained that he had committed more than he had confessed, he was to be arrested and judged as a false penitent.

By the 14th article, the accused was to be condemned as impenitent, if he persisted in his denials even after the publication of the testimony.

By the 15th, if a semi-proof existed against a person who denied his crime, he was to be put to the torture; if he confessed his crime during the torture, and afterwards confirmed his confession, he was punished as convicted; if he retracted he was tortured again, or condemned to an extraordinary punishment.

The 16th article prohibited the communication of the entire deposition of the witnesses to the accused.

The 17th article obliged the inquisitors to interrogate the witnesses themselves, if it was not impossible.

The 18th article decrees, that one or two inquisitors should be present when the prisoner was tortured, or appoint a commissioner if they were occupied elsewhere, to receive his declarations.

By the 19th article, if the accused did not appear when summoned, according to the prescribed form, he was condemned as an heretic.

The 20th article decrees, that if it is proved that any person died an heretic, by his writings or conduct, that he shall be judged and condemned as such, his body disinterred and burnt, and his property confiscated.

By the 21st, the inquisitors were commanded to extend their jurisdiction over the vassals of nobles; if they refused to permit it, they were to be censured.

The 22nd decreed, that if a man, burnt as an heretic, left children under age, a portion of their father's property should be granted to them under the title of alms, and the inquisitors shall be obliged to confide their education to proper persons.

By the 23rd, if an heretic, reconciled during the term of grace, without having incurred the punishment of confiscation, possessed property belonging to a condemned person, this property was not to be included in the pardon.

The 24th obliged the reconciled to give his Christian slaves their liberty, when his property was not confiscated, if the king granted the pardon on that condition.

The 25th prohibited the inquisitors, and other persons attached to the tribunal, from receiving presents, on pain of excommunication, deprivation of their employments, restitution, and a penalty of twice the value of the gifts received.

The 26th recommends to the officers of the Inquisition to live in peace together.

The 27th commands that they shall carefully watch the conduct of their inferior officers.

The 28th and last, commits to the prudence of the inquitors the discussion of all points not mentioned in the foregoing articles.

Ferdinand having convoked at Tarazona the Cortes of his kingdom of Arragon, decreed that the Inquisition should be reformed in a privy council. After this resolution, Torquemada named Gaspard Juglar, a dominican, and Peter Arbuès d'Epila, as inquisitors for the archbishopric of Saragossa. A royal ordinance commanded all the authorities to aid and assist them in their office, and the magistrate known by the name of Chief Justice of Arragon, took the oath with

several others. This circumstance did not prevent the resistance which the Arragonese opposed to the tribunal; on
the contrary it augmented, and rose to such a height, that it
might have been termed national.

The principal persons employed in the Court of Arragon
were descended from *New Christians;* among these were
Louis Gonzalez, the royal secretary for the affairs of the
kingdom; Philip de Clemente, prothonotary; Alphonso de
la Caballeria, vice-chancellor; and Gabriel Sanchez, grand
treasurer, who were all descended from Jews condemned, in
their time, by the Inquisition. These men, and many others
employed in the court, had allied themselves to the principal
grandees in the kingdom, and used the influence which they
derived from this circumstance, to engage the representatives
of the nation to appeal to the Pope and the king, against
the inquisitorial code. Commissioners were sent to Rome
and the Court of Spain, to demand the suspension of the articles relating to confiscation, as contrary to the laws of the
kingdom of Arragon. They were persuaded that the Inquisition would not maintain itself if this measure was abandoned. While the deputies of the Cortes of Arragon were
at Rome, and with the king, the inquisitors condemned several *New Christians* as Judaic heretics. These executions increased the irritation of the Arragonese; and when the deputies wrote from the Court of Spain, that they were not
satisfied with the state of affairs, they resolved to sacrifice
one or two of the inquisitors, with the hope that no one
would dare to take the office, and that the king would renounce his design. The project of assassination having been
approved by the conspirators, a voluntary contribution was
raised among all the Arragonese of the Jewish race; and it
was proved by the trials of Sancho de Paternoy and others,
that Don Blasco d'Alagon received ten thousand reals,
which were destined to reward the assassins of the Inquisitor
Arbuès. John de la Abadia, a noble of Arragon, but de-

scended from Jewish ancestors on the female side, took upon himself the direction of the enterprise. The assassination was confided to John d'Esperaindeo, to Vidal d'Uranso, his servant, to Matthew Ram, Tristande de Leonis, Anthony Gran, and Bernard Leofante. They failed several times in their attempts, as Peter Arbues, being informed of their design, took the necessary precautions to secure his life.

It appears, from the examination of some of the murderers, that the inquisitor wore a coat of mail under his vest, and a kind of helmet covered with a cap. He was at last assassinated in the metropolitan church during the performance of the matins, on the 15th of November, 1485. Vidal d'Uranso wounded him so severely in the back of the neck, that he died two days after. The next day the murder was known in the town, but its effects were different from what had been expected, for all the *Old Christians*, or those who were not of Jewish origin, persuaded that the *New Christians* had committed the crime, assembled to pursue them and revenge the death of the inquisitor. The disturbance was violent, and its consequences would have been terrible, if the young archbishop, Don Alphonso of Arragon, had not shewn himself, and assured the multitude that the criminal should be punished. Policy inspired Ferdinand and Isabella with the idea of honouring the memory of Arbuès with a solemnity which contributed to make him pass for a saint, and caused a particular worship to be addressed to him. This took place long after, when Pope Alexander VII. had beatified him as a martyr, in 1664. A magnificent monument was erected to his memory, by Ferdinand and Isabella. While the sovereigns were occupied in honouring the remains of Peter Arbuès, the inquisitors of Saragossa were labouring without ceasing to discover the authors and accomplices of his murder, and to punish them as Judaic heretics and enemies to the holy office. It would be difficult to enumerate the number of families plunged into misery through their vengeance; two hundred victims were soon sacrificed. Vidal d'Uranso, one of the assassins, revealed all he knew of the conspiracy, which was the cause of the discovery of its authors. There was scarcely a single family in the three first orders of nobility, which was not disgraced by having at least one of its members in the *auto-da-fé*, wearing the habit of a penitent.

Don James Diaz d'Aux Armendarix, lord of the town of Cadreita, a knight of Navarre, and ancestor of the Dukes of Albuquerque, was condemned to a public penance, for having concealed in his house, for one night, several persons who fled from Saragossa. The same punishment was inflicted on several other illustrious knights of the town of Tudela in Navarre, for having received and concealed other fugitives. Don James de Navarre (the son of Eleanor, Queen of Navarre, and Gaston de Foix) was imprisoned in the dungeons of the Inquisition, and was subjected to a public penance for having assisted several of the conspirators in their flight. The inquisitors knew, when they had the audacity to imprison him, that he was not beloved by Ferdinand, who always feared him, although he was not legitimate.

Don Lope Ximenez de Urrea, first count of Aranda; Don Louis Gonzalez, secretary to the king; Don Alphonso de la Caballeria, vice-chancellor of the kingdom; and many other persons of equal rank, were condemned to the same punishment. John de Esperaindeo and the other assassins of Arbuès, were hung, after having their hands cut off. Their bodies were quartered, and their limbs exposed in the highways. John de l'Abadia killed himself in prison the day before the execution, but his corpse was treated in the same manner as the others. The hands of Vidal d'Uranso were not cut off until he had expired, because he had been promised his pardon if he discovered the conspirators.

All the other provinces of Arragon made an equal resistance to the introduction of the new Inquisition. The sedi-

tions at Teruel were only quelled in 1485, by extreme severity. The town and bishopric of Lerida, and other towns
in Catalonia, obstinately resisted the establishment of the
reform, and were not reduced to obedience until 1487. Barcelona refused to acknowledge Torquemada or any of his
delegates, on account of a privilege which it possessed of
having an inquisitor with a special title. The king applied
to the Pope, who instituted Torquemada special inquisitor
of the town and bishopric of Barcelona, with the power of
appointing others to the office. The king was obliged to
employ the same method with the inhabitants of Majorca
and those of Sardinia, who did not receive the Inquisition
until 1490 and 1492. It is an incontestable fact in the history of the Spanish Inquisition, that it was introduced entirely against the consent of the provinces, and only by the
influence of the Dominican monks.

CHAPTER VII.

ADDITIONAL ACTS TO THE FIRST CONSTITUTION OF THE HOLY OFFICE; CONSEQUENCES OF THEM, AND APPEALS TO ROME AGAINST THEM.

THE inquisitor-general judged it necessary to augment the
laws of the holy office ; and added eleven new articles to
them: the substance of them is as follows :—

1st. That each inferior tribunal should consist of two inquisitors as civilians, an attorney, an alguazil, a recorder and
other persons, if necessary, who were to receive a fixed
salary. The same article prohibits the admission of the servants or creatures of the inquisitors into the tribunal.

2nd. That if any of the persons employed should receive
presents from the accused or his family, he should be immediately deprived of his office.

3rd. That the holy office should employ an able civilian at Rome, under the title of agent, and that this expense should be supported by the money arising from the confiscations.

4th. That the contracts signed before the year 1479, by persons whose property had since been seized, should be regarded as valid; but if it was proved that any deception had been used in the transactions, that the culprits should be punished by an hundred strokes of a whip, and branded on the face with a red hot iron.

5th. That the nobles who should receive fugitives in their estates, should be compelled to deliver up to government the property committed to their care; and if they claimed the fulfilments of contracts signed by the accused for their profit, that the attorney should commence an action to reclaim the property as belonging to the revenue.

6th. That the notaries of the Inquisition should keep an account of the property of the condemned persons.

7th. That the stewards of the holy office could sell the confiscated property, and receive the rents of the estates which might be let.

8th. That each steward should inspect the property belonging to his tribunal.

9th. That a steward could not sequestrate the property of a condemned person, without an order from the Inquisition, and even in that case, that he should be accompanied by an alguazil, and place the effects and an inventory of them in the hands of a third person.

10th. That the steward should pay the salaries of the inquisitors quarterly, that they might not be obliged to receive presents.

11th. That in all circumstances not foreseen in the new regulations, the inquisitors should conduct themselves with prudence, and apply to the government in all difficult cases.

The nature of these articles proves that the number of confiscations had been considerable. Ferdinand and Isabella often gave the property of the condemned persons to their wives and children, granted them pensions on the property, or a certain sum to be paid by the receiver-general.

These sums, and the care which people took to conceal their effects, diminished the funds of the Inquisition; besides which, most of the *New Christians* were merchants or artisans, and it often happened that the receivers who paid the royal gifts were unable to pay the salaries of the inquisitors. Torquemada, in 1488, decreed that the royal gifts should not be paid, until the salaries and other expenses of the Inquisition had been defrayed, and wrote to request the approbation of Ferdinand, who refused it. The inquisitor-general was then obliged to permit the inquisitors to impose pecuniary penalties on reconciled persons (which permission was afterwards revoked.) As experience shewed that the revenue of the Inquisition was never sufficient, on account of the great number of prisoners which it was obliged to maintain, and the expenses incurred by the agent at Rome, Ferdinand and Isabella requested the Pope to place at the disposal of the holy office, a prebendary in each cathedral in their dominions; to which he consented in 1501. The receivers finding themselves unable to defray the expenses of the administration, demanded restitution of many persons whom they accused of retaining estates belonging to the Inquisition. This conduct caused so many complaints, that the council of the Inquisition was obliged to prohibit the receivers from molesting the proprietors of estates which had been sold before the year 1479. It is not surprising that the receivers should employ such measures to augment the revenue, when the inquisitors contributed to impoverish it themselves, by disposing of it according to their caprices, and without the permission of the sovereigns. This abuse rose to such a height, that Ferdinand and Isabella complained to the Pope, who prohibited the inquisitors from disposing of their revenues without an order from the king, on pain of excommunication.   The inquisitors were afterwardsobliged to refund the sums which they had seized.

In 1488 the inquisitor-general formed, with the assistance of the supreme council, a new ordinance, which consisted of fifteen articles.

The 1st decreed that the regulations of 1484 should be followed in all things, except in regard to the confiscations, which were to be regulated by the rules of equity.

The 2nd enjoins the inquisitors to proceed in a uniform manner, on account of the abuses produced by a contrary system.

The 3rd prohibits inquisitors from delaying to pass sentence, on the pretence of waiting for the full proof of the crime.

The 4th imports, that as there are not in all the tribunals civilians of sufficient ability to be consulted in the preparation of the definitive sentences, the inquisitors shall send the writings of the trials to the inquisitor-general, in order to be examined by the civilians of the supreme council.

The 5th decrees that no person shall be allowed to hold any communication with the prisoners, except the priests, who were obliged to visit the prisons once in a fortnight.

The 6th commands that the testimony of witnesses shall be received in the presence of as small a number of persons as possible, that secrecy may not be violated.

The 7th, that the writings and papers belonging to the Inquisition shall be kept in the place of residence of the inquisitors, and locked up in a chest; the key of which shall be kept by the notary of the tribunal, who must not give it up on pain of losing his place.

The 8th article decrees, that if the inquisitors of a district arrest a man already pursued by another tribunal, all the papers relating to his trial shall be placed in the hands of the first.

The 9th article decrees, that if there are papers in the archives of a tribunal which may be of use to another, the expenses incurred in sending them shall be paid by it.

The 10th article declares, that as there are not prisons enough for all who are condemned to perpetual imprisonment, they shall be permitted to remain in their houses, but not to go out on pain of being punished with the utmost severity.

In the 11th, the inquisitors are recommended to execute rigorously all those laws which prohibit the children and grandchildren of condemned persons from exercising any honourable employment, and from wearing any garment of silk, or fine wool, or any ornament of gold, silver, or precious stones.

The 12th article decrees, that males cannot be admitted to reconciliation and abjuration before the age of fourteen years, or females before that of twelve ; if they had abjured before that age, a ratification was necessary.

The 13th prohibited the receivers from paying the royal gifts, until the expenses of the Inquisition were defrayed.

The 14th declares, that the holy office should petition the sovereigns to build a prison in each town where it was established, for the reception of those who might be condemned to that punishment.   It also recommends that the cells should be arranged in such a manner, that the prisoners might exercise their respective professions, and thus maintain themselves.

The 15th and last article obliged the notaries, fiscals, and alguazils, and other officers of the Inquisition, to perform their functions in person.

The inquisitor-general found that these regulations were not sufficient to prevent abuses ; he therefore convoked a junta of inquisitors at Toledo.   The decrees of this assembly were published at Avila in 1498, and were as follows :—

First, that each tribunal should be composed of two inquisitors, one a civilian, the other a theologian.   They were prohibited from inflicting imprisonment or torture, or communicating the charges made by the witnesses, without the consent of both.

Secondly, that the inquisitors should not allow their dependents to carry any defensive arms, except where their office obliges them to do so.

Thirdly, that no person should be imprisoned if his crime had not been sufficiently proved; and that when the arrest had taken place, his judgment should be immediately pronounced without waiting for fresh proofs.

Fourthly, that the Inquisition should acquit deceased persons, if sufficient proof was not produced, and not delay the trial to wait for fresh accusations, as it was injurious to the children, whose establishmemt was prevented, from the uncertainty of the result of the trial.

Fifthly, that the entire failure of the funds of the holy office should not occasion the imposition of a greater number of pecuniary penalties.

Sixthly, that the inquisitors should not change imprisonment, or any other corporeal punishment to a pecuniary penalty, but for the punishment of fasting, alms, pilgrimages, or other similar penances.

Seventhly, that the inquisitors should carefully examine into the expediency of admitting to reconciliation those who confessed their crimes after their arrest, since they might be considered as contumacious, as the Inquisition had been established many years.

Eighthly, that the inquisitors should punish false witnesses publicly.

Ninthly, that two men related in any degree should not be employed in the holy office, nor a master and his servant, even in case their functions should be entirely distinct.

Tenthly, that each tribunal should have archives secured by three locks, the keys of which should be placed in the hands of the two notaries and the fiscal.

Eleventhly, that the notary should receive the testimony of witnesses only in the presence of an inquisitor, and that the two priests commissioned to prove the truth of the deposition should not belong to the tribunal.

Twelfthly, that the inquisitor should establish the Inquisition in all towns where it did not already exist.

Thirteenthly, that in all difficult cases the inquisitors should consult the council.

Fourteenthly, that the women should have a prison separated from that of the men.

Fifteenthly, that the officers of the tribunal should perform their functions six hours in a day, and that they should attend the inquisitors whenever they were required.

Sixteenthly, that after the inquisitors had received the oath of the witnesses in presence of the fiscal, he should be obliged to retire.

Besides these ordinances, Torquemada established several particular regulations for each individual belonging to the tribunal : all the persons employed were obliged to take an oath that they would not reveal anything they might see or hear : the inquisitor was not allowed to remain alone with the prisoner ; the gaoler could not allow any person to speak with him, and was obliged to examine if any writings were concealed in the food which was given him. These were the last regulations framed by Torquemada, but Diego Deza, his successor, published a fifth *instruction* at Seville, in 1500.

Such were the laws of the holy office in Spain. This code caused the emigration of more than a hundred thousand families useful to the state, and the loss of many millions of francs which were spent at the court of Rome, either for the bulls which it expedited, or by those who repaired thither to solicit their absolution from the Popes. The holy see was far from complaining of this practice, as it brought immense sums to the treasury, and no person who presented himself with his money before the apostolical penitentiary, failed of obtaining the absolution he solicited, or an order for absolution elsewhere.

This conduct displeased the inquisitors: depending on the protection of Ferdinand and Isabella, they expostulated with the Pope, who annulled the absolutions already granted, thus deceiving those who had spent the greatest part of their fortunes in endeavouring to obtain them. He then promised new pardons on new conditions, contrary to the engagement he had entered into with Ferdinand, to abolish every means of appeal to the Court of Rome. Such was the constant practice of the holy see during thirty years after the establishment of the Inquisition in Spain.

CHAPTER VIII.

EXPULSION OF THE JEWS.—PROCEEDINGS AGAINST BISHOPS.—DEATH OF TORQUEMADA.

In 1492 Ferdinand and Isabella conquered the kingdom of Grenada. This event offered a multitude of victims to the holy office in the persons of the Moors, who were converted merely in the hope of obtaining consideration, and after their baptism returned to Mahometanism. John de Navagiero, in his travels in Spain, states, that Ferdinand had promised the Morescoes, (as those Moors were called who became Christians,) that the Inquisition should not interfere with them for the space of forty years, but that the Inquisition was established in the kingdom of Grenada, on the pretence that many Jews had taken refuge there. This statement is not exact; the sovereigns only promised that the Moorish Christians should not be prosecuted except for serious crimes, and the Inquisition was not introduced among them before 1526,

It was in the year 1492 that the unbaptized Jews were expelled from Spain.   They were accused of persuading those of their nation who had become Christians to apostatize, and of crucifying children on Good-Friday in mockery of the Saviour of the world, and of many other offences of the same nature.   The Jewish physicians, surgeons, and apothecaries, were also accused of having taken advantage of their professions, to cause the death of a great number of Christians, and among others, that of Henry III., which was attributed to his physician, D. Maïr.

The Jews, in order to avert the danger which threatened them, offered to supply Ferdinand with thirty thousand pieces of silver to carry on the war against Grenada ; they promised to live peaceably, to comply with the regulations formed for them, in retiring to their houses in the quarters assigned to them before night, and in renouncing all professions which were reserved for the Christians.   Ferdinand and Isabella were willing to listen to these propositions ; but Torquemada being informed of their inclinations, had the boldness to appear before them with a crucifix in his hand, and to address them in these words :—

" Judas sold his master for thirty pieces of silver, your highnesses are about to do the same for thirty thousand ; behold him, take him, and hasten to sell him."

The fanaticism of the Dominican wrought a sudden change in the minds of the sovereigns, and they issued a decree on the 31st of March 1492, by which all the Jews were compelled to quit Spain before the 31st of July ensuing, on pain of death, and the confiscation of their property ; the decree also prohibited Christians from receiving them into their houses after that period.   They were permitted to sell their stock, to carry away their furniture and other effects, *except gold and silver, for which they were to accept letters of change, or any merchandise not prohibited.*

Torquemada commissioned all preachers to exhort them

to receive baptism, and remain in the kingdom. A small
number suffered themselves to be persuaded ; the rest sold
their goods at so low a price, that Andrew Bernaldez (a contemporary historian) declares, in his history of the Catholic
Kings, that he saw *the Jews give a house for an ass, and a
vineyard for a small quantity of cloth or linen.*

According to Mariana, eight hundred thousand Jews
quitted Spain, and if the Moors, who emigrated to Africa,
and the Christians who settled in the New World, are added
to the number, we shall find that Ferdinand and Isabella
lost, through these cruel measures, two millions of subjects.
Bernaldez affirms, that the Jews carried a quantity of gold
with them, concealed in their garments and saddles, and even
in their intestines, for they reduced the ducats into small
pieces, and swallowed them. A great number afterwards
returned to Spain, and received baptism. Some returned
from the kingdom of Fez, where the Moors had seized their
money and effects, and even killed the women, to take the
gold which they expected to find within them. These cruelties can only be attributed to the fanaticism of Torquemada,
to the avarice and superstition of Ferdinand, and to the inconsiderate zeal of Isabella, who, nevertheless, possessed
great gentleness of character, and an enlightened mind.

The other European courts were not thus influenced by
fanaticism, and paid no attention to a bull of Innocent VIII.,
which commanded all governments to arrest, at the desire of
Torquemada, the fugitives whom he should designate, on
pain of excommunication ; the monarch was the only person
exempted from the penalty.

The insolent fanatic, Torquemada, while he affected
to refuse the honour of episcopacy through modesty, was
the first who gave the fatal example of subjecting bishops to
trial. Not satisfied with having obtained from Sixtus IV.
the briefs which prohibited bishops of Jewish origin from
interfering in the affairs of the Inquisition, he even wished to

put two on their trial, namely, Don Juan Arias Davila, Bishop of Segovia; and Don Pedro de Aranda, Bishop of Calahorra. He made his resolution known to the Pope, who informed him that his predecessor, Boniface VIII., had prohibited the Inquisition from proceeding against bishops, archbishops, or cardinals, without an apostolical commission; but if any prelate was accused of heresy, he charged Torquemada to send him a copy of the informations, that he might decide on the method to be pursued.

Torquemada immediately began to take secret informations of the conduct of the bishops, and the Pope sent Antonio Palavicini, Bishop of Tournai, to Spain, with the title of apostolical nuncio, when he received the informations of Torquemada, and returned to Rome, where the two bishops were cited to appear and defend themselves. Don Juan Arias Davila was the son of Diego Arias Davila, who was of Jewish origin, and was baptized after the preaching of St. Vincent Ferrier ; he afterwards became chief financier to the kings John II. and Henry IV. Henry IV. ennobled him, and gave him the lordship of the Castle of Pugnonrostro, and several other places which form the countship of Pugnonrostro, and the title of Grandee of Spain, which has been possessed by his descendants from the time of Pedro Arias Davila, the first count, and brother to the bishop, and who was also chief financier to Henry IV. and Ferdinand V. The rank of the bishop did not intimidate Torquemada ; informations were taken by his order, and the result was, that Diego Arias Davila died a Judaic heretic; the object which the inquisitor-general had in view, was to condemn his memory, confiscate his property, and to disinter his body, in order to burn it with his effigy. As, in all affairs of this nature, the children are cited to appear, Don Juan Arias Davila was obliged to repair to Rome in 1490, to defend his father and himself, although he had arrived at a great age, and had been Bishop of Segovia thirty years. He was well received by Alexander VI., who appointed him to accompany his nephew, the Cardinal Montreal, to Naples, when he went to crown Ferdinand II. Davila returned to Rome, and died there in 1497, after having cleared the memory of his father.

Don Pedro Aranda, Bishop of Calahorra, was not so fortutunate. He was the son of Gonzales Alonzo, a Jew, who was also baptized in the time of St. Vincent Ferrier, and who was afterwards master of a chapel. Gonzales had the pleasure of seeing both his sons attain the dignity of bishops : the eldest was Archbishop of Montreal in Sicily, the second was made Bishop of Calahorra, in 1478, and president of the Council of Castile in 1482; yet in 1488 he was the object of a secret instruction, directed by Torquemada, which however did not prevent him from convoking a synod in the town of Logrogna, in 1492. At that period Torquemada, and the other inquisitors of Valladolid, undertook the trial of Gonzales Alonzo, to prove that he had died a Judaic heretic. The inquisitors of Valladolid and the bishop of the diocese, could not agree on the sentence to be pronounced on the accused ; and his son, Don Pedro Aranda, obtained a brief from Alexander VI., by which this affair was referred to Don Inigo Manriquez, Bishop of Cordova, and John de St. John, prior of the Benedictines at Valladolid. They were commissioned to pronounce judgment and execute the sentence, without any interference on the part of the Inquisition. Their decision was favourable to Gonzales.

The bishop, his son, gained the esteem of the Pope, who made him chief major-domo of the pontifical palace, and sent him as ambassador to Venice, in 1494. These marks of favour did not cause the inquisitors to relax in their zeal : they proceeded in their trial against Don Pedro, for heresy : his judges were the archbishop, the Governor of Rome, and two bishops, auditors of the apostolical palace. Don Pedro called one hundred and one witnesses for his defence ; but unfortunately every one of them had something to advance against

him, on different points. The judges made their report to
the Pope, in a secret consistory, in 1498, who, with the cardinals, condemned the bishop to be deprived of his offices
and benefices, to be degraded from his episcopal dignity,
and reduced to the rank of a simple layman. He was confined in the Castle of Santangelo, where he died some time
after.

Thomas de Torquemada, first inquisitor-general of Spain,
died the 16th of November, 1498. The miseries which were
the consequences of the system which he adopted, and recommended to his successors, justify the general hatred which followed him to the tomb, and compelled him to take precautions
for his personal safety. Ferdinand and Isabella permitted him
to use an escort of fifty *familiars* of the Inquisition on horseback, and two hundred others on foot, whenever he travelled.
He also kept the horn of a unicorn on his table, which was
supposed to discover and neutralize poisons. It is not surprising that many should have conspired against his life,
when his cruel administration is considered : the Pope himself was alarmed at his barbarity, and the complaints which
were made against him ; and Torquemada was obliged to
send his colleague, Antonio Badoja, three times to Rome, to
defend him against the accusations of his enemies.

At last Alexander VI., weary of the continual clamours
of which he was the object, resolved to deprive him of his
dignity, but was deterred from so doing through consideration for the Court of Spain.   He therefore expedited a brief
in 1494, saying, that as Torquemada had arrived at a great
age, and suffered from many infirmities, he had named four
inquisitors-general, invested with the same powers which he
possessed.

The familiars of the holy office, who were employed as
the body-guard of the inquisitor-general, were the successors
of the familiars of the Old Inquisition. They were commissioned to pursue the heretics, and persons suspected of

heresy, to assist the officers of the tribunal in taking them to prison, and to do all that the inquisitors might require.

It has been shewn that the Spaniards received the Inquisition with reluctance; but as they were obliged to endure it when once established, some prudent persons thought they should be more secure from the danger of incurring suspicion, if they appeared devoted to the cause, which was the reason why several illustrious gentlemen offered to become *familiars of the holy office*, and were admitted into the congregation of St. Peter. Their example was followed by the inferior classes, and encouraged by Ferdinand and Isabella, who bestowed several immunities and privileges on them.

CHAPTER IX.

OF THE PROCEDURE OF THE MODERN INQUISITION.

AFTER the death of the inquisitor-general, Torquemada, Ferdinand and Isabella proposed Don Diego Deza, a Dominican, to the Pope, as his successor. Deza was Bishop of Jaen, and afterwards became Archbishop of Seville. The Pope signed his bulls of confirmation on the 1st of December, 1498, but limited his authority to the affairs of the kingdom of Castile. Deza was displeased at a restriction which did not exist in the bulls of his two colleagues, and refused to accept the nomination, until the Pope invested him with the same power over Arragon, in a bull, in 1499. The new inquisitor-general did not shew less severity in the exercise of his office than his predecessor; but, before I enter on this part of the history, it is necessary to give some account of the mode of proceeding of the holy office, as it was the work of Torquemada, the effect of the laws which he formed, and properly belongs to his history.

The processes in the Inquisition began by a denunciation, or some other information, such as a discovery accidentally made before the tribunal in another trial. When the denunciation is signed, it takes the form of a declaration, in which the informer, after having sworn to the truth of his deposition, designates those persons whom he presumes, or believes, to have anything to depose against the accused person. These persons are then heard, and their depositions, with that of the first witness, form the *summary of the information, or the preparatory instruction.*

Inquiry.

When the tribunal judged that the actions or words which were denounced were sufficient to warrant an inquiry to establish the proofs, the persons who had been cited as knowing the object of the declaration were examined, and were obliged to take an oath not to reveal the questions which were put to them. None of the witnesses were informed of the subject on which they were to make their depositions; they were only asked in general terms, *if they had ever seen or heard anything which was, or appeared, contrary to the Catholic faith, or the rights of the Inquisition.*

Personal experience has shewn me that the witnesses who were ignorant of the cause of their citation often recollected circumstances entirely foreign to the subject, which they made known, and were then interrogated as if their examination had no other object; this accidental deposition served instead of a denunciation, and a new process was commenced.

The declarations were written down by the commissary or notary, who usually aggravated the denunciation, as much as the arbitrary interpretation of the improper or equivocal expressions used by ignorant persons would permit. The declaration was twice read to the witnesses, *who did not fail to approve all that had been written.*

Censure of the Qualifiers.

When the inquisitors examine the preliminary *instruction*, if they find sufficient cause to proceed, they send a circular to all the tribunals in the province to inquire if any charges against the accused exist in their registers. This proceeding is called the *review of the registers.* Extracts are made of the propositions against the accused, and if each is expressed in different terms, which is almost always the case, they are sent as accusations advanced on different occasions. This writing was then remitted to the theologians, *qualifiers of the holy office,* who write at the bottom of the page if the propositions merit the *theological censure,* as heretical, if they give occasion to suppose that the person who pronounced them approved of any heresy, or if he is only suspected of that crime.

The declaration of the *qualifiers* determines the proceedings against the accused, until the trial is prepared for the definite sentence. The *qualifiers* were generally scholastic monks, almost entirely unacquainted with true dogmatic theology, and who carried fanaticism and superstition to such a height as to find heresy in everything which they had not studied: this disposition has often caused them to censure some of the doctrines of the fathers of the church.

Prisons.

When the qualification has been made, the procurator-fiscal demands that the denounced person shall be removed to the *secret prisons* of the *holy office.* The tribunal has three sorts of prisons, public, intermediate, and secret. The first are those where persons are imprisoned, who are not guilty

of heresy, but of some crime which the Inquisition has the
privilege of punishing: the second are destined for those servants of the holy office who have committed some crime
in the exercise of their functions, without incurring suspicion
of heresy. Those who are detained in these prisons are
permitted to communicate with others, unless they are condemned to solitary confinement. The secret prisons are
those where all heretics, or persons suspected of heresy, are
confined; they can only communicate with the judges of the
tribunal.

These prisons are not, as they have been represented,
damp, dirty, and unhealthy; they are vaulted chambers,
well lighted, not damp, and large enough for a person to
take some exercise in. The real horrors of the prisons are,
that no one can enter them without becoming infamous in
public opinion; and the solitude and the darkness to which
the prisoner is condemned for fifteen hours in the day during
the winter, as he is not allowed light before the hour of seven
in the morning, or after four in the evening. Some authors
have stated, that the prisoners were chained; these means
are only employed on extraordinary occasions, and to prevent them from destroying themselves.

First Audiences.

In the three first days following the imprisonment of the
culprit, he had three *audiences* of *monition,* or caution,
recommending him to speak the truth, without concealing
anything that he has done or said, or that he can impute to
others, contrary to the faith. He was told that if he followed this recommendation he would be treated leniently;
but in the contrary case, he would be proceeded against
with severity. Until then the prisoner is ignorant of the
cause of his arrest; he is only told that no person is taken
to the prisons of the holy office without sufficient proof that

he has spoken against the Catholic faith, and, therefore, it is for his interest to confess his crimes voluntarily. Some prisoners confessed themselves guilty of the crimes stated in the preparatory instruction; others acknowledged more, others less ; generally, the prisoners declared that their consciences did not reproach them, but that they would endeavour to recollect the faults which they had committed if the accusations of the witnesses were read to them.

The advantages of the confession were, that it lessened the duration of the trial, and rendered the punishments inflicted on the accused less severe when the reconciliation took place. Whatever promises might be made to the prisoners, they could not avoid the disgrace of the *san-benito* and *auto-da-fé*, or preserve their honour or their property, if they acknowledged themselves *formal* heretics.

Another custom of the Inquisition was to examine the prisoner on his genealogy and parentage, in order to discover by the registers of the tribunal if any of his family had been punished for heresy, supposing that he might have inherited the erroneous doctrines of his ancestors. He was also obliged to recite the *Pater*, the *Credo*, and other forms of Christian doctrine, because the presumption that he had erred in his faith was stronger, if he did not know them, had forgotten them, or if he made mistakes in the repetition. In short, the Inquisition employed every means, and neglected nothing in the trials of the prisoners, to make them appear guilty of heresy, and all this was done with an appearance of charity and compassion, and in the name of Jesus Christ.

Charges.

When the ceremony of the three first audiences is finished, the procurator-fiscal forms his act of accusation against the prisoner, from the preliminary instruction. Although a semi-proof only exists, he reports the facts in the depositions as if they were proved; and what is still more illegal, he does not reduce the articles of his *requisition* to the number of facts, but following the practice in forming the extracts of the propositions for the act of *qualification*, he multiplies them according to the variations in the statements; so that an accusation which ought to be reduced to one point, contains five or six charges, which appear to indicate that the accused has advanced so many heretical opinions on different occasions, without any foundation but the different manner in which each witness relates the conversation.

This mode of proceeding produces the worst effects; it confuses the prisoner where the charges are read to him, and if he has not coolness and intelligence, he imagines that several crimes are imputed to him, and replies, for instance, to the third article, and relates the facts in different words from those which he employed in answering the second; this variation taking place in each article, he sometimes contradicts himself, and thus furnishes the fiscal with fresh accusations against him, for he is accused of not adhering to truth in his replies.

Torture.

Although the prisoner has confessed all that the witnesses deposed against him in the first audiences, yet the fiscal terminates his *requisition* by saying, that he is guilty of concealment and denial, that he is, therefore, impenitent and obstinate, and demands that the question shall be applied to the accused.

It is true, that it is so long since torture has been inflicted by the inquisitors, that the custom may be looked upon as abolished, and the fiscal only makes the demand in conformity to the example of his predecessors, yet it is equally cruel to make the prisoners fear it.

In former times, if the inquisitors judged that the prisoner had not made a full confession, they ordered him to be tortured; the object was to make him confess all that formed the substance of the process. I shall not describe the different modes of torture employed by the Inquisition, as it has been already done by many historians: I shall only say that none of them can be accused of exaggeration. When the accused acknowledged the crimes imputed to them, during the torture, they were obliged the next day to ratify or retrac: their confession upon oath. Almost all confirmed their first statement, because they were subjected to the torture a second time if they dared to retract.

Requisition.

The requisition or accusation of the procurator-fiscal was never given to the prisoner in writing, that he might not reflect on the charges in prison and prepare his replies. The prisoner is conducted to the audience-chamber, where a secretary reads the charges, in the presence of the inquisitors and the fiscal; between each article he calls upon the prisoner to reply to it instantly, and declare if it is true or false.

It is evident that this proceeding is intended to embarrass the prisoner, by compelling him to reply without previous reflection. Such stratagems are allowed in other tribunals where the prisoners are guilty of homicide, theft, or other offences against society; but it must be allowed that it is against the spirit of Christianity to employ them where zeal for religion and the salvation of others seem to be the motives for acting.

Defence.

When the charges and the *accusation* have been read, the inquisitors ask the prisoner if he wishes to make a defence; if he replies in the affirmative, a copy of the *accusation* and the replies is taken. He is then required to select the lawyer whom he wishes to employ for his defence, from the list of those belonging to the holy office. Some prisoners required permission to seek a defender out of the tribunal, a pretension which is not contrary to any law, particularly if the lawyer has taken an oath of secrecy; yet this simple and natural right has seldom been granted by the inquisitors.

It is of little consequence to the accused to be defended by an able man, as the lawyer is not allowed to see the original process, or to communicate with his client. One of the notaries draws up a copy of the result of the *preliminary instruction*, in which he reports the deposition of the witnesses, without mentioning their names, or the circumstances of time or place, and (what is more extraordinary) without stating what has been said in defence of the prisoner. He entirely omits the declarations of the persons who, having been summoned and interrogated by the tribunal, have persisted in affirming that they knew nothing of the subject on which they were examined. This extract is accompanied by the censure of the *qualifiers*, and the demand of the fiscal for the examination, and the accusation, and the replies of the accused. This is all that is given to the defender in the audience-chamber, where the inquisitors have commanded him to attend. He is then obliged to promise to defend the prisoner if he thinks that it is just to do so; but, in the contrary case, that he will use all the means in his power to persuade him to solicit his pardon of the tribunal, by a sincere confession of his sins, and a demand to be reconciled to the church.

Those who have acquired any experience in criminal proceedings, are aware of the great advantages which may be derived from the comparison of the testimony of the witnesses in the defence of the accused; but the direction given to the proceedings by the Inquisition is such, that the lawyer can rarely find any means of defence but that which arises from the difference and variations in the depositions on the actions and words imputed to the prisoner.

As this is not sufficient, (because the semi-proof exists,) the defender generally demands to see the prisoner, that he may inquire if it is his intention to challenge the witnesses, to destroy either in part, or entirely, the proof established against him. If he replies in the affirmative, the inquisitors order proceedings to prove the irregularity of the witnesses.

Proof.

It is then necessary to separate all the original declarations of the witnesses from the process, and send them to the places which they inhabit to receive a *ratification*. This takes place without the knowledge of the prisoner, and as he is not represented by any person during this formality, it is impossible that the challenge of a witness should succeed, even if he was the greatest enemy of the prisoner. If the witness was at Madrid at the time of the instruction, and afterwards went to the Philippine Isles, the course of the trial was suspended, and the prisoner was obliged to wait till the ratification arrived from Asia. If he demanded an audience, to complain of the delay, he was answered with ambiguity, that the tribunal could not proceed with greater haste, as it was occupied with particular measures.

The prisoner made his challenge of the witnesses by naming those whom he considered as his enemies, giving his reasons for mistrusting them, and writing on the margin of each article the names of those persons who could attest the facts which are the causes of the challenge. The inquisitors decree that they shall be examined, unless some motive prevents it.

As the prisoner is not acquainted with the proceedings, he often accuses persons who have not been summoned as witnesses. The article in which they are mentioned is passed over with those of the witnesses who have not deposed against him, or who have spoken in his favour. Thus he encounters his accusers only by chance.

It sometimes happens that the procurator-fiscal secretly obtains the proof of the morality of the witnesses, in order to destroy the effect of the challenge; and as this is more easy to accomplish than the measures taken by the prisoner, they are generally rendered useless, because in doubtful cases the inquisitors are always disposed to depend upon the witness, if he is not known to be the declared enemy of the accused.

Publication of the Proofs.

When the proof is established, the tribunal publishes the state of the trial, the depositions, and the act of judgment. But these terms are not to be understood in the common sense, since the publication was only an unfaithful copy of the declarations and other facts contained in the extract formed for the use of the defender. A secretary reads it to the prisoner in the presence of the inquisitors; after each article he asks him if he acknowledges the truth of what he has just heard; he then reads the declarations, and if the prisoner has not yet alleged anything against the witnesses, that privilege is given him, because after hearing the deposition he is generally able to designate the person who has made it.

This reading is only a fresh snare, for if the least contradiction is perceived, he may be considered guilty of duplicity, concealment, or a false confession, and the tribunal may refuse to grant the reconciliation, although he demand it, and even condemn him to *relaxation*.

Definitive Censure of the Qualifiers.

After this ceremony the *qualifiers* are summoned, who receive the original writing of the sentence passed in the *summary* instruction, with the extract of the replies of the prisoner in his last examination, and the declarations of the witnesses which were communicated to him. They are commissioned to qualify the propositions a second time, to examine his explanation, and to decide if his replies have destroyed the suspicion of heresy which he had incurred, or if he had confirmed it, and was to be looked upon as a *formal* heretic.

Every one must be sensible of the importance of this censure, since it led to the definitive sentence; yet the *qualifiers* scarcely took the trouble to hear a rapid perusal of the proceedings; they hastily gave their opinion, and this was the last important act in the proceedings, as the rest was a mere formality.

Sentence.

The trial was then considered as finished. The diocesan in ordinary was convoked, that with the inquisitors he might decide upon the proper sentence. In the first ages of the holy office these functions were confided to *consulters:* these were doctors of law, but as they could only give their opinion, and as the inquisitors pronounced the definitive sentence, the latter always prevailed if they chanced to differ. The accused had the right of appealing to the *Supreme* Council, but appeals to Rome were more frequent. The inquisitors of the provinces were afterwards obliged to submit their opinion to the council before they pronounced the definitive sentence; the council modified and reformed it; their decision was sent to the inquisitors, who then established the judgment in their own names, although it might be contrary to their previous opinion. This proceeding rendered the office of the consultors useless, and it was discontinued.

Although the prisoner was acquitted, he was not acquainted with the names of his denouncers and the witnesses. He rarely obtained a more public reparation than the liberty of returning to his house with a certificate of absolution.

Execution of the Sentence.

The nature of the punishments inflicted by the Inquisition has been already described ; it is, therefore, only necessary to remark that the sentences were not communicated to the victims until the commencement of the execution, since the condemned were sent to the *autos-da-fé*, either to be reconciled or given over to secular justice ; on leaving prison the *familiars* attired them in the *san-benito*, with a paper mitre on their heads, a cord round their necks, and a wax taper in their hands.

When the prisoner arrives at the place of execution, his sentence is read, and he is then reconciled or *relaxed*, which means, that he is condemned to be burnt by the justice of the king.

San-benito.

The *San-benito* was a species of *scapulary*, which only descended to the knees, that it might not be confounded with those worn by some monks; this motive also made the inquisitors prefer common woollen stuff of a yellow colour with red crosses for the *San-benito*. Such were the penitential habits in 1514, when Cardinal Ximenez de Cisneros altered the common crosses for those of St. Andrew. The inquisitors afterwards had a different habit for each class of penitents.

Those who abjured as *slightly* suspected of heresy, wore the scapulary of yellow stuff without the cross. If he abjured as *violently suspected*, he wore half the cross ; if he was a *formal heretic* he wore it entire.   There were also three different kinds of garments for those who were condemned to death.   The first was, for those who repented before they were sentenced.   It was a simple yellow scapulary with a red cross, and a conical cap, denominated *Caroza*, which was formed of the same stuff as the *San-benito*, and decorated with similar crosses.

The second was destined for those who had been condemned to be burnt, but who had repented after their sentence, and before they were conducted to the *autos-da-fé*. The *San-benito* and the *Caroza* were made of the same stuff. On the lower part of the scapulary a bust was painted, in the midst of a fire, the flames of which were reversed, to shew that the culprit was not to be burnt until he had been strangled.   The *Caroza* was painted in the same manner.

The third was for those who were impenitent.   It was similar to the others, with a bust, and the flames in the natural direction, to shew that the person who wore it was to be burnt alive; grotesque figures of devils were also painted on the *San-benito* and *Caroza*.

CHAPTER X.

OF THE PRINCIPAL EVENTS DURING THE MINISTRY OF THE INQUISITORS DEZA AND CISNEROS.

THE new inquisitor-general was scarcely in possession of his office, when he began to establish regulations to increase the activity of the Inquisition.   In 1500 he published a constitution in seven articles ; and in 1504 four new articles relative to the confiscations.

To prove his zeal, Deza proposed to Ferdinand that the

Inquisition should be introduced into Sicily and Naples in its present form, and that it should be under the authority of the Spanish inquisitor-general, instead of being dependent on the Court of Rome. The king undertook to introduce it into Sicily by a decree in 1500; but the inhabitants made great resistance, and he was obliged to pursue the plan which had succeeded in Arragon, by commanding the viceroy and other magistrates to assist the inquisitors. Several seditions were quelled before the sub-delegated inquisitor-general, Don Pedro Velorade, Archbishop of Messina, could enter upon his office.

In 1516 the Sicilians, weary of the proceedings of the Inquisition, revolted and set all the prisoners at liberty. Melchior de Cervera, the inquisitor, only escaped death by a concurrence of extraordinary circumstances; the viceroy was also in the greatest danger. The islanders were thus freed from the yoke of this detested tribunal; but they did not long enjoy liberty, for they were not able to resist the power of Charles V., who obliged them to receive it a second time. Naples was more fortunate. Ferdinand in 1504 commanded the viceroy, Gonzales Fernandez de Cordova, surnamed *the great captain*, to assist the Archbishop of Messina with all his power, in establishing the Inquisition; but the Neapolitans opposed it so obstinately, that the viceroy judged it prudent to desist, and informed the king that it would be extremely dangerous to combat so decided a resistance.

In 1510 Ferdinand again attempted to introduce the new Inquisition, but his efforts were unavailing, and he was obliged to declare that he would be satisfied if the Neapolitans would banish all the *New Christians* who had taken refuge in their towns when they were driven from Spain.

Deza persuaded Ferdinand and Isabella to introduce the Inquisition into the kingdom of Grenada, although a promise to the contrary had been made to the baptized Moors.

The queen rejected the proposition, but granted one that differed little from it, namely, that the jurisdiction of the inquisitors of Cordova should extend over Grenada, but permitting them to prosecute only in cases of actual apostasy. From that period the Moors have been known in history by the name of *Morescoes.*

The principal inquisitor of Cordova was Don Diego de Lucero; the severity of his character caused great misery throughout the kingdom of Cordova.

The moderation and exhortations of Ximenez de Cisneros, Archbishop of Toledo, and Don Ferdinand de Talavera, had converted more than 50,000 Moors, and the conversions would have been still more numerous, if some priests had not treated the Moors with severity, and excited a general revolt.

In 1501 the sovereigns declared in an edict, that by the grace of God, there were no infidels in the kingdom of Grenada, and to render the conversions more secure, they forbade any Moors to enter the territory; they also prohibited the slaves of that nation from holding any communication with others, that their conversion might not be retarded, or with those who had been baptized, as they might induce them to apostatize. All who did not conform to these laws incurred the punishment of death.

In February, 1502, Ferdinand and Isabella commanded all the free Moors of both sexes, above fourteen and twelve years of age, to quit the kingdom of Spain before the month of May following; they were allowed to sell their goods as the Jews had been; but were prohibited from going to Africa, which was then at war with Spain. The states of the Grand Seignor and other countries were assigned to them as places of refuge : as several baptized Moors sold their property and went to Africa, a royal ordinance was published, importing that, for the space of two years, no person could sell his property, or leave the kingdom of Castile, except to

go into Arragon or Portugal, without a permission, which
would only be granted to those who gave a security for their
return when they had terminated their affairs.

Deza was not contented with exciting the zeal of Ferdinand and Isabella against the Moors; he also proposed
measures against the Jews on the occasion of the arrival of
different strangers in Spain, but who were not of those expelled in 1492. He obtained a royal ordinance in 1499,
which applied those measures to them which had been established against the first Jews. The council of the Inquisition
had already decreed that the converted Jews should be
obliged to prove their baptism, and that they lived with the
other Christians; that those who had been rabbins or masters
of the law should be obliged to change the place of their
residence; that they should appear every Sunday and on
festival days in the churches, and be carefully instructed in
the christian doctrine. Ferdinand permitted the inquisitors
of Arragon to take cognizance of usury and other crimes
foreign to their jurisdiction, contrary to the oath which he
had taken to observe the laws of that kingdom, which ordained that they should be punished by the secular judge.

Deza was at the head of the Inquisition eight years. If
the calculation of his victims is formed after the inscription
at Seville, we shall find that 38,440 persons were punished
during that time, of whom 2592 were burnt in person, 896
in effigy, and 34,952 condemned to different penances.
Among this crowd of persons who were persecuted by the
Inquisition, there were many distinguished by their birth,
their learning, their fortunes, and their offices. The
sanguinary inquisitor, Lucero, made the venerable Don
Ferdinand de Talavera, first Archbishop of Grenada,
the object of a shameful persecution. He became jealous
of the reputation for sanctity and charity which this prelate had acquired, and raised doubts of his faith, by reminding Isabella that he had opposed the establishment of

the Inquisition in 1478, and the following years; and by publishing that, although his father was noble, and of the illustrious family of Contreras, yet he was of Jewish origin by the mother's side. The Inquisitor concluded from these circumstances that he could commence a *secret instruction* against the holy prelate.   Deza commissioned the Archbishop of Toledo, Ximenez de Cisneros, to receive the preparatory informations on the faith of the Archbishop of Grenada; Cisneros informed the Pope of the commission which he had received, and the pontiff commanded his apostolical nuncio, the Bishop of Bristol, to take the affair under his direction, and prohibited Deza and the Inquisitors from pursuing it.   The Pope, in a Council of Cardinals and Bishops, acquitted the Archbishop of Grenada, who died in 1507, some months after this judgment, after three years of the greatest anxiety, as the inquisitor Lucero had caused many of his relations to be arrested, although they were all innocent.

The persecution suffered by the learned Antonio Lebrija was not less cruel; he had been tutor to Isabella, and was honoured by the friendship and protection of Ximenez de Cisneros: he was well acquainted with the Greek and Hebrew, and discovered and corrected in the Latin text of the Vulgate some errors which had been committed by the transcribers before the invention of printing.   He was accused by some scholastic theologians; his papers were seized, and after being treated with the greatest cruelty, he had the grief of seeing the suspicion of heresy established against him, and was obliged to live in that species of disgrace until he could write his apology under the protection of Ximenez de Cisneros.

The inhumanity of the inquisitor Lucero had still more serious consequences: as he declared almost all the accused persons guilty of concealment, and condemned them as *false penitents*, some persons added imaginary circumstances to

their confessions, and declared that synagogues were held
in different houses in Cordova, Grenada, and other towns;
they added, that even monks and nuns attended at them,
and went in procession from all parts of Castile; they also
affirmed that many Spanish families of *Old Christians,* whom
they named, assisted at the Jewish feasts. In consequence
of these declarations, Lucero arrested such an immense
number of persons, that Cordova was on the point of re-
volting against the Inquisition. The municipality, the
bishop, the chapter of the cathedral, and all the nobility
sent deputies to the inquisitor-general, to demand that Lucero
should be recalled. Deza refused to listen to their claim,
until the cruelties of which Lucero was accused were
proved. Lucero had then the audacity to note down as
favourers of Judaism, knights, ladies, canons, monks, nuns,
and respectable persons of every class.

At this period, 1506, Philip I. ascended the throne of
Castile; the Bishop of Cordova informed him of what was
passing, and the relations of the prisoners demanded that
they should be tried by another tribunal. Philip commanded
Deza to retire to his archbishopric of Seville, and to invest
Don Diego Ramirez de Guzman, Bishop of Catania, with
the powers of inquisitor-general; at the same time all the
papers relative to this affair were submitted to the Supreme
Council of Castile. Ramirez de Guzman suspended Lucero,
and the other inquisitors of Cordova, from their functions.
The affair would have terminated happily, but for the death
of the king in the same year.

Deza was no sooner informed of that event than he again
resumed his office of inquisitor-general, and annulled all that
had been done during his retirement. Ferdinand V. resumed the government of the kingdom, as father of Queen
Joanna, widow of Philip I., as her mind was disordered.
Some time elapsed, however, before he began to reign, as
he was at Naples at the time of the death of the King of

Spain. At this period, all the inhabitants of Cordova, and some members of the Council of Castile, declared against Deza, and published that he was of the race of *Marranos*, that is, a descendant of the Jews.

The Marquis de Priego excited the Cordovans to a revolt ; they forced the prisons of the holy office, and liberated an immense number of prisoners. They seized the persons of the procurator-fiscal, one of the notaries, and several other officers of the tribunal; Priego would also have arrested Lucero, but he escaped by means of an excellent mule. These events alarmed the inquisitor-general to such a degree, that he resigned his office, and retired to his diocese with the greatest precaution. This proceeding restored tranquillity in Cordova, but did not terminate the trials.

When the Regent of Spain arrived in that kingdom, he named Don Francisco Ximenez de Cisneros inquisitor-general for the crown of Castile, and Don Juan Enguera, Bishop of Vic, for that of Arragon. The Pope expedited their bulls in 1507, and made Cisneros a cardinal.

Ximenez de Cisneros began to exercise his new employment on the 1st October, when the conspiracy against the holy office had become almost general, on account of the events at Cordova, of which the Council of Castile took cognizance. All its members who had been of the party of Philip I. signalized themselves by their hatred against the Inquisition. This aversion made Ximenez de Cisneros feel the necessity of conducting himself with extreme caution, that he might not give occasion for a general convocation of the Cortes, which would have deprived him of the high office of governor of the kingdom, which he then possessed.

The events at Cordova forced a great number of persons to appeal to Rome. The Pope appointed two prelates to examine the trials, and made Cardinal Cisneros judge of appeals, with the power of bringing all the trials begun by the apostolical commissioners before him.

The cardinal immediately suspended the inquisitor Lucero, and sent him prisoner to Burgos; he also imprisoned all those witnesses who were suspected of having made false depositions, because some of the charges were so absurd that no one could believe them. The examination of the trials made the cardinal perceive, that an affair which implicated some of the most illustrious families of Spain could not be treated with too much delicacy: he, therefore, obtained the king's permission to form a junta, which he named the *Catholic Congregation;* it was composed of twenty-two respectable persons, namely, the inquisitor-general (who was the president); the inquisitor-general of Arragon; the Bishop of Ciudad Rodrigo; those of Calahorra and Barcelona; the mitred abbot of the Benedictines at Valladolid; the president of the Council of Castile, and eight of its members; the vice-chancellor and the president of the Chancery of Arragon; two councillors of the *Supreme;* two provincial inquisitors, and an auditor of the Chancery of Valladolid.

Their first assembly was held at Burgos, on Ascension-day, in 1508, and on the 9th of July they decreed that the characters of the witnesses were vile, contemptible, and unworthy of confidence; that their declarations were full of contradictions; that they contained things unworthy of belief, and contrary to common sense; that the prisoners were consequently at liberty, that their honour, and that of the prisoners who had died, was re-established; that the houses which had been destroyed, as having been used for synagogues, should be rebuilt; and that the judgment and the notes in the registers should be erased.

This decision of the *Catholic junta* was proclaimed at Valladolid on the 1st August, in the same year, in the presence of the king, and a multitude of nobles, and other inhabitants of all classes.

Cardinal Ximenez de Cisneros had genius, knowledge,

and was just, which he proved in the affair of Cordova, and in the protection which he granted to Lebrija and other learned men on different occasions. I shall here remark the error into which several writers have fallen, in accusing Cisneros of having taken a great part in the establishment of the holy office, when it is certain that, in concert with Cardinal Mendoza and Talavera, he endeavoured to prevent it. When he was chosen as chief of an institution which had more power and was better obeyed than many sovereigns, circumstances made it a duty to uphold and defend it, and he was obliged to oppose innovations in the manner of proceeding, although the events at Cordova had shewn him the inconveniences of the secrecy preserved by the tribunal.

The division of the kingdoms of Arragon and Castile, which took place at this time, and the idea that it was no longer necessary to have as many inquisitorial tribunals as bishoprics, were the reasons that induced Cisneros to distribute them by provinces. He established the holy office at Seville, Cordova, Jaen, Toledo, in Estremadura, at Murcia, Valladolid, and Calahorra, and determined the extent of territory for the jurisdiction of each tribunal: at this time he also sent inquisitors to the Canary isles. In 1513, the inquisition was introduced at Cuença; in 1524, at Grenada; under Philip II., at Santiago de Galicia; and under Philip IV., at Madrid. Cisneros also judged it necessary, in 1516, to have a tribunal at Oran, and soon after in America.

The inquisitor-general of Arragon adopted the same system, and sent inquisitors to Saragossa, Barcelona, Valencia, Majorca, Sardinia, and Sicily; and, at a later period, to Pampeluna, after the conquest of Navarre; but this kingdom being united in 1515 to that of Castile, its tribunal was subjected to the inquisitor-general of that kingdom, who suppressed it some time after, and transferred the territory to that of Calahorra.

During the eleven years of his ministry (which ended by his death in 1517), Cisneros permitted the condemnation of 52,855 individuals, 3564 were burnt in person, 1232 in effigy, and 4832 suffered different punishments. Although this number of executions is immense, yet it must be acknowledged that Cisneros had taken measures to relax the activity of the Inquisition ; the most important was, that he assigned particular churches to the *New Christians*, and charged the curates to increase their zeal in instructing them, and to visit them often in their own houses.

Offer made to the King to obtain the publicity of the Proceedings.

In 1512, a report being spread among the *New Christians* that Ferdinand intended to make war against his nephew, the King of Navarre, they offered him 600,000 ducats of gold towards the expenses of the war if he would consent to make a law that the trials of the Inquisition should be public ; the king was on the point of treating with the *New Christians*, when Cisneros placed a large sum of money at his disposal ; the king accepted it, though it was less than the first, and abandoned the idea of a reform.

After the death of that prince, and while Charles V. was in Flanders, in 1517, the *New Christians* again offered, on the same conditions, 800,000 ducats for the expenses of his journey to Spain. William de Croy, Duke d'Ariscot, the favourite governor of the young monarch, persuaded him to consult the colleges, universities, and learned men of Spain and Flanders ; they all replied that the communication of the names and the entire depositions of the witnesses was consonant to all rights natural, human, and divine. When the cardinal-inquisitor was informed of this decision, he sent deputies and wrote to the king to combat it ; he reminded him that a similar proposal had been refused by his grand-

father; but he did not tell him the most important circumstance, that he had refused it for a sum of money.
Charles V. left the affair undecided until his arrival in
Spain, but he terminated it according to the general hopes
after the death of Cisneros, in 1518.

The particular favour which Ferdinand granted to the
Inquisition did not prevent him from maintaining the rights
of his crown. In 1509, he published a law which prohibited,
on pain of death, any person from presenting to the inquisitors any bull, or writing of that nature, obtained from the
Pope, or his legates, without first applying to the king that
it might be examined by his council.

This right of the crown of Spain over the decisions of the
Pope has been lately renewed by a law of Charles III., yet
the law has often been impotent against the enterprises, the
decisions, and the briefs of the Popes.

Ferdinand named Don Louis Mercader inquisitor-general
for the kingdom of Arragon, after the death of the Bishop
of Vic. Mercader died in 1516, while the government was
in the hands of Charles of Austria, the grandson of Ferdinand, who died in the same year, leaving no children by
his second marriage.

Charles, his grandson, resided in Flanders, but he sent
into Spain several men who enjoyed his confidence: amongst
them were his governor, the Duke d'Ariscot, and Adrian de
Florencio, who was Dean of Louvain, and born at Utrecht.
As the two sovereignties of Castile and Arragon were now
united, it appeared natural that there should be but one
inquisitor-general for the monarchy, but Cisneros had too
much penetration to omit this opportunity of recommending
himself to the favourite, and, consequently, to the prince.
Instead of demanding this union, he wrote to the king to
represent that it appeared to him expedient to bestow the
bishopric of Tortosa and the office of inquisitor-general of

Arragon on the Dean of Louvain, and it was easy to obviate the difficulty of his being a foreigner by giving him letters of naturalization. This plan was executed, the double nomination was sent to Rome, and the Pope granted the bulls. Adrian took possession of Majorca on the 7th of February, 1517; this nomination was followed by one to the office of Cisneros, who died on the 6th November following. Although he was elected Pope on the 9th of January, 1522, he continued in his office until the 10th of September, in the following year, when he signed the bulls of his successor, Don Alphonso Manriquez de Lara, Archbishop of Seville.

During the period that the Inquisition remained separate from that of Castile, it was often violently attacked, and more than once was on the point of being abolished, or at least subjected to a reform, which would have left it without the power of exciting terror. Ferdinand having assembled the Cortes of the kingdom at Monzon, in 1510, the deputies of the towns and cities loudly complained that the inquisitors abused their powers, not only in matters of faith, but in several points which were not in their jurisdiction. The deputies also represented, that they interfered in the regulation of the contributions, and that the taxes were shamefully diminished by the reductions which they made in the lists; that their authority had made them so bold and insolent, that they created themselves judges in all doubtful cases; and where their competence was denied, they had recourse to excommunication; that they oppressed the magistrates, who feared that they should be obliged to do public penance in an *auto-da-fé*; that this misfortune had already happened to the viceroys and governors of Barcelona, Valencia, Majorca, Sardinia, and Sicily, and to several persons of high rank; in consequence, they entreated his majesty to maintain the execution of the laws and statutes of the kingdom of Arragon, and to oblige the officers of the

Inquisition to confine themselves to matters of faith, and to pursue them according to the rules of common law, in giving them the publicity of criminal proceedings.

This representation of the Cortes acquainted the king with the disposition of the public; yet he avoided giving a direct reply, and said that it was impossible to decide upon so important an affair without having acquired a profound knowledge of facts; that he requested them to collect all that came to their knowledge, and to lay them before him in the first assembly. This took place in the same town, in 1512. The resolutions which were then adopted form a treaty between the sovereign and his people: it contains twenty-five articles, all tending to restrain the extent of the jurisdiction of the inquisitors.

It was there stated that they could not interfere in trials for bigamy and usury, unless the culprits had fallen into the crime of heresy, in asserting that these offences were not sinful; nor in the proceedings instituted against blasphemers by other tribunals, unless the blasphemy was heretical; they were also prohibited from proceeding in a trial without the concurrence of the *ordinaire diocesan;* the inquisitor-general was likewise restrained from pronouncing judgment, in cases of appeal, without the consent of his counsellors; and that the execution of the sentence which had caused it should be delayed. No measures were taken for the publicity of the proceedings, or with regard to the confiscations; but it was agreed that the contracts and other engagements, signed by one who had the reputation of a good catholic, should be valid, although he should be afterwards proved to have been a heretic at the time of the transaction.

The king soon repented of having given his word to the Cortes; and, seconded by the intrigues of the inquisitors, he solicited and obtained a dispensation from his promise, on the 30th of April, 1513. One of the clauses of the dispensation reinstates the tribunals of the holy office in all the pri-

vileges which they had formerly possessed. This conduct of
the king caused a general revolt, and he was obliged to
request the Pope to confirm the regulations of the Cortes,
and subject those who did not conform to them to the
censure of the church. The Pope saw the necessity of compliance, and granted the bull in 1515.

CHAPTER XI.

AN ATTEMPT MADE BY THE CORTES OF CASTILE AND
ARRAGON TO REFORM THE INQUISITION.—OF THE PRIN-
CIPAL EVENTS UNDER ADRIAN, FOURTH INQUISITOR-
GENERAL.

THE Inquisition was never in so much danger as during the
first years of the reign of Charles V. When the young
monarch arrived in Spain, he was disposed to abolish the
Inquisition, or at least to regulate the proceedings according
to those of other tribunals. In 1518 a general assembly of
the Cortes was held at Valladolid, when the representatives
solicited that his highness would command the office of the
holy Inquisition to conform to the rules of the canons and
the common law. The Cortes likewise sent ten thousand
pieces of gold to the chancellor Selvagio, and promised the
same sum when the decree which they solicited should be
put in execution. The king replied that he would take
proper measures to remedy the evil of which they complained : in consequence he engaged the Cortes to publish
the abuses which had been introduced, and to indicate the
means of abolishing them.

When the assembly at Valladolid had terminated their
labours, Charles convoked the Cortes of Arragon at Saragossa, where he was accompanied by the chancellor Selvagio,
who had prepared a royal ordinance, to be published ac-

cording to the demand of the Cortes of Castile. It was composed of thirty-nine articles: the proceedings of the tribunal were regulated in it, with the ages, the rank, and salaries of the judges and subaltern officers.

The result of this new code was, that the inquisitors could not question a witness to obtain information on any subject but that for which he was summoned.

That each denouncer should be subject to a strict examination, to discover his motives for the accusation.

That the order for imprisonment could not be given without the concurrence of the diocesan in ordinary, or until they had examined each witness a second time.

That the prisons should be public, neat, and convenient.

That the prisoners should be allowed to see their relations, their friends, and their counsel.

That they might choose a lawyer or procurator in whom they placed confidence.

That the accusation should be immediately communicated to them, with the name of the place where, and the time when, the witnesses had declared the crime to have been committed.

That if the accused demanded a copy of the accusation and the examination, it should be given to him.

That when the proofs and the depositions were all received, they should be communicated entirely to the prisoner, *as in the present time there are no persons powerful enough to inspire the witnesses with fear, except in cases where the prisoner is a duke, marquis, count, bishop, or in possession of some other dignity of the church.*

That in this case, in order to conceal the names of the witnesses, the judge shall draw up a writing, declaring upon oath, that he believes this measure to be necessary for the preservation of the lives of the witnesses; that this act shall deprive the prisoner of his right of appealing against it.

That if it is considered absolutely necessary to make use

of the torture, it shall only be administered in moderation, and without recurring to the cruel inventions hitherto employed.

That it shall only be employed once for what personally concerns the accused; never to obtain from him information of other individuals; and only in the case of persons mentioned in the law.

That the definitive sentences, and even the interlocutory orders, shall be subject to the right of appeal, as to their double effect.

That when the preparatory examination of the judgment is commenced, the parties and their counsel may attend at this revision of the process, and demand that the reading may be made in their presence.

That if the proof of the crime is not then established, the prisoner shall be acquitted, without being liable to a punishment as being still suspected.

That if the accused desires to clear himself, on oath, he shall be allowed to seek witnesses, and to converse with them in private; and that their being descendants of the Jews shall not prevent their admission.

That the challenge of witnesses shall be permitted; and if one of those called by the procurator-fiscal is convicted of giving false testimony, he shall be subject to the punishment of retaliation, according to a law of Ferdinand and Isabella, in the beginning of their reign.

That when an accused person has been reconciled, he shall not be arrested for things which he has not confessed, because it is to be supposed that he forgot them.

That no persons shall be molested or imprisoned for a simple presumption of heresy, arising from their having been brought up among Jews or heretics.

That the San-benitos shall be taken out of the churches, and that they no longer be worn in the streets.

That the punishment of perpetual imprisonment shall be

abolished, *because the prisoners die of hunger, and cannot serve God.*

That the statutes recently established to prevent *New Christians* from being admitted into convents, shall be considered as null and void, because they are contrary to all laws, human and divine.

That where an individual is sentenced to imprisonment, an inventory shall be taken of his property, and they shall not be sequestrated or sold.

That he, and his wife, and children, shall possess his revenues during his detention, and shall be allowed to employ them to prepare his means of defence against the Inquisition.

That when a man is condemned, his children shall inherit his property.

That no donation shall be made on their property, until it has been definitively confiscated.

That the spirit and letter of the canons shall be complied with in all things, without regard to any particular custom previously in use.

That the king shall be supplicated to obtain a bull from the Pope to ratify these measures.

That until this bull is obtained, the king shall be requested to command the inquisitors to conform to these regulations, in the trials already commenced, and in those which may begin from this time.

This excellent code of laws was never put in execution, because the chancellor Selvagio, who framed it, died before its publication; and Cardinal Adrian so totally changed the ideas and inclinations of Charles V. that he became an ardent defender of the Inquisition.

Charles V. had sworn at Saragossa, in 1518, to respect the privileges and customs of the Arragonese, particularly the resolutions of the Cortes at Saragossa, Jarzona, and

Monzon, and consequently that he would not suffer the inquisitors to commence any trials for usury.

But a new assembly of the Cortes having been convoked at Saragossa, towards the end of the year 1518, the deputies of Arragon represented to the king, that the agreement of the Cortes at Monzon, in 1512, was not sufficient to remedy the abuses which the inquisitors had introduced; they therefore entreated his majesty to add to it thirty-one articles which they had adopted. These articles differed little from those of the Cortes of Castile.

The king, after having consulted his council, replied, " *that it was his pleasure that the holy canons, and the decrees of the holy see, should be conformed to in regard to all the articles which had been presented to him. That if difficulties or doubts should occur, which required explanation, they should apply to the Pope;* that if any person wished to accuse an inquisitor of abuse in the exercise of his office, he might do so by applying to the inquisitor-general, who would pronounce sentence according to equity; and that the king would cause them to be punished as an example; *that he engaged by oath to observe himself, and cause others to observe, the order and declaration which he addressed to the assembly, as well as the articles which the Pope might add to those of the Cortes;* that he also promised, upon oath, never to demand a dispensation from his promise; and that if one was addressed to him he would never make use of it, as he at that time renounced all the rights which might arise from it."

This reply induced the Cortes to believe that the king had granted all their requests; they considered that the trials would be there conducted as before other ecclesiastical tribunals. Persuaded that this was the king's intention, the Cortes resolved to show their gratitude by a voluntary conribution of money.

Some time elapsed before the agreement was approved by the Pope. The emperor wrote the following letter from Cologne, in 1520, to his ambassador at Rome :—" In regard to the transactions of the Cortes, it will be sufficient if his Holiness will approve an act sent to Don Louis Carroz, and afterwards to Don Jerome Vich, which is written by the hand of the venerable Cardinal of Tortosa, and that of the great chancellor, without any extension or interpretation, as I have often demanded earnestly."

The Arragonese, who did not even believe it possible to obtain this last point, entreated the inquisitor-general to command the inquisitors of Saragossa to conform immediately to the regulations of the agreement, without waiting for the confirmation of the Pope, because almost all the articles were the same as those in the convention of 1512, which the Pope had approved.

Cardinal Adrian complied with the request, and wrote to the inquisitors. They replied, that they thought themselves obliged to take the orders of the king before they obeyed him. Charles addressed an ordinance to them, in which he commanded them to execute all that he had promised and sworn in the preceding year.

At last the Pope confirmed the resolutions by a bull, which was proclaimed with great solemnity. However, it soon appeared that this publication would have no effect, because the promise of the king was, that the canons and apostolical ordinances should be strictly observed in regard to the articles, and in conforming to this they only executed the bull of 1515.

On the 21st of January, 1521, the emperor ordered the secretary of the Cortes to be set at liberty ; for although the inquisitor-general, in 1520, had decreed that he should be *relaxed*, and the prisoner had been informed of it, yet he refused to quit the prison, affirming that the decree which set him at liberty, tended more to make him appear guilty than innocent, by the use of the word *relaxed*.

Similar debates took place in Catalonia, where the king convoked a Cortes at Barcelona, in 1519, to take the oath of maintaining the privileges of the province. The Catalans, informed of the effect produced by the representations of the Cortes of Arragon, likewise demanded a reform of several abuses of their Inquisition relative to the taxes, as well as usury, bigamy, and other crimes of that class. The king, after having heard their remonstrances, made nearly the same reply as to the Cortes of Saragossa, and wrote to the Pope to demand a ratification of the articles. The Pope approved them a bull in 1520; but Charles did not wait for its arrival to enforce the execution of his promise, which is proved by his order to Don Diego de Mendoza, his lieutenant-general in Catalonia. Yet he declares in his letter to his lieutenant, that he only made these promises *on account of the importunities of some representatives* of towns, and some *men who were among the members of the Cortes.*

In consequence of some events in Arragon, during the period which elapsed before the bull of confirmation was issued, Leo X. was on the point of destroying the Inquisition, but intimidated by the policy of Charles V., he left the hydra in the same state.

John Prat, the secretary of the Cortes of Arragon, drew up the proposition of the representatives, and the reply of the king, to be addressed to the Pope; the chancellor of the king had done the same. This proceeding particularly displeased the inquisitors of Saragossa; and to avoid the danger which they believed themselves to be in, they began to intrigue at court, and soon succeeded in rendering the king averse to the cause of the deputies of Arragon. They insinuated that Prat had drawn up the act which was to be sent to Rome, in such a manner, as to represent the reply of the king as obligatory, not only in the literal sense of the words, but in supposing that he had admitted the articles as being conformed to the common law; and that they, consequently, only wanted the ratification of the Pope, which there was no doubt of obtaining, as it was known that the deputies of Arragon were supported by several cardinals, and had sent them considerable sums of money.

The papers which contained these details were sent to Cardinal Adrian, who communicated them to the king, and obtained permission to order the inquisitors of Saragossa to make an inquiry if this recital was true, when they would be authorized to arrest Prat. Everything happened according to the hopes of the inquisitors.

Prat was arrested on the 5th of May, 1509, and the next day the king wrote to the Pope to request that he would not expedite the bull. It was intended that the prisoner should be transferred to Barcelona, but the *permanent deputation* (who then represented the Arragonese during the intervals of the assembling of the Cortes) wrote to the king, that this proceeding was contrary to the statutes which he had sworn to maintain. The deputation also judged it necessary to convoke a new Cortes, who represented to the king the dangerous consequences of the removal of Secretary Prat, whose fidelity had been particularly remarked during the reign of Ferdinand, and entreated him to set Prat at liberty, not only because they believed him to be just, faithful, and loyal, but that it was impossible to levy the supply which had been offered to the king, unless this request was granted. The king prevented the removal of the prisoner, but would not liberate him.

The deputation of the Cortes sent commissioners to Barcelona, to say that the sum of money offered to the king was conditional, and at the same time convoked the *tiers-état*. Charles being informed of it, commanded the dissolution of the assembly, which replied, that the kings of Arragon had

no right to use so violent a measure, without the consent of
the people; it decreed that the levy should not be raised,
and applied to the Court of Rome for the ratification of the
articles of Saragossa.

Leo X. was at that time displeased with the Inquisition of
Spain, on account of its refusal to admit certain briefs of
inhibition in the tribunals of Toledo, Seville, Valencia, and
Sicily; and forgetting the consideration which he owed to
Charles (who was then Emperor of Germany), he resolved
to reform the holy office, and to compel it to submit to the
rules of common law.

In consequence of this resolution he expedited three briefs
addressed to the king, the cardinal inquisitor-general, and
the inquisitors of Saragossa, in which, after explaining his
intention, he decrees that the inquisitors shall be deprived
of their offices, and that the bishops and their chapters
should present two canons to the inquisitor-general, who
should appoint one; he added that this choice should be
confirmed by the holy see, and that these new inquisitors
should be subjected every two years to a judicial censure.

The deputies received these briefs, and immediately required the inquisitors to conform to them; they replied that
they would await the orders of their immediate chief. The
king wrote to his uncle Don Alphonso of Arragon, Archbishop of Saragossa, to enter into an agreement with the
deputies, and at the same time he sent an ambassador-extra-
ordinary to Rome to demand a revocation of the briefs. The
Arragonese then promised to levy the supply if the secretary
Prat was liberated, but protested that they would not admit any proposition contrary to the promise which the king
had made.

This prince instructed his ambassador to inform the Pope
of all that had passed in the Cortes of Castile, but to keep
silence on the most important circumstances, and to assure
his Holiness that no complaints had been made of the Inqui-

sition since Cardinal Adrian had been inquisitor-general. Charles also required that no brief should be expedited to cause the *San-benitos* to be removed from the churches, or to prohibit them from being worn in the streets.

The Pope, seeing the importance which Charles attached to these things, wrote to Cardinal Adrian, that although he was perfectly informed of all that was passing, and that he had resolved to do justice to the claims of the Cortes, yet he would not carry the affair further without the consent of the king, to whom he promised to make no innovations; but he requested him to pay great attention to what was passing, as he heard serious complaints every day from all parts of the kingdom, of the avarice and injustice of the inquisitors.

This brief offended the deputies, but they continued their importunities at the Court of Rome with so much ardour, that their credit balanced the power of Charles V.; and though they did not obtain the extension of the articles, they prevented the revocation of the reforming briefs, and Charles was obliged to be satisfied with that addressed to Cardinal Adrian.

Leo X. died on the 1st of December, 1521, and Cardinal Adrian succeeded him on the 9th of January, 1522; he did not quit his office of inquisitor-general until the 10th of September, 1523, when he bestowed it on Don Alphonso Manriquez, Archbishop of Seville.

According to the most moderate calculation from the inscription at Seville, it appears that 240,025 persons were condemned by the Inquisition during the five years of the ministry of Adrian; 1620 were burnt in person; 560 in effigy; and 21,845 subjected to different penances. If the year 1523, which may be considered as an interregnum until the inscription of Seville, which is of the year 1524, is added to this, the number of victims sacrificed by the Inquisition may be estimated at 234,526 persons, an immense number, though it is far below the truth.

CHAPTER XII.

CONDUCT OF THE INQUISITORS TOWARDS THE MORESCOES.

THE New Christians of Jewish origin, flattered themselves, at the commencement of the ministry of Don Alphonso Manriquez, that they should obtain the publication of the names and charges of the witnesses, as he had supported their request in 1516, but the inquisitors persuaded him that such a proceeding tended to the destruction of the holy office, and the triumph of the enemies of the faith; and that the appearance of two new sects of *Morescoes* and *Lutherans*, rendered a great degree of severity indispensable.

It has been already stated, that an order from Ferdinand and Isabella, in 1502, had compelled all those Moors who refused to become Christians, to quit Spain. Although this law was executed in Castile, it did not affect the Moors of Arragon, as the king had yielded to the solicitations of the nobles, who represented the immense injury which it would do them, in destroying the population of their domains, where there were scarcely any baptized inhabitants.

The two sovereigns renewed their promise in 1510, and Charles V. took an oath to the same effect in the Cortes of Saragossa in 1519.

A civil war soon after broke out in Arragon, similar to one in Castile, about the same time. The factious were almost all common people, who hated the nobles: they endeavoured to injure them as much as possible, and knowing that the Moors, who were their vassals, were obliged to serve them in a more laborious manner, on account of the difference of their religion, they baptized all the Moors who fell into their hands. Above sixteen thousand thus received baptism; but as they were forced to it, many afterwards returned to their former creed. The emperor punished the chiefs of the insurrection, and many Moors fearing the same fate, quitted Spain, and retired to the kingdom of Algiers, so that in 1523, more than five thousand houses were left without inhabitants.

Charles V., irritated at this conduct, persuaded himself that he ought not to suffer any Moors to remain in his dominions, and demanded a dispensation from his oath to the Cortes of Saragossa. The Pope at first refused, on account of the scandal of such a proceeding, but the emperor insisted, and it was granted in 1524; the Pope, however, engaged him, at the same time, to charge the inquisitors to accelerate the conversion of the Moors, by announcing, that if they did not become Christians within a certain period, they would be obliged to quit Spain, on pain of being reduced to slavery. Doubts were afterwards raised, of the validity of the baptism administered to the Moors in Valencia by the rebels; but Charles assembled a council, which, after many debates, decided on the 23d of March, 1525, that it was valid, as the infidels had not offered any resistance.

The greatest part of the Moorish people fled to the mountains and the Tierra de Bernia, and resisted the arms of Charles, until the month of August, when they surrendered, after obtaining an amnesty. The Moors of Almonacid refused baptism, and took up arms; their town was taken, and several put to death, and the rest became Christians.

In the borough of Correa, the Moors assassinated the lord of the district, and seventeen Christians, who endeavoured to compel them to embrace Christianity. At last the revolt became general throughout the kingdom of Valencia, where they formed nearly twenty-six thousand families; they fortified themselves in the town of the Sierra d'Espadan, and a considerable period elapsed before they were reduced by the royal army. They then implored the protection of Germaine de Foix, second wife to Ferdinand V., and who was

then married to Don Ferdinand of Arragon, Duke of Calabria. This princess granted a passport to twelve of their
deputies, whom they sent to court to learn the real intentions
of the emperor. They demanded a delay of five years before they became Christians, or left Spain by the port of
Alicant. These demands being refused, they offered to
become Christians, on condition that the inquisitors should
not be permitted to prosecute them for the space of forty
years; this was also cruelly refused them.

They then applied to the inquisitor-general Manriquez,
who received them graciously, and supposing that they would
freely consent to receive baptism, he offered to employ his
influence with the emperor. On the 16th of January, 1526,
they remitted a memorial to him, in which they demanded,
1st, that during forty years they should not be liable to be
prosecuted by the holy office; 2ndly, that they might be
allowed to preserve their language, and their manner of
clothing themselves; 3rdly, that they might have a cemetery
separate from that of the Old Christians; 4thly, that they
might be able to marry their relations during the space of
forty years, and that the marriages already contracted should
not be interfered with; 5thly, that the ministers of their religion should continue to receive the revenues of the mosques
converted into churches; 6thly, that they might be allowed
the use of arms like other Christians; 7thly, that the charges
and rents which they paid to their lords should not be
more burdensome than those of other Christians; 8thly, that
they should not be obliged to pay the municipal expenses
of royal towns, unless they were allowed to hold offices, and
enjoy the honours depending on them.

These articles being submitted to the emperor, they were
granted, with a few restrictions, and the Moors were all
baptized, with the exception of some thousands who fled to
the mountains, and resisted the royal force during the year
1526. When they were reduced, they received baptism, and

the punishment of slavery which they had incurred was commuted for a fine of twelve thousand ducats.

The Arragonese fearing that the Moors dispersed among
them would be subjected to the same laws as those of Valencia, represented to the emperor, through the medium of
his relation the Count de Ribagorza, that they had never
caused any trouble either in politics or religion; that they
could not have any communication with Africa, on account
of the distance of the countries ; and that many of them were
excellent workmen in the fabrication of arms, and, consequently, their banishment would occasion great loss to the
kingdom of Arragon. The representations of the Arragonese
were unavailing : the emperor commanded the inquisitors to
subject the Moors of Arragon to the same laws as those of
Valencia, and they were baptized without resistance in 1526.

In 1530 the Pope gave the inquisitor-general the necessary powers to absolve all the Moors of Arragon as often as
they should relapse into heresy and repent, without inflicting
any public penance or infamous punishments. The motives
expressed in the bull for this conduct, were, that they were
much sooner converted by gentle means than severity. It is
natural to inquire why a different policy was adopted with
respect to the Jews; they were all rich merchants, while
scarcely one in five thousand was found among the Moors.
Occupied in the cultivation of the ground and the care of
their flocks they were always poor ; sometimes workmen of
singular intelligence, talent, and address, were found among
them.

The Morescoes of Grenada also occupied the attention of
the emperor, although the events which passed among them
were of less importance.

When the emperor was at Grenada in 1526, a memorial
from the Morescoes was presented to him, by Don Ferdinand
Benegas, Don Michael d'Arragon and Diego Lopez Benax-
ara; they were all members of the municipality, and illus-

trious nobles, as they were descended in the direct male line from the Moorish kings of Grenada. They represented that the Moors suffered much from the priests, judges, notaries, alguazils, and other Old Christians. The emperor appeared touched by the recital, and commissioned a bishop to go into the countries inhabited by the Moors and examine into the state of religion. The bishop visited the kingdom of Grenada, and found that the Moors had reason to complain; but he also discovered that there were scarcely seven Catholics among all these people; all the others had returned to Mahometanism, either because they had not been properly instructed, or because they were permitted to exercise their old religion in public.

The emperor convoked a council, which decreed that the inquisitorial tribunal of Jaen should be transferred to Grenada. Several other measures were adopted and approved by the emperor; the most important was a promise of pardon to the Moors for all that had passed, and a notice that they would be treated with the utmost severity, if they again relapsed into heresy. The Morescoes submitted, and obtained for eighty thousand ducats the privileges of wearing the costume of their nation, and that the Inquisition should not be allowed to seize their property if they relapsed.

The inquisitors of Grenada celebrated an *auto-da-fé* in 1528 with the greatest ceremony, in order to inspire the Moors with more respect and fear. However no Moors were burnt, but only baptized Jews who had returned to Judaism.

The Moors still continued to emigrate to Africa, although they were treated with moderation. Philip II. obtained a brief from Paul IV., by which the confessors were authorized to absolve the Moors secretly, without imposing any penance or pecuniary penalty, on the condition that they demanded absolution voluntarily. The system of indulgence which had been adopted did not prevent Louis Alboacin from being condemned to the flames. After emigrating to Africa, he returned to Valencia with several other rene-gadoes, with the intention of exciting the Morescoes to a revolt; the plot was discovered, the conspirators disarmed, and Louis was burnt in 1562.

In 1567 the Pope expedited a brief in favour of the Mo-rescoes of Valencia, but those of Grenada revolted, and elected for their king Don Ferdinand de Valor, a descendant of their former sovereigns of the dynasty of Abenhumeyas. This rebellion continued for some time ; and Philip II. en-deavoured to quell it by issuing edicts of pardon even for those crimes which came under the jurisdiction of the Inqui-sition. An amnesty was granted to the Moors on condition that they came to solicit it, and many took advantage of the permission. To prevent emigration, the king remitted the penalty of confiscation, but the inquisitors, by means of the impenetrable secrecy which they always preserved, rendered the benevolent intentions of the sovereign of no avail. They did not publish the briefs of indulgence granted by the Court of Rome, knowing that a great number of the *relapsed* would take advantage of them ; these people, not being aware of their privileges, were condemned and burnt. These ex-amples of cruelty increased the hatred of the Moors for this sanguinary tribunal, and were the cause of many seditions, which, in 1609, led to the entire expulsion of the Moors, to the number of a million souls ; so that in the space of an hundred and thirty-nine years the Inquisition deprived the kingdom of Spain of three millions of inhabitants, Jews, Mo-rescoes, and Moors.

CHAPTER XIII.

OF THE PROHIBITION OF BOOKS AND OTHER ARTICLES.

THE opinions of Luther, Zuingle, Œcolampadius, Melancthon, Muncer, and Calvin, were first promulgated during the ministry of Don Alphonso Manriquez, the fifth inquisitor-general. These reformers were called *Protestants* after the imperial diet at Spire in 1529.

Leo the Xth had already condemned the opinions of Luther as heretical, which induced Manriquez to enact severe punishments for those who should openly maintain or write in favour of them.

In 1490 several Hebrew bibles and books written by Jews were burnt at Seville; at Salamanca more than six thousand volumes of magic and sorcery were committed to the flames. In 1502 Ferdinand and Isabella appointed the presidents of the Chanceries of Valladolid and Ciudad Real, the Archbishops of Seville, Toledo, Grenada, the Bishops of Burgos, Salamanca, and Zamora, to decide on all affairs relating to the examination, censure, printing, introduction, or sale of books. In 1521 the Pope wrote to the governors of the provinces of Castile during the absence of Charles V., recommending them to prevent the introduction of the works of Luther into the kingdom ; and Cardinal Adrian, in the same year, ordered the inquisitors to seize all books of that nature : this order was repeated in 1523.

In 1530 the *Supreme* Council wrote to the inquisitors during the absence of Cardinal Manriquez, on the necessity of executing the measures which had been ordained ; adding, that information had been received that the writings of Luther had been introduced into the kingdom under fictitious titles, or as works entirely composed by Catholic

54363

authors ; and in order to repress this intolerable abuse, they were commanded to visit all public libraries for those books, and to add to the edict of denunciations, a particular article, to oblige all Catholics to denounce any person who might read or keep them in their houses.   In 1535 Cardinal Manriquez addressed an order to the inquisitors, and another in the same year prohibiting the universities of the kingdom from explaining, reading, or even selling the *Colloquies of Erasmus.*   In 1528 he anathematised some other works of the same author, although he had defended him in 1527, in an assembly which met to examine his writings.

Erasmus was considered in Spain as a supporter of the Catholic faith against the doctrine of Luther, and his enemies were only a few scholastic theologians, who were not acquainted with the Greek and Hebrew tongues.   The Spanish theologians who wrote against him were, Diego Lopez de Zuñiga, Sancho de Carranza, professor of theology in the university of Alcala de Henarés, Brother Louis de Carjaval, a Franciscan, Edward Lee, the English ambassador, and Pedro Vittoria, a theologian of Salamanca.

After this first attack, in the Lent of the year 1527, two monks denounced several propositions in the works of Erasmus, as heretical.   Alphonso Manriquez (although he was then the friend of Erasmus) was obliged to submit these propositions to the examination of qualifiers; but he appointed the most learned men of the kingdom to that office.

This assembly of doctors lasted two months, when the plague, which then desolated some parts of the kingdom, obliged them to separate, before they had decided on the judgment to be pronounced ; it appears from several letters written by Erasmus about that time that he hoped it would be favourable to him *.

* Erasmus, letters 884, 907, 910.

But the Supreme Council qualified his *Colloquies*, his *Eulogy of Folly*, and his *Paraphrase*, and prohibited them from being read. In later times, this prohibition was extended to several other books of the same author, and the Inquisition recommended in its edicts that the works of Erasmus should be read with caution.

The emperor Charles V. commissioned the University of Louvain to form a list of dangerous books, and in 1539 he obtained a bull of approbation from the Pope. The index was published in 1546 by the university in all the states of Flanders, six years after a decree had been issued to prohibit the writings of Luther from being read or bought on pain of death*.

This severe measure displeased all ranks. The princes of Germany openly complained of it, and offered to assist Charles in his war against the Turks, if he would allow the people liberty in matters of religion. Charles paid no attention to their remonstrances, and this bad policy accelerated the progress of Lutheranism.

In 1549, the inquisitor-general, with the approbation of the Supreme Council, added some new works to the list of those which had been prohibited, and addressed two ordinances to the inquisitors, enjoining them in the first, not to allow any person to possess them, and in the second, commanding the consultors of the holy office neither to read nor keep them, though the execution of the decrees might throw them into their hands.

In 1546 the emperor commanded the University of Louvain to publish the index, with additions. This work appeared in 1550, and the prince remitted it to the inquisitor-general, and it was printed by the order of the Supreme Council, with a supplement composed of books prohibited in Spain; some time after the council framed another index, which was certified by the secretary.

* Sandoval. Hist. Charles V. B. 24, § 23.

All the Inquisitions received copies, and a bull from Julius III., which renewed the prohibitions and revoked the permissions contrary to the new bulls : he charged the inquisitors to seize as many books as they could ; to publish prohibitory edicts, accompanied by censures ; to prosecute those who did not obey them, as suspected of heresy ; and to give an account of the books which they had read and preserved.

The Pope added, that he was informed that a great number were in the possession of librarians and private persons, particularly the Spanish Bibles mentioned in the catalogue, and the Missal and Diurnal in the supplement.

The Council of Trent, after acknowledging the necessity of treating the writings of heretics with great severity, commissioned the celebrated Carranza to compose the catalogue. After having examined the great number of books submitted to the council, he sent all those which did not contain any thing reprehensible to the Dominican convent in the city of Trent, and caused the rest to be burnt, or torn, and thrown into the Adige*. Carranza soon after accompanied Philip II. to England, where he not only converted many Lutherans, but caused many bibles which had been translated to be burnt.

Some bibles, which had been introduced into Spain, and were not upon the list, were also prohibited ; and the inquisitors were commanded to publish the interdict, and to employ severe measures against those who refused to obey it. The ordinances of the Council of Castile, composed by the order of the king, and approved by him, were published in the same year ; they gave the council the privilege of permitting books to be printed, on the condition that they should be examined previously, if the subject of which they treated was important.

* Salazar de Mendoza, Life of Don Bartholomew Carranza, ch. vii.

Charles V. and Philip II. had regulated the circulation of books in their American states. In 1543 the viceroys and other authorities were commanded to prevent the introduction or printing of tales and romances.

In 1550 a new decree obliged the tribunal of the commerce of Seville, to register all the books destined for the colonies, to certify that they were not prohibited.

In 1556 the government commanded that no work relating to the affairs of America should be published without a permission from the council of the Indies, and that those already printed should not be sold unless they were examined and approved, which obliged all those who possessed any to submit them to the council. The officers of the customs in America were also obliged to seize all the prohibited books which might be imported, and remit them to the archbishops and bishops, who, in this case, possessed the same powers as the inquisitors of Spain.

Lastly, Philip II. in 1560 decreed new measures, and the *surveillance* was afterwards as strictly observed in the colonies of the New World as in the Peninsula.

Although Charles V. and Philip II. neglected nothing that could prevent the introduction of prohibited books into Spain, several which were favourable to the Lutheran heresy penetrated into the kingdom. In 1558 the inquisitor-general published an edict more severe than any of the preceding ; and also drew up an instruction for the use of the inquisitors ; importing, that all books mentioned in the printed catalogue should be seized ; that a public *auto-da-fé* should be made of those tending to heresy ; that the commentaries and notes attributed to Melancthon should be suppressed in all the treatises on grammar where they were introduced ; that the bibles marked as being suspected should be examined ; that no books should be seized except those mentioned in the list ; that all the books printed in Germany since 1519 without the name of the author should be examined; that the translation of *Theophylact* by *Œco-lampadius* should be seized; likewise some volumes of the works of St. John Chrysostom, which had been translated by that arch-heretic and *Wolfang Nusculus*; that the commentaries by heretics on works composed by catholics should be suppressed; and that a book on medicine might be seized, although it was not mentioned in the index.

When this edict was published, Francis Sanchez, professor of theology in the university of Salamanca, wrote to inform the Supreme Council, that he had occupied himself for several years in examining dangerous books, and gave his opinion on the course which ought to be pursued.

The council, in consequence, decreed that those theologians in the university who had studied the Oriental languages, should be obliged, as well as other persons, to give up their Hebrew and Greek Bibles to the commissaries of the holy office, on pain of excommunication; that the proprietors of Greek, Arabic, and Hebrew books, not mentioned in the list, should not be molested; that the order concerning the books printed without the name of the author, related only to modern productions; that the request made by some persons to be allowed to keep *Pomponius Mela*, with the commentary of *Nadicano*, should be refused; that these books should be remitted to the council to be examined; that the order to seize all works containing errors should only be applied to modern books; and that the *Summa Armata* of Durand, of Cajetan, Peter Lombard, Origen, Theophylact, Tertullian, Lactantius, Lucian, Aristotle, Plato, Seneca, and other authors of that class, should be allowed to circulate; that the council being informed that several catalogues of prohibited books existed, would unite them, and compose one general catalogue.

In the year 1558 the terrible law of Philip II. was published, which decreed the punishments of death and confiscation for all those who should sell, buy, keep, or read, the books prohibited by the holy office ; and, to ensure the execution of this sanguinary law, the index was printed, that the people might not allege ignorance in their defence.

A bull of 1559 enjoins confessors to interrogate their penitents on this subject, and to remind them that they were obliged to denounce the guilty on pain of excommunication. A particular article subjects the confessors to the same punishment if they neglected this duty, even if their penitents were of the highest rank.

This severe law was however mitigated in 1561, when the Cardinal of Alexandria, inquisitor-general of Rome, published a decree, announcing, in the name of Pius IV., that some of the prohibitions of books had been withdrawn. This decree also granted permission to read and possess some books which had been suppressed only because they were written by heretics.

Valdes, the Inquisitor-general of Spain, immediately wrote to the inquisitors of the provinces, to suspend the execution of the edict, until he had received the orders of the king, to whom he had represented the danger arising from a measure which annulled the punishment of excommunication ; but Valdes had another motive in this proceeding.

In 1559, this inquisitor had published a printed catalogue of prohibited books, which was much more extended than that of 1558, and in which, according to the advice of Francis Sanchez, he had introduced all the works mentioned in the catalogues of Rome, Lisbon, Louvain, and those of Spain of an earlier date. He divided them into six classes. The first consisted of Latin books ; the second of those written in Castilian ; the third of those in the Teutonic language ; the fourth of German books ; the fifth of French ; and the sixth of Portuguese. Valdes, in a note at the end of his index, gave notice that there were many books subject to the prohibition, not mentioned in the list, but that they would be added.   He appointed the punishment of excommunication, and a penalty of two hundred ducats, for those persons who should read any of these books, and in this number were included some which were permitted to be read by the last edict of the Pope.

Valdes had inserted in his catalogue some books which had not only been considered catholic, but were in the hands of everybody and full of true piety, particularly some works of Don Hernand de Talavera, the venerable Juan d'Arila, Bartholomew Carranza de Miranda, Archbishop of Toledo ; Hernand de Villegas, Louis de Granada, a Dominican ; and St. Francis Borgia.

The catalogue of Valdes contained other general prohibitions.   This proscription included all Hebrew books, and those in other tongues which treated of the Jewish customs ; those of the Arabs, or those which in any way treated of the Mahometan religion; all works composed or translated by an heretic, or a person condemned by the holy office; all treatises in the Spanish language with a preface, letter, prologue, summary, notes, additions, paraphrase, explanation, glossary, or writing of that nature added by an heretic ; all sermons, writings, letters, discourses on the Christian religion, its mysteries, sacraments, or the Holy Scriptures, if these works were inedited manuscripts.

Lastly, the same prohibition was extended to a multitude of translations of the Bible, and other books which had been written by men of great piety, and had always been considered as proper guides to virtue : of this number were the works of Denis, *the Carthusian ;* the author known by the name of *the Idiot;* the Bishop Roffnuse, and many other writers.

In the eighteenth session of the Council of Trent (which began on the 26th February, 1562), the bishops found that it was necessary to examine the books which were denounced as suspicious, on account of the complaints which had been made on the prohibition of the great number of works which had been unjustly enrolled in the decree of Paul IV. The council appointed commissioners to examine them, and they made a report of their labour in the last session in 1563 : they had drawn up a catalogue of the works which they considered necessary to be prohibited. It was submitted to Pius V., who published it in 1564, with ten general rules for the solution of any difficulties which might be discovered. A great number of books, which had been unjustly condemned by Valdes, were omitted in this index, and the Catechism of Carranza was declared to be orthodox by an assembly of theologians who had been appointed to examine it.

In 1565 the Doctor Gonzales Illescas published the first part of his *Pontifical History*. It was immediately seized by the holy office, and the second part, printed at Valladolid in 1567, shared the same fate. A short time after, Illescas was persecuted by the inquisitors of Valladolid ; and, to preserve himself from becoming their victim, was obliged to suppress his work and write another, omitting the articles against some of the popes : this work appeared in 1574. Although the holy office had so carefully suppressed the first edition, it was inserted in the index of 1583, as if some copies had been still in existence.

In 1567 the council commanded the theological works of Brother John Fero, a Franciscan of Italy, to be seized, with the notes and corrections of Brother Michael de Medina, and some other works of the same author, who ended his days in the dungeons of the Inquisition in 1578, before his sentence had been pronounced. After his death, his *Apology for John Fero* was inserted in the expurgatory index.

In 1568 the Supreme Council charged the officers of the Inquisition to watch the frontiers of Guiprescoa, Navarre, Arragon, and Catalonia, with the greatest vigilance, to prevent the introduction of prohibited books. This resolution was adopted, because information had been received that a great number of Lutheran books in the Castilian tongue were packed and sent in hogsheads of the wines of Champagne and Burgundy, with so much art, that the officers of the customs could not discover the deception.

In 1570 the council prohibited a work on the Pentateuch by Brother Jerome de Holcastro; and the *Petit Office*, printed at Paris in 1556. The motive for this suppression was singular: the frontispiece was decorated with a cross and a swan, with the motto, "IN HOC CIGNO VINCES." It is plain that the *Petit Office* was prohibited, because a C was used instead of the S in the word *signo*. The same severity was shewn in all cases where the books had this symbol, or any allegories of that nature.

In 1571 the inquisitors caused a Spanish Bible, printed at Baste, to be seized, and Philip II. wrote to the Duke of Alva, the governor of the Low Countries, to compose an index for the use of the Flemish people, with the assistance of the learned Arias Montanus. He presided in an assembly of theologians, who judged that the new index should only consist of the Latin prohibited by the Inquisition, or which it was necessary to correct. This measure was applied only to some well-known authors who were dead, and to some others, still living ; but more particularly to the works of Erasmus, and with circumstances which might lead to the supposition, that his books were the principal objects of the prohibition, and that of the other authors merely a pretext to conceal the injury done to him. This catalogue was printed at Antwerp in 1571, with a preface by Arias Montanus, a royal decree and a proclamation of the Duke of Alva enforcing the execution of it. This list is known by the name of the *Expurgatory Index of the Duke of Alva*. The holy office had no part in this affair, as the Flemings had refused to recognise their authority.

In 1582 the inquisitor-general, Don Gaspard de Quiroga,

published a new *Prohibitory Index*. It is remarkable *that the Index of his predecessor Valdes is mentioned in this list.*

That which was published in 1584 was drawn up by Juan de Mariana, who soon after had some of his own works prohibited. In 1611, a new index was formed under the inquisitor-general Don Bernard de Roxas of Sandoval.

The Cardinal Zapata, who succeeded Roxas, adopted one more extended in 1620, and it was used by his successor, Don Antonio de Sotomayor, in 1630. This catalogue was the first which the inquisitors presumed to publish from their own authority, and without being commissioned by government. Don Diego Savimiato Valladares, inquisitor-general in 1681, began to reprint it with additions, and it was finished by Don Vidal Marin, who published it in 1707.

Don Francis Perez del Prado, another inquisitor-general, commissioned the Jesuits Casani and Carrasco to compose a new catalogue. Although these monks were not authorized by the Supreme Council, they inserted in the list all the books which they supposed to be favourable to the Jansenists, Baius and Father Quesnel. Their conduct was denounced to the Supreme Council by the Dominican Concina, and some other monks; the Jesuits were examined, and defended themselves: the council, though it could not approve, did not carry the affair further; it had not sufficient power to balance the influence of the Jesuit Francis Rabago, who was confessor to Ferdinand VI.

Among the books which they prohibited were the works of Cardinal *Norris*, which were held in general estimation by the learned throughout Christendom. Benedict XIV., in 1748, addressed a brief to the inquisitor-general, commanding him to revoke the prohibition; as this order was not obeyed, the Pope complained to the king, but was unable to obtain his request until ten years after, when the Jesuit Rabago no longer directed the conscience of the monarch.

The index of the Jesuits also contained several treatises of the venerable Don Juan de Palafox y Mendoza, Archbishop and Viceroy of Mexico. The congregation of rites afterwards declared that there was nothing in them worthy of censure, and the inquisitor-general was obliged to revoke the prohibition in an edict, the copies of which were immediately bought up by some friends of the Jesuits. To give an idea of the criticism of Perez del Prado, it is sufficient to say that he bitterly lamented the misfortune of the age he lived in, saying, " *That some individuals had carried their audacity to the execrable extremity of demanding permission to read the Holy Scriptures in the vulgar tongue,* without *fearing to encounter mortal poison therein.*"

In 1792 a new index was published, without the consent, and even in opposition to the Supreme Council, by Don Augustine Rubin de Cevallos, inquisitor-general. It is this index which is still in force, but the prohibitions and expurgatory measures have since been multiplied.

The prohibitory decrees are preceded by *qualification.* The process is instituted before the supreme council; but as the information is generally laid before the inquisitors of the court, they appoint the qualifiers who censure the book. A copy of the work and the denunciation is sent to the first qualifier, and afterwards to the second, unsigned by the opinion of the first; if they do not accord, copies are sent a third time before it is submitted to the Supreme Council. The inquisitors of the provinces have likewise the privilege of receiving informations : they proceed in the same manner; but the council always commission the inquisitors of the court to censure books, because they were more sure of their qualifiers.

If any person presumed to buy, keep, or read prohibited books, he rendered himself liable to be suspected of heresy by the inquisitors, although it might not be proved that he became an heretic from such reading : he incurred the punishment of major excommunication, and was proceeded against by the tribunal: the result of this action was the absolution *ab cautelam*.

During the last years of the eighteenth century, no person has been imprisoned for reading prohibited books, unless he was convicted of having advanced or written heretical propositions. The punishment inflicted was merely a pecuniary penalty, and a declaration that the individual was slightly suspected of heresy; it must be acknowledged that this qualification was omitted, if there was any reason to suppose that the accused had erred from motives of curiosity, and not from a tendency to false doctrine. Nevertheless all these proceedings are arbitrary, and the inquisitors have the power of pursuing the infringers of this law as if they were heretics.

The permission to read prohibited books, rendered all actions instituted against those who violated the law ineffectual. The Pope granted it for a sum of money, without inquiring if the person who demanded it was capable of abusing the permission. The inquisitor-general of Spain acted with more prudence; he took secret informations on the conduct of the solicitor, and required him to state in writing the object of his demand, and the subject on which he wished to consult the prohibited books. Where the permission granted was general, the books mentioned in the edicts were excepted. In this sense the works of Rousseau, Montesquieu, Mirabeau, Diderot, d'Alembert, Voltaire, and several other modern philosophers, among whom was Filangieri, were excepted from the privilege. During the last years of the Inquisition, the permissions granted by the Court of Rome did not defend the persons who received them from the inquisitorial actions; they were subject to revision, and the inquisitor-general did not authorize the use of them without great difficulty, and as if the Court of Rome had never granted them.

The Inquisition also prohibited pictures, medals, prints,

and a number of other things, with as much severity as books. Thus fans, snuff-boxes, mirrors, and other articles of furniture, were often the cause of great troubles and difficulties to those who possessed them, if they happened to be adorned with a mythological figure which might be considered as indecent.

CHAPTER XIV.

PARTICULAR TRIALS FOR SUSPICION OF LUTHERANISM, AND SOME OTHER CRIMES.

Edicts against Lutherans, Illuminati, &c.

THE inquisitor-general, who perceived the necessity of arresting the progress of Lutheranism in Spain, decreed, in concert with the Council of the Inquisition, several new articles in addition to the annual edict. These articles oblige every Christian to declare, if he knows or has heard of any person who has said, maintained, or thought that the sect of Luther is good, or that his partisans will be saved, and approved nor believed any of his condemned propositions: for example, that it is not necessary to confess sins to a priest, and that it is sufficient to confess to God ; that neither the Pope or the priests have the power of remitting sins ; that the body of Jesus is not actually present in the consecrated host; that it is not permitted to pray to saints, or expose images in churches; that faith and baptism are sufficient for salvation, and that good works are not necessary ; that every Christian may, although not of the priesthood, receive the confession of another Christian, and administer the sacrament to him ; that the Pope has not the power of granting indulgences ; that priests and monks may lawfully marry; that God did not establish the regular religious orders ; that the state of marriage is better and more perfect than that of celibacy; that there ought to be no festivals but the sabbath, and that it is not sinful to eat meat on Friday, in Lent, or on other fast-days.

Alphonso Manriquez also gave permission to the inquisitors of the provinces to take any measures they might think proper, to discover those persons who had embraced the heresy of the *illuminati*, (*alumbrados*.) These people, who were also called *dejados* (*quietists*), formed a sect whose chief, it is said, was that *Muncer* who had already established that of the Anabaptists. Some time after, the Council of the Inquisition added several articles relative to the *illuminati* to those already mentioned.

I am of opinion, that the first Spaniards who followed the doctrines of Luther were Franciscan monks; for Clement VII., in 1526, authorized the general and provincials of the order of Minor Friars of St. Francis d'Assiz, to absolve those of the community who had fallen into that heresy, after they had taken an oath to renounce it for ever. Several monks of the same order had already represented to the Pope, that by the privileges granted to them in the bull *mare magnum,* and confirmed by other decrees of the holy see, no stranger had a right to interfere in their affairs, and that they did not recognise any judge but the judge of their institution, even in cases of apostasy and heresy.

Manriquez, embarrassed in his ministry by the pretensions of the Franciscans, wrote to the Pope, who expedited, in 1525, a brief, by which the inquisitor-general was empowered to take cognizance of these affairs, assisted by a monk, named by the prelate of the order, and that, in cases of appeal from judgment, the Pope should be applied to : but these appeals were afterwards ordered to be made before the inquisitor-general.

Trials of several Persons.

During the ministry of the inquisitor-general Mânriquez,

history points out several illustrious and innocent victims of the tribunal, who were suspected of Lutheranism: such was the venerable Juan d'Avila, who would have been beatified, if he had been a monk, but he was only a secular priest: he was called, in Spain, the *Apostle of Andalusia,* on account of his exemplary life, and his charitable actions. St. Theresa de Jesus informs us, in her works, that she derived much assistance from his counsels and doctrine. He preached the gospel with simplicity, and never introduced into his discourses those questions which at that time so disgracefully agitated the scholastic theologians. Some envious monks, irritated at his aversion for disputes, united to plan his ruin. They denounced some of his propositions to the Inquisition, as tending to Lutheranism and the doctrines of the *illuminati.* In 1534, Juan d'Avila was confined in the secret prison of the holy office, by an order of the inquisitors; they did not make their resolution known to the Supreme Council or to the ordinary, on the pretence that this measure was only ordained in case of a difference of opinion. Although this proceeding was contrary to the laws of the Inquisition, to the royal ordinances, and those of the Supreme Council, yet they contemned these violations, and even tacitly approved them, as no reprimand was addressed to the offenders. This act of the Inquisition, which took place at Seville, much affected the inquisitor-general: he occupied the see of that city, and had the greatest esteem for Juan d'Avila, whom he regarded as a saint, which was a fortunate circumstance for him, as the protection of Manriquez, as chief of the Inquisition, greatly contributed to prove his innocence; d'Avila was acquitted, and continued to preach with the same zeal and charity until his death.

This year was more fatal to two men, who are celebrated in the literary history of Spain—Juan de Vergara, and Bernardin de Tobar, his brother: they were arrested by the Inquisition of Toledo, and were not released from its dungeons, until they had been subjected to the abjuration (*de levi*) of the Lutheran heresy, to receive the absolution of censures *ad cautelam*, and to several penances. Juan de Vergara was a canon of Toledo, and had been secretary to Cardinal Ximenez de Cisneros, and to Don Alphonso de Fonseca, his successor in the see of that city. Nicholas Antonio has inserted, in his library, a notice of the literary productions of this Spaniard, and does justice to his virtue and merit. His profound knowledge of the Greek and Hebrew languages was the cause of his misfortune; he had remarked some faults in the translation of the vulgate, and thus gave the signal of persecution to some monks, who had only studied Latin and the jargon of the schools. The chapter of Toledo honoured his memory in placing on his tomb an epitaph, which is preserved by the author I have cited. Vergara had a claim on the gratitude of this community, for having composed the inscriptions which decorate the choir of their church.

Bernardin de Tobar is less known, but Peter Martyr d'Angleria mentions him among the learned men of the sixteenth century, and John Louis Vives, a learned man of that age, says in writing to Erasmus: " We live in a difficult time; it is dangerous either to speak or be silent; Vergara, his brother Bernardin de Tobar, and several other learned men, have been arrested in Spain *."

Among this number was one of whom Vives could not give a particular account. I speak of Alphonso Virues, a Benedictine, born at Olmedo, and one of the best theologians of his time. He had a profound knowledge of the oriental languages, and had composed several works. He was a member of the commission which judged the works of Erasmus in 1527, and preacher to Charles V., who listened to his discourses with so much pleasure, that he took him to

---

* Mayan's Life of John Louis Vives, in the introduction to the new edition of his works.

Germany, and on his return to Spain would not hear any other person. These distinctions excited the envy of the monks, and they would have succeeded in their endeavours to ruin him, but for the firmness and constancy of the emperor in protecting him.

Virues was suspected of being favourable to the opinions of Luther, and thrown into the secret prisons of the holy office at Seville. The emperor, who knew him well, both from his sermons, and the intercourse which took place during their travels in Germany, felt this blow acutely, and not doubting that Virues was the victim of an intrigue which the inquisitor-general ought to have prevented, he exiled Manriquez, who was obliged to retire to his archbishopric of Seville, where he died in 1538. Not content with this, Charles commanded the Supreme Council to address an ordinance to all the tribunals of the Inquisition, importing, that in case of a preliminary instruction sufficiently serious to cause the arrest of a monk, the decree of imprisonment should be delayed, and that the inquisitors should send an entire and faithful copy of the commencement of the proceedings to the Supreme Council, and wait for the orders which would be sent them after the examination of the writings.

The unfortunate Virues, nevertheless, suffered all the horrors of a secret imprisonment for four years. During this period, as he writes to Charles V., " he was scarcely allowed to breathe or to occupy himself with anything but charges, replies, testimonies, defences, libels, means, acts *(nomina quæ et ipso pœne timendo sono . . . . . words which cannot be heard without terrors)*, or with heresies, blasphemies, errors, anathemas, schisms, and other monsters, which, with labour that may be compared to those of Hercules, I have at last conquered with the aid of Jesus Christ, so that I am now justified through your majesty's protection *."

* Virues: *Philippics against Melancthon,* in the dedication of the edition of Antwerp, 1541.

One of the means employed by Virues for his defence, was
to demand that the tribunal should pay attention to the
points of doctrine which he had established, and prepared to
attack Melancthon and other Lutherans before the diet of
Ratisbon; but this demand did not gain the object which he
had in view, which was a complete absolution, because his
enemies had denounced propositions advanced in public.
Although he proved that they were extremely Catholic,
when examined with the text, yet he could not prevent them
from incurring the theological censure in the form given by
the denunciation: he was obliged to submit to an abjuration
of all heresies, particularly that of Luther and his adherents.
The definitive sentence was pronounced in 1537: he was
declared to be suspected of professing the errors of Luther,
and condemned to be absolved from the censures *ad cautelam;*
to be confined in a monastery for two years, and prohibited
from preaching the word of God for two years after his
release.

The emperor, when informed of these transactions, complained to the Pope, who, in 1538, addressed a brief to
Virues, which contained a dispensation from the different
penances to which he had been condemned: it also re-in-
stated him in his office of preacher ; and declared, that what
had passed could not exclude him from any office, not even
from episcopacy.

It is surprising that the affair of Virues, and many others,
did not make Charles V. perceive the nature of the Inquisition, and that he still continued to protect that institution.
However, the trial of his preacher, and several other crosses
which he experienced about that time, were the reasons why
he deprived the holy office of the royal jurisdiction in 1535,
and it was not restored until the year 1545. This favour
for Virues was so constant, that he soon after presented him
to the Pope for the bishopric of the Canaries, but the Pope
refused him, alleging that the suspicions raised against the

purity of his faith rendered him improper to be invested with
the dignity of a bishop, although the bull had declared him
to be eligible.   The emperor insisted, and the Pope at
length yielded to his pressing solicitations.   Virues was made
Bishop of the Canaries in 1540.

In 1527 the Inquisition of Valladolid was occupied by an
affair, of which it is necessary to give an account, that the
compassion and indulgence which the inquisitors always professed in their acts, and other forms of justice, may be justly
appreciated.

One Diego Vallejo, of the village of Palacios de Meneses,
in the diocese of Palencia, having been arrested for blasphemy by the Inquisition, declared, among other things, that
two months before, on the 24th of April, 1526, two physicians, named Alphonso Garcia and Juan de Salas, were
disputing on the subject of medicine, before him and Ferdinand Ramirez, his son-in-law : the first maintained his opinion on the authority of certain writers ; Salas affirmed that
these writers were deceived ; Garcia replied that his opinion
was proved by the text of the evangelists, which caused Salas
to say *that they had lied as well as the others*.   Ferdinand
Ramirez (who had also been arrested upon suspicion of Judaism) was examined the same day; his deposition was the
same as that of Vallejo, but he added, that Salas returned
to his house some hours after, and in speaking of what had
passed, said, *" What folly I have asserted !"*   When the
tribunal had finished the affair of Ramirez and Vallejo, they
arrested Juan de Salas.

The inquisitors (without the concurrence of the diocesan,
without consultors or qualifiers, and without communicating
with the Supreme Council) decreed the arrest of Juan de
Salas on the 14th of February, 1527, as if the declarations of
Ramirez and Vallejo had been sufficient.   The audiences of
admonition were granted, and the depositions were communicated without the names of the persons or place.   He

replied that the circumstances were not correctly stated. The other physician was then called, who declared, that in conversing with Salas on the evangelists, he heard him say, *that some of them had lied.* He was asked if any one had reproached Salas for this expression ; Garcia replied, that an hour after he had advised him to give himself up to the Inquisition, and that he had promised to do so. The inquisitor then asked if he was inimical to the accused ; the witness replied in the negative. On the 16th of April the ratification of Ramirez and Garcia took place. On the 6th of May the prisoner presented two requisitions or means of defence : in the first he protested against all that had been said contrary to his declaration, and pointed out the differences in the depositions of the witnesses ; the second was an *interrogatory* in thirteen questions, two of which tended to prove his orthodoxy, and the others to justify the motives of the challenge which he had presented against certain persons who had been called upon to depose in his trial. This piece contains, in the margin, the witnesses to be consulted for each question. It will be seen that the prisoner took advantage of the laws of the holy office in his defence ; but the inquisitors, instead of conforming to their own regulations, erased the names of several persons designated in the list of the accused as witnesses on his side, and would not hear them. Nevertheless, the facts mentioned in the interrogatory were proved by fourteen witnesses, and on the 25th of May the fiscal gave his conclusions.

The fact related by Ramirez ; the contradictions in the depositions of the witnesses ; the difference in the report of both, from that of the accuser ; the important advantages gained by the prisoner in justifying his challenge, in only having two witnesses against him (who had both been prosecuted, one for blasphemy, the other for Judaism), and in being accused of only one proposition ; lastly, the possibility that the accused had forgotten many things during the space

of a year, are circumstances which would make any one suppose that Juan de Salas would have been acquitted, or that
they would, at least, (if they supposed that he had denied
the truth,) have contented themselves with imposing the
penance of the suspicion *de levi* upon him; but instead of
this, the inquisitor Moriz, without the concurrence of his
colleague Alvarado, decreed that Salas should be tortured,
as guilty of concealment.   In this act the following deposition is found:—" We ordain that the said torture be employed in the manner and during the time that we shall think
proper, after having protested as we still protest, that, in
case of injury, death, or fractured limbs, the fault can only
be imputed to the said licentiate Salas."   The decree of
Moriz took effect: I subjoin the verbal process of the execution.

" At Valladolid, on the 21st of June, 1527, the licentiate
Moriz, inquisitor, caused the licentiate Juan de Salas to appear before him, and the sentence was read and notified to
him.   After the reading, the said licentiate Salas declared,
that *he had not said that of which he was accused;* and the
said licentiate Moriz immediately caused him to be conducted
to the chamber of torture, where, being stripped to his shirt,
Salas was put by the shoulders into the *chevalet,* where the
executioner, Pedro Porras, fastened him by the arms and
legs with cords of hemp, of which he made *eleven turns* round
each limb; Salas, during the time that the said Pedro was
tying him thus, was warned to speak the truth several times,
to which he always replied, *that he had never said what he
was accused of.*   He recited the creed, " Quicumque vult,"
and several times gave thanks to God and our Lady; and the
said Salas being still tied as before mentioned, a fine wet
cloth was put over his face, and about a pint of water was
poured into his mouth and nostrils, from an earthen vessel
with a hole at the bottom, and containing about two quarts:
nevertheless, Salas still persisted *in denying the accusation.*

Then Pedro de Porras *tightened the cords* on the right leg, and poured a second measure of water on the face ; the cords *were tightened a second time* on the same leg, but Juan de Salas still persisted in *denying that he had ever said any thing of the kind ;* and although pressed to tell the truth several times, *he still denied the accusation.* Then the said licentiate Moriz, having declared that *the torture was* BEGUN BUT NOT FINISHED, commanded that it should cease. The accused was withdrawn from the chevalet or rack, at which execution, I, Henry Paz, was present from the beginning to the end.—Henry Paz, notary."

If this execution was but the beginning of the torture, how was it to finish ? By the death of the sufferer ? In order to understand this statement, it is necessary to know that the instrument, which in Castilian is called *escalera* (and which has also the name of *burro,* and is translated into French by the word *chevalet*), is a machine of wood, invented to torture the accused. It is formed like a groove, large enough to hold the body of a man, without a bottom, but a stick crosses it, over which the body falls in such a position, that the feet are much higher than the head ; consequently, a violent and painful respiration ensues, with intolerable pains in the sides, the arms, and legs, where the pressure of the cords is so great, even before the *garot* has been used, that they penetrate to the bone.

If we observe the manner in which the people who carry merchandise on mules or in carts tighten the cords by means of sticks, we can easily imagine the torments which the unfortunate John de Salas must have suffered. The introduction of a liquid is not less likely to kill those whom the inquisitors torture, and it has happened more than once. The mouth, during the torture, is in the most unfavourable position for respiration, so much so, that a person would die if he remained several hours in it ; a piece of fine wet linen is introduced into the throat, on which the water from the vessel is poured so slowly, that it requires an hour to consume a pint, although it descends without intermission. In this state the patient finds it impossible to breathe, as the water enters the nostrils at the same time, and the rupture of a blood-vessel in the lungs is often the result.

Raymond Gonzales de Montes (who, in 1558, was so fortunate as to escape from the prisons of the holy office at Seville) wrote a book in Latin, on the Inquisition, under the name of *Reginaldus Gonsalvius Montanus**. He informs us that the cord was wound eight or ten times round the legs. Eleven turns were made round the limbs of Salas, besides those of the *garot.* We may form an idea of the humanity of the Inquisition of Valladolid, from the definitive sentence pronounced by the licentiate Moriz and his colleague, Doctor Alvarado, without any other formality, after they had taken (if we may believe them) the advice of persons noted for their learning and virtue, but without the adjournment which ought to have preceded it, and without the concurrence of the diocesan in ordinary. They declared that the fiscal had not entirely proved the accusation, and that the prisoner had succeeded in destroying some of the charges; but that on account of the suspicion arising from the trial, Juan de Salas was condemned to the punishment of the public *auto-da-fé*, in his shirt, without a cloak, his head uncovered, and with a torch in his hand; that he should abjure heresy publicly, and that he should pay ten ducats of gold to the Inquisition, and fulfil his penance in the church assigned. It is seen, by a certificate afterwards given in, that Juan de Salas performed his *auto-da-fé* on the 24th of June, 1528, and that his father paid the fine : the trial offers no other peculiarity. This affair, and several others of a simi-

---

* Reginaldus Gonzalvius Montanus, *Sanctæ Inquisitionis Hispanicæ, artes aliquot detectæ.* This work is now extremely rare; it was published in 8vo. at Heidelberg in 1567.

lar nature, caused the Supreme Council to publish a decree in 1558, commanding that the torture should not be administered without an order from the council.

Letter-Orders, relating to the Proceedings.

The abuse of the secrecy of the proceedings caused a number of complaints to be addressed to the Inquisitor-general. He usually referred them to the Supreme Council, which, during the administration of Manriquez, addressed several circulars to the provincial tribunals: it is necessary to make known the most important.

In one of these writings, dated March 14th, 1528, it is said, that if an accused person (when asked a general question) declares at first that he knows nothing on the subject, and afterwards, when questioned on a particular fact, confesses that he is acquainted with it (in case the inquisitors think proper to take down the second declaration, to make use of it against a third), they should insert the first question and the answer of the accused in the same verbal process, because it might assist in determining the degree of confidence to be placed in his declarations.

On the 16th of March, 1530, another instruction of the council appeared. It directed that the facts related by the witnesses in favour of the prisoner should be mentioned as well as those against him. This direction, however just, has not been strictly followed, since it was never observed in the extract of the publication of the depositions given to the accused and his defender; consequently, no advantage could be derived by the prisoner from the declarations in his favour.

Another circular of the 13th of May in the same year, says, that if an accused person challenges a witness, he must be interrogated on the foundation of the proceedings, as he might have facts to depose against the accused.

On the 16th June, 1531, the council wrote to the tribunals, that if the accused challenged several persons, on the supposition that they will depose against him, the witnesses whom he calls to prove the facts which caused the challenge, shall be examined on each individual, although they have not made any deposition, in order that the accused may not suppose at the time of the publication of the depositions, from an omission (if there should be any), that some have deposed against him, and that the others are not mentioned, or have not said anything.

Another instruction on the 13th of May, 1532, directs, that the relations of the accused shall not be admitted as witnesses in the proof of the challenge.

In another decree of the 5th March, 1535, it is ordained that the witness shall be asked if there is any enmity between them and the accused.

On the 20th of July, the council obliged the tribunals to insert in the extract of the publication of the depositions, the day, the month, and the hour when each witness gave his evidence.

In March, 1525, it was decreed, that when the extract was given to the accused, he was not to be informed that any witness had declared the fact to be known to others, because if they said nothing against him, it was not proper to inform the accused of it, as he would learn, from that circumstance, that some persons had spoken in his favour, or at least had declared that they knew nothing against him.

Another regulation of the 8th of April, 1533, prohibited the inquisitors from communicating the extract of the publication of the depositions to the accused, before the ratification of the declarations.

The council decreed, on the 22d December, 1536, that in transacting any business relating to circumstances which took place in the house of a person deceased, so that the corpse was still exposed to view, and that its position, figure, or other circumstance, might tend to discover if he died a heretic or not, the name of the defunct, his house, and other details, should be communicated to the witnesses, that they might be enabled to recollect the event, and to assist them in making their declaration.

Yet the council, on the 30th August, 1537, decreed that the time and place of the events should be inserted in the extract of the publication of the depositions, because it was of consequence to the interests of the accused; it would be done even in supposing that he would learn from it the names of the witnesses.

This rule is too contrary to the inquisitorial system, not to inspire a wish to seek for the principle and the cause-; it may be found in the bad reputation which the Inquisition had acquired by the proceedings against Alphonso Virues, which induced Charles V. to deprive it of the royal juris-diction: but although the council registered the order of the sovereign, he decreed, on the 15th of December, in this year, and on the 22nd of February, 1538, that the extract should not contain any article which could make known the wit-nesses; thus annulling the order imposed in the preceding year. During the last years of the Inquisition, neither the time nor place were indicated in the act of the publication of the depositions.

In June, 1537, the council being consulted by the Inqui-sition of Toledo, decreed, as general rules—1st, that all who *calmly* uttered the blasphemies, *I deny God, I abjure God,* should be punished severely; but those who uttered these words in anger, should not be subject to prosecution: 2nd, to punish all Christians accused of bigamy, if the guilty person supposed it permitted; and in the contrary case to abstain from prosecution; 3rdly, to ascertain, in cases of sorcery, if there had been any compact with the devil; if the compact had existed, the Inquisition was directed to judge the accused, if it had not, they were to leave the cause to the secular tribunals.

The second and third of these regulations are contrary to the system of the holy office, which leads me to suppose that the temporary disgrace and exile of Manriquez contributed to this moderation, which could not last long: the inquisitors have always proceeded against persons guilty of these crimes, on the pretence of examining if any circumstance might cause suspicion of heresy. The same spirit is found in another order of the 19th February, 1533 : it obliges the inquisitors to receive all the papers which the relations of the accused wish to communicate to them. The council made this rule, because these writings (though useless on the trial) might yet be serviceable in proving the innocence or guilt of the accused.

On the 10th May, 1531, the council decreed, that if bulls of dispensation from the use of the *San-benito,* imprisonment, or other punishments, were presented to the Inquisition, the procurator-fiscal should demand that they should be suppressed, as well as those obtained by the children and grandchildren of persons declared infamous by the holy office : the council supported this rule by alleging that children always followed the example of their heretical ancestors, and that it was a scandal to see them occupying honourable employments.

On the 22nd of March in the same year the council wrote to the tribunal of the provinces, that it had remarked, in one of the trials, that certain writings had not been digested in the places where the facts mentioned had happened ; whence they concluded that these formalities had not been fulfilled at the proper time, but at the moment when the proceedings were to begin : the council then recommended them to avoid these abuses, as contrary to the instructions. But the orders of the council were not obeyed : the same irregularity was renewed, and produced another still more dangerous, which during my time had the most serious consequences. In order to supply what might be omitted in the course of the trial, the inquisitors adopted the custom of writing each act, declaration, and deposition, on separate sheets of paper. As in these tribunals they did not make use of stamped paper, and as the pieces of the process were not numbered, it often happened that those which they wished to conceal from the council, the diocesan in ordinary, or other interested parties, were changed or suppressed. This manœuvre was employed by the inquisitors in the affair of the Archbishop of Toledo, Carranza, and I have myself seen several attestations of the secretary changed at the request of the inquisitors of Madrid.

The circular of the 11th of July in the same year is more remarkable, and had more success than the preceding. The inquisitors of the provinces were directed to refer to the Supreme Council all sentences pronounced without the unanimity of the inquisitors, the diocesan and the consulters, even supposing that there was only one dissentient voice. The inquisitors were afterwards obliged to consult the council on all the judgements which they passed; and I must confess that this measure was extremely useful, because, in a difference of opinion, the decisions of the *supreme* were much more just than those of the tribunals of the provinces, from being composed of a greater number of enlightened judges.

The council displayed the same love of justice in 1536, when it decreed that those convicted of making use of gold, silver, silk, or precious stones, should be punished by pecuniary fines, and not by fire, although they had been prohibited from so doing on pain of being *relaxed*.

The decree most contrary to the wisdom which ought to have animated the council, was that of the 7th of December, 1532, in which it was ordained that each provincial Inquisition should state the number and rank of the persons condemned to different punishments within their jurisdictions, since their establishment, and to deposit in the churches those *San-benitos* which had not been placed there, without even excepting those of persons who had confessed and suffered

their punishment during the term of grace. This direction
was executed with a severity worthy of the Inquisition; at
Toledo those San-benitos were renewed which had been
destroyed by time, and they were likewise sent to the parishes
of the condemned persons. The consequences of these proceedings were the ruin and extinction of many families, as the
children could not establish themselves according to the rank
they had possessed ; while the condemnation of their ancestors
by the Inquisition remained unknown. The council discovered too late the injustice it had committed in respect to
the *San-benito* since it revoked the decree seven years after,
in 1539.

It is not necessary to give the history of the quarrels which
took place between the Inquisition and the different civil
authorities, during the administration of Manriquez : a scandalous enterprise of the Supreme Council ought nevertheless
to be mentioned; in 1531, it presumed to condemn the
president of the royal court of appeals, in Majorca, to ask
pardon of the holy office, to attend mass (as a penitent), with
a wax taper in his hand, and to receive the absolution of
censures, for having defended the jurisdiction of the criminal
tribunal in an affair which involved several persons, among
whom was one Gabriel Nebel, a servant of the summoner of
the holy office.

CHAPTER XV.

PROSECUTIONS OF SORCERERS, MAGICIANS, ENCHANTERS,
NECROMANCERS, AND OTHERS.

Under the administration of the inquisitor-general Manriquez
the Inquisition was particularly occupied by the sect of
sorcerers.

Pope Adrian VI. (who had been inquisitor-general in Spain), published a bull on the 20th July, 1523, in which he says, that in the time of his predecessor Julius II. a numerous sect had been discovered in Lombardy, which abjured the christian faith, and abused the ceremonies of religion and the eucharist. These sectarians acknowledged the devil as their patron, and promised obedience to him.

They sent maladies to animals and destroyed the fruits of the earth by their enchantments. An inquisitor having attempted to arrest and bring them to punishment, the ecclesiastical and secular judges opposed him, which led Julius II. to declare that these crimes were within the jurisdiction of the Inquisition, as well as all other heresies. In consequence Adrian VI. reminded the different inquisitions of their duty in this respect.

This bull was not necessary in Spain, as the Inquisition of Arragon had taken cognizance of magic and sorcery, since the pontificate of John XXII.

It appears that the Inquisition of Calahorra, burnt more than thirty women as sorceresses and magicians in the year 1507. In 1527, a great number of women who practised magic were discovered in Navarre.

These crimes increased so much in the province of Biscay, that Charles V. found it necessary to notice it. Persuaded that the ignorance in which the people were left by the priests, was the cause of these superstitions, he wrote in December, 1527, to the Bishop of Calahorra, and to the provincials of the Dominicans and Franciscans, to select a number of able preachers from their communities, to teach the doctrine of the christian religion on this point. But these ministers of the gospel, even those who had acquired a reputation for learning, believed as well as the enchanters in these illusions.

Nevertheless, Father Martin de Castanaga, a Franciscan monk, composed in that time, a book in Spanish, entitled,

A Treatise on Superstitions and Enchantments. I have read this work, and I acknowledge (with the exception of a few articles in which the author appears too credulous), that it would be difficult even in the present time to write with more moderation or discernment. The Bishop of Calahorra, Don Alphonso de Castilla, having read this treatise had it printed in quarto, and sent it to the priests in his diocese, with a pastoral letter, in 1529.

The Inquisition of Saragossa condemned several sorceresses who had formed part of the association in Navarre, or had been sent into Arragon to gain disciples. The inquisitors, the ordinary, and the consulters, were not of the same opinion ; the greatest number voted for the sorceresses, the others for reconciliation and perpetual imprisonment. The minority gave up their opinion in deference to the greater number, and thus relaxation was pronounced unanimously, without any of the formalities prescribed, and the unfortunate women perished in the flames. The *Supreme* Council which was informed of this event by one of its members, who had learnt it from an inquisitor of Saragossa, addressed a circular on the 23d of March, 1536, to all the tribunals, stating the Inquisition of Saragossa had failed in its duty, in not having consulted the council, after having found that the opinions of its members were different.

The inquisitor-general Manriquez, being informed that the sect of sorcerers made great progress in different parts of the Peninsula, added several articles to the edict of denunciation, the substance of them was that all Christians were obliged to declare to the Inquisition :

First, If they had heard that any person had familiar spirits, and that he invoked demons in circles, questioning them and expecting their answer, as a magician, or in virtue of an express or tacit compact; that he had mingled holy things with profane objects, and worshipped in the creature that which belongs only to the Creator.

Secondly, If he had studied judicial astrology to discover the future, by observing the conjunction of the stars at the birth of persons.

Thirdly, If any person in order to discover the future, had employed *geomancy*, *hydromancy*, *aëromancy*, *piromancy*, *onomancy*, *necromancy*, or sorceries by beans, dice or wheat.

Fourthly, If a Christian had made an express compact with the devil, practised enchantments by magic, with instruments, circles, characters, or diabolical signs; by invoking and consulting demons, with the hope of a reply, and placing confidence in them; by offering them incense, or the *smoke* of good or bad substances; by offering sacrifices to them; in abusing sacraments or holy things; by promising obedience to them, and adoring or worshipping them in any manner.

Fifthly, If any one constructed, or procured mirrors, rings, phials, or other vessels, for the purpose of attracting, enclosing, and preserving a demon, who replies to his questions, and assists him in obtaining his wishes; or who had endeavoured to discover the future, by interrogating the demons in possessed people; or tried to produce the same effect by invoking the devil under the name of *holy angel*, or *white angel*, and by asking things of him with prayers and humility; by practising other superstitious ceremonies with vases, phials of water, or consecrated tapers; by the inspection of the nails, and of the palm of the hand rubbed with vinegar; or by endeavouring to obtain representations of objects by means of phantoms, in order to learn secret things, or which had not then happened.

Sixthly, If any one had read or possessed, or read or possessed at present, any manuscript or book on these matters, or concerning all other species of divination, which is not performed by natural and physical effects.

Although the edicts and punishments for sorcery were extremely severe, they have appeared from time to time in

different parts of Spain.   The history of the sorceresses of
the valley of Bastan, in Navarre, has been particularly
celebrated.   These women were taken before the Inquisition
of Logrono, and confessed the greatest extravagances.   They
were condemned to an *auto-da-fé*, in 1610 ; their history was
published at Madrid, in 1810, with very pleasant remarks
by the Moliere of Spain, who deserves a better fate than he
experiences.

History of a famous Magician.

The history of Doctor Eugene Torralba, a physician of
Cuença, ought not to be passed over, as it offers several remarkable events, and is mentioned in the *History of the
famous knight, Don Quixote de la Mancha.*   This person
is also introduced in different parts of a poem, entitled,
*Carlos Formoso**, composed by Louis Zapata, dedicated to
Philip II. and printed at Valencia, in 1566.

The author of *Don Quixote* in the adventure of the
Countess Trifaldi, represents that famous knight as mounted
upon *Clavileno*, with Sancho Panza behind him, having their
eyes covered; the squire wishes to uncover his eyes to see if
they had arrived at the region of fire.   Don Quixote says,
"Take care not to do it, and remember the true history of
the licentiate Torralba, who being mounted on a cane, with
his eyes covered, was conveyed through the air by devils,
and arrived at Rome in twelve hours, and descended on the
tower of Nona, which is in a street of that city, where he
saw the tumult, assault, and death of the constable de Bourbon, and returned to Madrid before morning, where he gave
an account of what he had seen.   He also related that while
he was in the air, the devil told him to open his eyes, and
that he saw himself so near the moon that he might have

* Charles V. is the hero of this Poem.

touched it with his hand, and that he did not dare to look towards the earth for fear of fainting."

The Doctor Eugene Torralba, was born in the town of Cuença. In an examination he stated that at the age of fifteen he went to Rome, where he was made a page of Don Francis Soderini, Bishop of Volterra, who was made a cardinal in 1503. He studied medicine under several masters, who in their disputes attacked the immortality of the soul, and though they did not succeed in convincing him, caused him to incline to pyrrhonism. Torralba was a physician in 1501, at which period he became intimately acquainted with Master Alphonso of Rome, who had renounced the law of Moses for that of Mahomet, which he quitted for the Christian doctrine, and finished by preferring natural religion. Alphonso told him that Jesus Christ was only a man, and supported his opinion with several arguments : this doctrine did not entirely eradicate the faith of Torralba, but he no longer knew on which side the truth lay.

Among the friends he acquired at Rome, was a monk of St. Dominic, called Brother Peter. This man told him one day that he had in his service one of the good angels, whose name was *Zequiel,* so powerful in the knowledge of the future, that no other could equal him ; but that he abhorred the practice of obliging men to make a compact with him ; that he was always free, and only served the person who placed confidence in him through friendship, and that he allowed him to reveal the secrets he communicated, but that any constraint employed to force him to answer questions made him for ever abandon the society of the man to whom he had attached himself. Brother Peter asked him if he would not like to have *Zequiel* for his friend, adding that he could obtain that favour on account of the friendship which subsisted between them ; Torralba expressed the greatest desire to become acquainted with the spirit of Brother Peter.

Zequiel soon appeared in the shape of a young man, fair,

with flaxen hair, dressed in flesh colour, with a black surtout; he said to Torralba, *I will belong to thee as long as thou livest, and will follow thee wherever thou goest*. After this promise *Zequiel* appeared to Torralba at the different quarters of the moon, and whenever he wished to go from one place to another, sometimes in the figure of a traveller, sometimes like a hermit. *Zequiel* never spoke against the Christian religion, or advised him to commit any bad action ; on the contrary, he reproached him when he committed a fault, and attended the church service with him; he always spoke in Latin or Italian although he was with Torralba in Spain, France, and Turkey; he continued to visit him during his imprisonment but seldom, and did not reveal any secrets to him, and Torralba desired the spirit to leave him, because he caused agitation and prevented him from sleeping, but this did not prevent him from returning and relating things which wearied him.

Torralba went to Spain in 1502. Some time after he travelled over all Italy, and settled at Rome under the protection of Cardinal Volterra ; he there acquired the reputation of a good physician, and engaged the favour of several cardinals. He studied chiromancy, and acquired some knowledge of the art. *Zequiel* revealed to Torralba the secret virtues of several plants in curing certain maladies; having made use of this information to procure money, *Zequiel* reproached him for it, saying, that as these remedies had cost him no labour, he ought to bestow them gratuitously.

Torralba having appeared sad sometimes because he was in want of money, the angel said to him, *Why are you sad for want of money ?* Some time after Torralba found six ducats in his chamber, and the same thing was repeated several times, which made him suppose that *Zequiel* had placed them there, although he would not acknowledge it when questioned.

The greatest part of the information which *Zequiel* com-municated to Torralba related to political occurrences, Thus, when Torralba returned to Spain in 1510, being at the court of Ferdinand the Catholic, *Zequiel* told him that this prince would soon receive disagreeable news. Torralba hastened to inform the Archbishop of Toledo, Ximenez de Cisneros, and the great captain Gonzales Fernandez de Cordova, and the same day a courier brought letters from Africa, which announced the failure of the expedition against the Moors, and the death of Don Garcia de Toledo, son of the Duke of Alva, who commanded it.

Ximenez de Cisneros having learnt that the Cardinal de Volterra had seen *Zequiel*, expressed a wish to see him also, and to become acquainted with the nature and qualities of this spirit. Torralba, to gratify the archbishop, entreated the angel to appear to him under any human form : *Zequiel* did not think proper to do so ; but to soften the severity of his refusal, he commissioned Torralba to inform Ximenez de Cisneros that he would be a king, which was in a manner verified, as he became absolute governor of the Spains and the Indies.

Another time when he was at Rome, the angel told him that Peter Margano would lose his life if he went out of the city. Torralba had not time to inform his friend, he went out and was assassinated.

Zequiel told him that Cardinal Sienna would come to a tragical end, which was verified in 1517, after the sentence which Leo X. pronounced against him.

When he returned to Rome in 1513, Torralba had a great desire to see his intimate friend Thomas de Becara, who was then at Venice. *Zequiel*, who knew his wish, took him to that city, and brought him back to Rome in so short a time, that the person with whom he was in the habit of associating, did not perceive his absence.

The Cardinal de Santa Cruz, in 1516, commissioned Tor-

ralba to pass a night with his physician, Doctor Morales, in
the house of a Spanish lady named *Rosales,* to ascertain if
what this woman related of a phantom which she saw every
night in the form of a murdered man, was to be believed;
Doctor Morales had remained a whole night in the house,
and had not seen anything, when the Spanish lady announced
the presence of the ghost, and the Cardinal hoped to discover something by means of Torralba.   At the hour of one
the woman uttered her cry of alarm; Morales saw nothing,
but Torralba perceived the figure, which was that of a dead
man, behind him appeared another phantom with the fea-
tures of a woman. Torralba said to him with a loud voice,
What dost thou seek here? The phantom replied, *a treasure,*
and disappeared.   *Zequiel,* on being questioned, replied that
under the house there was the body of a man who had been
assassinated with a poignard.

In 1519, Torralba returned to Spain, accampanied by
Don Diego de Zuñiga, a relation of the Duke de Bejar, and
brother to Don Antonio, grand prior of Castile, who was his
intimate friend.   At Barcelometta, near Turin, while they
were walking with the secretary Acebedo (who had been
marshal of the camp in Italy and Savoy), Acebedo and
Zuñiga thought they saw something pass by Torralba which
they could not define; he informed them that it was his
angel *Zequiel* who had approached to speak to him.   Zuñiga
wished much to see him, but *Zequiel* would not appear.

At Barcelona, Torralba saw in the house of the Canon
Juan Garcia, a book on chiromancy, and in some notes a
process for winning money at play.   Zuñiga wished to learn
it, and Torralba copied the characters, and told his friend to
write them himself on paper with the blood of a bat, and
keep them about his person while he played.

Being at Valladolid in 1520, Torralba told Don Diego
that he would return to Rome because he had the means of
getting there in a short time, by being mounted on a stick

and guided through the air by a cloud of fire. Torralba really went to that city, where Cardinal Volterra and the grand prior requested him to give up his *familiar spirit* to them. Torralba proposed it to *Zequiel*, and even entreated him to consent, but without success.

In 1525 the angel told him that he would do well if he returned to Spain, because he would obtain the place of physician to the infanta Eleonora, queen dowager of Portugal, and afterwards married to Francis I. King of France. The doctor communicated this affair to the Duke de Bejar, and to Don Stephen-Manual Merino, Archbishop of Bari; they solicited and obtained for him the place which he aspired to.

Lastly, on the 5th of May in the same year, *Zequiel* told the doctor that Rome would be taken by the imperial troops the next day. Torralba entreated his angel to take him to Rome to witness this important event; he complied, and they left Valladolid at the hour of eleven at night : when they were at a short distance from the city, the angel gave Torralba a knotted stick and said to him, *Shut your eyes, do not fear, take this in your hands, and no evil will befal you.* When the moment to open his eyes arrived, he found himself so near the sea, that he might have touched it with his hand; the black cloud which surrounded them was succeeded by a brilliant light, which made Torralba fear that he should be consumed. *Zequiel* perceiving his fear, said, *Reassure yourself, fool!* Torralba again closed his eyes, and when *Zequiel* told him to open them, he found himself in the tower of Nona in Rome. They then heard the clock of the Castle St. Angelo sound the fifth hour of the night, which is midnight according to the manner of computing time in Spain, so that they had been travelling one hour. Torralba went all over Rome with *Zequiel*, and afterwards witnessed the pillage of the city; he entered the house of the Bishop Copis, a German who lived in the tower of

St. Ginia; he saw the Constable de Bourbon expire, the
Pope shut himself up in the Castle of St. Angelo, and all the
other events of that terrible day. In an hour and a half
they had returned to Valladolid, where *Zequiel* quitted him,
saying, *Another time you will believe what I tell you.* Torralba published all that he had seen, and as the court soon
received the same news, Torralba, (who was then physician
to the Admiral of Castile), was spoken of as a great
magician.

These rumours were the cause of his denunciation; he was
arrested at Cuença by the Inquisition in the beginning of
the year 1528. He was denounced by his intimate friend
Diego de Zuñiga, who after having been as foolishly capti-
vated as Torralba, with the miracles of the good angel,
became fanatical and superstitious. Torralba at first confessed all that has been related of *Zequiel,* supposing that
he should not be tried for the doubts he had expressed of the
immortality of the soul and the divinity of our Saviour.
When the judges had collected sufficient evidence, they
assembled to give their *votes,* but as they did not accord,
they applied to the council, which decreed that Torralba
should be tortured, *as much as his age and rank permitted,*
to discover his motives in receiving and keeping near him the
spirit *Zequiel;* and if he believed him to be a bad angel,
as a witness declared that he had said so; if he had made a
compact with him, what had passed at the first interview;
if at that time or afterwards he had employed conjurations
to invoke him ; immediately after this the tribunal was to
pronounce the definitive sentence.

Torralba had never varied, until that time, in his account
of his familiar spirit, whom he always affirmed to be of the
order of good angels, but the torture made him say, that he
now perceived him to be a bad angel, since he was the cause
of his misfortune. He was asked if *Zequiel* had told him
that he would be arrested by the Inquisition; he replied that

he had told him of it several times, desiring him not to go
to Cuença, because he would meet with a misfortune there,
but that he thought he might disregard this advice.   He
also declared that there was no compact between them, and
that every circumstance had passed as he had related it.

The inquisitors considered all these details to be true,
and after taking a new declaration from Torralba, they
suspended his trial for the space of one year, from motives
of compassion, and with the hope of seeing if this famous
necromancer would be converted, and confess the compact
and sorcery which he had constantly denied.

A new witness recalled the memory of his dispute, and
his doubts of the immortality of the soul, and the divinity
of Jesus Christ, which caused another declaration of the
Doctor in January, 1530. The council being informed of it,
commanded the Inquisition to commission some pious and
learned persons to endeavour to convert the accused.
Augustin Barragan, prior of the Dominican Convent at
Cuença, and Diego Manriquez, a canon of the cathedral,
undertook this task, and exhorted him vehemently. The
prisoner replied that he sincerely repented of his faults, but
that it was impossible for him to confess what he had not
done, and that he could not follow the advice given him, to
renounce all communication with *Zequiel* because the spirit
was more powerful than he was ; but he promised that he
would not desire his presence, or consent to any of his
propositions.

On the 6th of March, 1531, Torralba was condemned to
the usual abjuration of all heresies, and to suffer the punishment of imprisonment and the *San-benito* during the pleasure of the inquisitor-general ; to hold no further communion with the spirit *Zequiel*, and never to attend to any
of his propositions ; these conditions were imposed on him
for the safety of his conscience and the good of his soul.

The inquisitor soon put an end to the punishment of Tor-

ralba, in consideration, as he said, of all that he had suffered
during an imprisonment of four years ; but the true motive
of the pardon granted to Torralba was the interest which
the Admiral of Castile took in his fate, he retained him as
his physician for several years after his judgment.

The truth of the marvellous facts related by Torralba,
rests solely upon his confession, and the report of the
witnesses whom he had induced to believe all that he had
told them.   Torralba cited none but deceased persons in
eight declarations which he made, except Don Diego de
Zuñiga.   It was necessary to remark this to shew the
degree of confidence to be placed in some parts of his narration.   It may be supposed that a great number of different
accounts of this affair were spread, to which I attribute the
additions and alterations in some circumstances which Louis
Zapata introduced into his poem of *Carlos Famoso*, thirty
years after the sentence passed on Torralba, and of those
details which Cervantes eighty years later thought proper
to put in the mouth of Don Quixote.

I terminate, by this account of Doctor Torralba, the
history of the administration of Cardinal Don Alphonso
Manriquez, Archbishop of Seville, who died in that city on
the 28th of September 1538, with the reputation of being a
friend and benefactor to the poor.   His charity and some
other qualities worthy of his birth have gained him a place
among the illustrious men of his age.   He had several
natural children before he entered into orders ; Don Jerome
Manriquez is cited as having been most worthy of his father,
he successively attained the dignities of Provincial Inquisitor,
Counsellor of the *Supreme*, Bishop of Carthagena and
Avila, president of the Chançery of Valladolid, and, lastly,
Inquisitor-general.

At the death of Don Alphonso Manriquez, there were
nineteen provincial tribunals; they were established at
Seville, Cordova, Toledo, Valladolid, Murcia, Calahorra,

Estremadura, Saragossa, Valencia, Barcelona, Majorca, in the Canaries, at Cuença, in Navarre, Grenada, Sicily, Sardinia, in Tierra Firma, and the isles of the American Ocean. The Inquisition of Jaen had been united to that of Grenada.

The Inquisition had afterwards three tribunals in America, at Mexico, Lima, and Carthagena. In the Indies they had been decreed but not organized.

By omitting the tribunals of America, Sardinia, and Sicily, we shall find that there were fifteen in Spain, which respectively burnt, annually, about ten individuals in person, five in effigy, and subjected fifty to different penances; so that in all Spain one hundred and fifty persons were burnt every year; sixty-five in effigy, and seven hundred and fifty suffered different canonical penances, which, multiplied by the fifteen years of the administration of Manriquez, shews that two thousand two hundred and fifty individuals were burnt, one thousand one hundred and twenty-five in effigy, and eleven thousand two hundred and fifty condemned to penances; in all fourteen thousand, six hundred and twenty-five condemnations. This number scarcely deserves to be mentioned in comparison with those of preceding times, but still it appears enormous, particularly if the excessive abuse of the secret proceedings is considered.

CHAPTER XVI.

OF THE TRIAL OF THE FALSE NUNCIO OF PORTUGAL, AND OTHER IMPORTANT EVENTS DURING THE TIME OF CARDINAL TABERA, SIXTH INQUISITOR-GENERAL.

Quarrels of the Inquisition with the Court of Rome.

CHARLES V. appointed Cardinal Don Juan Pardo de Tabera, Archbishop of Toledo, to succeed Cardinal Manriquez, in the office of inquisitor-general; his bulls of institution were expedited in September 1539, and a month after he entered upon his office, so that the *Supreme* Council governed the Inquisition for the space of one year.

It was under the inquisitor Tabera, that the congregation of the holy office was founded at Rome, on the 1st of April, 1543. It gave the title and privilege of inquisitors-general of the faith, for all the christian world, to several cardinals; two of the number were Spaniards, Don Juan Alvarez de Toledo, Bishop of Burgos, a son of the Duke of Alba, and Don Thomas Badia, cardinal-priest of the title of St. Silvestre, and master of the sacred palace. These two cardinals were of the order of St. Dominic.

This new creation alarmed the Inquisition of Spain for its supremacy, but the Pope formally declared that it was not his intention to alter anything that had been established, and the institution of the inquisitors-general, would not interfere with the privileges of the other inquisitors. Yet the general Inquisition attempted several times to give laws to that of Spain, particularly in the prohibition of some writings which had been proscribed at Rome. The inquisitors-general wrote to those of Spain, to register the censure of the theologians, because they were to be looked upon as the most learned of the Catholic church, and because their opinion was supported by the confirmation of the supreme head of the church, whom the cardinals asserted to be infallible when he acted (as in this case) as sovereign pontiff. He approved and commanded the decrees of the congregation of cardinals, to be received and executed with submission.

These pretensions of the Court of Rome, did not inspire the inquisitors of Spain with any awe; they have always defended their privileges with so much vigour, that they often refused to execute the apostolical briefs, when they were contrary to the decisions they had made conjointly with the *Supreme* Council. We find examples of this resistance under

Urban VIII., in the condemnation of the works of the Jesuit, John Baptist Poza, which had been pronounced at Rome ; and under Benedict XIV., when the inquisitor-general, Don Francis Perezdel Prado, Bishop of Teruel, refused to enter upon the *prohibitory index*, the works of Cardinal Noris, in opposition to the request, and even the formal demand, of that great Pope.

Although the inquisitors of Spain pretended that their an-thority was canonical and spiritual, and had been delegated to them by the sovereign pontiff, who is infallible when he pronounces *ex cathedrâ*, yet they always opposed this infal-libility in fact, and refused to submit to his decrees, when contrary to their particular system. The inquisitors would have acted differently, if they had not been certain that by applying to the king and interesting his policy, they would force the royal authority to take a part in their quarrels, and oppose the measures of the pontiff, who, if they had not pos-sessed that powerful support, would have treated them as rebels, and degraded them to the rank of simple priests by depriving them of their employments.

History of the Viceroys of Sicily and Catalonia.

In 1535, Charles V., had deprived the Inquisition of the royal jurisdiction, and it was not restored to them till 1545; consequently, in 1543, they had not the privilege of trying their officers, familiars, or other secular attendants of the holy office, for matters not relating to religion. This royal decree was known to the Captain-general of Catalonia, Don Pedro Cardona, when he commenced proceedings against the gaoler, a familiar and a servant of the grand-serjeant of the Inquisition of Barcelona, for carrying arms, which was pro-hibited in his government.

The inquisitors of Barcelona had become insolent, from having always prevailed in affairs of this nature, and they instituted proceedings against Don Pedro Cardona, as a rebel against the holy office; without respecting his high situations of captain-general, and military governor of the province, or the rank and name of his illustrious family. Being informed that the emperor was only nine leagues from Barcelona, they denounced the act of his lieutenant to him, and represented, through Cardinal Tabera, that if Cardona was not condemned to make a public reparation, the people would lose all respect for the Inquisition, and an incalculable injury be done to the catholic religion throughout the kingdom.

The emperor, blinded by fanaticism, not only favoured the inquisitors against all justice, and in contempt of his own ordinance of 1535; but he wrote to Cardona, that the interests of the faith required that he should submit to receive the absolution *ad cautelam*. This order deeply afflicted Don Pedro, but he resolved to obey his master, and demanded absolution. The inquisitors, to render their triumph greater, celebrated an *auto-da-fé*, in the cathedral of Barcelona, where Cardona was compelled to attend, standing without a sword, and with a taper in his hand, during the celebration of mass, and the ceremony of his absolution.

Charles V. had also deprived the Inquisition of Sicily of the royal jurisdiction, for the space of five years, and afterwards prolonged it to ten; but the inquisitors represented, through Cardinal Tabera, that the inconveniences arising from this measure were so great, that Don Ferdinand Gonzaga, Prince de Malfeta, the viceroy and captain-general of the island, was informed that the suspension was to be revoked at the expiration of the tenth year, without a particular order. The Marquis de Terranova had been viceroy and governor-general; he was constable and admiral of Naples, a grandee of Spain of the first class, and related to the emperor through the house of Arragon. Two familiars of the Inquisition had been taken before the civil tribunal, by his orders, for some crimes which they had committed.

Philip of Austria, Prince of Asturias, the eldest son of Charles V., then aged sixteen, governed the Spanish dominions during the absence of his father; and as he was not less superstitious, his conduct towards the Marquis de Terranova was the same as that of the emperor to Don Pedro Cardona. I consider it necessary to give the letter of the Prince to the Marquis de Terranova; it was as follows:—

"I, the Prince. Honourable marquis, admiral and constable, our dear counsellor: you know what happened when you commanded two familiars of the holy office to be whipped, (while you were governor of this kingdom, and not well informed of the affair.) So great a contempt for that holy tribunal has been the result, that it has been impossible for it to command anything with the success which it formerly obtained. On the contrary, several persons of this kingdom have presumed to insult and use violence towards the officers of the Inquisition, and to prevent and disturb them in the exercise of their office, according to the complaints and informations which we have received on this affair. The reverend Cardinal of Toledo, inquisitor-general, and the members of the council of the general Inquisition, have deliberated with his majesty, and it has been found proper and convenient that you should do penance for the fault you have committed; saving that it should be gentle and moderate, in consideration of the services you have rendered his majesty. In consequence, the inquisitor-general and the council, guided by their esteem for your person, have commanded the inquisitor Gongora to speak to you, and represent your fault, that you may accomplish the penance imposed, which (according to the nature of the fact, and the evil which has been the result) ought to have been much more severe, as you will learn from what the inquisitors have been commanded to say to you. As to the rest, this has only been decreed for the glory of God, the honour of the holy office, and the good of your conscience. We require and charge you, for the sake of the good example which you owe to others, to accept and accomplish this penance, with the submission which is due to the church, and without waiting to be compelled by means of excommunication and ecclesiastical censures; the submission which we ask of you will not affect your honour, but will be profitable to you in freeing you from all inquietude and vexation; it is approved by his majesty, will give us pleasure, and we undertake to treat you in all that concerns you with the favour that we have used towards you, and which we will shew whenever there is an opportunity. Given at Valladolid, 15th December, 1543. I, the Prince." This letter is marked by several members of the council, and countersigned *Juan Garcia, pro-secretary.*

The silence which is observed on the nature of the penance imposed on the viceroy is remarkable; but whatever gentleness and moderation was affected, it was the same as that of Don Pedro Cordona. The only difference to be observed was, that it did not take place in the cathedral, but in the church of the Dominican convent; it was also thought necessary, by way of compensation, to prevent the Marquis from kneeling, except during the elevation of the host, that he might be more exposed to the sight of the people, and to condemn him to pay an hundred ducats to the familiars whom he had punished.

History of the False Nuncio of the Pope in Portugal.

The history of the quarrels of the Inquisition with the royal authority affords another conflict of jurisdiction. I speak of the affair of the famous Juan Perez de Saavedra mentioned in histories, romances, and dramatic pieces, under the name of *the False Nuncio of Portugal*, and who generally passes for the founder of the Inquisition in that kingdom. The critic Feijoo has supposed that the history of this affair was fabulous. The narration of Saavedra, which

Feijoo quotes, contains fables, but it also contains truths belonging to the history of the Inquisition. It is necessary to enter into the details of this history : I shall first relate the facts according to the narrative which Saavedra wrote for the Cardinal Espinosa in 1567; I shall afterwards establish the truth on some points which that impostor contrived to obscure.

Juan Perez de Saavedra was born at Cordova. His father was a captain in a regiment of infantry, and a perpetual member of the municipality of that city, from a privilege acquired by his family; his mother, Anne de Guzman, was descended from a family as noble as that of her husband. Saavedra, who was possessed of great talents and information, employed himself for some time in forging apostolical bulls, royal ordinances, regulations of councils and tribunals, letters of change, and the signatures of a great number of persons : he imitated them so perfectly, that he made use of them without exciting any doubts of their authenticity, and passed for a knight commander of the military order of St. Jago, and received the salary, which was three thousand ducats, for the space of a year and a half. In a short time, by means of the royal orders which he counterfeited, he acquired three hundred and sixty thousand ducats, and the secret of this great fortune would never have been revealed (as he expresses himself in his confession) *if he had not clothed himself in scarlet*, that is, if he had not taken it into his head to feign himself a cardinal, in order to exercise the functions of a legate à *latere*.

He says, that being in the kingdom of Algarves, a short time after the institution of the Jesuits had been confirmed by Paul III., a priest of that society arrived in the country, furnished with an apostolical brief, which authorized him to found a college of the order in the kingdom of Portugal; that having heard him preach on St. Andrew's Day, he was so pleased with him, that he invited him to dinner, and kept him several days in his house. The jesuit, having discovered his talent during this period, expressed a wish to have a *fac-simile* of his brief, containing a eulogy on the Society of Jesus. He performed this task with so much success, that the brief might have been taken for the original, and they at last agreed that, to complete the good which would accrue to Portugal from the establishment of the Society of Jesus, it would be proper to introduce the Inquisition on the same plan as that of Spain. Saavedra then went to Tabilla, a town in the same province, where, with the assistance of the jesuit, he made the apostolical bull which was necessary for their purpose, and forged letters from Charles V. and Prince Philip his son, to the King of Portugal, John III. This bull was supposed to have been sent to Saavedra, as legate, to establish the Inquisition in Portugal, if the king consented.

Saavedra afterwards passed the frontier, and went to Argamonte, in the kingdom of Seville. The Provincial and Franciscan monks of Andalusia had lately arrived there from Rome. Saavedra thought he would try if the bull would pass as authentic : he told the Provincial that some individual going to Portugal had dropped a parchment on the road, which he shewed him, and begged to know if it was of importance, as, in that case, he would lose no time in restoring it to the person who had dropped it. The Provincial took the parchment for an original writing and true bull ; he made the contents known to Saavedra, and expatiated on the advantages which Portugal would derive from it.

Saavedra went to Seville, and took into his service two confidants, one of whom was to be his secretary, the other his major-domo ; he bought litters and silver-plate, and adopted the dress of a Roman Cardinal ; he sent his confidants to Cordova and Grenada to hire servants, and commanded them to go with his suite to Badajoz, where they gave out that they were the familiars of a Cardinal from Rome, who would pass through the city in his way to Portugal, to establish the Inquisition by the order of the Pope; they also announced that he would soon arrive, as he travelled post.

At the appointed time Saavedra appeared at Badajoz, where his servants publicly kissed his hand as the Pope's Legate. He left Badajos for Seville, where he was received into the archiepiscopal palace of Cardinal Loaisa, who resided at Madrid in the quality of apostolical commissary-general of the holy crusade. He received the greatest marks of respect and devotion from Don Juan Fernandez de Temiño, the vicar-general. He remained eighteen days in this city, and during that time obtained, by false obligations, the sum of eleven hundred and thirty ducats from the heirs of the Marquis de Tarifa. He afterwards took the road to Llerena (where the Inquisition of Estremadura had been established) after going to different towns in the province; he was lodged in part of the buildings of the Inquisition, which was then occupied by the Inquisitors Don Pedro Alvarez Becerra and Don Louis de Cardenas, to whom he said that he meant to visit the Inquisition of Llerena in his quality of legate; and, after having fulfilled that part of his mission, he should proceed to Portugal, where he should establish the holy office on the plan of that of Spain.

Saavedra then returned to Badajoz, from whence he sent his secretary to Lisbon with his bulls and papers, that the court being informed of his arrival, might prepare to receive him. The mission of this agent caused great doubts and agitation at the court, where such a novelty was little expected: nevertheless the king sent a nobleman to the frontier to receive the Cardinal Legate, who made his entry into Lisbon, where he passed three months, and was treated with every mark of respect: he then undertook a long journey into different parts of the kingdom, going over the dioceses, and taking a detailed account of them ; it would have been difficult to discover the aim of his apostolical solicitude, if some unforeseen circumstances had not put an end to his imposture.

The Inquisition of Spain discovered this intrigue through the address of Cardinal Tabera, who shared the cares of government with the Prince of Asturias, at the time when Charles V. was absent in France. In consequence of the measures concerted between the cardinal and the Marquis de Villaneuva de Barcarrota, the governor of Badajoz, Saavedra was arrested at Nieva de Guadiana in the Portuguese territory, on the 23rd of January, 1541, where he was at table with the curate of the village, who had entreated that he would do him the honour of visiting his parish, as he had the others in the diocese. This request was only a snare, in order to arrest the impostor with more safety.

Saavedra says that, when he was arrested, three treasures which he had with him were seized; one of twenty thousand ducats, the produce of the fines of the condemned, destined for the holy office; the second of an hundred and fifty thousand ducats, which, he said, he intended to apply to the use of the church, and other good works; the third of ninety thousand ducats, which belonged to himself. Saavedra was taken to Madrid by the order of the procurator-general of the kingdom, and there imprisoned. The alcaldes of the court went to him, and received his declaration, which was necessary to the trial. The tribunal of the Inquisition had not then been established at Madrid, which was subject to that of Toledo. The inquisitors pretended that this affair ought to come before them, because it was to be presumed that the prisoner had renounced the Catholic religion, from the fictions which he had invented to procure money; as if Catholics did not commit greater crimes every day!

As the inquisitor-general was the lieutenant of the prince, the holy office was sure to prevail. Tabera, wishing to satisfy

both parties, decreed that the alcaldes should remain in possession of the person of Saavedra, and proceed against him
for his exactions, forgeries, and other political crimes, and
that the holy office should take cognizance of the crimes
against the faith which he had been guilty of, under the title
of a cardinal.

The inquisitor reflected that Saavedra was a man of great
talent, and that he therefore should be treated with moderation ; besides that, he had always conducted himself like a
real Judge, except that he only condemned the accused to
pay fines.

Saavedra declared that these reasons made the inquisitor-
general wish to be personally acquainted with him; that he
caused him to be brought before him, heard him with interest,
and offered to protect him, promising to give him for a judge
any one that he named : that he then expressed a wish to be
judged by Doctor Arias, inquisitor at Llerena; this was
granted, and caused great murmurs against the cardinal and
the court at Madrid, where it was whispered that Tabera
had appropriated the ninety thousand ducats which had been
taken from Saavedra : that Doctor Arias condemned him to
serve ten years in the king's galleys; that, after a detention
of two years, the alcaldes of Madrid pronounced his definitive
sentence, one of the principal parts of which was, that after
having fulfilled the inquisitorial sentence, he could not be set
at liberty, or quit the galleys without the permission of his
majesty, on pain of death; that he was sent to the galleys in
1544; that in 1554, although the period of his punishment
had expired, he could not obtain his liberty: then, persuaded
that his affair depended more on the Inquisition than the alcaldes of the court, he endeavoured to interest the Pope in
his fate, representing that he had done several things extremely useful to religion and the state, in the exercise of his
false legation; that Paul IV. sent him a brief, which was
addressed to the inquisitor-general Don Ferdinand Valdes,

whom his holiness charged to obtain Saavedra's liberty; that
he received this brief when the king's galleys were in the
port of St. Mary; that he immediately forwarded it to the
bishop coadjutor of Seville, and he sent it to the inquisitor-
general, who was his archbishop. Valdes having communicated the affair to Philip II., that prince gave orders that
Saavedra should be set at liberty, that he might immediately
repair to court. Saavedra arrived there in 1562, after having
passed nineteen years in the galleys. He was presented to
the king, who desired to hear his history from his own lips,
and to have it in writing; while Saavedra related it to the
king, Antonio Perez wrote down the singular events of his
life; lastly, Saavedra himself wrote it in 1567, for the inquisitor-general, Don Diego Espinosa.

The history of Saavedra has furnished the subject for a
Spanish comedy, entitled the " *False Nuncio of Portugal*,"
in which not only all the unities of time, place, and action
are wanting, but the rule which only admits probable events
is infringed; but this ought not to surprise in poets, since the
hero himself has taken the same liberty in the narrative which
he composed for the amusement of Cardinal Espinosa. It is
certain that he was imprisoned on the 25th of January, 1541,
as he states in his history. But this point, so well established, proves that he imposed in other circumstances; for
example, if what he relates of the Jesuit in Algarves is true,
it could not have happened until the year 1540, because
Paul III. only expedited his bull of approval for the
Society of Jesus, on the 27th of September, 1540; now
the sermon preached by the Jesuit on St. Andrew's day
corresponds with the 30th of November in the same year,
that is, on the fifty-second day before his imprisonment; this
interval would not be sufficient for his journeys to Ayamonte,
Llerena, Seville, Badajoz, and in Portugal. Thus Saavedra
did not speak truth, either in stating the period of his appearing to the world as a Cardinal, and the motives which

induced him to enter into the intrigue with the Jesuit ; or when he said that he sustained his part for three months at Lisbon, and during three months which he employed in visiting different towns in the kingdom.

Besides, the number and names of the disciples of St. Ignatius were known at that period; and it is certain that before the bull of approbation was obtained, the founder of the order had appointed St. Francis Xavier and Simon Rodriguez, a Portuguese, to preach in Portugal ; and that these monks left Rome on the 15th of March, 1540, with the Portuguese ambassador; that on their arrival at Lisbon, John III. wished to receive them into his palace ; that they refused that honour, and lodged in the hospital ; that St. Francis Xavier embarked for the East Indies, with the new governor, on the 8th of April, 1541, and that Rodriguez remained in Portugal to preach, as he had already done, to the great satisfaction of the inhabitants, who had a high opinion of his virtues: these circumstances render it improbable that the Jesuit would ask for a forged brief, and enter into an intrigue with a layman.

Saavedra says, that the court of Lisbon was disturbed at the news of the arrival of a nuncio in Portugal. This would not be extraordinary, as neither the Pope nor any other person had written to the court on the subject, and as the Pope had appointed Don Henry, archbishop of Braga, the king's brother, inquisitor-general in the preceding year. But if the arrival of the legate caused so much surprise, it was natural that the king should write to the pope, whose answer would have arrived two months afterwards, and Saavedra would have been detected before the end of the third month, and thus there would have been no necessity for the king of Spain to arrest him.

It is not more certain that Saavedra established the Inquisition in Portugal. The expulsion of the Jews took place in 1492 ; many of them retired to Portugal: among them were some that had been baptized, and John II. consented to receive them into his states, if they would behave like faithful Christians. King Manuel ordered them to quit the kingdom, and to leave all their children under the age of fourteen, who were to be made Christians ; they offered to receive baptism, if the king would promise not to establish the Inquisition for twenty years ; the king granted their request, and also that the names of the witnesses should be communicated to them, if they were accused of heresy after that period, besides the power of bequeathing their effects if they were condemned. In 1507, Manuel confirmed these privileges, prolonging the first twenty years, and rendering the others perpetual; in 1520, John renewed the first con- cession for another twenty years.

Clement VII., being informed that the baptized Jews in Portugal did not shew much attachment to the Christian religion, and that the Protestant and Lutheran heresies made great progress in the kingdom, appointed Brother Diego de Silva inquisitor for that country. He attempted to exercise his functions, but the new Christians claimed their rights, which were to last for several years; a trial was the result of this opposition. Clement VII. died, and his successor, Paul III., granted to the New Christians a privilege which they could not obtain in Portugal; that they might confide, to persons chosen by themselves, their defence before the prince of the sense to be given to the dispositions of their privileges, which had been interpreted to their prejudice. In the same year, the Pope granted them a pardon for all that had passed.

The king afterwards represented that the converted Jews abused their privileges, some returning to Judaism, and others adopting the errors of the Protestants. This circum- stance induced the Pontiff to publish another bull on the 25th of March, 1536, which is considered as the foundation of the Inquisition in Portugal. The Pope appointed as inquisitors, the Bishops of Coïmbra, Lamego, and Ceuta; and decreed at the same time, that another bishop or priest of the king's nomination should be associated with them. The Pope granted to each inquisitor the power of proceeding against heretics and their adherents, in concert with the diocesan in ordinary, or alone, if he refused to assist; they were likewise obliged for the first three years, in the proceedings against heretics, to conform to the manner of proceeding in cases of theft or homicide, and after that period to the rules of common law; the practice of confiscation was abolished, and the heirs of the condemned could inherit as if he died intestate. Lastly, the Pope commanded that a sufficient number of tribunals should be instituted, for the execution of these measures *. The king appointed Don Diego de Silva, bishop of Ceuta, first inquisitor-general.

Such was the origin of the Inquisition in Portugal, four years before Saavedra arrived in that country. In 1539, the Pope appointed Don Henry, archbishop of Braga, to succeed the first inquisitor-general. The third grand inquisitor was Don George de Almeida, archbishop of Lisbon.

All that I have now stated is taken from authentic documents. I conclude from them that Juan Perez de Saavedra forged his brief of cardinal à latere, presented it in December, 1540, and succeeded in concealing his forgery; that what he related of the Jesuit was not true, or happened differently; that seeing the Inquisition established in a manner contrary to his opinions, he insinuated that it would be better to take that of Spain as a model, which was well known to the inquisitors of Llerena, and that he would visit the different parts of the kingdom, to facilitate this design; that he travelled through part of the kingdom in the month of December, and continued his journeys in January in the following year, when he was arrested, before the court of Lisbon received informa-

* Don Antonio Cajetan de Souza has inserted this bull in his genealogical History of the Royal House of Portugal; Vol. II.

tion of his imposture. I have no doubt that Saavedra amassed great sums, but I am far from thinking that they were as considerable as he affirmed them to be.

Cardinal Tabera, sixth inquisitor-general, died on the 1st of August, 1545: at his death the number of tribunals was the same as when he was placed at the head of the Inquisition: he had re-established that of Jaen, but the tribunal of Navarre was united with that of Calahorra.

The number of victims, calculated as it was for the time of Manriquez, affords, for the seven years of Cardinal Tabera's ministry, seven thousand, seven hundred, and twenty individuals condemned and punished; eight hundred and forty were burnt in person, four hundred and twenty in effigy; the rest, in number five thousand, four hundred, and sixty, were subjected to different penances. I firmly believe that the number was much more considerable; but faithful to my system of impartiality, I have stated the most moderate calculation.

CHAPTER XVII.

OF THE INQUISITIONS OF NAPLES, SICILY, AND MALTA, AND OF THE EVENTS OF THE TIME OF CARDINAL LOAISA, SEVENTH INQUISITOR-GENERAL.

Naples.

CHARLES V. appointed, to succeed Cardinal Pardo de Tabera, Cardinal Don Garcia de Loaisa, Archbishop of Seville, who was the seventh inquisitor-general. This prelate had arrived at a great age, since he had signed different ordinances of the Supreme Council in 1517. He had been the confessor of Charles V., prior-general of the order of St. Dominic, Bishop of Osma and Siguenza, and apostolical commissary of the Holy Crusade. The Court of Rome expedited his bulls of confirmation on the 18th of February, 1546, and he died on the 22nd of April, in the same year.

In 1546, Charles V. resolved to establish the Inquisition at Naples, although his grandfather had failed in the attempt in 1504 and 1510. He commissioned his viceroy, Don Pedro de Toledo, Marquis of Villa Franca del Bierzo, to select inquisitors and officers from among the inhabitants, to send to the government a list of the persons chosen, and all the necessary documents, that the inquisitor-general might be able to delegate the necessary powers to the new inquisitors; when these measures had been taken, the tribunal was to be established with all the forms of the inquisitorial jurisdiction.

Frederic Munter, professor of theology in the literary academy at Copenhagen, has supposed that the intrigues of Don Pedro de Toledo were the causes of the introduction of the Inquisition ; but he was not able to consult the original documents, which are now in my hands, and this impossibility was the cause of his errors in his history of the Sicilian Inquisition.

The efforts of Charles V., to establish the Inquisition at Naples, arose from the progress which Lutheranism made in Germany, and his fear that it would penetrate into other countries. His inclinations were fostered by Cardinal Loaisa, and the councillors of the Inquisition : the only part that Don Pedro took in this affair, was, that he was the first person to whom the emperor confided his intentions, and the only one who had sufficient wisdom to advise his master to relinquish his designs, when he found the evil they would cause. The orders of the emperor were executed without meeting any opposition, but scarcely was it known that some persons had been arrested by the new Inquisition, than the people rebelled, crying, " *Long live the Emperor ! Perish the Inquisition !*" The Neapolitans flew to arms, they compelled the Spanish troops to retire to the fortresses, and Charles V. was obliged to abandon his enterprise.

It is worthy of remark, that Paul III. openly protected the Neapolitan rebels ; being displeased that the Inquisition of Naples should depend on that of Spain, he complained that his predecessors, Innocent VIII., Alexander VI., and Julius II., had done much evil in not making the inquisitors entirely dependant on the Popes, and in allowing an intermediate authority, which rendered that of the holy see of no effect.

Paul III., without communicating these motives to the Neapolitans, told them that they were right in resisting the will of their master, since the Spanish Inquisition was extremely severe, and did not follow the example of that of Rome, which had been established three years, and of which no complaints had been made.

In 1563, Philip II. attempted to introduce his favourite tribunal at Naples, but the inhabitants had recourse to their usual method, and the despot was obliged to yield.

Sicily and Malta.

The holy office of Sicily triumphed in the same year still more completely than it had done in 1543.   In 1500, Ferdinand V. endeavoured to establish the Spanish Inquisition in that kingdom, after having suppressed that of the Popes, which was confided to the monks of St. Dominic, but all his efforts failed, until the year 1503.   In 1520, Charles V. wrote to the Pope to request that he would not admit any appeals from persons condemned by the Sicilian Inquisition, because they could apply for that purpose to the inquisitor-general of Spain, in virtue of apostolical concessions granted by his predecessors, and confirmed by himself.

This proceeding, and the particular favour which the emperor bestowed on the holy office, singularly increased the pride of the inquisitors, and their audacity in abusing the secrecy of their trials.   But the hatred of the people for the

Inquisition, and their rebellion in 1535, compelled Charles V. to revoke the privileges which he had granted, and deprive it of the royal jurisdiction for five years.

This measure humiliated the inquisitors, but they contrived to re-establish their authority in 1538, when the inquisitor Don Arnauld Albertius was viceroy *ad interim :* his presence emboldened them to persecute all who offended them; but their despotism was not of long duration. The viceroy returned to Sicily, and finding that the aversion of the inhabitants for the Inquisition was still the same, he communicated it to the emperor, who, as an indispensable measure, prolonged the suspension of their privileges for a fresh term of five years. The aversion inspired by the holy office was not without a cause, as will be seen in the following affair, which happened in 1532.

Antonio Napoles, a rich inhabitant of the island, had been thrown into the secret prisons of the Inquisition ; Francis Napoles, his son, applied to the Pope, and described this act of authority as the result of a miserable intrigue of some men of the lowest class, of whom the inquisitors had been the dupes, and had granted them a degree of confidence which nothing could justify, since his father had acted like a good Catholic from his infancy. He represented that the dean of the inquisitors had leagued with his father's enemies, and detained him in prison five months, to the scandal and discontent of the inhabitants of Palermo, and without affording him any means of defence ; Francis entreated his holiness not to allow the inquisitor to judge his father. The Pope referred the affair to his commissioners in Sicily, Don Thomas Guerrero and Don Sebastian Martinez. Scarcely had the inquisitors of Madrid received information of this event, than they pressed the emperor and Cardinal Manriquez to write to the Pope, and represent to him that the existence of this commission destroyed the privileges of the Spanish Inquisition, on which that of Sicily depended. The weak

Clement VII. hastened to suppress the commission, and caused Guerrero to send all the writings of the process to the Spanish inquisitor-general. He appointed Doctor Don Augustin Camargo, inquisitor of Sicily, to continue the trial, or in his place any other inquisitor, so that Antonio Napoles fell into the hands of his enemy. He was condemned as an heretic, his property confiscated, (although he was admitted to reconciliation,) and to be imprisoned for life. What can justify the conduct of the Pope, the cardinal, and the judges?

The inquisitors of Sicily depended on the protection of the Court of Madrid, and supposed, that when all fear of rebellion had ceased, their privileges would be restored: this was really the case; the emperor, in 1543, signed a royal ordinance, which annulled the suspension at the end of the tenth year. This event inspired the inquisitors with the boldness to signify to the Marquis de Terranova, that he must accomplish the penance to which he had been condemned.

An act appeared on the 16th of June, 1546, renewing the former concessions, and granting new ones. The Inquisition resolved to celebrate its victory; a solemn *auto-da-fé* was celebrated, in which four contumacious persons were burnt in effigy. Similar ceremonies took place in 1549 and 1551. The inquisitors now become as insolent as formerly, treated the Sicilians of all classes with so much severity, that a new sedition was excited in Palermo against the holy office, at the time when the edict *of the faith* was about to be published. The viceroy succeeded in restoring tranquillity, and the inquisitors appeared more moderate, at least while they were under the influence of fear, and instead of the solemn *autos-da-fé* which had caused so much indignation, satisfied themselves with celebrating them, from time to time, privately in the hall of the tribunal; but in 1569 they ordained one which was general, and gave rise to a circumstance which deserves to be recorded.

Among the prisoners of the Inquisition, was an unfortunate creature who had inspired the Marchioness of Pescara, the wife of the viceroy, with some interest. The inquisitors, thinking it necessary to conciliate the first magistrate of the island, remitted his punishment at the request of the mar-chioness, but at the same time informed the inquisitor-general of the circumstance, to avoid all reproach. The Supreme Council having deliberated on the affair, addressed a severe reprimand to the inquisitors, for having assumed a right which they did not possess, *because, in affairs of that nature, intercession could not be admitted.*

When the Island of Malta belonged to the Spanish-monarchy, it was subject to the Inquisition of Sicily ; but when it was given to the knights of St. John of Jerusalem, it would have been contrary to the dignity of the grand-master to permit the exercise of foreign jurisdiction in it, after having received that of ecclesiastical power from the Pope.

A man was arrested in the Island as an heretic, and the Inquisition of Sicily took informations on the affair. The grand-master wrote to demand them ; the inquisitors consulted the council, which directed them, in 1575, not only to refuse them, but to claim the prisoner. The grand-master, resolved to defend his privileges, caused the man to be tried in the island, and he was acquitted. This act displeased the inquisitors, who, to revenge themselves, took advantage of an occurrence which took place in the following year.

Don Pedro de la Roca, a Spaniard, and a knight of Malta, killed the first alguazil of the Sicilian Inquisition in the city of Messina. He was arrested and conducted to the secret prisons of the holy office. The grand-master claimed his knight, as he alone had a right to try him. The council being consulted, commanded the inquisitors to condemn and punish the accused as an homicide. The inquisitor-general communicated this resolution to Philip II., who wrote to the grand-master to terminate the dispute.

The quarrels between the secular powers and the Inquisition were not less violent in Sicily: in 1580 and 1597 attempts were made to appease them, but without success; and in 1606 the Sicilians had the mortification of seeing their viceroy, the Duke de Frias, constable of Castile, prosecuted and subjected to their censures.

In 1592 the Duke of Alvà, who was then viceroy, endeavoured by indirect means to repress the insolence of the inquisitors. Perceiving that the nobility of all classes were enrolled among the *familiars* of the holy office, in order to enjoy its privileges, and to keep the people in greater order, he represented to the king that the power of the sovereign and the authority of his lieutenant were almost null, and would be entirely so in time, if these different classes continued to enjoy privileges which had the effect of neutralising the measures of government. Charles II. acknowledged that this state of things was contrary to the dignity of his crown, and he decreed that no person employed by the king should possess those prerogatives, even if he was a *familiar* or officer of the Inquisition. The people then began to feel less respect for the tribunal, and this was the commencement of its decline.

In 1713, Sicily no longer formed a part of the Spanish dominions, and Charles de Bourbon in 1739 obtained a bull, which created an inquisitor-general for that country, independent of Spain; and in 1782 Ferdinand IV., who succeeded Charles, suppressed this odious tribunal. During the two hundred and seventy-nine years of its existence, the solemn and general *autos-da-fé* were celebrated of which Munter speaks, and several others which were performed in the hall of the tribunal.

In the year 1546, which corresponds with the administration of Cardinal Loaisa, the number of condemned in the fifteen Spanish tribunals amounted to seven hundred and eighty individuals.

CHAPTER XVIII.

OF IMPORTANT EVENTS DURING THE FIRST YEARS OF THE
ADMINISTRATION OF THE EIGHTH INQUISITOR-GENERAL;
RELIGION OF CHARLES V. DURING THE LAST YEARS OF
HIS LIFE.

Trials during the first years of the ministry of Valdés.

DON FERDINAND VALDES was the successor of Cardinal
Loaisa in the archbishopric of Seville, and the office of
inquisitor-general. At the time of his appointment he was
bishop of Siguenza, and president of the royal Council of
Castile, after having been successively a member of the grand
College of St. Bartholomew de Salamanca, of the Council
of Administration for the archbishopric of Toledo, for
the Cardinal Ximenez de Cisneros, visitor of the Inquisition
of Cuença and of the Royal Council of Navarre, a member
of the Council of State, canon of the metropolitan church
of Santiago de Galicia, counsellor of the Supreme Inquisition, bishop of Elna, Orensa, Oviedo and Leon, and president of the Royal Chancery of Valladolid. So many honours
could not render him insensible to the mortification of not
being a cardinal like his predecessors, and of seeing Bartholomew Carranza elevated to the see of Toledo. This was
the true cause of his cruel persecution of Carranza.

The Pope approved the nomination of Valdés in January,
1547, and he took possession of his office in the following
month. Valdés displayed an almost sanguinary disposition
during his administration. It led him to demand from the
Pope the power of condemning Lutherans to be burnt, even
though they had not relapsed, and had desired to be reconciled. I shall here make known the most illustrious of the
victims sacrificed before the abdication of Charles V., as it is

necessary to make a separate article for the events of that nature under the reign of Philip II.

Among the condemned persons who appeared in the *auto-da-fé* of Seville in 1552, was *Juan Gil*, a native of Olvera, in Arragon, and a canon in the metropolitan church of that city ; he is better known by the name of Doctor *Egidius*. He was first condemned, as violently suspected, to abjure the Lutheran heresy, and to be subjected to a penance ; but four years after his death, in 1556, he was condemned, and, as having relapsed, his body was disinterred, and burnt with his effigy ; his memory was declared infamous, and his property confiscated, for having died as a Lutheran. Raynald Gonzales de Montes was his companion in prison, but succeeded in escaping, and was burnt in effigy. In a work written on the Spanish Inquisition, he has introduced several particulars relating to the life of *Juan Gil*. He informs us that Egidius studied theology at Alcala de Henares, and there obtained the title of Doctor. He acquired so great a reputation, that he was compared to Peter Lombard, to St. Thomas d'Aquinas, to John Scott, and other theologians of the greatest merit. His talents induced the chapter of Seville to offer him unanimously the office of preacher to the cathedral. Egidius had very little talent for preaching, and the canons soon repented of having appointed him.

Rodrigo de Valero told Egidius that the books from which he derived his knowledge were worth nothing, and that his preaching would never be admired, if he did not study the Bible. Egidius took his advice, and in time acquired a style of preaching extremely agreeable to the people, but his success raised him many enemies.

The emperor gave him the Bishopric of Tortosa in 1550, which increasing the envy and hatred of his enemies, they denounced him to the Inquisition of Seville as a Lutheran heretic, for some propositions which he had advanced in his sermons, and which they separated from the other parts, to give them a different sense from what they would otherwise have had; they took advantage of the favour he shewed to Rodrigo Valero in 1540 during his trial, and of some other circumstances, to injure him.

Egidius was taken to the secret prisons of the holy office in 1550 : he made use of this opportunity to compose his apology, which rendered the storm his enemies had raised still more violent. His simplicity had made him, in his apology, establish as certain principles, some propositions which the scholastic theologians looked upon as erroneous, and tending to heresy. The conduct and morals of Egidius were so pure, that the emperor wrote in his favour, the chapter of Seville followed his example, and (what is still more remarkable) the licentiate, Correa, Dean of the inquisitors, was touched by his innocence, and undertook to defend him against his colleague, Pedro Diaz, who bore the greatest hatred to the accused. This circumstance was particularly mortifying to Egidius, as his enemy had formerly possessed the same opinions, and had likewise studied in the school of Rodrigo Valero.

The interest which Egidius had inspired induced the inquisitors to accede to his proposal of a discussion between him and some learned theologians. Brother Garcia de Arias, of the convent of St. Isidore of Seville, was chosen, but his opinion was not deemed sufficient, and Juan Gil demanded that the Dominican friar, Dominic Soto, should be summoned to the conference. This incident retarded the trial, but Soto arrived at Seville.

According to Gonzales de Montes, this theologian held the same opinions as Egidius; but to prevent the suspicions which might arise from this circumstance, he persuaded Egidius to draw up a sort of confession of faith. They agreed that both should write their opinions, and only communicate them to each other in public. This author states that these confessions of faith were compared, and found to accord perfectly.

The inquisitors being informed of this arrangement, declared that, as the reputation of a bishop was concerned, it was necessary to convoke a public assembly, where Dominic Soto should explain the object of the meeting in a sermon, and read his confession of faith; that Egidius should afterwards read his, that the assembly might judge of the conformity of their opinions. The inquisitors caused two pulpits to be prepared, but either by chance, or from a private order, they were so far apart, that Egidius could not hear what Soto said.

Soto* read an exposition of his principles entirely different from that on which they had agreed in their private conferences; and as Egidius did not hear him, and supposed that he was reading the same confession which he had approved, he consequently made signs with his head and hands that he accorded with his propositions. Egidius then began to read his confession of faith, but those who understood the subject, soon perceived that there was not the slightest resemblance between them, and that Egidius held several opinions entirely opposite to some propositions advanced by Dominic Soto, and acknowledged as dogmatical by *the tribunal of the faith;* this circumstance effaced the favourable impressions produced by the gestures of Egidius. The inquisitors added these writings to those of the trial, and passed judgment upon Egidius according to the advice of Soto. He was declared violently suspected of the Lutheran heresy, and condemned to three years' imprisonment; he was prohibited from preaching, writing, or explaining theology for the space of ten years, and never to leave the kingdom on pain of being considered and punished as a formal heretic.

Egidius remained in prison until 1555; he was at first extremely astonished at his situation, after having perfectly agreed with the Dominican on all the points in question. He

* Continued from Gonzales de Montes.

was not undeceived, until some of his fellow-prisoners informed him of the difference of his articles with those of
Soto, and the treachery of that monk.

Egidius took advantage of the short interval of liberty
which followed his imprisonment to go to Valladolid, where
he had an interview with Doctor Cazalla and other Lutherans in that city ; on his return to Seville he fell sick, and
died in 1556. The tribunal being informed of his intercourse
with heretics, instituted another trial, and pronounced that
he died an heretic ; his body was disinterred, and burnt with
his effigy, in a solemn *auto-da-fé*, his memory declared infamous, and his property confiscated : this sentence was executed in 1560.

It will be necessary here to quote a letter of Don Bartholomew Carranza to Brother Louis de la Croix, a Dominican,
and his disciple. The archbishop mentions as a well-known
circumstance, that his catechism having been presented to the
holy office, Brother Melchior Cano and Dominic Soto had
been commissioned to censure it, and that they had judged
unfavourably of his work. He complained much of this conduct in Soto ; he said he could not comprehend such scruples
*in a man who had been so indulgent to the Doctor Egidius
who was considered as an heretic, while, on the contrary, the
author of the Catechism had combated the opinions of the
heretics of England and Flanders ;* that Soto had judged the
book of a Dominican monk no less favourably, while he
treated an archbishop, whom he was bound to respect, without consideration ; that he would, in consequence, write to
Rome and Flanders, where he hoped that his propositions
would be more favourably received than at Valladolid ; but
that, at all events, Pedro de Soto, confessor to the emperor,
would write to Dominic, and he hoped that the Almighty
would allay the tempest which had been raised around him.

Brother Pedro wrote to Dominic Soto, and a correspondence ensued between him and the archbishop Carranza, on

the censure of the catechism, and other works. These letters were found among the papers of Carranza, when he was arrested by the Inquisition. They proved, that Dominic Soto had violated the secrecy which he had sworn to maintain before the Inquisition : some details were found in them relating to the violence which had been used to make him condemn the catechism of Carranza ; he was arrested by the Inquisition of Valladolid, on account of these expressions.

It appears from the archbishop's letter, that the censure of Brother Dominic on Egidius was mild and conciliating, which does not accord with the substitution of the false exposition of his principles mentioned by Gonzales de Montes. I must observe that this author writes like a man blinded by his hatred of his enemies, whom he calls papists, hypocrites, and idolaters ; he even carries his fanaticism so far as to look upon the deaths of the three judges of Egidius during his lifetime as a particular effect of divine justice.

As the affair of Juan Gil is connected with the history of Rodrigo Valero, I shall here relate it. He was born of a good family in Lebrija. In his youth he was extremely irregular and dissipated, but all at once he quitted society, and shut himself up to study the Scriptures with so much ardour, that his conversation, and his contempt for food and clothing, made him pass for a madman.

He endeavoured to persuade priests and monks, that the Roman church was far from holding the pure doctrine of the Evangelists, and became one of the sect of Luther. His attachment to their doctrine was so great, that when he was asked from whom he held his mission, he replied from God himself through the inspiration of the Holy Spirit.

This fanatic was denounced to the holy office, which paid no attention to it, being persuaded that Rodrigo was mad. But as he continued to preach in the streets in favour of Lutheranism, and as no part of his conduct shewed that he was deranged, he was arrested, and would have been condemned to be delivered over to secular justice, if the inquisitors had not persisted in believing him to be mad, and if his disciple Egidius, whose opinions were not then known, had not undertaken his defence. Nevertheless he was condemned in 1540 as an heretic and *false apostle;* he was admitted to reconciliation, deprived of his property, condemned to the *San-benito,* to perpetual imprisonment, and to assist on every Sunday at the grand mass of St. Saviour of Seville.

Several times, when he heard the preacher advance propositions contrary to his own, he raised his voice, and reproached him for his doctrine : this boldness confirmed the inquisitors in the opinion that he was deprived of reason : he was shut up in a convent in the town of San Lucar de Barrameda, where he died at the age of fifty. Gonzales de Montes considers him as a man miraculously sent by God to preach the truth : he adds, that his *San-benito* was suspended in the metropolitan church of Seville, where it excited great curiosity, as he was the first person condemned as a *false apostle.*

Although, during the period of which I have related the history, there were fewer Judaic heretics than in former times, yet there were many more than might be supposed. Of this number was *Mary de Bourgogne,* who was born at Saragossa : her father-in-law was a native of Burgundy, of Jewish extraction. A *New Christian* slave, (who had renounced the law of Moses, to obtain his liberty, and was afterwards burnt for having relapsed,) in 1552, denounced Mary de Bourgogne, who resided in the city of Murcia, and had attained her eighty-fifth year. This man deposed that, before his conversion, some person asked him if he was a Christian ; he replied that he was a Jew, and that Mary then said to him: *You are right, for the Christians have neither faith nor law.* It will no doubt appear incredible, but the trial proves that in 1557 she was still in prison, waiting until sufficient proof was found to condemn

her. After having waited in vain, the inquisitors commanded that Mary should be *tortured, though she was then ninety
years old,* and the council had decreed that in such cases the
criminal should only be intimidated by the preparations.
The inquisitor Cano says, that the *moderate* torture was
applied, but such were the effects of this gentle application,
that the unfortunate Mary ceased to live and suffer in a few
days after.

The inquisitors took advantage of some expressions which
escaped from the unfortunate woman during the torture, to
condemn her as a Judaic heretic, in order to confiscate her
property, which was considerable. Her memory, her children, and her descendants in the male line were declared infamous, her bones and effigy were burnt, and her property
confiscated.

The Supreme Council shewed a certain degree of moderation in another affair, before the tribunal of Toledo. Michael
Sanchez died in prison, before his sentence, which was a
pecuniary penalty, could be announced to him : the inquisitors were uncertain if his property was liable for this
penalty; they applied to the council, which replied in the
negative.

I now terminate the history of the remarkable events of
the reign of Charles V. After a reign of forty years, this
prince abdicated the crown in favour of his son Philip II.,
on the 16th of January, 1556. He did not long survive his
abdication; he died in the convent of the Jeronimites, at
Yuste in the province of Estremadura, on the 21st of September, 1558, aged fifty-seven years and twenty-one days.
He had made his will at Brussels on the 16th of June, 1554,
and a codicil in the monastery of Yuste, twelve days before
his death.

Religion of Charles V.

Some historians have asserted, that Charles V. adopted,

in his retreat, the opinions of the German protestants; that
in his last illness he confessed himself to Constantine Ponce
de la Fuente, his preacher, who was afterwards known to
be a Lutheran; that after his death Philip II. commissioned
the inquisitors to examine the affair, and that the holy office
took possession of the emperor's will, to examine if it contained anything contrary to the true faith. These statements
compel me to enter into some details which will elucidate
this point of history.

To ascertain that the report on the religion of Charles V.
is only an invention of the protestants and the enemies of
Philip II., it is sufficient to read the life of that prince, and
that of his father, composed by Gregorio Leti. Although
this historian has made use of the least authentic documents,
in his work, he is entirely silent on this point. He enters
into a minute detail of the life and occupations of Charles V.
in his retreat, and he relates many decisive proofs of his
attachment to the catholic faith, and his zeal in wishing that
it might triumph over the Lutheran heresy; and though no
dependance can be placed on what he says concerning the
conversations of the emperor with the Archbishop Carranza, (since there is nothing relating to them in his trial,
which I have read,) yet it must be confessed that his recital
is otherwise very exact.

It is not true that Constantine Ponce de la Fuente attended the emperor in his last moments, either as his preacher,
(which office he had filled in Germany,) or as a bishop, since
he did not possess that dignity, as foreign authors have asserted
without any foundation, or as his confessor, since he had
never directed his conscience, though the emperor had
always looked upon him as one of the most learned and
respectable priests in his kingdom. Lastly, Ponce de la
Fuente could not assist Charles V. in his last moments, since
it appears from his trial before the Inquisition of Seville,
that he was in the secret prisons of the holy office long before

the illness of the emperor. Don Prudent de Sandoval, Bishop
of Tui and Pampeluna, speaking of the last circumstances of
the life of Charles V., relates that when that prince heard of
the imprisonment of Ponce, he said, *Oh! if Constantine is
an heretic, he is a great heretic:* an expression very different
from that which he used on hearing that a monk named
Dominic de Guzman had been arrested in the same city :
They might rather imprison him as a fool than an heretic.

In his codicil, written twelve days before his death,
Charles V. thus expresses himself : " When I had been informed that many persons had been arrested in some provinces, and that others were to be taken, as accused of
Lutheranism, I wrote to the princess my daughter, to inform
her in what manner they should be punished, and the evil
remedied. I also wrote afterwards to Louis Quixada, and
authorized him to act in my name in the same affair ; and
although I am persuaded that the king my son, the princess
my daughter, and the ministers, have already, and will
always, make every possible effort to destroy so great an
evil, with all the severity and promptitude which it requires, yet considering what I owe to the service of our
Lord, the triumph of his faith, the preservation of his
church and the Christian religion, (in the defence of which I
have performed such painful labours at the risk of my life,
as every one knows;) and particularly desiring, above all,
to inspire my son, whose catholic sentiments I know, with
the wish of imitating my conduct, and which I hope he will
do, from knowing his virtue and piety, I beg and recommend
to him very particularly, as much as I can and am obliged
to do, and command him moreover in my quality of father,
and by the obedience which he owes me, to labour with
diligence, as in a point which particularly interests him, that
the heretics shall be prosecuted and chastised with all the
severity which their crimes deserve, *without permitting any
criminal to be excepted, without any respect for the entrea-*

ties, or rank, or quality of the persons; and that my intentions may have their full and entire effect, I desire him to
protect the holy office of the Inquisition, for the great numbers of crimes which it prevents or punishes, *remembering
that I have charged him to do so in my will*, that he may
fulfil his duty as a prince, and render himself worthy that
the Lord should make his reign prosperous, conduct his
affairs, and protect him against his enemies, to my consolation *."

I have already stated, that no dependance can be placed
on the account given by Gregorio Leti of the conversations
of the emperor with Don Bartholomew Carranza de Miranda,
archbishop of Toledo.   It is certain that the emperor had a
great esteem for Carranza, which induced him to give him
the bishopric of Cusco in America, in 1542, and of the
Canaries in 1549; to send him as theologian of the emperor
to the Council of Trent, in 1545 and 1551 ; and to London
with his son Philip II., king of Naples and England, in 1554,
to preach against the Lutherans. Nevertheless, when he was
informed, in his retreat at Yuste, that Carranza had accepted the archbishopric of Toledo, to which King Philip had
appointed him, he began to feel less esteem for him, because
he did not know that Carranza had refused that dignity, and
named three persons whom he considered more worthy to
occupy it.   Philip was not only displeased at this refusal,
but he commanded him to obey the will of his sovereign, and
wrote to the Pope, who supported his order by a particular
brief addressed to Br. Bartholomew.

Charles V., at this period, had Br. Juan de Regla, a
Jeronimite, and a learned theologian, for his confessor. He
had assisted at the Council of Trent with Carranza, whom
he always treated as an enemy, because he was jealous of his
great reputation. I shall hereafter prove the disposition of
Juan de Regla towards Carranza; at present I shall only

* Sandoval's History of Charles V. vol. II.

shew that he had great part in his disgrace with the emperor, for being suspected of professing the same doctrines as
Egidius, Constantine, Cazalla, and others.   Regla became
more fanatic than charitable, during the persecution which
he suffered from the Inquisition of Saragossa, when he was
prior of the Convent of Santa Fè ; he was condemned to abjure
eighteen Lutheran propositions, of which the Inquisitors declared him to be suspected. The emperor was also informed,
through the private correspondence of his children, that the
Inquisition was occupied in preparing the trial of the archbishop for heresy, when he came to visit him in his last illness ; and his presence was so disagreeable, that, instead of
conversing with him, as Leti affirms, he did not speak one
word.   Sandoval, with more probability, thus expresses
himself : " This evening the archbishop of Toledo, Carranza,
arrived, but he could not see the emperor.   This prince had
waited for him with much impatience since he had quitted
England, because he wished to have an explanation on certain
things which had been reported of him, and seemed to shew
that his faith was suspected ; for that of the prince was extremely lively, and anything which appeared contrary to
sound doctrine gave him great pain.   The archbishop returned on another day ; the emperor who wished much to
hear him, admitted him into his presence, and told him to sit
down, but did not talk to him, and on that night he became
much worse*."

The animosity of Juan de Regla against the archbishop of
Toledo, was soon manifested in two voluntary informations
before the Inquisitor-General Valdes, on the 9th and 23rd
of December, in 1558, at Valladolid. I shall at a future
period explain all the articles of the denunciation of Juan de
Regla, but it is necessary to anticipate the order of time in
affairs, to prove that Charles V. was not disposed to favour
Carranza in the latter part of his life.

* Sandoval's History of Charles V. tom. II.

The first denunciation took place on the 9th of December: it imported, that on the day before the death of the emperor, the archbishop of Toledo kissed his majesty's hand, and left the room ; that he soon after returned ; and that he did so several times, *though the emperor shewed very little desire to see him,* and that he gave him absolution before he confessed him ; which Juan de Regla imputed to the archbishop as a sign of contempt or neglect of the sacrament : that in one of these visits he said to the emperor, *Your majesty may be full of confidence, for there is not, nor ever has been any sin, the death of Jesus having sufficed to efface it;* that this discourse appeared bad to him, and that there were present Br. Pedro de Sotomayor and Br. Diego Ximenez, Dominicans, Br. Marc Oriols de Cardona and Br. Francis Villaba, monks of St. Jerome : the last was his majesty's preacher; the Count de Oropesa and Don Diego de Toledo his brother ; Don Louis d'Avila Zuñiga, grand commander of the military order of Alcantara, and Don Louis de Quixada, major-domo to the emperor.

The inquisitor-general would not admit the Dominican monks as witnesses, because he supposed them subject to the archbishop : the evidences of Count Oropesa and his brother were likewise rejected, because they were his friends. The monk of St. Jerome declared that the archbishop arrived at Yuste on a Sunday, two days before the death of the emperor ; that this prince *would not see him or allow him to enter,* but his major-domo, Don Louis de Quixada, undertook to introduce him ; that Carranza threw himself on his knees in the chamber, and that the emperor, *without saying a word to him,* fixed his eyes upon him, like a person who wishes to express himself by a look: that the persons who were present retired : that when the archbishop came out of the chamber he appeared discontented, and he the witness believed that he was so, having heard from William, the emperor's barber, that on the day when the news of the nomination of Carranza to the archbishopric of Toledo arrived, his majesty said, *When I gave him the bishopric of the Canaries he refused it ; now he accepts the archbishopric of Toledo ; we shall see what we are to think of his virtue ;* that their private interview lasted a quarter of an hour, and the archbishop called in the attendants. When they entered, the archbishop threw himself on his knees, and his majesty made a sign for him to sit down, and repeat some words of consolation ; that the prelate again threw himself on his knees, and repeated the four first verses of the psalm *De profundis*, not literally, but paraphrasing the text. His majesty made him a sign to stop, and Carranza then retired with the other attendants ; that on another day, about the hour of ten in the evening, just before the emperor expired, Carranza visited him, because he had been informed of his danger, and gave him the crucifix to kiss, and at the same time addressed some words of consolation to him, at which the monks Juan de Regla, Francis de Villaba, Francis Angulo, prior, and Louis de St. Gregoria, were scandalized. These persons conversed together afterwards, and said that the prelate ought not to have spoken thus ; but the witness could not recollect what the words were. They were repeated to him, and he replied that he believed they might be the same, but that he could not be certain, as he was reading the passion of our Saviour, *according to St. Luke*, at the time ; he only remarked that the monks looked at one another with a kind of mystery.

Neither Francis Angulo, nor Louis de St. Gregoria were examined, perhaps they were dead. Francis de Villaba, preacher to the emperor, declared, that he had not heard anything in the emperor's apartment which was worthy of being reported to the Inquisition. Being questioned as to what he thought of the discourse which the archbishop had addressed to the emperor, he replied that he was only present once, when the prelate recited some verses of the *De pro-*

fundis; that Don Louis d'Avila afterwards requested him to speak to the emperor, and that he made him an exhortation. When examined on the subject of the words and the scandal, he replied that he did not hear or see anything that could offend him.

Don Louis d'Avila y Zuñiga cited the entrance of the prelate ; and that he took a crucifix and knelt down, saying with a loud voice, *behold him who answers for all ; there is no longer any sin, all is pardoned.* The witness did not recollect if the archbishop said, *and however numerous the sins may be, they are all pardoned :* that these words did not appear proper to him, and he requested the emperor's preacher to make him an exhortation, who afterwards told him that his majesty appeared satisfied.

Don Louis de Quixada deposed that the archbishop was with the emperor three times before his death, that he saw him take a crucifix, and that he pronounced some words on the subject of Jesus Christ dying for our sins, but he could not recollect them, because his employment as major-domo occupied him at the time.

These circumstances shew that Charles V. was far from being inclined to Lutheranism at his death. It is equally false that the inquisitors took his will, to examine if it contained any sentiments tending to heresy. I have read or consulted a multitude of books and papers in the archives of the Inquisition, and could not discover anything to support the opinion; so that nothing now remains but to seek the origin of this fable.

A number of circumstances may have caused the Inquisition to be mentioned in relating the death of Charles V. The first is, that Carranza, who attended him at his death, was soon after arrested by the holy office ; the second, that his two preachers, Constantine Ponce and Augustine Cazalla, were condemned by that tribunal ; the third, that his confessor, Juan de Regla, was obliged to abjure certain propositions;

the fourth, that the emperor himself had been threatened with excommunication three years before, as a favourer of heretics, by Paul IV.; the fifth, that Philip II. made use of the Inquisition in a variety of circumstances entirely political.

Charles V. died a Catholic; and it is only to be regretted that he associated so many superstitions with his Catholicism, and shewed so much attachment to the Inquisition during his life.

CHAPTER XIX.

OF THE PROCEEDINGS AGAINST CHARLES V. AND PHILIP II. AS SCHISMATICS AND FAVOURERS OF HERESY.—PROGRESS OF THE INQUISITION UNDER THE LAST OF THESE PRINCES—CONSEQUENCES OF THE PARTICULAR FAVOUR WHICH HE SHEWED TOWARDS IT.

Trials of Charles V., Philip II., and the Duke of Alva.

In 1555, John Peter Carafa, a noble Neapolitan, and as such the subject of Charles V. and Philip II., was elevated to the holy see, under the name of Paul IV. at the age of seventy-nine years. Charles V. had then renounced the crown of Sicily, in favour of Prince Philip, who was about to marry the Queen of England. The new Pope mortally hated the emperor, not only because he could not bear to be a subject to the house of Austria, but because this prince and his son favoured the families of *Colonna and Sforza,* which he looked upon as the rivals of his house. The kingdom of Naples passed at that time for a fief of the holy see. Paul IV. undertook to deprive Charles of the imperial purple, and his son of the crown of Sicily, and to dispose of it in favour of one of his nephews, with the assistance of the King of France, or to give the kingdom to some French prince.

He commenced the proceedings against Charles V. and Philip, by the preparatory instruction, to shew that they were enemies of the holy see, particularly in protecting the families of *Sforza* and *Colonna*, whose hatred for the Pontiff was well known.

To these reasons it was to be alleged that Charles V. was a favourer of heretics, and suspected of Lutheranism, since the publication of the imperial decrees at the diet of Augsburg, in 1554. The fiscal of the apostolical chamber then demanded that the Pope should declare Charles V. to be deprived of the imperial crown, and that of Spain and its dependencies, and Philip of the throne of Naples ; that bulls of excommunication should be issued against them, and the people of Germany, Spain, Italy, and particularly of Naples, released from their oath of fidelity. Paul IV. suspended the trial at this stage of the proceedings, to continue it when he judged it convenient. He revoked at the same time all the bulls which his predecessors had expedited in favour of the Spanish monarchs, for the collection of the annual subsidy imposed on the clergy, and for the funds destined for the *holy crusade.* The Pope was not content with this hostile measure ; he entered into an alliance with Henry II., King of France, to make war upon the house of Austria, until its princes were deprived of their kingdoms.

Charles V. was then at Brussels, occupied in ceding the empire of Germany to his brother Ferdinand, King of Hungary and Bohemia, and in making over the crown of Spain and the countship of Flanders to his son. This policy was useful to Charles V., as it threw the weight of the embarrassment on Philip, who had just arrived from England to receive his father's instructions how to govern Spain. The circumstances in which they found themselves required the greatest prndence, for they not only had to fear the abuse which the Pope might make of his apostolical and temporal power, but also the consequences of the alliances which his holiness had just signed with the King of France.

Besides the Council of State (which Charles and Philip always consulted before they decided on any subject) they deemed it necessary to have judgments of *conscience*, to balance the authority of the supreme head of the Catholic Church. On the 15th of November, 1555, the famous consultation of Brother Melchior Cano was framed at Valladolid, which was published at Madrid in 1809, in my *collection of different papers, ancient and modern, on matrimonial dispensations, and other ecclesiastical dispensations.* The decision of Cano was, that in all similar cases the only and proper remedy is not only to deprive the temporal sovereign of Rome of the power of injuring, but to reduce him to the necessity of accepting reasonable terms, and of acting with more prudence in future. Other theologians decided that the concessions made by the Court of Rome were irrevocable, and had the force of a true contract passed for the benefit of an empire or kingdom.

The Pope, informed of these decisions, commanded the inquisitor-general to punish the authors of it; he was supported by most of the prelates of the kingdom, at the head of whom was the Cardinal Siliceo, Archbishop of Toledo, who had been the king's preceptor. Philip, who had been King of Spain from January, 1556, wrote from London, in the month of July following, the letter to his sister, the governess of the kingdom, which I have inserted in my diplomatic collection. It is as follows:—

"Since I informed you of the conduct of the Pope, and of the news received from Rome, I have learnt that his holiness proposes to excommunicate the emperor and me, to put my states under an interdict, and to prohibit the divine service. Having consulted learned men on this subject, it appears that it is not only an abuse of the power of the sovereign pontiff, founded only on the hatred and passion, which, certainly, has not been provoked by our conduct, but that we are not obliged to submit to what he has ordained in respect to our persons, on account of the great scandal which would be caused by our confessing ourselves guilty, since we are not so, and the great sin which we should commit in so doing. In consequence, it has been decided, that if I am interdicted from certain things, I am not obliged to deprive myself of them, as those do who are excommunicated, although a censure may be sent to me from Rome, according to the disposition of his holiness. For after having destroyed the sects in England, brought this country under the influence of the church, pursued and punished the heretics without ceasing, and obtained a success which has always been constant, I see that his holiness evidently wishes to ruin my kingdom, without considering what he owes to his dignity; and I have no doubt that he would succeed if we consented to his demands, since he has already revoked all the legations which Cardinal Pole received for this kingdom, and which had produced so much benefit. These reasons, other important considerations, the necessity of preparing for all events, and of protecting our people from being surprised, have induced us to draw up, in the name of his majesty, and in our own, an act of recusation in form, of which I intended to send you a copy; but as this piece is very long, and the courier is setting out for France, it could not be done, and I will send it by the courier going by sea, who will soon set out. When you receive it, you must write to the prelates, the grandees, to the cities, universities, and the heads of orders, and inform them of all that has passed: you must direct them to look upon the censures and interdict sent from Rome as non-existent, because they are null, unjust, and without foundation, for I have taken counsel on what is permitted in these circumstances. If any act of the Pope should arrive in the interim, it will be sufficient to prevent it from being received, accepted, or executed; but to preclude the necessity of coming to this extremity, you must cause the frontiers to be strictly guarded, as we have

done in England, that none of these pieces should be notified
or delivered, and *punish very severely any person who shall
dare to distribute them, because it is not to be permitted that
we should continue to dissimulate.* If it is impossible to
prevent their introduction, and if any one attempts to put
them in force, you must oppose their execution, as we have
powerful motives for this command; and this prohibition
must extend to the kingdom of Arragon, to which you must
write if it is necessary. It has been since known, that in
the bull published on Holy Thursday, the Pope has excommunicated all those who have taken or shall take the property of the church, *whether they are kings or emperors,*
and that on Good Friday, he commanded the prayer for his
majesty to be omitted, although the Jews, Moors, heretics,
and schismatics, are prayed for on that day. This proves that
the evil is becoming serious, and induces us to recommend
more particularly the execution of the measures which we
have prescribed, and of which we shall give an account to
his majesty *."

Philip, for the time, prevented the inquisitor-general from
trying any of those persons who had been marked as suspected of heresy, among whom were not only the theologians
and canonists who had been consulted, but many councillors
of state who supported their opinion against Cardinal Siliceo
and his adherents †.

The Pope was obstinate in his resolutions, and deceived by
the tranquillity which Philip suffered him to enjoy in Rome,
he placed himself at the brink of the precipice. The Duke
of Alva, who was viceroy of Naples (and whose character
was at least as harsh as that of the Pope), in September
1556, left his government, and occupied the states of the
holy see, even to the gates of Rome; and Paul IV., finding
that the republic of Venice had deserted him, and being

* Cabrera, Hist. Philip II., Book 2. chap. vi.
† Cabrera, Ibid. B. 1. chap. viii. and ix.

pressed by the cardinals and people, demanded an armistice, which was granted. Instead of taking advantage of this favour to make peace on reasonable terms, the Pope confirmed his alliance with Henry II., and raised a war between that monarch and the King of Spain, although Charles V. had, in 1555, signed a truce of five years with that prince. Henry, having lost the famous battle of St. Quentin, on the 10th of August, 1557, the Pope became so alarmed, that he demanded a peace at the time when the Duke of Alva was preparing to enter Rome at the head of his army. The viceroy renounced his design, but had the boldness to tell the Pope that he would not make peace until he had asked pardon of the king, his master, for having treated him with so little respect. This message increased the alarm of the old pontiff, who had recourse to the mediation of Venice. The Pope refused to negotiate with the Duke of Alva, but said, that he would consent to any proposal from the King of Spain, as he was persuaded that he would not impose any condition on him contrary to his honour, or to the dignity of the holy see.

The Duke of Alva wrote to Philip to request, that in this instance, he would display the severity necessary to prevent new divisions. But this prince (who had signed on the 10th of July, 1556, the excellent letter already quoted) had no person in the following year to inspire him with sufficient energy to follow the advice of his viceroy. He wrote to command him to conclude a peace immediately, " as he would rather lose the privileges of his crown, than infringe those of the holy see in the slightest degree."

The Duke of Alva was extremely displeased at this resolution, but he immediately obeyed his master, and this singular peace was signed on the 14th of September, 1557, by the Duke of Alva, and Cardinal Carafa, nephew and plenipotentiary to the Pope. The envoy made no reparation to Philip II., and the following singular article is part of the treaty :—" His holiness will receive from the Catholic king, through his plenipotentiary, the Duke of Alva, all the necessary submissions to obtain the pardon of his offences, without prejudicing the engagement of the king to send an ambassador extraordinary for the particular object of the pardon which he demands, it being understood that his holiness will restore him to favour as a submissive son, and worthy to share the benefits which the holy see is accustomed to bestow on its children and the other Christian princes."

The haughty pontiff acknowledged that he had obtained more than he had hoped for, and to shew his satisfaction, bestowed the highest honours on the Duke of Alva; he invited him to eat at his own table, and received him in the palace of the Vatican.

Gregorio Leti is right in attributing all the evils that have since arisen from the excessive authority which the priests have arrogated over laymen, to this conduct of Philip II. Paul IV. soon displayed his contempt for Philip II. and his father, since, in five months after the treaty, on the 13th of February, 1558, he addressed a brief to the inquisitor-general Valdés, in which he revived all the regulations of the councils and pontiffs against heretics and schismatics. He commanded him to prosecute them, and punish them according to the constitutions, and, above all, to deprive all such persons of their dignities and offices, whether they were bishops, archbishops, patriarchs, cardinals, or legates, *barons, counts, marquises, dukes, princes, kings, or emperors*. Fortunately, neither Charles V. nor his son had embraced the opinions of Luther, yet it was certainly the intention of the Pope to subject them to the dispositions of his bull.

Of the Inquisitions of Sardinia, Flanders, Milan, Naples,
Galicia, America, and the Sea.

In 1562, Philip II. commanded the Inquisition of Sardinia

to conform rigorously to the rules of the holy office of Spain in prosecuting the accused, although it was represented to him that they had hitherto only known those of Ferdinand V., which were less severe.

Philip did not treat his Flemish subjects with less rigour. In 1522 Charles V. appointed Francis de Hult, a lay counsellor of Brabant, inquisitor-general for the states of Flanders; and Adrian VI. invested him with the apostolical jurisdiction, on the condition that he had priests and theologians for assessors. Soon after three provincial inquisitors were appointed, the overseer of the regular canons of Ypres for Flanders and its dependencies; the overseer of the clergy of Mons for Hainault, and the Dean of Louvain for Brabant, Holland, and the other provinces. The inquisitors-general appointed by Clement VII. were Cardinal Everard de la Marche, Bishop of Liege, and Francis de Hult, before mentioned. This measure did not deprive the other inquisitors of their privileges; those of Louvain in 1527, celebrated several *autos-da-fé*, and condemned sixty persons to different punishments. In 1529 terrible edicts were issued against heretics, which were renewed in 1531, but with some mitigation.

At the death of the Dean of Louvain, Paul III., in 1537, appointed as inquisitor-general for the Low Country the successor in the deanery, and the canon Douce; they were approved by Charles V. In 1555 Julius III. authorized the sub-delegates of the dean and canon; Paul IV. did the same in 1560 for the overseer of Valcanet, and the theological doctor of Louvain, Michael Bayo. All these men took the title of *ecclesiastical ministers* from the year 1550, when Charles V. prohibited them from ever taking the name of *inquisitors*, because it was obnoxious to the people. The Flemish Inquisition was extremely severe in the first period of its existence; it inflicted the same punishments as that of Spain, but applied them to a greater number of cases.

Philip II. moderated the action of this tribunal by an edict in 1556.

Such was the state of the Flemish Inquisition in 1559, when a bull of Paul IV. was received from Rome, by which three ecclesiastical provinces were created, the bishoprics of which were subjected to the jurisdiction of the Archbishops of Malines, Cambray, and Utrecht: twelve canons were instituted for each cathedral, three of whom were to be inquisitors for life.   This measure caused the first indication of the rebellion which raged in Holland and the United Provinces in 1562.   The people maintained that they had only tolerated the inquisitors since 1522, because they considered them as temporary agents; but that they would never allow the permanent establishment of an institution so obnoxious to the provinces. This opposition increased when it was known that Philip II. intended to organize the eighteen Inquisitions of Flanders, on the plan of that of Spain, which had long been regarded as a sanguinary tribunal.

This project was the more dreaded, as many Spaniards had fled from the Inquisition to Holland. These emigrations were most numerous after the year 1550, when several Bibles, which had been printed in the Spanish language in the Low Countries, were prohibited as containing the opinions of the new heretics.   Notwithstanding the obstinacy with which the King of Spain pursued the establishment of the Inquisition in Flanders, he failed in his enterprise, and also in his attempt to force the Low Countries to receive the regular tribunal. The Flemings persisted in opposing everything resembling the Inquisition, and their resistance was the cause of the long and bloody wars which exhausted the treasures and armies of Spain during half a century.

In the following year, 1563, Philip II. decreed the necessary measures to establish the Inquisition at Milan.   He communicated his design to the Pope, who appeared to approve it, but was really displeased, because it tended to

diminish the power of the holy see. The Milanese immediately protested against the introduction of a tribunal, of
which they had formed the most unfavourable opinion. The
bishops of Lombardy were not less averse to it, as they
knew that in Spain the bishops were not only deprived of all
power, but had fallen into contempt from the despotism of
the inquisitors, who had taken possession of the episcopal
privileges, and enjoyed them in peace under the protection
of the sovereign, who had no adviser in these affairs but the
inquisitor-general.

The city of Milan sent deputies to the Pope (who was a
native of that place), to entreat him to preserve his country
from the danger which threatened it. They also sent
deputies to Madrid to demand that things should remain in
the same state, and applied at the same time to the Milanese
bishops at the Council of Trent to support their cause before
that celebrated assembly. Pius IV. told the deputies that
he would never allow the Spanish Inquisition to be established in Milan, *as he knew its extreme severity*, and promised that their tribunal should be dependant on the Court
of Rome, whose decrees were extremely mild, and gave the
accused every facility in their defence.

During the course of this negotiation, the Duke de Sesa,
wishing to execute his master's private orders, established
the tribunal of the Inquisition in the city of Milan, of which
he was the governor, and published the names of the sub-
delegated inquisitors. This declaration displeased the Milanese, who began to excite popular commotions, and cried
Long live the king ! perish the Inquisition!

The Milanese bishops at the Council of Trent disinclined
all the Italian prelates to the Spanish Inquisition ; the
legates of the Pope who presided at the council, declared in
favour of the Milanese, and Cardinal S. Charles Borromeo
pleaded the cause of his countrymen in the college of cardinals, and placed them under their protection. The Duke

de Sesa, who observed all that passed, foresaw that the result would be disagreeable to his master, and wrote to Philip, who abandoned his design*.

These events did not prevent Philip II. from attempting to introduce the Inquisition at Naples, although both Ferdinand V. and Charles V. had failed in the enterprise; but his efforts only served to disgrace him and destroy his authority in Naples, as they had before done in Flanders and Milan.

It may be supposed that Philip did not forget his American dominions. Ferdinand V. having resolved to establish the Inquisition in the New World, charged Cardinal Ximenez de Cisneros with the conduct of the affair, and in 1516 he appointed Don Juan Quevedo, Bishop of Cuba, the *delegated* inquisitor-general, for the Spanish colonies then known by the name of the *kingdom of Terra Firma*, and gave him the power of appointing judges and officers for the tribunal. Charles V. wished to extend the benefits of this *pious* institution, and Cardinal Adrian, by his order, appointed on the 7th of January, 1519, Don Alphonso Manso, Bishop of Porto Rico, and Brother Pedro de Cordova, inquisitors for the *Indies and Isles of the Ocean*, and gave them the requisite powers to establish the tribunal.

The new inquisitors began to prosecute the baptized Indians, who still retained some idolatrous practices. The viceroys informed the King of Spain of the evils produced by this system; in fact the Indians fled into the interior, and joined the savage tribes, which considerably retarded the progress of population in those vast countries. Charles V. in 1538 prohibited the inquisitors from prosecuting the Indians, who were to be under the jurisdiction of the bishops. The inquisitors of America were not more submissive than

* Leti, Life of Philip II. Book 17.—Reinaidi, Annales Eccles. An. 1563, No. 146.—Palavicini, Hist. Council of Trent, Book 22, Chap. viii. —Sarpi, Hist. Council of Trent, Book 8. No. 42.

those of Spain, which obliged the prince to renew his orders
in 1549. Philip II. undertook to organize the tribunal on
the plan of that of Spain. In 1553 and 1565 he renewed
his father's injunctions to leave the Indians under the jurisdiction of the bishops; and in 1569 he published a royal
ordinance, importing that the inquisitor-general had appointed inquisitors, and commanding the viceroys and governors to give them every assistance in their establishment.
These inquisitors were received with great ceremony at
Panarma and Lima, when they first formed the tribunal.

In 1570 Philip II. appointed an Inquisition at Mexico,
and in 1571 established three tribunals for all America; one
at Lima, one at Mexico, and the other at Carthagena,
assigning to each the extent of territory which they were to
possess, and subjecting them to the authority of the inquisitor-general and the Supreme Council.

The first *auto-da-fé* in Mexico took place in 1574; it was
celebrated with so much pomp and splendour, that eye-
witnesses have declared that it could only be compared to
that of Valladolid in 1559, at which Philip II. and the royal
family attended. A Frenchman and an Englishman were
burnt as impenitent Lutherans; eighty persons were reconciled, and subjected to different penances. The Inquisition
of Carthagena was not established at this period; it was
founded in 1610 by Philip III.

The great fleet of the Catholic league against the Emperor
of Constantinople, which gained the famous battle of
Lepanto, inspired Philip II. with the project of creating an
Inquisition for heretics who might be found in ships. As
the authority of the inquisitor-general did not extend beyond the dominions of the King of Spain, it was considered
necessary to apply to the Pope, who in 1571 granted the
brief, which was demanded, authorizing the inquisitor-
general to create the new tribunal, and appoint judges and
officers. It was first known by the name of the *Inquisition*

of the Galleys, but was afterwards called the *Inquisition of the Fleets and Armies* ; it existed but for a short period, as it was found to impede the progress of navigation.

The Inquisition was unknown in Galicia for more than a century before this period. This province formed part of the district subject to the holy office of Old Castile and the kingdom of Leon ; it had escaped this scourge, but at last Philip II. resolved that it should have an Inquisition to superintend the sea-ports, in order to prevent the introduction of pernicious books, and the entrance of persons who would teach the doctrines of the Protestants. The royal ordinance which established the Inquisition in Galicia was expedited in 1574, and the tribunal was organized in the same year.

Disputes with the Inquisition of Portugal.

The establishment of the power of Philip II. in Portugal, after the death of the Cardinal Don Henry, who had occupied the throne until 1580, gave that prince another opportunity of signalizing his zeal for the Inquisition. I have already indicated the period of its institution, and the attendant circumstances*. Don Henry was inquisitor-general from 1539 to 1578, when he succeeded to the crown of Portugal, after the death of his nephew Don Sebastian. He bestowed the archbishopric of Lisbon, which he occupied at the time of his accession, on Don George Almida, and likewise appointed him the third inquisitor-general of the kingdom.

In 1544, Don Henry (who then occupied the see of Evora), and Cardinal Don Juan Pardo de Tabera, inquisitor-general of Spain, with the consent of their respective sovereigns, published a circular, in which they announced, that as the two states were so near each other, and the extent of the frontier favoured the flight of the persons

* See Chapter XVI.

prosecuted by the Inquisition, they had agreed, 1st, to communicate reciprocally everything which might interest the Inquisition; 2nd, to arrest in their respective jurisdictions those subjects who were designated; 3rdly, to keep them prisoners, and to claim the writings of the trial, because this measure was less inconvenient than the exchange of the prisoners.

This convention was obscured several times; but in 1588 the inquisitors of Lisbon sent a requisition to those of Valladolid, to deliver up to them Gonzales Baez, who had been arrested at Medina del Campo: they replied that this demand could not be admitted, as it was contrary to the convention. The inquisitors of Portugal acknowledged the justice of this claim; but those of Spain, who in 1568 found themselves in the same situation, refused to conform to the measure, because they had at their head Cardinal Espinosa, who was all-powerful with Philip. The cardinal informed Don Henry that he had not ratified the convention, and that he considered it more proper that the prisoner should be given up to the tribunal which had instituted the trial. He requested Cardinal Henry to apply to both their sovereigns, and promised to propose to the King of Spain a measure which should be a general rule for all cases in future.

Don Henry commissioned Francis Pereira, the Portuguese ambassador at Madrid, to terminate this dispute with Cardinal Espinosa. While this affair was being negotiated, several Spaniards who had been condemned by the tribunal of Llerena to be burnt in effigy as contumacious, were arrested in Portugal by the inquisitors of Evora, who immediately demanded the writings of the trial according to the convention of 1544. The tribunal of Llerena replied that it was impossible not to follow the example of Cardinal Espinosa. Almost at the same time these inquisitors arrested some Portuguese who had escaped from their country. The Bishop of Portalegre, inquisitor of Evora, reclaimed the prisoners, but the tribunal refused to give them up, if the inhabitants of Albuquerque, who had been arrested by the Inquisition of Evora, were not returned. Cardinal Henry yielded to the Spanish Inquisition, but wrote to them on the 5th of December to address a formal requisition on this subject, while the Inquisition of Evora would do the same to Cardinal Espinosa. The Supreme Council consented to this arrangement, and the prisoners were exchanged.

The inquisitor-general, Don Henry, died in 1580. The crown of Portugal then descended to Philip II., as being the son of the Empress Isabella, the sister of John III., King of Portugal. As the office of grand-inquisitor was vacant, he wished to suppress it, and place Portugal under the dominion of that of Spain. He represented to the Pope that there would be more unity in the proceedings: but this attempt was unsuccessful, as he had only been acknowledged king on condition that the crown should continue independent of that of Spain.

When the Duke of Braganza was proclaimed King of Portugal in the reign of Philip IV., Don Francis de Castro grand inquisitor, and Don John de Vasconcellas, a member of the council of the Inquisition, remained faithful to the King of Spain. The new sovereign (who had taken the name of John IV.) wished to increase his party. Influenced by the advice of England, which had favoured the insurrection, he resolved to restore to the Jews the liberty which they enjoyed before the establishment of the Inquisition; but he was opposed by the two inquisitors above mentioned. The council even condemned a decision of the university of Paris, in which it was said that the king could appoint and consecrate bishops without bulls from Rome, if Pope Innocent X. refused to grant them. John IV. threatened the inquisitors with imprisonment, and even with death, but they were ready to suffer anything rather than consent to the emancipation of the Jews. Don Francis de Castro died, and it was necessary to appoint another inquisitor-general; but the bulls of confirmation were not less difficult to obtain than those for bishops, as the Popes, Urban VIII., Innocent X., and Alexander VII., avoided declaring in favour of either the King of Spain or the Duke of Braganza. At last Portugal triumphed over the efforts of Spain, and the Inquisitions of the two kingdoms seldom had any communication.

That I may not pass over any event tending to prove the attachment of Philip II. for the Inquisition, I shall here mention a project for a military order of the holy office, which would never have been conceived, if the partiality of the monarch for this tribunal had not been generally known.

Some fanatics thought to please him by founding a new military order under the name of *St. Mary of the White Sword.* The object of this institution was to defend the Catholic religion, the kingdom of Spain, its frontiers, and forts, from any invasion ; to prevent the ingress of Jews, Moors, and heretics ; and to execute any measures which the inquisitor might command. To be a member of this order it was necessary to produce proofs and witnesses that they descended neither from Jews, Moors, or any Spaniard condemned and punished by the holy office; nobility was not necessary. The members of this association were independent of the jurisdiction of the bishops and civil authorities ; they were all to take the field and fight in defence of the frontier towns, but they acknowledged no chief but the inquisitor-general.

This scheme was adopted by the provinces of Castile, Leon, the Asturias, Arragon, Navarre, Galicia, Guipuscoa, Alava, Biscay, Valencia, and Catalonia. The statutes of the order received the approbation of the inquisitor-general and the Supreme Council ; the founders and the representatives of the metropolitan churches of Toledo, Seville, Santiago, Gre-

nada, Tarragona, Saragossa, Valencia, and forty-eight noble
families known for having never mixed their blood with that
of the New Christians, addressed an humble supplication to
the king to obtain the confirmation of them. They represented that the order of the *White Sword* offered the greatest
advantages to Spain ; that it would increase the army without
any expense of public treasure; that its services would reform and ameliorate the morals of the people ; lastly, that it
would shed fresh lustre on the nobility of the kingdom.

Philip commissioned his Sovereign Council to examine the
plan of this institution, which was likewise discussed in
several assemblies appointed by his majesty. The opinions
were various, but I shall make known that of a Spanish
gentleman, as it deserves to be recorded.

Don Pedro Venegas, of Cordova, represented to the king,
that the new order was not necessary, as the Inquisition had
not found the want of it in the most difficult circumstances ;
that the bishops reformed the morals of the people as much
as could be expected from human nature ; that Spain had
never wanted troops even when part of the Peninsula was
occupied by enemies; that other military orders existed,
who were obliged to obey their respective grand-masters ;
that these dignities were now possessed by the monarch in
virtue of apostolical bulls; that the new establishment
might one day attack the authority of the sovereign, if the
inquisitor-general made a bad use of the troops at his disposal; that several similar instances had been known of the
grand-masters of the orders above mentioned ; that this
institution would create two parties in the kingdom, that of
the Old Christians and that of the new, and that the distinction granted to the first would cause murders and civil
wars, and threaten the monarchy with ruin.

Philip II. thought seriously on what the grand-masters of
the military orders had done, and being jealous of his authority, he was not disposed to place an army in the power

of the inquisitor-general, who might follow their example ; he therefore commanded that the proceedings should be suspended, and the interested persons informed that it had not been found necessary to create a new order.

CHAPTER XX.

THE INQUISITION CELEBRATES AT VALLADOLID, IN 1559, TWO AUTOS-DA-FE AGAINST THE LUTHERANS, IN THE PRESENCE OF SOME MEMBERS OF THE ROYAL FAMILY.

First Auto-da-fé.

THE trial of Juan Gil, Bishop of Tortosa, so much alarmed many Lutherans, that they quitted the kingdom. Of this number were Cassiodorus de Beina, Juan Perez de Pineda, Cyprian de Valera, and Julian Hernandez ; the three first published catechisms, translations of the Bible, and other works written in the Castilian tongue, in foreign countries *. Juan Perez published his at Venice in 1556, and they were soon after introduced into Spain by Hernandez, who was arrested by the Inquisition. The citations and inquiries made in consequence of the trial of Hernandez, in order to discover the religious opinions of the persons with whom he associated, caused an infinite number of trials to be instituted during the fifteen years following, in all the tribunals of Spain, particularly in those of Seville and Valladolid. In 1557 and 1558, the Inquisition arrested a great number of persons distinguished by their birth, their offices, or their doctrine. Some indications found in the writings of the trials, of a vast scheme tending to the propagation of the

* Pellecyr, Ensago de Biblioteca de Traductores Españoles. Articles, *Reina, Perez,* and *Valera.*

opinions of Luther, persuaded Philip II. and the inquisitor
Valdés that it was necessary to treat all the convicted
persons with the utmost severity.   Philip wrote to Rome on
the subject on the 4th January, 1559.   The Pope addressed
to Valdés a brief, in which he authorized him to give over
to secular justice all dogmatizing Lutherans, even those who
had not relapsed, and who, to avoid capital punishment, had
given equivocal signs of repentance.   If history had nothing
to allege against Philip II. and the inquisitor Valdés, but
the solicitation for this bull, it would be sufficient to devote
their names to infamy.

On the 5th of January, 1559, a second bull revoked all
the permissions granted for reading prohibited books, and
charged the inquisitor-general to prosecute all who should
read or keep them in their houses; and as his Holiness was
informed that a great number of writings which tended to
propagate the Lutheran doctrines were circulating in Spain,
the bull commanded the confessors to ask their penitents if
they knew or had heard of any persons possessing, reading, or
dispersing them; that they should also impose upon them the
obligation of communicating such circumstances to the holy
office on pain of excommunication; and that the confessors
who omitted this duty should be punished as guilty, even if
persons they absolved were bishops, archbishops, patriarchs,
cardinals, *kings*, or *emperors*.   It is easy to perceive how
much these measures must have increased the number of accusations; and to encourage the informers, Philip renewed
the edict of Ferdinand V., published at Toro in 1505, by
which they were entitled to the fourth part of the confiscated
property.

The multitude of accusations caused by these bulls, induced
the inquisitor-general to delegate his powers to Don Pedro
de la Gasca, Bishop of Palencia, who established himself at
Valladolid, and to Don Juan Gonzales de Munebrega,
Bishop of Tarragona, who repaired to Seville.   Valdés at

the same time executed the dispositions of another bull, which granted to the holy office, on account of its increased expenses in travelling and maintaining so great a number of prisoners, the revenues of a canonship in each metropolitan church, cathedral, and college, in the kingdom. Another brief granted them a subsidy of one hundred thousand ducats of gold, to be imposed on the ecclesiastical revenues of the kingdom, to pay the debts contracted from the same cause. It is surprising that after eighty years of confiscation, the establishment should complain of distress. These bulls however were not sufficient to procure money, owing to the resistance of several chapters, particularly that of Majorca. In 1574 they still remained unexecuted, when Gregory XIII. confirmed them, and the King of Spain was obliged to force the rebel canons to submit.

The arrest and trial of so great a number of Spaniards necessarily caused an *auto-da-fé* to be celebrated in many tribunals; but as the victims in those of Valladolid and Seville were persons distinguished, some for their nobility, others for their doctrine, and all for the purity of their lives, the ceremonies in these cities were more noted than the others;. and I do not hesitate in affirming that all that has been written against the Spanish Inquisition in Germany and France was only caused by the treatment of the Lutherans at Seville and Valladolid (for, until then, scarcely anything had been written on the subject), though the number of Lutherans who perished was small, when compared to the enormous and almost incredible number of those who had suffered as Jews or Mahometans.

The first solemn *auto-da-fe* of Valladolid, was celebrated on the 21st of May, 1559, in the grand square, and in the presence of the Prince Don Carlos, and the Princess Juana, of the civil authorities, and of a considerable number of the grandees of Spain, besides an immense multitude of people. The arrangement of the scaffolds and seats have been already described in several works, and represented in prints. Fourteen persons were relaxed, the bones and effigy of a woman burnt, and sixteen individuals were admitted to reconciliation with penances. Some details of the principal persons may be found interesting.

Dona Eleonora de Vibero (the wife of Pedro Cazalla, who held an office in the Treasury), daughter of Juan de Vibero, who had a similar employment, and Constance Ortiz, was proprietress of a chapel in the Benedictine convent of Valladolid. She had been interred without any doubt of her orthodoxy; but she was accused of Lutheranism by the fiscal of the Inquisition, though he said she had concealed her opinions, by receiving the sacraments and the eucharist at her death. He supported his accusation by the testimony of several witnesses who had been tortured or threatened, the result of which was that the house of Eleonora de Vibero had been used as a temple by the Lutherans. Her memory and her posterity were condemned to infamy, her property confiscated, her body disinterred and burnt with her effigy, and her house razed to the ground, and prohibited from being rebuilt; a monument with an inscription relating to this event was placed on the spot. I have seen the column and the inscription; I have heard that it was destroyed in 1809.

The other principal persons who perished in this *auto-da-fé* were, Doctor Augustin Cazalla, priest and canon of Salamanca, almoner and preacher to the king and emperor; he was the son of Pedro Cazalla and Eleonora de Vibero, and descended from the Jews both by his father and mother. He was accused of professing the Lutheran heresy; of having dogmatized in the Lutheran conventicle of Valladolid, and corresponded with the heretics of Seville. Cazalla denied the facts imputed to him in several declarations on oath, and in others which he presented when the *publication of the proofs* took place. The torture was decreed: Cazalla, on the 4th of March, was conducted to the dungeon where it was to be inflicted, but it did not take place, as the prisoner promised to make a confession. He gave it in writing, and ratified it on the 16th, acknowledging that he was a Lutheran, but denied having taught the doctrine. He explained the motives which had prevented him from making this declaration before; and promised to be a good catholic for the future, if reconciliation was granted him: but the inquisitors did not think proper to spare him the capital punishment, as the witnesses affirmed that he had dogmatized. Cazalla, however, continued to give every possible proof of conversion until his execution : when he saw that death was inevitable, he began to preach to his companions in misfortune. Two days before his death, he related some particulars of his life. He was born in 1510 : at the age of seventeen he had Bartholomew Carranza de Miranda for his confessor, in the college of St. Gregory at Valladolid ; he continued his studies at Meala de Henares, where he remained till 1536. In 1545 Charles V. made him his preacher, in the following year he accompanied that prince to Germany, and stayed there till 1552, preaching against the Lutherans; he returned in that year to Spain, and retired to Salamanca, where he lived for three years, going sometimes to Valladolid. He once attended, by the emperor's order, at an assembly where Don Antonio Fonseca, president of the Royal Council of Castile, presided, and at which the Licentiate Otalora, the Doctors Ribera and Velasco, auditors of the council and chancery, and Brothers Alphonso de Castro, and Bartholomew Carranza, assisted. The object of the meeting was to decide on the course to be pursued on the occasion of certain briefs which the Court of Rome had expedited against those who approved of the decrees of the Council of Trent, which continued to assemble in that city, though the Pope had commanded that it should be transferred to Bologna. Cazalla declared that all the members of the junta acknowledged that the Pope only acted from motives of personal interest ; and that Bartholomew Carranza particularly distinguished himself by inveighing against the abuses of the Court of Rome. On the 20th of May, the day before his death, he received a visit from Brother Antonio de la Carrera, a monk of St. Jerome, who was sent to him by the inquisitors, to inform him that they were not satisfied with his declarations, and to exhort him, for the good of his conscience, to confess all that he knew of himself and others. Cazalla answered, that he could not say more, without bearing false-witness. The monk replied, that he had always denied that he had dogmatized, though the contrary was proved by the witnesses. He said, that this crime had been unjustly imputed to him ; that he was guilty of not having undeceived those who held bad doctrines; but that he had only spoken of his opinions to persons who thought as he did : Brother Antonio then exhorted him to prepare for death on the following day. This information was a thunderbolt to Cazalla, who had expected to be admitted to a reconciliation. He demanded if his punishment might not be commuted : Carrera told him, that if he confessed what he had hitherto concealed, he might hope for mercy. *Well then,* said Cazalla, *I must prepare to die in the grace of God ; for it is impossible that I should add anything to what I have already said, unless I lie.* He then began to encourage himself to suffer death ; he confessed several times in the same night, and the next day to Antonio de la Carrera. When he arrived at the place of the *auto-da-fé,* he asked permission to preach to those who were to suffer with him ; he could not obtain it, but he addressed a few words to them : as he was a penitent, he was strangled before he was burnt. When he was fastened to the stake, he confessed for the last time, and his confessor was so affected by all that he had seen and heard during the last twenty-four hours, that he afterwards wrote, " that he had no doubt that Doctor Cazalla was in Heaven."

Francis de Vibero Cazalla, brother to Augustin, a priest, and Curate of Hormigos in the diocese of Palencia, at first denied the charges, confessed them when tortured, ratified his confession, and demanded to be admitted to reconciliation. This was refused, as it was supposed that he had only confessed from the fear of death. In fact he ridiculed his brother's exhortations on the scaffold, and expired in the flames without shewing any signs of repentance. He was degraded from the priesthood, as well as his brother, before he ascended the scaffold.

Donna Beatrice de Cazalla, sister to the above-mentioned persons, and Alphonso Perez, at first denied the charges, confessed during the torture, demanded reconciliation, but were strangled and burnt.

Don Christobal de Ocampo, of Seville, a knight of the order of St. John, and almoner to the Grand Prior of Castile and Leon, and Don Christobal de Padilla, a knight and inhabitant of Zamora, were condemned to the same punishment for Lutheranism.

The licentiate Antonio Herrezuelo, a lawyer of the city of Toro, condemned as a Lutheran, died without any signs of repentance. Doctor Cazalla addressed some words to him in particular ; Antonio ridiculed his discourse, although he was already fastened to the stake. One of the archers, furious at so much courage, plunged his lance into the body of Herrezuelo ; he died without uttering a word.

Juan Garcia, a goldsmith of Valladolid, and the licentiate Perez de Herrera, judge of the court against smugglers, in Logrono, suffered as Lutherans. Gonzalez Baez, the Portuguese mentioned in the preceding chapter, suffered as a Judaic heretic.

Donna Catherine de Ortega, widow of the commander Loaisa, and daughter to Hernand Diaz, fiscal of the Royal Council of Castile, was condemned as a Lutheran, and made her confession. She suffered the same fate with Catherine

Roman de Pedrosa, Isabella d'Estrada, and Jane Blazquiez, a servant of the Marchioness d'Alcanizes. None of these persons had dogmatized, none had relapsed, but they were condemned because they only confessed during the torture.

Among the persons reconciled were distinguished, Don Pedro Sarmiento de Roxas, a knight of the order of St. Jago, commander of Quintana, and the son of the first Marquis of Poza. He was condemned as a Lutheran, deprived of his orders, clothed in the perpetual *San-benito*, imprisoned for life, devoted to infamy, and his property confiscated.

Don Louis de Roxas, nephew of the above, was charged with the same crime ; he was exiled from Madrid, Valladolid, and Palencia, and prohibited from leaving Spain ; his property was confiscated, and he was declared incapable of succeeding to the marquisate of Poza, which passed to his youngest brother.

Donna Mencia de Figueroa, wife of Don Pedro Sarmiento de Roxas, and an attendant of the Queen of Spain, was condemned, for Lutheranism, to wear the *San-benito*, to imprisonment for life, and the confiscation of her property.

Donna Anna Henriquez de Roxas, daughter of the Marquis d'Alcanizes, and the wife of Don Juan Alphonso de Fonseca Mexia, was condemned as a Lutheran. She appeared in the *auto-da-fé* with the *San-benito*, and was afterwards shut up in a monastery. She was twenty-four years of age, was perfectly acquainted with the Latin tongue, and had read the works of Calvin, and those of Constantine Ponce de la Fuente.

Donna Maria de Roxas, a nun of the convent of St. Catherine of Valladolid, and daughter to the first Marquis de Poza. She was condemned as a Lutheran, conducted to the *auto da fé* with the *San-benito*, and secluded for life in her convent. The Inquisition commanded that she should be treated as the lowest in the community in the choir and refectory, and deprived of the power of voting.

Don Juan de Ulloa Pereira, a knight commander of the order of St. John of Jerusalem. He was son and brother to the Lords de la Mota, who were soon after made Marquisses, and an inhabitant of Toro. He was condemned, for Lutheranism, to wear the *San-benito*, to be imprisoned for life, and to be deprived of his property. He was declared infamous, incapable of obtaining dignities, stript of the habit and cross of his order, and banished from Madrid, Valladolid, and Toro, but was prohibited from quitting the kingdom. In 1565, Ulloa represented his situation to the Pope, reminding him of his services in fighting against the Turks, particularly when he took five ships of the pirate Caramani Arraez; he added that the inquisitor-general had remitted the continuation of his penance for more than a year, but that he wished to regain his rank as a knight, as he was still capable of serving. The Pope granted a brief in favour of Ulloa, rehabilitating him in his privileges as a knight, with a particular clause, stating that what had passed could not prevent him from attaining the superior dignities of his order, provided the inquisitor-general and the grand master of Malta approved the decree. Ulloa was then reinstated in his commandery.

Juan de Vibero Cazalla, a brother of Augustin, and Donna Juana Silva de Ribera, his wife, were condemned as Lutherans, to be deprived of their liberty and their property, and to wear the *San-benito*.

Donna Constance de Vibero Cazalla, sister of Augustin, and widow of Hernand Ortiz, was condemned to wear the *San-benito*, to perpetual imprisonment, and the confiscation of her property. When Augustin saw his sister pass, he turned to the princess governess, and said to her: *Princess, I entreat your highness to have compassion on that unfortunate woman, who will leave thirteen orphans.*

Eleonora de Cisneros, aged twenty-four, the wife of Antonio Herrezuelo, and Donna Francisca Zuñiga de Baeza, were condemned to the *San-benito*, imprisonment, and confiscation.

Marina de Saavedra, the widow of Juan Cisneros de Soto, a distinguished gentleman, Isabella Minguez, a servant of Donna Beatrice Cazalla, and Antonio Minguez, the brother of Isabella, suffered the same punishment.

Anthony Wasor, an Englishman, servant to Don Louis de Roxas, was condemned to wear the *San-benito*, to lose his property, and be confined in a convent for one year.

Daniel de la Quadra lost his liberty and property, and took the perpetual *San-benito*, as a Lutheran.

The sermon on the faith was preached by the celebrated Melchior Cano, after all the assembly had witnessed a scandalous transaction. When the court and all the other attendants had taken their places, Don Francis Baca, Inquisitor of Valladolid, advanced towards the Prince of Asturias, Don Carlos, and his aunt, the princess Juana, to demand and receive from them an oath to maintain and defend the Inquisition, and to reveal to it all that might have been said against the faith by any person within their knowledge. It had been decreed at the establishment of the Inquisition, that the magistrate who presided at an *auto-da-fé* should take a similar oath, but sovereigns cannot be considered as magistrates. Don Carlos and his aunt took the oath, but succeeding events shew how much he was displeased at the boldness of this inquisitor : he was then aged fourteen years.

Second Auto-da-fé.

The second *Auto-da-fé* of Valladolid took place on the 8th of October, in the same year, 1559 ; it was still more splendid than the first, on account of the presence of Philip II. The inquisitors had waited his return from the Low Countries, to do him honour in this grand festival.

Thirteen persons, with a corpse and an effigy, were burnt,

and sixteen admitted to reconciliation. The king was accompanied by his son, his sister, the Prince of Parma, three ambassadors from France, the Archbishop of Seville, the Bishops of Palencia and Zamora, and other bishops elect; there were also present, the constable and admiral, the Dukes de Naxara and d'Arcos, the Marquis de Denia, afterwards Duke of Lerma, the Marquis d'Astorga, and the Count de Uregna, afterwards Duke of Ossuna, the Count de Benavente, the Count de Buendia, the last grand-master of the military order of Montesa, Don Louis Borgia, the Grand Prior of Castile and Leon, a knight of the order of St. John of Jerusalem, Don Antonio de Toledo, son and brother to the Dukes of Aloa; several other grandees of Spain, not named in the verbal-process of this execution, and many persons of lower rank; the Countess de Ribadabia, and other ladies of distinction, besides the councils, the tribunals, and other authorities.

The sermon on the faith was preached by the Bishop of Cuença: the Bishops of Palencia and Zamora degraded the condemned priests; and the inquisitor-general, the Archbishop of Seville, demanded and received from the king the same oath which had been administered to Don Carlos. The condemned persons were:—

Don Carlos de Seso, a noble of Verona, son to the Bishop of Placenza in Italy, and of one of the most noble families in the country; he was forty-three years of age, passed for a learned man, who had rendered great services to the emperor, and had held the office of Corregidor of Toro. He married Donna Isabella de Castilla, daughter of Don Francis de Castilla, who were descended from the king Don Pedro *the Cruel*. After his marriage he settled at Villamediana, near Logroño. He there openly preached heresy, and was the principal author of the progress of Lutheranism at Valladolid, Palencia, Zamora, and the boroughs depending on those cities. He was arrested at Logroño, and taken to the

secret prisons of Valladolid. He answered the requisition of
the fiscal on the 28th of June, 1558. His sentence was communicated to him on the 7th of October, 1559, and he was
told to prepare to suffer death on the following day. De
Seso asked for ink and paper, and wrote his confession, which
was entirely Lutheran; he said that this doctrine, and not
that taught by the Roman Church, which had been corrupted for several centuries, was the true faith of the
gospel ; that he would die in that belief, and that he offered
himself to God in memory of the passion of Jesus Christ. It
would be difficult to express the vigour and energy of his
writing, which filled two sheets of paper. De Seso was exhorted during the night, and on the morning of the 8th, but
without success ; he was gagged that he might not have the
power of preaching his doctrine. When he was fastened to
the stake, the gag was taken from his mouth, and he was
again exhorted to confess himself; he replied with a loud
voice and great firmness: " If I had sufficient time, I would
convince you that you are lost, by not following my example.
Hasten to light the wood which is to consume me." The
executioners complied, and De Seso died impenitent.

Pedro de Cazalla, curate of the parish of Pedrosa, he was
the brother of Augustin Cazalla, and aged thirty-three. He
was arrested on the 23rd of April, 1558, and confessed that
he was a Lutheran. He demanded to be reconciled, but
was sentenced to be *relaxed* because he had preached the heretical doctrine. On the 7th of October, he was informed of
his sentence, but refused to confess; when he was fastened
to the stake, he asked for a confessor, and was then strangled,
and afterwards burnt.

Dominic Sanchez, a priest of Villamediana, adopted the
Lutheran heresy, after having heard De Seso and read his
books. He was condemned to be burnt, and followed the
example of Pedro de Cazalla.

Dominic de Roxas, a Dominican priest; he was a disciple

of Bartholomew Carranza. His father was the Marquis de Poza, who had two children punished in the first *auto-da-fé*. Brother Dominic was forty years of age. He was taken at Calahorra disguised as a layman ; he had taken the habit to conceal himself from the agents of the Inquisition, until he could escape to Flanders, after an interview which he wished to have with Don Carlos de Seso. He made his first declaration before the Holy Office, on the 13th of May, 1558 ; he was obliged to make several others, because he retracted in one what he advanced in another ; he was condemned to the torture for these recantations. Brother Dominic intreated that he might be spared the horrors of the question, as he dreaded it more than death. This request was granted on condition that he would promise to reveal what he had hitherto concealed ; he consented, and added several new declarations to the first ; he afterwards demanded to be reconciled. On the 7th of October, he was exhorted to prepare for death, he then made some discoveries in favour of persons against whom he had spoken in the preceding examinations; but he refused to confess, and when he descended from the scaffold of the *auto-da-fé*, he turned towards the king, and exclaimed, that he was going to die for the true faith, which was that of Luther. Philip II. commanded that he should be gagged. He was still in that situation when he was fastened to the stake ; but when they began to light the fire his courage failed, he demanded a confessor, received absolution, and was strangled.

Juan Sanchez, a servant of Pedro de Cazalla, and Donna Catherine Hortega ; he was thirty-three years of age. The fear of being arrested by the Inquisition induced him to go to Valladolid, in order to escape to the Low Countries, under the forged name of Juan de Vibar. The inquisitors were informed of his intention by his letters written at Castrourdiales, addressed to Donna Catherine Hortega, while she was in prison. The inquisitors gave information to the king, who commissioned Don Francis de Castilla Alcalde, of the court, to arrest him.   Sanchez was taken at Turlingen, and transferred to Valladolid, where he was condemned to *relaxation*, as a dogmatising and impenitent Lutheran.   He was gagged until he was fastened to the stake.   As he did not ask for a confessor, the pile was lighted, and when the cords which held him were burnt, he darted to the top of the scaffold, from whence he could see that several of the condemned confessed, that they might avoid the flames.   The priests again exhorted him to confess, but seeing that De Seso remained firm in his resolution, he returned and told them to add more wood, for that he would die like Don Carlos de Seso.   The archers and executioners obeyed his injunctions, and he perished in the flames.

Donna Euphrosyne Rios, a nun of the order of Santa Clara of Valladolid, was convicted of Lutheranism by twenty-two witnesses; she continued impenitent until she was fastened to the stake, when she confessed, and was strangled and burnt.

Donna Marina de Guevara, a nun of the convent of Belen at Valladolid, of the order of Citeaux; she was related to the family of Poza.   Marina confessed the facts, but could not avoid her condemnation, though she demanded to be reconciled.   This was the more surprising, as the inquisitor-general made great efforts to save her life; he was the intimate friend of several of her relations, and being informed that the inquisitors of Valladolid intended to condemn her, he authorized Don Alphonso Tellez Giron, Lord of Montalban and cousin to Marina, and the Duke of Ossuna, to visit the accused, and press her to confess what she denied and the witnesses affirmed; but Marina said that she could not add anything to what she had already declared.

She was condemned to be *relaxed,* but the sentence was not immediately published, as it was the custom to do so only on the day before the *auto-da-fé;* and as the rules of

1541 allow the sentence of death to be revoked if the criminals repent before they are given up to secular justice. the inquisitor-general sent Don Alphonso Giron a second time to his cousin, to exhort her to confess all, and avoid death. This conduct of Valdés displeased the inquisitors of Valladolid, who spoke of it as a singular and scandalous preference. Valdés applied to the Supreme Council, which commanded that the visit should be made in the presence of one or two inquisitors. This last attempt did not succeed better than the first; Marina persisted in her declaration, and was burnt.

Donna Catherine de Reinoso, a nun in the same convent, Donna Margaret de St. Etienne, and Donna Maria de Miranda, nuns of Santa Clara at Valladolid were likewise strangled and burnt as Lutherans.

Pedro de Sotelo and Francis d'Almarzo suffered the same punishment for Lutheranism, with Francis Blanco a New Christian, who had abjured Mahometanism, and had afterwards fallen into error.

Jane Sanchez, of the class of women called Beates, was condemned as a Lutheran; when she was informed of her sentence she cut her throat with a pair of scissors, and died impenitent some days after in the prison. Her corpse was taken to the *auto-da-fé* on a bier, and burnt with her effigy.

Sixteen persons were condemned to penances. I shall only mention those distinguished for their rank or the nature of their trials.

Donna Isabella de Castilla, the wife of Don Carlos de Seso, voluntarily confessed that she had adopted some of her husband's opinions; she was condemned to wear the *sanbenito*, to be imprisoned for life, and to be deprived of her property.

Donna Catherine de Castilla, the niece of the above, suffered the same punishment.

Donna Francisca de Zuñiga Reinoso, sister to Donna Catherine, who was burnt in the same *auto-da-fé*, and a nun in the same convent, was condemned with Donna Philippina de Heredia and Donna Catherine d'Alcaraz, two of her companions, to be deprived of the power of voting in her community, and prohibited from going out of the convent.

Antonio Sanchez, an inhabitant of Salamanca, was punished as a false witness; it was proved that he had deposed falsely for the purpose of causing a Jew to be burnt: he was condemned to receive two hundred stripes; was deprived of half his property, and sent to the galleys for five years. The compassion of the inquisitors for this sort of criminals is an incontestable fact, although they did not hesitate to condemn heretics to death, if they had only concealment, or an insincere repentance to reproach them with.

Pedro d'Aguilar, a shearer, born at Tordesillas, pretended to be an alguazil of the Inquisition, and appeared at Valladolid with the *wand* of the Holy Office on the day of the celebration of the first *auto-da-fé*; he afterwards went to a town in the province of Campos, where he said that he was commissioned to open the tomb of a bishop, and take the bones to be burnt in an *auto-da-fé*, as belonging to a man who had died in the Judaic heresy. Pedro was condemned to receive four hundred stripes, to have his property confiscated, and to be sent to the galleys for life. This affair proves that the inquisitors considered it a much greater crime to pretend to be an alguazil of the Holy Office, than to bear false-witness, and to cause the death of a man, the confiscation of his property, and the condemnation of his posterity to infamy!

Such is the history of the two celebrated *autos-da-fé* of Valladolid, of which so much has been said, although nothing certain was known of them. It is an interesting circumstance that the Inquisition was at the same time proceeding against forty-five persons distinguished for their rank or personal qualities; of these forty-five persons, ten had been arrested. It is not to be supposed that the inquisitors only prosecuted

these persons: the trial of Carranza Archishop of Seville
was the origin of a great number against bishops and other
distinguished individuals. I have confined myself to those
of which I could consult the papers; it would be a task beyond the strength of one man to read all that have accumulated in the archives.

CHAPTER XXI.

HISTORY OF TWO AUTOS-DA-FE, CELEBRATED AGAINST THE LUTHERANS IN THE CITY OF SEVILLE.

AN *auto-da-fé* was celebrated on the 24th of September,
1559, in the place of St. Francis, at Seville, not less celebrated for the rank of the condemned, than for the nature
of their trials. Four bishops attended at it; the coadjutor
of Seville, those of Largo and the Canaries, who happened
to be in the city, and of Tarrazona, whom the king had authorized to reside at Seville as vice-inquisitor-general.

The inquisitors of the district of Seville were Don Michel
del Carpio, Don Andrea Gasco, and Don Francis Galdo;
Don Juan de Obando represented the archbishop. I make
this remark, to shew that none of the judges were named
Pargas, as the author of a romance entitled *Cornelia Bororquia*, has asserted.

This *auto-da-fé* was celebrated before the royal court of
justice, the chapter of the cathedral, some grandees of Spain,
and a great number of titled persons and gentlemen; the
Duchess of Bejar was present with several ladies, and an
immense concourse of people. Twenty-one persons were
relaxed, with an effigy of a contumacious person, and eighty
persons condemned to penances, the greatest number of whom
were Lutherans; I shall mention the most remarkable instances.

The effigy was that of Francis Zafra, the beneficed priest
of the parish of St. Vincent of Seville, who was condemned
as a Lutheran, but had made his escape. Reynald Gonzalez
de Montes gives a long account of this man, which I found
to be correct, on examining the papers of the holy office. He
says that Francis Zafra was well versed in the scriptures ;
for some time he succeeded in concealing his inclination to
Lutheranism, and was employed by the inquisitors to qualify
denounced propositions, and that he was thus enabled to
save many persons from being condemned. He had received
into his house one of the women called *Beates,* who (after
obstinately supporting the new doctrines) became so much
deranged, that he was obliged to confine and scourge her,
to calm her violence. In 1555, this woman escaped, and
denounced three hundred persons as Lutherans to the Inquisition: the inquisitors drew up a list of them; Francis
Zafra was summoned, and although he was mentioned as
one of the principal heretics, proved that they could not
receive the evidence of a person whose mind was so much
disordered *. As the holy office never neglected anything
that could assist in discovering heresy, this list caused the
conduct of many persons to be strictly observed, and more
than eight hundred were arrested; Francis Zafra was one of
the prisoners, but he contrived to escape, and was burnt in
effigy as contumacious.

The first person I shall mention as condemned to relaxation, was Donna Isabella de Baena, a rich lady of Seville.
Her house was razed to the ground for having served as a
temple to the Lutherans.

I find, among the other victims at Seville, Don Juan
Ponce de Leon, youngest son to the Count de Baylen ; he
was cousin-german to the Duke d'Arcos, and related to the
Duchess de Bejar, who were both present at his *auto-da-fé.*

* Regnialdus Gonzalirus Montanus, *Sanctæ Inquisitionis Hispanicæ
artes aliquot detectæ,* in the rubric *Publicato testium,* p. 50.

He was condemned as an impenitent Lutheran : he at first denied the charges, but confessed during the torture : the inquisitors sent a priest, with whom he was well acquainted, to persuade him that it would be to his advantage if he confessed the truth.   Ponce was deceived, and made the confession they required ; but on discovering his mistake, the day before the *auto-da-fé*, he made one truly Lutheran, and treated the priest who attended him with contempt.   Gonzalez de Montes pretends that he persisted in his sentiments, but he is mistaken, for Ponce confessed when he was fastened to the stake, and was strangled before he was burnt.

Don Juan Gozalez, a priest of Seville, and a celebrated preacher of Andalusia, embraced Mahometanism at twelve years of age, because his parents were Moors, but he was reconciled by the Inquisition.   Some time after he was imprisoned as a Lutheran, but obstinately persisted in refusing to confess, even when tortured ; affirming that his opinions were founded on the Holy Scriptures, and that, consequently, he could not be a heretic.   This example was imitated by his two sisters, who suffered in the same. *auto-da-fé*. When the gags were taken from their mouths, Don Juan told them to sing the 106th psalm.   They died (say the Protestants) in the faith of Jesus Christ, and detesting the errors of the *Papists*.

Brother Garcia de Arias (surnamed the *White Doctor*, on account of the extreme whiteness of his hair) was a Jeronimîte of the Convent of St. Isidore, at Seville; he was condemned as an impenitent Lutheran, and perished in the flames.   He had professed the doctrines of Luther for several years, but his sentiments were known only to the principal partisans of the heresy, such as Vargas, Egidius, and Constantine ; his prudence was so great, that he was looked upon as an orthodox theologian and of the greatest piety : he even carried his dissimulation so far as to profess to be an enemy to the Lutherans.   He was several times employed to

qualify heretical propositions, and appeared to be so devoted
to the inquisitorial system, that though he was denounced
several times, the inquisitors declared that the informers
acted out of hatred to him.   However, the informations were
communicated to him, that he might be more cautious in his
conversations with suspicious persons.

His conduct towards Gregorio Riuz ought to be recorded.
Riuz was denounced for some explanations of doctrine in a
sermon; being obliged to appear and defend his doctrine
before theologians, he applied to his friend, the White
Doctor, who wished to hear his exposition of the principles
he intended for his defence, and the solutions he had prepared for the difficulties which he might meet with.   When
the assembly took place, the inquisitors commissioned Arias
to argue against Riuz, who was much surprised to see him
at this conference, and still more so, when he heard him
speak in such a manner, that the answers he had prepared
were entirely useless.   Riuz sunk under this attack, and the
doctor Arias was severely reproached for his treachery by
the Lutheran doctors, Vargas, Egidius, and Constantine.

Arias taught the Lutheran doctrine to some monks of his
convent : one of them (Brother Cassiodorus) made so much
progress in it, that he converted almost all the monks of
the community, so that the monastic exercises were no longer
practised.   Twelve of these persons being alarmed at this
state of things, fled to Germany ; the rest who remained at
Seville, were condemned by the Inquisition.   The same fate
awaited Garcia d'Arias ; the depositions against him continued to multiply, and he was at last arrested.   Foreseeing
the result of his trial, he made a confession of his faith, and
undertook to prove, that the opinions of Luther were founded on the gospel.   He persevered in his impenitence, and no
Catholic could convert him, because he understood doctrine
better than those who disputed with him.

Donna Maria de Virues, Donna Maria Cornel, and Donna

Maria Bohorques, also perished in this *auto-da-fé*. They were all young, and of the highest class of nobility. The history of the last of these ladies ought to be made known, on account of some circumstances in her trial, and because a Spaniard has composed a *novel* under the title of *Cornelia Bororquia*, which he affirms to be rather a history than a romance, although it is neither the one nor the other, but a collection of scenes and events badly conceived, in which he has not even given the actors their true names, from not having understood the History of the Inquisition by Limborch. This historian has mentioned two of the ladies by the names of *Cornelia* and *Bohorquia*, which means *Donna Maria Cornel*, and *Donna Maria Bohorquia*. The Spanish author has united these names, to designate *Cornelia Bororquia*, an imaginary person. He has supposed a love intrigue between her and the inquisitor-general, which is absurd, since he was at Madrid. He has also introduced examinations, which never took place in the tribunal ; in short, the intention of the author was to criticise and ridicule the Inquisition, and the fear of being punished for it, induced him to fly to Bayonne. A good cause becomes bad when falsehood is employed in its defence: the true history of the Inquisition, is sufficient to shew how much it merits the detestation of the human race, and it is therefore useless to employ fictions or satire. The same may be said of the *Gusmanade*, a French poem, containing assertions false and injurious to the memory of St. Dominic de Guzman, whose personal conduct was very pure, though he may be blamed for his conduct to the Albigenses.

Donna Maria de Bohorques, was the natural daughter of Pedro Garcia de Xerez Bohorques of one of the first families of Seville, and from which sprung the Marquises de Ruchena, grandees of the first class. She was not twenty-one years of age when she was arrested as a Lutheran. She had been instructed by the doctor, Juan Gil (or Egidius), was perfectly acquainted with the Latin language, and understood Greek; she had many Lutheran books, and had committed to memory the Gospels, and some of the principal works which explain the text in a Lutheran sense. She was conducted to the secret prisons, where she acknowledged her opinions, and defended them as catholic. She said that some of the facts and propositions contained in the depositions were true, but denied the others, either because she had forgotten them, or was afraid to compromise others. She was then tortured, and confessed that her sister, Jane Bohorques, was acquainted with her sentiments, and had not disapproved them. The fatal consequences of this confession will be shewn hereafter. The definitive sentence was pronounced, and Maria Bohorques was condemned to *relaxation*. As the sentence was not communicated to the prisoner till the day before the *auto-da-fé*, the inquisitors desired that Maria should be exhorted during the interval. Two Jesuits and and two Dominicans were successively sent to her. They returned full of admiration at the learning of the prisoner, but displeased at her obstinacy, in explaining the texts of Scripture which they proposed, in a Lutheran sense. On the day before the *auto-da-fé*, two other Dominicans went with the first, to make a last effort to convert Maria, and they were followed by several other theologians of different religious orders. Maria received them with as much pleasure as politeness, but she told them that they might spare themselves the trouble of speaking to her of their doctrines, as they could not be more concerned for her salvation than she was herself; that she would renounce her opinions if she felt the least uncertainty; but that she was still more convinced that she was right, since so many *popish* theologians had not been able to advance any arguments, for which she had not prepared a solid and conclusive answer. At the place of execution, Don Juan Ponce de Leon, who had abjured heresy, exhorted Maria to do the same. She received his advice very ill, and called him *ignorant, an idiot, and a babbler :* she added, that it was no longer a time to dispute, and that the few moments they had to live ought to be employed in meditating on the passion, and death of their Redeemer, to reanimate the faith by which they were to be justified and saved.   Although she was so obstinate, several priests, and a great number of monks, earnestly entreated that she might be spared, in consideration of her extreme youth and surprising merit, if she would consent to repeat the *Credo.* The inquisitors granted their request ; but scarcely had Maria finished it, than she began to interpret the articles on the catholic faith, and the judgment of the quick and the dead, according to the opinions of Luther: they did not give her time to conclude, the executioner strangled her, and she was afterwards burnt.   Such is the true history of Maria Bohorques, according to the writings of the Inquisition.

Paul IV. died at Róme on the 18th of August, 1559, a few days before the *auto-da-fé* at Seville. When the people learnt this event, they went in crowds to the Inquisition, set all the prisoners at liberty, and burnt the house and the archives of the tribunal.   It cost much money and trouble to prevent the enraged populace from burning the convent *De la Sapienza* of the Dominicans, who conducted all the affairs of the Roman Inquisition.   The principal commissioner was wounded, and his house burnt.   The statue of Paul IV. was taken from the capitol and destroyed ; the arms of the house of Carafa were everywhere defaced, and even the mortal remains of the Pope would have been abused, if the Canons of the Vatican had not interred him secretly, and if the guards had not defended the pontifical residence*.   This revolt of the Romans did not alarm the inquisitors of Spain, where the people had been brought up by the monks in different principles from those professed by their ancestors under the reign of Ferdinand, and the first ten years of that of Charles V.

* Fleury, Hist. Eccles. liv. 154, ann. 1559, No. 14.

Auto-da-fé of the year 1560.

The inquisitors of Seville, who had perhaps depended on the presence of Philip II., prepared another *auto-da-fé* for him similar to that of Valladolid. When they had lost all hope of that honour, the ceremony was performed : it took place on the 22nd of December, 1560. Fourteen individuals were burnt in person (*i. e.* relaxed), and three in effigy ; thirty-four were subjected to penances, and the reconciliation of three other persons was read before the *auto-da-fé*. The effigies were those of the Doctors Egidius, Constantine, and Juan Perez.

Constantine Ponce de la Fuente was born at *San Clemente de la Mancha*, in the diocese of Cuença ; he finished his studies at Alcala de Henares, with the Doctor Juan Gil, or *Egidius ;* and with Vargas, who died during his trial. These three theologians were the principal chiefs of the Lutherans at Seville, whom they secretly directed, enjoying at the same time the reputation of good catholics and virtuous priests. Egidius preached much in the metropolitan church; Constantine was less ardent in his zeal, but he obtained as much applause ; Vargas explained the Scriptures in the pulpit of the municipality. Constantine refused the dignity of magisterial canon, which was offered to him both by the Chapter of Cuença and that of Toledo. Charles V. appointed him his almoner and preacher ; in this quality he took him to Germany, where he made a long stay. On his return to Seville, he directed the college *De la Doctrina*, and there established a pulpit to preach the Holy Scriptures, of which he appointed the salary : he undertook to fill the office, and during this period the Canons' corporation offered him the place of magisterial canon, exempting him from the usual competition. Some of the canons recollecting the unfortunate consequences of the election of Juan Gil (who was appointed in the same manner), wished that the competition should take place. Constantine was requested to submit to it, and assured that he would triumph over the competitors. This, in fact, took place in 1556, in opposition to the appeals and intrigues of the only person who had the courage to compete with him. While Constantine continued to enjoy general esteem, the declarations of a great number of prisoners who were arrested for Lutheranism, caused his arrest in 1558, some months before the death of Charles V. During the time that he was preparing his defence, an accident happened which rendered it useless.

Isabella Martinez, a widow of Seville, was arrested as a Lutheran. Her property was sequestrated ; but it was soon found, that Francis Beltran, her son, had concealed several chests of valuable effects before the inventory was taken. Constantine had committed some prohibited books to the care of this woman, who concealed them in her cellar. The inquisitors sent Louis Sotelo, the alguazil of the holy office, to Francis Beltran, to claim the effects which he had concealed. Francis, on seeing the alguazil, did not doubt that his mother had declared the concealment of the books given to her care by Constantine, and without waiting until Sotelo should tell him the cause of his visit, he said, *Señor Sotelo, I suppose that you come for the things deposited in my mother's house. If you will promise that I shall not be punished for not giving information of them, I will shew you what there is hidden there.* Beltran then conducted the alguazil to his mother's house, and pulled down part of the wall, behind which the Lutheran books of Constantine had been concealed ; Sotelo, astonished at this sight, told him that he should take possession of the books, but that he did not consider himself bound by his promise, as he only came to claim the effects which he had concealed. This declaration increased the alarm of Beltran, and he gave everything up to the alguazil, on condition that he might remain free in his house. This denunciation had been made by a servant, who hoped to obtain the benefit of the act of Ferdinand V., which assigns the fourth part of the concealed effects to the informer.

Among the prohibited books, were found several writings by Constantine Ponce de Fuente, which treated of the true church according to the principles of the Lutherans, and proved in their manner, that this church was not that of the *papists*: he also discussed in them several other points on which the Lutherans differed from the Catholics. Constantine could not deny these papers, as they were in his own handwriting; he confessed that they contained the profession of his faith, but refused to name his accomplices and disciples. The inquisitors, instead of decreeing the torture, plunged him into a deep, humid, and obscure dungeon, where the air, impregnated with the most dangerous miasma, soon altered his health. This situation could not last long, Constantine fell sick, and died of a dysentery: it was reported, when the *auto-da-fé* was celebrated, that he had killed himself to avoid his punishment. His trial was as celebrated as his person. The inquisitors caused the *merits* or charges against him to be read in a pulpit close to their seats, where the people could not hear them; the Corregidor Calderon remarked the circumstance twice, and they were obliged to begin it again where those of the other trials were read. Constantine had published the first part of a catechism; the second was not printed. The following works of Constantine were inserted in the prohibitory Index, published in 1559, by Don Ferdinand Valdés: An Abridgment of the Christian Doctrine; a Dialogue on the same subject, between a Master and his Disciple. The Confession of a Sinner to Jesus Christ. A Christian Catechism. An Exposition of the Psalm, *Beatus qui non abiit in concilio impiorum.* Alphonso de Ulloa, in his Life of Charles V., gives the highest praise to the works of Constantine, particularly his Treatise on the Christian Doctrine, which was translated into Italian*. The effigy of Constantine was not like those of the other condemned persons (which were an unformed mass surmounted by a head); it was an

---

* Ulloa, *Vita di Carlos V.* edition of Venice, 1589, p. 237.

entire figure with the arms spread, as Constantine was accustomed to do when preaching, and was clothed in garments
which appeared to have belonged to him. After the *auto-
da-fé*, this figure was taken back to the Holy Office, and a
common effigy was burnt with the bones of the condemned.

Another prisoner died in the dungeons of the Inquisition ;
he was (according to Gonzalez de Montis) a monk of the
Convent of St. Isidore, named Ferdinand. The same author
affirms, that one Olmedo, a Lutheran, was likewise carried
off by an epidemic disease which ravaged the prisons, and that
he uttered groans similar to those of Constantine when he
was dying. I have not found that any Inquisition in Spain
has, of late years, condemned any person to this sort of
dungeon, unless the torture was decreed ; the inquisitors of
that time cannot be pardoned for making them a common
prison.

The Doctor Juan Perez de Pineda, whose effigy was the
third in the *auto-da-fé*, was born at Montilla in Andalusia :
he was placed at the head of the College *de la Doctrine*, in
which the young people of Seville were educated.

He made his escape when he was informed that the inquisitors were about to arrest him as suspected of Lutheranism.
Proceedings were instituted against him as contumacious, and
he was condemned as a formal Lutheran heretic. He had
composed several works : the Index prohibited the following :
The Holy Bible, translated into the Castilian tongue; a Catechism, printed at Venice in 1556, by Pedro Daniel : The
Psalms of David in Spanish; and a Summary of the Christian
Doctrine. Juan Perez had attained a great age when he
was condemned. Of the fourteen persons who were reconciled in the second *auto-da-fé*, the most remarkable were :—

Julian Hernandez, surnamed the *Little*, a native of Villa-
verdè. The wish to promulgate Lutheran books in Seville
induced him to go to Germany. He gave the books to Don
Juan Ponce de Leon, who undertook to distribute them.

He passed more than three years in the prisons of the Holy Office, and was tortured several times, to force him to discover his accomplices. He bore the torture with a fortitude far above his physical strength, and remained faithful to his creed. When he arrived at the stake he arranged the wood around him so as to burn quickly ; the Doctor Ferdinand Rodriguez, who attended him, demanded that the gag should be taken from his mouth, that he might make his confession, but Julian opposed it, and he was burnt.

Nicholas Burton, born in England, was condemned as an impenitent Lutheran heretic. It is impossible to justify the conduct of the inquisitors to this Englishman, and several other foreigners who had not settled in Spain, and were merely returning to their respective countries after having transacted their commercial affairs. This man came to Spain in a vessel laden with merchandise, which, he said, was all his own property, but of which some part belonged to John Fronton, who was reconciled in this *auto-da-fé*. Burton refused to abjure, and was burnt alive ; the inquisitors seized his vessel and its freight, thus proving that avarice was the principal motive of the Inquisition. The inquisitors were guilty of a great cruelty in this instance, and the commerce of Spain would perhaps have been destroyed, if the violence committed against Burton, and some others, had not been protested against by the different powers, which induced Philip IV. to prohibit the inquisitors from molesting foreign merchants and travellers, if they did not attempt to promulgate heretical opinions ; but the inquisitors eluded this order, by pretending that they brought prohibited books into the kingdom, or spoke in favour of heresy.

Gonzalez de Montis speaks of the arrival in Spain of a very rich stranger, named Rehukin, whose vessel was finer and better built than any that had ever appeared at San-Lucar de Barrameda. The Inquisition arrested him as an heretic, and confiscated his property ; the merchant proved that the vessel did not belong to him, and that it could not be included in the confiscation ; but his efforts to recover it were useless.

Two other foreigners shared the fate of Burton. One was an Englishman named William Brook, born at Sarum, and a sailor ; the other was a Frenchman of Bayonne, named Fabianne, whose trade required his presence in Spain.

The *Beata* protected by Francis Zafra, who had recovered her senses, but persisted in her heresy, was burnt in this *auto-da-fé*, with five women of her family. Thirty-four persons were condemned to penances. The most remarkable instances were :—

John Fronton, an Englishman of the city of Bristol, who came to Seville, where he was informed of the arrest of Nicholas Burton. He was the proprietor of a considerable part of the merchandise taken from Burton, and after proving this fact by documents which he brought from England, he claimed restitution. He was subjected to great delays and expenses, but as it was impossible to deny his rights, the inquisitors promised to restore the merchandise; in the mean time they contrived that witnesses should appear and depose that John Fronton had advanced heretical propositions, and he was taken to the secret prisons. The fear of death induced Fronton to say everything that the inquisitors required, and he demanded reconciliation. He was declared to be *violently suspected* of the Lutheran heresy. This was sufficient to authorize the inquisitors to seize his property, and he was reconciled, condemned to forfeit his merchandise, and to wear the *san-benito* for the space of one year. This is a remarkable proof of the mischief produced by the secrecy of the inquisitorial proceedings. If the affair of John Fronton had been made public, any lawyer would have shewn the nullity and falsehood of the *instruction.* Yet there are Englishmen who defend the tribunal of the holy office, as a useful institution, and I have heard an *English Catholic priest*

speak in its defence. I represented that he did not understand the nature of the tribunal ; that I was not less attached
to the Catholic religion than he, or any inquisitor might be ;
but that if the spirit of peace and charity, humility and
disinterestedness, inculcated by the Holy Scriptures, is compared with the system of severity, craft, and malice, dictated
by the laws of the holy office, and the power possessed by
the inquisitors (from the secrecy of their proceedings) of
abusing their authority in defiance of natural and divine laws,
the orders of the Popes and the royal decrees, it will be impossible not to detest the tribunal as only tending to produce
hypocrisy.

Gaspard de Benavides was an alcalde of the prison of the
Inquisition, and appeared in the *auto-da-fé* with a flambeau ;
he was banished for life from Seville, and lost his place, for
having failed in zeal and attention in his employment. Let
this qualification and the sentence be compared with the
crime of which he was accused. He purloined part of the
small rations of the prisoners, the food which he gave them
was of a bad quality, and he made them pay for it, as if it
was superior ; he did not take care to prepare it properly, it
was badly cooked and seasoned ; he deceived them in the
price of wood, and made false bills of expenditure. If any
of the prisoners complained, he removed them to a dark and
humid dungeon, where he left them for a fortnight or even
longer, to punish them for murmuring ; he did not fail to
tell them that he did this by the order of the inquisitors, and
that they were released at his intercession. When any
prisoner demanded an audience, Gaspard (fearing that they
would denounce him) did not inform the inquisitors of the
request, and told the prisoner the next day, that the inquitors were so much occupied that they could not grant
audiences. In short, there was no sort of injustice which he
did not commit, until the moment when his conduct was discovered by chance.

Maria Gonzalez, a servant of this man, was condemned to receive two hundred stripes, and to be banished for ten years. Her crime was, having received money from some prisoners, and having permitted them to see and converse with each other.

Donna Jane Bohorques was declared innocent. She was the legitimate daughter of Don Pedro Garcia de Xeres y Bohorques, and the sister of Donna Maria Bohorques, who perished in a former *auto-da-fe*. She had married Don Francis de Vargas, lord of the borough of Higuera. She was taken to the secret prisons, when her unfortunate sister declared that she was acquainted with her opinions, and had not opposed them; as if silence could prove that she had admitted the doctrine to be true. Jane Bohorques was six months gone with child; but this did not prevent the inquisitors from proceeding in her trial, a cruelty which will not surprise, when it is considered that she was arrested before any proof of her crime had been obtained. She was delivered in the prison, her child was taken from her at the end of eight days, in defiance of the most sacred rights of nature, and she was imprisoned in one of the common dungeons of the holy office. The inquisitors thought they did all that humanity required in giving her a less inconvenient cell than the common prison. It fortunately happened that she had as a companion in her cell a young girl who was afterwards burnt as a Lutheran, and who pitying her situation, treated her with the utmost tenderness during her convalescence. She soon required the same care; she was tortured, and all her limbs were bruised and almost dislocated. Jane Bohorques attended her in this dreadful state. Jane Bohorques was not yet quite recovered, when she was tortured in the same manner. The cords with which her still feeble limbs were bound penetrated to the bone, and several blood vessels breaking in her body, torrents of blood flowed from her mouth. She was taken back to her dungeon in a dying state, and expired a few days after. The inquisitors thought they expiated this cruel murder, by declaring Jane Bohorques innocent, in the *auto-da-fé* of this day. Under what an overwhelming responsibility will these monsters appear before the tribunal of the Almighty !

CHAPTER XXII.

OF THE ORDINANCES OF 1561, WHICH HAVE BEEN FOL-
LOWED IN THE PROCEEDINGS OF THE HOLY OFFICE,
UNTIL THE PRESENT TIME.

THE ancient laws of the holy office had been almost entirely forgotten, and the inquisitors merely followed a kind of routine in transacting their affairs. The inquisitor-general Valdés found it necessary to remedy this evil, and as a mul. titude of extraordinary cases had occurred since the publication of the Codes of Torquemada and his successor Deza, which had obliged the inquisitors to publish supplements and new declarations, he resolved to frame a new code, composed of those laws which experience had shewn to be useful. This edict was published at Madrid, on the 2nd of September, 1561 ; it was composed of eighty-one articles, which have been, till the present time, the laws by which the proceedings of the Inquisition have been regulated.

Preamble. " We, Don Ferdinand Valdés, by the grace of God, Archbishop of Seville, apostolical inquisitor-general against heresy and apostacy in all the kingdoms and domains of his majesty, &c. ; we inform you, venerable apostolical inquisitors, that we understand, that although it has been provided by the ordinances of the holy office, that the same manner of proceeding should be exactly followed in all the Inquisitions, there are, nevertheless, some tribunals where this measure has not been, and is not well observed. In order to prevent any difference for the future, in the conduct of the tribunals, and the forms which should be followed, it has been resolved, after communicating and consulting with the council of the general Inquisition, that the following order shall be observed by the tribunals of the holy office:—

1st. When the inquisitors admit an information, which shews that propositions have been advanced which ought to be denounced to the holy office, they must consult theologians of learning and integrity, and capable of qualifying the said propositions; they shall give their opinion in writing, accompanied by their signature.

2nd. If it is certain from the opinion of the theologians that the object of their examination is a matter of faith, or if it is apparent without consulting them, and the denounced fact is sufficiently proved, the procurator-fiscal shall denounce the author of it, and the individuals implicated, if there are any, and shall require that they be arrested*.

3rd. The inquisitors shall be assembled to decide if imprisonment should be decreed; in doubtful cases, they shall summon consultors, if they find it necessary †.

4th. When the proof is not sufficient to cause the arrest of the denounced person, the inquisitors shall not cite him to appear, or subject him to any examination, because experience has shewn, that an heretic who is at liberty will not confess, and this measure only makes him more reserved and attentive in avoiding everything that may increase the suspicions or the proofs brought against him.

---

* The *informer* is admitted as a witness, in contempt of the rule of right, and the punishment due to a false witness is not inflicted, if he is discovered to be such.

† They never found this measure necessary. The old bulls and the Cortes had provided that the interlocutory act of arrest should be consented to, and signed by the inquisitor in ordinary of the diocese. Reason dictated this measure, because the decree for an arrest does not permit the summons.

5th. If the inquisitors are not unanimous in decreeing an arrest, the writings of the trial shall be sent to the council, and this must likewise take place even when they are unanimous in their decisions, if the individuals to be arrested are persons of quality and consideration.

6th. The inquisitors shall sign the decree of arrest, and address it to the *grand alguazil* of the holy office. When it relates to a formal heresy, this measure shall be immediately followed by the sequestration of the property of the denounced person. If several persons are to be imprisoned, a decree of arrest shall be expedited for each individual, distinct and independent of each other, to be separately executed; this precaution is necessary to ensure secrecy, in case one *alguazil* cannot arrest all the criminals. A note shall be entered in the trial, stating the day on which the decree of arrest was delivered, and the person who received it.

7th. The *alguazil* shall be accompanied, in the execution of the decree of imprisonment, by the recorder of the sequestrations, and the stewards. He shall appoint a depositary, and if the steward does not approve of the person mentioned, he shall appoint another himself, as he is responsible for the property.

8th. The recorder of the sequestrations shall note all the effects separately, with the day, the month, and year of the seizure; he shall sign it with the *alguazil*, the steward, the depositary, and the witnesses; he shall give a copy of this writing to the depositary; but if the others demand copies, he is permitted to require payment for them.

9th. The *alguazil* shall deduct from the sequestrated property a sufficient portion to defray the expenses of the food, lodging, and journey of the prisoner; he shall give an account of what he received when he arrives at the Inquisition. If any money remains he shall give it to the cashier, to be employed in the maintenance of the prisoner.

10th. The *alguazil* shall require the prisoner to give up his money, papers, arms, and everything which it might be dangerous for him to be in possession of; he shall not allow him to have any communication, either by speech or writing with the other prisoners, without receiving permission from the inquisitors. He shall remit all the effects found upon the person of the prisoner to the goaler, and shall take a receipt, with the date of the day on which the remittance took place. The goaler shall inform the inquisitors of the arrival of the prisoner, and he shall lodge him in such a manner, that he cannot have at his disposal anything which might be dangerous in his hands, unless they are confided to him, and he is obliged to be responsible. One of the notaries of the holy office shall be present, and shall draw up the verbal process of the decree of imprisonment and its execution; even the hour when the prisoner entered the prison must be mentioned, as this point is important in the accounts of the cashier.

11th. The goaler shall not lodge several prisoners together, he shall not permit them to communicate with each other, unless the inquisitors allow it.

12th. The goaler shall be provided with a register, in which all the effects in the chamber of the prisoner, with the clothes and food which he receives from each detained person, shall be noted; he shall sign the statement with the recorder of the sequestrations, and shall give notice of it to the inquisitors; he shall not remit any food or clothing to the prisoners without examining them with great attention, to ascertain if they contain letters, arms, or anything of which they might make a bad use.

13th. When the inquisitors think proper, they shall order the prisoner to be brought into the chamber of audience; they shall cause him to sit on a bench or small seat, and take an oath to speak the truth, at this time, and on all succeeding audiences; they shall ask him his name, his surname, his age, his country, the place where he dwells, his profession and rank, and the time of his arrest; they shall treat him with humanity, and respect his rank, but without derogating from the authority of judges, that the accused may not infringe the respect due to them, or commit any reprehensible act towards their persons. The accused shall stand while the act of denunciation by the fiscal is read.

14th. The accused shall be afterwards examined on his genealogy. He shall be asked if he is married : if more than once, what woman he married : how many children he had by each marriage, their age, as well as their rank and place of dwelling. The recorder shall write down these details, paying attention to place each name at the beginning of a line, because this practice is useful in consulting registers, to discover if the accused is not descended from Jews, Moors, heretics, or other individuals punished by the holy office.

15th. When the preceding ceremony has passed, the accused shall be required to give an abridged history of his life, mentioning those towns where he has made a considerable stay, the motives of his sojourn, the persons he associated with, the friends he acquired, his studies, the masters he studied under, the period when he began them, and the time that he continued them ; if he had been out of Spain, at what time and with whom he had quitted the country, and how long he had been absent. He shall be asked if he is instructed in the truths of the Christian religion, and shall be required to repeat the *Pater-noster*, the *Ave Maria*, and the *Credo*. He shall be asked if he has confessed himself, and to what confessors. When he has given an account of all these things, he shall be asked if he knows or suspects the cause of his arrest, and his reply shall regulate the questions put to him afterwards. The inquisitors shall avoid interrupting the accused while he is speaking, and shall allow him to express himself freely while the recorder writes down his declarations, unless they are foreign to the trial. They shall ask all necessary questions, but shall avoid fatiguing him by examining him on subjects not relating to the trial, unless he gives occasion for it by his replies.

16th. It is proper that the inquisitors should always suspect that they have been deceived by the witnesses, and that they shall be so by the accused, and that they should not take either side ; for, if they adopt an opinion too soon, they will not be able to act with that impartiality which is suitable to their station, and on the contrary will be liable to fall into error.

17th. The inquisitors shall not speak to the accused during the audience, or at other times, of any affair not relating to his own. The recorder shall write down the questions and replies ; and, after the audience, he shall read it to the accused, that he may sign it. If he wishes to add, retrench, alter, or elucidate, any article, the recorder shall write after his dictation, without suppressing or certifying the articles already written.

18th. The fiscal shall present his act of accusation within the time prescribed by the ordinances ; he shall accuse the prisoner of being an heretic in general terms, and afterwards mention, in particular, the facts and propositions of which he is charged. The inquisitors have not the right of punishing an accused person for crimes which do not relate to matters of faith ; but if the preparatory instruction mentions any, the fiscal shall make it the object of an accusation, because this circumstance, and that of his general good or bad conduct, assists in determining the degree of credence to be given to his replies, and serves for other purposes in his trial.

19th. Although the accused may confess all the charges brought against him in the first audiences of *admonition*, yet the fiscal shall draw up and present his act of accusation, because experience has shewn, that it is better that a trial, caused by the *denunciation* of a person who is a party in the cause, should be continued and judged at the prosecution of the *denunciator ;* that the inquisitors may be at liberty to deliberate on the application of punishments and penances, which would not be the case if they proceeded *officially.*

20th. Whenever the accused shall be admitted to an

audience, he shall be reminded of the oath which he has taken to speak the truth.

21st. At the end of his requisition, the fiscal shall introduce a clause, importing, that if the inquisitors do not think his accusation sufficiently proved, they are requested to decree the torture for the accused, because, as it cannot be inflicted without previous notice, it is proper that the accused should be informed that it has been required; and this moment appears the most convenient, because the prisoner is not prepared for it, and he will receive the notice with less agitation.

22nd. The fiscal shall himself present his requisition, or demand in accusation, to the inquisitors; the recorder shall read it in the presence of the prisoner, the fiscal shall make oath that he does not act from bad intentions, and retire; the accused shall then reply successively to all the articles of the act, and the recorder shall write down his answers in the same order, even if they are only denials.

23rd. The inquisitors shall give the prisoner to understand that it is of great consequence to him to speak the truth. One of the advocates of the holy office shall be appointed to defend him, who shall communicate with him in the presence of an inquisitor, in order to prepare himself to reply in writing to the accusation, after swearing fidelity to the accused, and secrecy to the tribunal, although he had already taken that oath at the time that he was appointed the *advocate of the prisoners of the holy office*. He must endeavour to persuade the accused that it is of the greatest consequence to be sincere, to ask pardon and submit to a penance if he acknowledges his guilt. His reply shall be communicated to the fiscal, who, with the prisoner and his advocate, shall be present at the audience, and shall demand the proofs. The inquisitors shall admit the requisition, but without naming the day or informing the parties of it, because neither the accused nor any other person in his name has the right of being present when the witnesses take their oaths.

24th. The recorder shall read to the advocate all that the accused has declared relating to himself, but shall omit all that he has said concerning others; this communication is necessary to the advocate, that he may establish the defence of his client. If he wishes to make any additions to his declaration, the advocate must be obliged to retire.

25th. If the accused has attained the age of twenty-five years, a guardian shall be appointed for him before the accusation is read. The advocate may fill that office, or any other person of known honour and integrity. The prisoner, with the approbation of his guardian, shall ratify all that he has declared in former audiences; and he shall afterwards be attended by the same person in all the circumstances of the trial.

26th. Where the proof has been admitted, the fiscal shall announce in the presence of the accused, that he reproduces and presents the witnesses and the proofs which existed in the writings and the registers of the holy office; he shall demand that they proceed to the *ratification* of the witnesses who have been examined in the preparatory instruction, that the witnesses shall be confronted and the depositions published. If the accused or his advocate speak at this time, the recorder shall write down all that they say.

27th. If the accused confesses himself guilty of another crime, after the proof is admitted, the fiscal shall accuse him of it, and he shall be prosecuted according to the ordinary forms. If the proof of the first crime is increased, it will be sufficient to inform the prisoner of the circumstance.

28th. In the interval between the proof and the publication, the prisoner may demand audiences, through the gaoler. The inquisitors must grant them without delay, in order to profit by the inclination of the accused, which may change from day to day.

29th. The inquisitors must not neglect to cause the *ratification* of the witnesses, or to take any measures to discover the truth.

30th. The *ratification* of the witnesses shall take place before responsible persons, such as two priests, Christians of an ancient race, and of a pure life and reputation. The witnesses shall be asked in their presence if they recollect having deposed in any trial before the Inquisition : if they reply in the affirmative, they shall be questioned on the circumstances, and the persons interested in it. When they have given satisfaction on this article, they shall be informed that the fiscal has presented them as witnesses in the trial of the prisoner. Their first declaration shall be read to them, and if they say that they have attested those facts, they shall be required to ratify them, making any additions, suppressions, explanations, and alterations, which they may think proper. These shall all be mentioned in the verbal process : it shall also be stated if the witness is at that time at liberty or detained in the chamber of audience, or in his chamber, and why he has not appeared in the ordinary place.

31st. When the ratification of the witnesses is concluded, the publication shall be prepared, taking a copy of each deposition ; it shall be literal, except in all that may tend to discover the witnesses to the accused. If the declaration is too long, it shall be divided into several chapters. At the publication of the depositions, they shall not be read to the accused all at once, nor all the articles of a long declaration. The first head of the deposition of the first witness shall be read to him, that he may reply to it with more precision and facility ; they shall then pass to the second chapter, then to the third, following the same order in all the depositions. The inquisitors shall hasten, as much as possible, the publication of the depositions, to spare the accused the anxiety of a long delay ; they shall avoid all that may lead him to suppose that new charges have been brought against him, or that those already made are more extended than in their own declarations; and although such circumstances may have occurred, and the accused has denied the charges, they shall cause the delay of the formalities and the conclusion of the trial.

32nd. The inquisitors shall fulfil the form of the *publication*, dictating to the recorder all that is to be written in the presence of the accused, or they shall write it themselves and sign it. This writing shall be dated with the year, the month, and the day, when the witness deposed, provided that it is not inconvenient to do so; it would be improper if the deponent was in prison. They shall also mention the time and place when the facts occurred, because this is useful to the accused in his defence; but the place must only be designated in general terms. In the copy of the deposition the *third person* shall be used, although the witness spoke in the *first*. Thus it must be said: The witness has seen or heard the accused conversing with an individual, &c.*

33rd. If an accused, who has made declarations in several sittings, reveals crimes committed by persons whom he named, and afterwards makes new declarations, only cites these persons in a vague and general manner, employing for example, the words, *all those whom I have named*, or a similar expression; these accusations cannot be brought against any accused person, as they do not apply in a direct manner; this must oblige the inquisitors to pay attention to the prisoner who speaks of different individuals, and cause him to name them one after the other, and afterwards to state the facts or words which he imputes to them.

34th. Although the accused has denied the charges, the publication of the depositions must be read to him, that he

---

* This form is very prejudicial to the prisoner, when the conversation takes place with one person, because the manner of relating the fact supposes three, the accused, the interlocutor, and the individual who has seen or heard.

may not call in question the regularity of the proceedings of the tribunal which has arrested him, and that the judges may rely with more confidence on the law when they pass sentence; for this discretionary power exists only if the accused is convicted and confesses himself guilty; otherwise, the charges brought against him by the witnesses, whose declarations have not been mentioned to him, cannot be of any value, particularly in a trial of this kind, when the accused is not present at the oath of the witnesses.

35th. When the accused has replied to the publication of the depositions, he shall be permitted to consult with his advocate, in the presence of an inquisitor and the recorder, that he may prepare his defence. The recorder shall write down the particulars of the conference which he considers worthy of attention. Neither the inquisitor nor recorder, still less the advocate, shall remain alone with the accused. It shall be the same with all other persons, except the gaoler or his deputy. It is sometimes eligible that learned and pious persons should visit the accused, to exhort them to confess what they obstinately deny, though they have been convicted. These interviews can only take place in the presence of the recorder or an inquisitor. Procurators shall not be permitted to be appointed for the prisoner, though the *old instructions* have established this measure, because experience has shewn that great inconvenience arises from it*; besides which the accused derives little advantage from it†. If any unforeseen circumstance renders this measure necessary, the advocate may be appointed to fill the office.

36th. If the accused wishes to write, to fix the points of

---

* This inconvenience was the danger to which the secrecy of the holy office was exposed from the activity of these procurators.

† This is false; the advantages on the contrary were very important, because the procurators who knew the persons capable of proving the challenge of presumed witnesses, informed them of it, in order to favour the accused.

his defence, he shall be furnished with paper : but the sheets shall be counted and numbered by the recorder, that the accused may give them back again either written upon or blank.   When his work is finished, he shall be allowed to converse with his advocate, to whom he may communicate what he has written, on condition that his defender restores the original without taking a copy when he presents his address to the tribunal.   When there is an examination in the defence of the prisoner, he shall be required to name, on the margin of each article, the witnesses he wishes to call, that those who are the most worthy of credit may be examined.   He must also be required to name as witnesses none but Christians of an ancient race, who are neither his servants nor relations, unless it is a case when the questions can only be answered by them*.   Before the address is presented by the advocate, if the accused requires it, it shall be communicated to him, and the inquisitors shall desire the advocate to confine himself to the defence of the accused in what he has to say, and to observe a strict silence on everything said in the world, as experience has shewn the inconvenience of this sort of revelations, even in respect to the accused persons ; they shall cause him to restore all the papers, without taking copies of them, or even of the address, of which he must give up the notes, if there are any.

37th. Whenever the prisoner is admitted to an audience, the fiscal shall examine the state of the trial, to ascertain if he has declared anything new of himself or others; he shall receive his declaration judicially, and mark the names of the persons of whom he has said anything, and all the other points which might elucidate the affair, in the margin.

* The New Christians, the relations, the servants, malefactors, infamous persons, in fact every man, a wife, a child, are admitted to depose against the accused, and he cannot call as a witness any person who is a relation or a servant !

38th. The inquisitors shall receive the informations relative to the defence of the accused, the depositions in his favour, the indirect proofs and challenges of the witnesses, with as much care and attention as they receive those of the fiscal; that the detention of the prisoner, which prevents him from acting for himself, may not be an obstacle to the discovery of the truth.

39th. When the inquisitors receive important information in defence of the prisoner, he shall be brought before the tribunal accompanied by his advocate; they shall inform him that the proofs of all the circumstances which might mitigate his crime have been received, and that they can conclude the trial, unless any other demand occurs on their part, in which case they will do everything which may be permitted for the prisoner. If he declares that he has nothing more to say, the fiscal may give in his conclusions. It will be proper, however, that he should not do it immediately, that he may take advantage of every circumstance that may take place. If the accused demands the publication of the depositions in his defence, it must be refused, as it may tend to discover the persons who have deposed against him*.

40th. When the trial is so far advanced that the sentence may be passed, the inquisitors shall convoke the ordinary and the consulters. As there is no reporter, the dean of the inquisitors shall report the trial, without giving any opinion, and the recorder shall read it in the presence of the inquisitors and the fiscal, who shall sit by the consultors, and retire when he has heard the report, before the judges give their votes. The consultors shall give their votes first, and then the ordinary, the inquisitors after him, and the dean the last. Each voter shall be at liberty to make any obser-

---

* This is an injustice. If an accused person had seen the proved articles of the examination in his defence, or if they had been communicated to his lawyer, he would have often derived conclusive arguments from them against the depositions for the prosecution.

vations which he thinks proper in giving his vote, without being interrupted or prevented. If the inquisitors give different votes, they shall explain their motives, to prove that there is nothing arbitrary in their conduct. The recorder shall write each opinion in a register prepared for the purpose, and shall afterwards join it to the trial, to give testimony of it.

41st. When the accused confesses himself guilty, and his confessions have the required conditions, if he is not relapsed, he shall be admitted to reconciliation; his property shall be seized; he shall be clothed in the habit of a penitent, or a *San-benito* (which is a scapulary of linen or yellow cloth, with two crosses of St. Andrew of another colour), and he shall be confined in the prison for those who are condemned to perpetual imprisonment, namely, that of *Mercy*. As to the colours of the habit he is to wear, and the confiscation of his property, there are *Fueros* and privileges existing in some provinces of Arragon, and other rules and customs which must be conformed to, in acquitting the criminal, and restoring his ordinary garments to him, according to the sentence. If it is proper that he should remain in prison for an unlimited time, it shall be said in his sentence, that his punishment shall last as long as the inquisitors think proper. If the accused has really relapsed, after abjuring a *formal* heresy, or is a *false penitent* when he has abjured as *violently* suspected, and is convicted in the present trial of the same heresy, he shall be given up to the common judge according to the civil law, and his punishment shall not be remitted, although he may protest that his repentance is sincere, and his confession true in this case.

42nd. The abjuration must be written after the sentence, and signed by the accused; if he is incapable of signing it, this ceremony must be performed by an inquisitor and the recorder; if the condemned abjures in a public *auto-da-fé*, the abjuration must be signed the next day, in the chamber of audience.

43rd. If the accused is convicted of heresy, bad faith, and obstinacy, he shall be *relaxed*, but the inquisitors must not neglect to endeavour to convert him, that he may die in the faith of the church.

44th. If an accused who has been condemned, and informed of his sentence on the day before the *auto-da-fé*, repents during the night and confesses his sins, or part of them, in a manner that shews true repentance, he shall not be conducted to the *auto-da-fé*, but his execution shall be suspended, because it might be improper to allow him to hear the names of the persons condemned to death, and those condemned to other punishments, for this knowledge and the report of the offence might assist him in preparing his judicial confession. If the accused is converted on the scaffold of the *auto-da-fé*, before he has heard his sentence, the inquisitors must suppose that the fear of death has more influence in this conversion than true repentance; but if, from different circumstances and the nature of the confession, they wish to suspend the execution, they are permitted to do so, considering at the same time that confessions made in such circumstances are not worthy of belief, and more particularly those which accuse other individuals.

45th. The inquisitors must maturely consider motives and circumstances before they decree the torture; and when they have resolved to have recourse to it, they must state the motive ; they must declare if the torture is to be employed *in caput proprium*, because the accused is subjected to it as persisting in his denials, and incompletely convicted in his own trial; or if he suffers it *in caput alienum*, as a witness who denies, in the trial of another accused, the facts of which he has been a joint witness. If he is convicted of bad faith in his own cause, and is consequently liable to be *relaxed*, or if he is equally so in any other affair, he may be tortured, though he must be given up to the secular judge for what concerns him personally. If he does not

reveal anything in being tortured as a witness, he shall
nevertheless be condemned as an accused; but if the question
forces him to confess his crime, and that of another person,
and he solicits the indulgence of his judges, the inquisitors
shall conform to the rules of right.

46th. If only a semi-proof of the crime exists, or if ap-
pearances will not admit of the acquittal of the prisoner, he
shall make an abjuration as being either *violently* or *slightly*
suspected. As this measure is not a punishment for the past,
but a precaution for the future, pecuniary penalties shall be
imposed ; but he shall be informed that if he again commits
the crime for which he was denounced, he will be considered
as having *relapsed*, and be delivered over to the secular
judge; for this purpose he shall sign his act of abjuration.

47th. In cases where only the semi-proof, or some indications
of a crime exist, the accused has been sometimes permitted
to clear himself canonically before the number of persons
appointed in the ancient instructions ; the inquisitors, the
ordinary, and the consultors, may therefore allow it if they
think proper, but they must observe that this proceeding is
very dangerous, not often used, and can only be employed
with great caution*.

48th. The third manner of proceeding in this case is to
employ the *question*. This measure is thought to be dangerous and not certain, because its effects depend upon the
physical strength of the subject; consequently no rule can

---

* *It was not often used,* because the inquisitors were unwilling to reveal the secret of their irregular proceedings ; they considered it *dangerous,* because it was favourable to the accused, in the few cases where it
had been employed; they wished it to be used with great caution, because
they felt that those who are not inquisitors act like judges. The canonical proof takes place in the presence of twelve persons, who declare upon
oath whether they believe the accused to be innocent or guilty. They
were a kind of jury, to whom the inquisitors were obliged to show the
original process, and thus the accused depended more upon the jury than
on the inquisitors.

be prescribed on this point, but it is left to the prudence and equity of the judges. Nevertheless the question shall only be decreed by the ordinary, the consultors, and the inquisitors, or applied without their concurrence, as circumstances may occur, when their presence would be necessary *.

49th. When it is necessary to decree the torture, the accused shall be informed of the motives for employing it, and the offences for which he is to suffer it; but after it has been decided he shall not be examined on any particular fact, he shall be allowed to say what he pleases. Experience has shown that if he is questioned on any subject when pain has reduced him to the last extremity, he will say anything that is required of him, which may be injurious to other persons, in making them parties concerned, and producing other inconveniences.

50th. The question shall not be decreed until the process is terminated, and the defence of the accused has been heard. As the sentence of recourse to the question admits of an appeal, the inquisitors shall consult the council, if the case is doubtful; if the accused can maintain his appeal, it shall be admitted. But if the point of law is clear, the inquisitors are not required to consult the council, or to admit the application of the accused; they are at liberty to proceed immediately to execution, as if it had not been made.

51st. If the inquisitors think that the appeal ought to be admitted, they shall send the writings of the process to the Supreme Council, without informing the parties, or any individual not belonging to the tribunal, because the council will send an order to the inquisitors, if it is considered proper that they should be made acquainted with it.

52nd. If an inquisitor is challenged, and there is another

* I have not read any process which proves that more than one inquisitor has assisted at this execution; I have never seen either the ordinary, or the consultors present at it; the question was only applied in the presence of the inquisitor, the notary, and the executioners.

in the tribunal, the first shall abstain from performing his office, and the second shall take his place, after the council has been informed of the circumstance. If there is only one inquisitor in the tribunal, the proceedings shall be suspended until the decision of the Supreme Council has been received; the same course shall be pursued if there are several inquisitors, and they are all challenged.

53rd. Twenty-four hours after the accused has been put to the question, he shall be asked if he persists in his declarations, and if he will ratify them. The notary of the tribunal shall appoint the time for this formality, and likewise that for the application of the question. If at this moment the accused confesses his crimes, and afterwards ratifies his declarations in such a manner that the inquisitors may believe him to be converted, repentant, and sincere in his confessions, he may be admitted to reconciliation, notwithstanding the article in the ordinance of Seville, in 1484. If the accused retracts his declarations, the inquisitors shall proceed according to rule.

54th. When the inquisitors, the ordinary, and the consultors decree the question, they shall not decide on what is to be done after it has been administered, as the result is uncertain, nothing being regulated on this point. If the accused resists the torture, the judges shall deliberate on the nature, form, and quality of the torture which he has suffered, on the degree of intensity with which it was inflicted, on the age, strength, health, and vigour of the patient; they shall compare all these circumstances, with the number, the seriousness of the indications which lead to the supposition of his guilt, and they shall decide if he is already cleared by what he has suffered; in the affirmative they shall declare him free from prosecution, in the other case he shall abjure according to the nature of the suspicion.

55th. The judges, notary, and the executioners shall be present at the torture; when it is over, the inquisitors shall cause an individual who has been wounded to be properly attended, without allowing any suspected person to approach him, until he has ratified his declarations.

56th. The inquisitors shall take every precaution that the goaler shall not insinuate anything to the accused relating to his defence, that he may only follow his inclination in all that he says. This measure does not allow the goaler to fill the office of guardian or defender to the prisoner, or even representative of the fiscal; he may however serve as a writer for the accused, if he does not know how to write; in this case he shall be prohibited from substituting his own ideas for those of the accused.

57th. The affair being for the second time in a state for passing sentence, there shall be a new audience of the inquisitors, the ordinary, the consultors, the fiscal and the notary. The fiscal shall hear the report of the last incidents, to ascertain if it contains anything important relating to his office; after it has been read he shall retire, that the judges may remain alone when they proceed to vote.

58th. When the inquisitors release an accused person from the secret prisons, he shall be conducted to the chamber of audience; they shall there ask him if the goaler treated him and the other prisoners well, or ill; if he has communicated with him or other persons on subjects foreign to the trial; if he has seen or known that other prisoners conversed with persons not confined in the prison, or if the goaler gave them any advice. They shall command him to keep secret these details, and all that has passed since his detention, and shall make him sign a promise to this effect, if he knows how to write, that he may fear to break it.

59th. If a prisoner dies before his trial is terminated, and his declarations have not extenuated the charges of the witnesses, so as to give a sufficient cause for reconciliation, the inquisitors shall give notice of his death to his children, his heirs, or other persons who have the right of defending his memory and property; and, if there is cause to pursue the trial of the deceased, a copy of the depositions and the act of accusation shall be remitted to them, and all that they advance in defence of the accused shall be received.

60th. If the mind of an accused person becomes deranged before the conclusion of the trial, a guardian or defender shall be appointed for him; if the children or relations of the accused present any means of defence in his favour to the tribunal, when he is in possession of his senses, the inquisitors shall not permit them to be joined to the other writings of the process, because neither the children nor relations of the accused are lawful parties; yet in a distinct and separate writing they may decree what they think fit, and take measures to discover the truth, without communicating with the prisoner, or the persons who represent him.

61st. When sufficient proof exists to authorize proceedings against the memory and property of a deceased person, according to the *ancient instruction*, the accusation of the fiscal shall be signified to the children, the heirs, or other interested persons, each of whom shall receive a copy of the notification. If no person presents himself to defend the memory of the accused, or to appeal against the seizure of his goods, the inquisitors shall appoint a defender, and pursue the trial, considering him as a party. If any one interested in the affair appears, his rights shall be admitted, although he should be a prisoner in the holy office at the time; but he shall be obliged to choose a free person to act for him. Until the affair is terminated, the sequestration of the property cannot take place, because it has passed into other hands: yet the possessors shall be deprived of it, if the deceased is found guilty.

62nd. If a person is found not liable to prosecution, this resolution of the tribunal shall be announced in the *auto-da-fé* by a public act, in any manner most suitable to the interested party; the errors with which he was charged shall not be designated, if the accusation is not proved. If a deceased person is pronounced free from prosecution, the judgment shall be formally published, because the action was public and notorious.

63rd. When a defender is appointed for the memory of a person accused after his death, in default of interested persons to take his defence, the choice must only fall on a person not belonging to the Inquisition; but he must be required to keep all the proceedings secret, and not to communicate the *depositions* and the accusations to any but the lawyers of the prisoners, unless a decision of the inquisitors authorise him to make them known to other persons.

64th. When absent individuals are to be tried, they shall be summoned to appear, by three public acts of citation at different intervals, according to the known or supposed place of their residence.   The fiscal shall denounce them contumacious, at the end of each citation.

65th. The inquisitors may take cognizance of several crimes which occasion suspicion of heresy, although they do not consider the accused an heretic, on account of certain circumstances; such as bigamy, blasphemy, and suspicious propositions.   In these cases the application of the punishments depends upon the prudence of the judges, who ought to follow the rules of right, and consider the gravity of the offence.   However, if they condemn the accused to corporeal punishment, such as whipping, or the galleys, they shall not say that it may be commuted for pecuniary penalties; for this measure would be an extortion, and an infringement of the respect due to the tribunal.

66th. If the inquisitors and the ordinary differ in opinion when they assemble to give their votes on the definitive sentence, the trial shall be referred to the Supreme Council; but if the division is produced by the manner in which the consultors have voted, the inquisitors may pass them over, (although they may be more numerous,) and establish the definitive sentence on their own votes, and that of the ordinary, unless the importance of the case compels them to apply to the council, even if the inquisitors, the consultors, and ordinary are unanimous*.

67th. The *secret notaries* shall draw up as many literal and certified copies of the declarations of the witnesses, and the confessions of the accused, as there are persons designated as guilty, or suspected of the crime of heresy, that there may be a separate proceeding against each; for the writings which contain the original charges are not sufficient, since experience has shewn that it always causes confusion, and the prescribed method has been employed several times, although it increases the labour of the notaries.

68th. When the inquisitors are informed that any of the prisoners have communicated with other detained persons, they shall ascertain the truth of the fact, inform themselves of the name and quality of the denounced persons, and if they are accused of the same species of crime. These details shall be mentioned in the process of each prisoner. In these cases little credit can be given to any subsequent declarations made by these persons, either in their own cause, or in the trial of another.

69th. Where a trial has been suspended by the inquisitors, if another commences, though for a different crime, the charges of the first shall be added to those of the second, and the fiscal shall maintain them in his act of accusation, because they aggravate the new crime of which the prisoner is accused.

70th. When two or more prisoners have been placed in the same prison, they shall not be afterwards separated, or introduced to other companions; if extraordinary circumstances make it impossible to comply with this order, they shall be stated in the process of each person, and this incident

* It was afterwards regulated that this should be done in all definitive sentences.

ought to diminish the weight of their declarations after the change ; for it is certain that each prisoner will tell his companions all that he knows and has seen, and that these reports will influence the other prisoners in the recantations which they sometimes oppose to their first confessions.

71st. If a prisoner falls sick, the inquisitors must carefully provide him with every assistance, and more particularly attend to all that relates to his soul.   If he asks for a confessor, the inquisitors shall summon a learned man, worthy of possessing their confidence; they shall recommend that he shall not undertake any commission for any person, during the sacramental confession ; and if the accused gives him one out of the tribunal of penance, that he shall communicate to the Inquisition everything relating to his trial.   The confessor shall be required to inform the accused that he cannot be absolved in the sacrament of penitence, unless he confesses the crime of which he is accused.   If the sick person is in danger of dying, or is a woman about to be delivered, the rules appointed for such cases shall be followed.   If the accused does not ask for a confessor, and the physician declares that he is in danger, he shall be induced to make the request, and to confess himself.   If the accused makes a judicial confession of his crime, agreeing with the charges, he shall be reconciled, and when he has been acquitted by the tribunal, the confessor shall give him absolution.   In case of death, ecclesiastical sepulture shall be granted, but secretly, unless it is inconvenient.   If the accused demands a confessor when he is in good health, it may be useful to refuse it, as he cannot be absolved until after his reconciliation ; unless he has already judicially confessed enough to justify the charges ; in that case the confessor may encourage him to be patient.

72nd. The witnesses in a trial shall not be confronted, because experience has shewn that this measure is useless and inconvenient, independently of the infringement of the law of secrecy which is the result.

73rd. When an inquisitor visits the towns of the district of his tribunal, he shall not undertake any trial for heresy, or arrest any denounced person, but he shall receive the declarations, and send them to the tribunal. Yet if it is the case of a person whose flight may be apprehended, he may be arrested and sent to the prisons of the holy office; the inquisitor may also decide upon affairs of small consequence, such as heretical blasphemies, which may be judged without arresting the parties. The inquisitor shall not exercise this authority without being empowered by the ordinary.

74th. In the definitive sentence pronounced against an individual declared guilty of heresy, and condemned to be deprived of his property, the period when he first fell into heresy shall be indicated, because this knowledge may be useful to the steward of the confiscations; it shall likewise be mentioned if this declaration is founded on the confession of the accused, on the depositions of the witnesses, or on both. If this formality is omitted, and the steward demands that it shall be fulfilled, the inquisitors shall comply; if it cannot be done by all together, it shall at least be executed by one of them, or the consultors.

75th. An account shall be given by the gaoler of the common and daily nourishment of each prisoner, according to the price of the eatables; if there is in the prison a person of quality, or who is rich and has several domestics, he shall be supplied with the quantity of food which he requires, but only on condition that the remnants be distributed to the poor, and not given to the gaoler.

76th. If the prisoner has a wife or children, and they require to be maintained from his sequestrated property, a certain sum for each day shall be allowed them, proportioned to their number, age, quality, and the state of their health, as well as to the extent and value of these possessions. If any of the children exercise any profession, and can thus provide for themselves, they shall not receive any part of the allowance.

77th. When any trials are terminated and sentences passed, the inquisitors shall fix the day for the celebration of an *auto-da-fé*. They give notice of it to the ecclesiastical chapter and the municipality of the town, and likewise to the president and the judges of the royal court, if there is one, that they may assemble with the tribunal, and accompany it to the ceremony according to custom. They shall use proper means that the execution of those who are to be *relaxed* shall take place before night, in order to prevent accidents.

78th. The inquisitors shall not permit any person to enter the prisons on the day before the *auto-da-fé*, except the confessors and the *familiars* of the holy office when their employments make it necessary. The *familiars* shall receive the prisoner and be responsible for him, after the notary has taken evidence of it in writing, and shall be required to take him back to the prisons after the ceremony of the *auto-da-fé*, if he is not given over to the secular judge; they shall not allow any person to speak to him on the road, or inform him of anything that is passing.

79th. On the day after the *auto-da-fé*, the inquisitors shall cause all the reconciled persons to be brought into their presence. They shall explain to each the sentence which had been read the day before, and shall tell him to what punishment he would have been condemned if he had not confessed his crime; they shall examine them all, particularly on what passes in the prisons, and they shall afterwards give them into the custody of the gaoler of the *perpetual* prisons, who shall be commissioned to observe that they accomplish their penances, and to inform them when they fail. He shall also be required to supply the prisoners with everything they want, and to procure work for those who can occupy themselves, that they may contribute to their subsistence, and be able to alleviate their misery.

80th. The inquisitors shall visit the *perpetual* prisons from time to time, to observe the conduct of the prisoners

and if they are well treated. In those places where there
is no *perpetual* prison a house shall be provided instead,
for without this precaution it is impossible to inflict the
punishment of imprisonment on those who are condemned
to it, or to ascertain if they faithfully accomplish their
penances.

81st. The *San-benitos* of all those persons who have been
condemned to *relaxation*, shall be exposed in their respective
parishes, after they have been burnt in person or in effigy ;
the same shall be done with the *San-benitos* of the reconciled
persons, after they have left them off : no *San-benitos* shall
be suspended in the churches for those individuals who have
been reconciled before the term of grace, as they have not
been condemned to wear them. The inscription for the
San-benito shall consist of the names of the condemned
persons, a notice of the heresies for which they were
punished, and of the time when they suffered their penance,
in order to perpetuate the disgrace of the heretics and their
descendants.

As this formulary is still in force in the tribunals of the
holy office, it appeared to me useless to follow minutely the
details of the events of the reign of each inquisitor-general,
since the nature of the institution may be known by the
picture I have given of its laws and ordinances, and by the
observations which I shall have occasion to make in the re-
mainder of the history.

I shall only say, that Don Ferdinand Valdés was, in 1566,
succeeded by Don Diego Espinosa, Bishop of Siguenza and
President of the Council of Castile. Espinosa died on the 5th
of September, 1572. Don Pedro Ponce de Leon, Bishop of
Placentia and Estremadura, was the next inquisitor-general,
but he died before he had entered on his office.

The king appointed the Cardinal Gaspard de Quiroga,
Archbishop of Toledo, to be the eleventh inquisitor-general :
he died on the 20th November, 1594.

Don Jerome Manriquez de Lara succeeded Quiroga; he was Bishop of Avila, and the son of Cardinal Manriquez, who had filled the same office under Charles V.

Don Jerome died in September, 1595, and after him Don Pedro Portocarrero, Bishop of Cordova, was at the head of the Inquisition.

The fourteenth inquisitor-general was the Cardinal Don Ferdinand Niño de Guevara, Archbishop of Seville, who took possession in December, 1599, during the reign of Philip III.

It was under Philip II. that the Inquisition committed the greatest cruelties, and the reign of this prince is the most remarkable period of the history of the holy office.

CHAPTER XXIII.

OF SOME AUTOS-DA-FE CELEBRATED IN MURCIA.

THE opinions of Luther, Calvin, and the other Protestant reformers, were not disseminated in the other cities in Spain with the same rapidity as at Seville and Valladolid; but there is reason to believe that all Spain would soon have been infected with the heresy, but for the extreme severity shewn towards the Lutherans. From 1560 till 1570 at least one *auto-da-fé* was celebrated every year in every Inquisition of the kingdom, and some heretics of the new sect always appeared among the condemned persons. Yet the progress of Lutheranism cannot be compared to that of Judaism and Mahometanism, because these religions had been long established, and the ancestors of a great number of Spanish families had professed them. An opinion may be formed of what passed in the other tribunals from some notices of the proceedings of that of Murcia.

On the 7th of June, 1557, a solemn *auto-da-fé* was celebrated at Murcia, where eleven individuals were burnt, and forty-three were reconciled. On the 12th of February, 1559, thirty victims were burnt with five effigies, and forty-three were reconciled. On the 14th February, in the same year, 1560, fourteen persons were burnt, and twenty effigies: twenty-nine persons were subjected to penances.

On the 8th of September, in the same year, sixteen individuals perished in the flames, and forty-eight were condemned to penances.

On the 15th of March, 1562, another *auto-da-fé* took place, composed of twenty-three persons, who were burnt, and of sixty-three who were condemned to penances. They were all punished as Judaic heretics; among the first may be remarked, Fray Louis de Valdecagnas, a Franciscan, descended from the ancient Jews; he was condemned for having preached the law of Moses; Juan de Santa-Fé, Albert Xuarez, and Paul d'Ayllon, aldermen or sheriffs; Pedro Gutierrez, a member of the municipality; and Juan de Leon, syndic of the city.

An *auto-da-fé* was celebrated in the same town on the 20th of May, 1563; seventeen persons were burnt in person, and four in effigy; forty-seven others were subjected to penances. I shall mention those distinguished by their rank or some particularity in their trials.

Don Philip of Arragon, son of the Emperor of Fez and Morocco, came to Spain while he was very young, and became a Christian; he had for his godfather Ferdinand of Arragon, Viceroy of Valencia, Duke of Calabria, and eldest son of the King of Naples, Frederic III. Neither his rank, as the son of an emperor, nor the advantage of having a prince for his godfather, were sufficient to prevent the inquisitors from exposing him to the disgrace of appearing in a solemn *auto-da-fé;* he was introduced in the ceremony with the paper mitre on his head, terminated by long horns, and covered with figures of devils. In this state he was admitted to public reconciliation, after which he was to be imprisoned for three years in a convent, then banished for ever from the

town of Elche where he had settled, and from the kingdoms
of Valencia, Arragon, Murcia, and Grenada. The inquisitors boasted much of the lenity of this sentence, and informed the public that it was occasioned by Don Philip's
having given himself up, instead of taking flight as he might
have done. It appears that, after his baptism, he had shewn
some interest and inclination to the sect of Mahomet; he had
also given assistance to some apostates, and had shewn himself a favourer and concealer of heretics. He was also accused of having made a compact with the devil, and having
practised sorcery.

The licentiate Antonio de Villena, a native of Albacette,
and a priest and preacher much esteemed at court, appeared
in the *auto-da-fé* in his shirt, with his head uncovered and a
flambeau in his hand; he abjured heresy as slightly suspected. He was reconciled, and condemned to one year's
imprisonment, without the privilege of celebrating the holy
mysteries; deprived for ever of the power of preaching,
banished from Madrid for two years, and obliged to pay five
hundred ducats towards the expenses of the holy office. His
crime was having spoken ill of the Inquisition, and of the
inquisitor-general Valdés, saying that he persecuted him,
and that he would find an opportunity of complaining to the
king. He had also been unfortunate enough to betray the
system of the prisons of the holy office, after having been detained there twice for suspicious propositions.

Juan de Sotomayor, of Jewish origin, and a native of the
town of Murcia, appeared in the *auto-da-fé* as a penitent,
with the gag and the cord round his neck. He was condemned to receive two hundred stripes, to wear the *San-
benito*, and to be imprisoned in the *House of Mercy* for life,
with a threat that he should be treated with still greater severity, if he presumed to converse with any one on the affairs
of the Inquisition. Juan de Sotomayor had already been
arrested and condemned to a penance, as suspected of

Judaism. When he was set at liberty, he conversed with several persons on the subject, repeated the confession he had made, and some other circumstances. This was the crime for which he was condemned to receive two hundred stripes, and to be imprisoned for life!

Francis Guillen, a merchant, of Jewish origin, appeared in the *auto-da-fé*, with several persons condemned to be *relaxed*, in virtue of a definitive sentence confirmed by the Supreme Council, which was to be read during the ceremony, with the charges against him. In the midst of the *auto-da-fé* Francis announced that he had new declarations to make. Immediately Don Jerome Manriquez (son of the Cardinal of that name, and who was afterwards inquisitor-general,) descended from the tribunal, took off the insignia of *relaxation*, and gave Francis those belonging to a person intended to be reconciled.

The history of this trial proves the arbitrary conduct, and the disorder with which the inquisitors pursued ard judged the causes, and executed their sentences.

More than twenty witnesses deposed that Francis Guillen had attended assemblies of the Jews in 1551, and the following years. He was sent to the secret prisons, and his sentence of *relaxation* was pronounced in December, 1561. The process having been sent to the Supreme Council, the Council remarked that two new witnesses having been heard before the end of the trial, their depositions had not been communicated to the condemned; in consequence they commanded that this formality should be fulfilled, and that the votes should be afterwards given, according to law. The inquisitors obeyed, but they did not agree on the sentence; some voted for relaxation, the others, that the trial should be suspended, and that the accused should be induced to acknowledge that which was admitted to be true, from the state of the depositions. Francis had three audiences, in which he confessed several other facts which related to himself, or concerned other persons ; the inquisitors then voted a second time for the definitive sentence. Francis was unanimously declared to be a false penitent, for having confessed only a part of his crimes, and he was condemned to be *relaxed*: but it was agreed that as he had concealed facts concerning persons of consideration, he should be induced to make a more extended declaration.

On the 27th of April, Guillen named twelve accomplices in his heresy, and ratified his declaration. On the 9th of May it was decreed that he should be told to prepare to die the next day. Francis inquired if his life would be spared supposing that he revealed all he knew: they replied that he might depend upon the clemency of his judges. He demanded another audience, named a great many persons as his accomplices, and designated Fray Louis de Valdecagnas, as the principal preacher of the party. Some time after he accused other persons. On the night of the 19th the inquisitors assembled, with the ordinary and consultors, and decided that Francis should appear in the *auto-da-fé* with the habit of the *relaxed* persons, in order to make him suppose that he was condemned to die; but that he should be reconciled, with the punishment of the *san-benito*, perpetual imprisonment, and confiscation.

When he was placed among those destined to the flames, Francis demanded an audience. The inquisitor Manriquez then informed him of his sentence; and when he was taken back to the prison, he made a new declaration against nine persons, alleging that he had forgotten them in his other depositions: he ratified these on the 22nd of the same month.

Some days after the inquisitor-general caused the tribunal to be visited; the visitor declared that the judges had acted contrary to the laws in conducting Francis to the *auto-da-fé* in the habit of a relaxed person, when they had decided on his reconciliation. The inquisitors endeavoured to justify themselves by saying that they thought it would frighten the accused into making new declarations. The visitor commanded that Francis should be reconciled and taken to the prison of the *Penitents*, likewise called that of *Mercy*.

Francis, who was probably a little deranged, declared several times that he had deceived the inquisitors by accusing some persons as heretics who were innocent, because he hoped that he should escape death by this proceeding. These words were reported to the inquisitors, and Francis was taken to the secret prisons. There was an act of accusation against him; he acknowledged all the articles of the fiscal, and affirmed upon oath that all his declarations were true; he ratified them, and begged that he might be pardoned. On the 19th of January, 1564, he was condemned to appear in the *auto-da-fé* with the gag, to receive two hundred stripes, and to pass three years in the house of *Penitence*. Francis suffered the stripes, but they did not render him more prudent, for he declared, even in the prison, that he was unjustly treated, for all that he had said was false, and dictated by fear.

In 1565, the Inquisition of Murcia received the visit of a new commissary, who obliged Francis to appear before him as a witness, to ratify a declaration which he had made against Catherine Perez, his wife, for Judaism. The following dialogue took place between the visitor and the witness:—

Do you remember making a declaration against Catherine Perez, your wife?—Yes.

What was that declaration?—It will be found in the writings of the trial. (The declaration was here read to Francis.)

Is what you have just heard true?—No.

Why then did you affirm that it was so?—Because I heard an inquisitor say it.

Are the declarations against other persons true?—No.

Why did you make them?—Because I perceived in the *auto-da-fé* at which I assisted, that the contents were read in the publication of the depositions, and I thought that if I declared it to be true, I should avoid death as being a good penitent.

Why did you make your ratification after the *auto-da-fé*, when the fiscal presented you as a witness against your wife, and other persons ?—For the same reason.

After this conversation, Francis was sent back to the prison, where he wrote a kind of memorial, in which he said that none of the witnesses were admissible against him, because they differed and contradicted each other in their declarations.

When the visitor was gone, the inquisitors recommenced their prosecution; the fiscal accused Francis Guillen of the crime of *revocation*, saying that he had imposed on them from fear, ignorance, or some other motive. When Francis again found himself in danger, he, as might have been expected, declared that his first depositions were true, and that the cause of his retracting was a mental indisposition, with which he had been affected. On the 10th November, 1565, Francis was condemned to appear in the *auto-da-fé* to receive three hundred stripes, and to pass the rest of his life in a prison. The punishment of imprisonment was commuted for that of serving in the galleys, as long as the strength and health of Francis allowed of it. The judges reserved the right of deciding this point themselves. The prisoner was conducted to the *auto-da-fé* on the 9th of December, and suffered the punishment of whipping; he was then transferred to the common royal prison.

After he arrived there, he wrote to his judges, declaring himself incapable of serving in the galleys. The tribunal revised the judgment, and sent him to the house of *Mercy*. This proceeding displeased the fiscal, who protested against it, saying, that the office of the judges did not extend beyond the sentence, and that they had not the right of commuting the punishment, without the consent of the inquisitor-general;

the affair stopped here, and Francis had been sufficiently punished for his indiscretion to render him more cautious for the future.

The irregularity and disorder of the proceedings of this tribunal may be seen still more clearly in another trial before the Inquisition of Murcia, about the same time, and which was undertaken in consequence of the depositions of Guillen. It was instituted against *Melchior Hernandez*, a merchant of Toledo, which he afterwards left to establish himself at Murcia. As he was descended from the Jews, he was suspected of being attached to the religion of his ancestors. After being taken to the secret prisons from the informations of seven witnesses, he had his first audience of *admonition* on the 5th of June, 1564 ; he was accused of having frequented a clandestine synagogue in Murcia, from 1551 to 1557, when the assembly was discovered ; and of having acted and discoursed in a manner that proved his apostasy. Two witnesses afterwards appeared, and the accused having denied all the charges, the publication of the nine deponents was given to him : he persisted in his denial, and by the advice of his defender, alleged that the evidence of the witnesses could not be admitted, as they contradicted each other, and several of them were known to be his enemies.

To prove this, and to challenge some other persons, he presented a memorial which was admitted, although it was afterwards considered to have failed in disproving the charges.

A new witness was heard, when Melchior fell dangerously ill. On the 25th of January, 1565, he made the sacramental confession, and on the 29th demanded an audience, when he said that his memory was bad, but he remembered being in a house in 1553, where a number of persons, whom he named, were assembled ; he denied having uttered anything concerning the law of Moses, and that the only thing he could reproach himself with, was not having declared that the others had made it the subject of conversation.

Four days after he declared that all that had been said in the assembly was spoken in jest. Several days after this he said that he had not heard what these persons said; and that he had affirmed the contrary, because the witnesses had deposed to that effect.

Another witness, who was in the prison, was produced, who deposed, that after Melchior had written his memorial, he formed a plan of escaping, and endeavoured to induce his companions to accompany him. The procurator-fiscal read to him the act of accusation, and he denied all that it contained.

At this period, the visitor Don Martin de Coscojales arrived, and examined the prisoner, who affirmed that if he had said anything, he was induced to do it from the fear of death. The advocate made his defence; Melchior wrote a memorial, which he read to his judges, in which he challenged several persons as if they had deposed against him.

On the 24th September, 1565, Melchior suffered the *question in caput alienum*, with the view of making him confess what he knew of some suspected persons, but he bore it without speaking. On the 18th of October he was declared to be a Jewish heretic, guilty of concealment in his judicial confession, and condemned to *relaxation*, as a false penitent and obstinate heretic.

Although the sentence was pronounced, it was resolved to press Melchior once more to reveal the truth. The *auto-da-fé* was to be celebrated on the 9th of December, 1565; he was exhorted on the 7th; he replied that he had confessed all he knew; yet, when he was told on the 8th to prepare for death, he demanded an audience, and declared that he had seen and heard the suspected persons and several others, and that they spoke of the law of Moses, but that he considered these conversations to be of no consequence, and a mere pastime.

On the 9th before daylight, Melchior was dressed in the

garb of the *relaxed* persons, when perceiving that his confessions were not sufficient to save him, he demanded an
audience, and mentioned the persons designated in the information, as forming part of the assembly, besides twelve
other individuals who had not been named to him; but he
added that he did not approve of their doctrine.

Some minutes after, finding that the marks of condemnation were not taken from him, he added the names of two or
three accomplices, declared the name of the person who had
preached on the Law of Moses, and even confessed that he
approved of some of the things which he had heard.

Lastly, when his confessions did not produce the effect he
wished, he said, that he really believed in what was preached
in the synagogue, and persisted in this belief for a year; but
that he had not confessed, because he thought there was no
proof of his heresy in the depositions of the witnesses. The
inquisitors decreed that Melchior should not appear in the
auto-da-fé of this day, and that they would consult on the
proper measures to be taken.

On the 14th of December, Melchior ratified his propositions of the 9th, but on the condition that all that had passed
should not separate him from the Catholic communion, or
cause him to be considered as a Judaic heretic. On the 18th
he desired another audience, and again confessed that he
believed in the Law of Moses. Yet on the 29th of June,
1566, he declared that the Holy Scriptures were read in the
assembly, that he believed part of what he heard, and had
consulted a priest on the subject; that the priest told him
it ought to be held in contempt, and that this decision had
regulated his subsequent conduct.

On the 6th of May, 1566, the tribunal assembled to
decide whether the definitive sentence pronounced against
Melchior should be executed. Two of the consultors voted
in the affirmative; the inquisitors, the ordinary, and the other
consultors agreed that Melchior had confessed enough to

entitle him to reconciliation.   In an audience on the 28th of May, the accused again asked pardon, alleging that he had only believed what he heard, until he was undeceived by the priest.   On the 30th he declared that he thought all he had heard necessary to salvation.

In the October following, he was again admitted to an audience, where he spoke against the inquisitor, who had received his confession on the day of the *auto-da-fé* (this was Don Jerome Manriquez); he complained of the ill treatment he had been subjected to, in order to obtain new declarations.   He acknowledged that his confessions on that day were true, but added that the presence of two inquisitors was necessary to prevent the abuse of authority which took place in his case.

The fiscal protested against the act of reconciliation granted to Melchior on the 6th of May, 1566, and demanded that the sentence of *relaxation* pronounced on the 8th of October, 1565, should be executed, because the accused had shewn no signs of true repentance, and would not fail to seduce others into heresy if he was pardoned.   The inquisitors consulted the Supreme Council, which decided that the prisoner should be examined again before the ordinary and consultors, and the affair submitted to the Council.   The sentence was pronounced on the 9th of May, 1567; three of the judges voted for the *relaxation*, and two for the *reconciliation* of the accused.

The Supreme Council decreed on the 6th of May, that Melchior should be *relaxed*, and the tribunal of Murcia pronounced a second definitive sentence according to the orders which they received.   The execution was to take place on the 8th of the following month.

In contempt of the rules of common law, Melchior was called up on the 5th, 6th, and 7th of June, and exhorted to discover his accomplices; as he did not know that he was already sentenced, he referred them to what he had confessed before. But when he found that he was to be arrayed in the habit of a *relaxed* person, he declared that he could name other accomplices. The inquisitor went to the prison, and Melchior designated another house where the Jews assembled, and named seven persons, whom he said he had seen there ; he also wrote a list of seven synagogues, and of fourteen persons who frequented them. He afterwards named another house of Judaic heretics.

He was conducted to the *auto-da-fé* with the other persons condemned to be burnt ; when he arrived at the place of execution, he demanded another audience, in which he named two other houses, and twelve heretics ; on being told that this declaration was not sufficient to confirm the result of the trial, he said he would endeavour to recollect others, and a few minutes after he denounced seven persons. Before the conclusion of the *auto-da-fé*, he desired to make a third confession, and named two houses and six individuals ; the inquisitors then agreed to suspend the execution, and to send Melchior back to the prison. This was what he wished, and on the 12th of June he signed his ratification, but when told that he was suspected of having other accomplices, he replied that he did not remember any other.

On the 13th, Melchior declared that he was mistaken in naming a certain person among his acomplices, but pretended to remember another house, and two persons whom he named.

The procurator-fiscal again spoke in favour of the *relaxation* of the accused, alleging that he had been guilty of concealment ; Melchior, supposing that his death was resolved upon, demanded an audience on the 23rd of June, and endeavoured to excite the compassion of his judges. " What more could I do," he exclaimed, " than accuse myself falsely. Know that I have never been summoned to any assembly, that I never attended them for any purposes but those of commerce."

Melchior was summoned to fifteen audiences during the months of July, August, and September; his replies were always the same. On the 16th of October another witness appeared, but Melchior denied his statement, as well as that of a witness who was examined on the 30th of December. Melchior wrote his defence, and demanded that his own witnesses should be heard, in order to prove that he was not at Murcia, but at Toledo, at the time specified by his accusers; but the inquisitors did not think the evidence offered by the accused sufficient to invalidate that of the witnesses against him.

Melchior was at last sentenced to *relaxation* for the third time, on the 20th of March; he, however, had not forgotten the means he had formerly used to save himself, and returned from the *auto-da-fé*. In five subsequent audiences, he made a long declaration against himself, and denounced a great number of persons. He was then told that he was still guilty of concealment in not mentioning several persons not less distinguished and well known than those he had already denounced, and that he could not be supposed to have forgotten them.

This proceeding destroyed the tranquillity which Melchior had hitherto shewn; and after a long invective against the inquisitors and all who had appeared on the trial, he said, "What can you do to me? burn me? well then be it so; I cannot confess what I do not know. Nevertheless know that all I have said of myself is true, but what I have declared of others is entirely false. I have only invented it, because I perceived that you wished me to denounce innocent persons; and being unacquainted with the names and quality of these unfortunate people, I named all whom I could think of in the hope of finding an end of my misery. I now perceive that my situation admits of no relief, and I therefore retract all my depositions, and now I have fulfilled this duty, burn me as soon as you please."

The trial was sent to the Supreme Council, which confirmed the sentence of *relaxation* for the third time, and wrote to reprimand the tribunal for having *summoned* the accused before them after passing the sentence, since an audience should only take place at the request of the accused.

Instead of submitting to this opinion, the inquisitors called Melchior before them on the 31st of May, and asked him if he had nothing else to communicate; he replied in the negative : they then represented to him that his declarations contained many contradictions, and that it was necessary for the good of his soul, that he should finally make a confession of the truth, respecting himself and all the guilty persons he was acquainted with.

These words shew the cunning of the inquisitors; their object was to induce the accused to retract his last declaration : but Melchior, knowing the character of the inquisitors, replied, that if they wished to know the truth, they would find it in the declaration which he made before the Señor *Ayora*, when he visited the tribunal. This writing was examined, and it was found that Melchior had said, *that he knew nothing of the subject on which he was examined.* The following conversation then took place :—

" How can this declaration be true, when you have several times declared that you have attended the Jewish assemblies, believed in their doctrines, and persevered in the belief for the space of one year, until you were undeceived by a priest ?"—" I spoke falsely when I made a declaration against myself."

" But how is it that what you have confessed of yourself, and many other things which you now deny, are the result of the depositions of a great many witnesses ?"—"I do not know if that is true or false, for I have not seen the writings of the trial ; but if the witnesses have said that which is imputed to them, it is because they were placed in the same situation as

I am. They do not love me better than I love myself; and I have certainly declared against myself both truth and falsehood."

"What motive had you for declaring things injurious to yourself, if they were false?"—"I did not think it would be injurious to me; on the contrary, I expected to derive great advantages from it, because I saw that if I did not confess anything, I should be considered as impenitent, and the truth would lead me to the scaffold. I thought that false-hood would be most useful to me, and I found it so in two *autos-da-fé*."

On the 6th of June Melchior Hernandez was informed that he must prepare for death on the following day. He was clothed in the habit of the persons condemned to be burnt, and a confessor was appointed for him. At two o'clock in the morning he demanded an audience, saying that he wished to acquit his conscience. An inquisitor, attended by a secretary, went to his cell; Melchior then declared "that at the point of appearing before the tribunal of the Al-mighty, and without any hope of escaping from death by new delays, he thought himself bound to declare that he had never conversed with any person on the Mosaical Law; that all he had said on this subject was founded on the wish to preserve life, and the belief that his confessions were pleasing to the inquisitors; that he asked pardon of the persons im-plicated, that God might pardon him, and that no injury might be done to their honour and reputation."

The inquisitor represented that he ought not to speak falsely, even from a motive of compassion for the denounced persons; that the declarations of the witnesses had every appearance of truth, and he therefore entreated him, in the name of God, not to increase his sins at the hour of death. Melchior merely repeated that all his former declarations were false. The royal judge condemned him to be strangled, and his body was afterwards burnt.

Some doubts may be entertained of the sincerity of the last declarations of Melchior Hernandez, but the extreme irregularity of the proceedings of the tribunal must be evident to every one. The intervention of the Supreme Council proves that the same system was pursued in the other tribunals, since it approved of their proceedings, and exercised the rights of revocation and censure.

In 1564 another *auto-da-fé* took place at Murcia, one person and eleven effigies were burnt; there were also forty-eight penitents, but the following circumstance was the cause of this ceremony being more particularly remembered. Pedro Hernandez had been reconciled in 1561, as suspected of Judaism. In 1564 he fell sick, and through the mediation of his confessor demanded an audience of the inquisitors. One of them went to his house, and Pedro told him that he had denied the crime of which he was accused, and had afterwards made a confession, alleging as an excuse for this conduct, that a French priest had given him absolution. He now confessed that this was not true, and that he wished to relieve his conscience by acknowledging it before he died. The inquisitors presented this declaration to the tribunal, which immediately caused Pedro to be taken from his bed, and conveyed to their prisons, where he died three days after.

Three other *autos-da-fé* took place at Murcia in the years 1565, 1567, and 1568, in which thirty-five persons were burnt, and a considerable number condemned to penances.

CHAPTER XXIV.

OF THE AUTOS-DÀ-FE CELEBRATED BY THE INQUISITIONS
OF TOLEDO, SARAGOSSA, VALENCIA, LOGRONO, GRE-
NADA, CUENCA, AND SARDINIA, DURING THE REIGN
OF PHILIP II.

Inquisition of Toledo.

On the 25th of February, 1560, the inquisitors of Toledo
celebrated an *auto-da-fé*, in which several persons were
burnt, with some effigies, and a great number subjected to
penances. This *auto-da-fé* was performed to entertain the
new queen, Elizabeth de Valois, the daughter of Henry II.,
King of France. It is rather surprising that this melancholy
ceremony was chosen to amuse a royal princess of thirteen
years of age, and who in her native country had been accustomed to brilliant festivals, suitable to her rank and age.
The Cortes general of the kingdoms was also assembled at
Toledo at the same time, to swear allegiance to the heir-pre-
sumptive, Don Carlos, so that this *auto-da-fé*, with the exception of the number of victims, was as solemn as any of
those in Valladolid.

In 1561, another *auto-da-fé* took place in the same town;
four impenitent Lutherans were burnt, and eighteen reconciled. Among those condemned to penances was one of the
king's pages, a native of Brussels, named Don *Charles Es-
trect*, but the young queen Elizabeth obtained his pardon.

On the 17th of June, 1565 (which was Trinity Sunday),
an *auto-da-fé* of forty-five persons was celebrated; eleven
were burnt, and thirty-four condemned to penances. Some
of these were Lutherans, but the greater number were Jews.
Among those designated as Protestants, some were called

Lutherans, others the *Faithful;* there was a third class called *Huguenaos,* after *Huguenots.*

Although the Inquisition of Toledo celebrated as many *autos-da-fé* as the other tribunals, I do not find any persons of distinction among the victims, until the *auto-da-fé* of the 4th of June, 1571, when two men were burnt in person, and three in effigy, for Lutheranism, and thirty-one individuals were condemned to penances. One of the men who were burnt ought to be particularly mentioned. He was called the *Doctor Sigismond Archel,* of Cagliari, in Sardinia. He had been arrested at Madrid, in 1562, as a dogmatizing Lutheran, and after remaining for a long time in the prisons at Toledo, he contrived to make his escape. He had not time to get out of the kingdom; descriptions of his person were sent to all parts of the frontier, and he was again arrested, and fell into the hands of his judges. He persisted in denying the facts imputed to him, until the *publication of the witnesses,* when he confessed, and maintained not only that he was not a heretic, but that he was a better Catholic than the *Papists.* He was condemned to be burnt, but persevered in his system, and declared that he was a martyr; he insulted the priests when they exhorted him, and was then gagged until he was fastened to the stake. The archers perceiving that he pretended to the glory of martyrdom, pierced him with their lances, while the executioners were lighting the fagots.

Inquisition of Saragossa.

The Inquisition of Saragossa also celebrated an *auto-da-fé* every year, when several people were burnt, and about twenty reconciled. Most of these were *Huguenots* who had quitted Bearn, to establish themselves as merchants in Saragossa, Huesca, Barbastro, and other cities. The progress which the Calvinistic doctrines had made in Spain, is proved by an ordinance of the Supreme Council, in which we read, that "Don Louis de Benegas, the ambassador of Spain at Vienna, informed the inquisitor-general, on the 14th of April, 1568, that he had learnt from particular reports, that the Calvinists congratulated each other on the peace signed between France and Spain, and that they hoped that their religion would make as much progress in Spain as in England, Flanders, and other countries, because the great number of Spaniards who had secretly adopted it might easily hold communication with the Protestants of Bearn, through Arragon." These, and other reports, induced the council to recommend additional vigilance to the inquisitors.

The following circumstance shews the injustice and cruelty of the Inquisition in a strong light. In 1578, a man was condemned, on suspicion of heresy, to receive two hundred stripes, to be sent for five years to the galleys, and to pay an hundred ducats. This crime was sending Spanish horses into France. Since the reign of Alphonso XI., in the fourteenth century, the introduction of Spanish horses into France was prohibited, on pain of death and confiscation; the particular circumstances which caused so disproportionate a punishment to the crime to be established are not known; it was however renewed in 1499, by Ferdinand the Catholic. No one will deny that the officers of the customs were the proper persons to arrest these smugglers, but when the civil wars broke out between the Catholics and Protestants in France, Philip thought proper to employ the Inquisition in repressing the practice, pretending, according to the Papal bull, that those who furnished the Protestants with arms, ammunition, &c., were favourers of heretics, and liable to suspicion of heresy. Philip II. commissioned the Inquisition of Logroño, Saragossa, and Barcelona, to take cognizance of all the crimes relating to the introduction of Spanish horses into France.

The Council of the Inquisition added a clause to the annual edict of denunciations, which obliged every Spanish Catholic Christian to denounce persons known to have bought horses to send to France, for the use of the Protestants. Besides these motives of religion, the zeal of the inhabitants was excited by the promise of a reward.

In 1575, the punishment of whipping was decreed for this crime ; but though the law is expressed in general terms, the following event shews that it was only inflicted on those whose power and credit were small. In 1576, a Commissary of the Inquisition met a servant of the viceroy of Arragon going into France with two horses ; he seized the horses, but allowed the servant to go away. He gave an account of his proceedings to the inquisitors, who approved of his conduct in not arresting the servant ; their opinion was confirmed by the Supreme Council. The inquisitors were on the point of writing to the viceroy, to demand an explanation of the conduct of his servant, and the destination of the horses, when the council ordered them to desist, if they thought it would be disagreeable to the viceroy.

This law was afterwards applied to those who were suspected of smuggling, and to those who favoured the practice. In 1607, Philip III. ordered the inquisitors to offer rewards to those who intercepted this trade, and the people were at last inspired with so great a horror of it, and those who practised it became so odious, that the government was obliged to declare that the misfortune of being convicted and punished for this crime, did not exclude a person from enjoying honours and offices.

The inquisitors, always eager to extend their jurisdiction, wished to have the right of undertaking the trials for smuggling saltpetre, sulphur, and gunpowder ; this attempt did not succeed, and was in fact the cause of their being deprived of the powers bestowed on them by Philip, respecting the introduction of horses into France.

Inquisition of Grenada.

In the yearly *autos-da-fé* of the Inquisition of Grenada,

there generally appeared about twenty condemned persons ; for although the Morescoes who denounced themselves were treated with great clemency, yet there were many who refused to accuse themselves, either from the fear which the severity of the Inquisition inspired, or because they were persuaded that those who declared they had been treated with great gentleness, did not dare to assert the contrary, and others after having emigrated to Africa, had returned to Spain, without considering the danger they were in of being arrested by the Inquisition.

On the 27th of May, 1593, a grand *auto-da-fé* took place at Grenada, five individuals were burnt in person, and five in effigy ; eighty-seven were condemned to penances. The only considerable person among these, was Donna Inez Alvarez, the wife of Thomas Martinez, alguazil to the royal chancery. She was condemned to be burnt, but making a confession on the scaffold, she was reconciled.

The proceedings were the same in the Inquisition of Valencia. The number of Morescoes who relapsed into Mahometanism, and refused to accuse themselves, was so considerable, that many appeared in every *auto-da-fé*, either to be burnt as *impenitent*, or to suffer different penances.

Inquisition of Logroño.

The Inquisition of Logroño was not less active in prosecuting heretics. An *auto-da-fé* was celebrated every year, composed of about twenty persons condemned for Judaism, and some others for different heresies, particularly Lutheranism, for after the time of Don Carlos de Seso, corregidor of Toro (who was arrested at Logroño, in 1558, and burnt in the following year at Valladolid), there were always some individuals to be found who professed his opinions, and succeeded in obtaining Lutheran books. The council which was informed of this circumstance, wrote to the inquisitors in

1568, enjoining them to redouble their vigilance, in preventing the introduction of heretical books, and informed them, that Don Diego de Guzman, ambassador to England, had written that the Protestants of that country, boasted that their doctrine was well received in Spain, particularly in Navarre, and that it was even preached there.

While the inquisitors of Logroño were preparing for the the *auto-da-fé* of 1570, they had the mortification of being blamed for their conduct in two instances by the Supreme Council. One was in the case of Lope de Arguinaraz, and the other in that of Juan Floristan Maestuz, who were accused of Judaism. Arguinaraz denied the fact, was tortured, and then confessed having committed the actions, but asserted that he did not do them with the sentiments and belief that he was accused of. He ratified his confession some days after, and demanded reconciliation. The judges when they assembled to vote for the definitive sentence, resolved to refer the case to the Supreme Council, which pronounced, that they had not sufficiently examined the accused on the sentiments and intentions which he entertained in committing the actions he had confessed, and commanded them to return to that stage of the trial and vote according to the result. The inquisitors sent an account of the motives of their conduct, and gave notice that they should wait until the council had considered their observations, before they proceeded further. The reply to this message enjoined the inquisitors to execute the orders they had received, immediately, and harshly reproached them for not having obeyed them in silence, and for having failed in their duty, in the interrogation; when they ought to have examined the accused on his doctrine.

In the other affair of Juan Floristan Maestuz, the council expressed its surprise, that the inquisitors did not examine the accused on some heretical propositions which were proved against him, though he refused to confess even during the torture ; and above all, that the inquisitor, who had qualified the accused as *negatively* perjured, had voted for his reconciliation, since the constitutions of the holy office prohibited the reconciliation of those who persisted denying the charges proved against him.   The reconciliation of the two prisoners took place in the *auto-da-fé*.

An *auto-da-fé* took place at Logroño, on the 14th of November 1593, where forty-nine persons appeared; five were burnt in person, seven in effigy ; the others were subjected to penances.

The custom of celebrating one *general auto-da-fé* every year, was so well established, that when the inquisitors of Cuença, in 1558, gave up a man to secular justice, in a *particular auto-da-fé*, it was doubted if the rules of the holy office permitted it; and though the council decided in the affirmative, the custom of reserving all the condemned persons for the general *auto-da-fé*, prevailed, unless any very particular circumstance, made it necessary to deviate from it.

Inquisition of Sardinia.

I have already stated, that Philip II. introduced the Spanish constitution into Sardinia, in 1562.   Don Diego Calvo first began to put it into execution, but the novelty made so great an impression on the inhabitants, that they demanded that the tribunal should be visited.   This commission was confided by the inquisitor-general, to the licentiate, Martinez del Villar, who fulfilled it in 1567.   He received so many complaints, against the inquisitor Calvo, that he was recalled, and Martinez took his place ; he however did not remain there long, but was succeeded by Don Alphonso de Lorca.

In 1575, an appeal was made to Rome against the tribunal of Sardinia, and Philip II. interposed in its defence.   Don Francis Minuta, a Sardinian gentleman, had been subjected to a penance for bigamy, and condemned to serve for three years as a common soldier in the galleys of Spain, and without the liberty of going out of the Goletta, in Malta. He had not been there a month, before he contrived to escape, and returned to Sardinia; the inquisitor-general then ordered him to be again arrested, and doubled his punishment; Minuta was taken back to the Goletta, whence he escaped a second time, and fled to Rome. He represented to the Pope that he was not guilty of bigamy, and that the manner in which the inquisitor-general had treated him, was unjust, since he had left the fort with the permission of the governor. Don Francis demanded, and obtained of the Pope, two briefs of commission: the first for the examination of the principal question, that of bigamy; the other to judge of the reasons which he advanced against the sentence, which prolonged his detention. In the interim, the inquisitor of Sardinia, declared him a contumacious fugitive, and condemned him to eight years labour in the galleys. The apostolical judge required the inquisitor to suspend the proceedings, he informed the inquisitor-general, who applied to the king; whose interference they had never requested in vain. Philip II. wrote to Don Juan de Zuñiga, his ambassador at Rome, to demand a revocation of the briefs of commission, and to obtain permission for the inquisitor of the island to continue the prosecution, or that it might at least be referred to the inquisitor-general, to whom the right of judging the cause belonged. The Pope revoked his bulls to please the King of Spain, and the unfortunate Don Francis Minuta, experienced the fate which he might have expected; for in cases of this nature, the inquisitor-general always delegates one of the members of the accused tribunal, to be the examining judge, on pretence that they are in possession of the writings of the trial.

Don Andrea Minuta, brother to Don Francis, was also condemned to the same punishment for three years. He fled to Rome, and appealing to the Pope, obtained a brief of commission for a bishop of Sardinia. Philip II. made the same request to the Pope, and Andrea was treated in the same way as his brother.

Don Pedro Guisa, Baron de Casteil, in Sardinia, was prosecuted and condemned for the same crime of bigamy ; but having learnt what had happened to the two brothers Minuta, he had recourse to entreaties and humiliations, to appease the inquisitor-general and obtain a commutation of his punishment.

CHAPTER XXV.

OF THE LEARNED MEN WHO HAVE BEEN PERSECUTED BY THE INQUISITION.

AMONG the many evils which the Inquisition has inflicted on Spain, the obstacles which it opposes to the progress of the arts and sciences, and literature, are not the least deplorable. The partisans of the holy office have never allowed this, yet it is a certain truth. The apologists, of whom I speak, maintain, that the Inquisition only opposes the invasion of heretical opinions, and leaves those who do not attack the doctrines of the faith, in perfect liberty,—consequently, that it does not influence the arts and sciences. If this pretension was just there are many excellent works which might be read, and which are only prohibited because they contain doctrines opposed to the opinions of the scholastic theologians.

St. Augustine was certainly a very zealous partisan of religion in its greatest purity, yet he made a great distinction between a dogmatic proposition and one not defined. He acknowledged that in the second case a Catholic was free to maintain the argument for, or against, according to the dictates of his reason. St. Augustine did not suppose that the freedom of opinion would be opposed by such theological censures, as the qualifiers of the holy office have established in modern times. They have had great influence on the prohibition of books, and even on the condemnation of their authors. They are employed against the first, on pretence that they contain propositions *favourable to heresy, ill sounding, savouring of heresy, fomenting heresy, or tending to heresy ;* against the authors in declaring them suspected of having adopted heresy in their hearts.

In the present time the qualifiers have extended the prohibitions, by saying that the books contained propositions *offensive to persons of high rank, seditious, tending to disturb public tranquillity, contrary to the government of the state, and opposed to the obedience which has been taught by Jesus Christ and his apostles.*

These censures are generally passed by scholastic theologians. The work of *Filangieri,* entitled, *The Science of Legislation,* was censured by Fray Joseph de Cardenas, a Capuchin, who thought himself competent to do it, though he had only read the first volume of the Spanish translation, which contained only half of that of the original.

The prohibition applies most to those books which treat of theology, and the canonical laws, particularly if they are well written, and contain the doctrines taught by the fathers, the councils, and even by the popes who reigned in the seven first centuries, but which have been forgotten or opposed by the theologians of the barbarous times, who wished to establish the system of the union of the two powers in the person of the sovereign pontiff.

The theological censures likewise attack works on philosophy, on civil and natural law, and on the people. Those books which have been published on mathematics, astronomy, physic, and other subjects which depend upon these, have not been more highly favoured. The Spaniards have, consequently, been deprived of the advantages which other nations have derived from all the recent discoveries.

Since the establishment of the holy office, there has scarcely been any man celebrated for his learning, who has not been prosecuted as a heretic. In the list which follows, I shall not (unless particular circumstances render it necessary) include any learned man who has been prosecuted for having embraced Judaism, Mahometanism, or any sect equally prohibited by the Catholic religion. Those only will be mentioned who suffered in their liberty, honour and fortunes, from not having adopted erroneous scholastic opinions.

The names are disposed in an alphabetical order, that the reader may be enabled to find the article he wishes to consult more quickly.

Abad-la-Sierra (D. Augustin), bishop of Barbastro. See Chapter 29.

Abad-la-Sierra (D. Manuel), Archbishop of Selimbria, *ibid.*

Almodobar (Duke of). See following Chapter.

Aranda (Count d'). *Ibid.*

Arellano (D. Joseph Xavier Rodriguez d'), Archbishop of Burgos. See Chapter 29.

Avila (the venerable Juan d'), secular priest, born at Almodovar del Campo, surnamed the Apostle of Andalusia. See Chapter 13 and 14.

Azara (Doctor Nicholas d'). See the following Chapter.

Balvoa (Doctor Juan de), doctoral canon of the cathedral of Salamanca, and law professor in the university of that city. He was one of the most distinguished literati of his age. Nicolas Antonio only mentions one of his works, entitled *Salmantine Lessons.* He composed several others, one of which would have caused him to be arrested by the Inquisition, if he had not been protected by the inquisitor-general, Cardinal Don Antonio Zapata, and by some of the councillors of the tribunal. It was a memoir which he had drawn up and presented in 1627, to Philip IV., in the name of the Universities of Salamanca, Valladolid and Alcala. The object of this memoir was to induce the king to refuse the permission which the Jesuits had requested, to change the *Imperial* College of Madrid into a university.

The Jesuits denounced the work, and qualified some of the propositions as *erroneous, offensive to pious ears, scandalous and injurious to the government, and to the regular ecclesiastics of the Society of Jesus.*

The council caused the memoir to be examined by *qualifiers,* who declared that it did not merit theological censure, and the council abandoned the affair.   The Jesuits then employed the influence of the Count Duke d'Olivarez with the king, but the attempt was unsuccessful.   The other work which is attributed to Balvoa, is perhaps that which was printed at Rome in 1636, in the printing-office of the apostolic chamber. It is written in Latin in quarto, and bears the name of Alphonso de Vargas de Toledo, with this title, *An Exposition made by Alphonsa de Vargas to the Christian Kings and Princes, of the Stratagems and political Artifices which the Members of the Society of Jesus employ to establish a universal Monarchy in their favour, a Work which proves the deceit of the Jesuits towards the Kings and Nations who have received them favourably ; their Perfidy and Disobedience, even to the Pope, and the immoderate Desire of Innovation which they have always shewn in Matters of Religion.*   It has been said that this work was printed at Frankfort, with the exception of the justificatory pieces.   The author advances and proves heavy charges against the Jesuits.

Bails (D. Benedict), professor of mathematics at Madrid, and author of a work on that science, used in the schools. The Inquisition instituted his trial towards the end of the reign of Charles III., as suspected of atheism and materialism. Bails was deprived of the use of his limbs, and incapable of attending to his affairs; yet he was arrested and taken to the prisons of the holy office, with one of his nieces, who obtained permission to share his captivity, that she might continue to

render him the assistance which his situation rendered necessary. He prepared his defence in the best manner he was
able, and before the publication of the depositions, he acknowledged enough to shew that he was sincere in his confession and repentance. When he was examined on his in-
ternal belief, he declared that he had had some doubts on
the existence of a God, and the immortality of the soul, but
that he had never actually been an atheist, or a materialist;
that during his solitude in the prison, he had reflected on the
subject, and was ready to abjure all heresies, and particularly
those of which he was suspected. He demanded reconciliation, and a penance, which he promised to accomplish as well
as his health would allow him. His situation was considered;
and instead of sending him to a convent, whither his niece
could not have followed him, he was kept for some time in
the secret prisons of the holy office: he was afterwards removed to his own house, which served for his prison, and he
was obliged to pay for his food during his imprisonment, and
subjected to several other penances, one of which, was being
obliged to confess to a priest, who was appointed, three
times in the year; at Christmas, Easter, and Pentecost.

Balza (Francis), Franciscan, and a celebrated preacher in
the reign of Charles III. When the Jesuits were driven
from Spain, he openly preached against the relaxed morals
of the age; he inveighed against the authors who had introduced and propagated them, and endeavoured to inspire
people with a horror of reading their works. As some of
these authors were Jesuits, he declaimed violently against
those persons who blamed the king for the measures he had
taken, to drive them out of the kingdom. Balza was denounced at Logroño, and the inquisitors gave him to understand, that he would be treated with severity if he did not
change his tone.

Barriovero (Doctor Ferdinand de), theologist of the church
of Toledo, and a professor in the university. He was tried

in 1558, for approving the doctrine of the Catechism of Don Bartholomew Carranza. He allayed the storm by retracting, when he received the king's order to do so, and by sending his recantation to the Pope, when the Archbishops of Granada and Santiago, and the Bishop of Jaen adopted that measure.

Belando (Fray Nicolas de Jesus), Franciscan: he was prosecuted on account of his *Civil History of Spain*. In this work he gives an account of all the events from the accession of Philip IV. to 1733. The inquisitors prohibited this book entirely from political motives, and not from anything relating to doctrine; their judgment against Belando was given on the 6th of Dec. 1774. The inquisitors had no respect either for the license at the beginning of the book, the dedication to Philip V., or for the favourable opinion of an enlightened member of the Council of Castile, who was commissioned by his majesty to examine it, before he allowed it to be dedicated to him. The author appealed against the sentence and demanded to be heard: he offered to reply to all the observations, and to make any alterations or suppressions in his work, which the tribunal should suggest. This attempt of Belando to defend his book was considered as a crime, and he was confined in the dungeons of the holy office, where he suffered the harshest treatment. He only left them to be imprisoned for life in a convent, and he was prohibited from ever composing another work. He was stripped of the honours which distinguished him in his order, and more severe penances were inflicted on him than if he had been an heretic.

Bercial (Clement Sanchez del), priest, archdeacon of Valderas, and dignitary of the church of Leon. He was prosecuted and punished in the time of Charles V. for Lutheranism. He was condemned for some propositions in a work called *Sacramental*. In 1559, the inquisitor-general Valdez placed this book in the *Index*.

Berroçosa (Fray Manuel Santos), author of a work called *Essays on the Theatre of Rome.* He was imprisoned by the Inquisition of Toledo, because he spoke of the court of Rome in his Essays, in a manner displeasing to the Jesuits and inquisitors. The proceedings in this trial were so arbitrary, that the work in question was not examined until the affair was nearly finished. The writings of this trial were taken from the archives of the Inquisition, for some unknown reason. In 1768 they were laid, by the king's order, before the council extraordinary of bishops, who were assembled to consider the affairs of the Jesuits.

Blanco (Don Francis), archbishop of Santiago. See Chapter 29.

Brozas (Francis Sanchez de Las), generally called *el Brocense;* he was born in the village of Las Brozas, from whence he took his name. He was one of the greatest *humanists* of his age, and the most distinguished Spaniard of that party in the time of Philip II. During this reign he published several works, which are mentioned by Nicolas Antonio in his catalogue. The severe *Justus Lipse* calls him the *Mercury and Apollo of Spain*, and Gaspard Scioppius, the *divine man.* He was prosecuted by the Inquisition of Valladolid several times for some propositions contained in his works, but principally in a book in octavo, entitled: *Escolias à las quatro Sylvas escritas en verso heroico por Angelo Policiano, intituladas Nutricia, Rustico, Manto y Ambra*, viz. " Commentaries on the four *Sylvas*, written in heroic verse by Angelo Politiano, called *Nutricia, Rustico, Manto*, and *Ambra. El Brocense* completely satisfied the qualifiers, and his work was not inscribed on the Index.

Barruaga (Don Thomas Saenz), archbishop of Saragossa. See Chapter 29.

Cadena (Louis de la), second chancellor of the university of Alcala de Henares, and nephew of Doctor Pedro de Lerma, who was the first who possessed that dignity. Cadena was

one of the most learned men of his time ; he understood
Hebrew, Greek, Arabic, and other eastern languages; he
wrote Latin with the greatest elegance, and enjoyed a high
reputation among the literati. The learned Alvaro Gomez
de Castro says, in his *History of Cardinal Ximenez de Cisneros*, that he had formed the design of destroying the bad
scholastic taste which reigned in the universities. This enterprise cost Cadena dear : those who were attached to the
opinions of the schools denounced him to the Inquisition of
Toledo, as suspected of Lutheranism ; the archbishops Ximenez de Cisneros and Fonseca, who protected the persecuted
members of the university of Alcala, were no more, and Cadena was obliged to follow the example of his uncle, and fly
to Paris to escape the dungeons of the holy office. He was
received as a doctor in the Sorbonne, and died a professor
in that celebrated house.

Campomanes. See following Chapter.

Cano (Melchior), Bishop of Canary. See Chapter 29.

Cañuelo (Don Louis), advocate of the king's council
during the reign of Charles III. He was subjected to a
penance, and abjured, *de levi*, for having inserted certain
propositions in some numbers of a periodical work called
The Censor, which appeared without the name of the author.
Cañuelo often published declamations against superstition in
the *Censor*, in which he proved the evil which might be produced by a blind and vain confidence in the indulgences and
pardons obtained by those who wore the scapulary of our
Lady of Mount Carmel, in reciting *neuvaines*, and in the
other outward exercises of devotion, which he said were de-
trimental to the purity of religion. He also presumed to
ridicule the pompous titles given by the monks to the saints
of their orders : thus St. Augustine was called the *Eagle of
Doctors;* St. Bernard, *Honied ;* St. Thomas, *Angelic;* St.
Buonaventure, *Seraphic ;* St. John de la Croix, *Mystic ;* St.
Francis, *Cherubim ;* and St. Dominic, *Burning*. He one

day offered a recompense to any one who would apply the name of *Cardinal* to St. Jerome, and that of *Doctor* to St. Theresa de Jesus. The monks whom he ridiculed could not forgive his boldness, and they persecuted him with virulence. The numbers of his work were prohibited, although they were already published ; and he was forbidden to write on any subject which had the least relation to doctrine, morals, or the received opinions on piety and devotion.

Cantalapiedra (Martin Martinez de), professor of theology, and very learned in the Oriental tongues. He was prosecuted during the reign of Philip II. for publishing a book called *Hippotiposeon*, &c. ; it was prohibited, and inserted in the *Index* of Cardinal Quiroga in 1583. This author was suspected of Lutheranism from having too much enforced the necessity of consulting the original books of the Holy Scriptures, in preference to the interpretations: he abjured *de levi*, submitted to a penance, and was forbidden to write again. This example gives us an idea of the judgment and discrimination of the judges and qualifiers.

Carranza (Don Bartholomew), archbishop of Toledo. See Chapters 32, 33, and 34.

Casas (Don Fray Bartholomew de Las), a Dominican, bishop of Chiapa and afterwards of Cuzco, resigned his see to live in Spain; he was the defender of the right and liberty of the native Indians. He wrote several excellent works which are mentioned by Nicolas Antonio. In one of these, he endeavours to prove that the kings have not the power of disposing of the property and liberty of their American subjects, and of giving them to other masters, either under a feodal tenure, or from a right of conquest. This work was denounced to the Inquisition as opposed to the declarations of St. Paul and St. Peter, concerning the submission of serfs and vassals to their lords. The author was much grieved when he heard that it was intended to prosecute him ; but the council only required of him, in an official manner, the remittance of the work and the manuscript. It was afterwards printed several times in other countries, which is mentioned by M. Peignot in his, *Dictionnaire Critique, Littéraire et Bibliographique des Livres remarquables qui ont été brulés, supprimées ou censurés.* Casas died at Madrid in 1566 at the age of ninety-two. He had the pleasure of seeing another of his works in favour of the Americans, approved by the censors, although it had been criticised by Juan Gines de Sepulveda. Charles V. ordered this writing to be suppressed, although it was favourable to the royal authority : he likewise made several ordinances in favour of the Americans, and if they had been executed, fewer reproaches would have been bestowed on the Spaniards who governed the new world.

Castillo (Fray Ferdinand del), a Dominican and one of the most illustrious men of his order. He was implicated in the proceedings against the Lutherans at Valladolid in the year 1559. Fray Dominic de Roxas, Pedro Cazalla, and Don Carlos de Seso, wishing to prove that their opinions on *justification* were orthodox, declared that they were the same as those of Fray Ferdinand del Castillo, who was universally acknowledged to be eminent for virtue and wisdom ; he had been a member of the College of St. Gregory at Valladolid, afterwards professor of philosophy and theology at Grenada : he was at this time a preacher of great eminence at Madrid. The three witnesses ratified their declarations on the 3rd, 4th, and 5th, of October, 1559 ; they were to be burnt on the 8th of the same month. Fortunately for Fray Ferdinand, the three witnesses had not positively asserted that he had maintained the doctrine of *justification* in the manner that they did, or in the same sense, but that he had expressed himself in such a manner that it might be supposed. Fray Ferdinand was ordered to repair to Valladolid, where he was confined in the College of St. Gregory, and was summoned to appear before the tribunal. He cleared himself

from the charges brought against him, and even obtained a
certificate of his acquittal, that his honour and reputation
might not be affected. He returned to Madrid, where he
was made a prior, and was afterwards sent to Medina with
the same dignity; lastly he was appointed preacher to Philip
II. This prince often consulted him on difficult affairs, and
appointed him to accompany the Duke of Ossuna in his
embassy to Lisbon. Castillo was one of those who took
the greatest part in inducing the Cardinal King, Don Henry,
to call Philip II. to succeed him on the throne of Portugal,
and he was subsequently made preceptor to the infant Don
Ferdinand. He wrote the history of the order of St.
Dominic, a work which is much esteemed by the learned of
the present day. Castillo died on the 29th of March, 1593:
his life had been a model of austerity, and he fasted on bread
and water three times a week.

Centeno (Fray Pedro), an Augustine monk. He was
one of the most learned men of his order, and one of the most
distinguished literati in Spain, during the reigns of Charles
III. and Charles IV. Centeno incurred the hatred of all the
monks, priests, and seculars, by his periodical work, entitled,
The Universal Apologist for all unfortunate Authors. Centeno attacked the bad taste which predominated in literature,
with the most delicate irony, so that the scholastic theologians, who knew nothing of good taste, dreaded to come
under his examination. The ironical praise which he lavished
on them, was more to be feared than his sharpest satire : his
papers were universally read with pleasure, and his decisions
generally adopted by his readers. The prejudices which prevailed in Spain did not fail to create him many enemies. He
relied on the purity of his religious opinions, and the extent
of his knowledge; but he was denounced at the holy office,
and the denunciations were as different as the stations and characters of those who attacked him. He was accused of *impiety* (a crime then considered in Spain as equal to *atheism,*

or *materailism*), at the same time that others accused him of being a Lutheran and a Jansenist. The great reputation enjoyed by the accused, the protection which the Count de Florida Blanca, first secretary of state, afforded him, the fear that hatred, envy and resentment had induced the accusers to invent calumnies, and the impossibility that Centeno could be at the same time an atheist and a Lutheran, prevented the tribunal from sending him to their dungeons; they therefore confined him in the Convent of St. Philip, where he dwelt, commanding him to appear before the tribunal when summoned. His great knowledge of doctrine, enabled him to defend himself with advantage : if his discourse had been printed, his fame must have much increased by it ; yet he was condemned as *violently* suspected of heresy, and was compelled to abjure and perform different penances. This treatment plunged Centeno into a profound melancholy, which alienated his reason ; he died in this state in the convent of Arenas, where he was confined.

The principal accusations against him were, 1st. That he had disapproved of the *Novenas*, the rosaries, processions, stations, and other pious exercises. This charge was supported by a quotation from the funeral oration of a nobleman, in which he had said, that beneficence was the favourite virtue of the deceased ; that it was in the constant practice of it, that true devotion consisted, and not in the mere exterior exercises of religion, which required neither care nor trouble, or any sacrifices of money, or other things. 2d. That he denied the existence of *limboes*, places destined to receive the souls of those who die before the age of reason, without receiving baptism : the argument brought to support this charge was the suppression of the question and answer on the article *Limbo*, which he had obliged the author of the Catechism to make. This work had been printed for the use of the charity-schools at Madrid, of which he had been appointed censor ; the accused replied to the first accusation, by giving clear and perfect explanations, founded on the texts of Scripture and the Holy Fathers, and on the principles of true devotion: he proved the perfect connexion of his defence with the expressions he had used in the sermon, of which he produced the original copy as a proof of his innocence. On the second charge, he said that the existence of *Limbus* was not defined as an article of faith ; that it ought not to be mentioned in a catechism, where, according to his opinion, nothing ought to be considered but *doctrine ;* and that he had suppressed the question, that the Christians might not confound this subject which was still an object of discussion among the Catholics, with those already decided by the Church. He was formally summoned to declare whether he believed in the existence of *Limbus;* he replied that he was not obliged to answer, because it did not relate to an article of faith ; but that as he had no motives to conceal his opinions, he would confess that he did not believe in the existence. He demanded permission to compose a theological treatise, in which he offered to demonstrate the truth of what he advanced, humbly submitting to the decisions of the Church: this permission being granted, he wrote an hundred and twenty pages in folio, in close lines, so that it would form an octavo volume. I had the curiosity to read it, and was astonished at his immense and profound erudition: this writing contains all that the Fathers and the great theologians have said since the time of Jesus Christ, particularly since St. Augustine, on the future lot of those who die without receiving baptism, and before they have committed any mortal sin. His defence could not save him. A barefooted Carmelite and a Minime were the principal qualifiers, who censured Centeno as *violently suspected of heresy.*

Cespedes (Doctor Paul de), born at Cordova, prebendary of the Cathedral in that city, and residing at Rome. The Inquisition of Valladolid tried him in 1560, for some letters which he had written to Don Bartholomew Carranza, Archbishop of Toledo, and which were found among the papers of that prelate, with the copies of his replies. In one of these letters dated from Rome, on 17th of February, 1559, he gives him an account of his proceedings in his favour, and allowed himself to speak ill of the inquisitor-general and the Inquisition of Spain. Cespedes was a great literati, a great painter, and poet, and a very clever modeller in wax: he composed a poem, in stanzas of eight verses, on *Repentance.* Juan de Verzosa and Francis Pacheco, (both mentioned with approbation by Nicolas Antonio, have highly praised this poem. Cespedes continued to reside at Rome, and thus the inquisitors of Valladolid could not execute their projects of vengeance.

Chumacero (Don Juan de). See the following Chapter.

Clavijo y Faxardo (Don Joseph de), principal director of the museum of natural history at Madrid, and a learned man, who had a great taste for science. The Inquisition of the *Court* tried him on the suspicion that he had adopted the antichristian principles of modern philosophy. He was confined to the city of Madrid, which was fortunate for him, as he thus preserved his honour and his office ; he appeared privately before the tribunal, and was only condemned to private penances ; he also made his abjuration, *de levi,* with closed doors, in the hall of the tribunal. It is true that the proofs against him were weak, and he gave to his propositions an air of Catholicism. He had lived for some time in Paris, where he had been intimate with Buffon and Voltaire. He edited a journal, called, *The Thinker.* M. Langle, in his *Travels in Spain,* says, that this work is without merit; if this author judged truly, it would, perhaps, be the only truth in his book. Clavijo was appointed editor of the *Mercury,* by the government, he also published a translation of " Buffon's Natural History," with notes. As this book is written with great purity of style, and without gallicisms, it is an important acquisition to those who seek a work rich in the beauties of the Spanish language. The Count d'Aranda also gave him the direction of a company of tragic actors: Clavijo endeavoured to fulfil the intentions of the minister, but religious fanaticism arrested the progress of the design.

Clement (Don Joseph), bishop of Barcelona. See the following Chapter.

Corpus Christi (Fray Mancio de), Dominican, doctor and professor of theology in the university of Alcala de Henares. He was tried by the Inquisition of Valladolid for having given a favourable opinion of the Catechism of Carranza. On the 21st of February, 1559, he remitted those of the doctors of his university, who had carefully examined some propositions of a doubtful nature, and of which they acknowledged the orthodoxy. He escaped the dungeons, by retracting, at the request of Philip II. A brief of Gregory XIII. obliged him to restore the definitive sentence which he had passed on the Catechism and other works of Carranza, and in which he had condemned an hundred and thirty-one propositions of that prelate. On the 17th of October, 1559, he addressed a letter to the inquisitor-general, in which he asked pardon, and submitted toa ny penances which might be imposed on him.

Cruz (Father Louis de la), Dominican, disciple of Don Bartholomew Carranza de Miranda, a member of the college of St. Gregory, at Valladolid, and extremely well versed in doctrine and theology. He was imprisoned in the dungeons of the Inquisition of Valladolid, for being implicated in the affair of Cazalla and his companions. The quotations made by the friends of Cazalla from his works, created a suspicion that he was a Lutheran: it is true that he had held a regular correspondence with Carranza, and had given him his opinion of his Catechism. He was accused of having bribed the minister of the holy office to obtain information of his old master; but he vindicated himself by proving that he had acquired some knowledge of the affair, in his conversations with Melchior Cano, and with one of the condemned Lutherans whom he had exhorted. Fray Louis was arrested in the month of June, 1559, and on the 7th of August he drew up a writing of six pages, in which he made many confessions. He soon became subject to fits of insanity, owing to his anxious thoughts during his trial. In June, 1560, he was removed to the ecclesiastical prison of the bishop, that he might be taken care of. It was impossible to prove any of the charges against him, yet the Inquisition kept him in prison until Carranza was released. At last, after five years of captivity, he abjured, *de levi*, and was sentenced to a seclusion of a few years as a penance.

Cuesta (Don Andrea de la). See Chapter 29.

Cuesta (Don Antonio de la), archdeacon of the cathedral of Avila. The Inquisition of Valladolid ordered him to be arrested in 1801, as suspected of Jansenism and heresy; but he fled to Paris, where he lived during the five years of his trial : it would have been much longer if government had not interposed, as will be seen in the following article.

Cuesta (Don Jerome de la), penitentiary canon of the cathedral of Avila. He was arrested for Jansenism, and heresy, while his brother Antonio was pursued, to whom he furnished the means of flight, at the expense of his own safety. He passed five years in the prisons of the Inquisition, and he would have been detained for a much longer time, but for the solicitations addressed to Charles IV., by persons of the highest rank, who obtained permission to cause the original writings of the trial to be laid before his majesty. Don Jerome proved that the prosecution of himself and his brother originated in the intrigues of Don Raphael de Muzquiz, bishop of Avila, and formerly confessor to the queen, and archbishop of Santiago, and of Don Vincent Soto de Valcarcel, bishop of Valladolid. When the depositions of the witnesses were read to Don Jerome, his great penetration enabled him to recognise them, and he clearly proved their injustice. The Archbishop of Santiago, made many representations to the king against the two brothers, the Inquisitors of Valladolid, and some members of the Supreme Council; he did not even spare Don Raymond Joseph de Arce, archbishop of Saragossa, patriarch of the Indies, and inquisitor-general: he accused them all of partiality in favour of the two brothers, who were besides, countrymen of the chief of the holy office. The tribunal of Valladolid, pronounced Don Jerome innocent; the votes were divided in the council: the king then examined the writings, and declared, that from the reports he had received, the two brothers were innocent of the crimes of which they were accused. He authorized Don Antonio to return to Spain, created him and his brother, knights of the order of Charles III., and commanded the inquisitor-general to appoint them honorary inquisitors. Don Manuel Gomez de Salazar, bishop of Avila, (who in quality of Inquisitor of Valladolid, and member of the council, had taken a great part in this intrigue,) received an order from his majesty to reinstate the brothers in their stalls. This is one of the very rare instances, where the King of Spain took an active part in the affairs of the Inquisition, and one of the still more rare occurrences where innocence has triumphed.

Delgado (Don Francis), archbishop of Santiago. See Chapter 29.

Feyjoo (Benedict), Benedictine, born in the Asturias, and a distinguished literati. He was one of the first who restored good taste in Spain: the works which he has composed, have been enumerated by Don Juan Sempere y Guarinos in the *Catalogue of the Authors who flourished during the Reign of Charles III.* This learned man was denounced at the different tribunals of the Inquisition, as being suspected of the different heresies of the fifteenth century, and of that of the ancient Iconoclasts; most of his accusers were

ignorant and prejudicial monks, of whom he had made enemies by the arguments in his *Critical Theatre* against false
devotion, false miracles, and some superstitious customs.   It
was fortunate for the author that the council of the Inquisition was well acquainted with the purity of his principles
and Catholicism.   Although the progress of knowledge has
been extremely slow in Spain, it must be confessed that it
has even penetrated into the interior of the *Holy House* during
the last part of the eighteenth century.

Fernandes (Juan), doctor of theology, prior of the cathedral of Palencia.   He was prosecuted from the declarations of
some Lutherans who were executed in 1559, particularly
that of Fray Dominic de Roxas, who quoted several propositions of Fernandez, in which he pretended to find, especially on the subject of justification, the same opinions as his
own.   The fiscal presented Fray Dominic as a witness in the
trial of Fernandez : he persisted in his declaration (he was
already condemned to *relaxation*, but did not know it), and
expected to be reconciled as a penitent.   Fernandez, however only received a reprimand for not having observed in
his discourse, the prudence which became a doctor of theology, at a period when heresy was so common in the kingdom.

Frago (Don Pedro), bishop of Jaca.   See Chapter, 29.

Gonzalo (Don Vittoriano Lopez), bishop of Murcia. *Ibid.*

Gorrionereo (Don Antonio), bishop of Almeria. *Ibid.*

Guerrero (Don Pedro), archbishop of Grenada.   *Ibid.*

Grenada (Fray Louis de), *Ibid.*

Gracian (Fray Jerome), Carmelite, born at Valladolid, and
the son of Diego Gracian, secretary to Charles V., and Jane
Dantisque, daughter of the ambassador of Poland, at the
court of the emperor.   He was a doctor of theology, and
professor of philosophy, at the university of Alcala.   He
wrote several works of a mystical nature, and some others on
literary subjects, which are mentioned by Nicolas Antonio.
He was prior of a convent of barefooted Carmelites at

Seville, which he founded when St. Theresa and her community, of whom he was the director, were attacked by the Inquisition. The tribunal of Seville prosecuted him as a heretic, of the sect of the *Illuminati*; but his trial failed for want of proof. Father Jerome experienced many vicissitudes; but as they have been related by historians it is unnecessary to mention them here.

Gudiel de Peralta. See the following Chapter.

Gonzalez (Gil), Jesuit, born at Toledo in 1532. He was prosecuted by the Inquisition of Valladolid, in 1559, for having begun a Latin translation of the Catechism of Carranza. When this prelate was informed that his work was to be translated into the language of theologians, he made some corrections in it, thinking it not sufficiently clear, and in July requested Gil Gonzalez to undertake the task. St. Francis de Borgio, having heard of the trial of the archbishop, commanded Gonzalez to communicate to the Inquisition all that he had been requested to do. He obeyed; and in August informed the inquisitor-general of the order he had received, and his promptitude in submitting to it. In September he renewed his declarations, gave up the Castilian copy of the Catechism, with the corrections of Carranza, and all that he had written of the translation. He thus escaped persecution, and died in peace at Madrid in 1596.

Illescas (Gonsalvo de). See Chapter 13.

Iriarte (Don Thomas), born in the island of Canary, master of the archives of the minister for foreign affairs, and of the first secretary of state, author of a poem on *Music*, a volume of *Fables*, and other poetical works. He was prosecuted by the Inquisition of Madrid, during the last years of the reign of Charles III., as suspected of professing the antichristian philosophy. He was confined to the city, and received an order to appear when he was summoned: the proceedings were private, and he replied in a satisfactory manner to the accusations, but the inquisitors did not think fit to acquit him; they declared him to be *slightly suspected* : he abjured and obtained absolution in private, the penance imposed was likewise private, and few persons knew that he had been tried. Don Thomas Iriarte, had two brothers, one called Don Dominic, who concluded a treaty of peace with the French Republic at Basle; and the other, Don Bernard, counsellor of the Indies, and knight of the order of Charles III.

Isla (Francis de), Jesuit. He was the author of several works, during the reign of Charles III.; and also published under a feigned name, the *History of the famous Preacher Fray Gerund de Campazas otherwise called Zotes, written at Madrid in 1750 and 1770, by the Licentiate Don Francis Lobon de Salazar.* This work is a fine satire, in two volumes, against the preachers who make a bad use of texts by quoting them in the wrong place, and distorting their meaning to support an extravagant proposition. This work produced very beneficial effects in Spain; all the preachers dreaded the epithet of *Fray Gerund.* This fictitious hero might be called the Don Quixote of the pulpit, since the effects of this romance were the same as those of Don Quixote de la Mancha, which was intended to cure the Spaniards of their ridiculous mania for books of chivalry. The monks united against this work ; they declared it to be impious, injurious to the ecclesiastical state, and the author suspected of all the heresies of those who speak with contempt of mendicant friars. The holy office received an infinite number of denunciations against this work. The qualifiers were of opinion that it ought to be prohibited, because the author, in ridiculing those who made a bad use of the sacred text, had fallen into the same error in composing the sermons preached by his hero. These volumes were consequently forbidden, but a publisher at Bayonne reprinted them with a third volume composed of the different essays which had appeared in Spain, either for or against the history of Fray Gerund.

The true author did not put his name to the work, but he was known, and the Inquisition having arrested him, reproached him for what he had done. Isla alleged his laudable intention of correcting the defects which had been introduced into the pulpit by bad preachers, and the affair finished there. The Jesuits at that time had still some power at Madrid, and many of their society were judges of the holy office.

Jesus (St. Theresa de). See Chapter 27.

Jovellanos. See Chapter 43.

Joven de Salas (Don Joseph Ignacio), born in one of the towns of the Pyrenees, advocate to the king's councils, and a very learned man. He was chosen by several grandees of Spain to defend the right of their families to the succession of the elder branches, and for other interesting trials. He was denounced to the Inquisition for having read prohibited books : the inquest did not furnish sufficient proofs to authorize imprisonment. His aversion for popular commotions, his love for social order, the absence of all the royal family, and the impossibility of resisting the invasion, induced him in 1808 to submit to the conqueror. The great merit of Joven obtained him the office of a counsellor of state under King Joseph : for this reason the political inquisitors who surround the throne of Ferdinand VII., induced him to banish this respectable old man, who lives at Bordeaux full of years and virtues.

Lainez (Diejo). See Chapter 29.

Laplane (Don Joseph), bishop of Tarrazona. *Ibid.*

Lara (Don Juan Perez de). See the following Chapter.

Lebrija (Antonio de). See Chapter 10.

Ledesma (Fray Juan de), Dominican, professor of theology in the college of St. Peter Martyr, at Toledo. He was tried by the Inquisition of Valladolid in 1559, for having expressed a favourable opinion of the Catechism of Carranza ; the proceedings were transferred to the tribunal of Toledo, which continued the trial without imprisoning Fray Juan, who was only confined to his college. Fray Juan declared that he had not perceived the heresies in Carranza's work, for that relying on the learning, virtue, and zeal of the author, he had read it without examining it particularly; he added, that as he had not fallen into any error knowingly, which he acknowledged as such, he abided by the censures of the qualifiers. He abjured *de levi;* a small private canonical penance was imposed on him to be performed in secret, and he received the absolution *ad cautelam.*

Leon (Fray Louis de), an Augustine. He was born in 1527, of Lope de Belmonte, a judge and member of the chancery of Grenada, and of Donna Inez de Valera, his wife. He distinguished himself by the purity of his language and the beauty of his verses, which are looked upon as models of elegance. He took the monastic habit at Salamanca in 1544. His discernment was very great, and his knowledge of theology was so profound, that he was not surpassed by any of his contemporaries, and had very few rivals. He understood the Greek and Hebrew languages sufficiently to read them, and wrote Latin with peculiar elegance. He composed several works in verse and prose, which are mentioned by Nicolas Antonio. Experience has shewn that it is impossible to possess superior talents without exciting envy; it is not therefore surprising that he was denounced to the holy office of Valladolid as being suspected of Lutheranism, at the time that he was professor of theology at Salamanca. Although he was innocent, he was kept in prison for five years. The solitude in which he lived during this period was so painful to him, that he could not help commemorating it in one of his works, taking for his text the 26th Psalm. Having been acquitted, he resumed his professorship; but his long captivity, the inaction in which he had lived, and his grief at being dishonoured, had

considerably injured his health.   He however had still sufficient strength to compose in 1558, rules for the use of his
order.   He died at Madrid on the 23rd of August, 1591,
during the chapter of which he was named vicar-general.

Lerma (Pedro de), doctor, professor of theology and first
chancellor of the university of Alcala.   He was very learned
in the oriental languages, which he had studied at Paris,
where he had obtained the degree of Doctor in Theology :
he was also one of the Junta convoked at Valladolid in 1527,
by the inquisitor-general Manriquez, to examine the works
of Erasmus.   He endeavoured to revive good taste in ecclesiastical literature in the university of Alcala, exhorting
every one to take their opinions from the ancient sources.
The scholastic theologians who did not understand the oriental languages, and who were accustomed to read the councils and the Holy Fathers only in the quotations of other
authors, adopted the usual resource of the envious; they
denounced him to the Inquisition of Toledo as suspected of
Lutheranism.   Pedro being informed that he would be
arrested, fled to Paris, where he died dean of the doctors of
the Sorbonne, and professor of theology in that school.

Ludona (Fray Juan).   See Chapter 29.

Linacero (Don Michael Raymond), canon of Toledo,
preceptor of the archbishop of that city, the Cardinal de
Bourbon.   In 1768 he received an admonition from the
holy office, while he was only curé of Ugena, because he had
in his possession the *Ecclesiastical History* written by
Racine.   This work had not yet been prohibited; but an
order of the king forbade any person to read it, and the
inquisitors compelled Linacero to give it up.   After the
king's death the tribunal prohibited this work as infected
with Jansenism.

Melendez Valdéz (Don Juan), a native of Estremadura ;
after having been a professor at Salamanca, he was appointed judge of the royal court of appeal at Valladolid,

by Charles III. Charles IV. promoted him to the office of the king's attorney in the royal Council of Castile, the chamber of the alcades of the royal house and of the Court of Madrid. He was the Spanish Anacreon of the nineteenth century, and the fame of his odes will last while good poetry is made. One of these gave rise to several denunciations in 1796, and Melendez was accused of conversing like a man who had read prohibited books, such as Filangieri, Puffendorf, Grotius, Rousseau, Montesquieu, and others. This attack failed from want of proof. In 1808 Melendez was barbarously treated by assassins of the same description as those who massacred the Marquis de Perales and the intendant Truxillo, at Madrid ; the Marquis del Socorro, at Cadiz ; the Count del Aguila, at Seville ; the Count de Torre del Fresno, at Badajoz, and many distinguished Spaniards in other places. Melendez survived almost by a miracle, and sought safety in the French army. King Joseph appointed him a counsellor of state. Melendez accepted the place for the same reasons as *Joven de Salas;* he afterwards incurred the same fate, and died at Montpellier in 1817. The *Mercury* of France and the other Parisian journals have published his panegyric. I shall therefore only add that at Valladolid in 1788 he gave me a small poem of his own composition to read ; it was called *The Magistrate.* When the second edition of his poems appeared, this poem was inserted, and on my inquiring the reason, he gave me the following account of it. " As I was always much occupied in composing poetry, even after I was appointed judge of the royal court of appeal, some of my colleagues harshly censured my conduct, saying that the composition of lyric and amatory verses was very unbecoming the dignity of the magistracy : one of them said maliciously, that I might perhaps know what a troubadour was, but not what a magistrate should be. I then composed this poem, and intended to publish it, but afterwards changed my mind, that it

might not occasion a suspicion that I wished to revenge
myself." This poem in my opinion has much merit, and I
hope it will be included in the first edition of the poems of
Melendez.

Macanaz, (Don Melchior de).   See the following Chapter.

Mariana (Juan de), Jesuit.   He was a natural son of
Juan Martinez de Mariana, afterwards canon and dean of
the college of Talavera de la Reyna, where Mariana was
born in 1536.   When he had finished his studies at Alcala,
and had become well skilled in the oriental tongues and in
theology, he quitted Spain to travel in foreign countries: he
professed theology in Rome, Sicily, and at Paris.   When he
returned he wrote his history of Spain, and was often consulted by the government in affairs of a difficult and delicate
nature.   He was chosen as an arbitrator in the great question concerning the royal Polyglott Bible of Antwerp, and,
contrary to the wishes and intrigues of his brethren, he
decided in favour of Benedict Arias Montanus.   In 1583 he
was commissioned to form an Index, in which he left out the
work of St. Francis Borgia.   The Jesuits, who are not
accustomed to forgive such conduct, did not afterwards
treat him with the consideration to which he was entitled.
He proved the vices of the government of their society in a
work called, *Of the Maladies of the Society of Jesus.*   This
work was not published till after the death of the author;
but his brethren were acquainted with some parts of it
which increased their hatred towards him.   In 1599 he
published and dedicated to Philip III. his treatise *de Rege
et Regis institutione*, which was burnt at Paris by the common executioner.   He also published in 1609, seven treatises in one folio volume, one of them, is on the *Exchange of
Money*, and another on *Death and Immortality*.   These
works exposed him to prosecutions from the government and
the holy office.   I have read his defence, and the doctrine he
professed is so pure and solid, that I am persuaded it would

be favourably received if it was printed. The sentence of
the king was more lenient than he could have expected,
after having, in his dedication to that monarch, shewn himself the advocate of the *regicide*, disguised under the name
of the *tyrannicide*. He did not escape so well from the
inquisitors : they made some retrenchments in his work on
the *Exchange of Money*, and it was prohibited until he had
been punished. A penance was imposed on the author, and
he was confined a long time in his college. He died at
Toledo in 1623, at the age of eighty-seven. Nicolas Antonio mentions other works by the same author. In the
Dictionnaire of Peignot there are some details which might
be interesting to a literary person.

Medina (Fray Michel de). See Chapter 29.

Meneses (Fray Philip de), Dominican, and professor of
theology at Alcala de Henares ; he gave a favourable opinion of the Catechism of Carranza. The Inquisition of
Toledo received from that of Valladolid the writings of his
trial, summoned Fray Philip, and condemned him to the
same punishment as Fray Juan de Ludeña.

Merida (Pedro de), canon of Palencia : he was commissioned by Carranza to take possession of the see of Toledo in his name, and administer to the archbishopric. He
was mentioned by Pedro Cazalla and others, as partaking
their sentiments on the subject of *justification*. He corresponded with Carranza, and in his trial the Inquisition took
advantage of several letters in which he spoke ill of the holy
office. He was arrested at Valladolid, abjured *de levi*, was
subjected to a penance and a pecuniary penalty.

Moñino (Don Joseph). See the following Chapter.

Molina (Don Michel de), bishop of Albaracin. See
Chapter 29.

Montanus (Benedict Arias). *Ibid.*

Montemayor (Prudence de), Jesuit, born at Ceniecros,
in Rioja, and professor of theology at Salamanca. He com-

posed several works, which are mentioned by Nicolas Antonio. The Inquisition of Valladolid tried him on suspicion
of Pelagianism, arising from some theological conclusions
which he maintained and printed in 1600. He defended himself and explained what he had advanced like a true Catholic. The inquisitors ceased to prosecute him personally,
but they prohibited his conclusions. The Jesuits have
always been reproached with their adherence to the system
of the heresiarch Pelagius, on the subject of grace and free
will. Montemayor afterwards endeavoured to vindicate his
honour and that of his order, in a discourse entitled, *A Reply
to the Five Calumnies invented against the Society of Jesus,
and promulgated in the City of Salamanca.* He died in
that city in 1641, at a very advanced age.

Montijo (Donna Maria-Frances Portocarrero, Countess
of), a grandee of Spain : she deserves a distinguished rank
among the literati of Spain. Her claims to celebrity are not
only supported by her translation of the *Christian Instructions on the Sacrament of Marriage,* by M. Le Tourneux,
but by her great love for good literature, and by her efforts
to render the taste for it more common. Her amiable and
benevolent character made her house a favourite resort for
many virtuous and enlightened ecclesiastics : among these
may be distinguished Don Antonio de Palafox, bishop of
Cuença, and brother-in-law to the Countess; Don Antonio
de Tabira, bishop of Salamanca; Don Joseph de Jeregui,
preceptor to the Infants of Spain; Don Juan Antonio Rodrigalvarez, archdeacon of Cuença; Don Joachim Ivarra,
and Don Antonio de Posada, canon of St. Isidore at Madrid.
All these ecclesiastics, and the Countess herself, were the
victims of the calumnies of fanatical priests and monks, who
were the partisans of the Jesuists and of their maxims on discipline and morals; they were accused of Jansenism. The
hatred of their enemies was so great, that Don Balthazar
Calvo, canon of St. Isidore, and Fray Antonio de Guerrero,

a Dominican, declared in the pulpit, that there existed in one of the first houses in the capital a conventicle of Jansenists, protected by a lady of distinction: they took care to speak of her in such a manner that the person could not be mistaken. The nuncio of the Court of Rome informed the Pope of all these circumstances, and his Holiness immediately addressed letters of thanks to these two preachers and some other individuals, for the zeal they had shewn in defending the faith. These letters were, in a manner, the signal for a denunciation against all persons suspected of Jansenism, and did not fail to produce that effect. Besides the suspicion of Jansenism, the Countess of Montijo was accused of holding a religious and literary corrspondence with Monsignor Henri Gregoire, then bishop of Blois, and one of the most catholic and learned men in France, a Member of the Institute, and author of several works, one of which was a *Letter to the Inquisitor-general of Spain*, in which he invites him to propose the suppression of the Inquisition of which he is the head. The accusers supposed Monsignor Gregoire to be the head of the Jansenists in France; but they concealed the fact that this bishop had several times exposed himself to death to give the victims of the revolution the last spiritual aid, and to maintain the Catholic religion when Robespierre endeavoured to destroy it. The accusers, who dwelt upon the mention which had been made of the Countess in the national council of France, held by the bishops who had taken the oaths, and of which Monsignor Gregoire was a member. The inquisitors received secret informations of this affair; but no facts or heretical propositions were proved, and they had not courage to issue the orders for an arrest. The rank and birth of the accused gave them the means of putting an end to the persecution: a sort of court intrigue, however, caused the Countess to be sent from Madrid. She retired to Logroño, where she died in 1808, with the reputation of being virtuous, and charitable to the poor.

Mur (Don Joseph de). See following Chapter.
Olavide (Don Paul). *Ibid.*
Palafox y Mendoza (Don Juan de). See Chapter 30.
Palafox (Don Antonio de), bishop of Cuença. He was prosecuted by the Inquisition of Madrid on suspicion of Jansenism, but his trial did not proceed further than the *preparatory instruction*, as nothing but conjectures could be brought against him. He was tried at the same time with his sister-in-law, the Countess de Montijo. This prelate made a learned and energetic representation to the king, in which he proved that the ex-jesuits who had returned to Spain were the authors of the prosecutions against himself and his friends; and they left nothing undone to ruin those who were not of their party.

Pedroche (Fray Thomas de), Dominican, and a professor at Toledo; he gave a favourable opinion of the Catechism of Carranza, and received the same treatment as Fray Juan de Ledesma.

Peña (Fray Juan de la), Dominican, director of the studies of the college of St. Gregory at Valladolid, and a professor of Salamanca. In 1558 he gave a favourable opinion of the Catechism of Carranza. He was summoned by the inquisitors on the 15th of March, 1559, to qualify twenty propositions of an author whose name they concealed from him; on the 5th of April following, he gave his reply, containing nineteen pages of writing. He declared that the propositions were Catholic; that some of them were ambiguous, which might cause them to be considered as tending to Lutheranism, but that it did not appear that the author had advanced them with any bad intention. The Archbishop Carranza, being thrown into prison on the 22nd of August in the same year, De la Peña became alarmed, and wrote to the Inquisition, saying, that he had been intimate with that prelate, because he believed him to be a good Catholic; that this reason had also prevented him from denouncing a favour-

able opinion which he had expressed of one Don Carlos de
Seso, one of the Lutherans who were tried in this year; that
Carranza had not condemned him, because he did not think
him an heretic, although he had advanced propositions which
were tinctured with Lutheranism. De la Peña added, that,
seeing the archbishop arrested, he had confessed this, lest his
silence might be construed into a crime. His precaution was
unavailing. De la Peña appeared guilty, from the opinion he
had given of the Catechism, and two other accusations were
brought against him: the first was, that he had said that
there was no foundation for denouncing the proposition of
Carranza, which states, *that it is not yet decided if faith
was lost in committing a mortal sin;* the second, that he
had asserted when the archbishop was arrested, *that even if
he was an heretic, the holy office ought to overlook it, lest the
Lutherans in Holland should acknowledge him as a martyr,
which they had already done to several individuals who had
been punished.* De la Peña's reply displeased the inquisitors; they sharply reproved him, condemned him to several
penances, and commanded him to be more cautious for the
future.

Perez (Antonio), secretary of state. See Chapter 35.

Quiros (Don Joseph), priest, advocate to the king's council
at Madrid. Being informed of the persecution of Belando
by the Inquisition, on account of his *Civil History of Spain,*
he drew up a writing, in which he endeavoured to prove
that the inquisitors ought to have examined the author before they condemned his work. This liberty cost him dear;
although he was seventy years old, and his legs swelled
continually, he was sent to the secret prisons, and as if this
was not sufficient, he was kept during the months of February
and March in a cold damp chamber, where he was obliged
to endure all the rigour of the season and nearly sunk under
it. Philip V. was at last informed of the state to which
Quiros was reduced, and he obtained his liberty after forty-

four days of suffering, on the condition of never again writing on the affairs of the Inquisition, unless he wished to experience greater severity.

Ramos de Manzano (Don Francis). See following Chapter.

Regla (Fray Juan de). See Chapter 29.

Ricardos (Don Antonio), Count de Trullas in his own right, and of Torrepalma in that of his wife and cousin : captain-general of the royal armies, and commander-in-chief of that of Roussillon against the French republic in the years 1793 and 1794. He was suspected of being an *esprit fort*, or an incredulous philosopher, and the dean of the inquisitors invited him to attend the *auto-da-fé* of Don Paul de Olavide ; they thought that he might consider some of the declarations as relating to himself, though his name was not mentioned, particularly as he had been very intimate with Olavide, and their religious sentiments were very similar on some points. This was the only mortification which the Inquisition could inflict upon Ricardos, as they had not sufficient proof to authorize a prosecution.

Ripalda (Jerome de), Jesuit, born at Teruel in Arragon towards the end of the sixteenth century and the beginning of the seventeenth. He was one of the most learned theologians of his order ; he professed theology, and wrote two Treatises, one mystic and the other on *Christian Doctrine,* which has been used by the schools for near a century, with the exception of some alterations which have been made in the new editions of his Catechism. Nicolas Antonio says that he died, with the reputation of being a saint, in 1618, aged eighty-four. He had been for some time director to St. Theresa de Jesus. It is possible that the forty-four last years of Ripalda's life may have been exemplary, but the impartiality of an historian compels me to say, that Jerome Ripalda was tried by the Inquisition of Valladolid as an *illuminati*, or *quietest*, and tinctured with the heresy of *Molinos;* that he confessed some of the charges, asked pardon, and implored his judges to be merciful ; and that a penance was imposed on him in 1574, as being *suspected de vehementi.* The sincere repentance which he shewed induced the inquisitor-general, Quiroga, to shorten the duration of his penance ; I must add that the purity of Ripalda's faith and morals after this event were such as to render him worthy of the esteem and respect of mankind.

Ribera (Don Juan de). See Chapter 30.

Roda (Don Manuel de.) See following Chapter.

Rodrigalvarez (Don Juan Antonio), priest, canon of St. Isidore at Madrid, afterwards archdeacon of Cuença, and provisor and vicar-general of that diocese ; he wrote several historical works. Rodrigalvarez was implicated in the denunciation of Don Balthazar Calvo, his colleague, who giving way to personal considerations, and instigated by the ex-jesuits lately arrived from Italy, inflicted such cruel mortifications on Rodrigalvarez and Posada his colleague, that they were obliged to complain to the Prince of Peace, and to implore his assistance. The trial begun by the Inquisition did not furnish sufficient proof of their guilt, and it was not continued. The trials of Don Antonio Posada, and Don Joachim Ibarra, mentioned in the article *Montijo,* finished in the same manner.

Roman (Fray Jerome), an Augustine, born at Logroño. He was very learned in the oriental languages, and directed his attention towards the study of sacred and profane history. In prosecuting this design, he travelled over a part part of Europe, examining the different archives, and making extracts of all that appeared likely to increase the success of the great works which he had projected. Being appointed historian to his order, he published the history of it from the year 1569: in it he gives an account of the lives of the saints and illustrious men who had belonged to it, with many interesting details. His wish to publish the historical facts which he had collected during his travels, induced him to write a book called the *Republics of the World;* in this work he treats very learnedly of the ancient and modern republics : it was printed at Medina del Campo, in 1575, and again in 1595 at Salamanca.   Unfortunately for the author it contained several truths which displeased some persons powerful enough to injure him ; he experienced some persecution, and the Inquisition of Valladolid reprimanded him, and ordered his work to be corrected.   He died in 1597, leaving some MSS. which are mentioned by Nicolas Antonio.

Salazar (Fray Ambrose de), Dominican, and professor of theology at Salamanca.   The Inquisition of Valladolid tried him in 1559, on two accusations : the first was founded on the declarations of Fray Dominic de Roxas and Fray Louis de la Cruz, during their imprisonment : they imputed to Fray Ambrose some propositions which tended to Lutheranism ; the second charge was founded on the favourable opinion which he had given of the Catechism of Carranza. The trial was not continued, on account of the death of Fray Ambrose in 1560, in the thirty-eighth year of his age : it was supposed that fear, and his imprisonment in the holy office, where Carranza was detained, hastened his death. He left, in order to be printed, some *Commentaries on the first part of the Sum of St. Thomas.*

Salas (Don Raymond de), born at Belchite in Arragon, was a professor at Salamanca, and one of its greatest literati : he was prosecuted in 1796 by the Inquisition of Madrid, on suspicion of having adopted the principles of the modern philosophers, Voltaire, Rousseau, and others, whose works he had read.   He acknowledged that he was acquainted with their works, but added that he had only read them in order to refute them, which he had done in several public theses, maintained at Salamanca by some of his pupils, under his direction.   All these theses were introduced in the trial.

He replied in a satisfactory manner to all the allegations, and the qualifiers did not find anything in his writings which deserved theological censure. The judges not only acquitted him, but on being informed that Father Poveda, a Dominican, had intrigued against him, thought that he had a right to a public reparation. On the 22nd of October, in the same year, they sent their sentence and the writings of the trial, together with the considerations and the points of doctrine on which they were founded, to the Supreme Council, at the same time expressing their opinion on the right of Salas to a reparation.

Father Poveda, by his intrigues, caused the trial to be sent back to the inquisitors, with an order to make fresh inquiries, which was done, but the qualifiers and judges persisted in their first sentence. The intrigues again began in the council, which returned the trial to the Inquisition a second time, with an order to make another inquest extraordinary: a third qualification, and a third sentence were the result, confirming the innocence of Salas. This was not what was intended, the accused had a powerful enemy in the council: this was Don Philip Vallejo, archbishop of Santiago, and governor of the Council of Castile; he had been inimical to Salas, from having had certain literary discussions with him at the university of Salamanca, when he was bishop of that see. The trial was suspended, to afford time for the archbishop to procure new denunciations, to add to those he had already obtained. Salas requested that his imprisonment might be ameliorated, and that he might only be confined to the city of Madrid. The council refused this favour; he then demanded permission to apply to the king, but this was also refused. He was at last condemned to abjure *de levi ;* received the absolution and censures *ad cautelam ;* and was banished from the capital. He retired to Guadalaxara, and there complained to his sovereign of the injustice of the Council of the Inquisition. Charles IV. ordered the writings of the trial to be sent to his minister of justice. Cardinal de Lorenzana, inquisitor-general, endeavoured to prevent it, but his efforts were ineffectual. When the affair was examined by the minister, the intrigue was discovered, and a resolution was formed to expedite a royal ordinance, forbidding the inquisitors to arrest any individual for the future, without first informing the king of their intention. The decree was drawn up by Don Eugene Llaguno, minister of justice, and he presented it to his majesty for signature: the king told him that it must first be shewn to the Prince of Peace, as he had taken part in the deliberation, and would see if it was properly drawn up. Unfortunately for mankind, this delay of one day gave Vallejo time to renew his intrigues, so that the Prince of Peace changed his mind, and the royal decree was so different from what was expected, that the affair was ordered to be left in the same state.

St. Ambrose (Fray Ferdinand de), Dominican; he was a learned man, and well-skilled in the conduct of affairs. The Inquisition of Valladolid tried him in 1559: he was accused of having taken measures in favour of Carranza; of having profited by his sojourn at Rome in the same year, to prejudice his Holiness against the tribunal, to engage him to cause the trial to be transferred to Rome, and not to allow the archbishop to be arrested. The prosecutions soon ceased, because the accused remained at Rome.

Salcedo. See following Chapter.

Salgado. Ibid.

Samaniego (Don Felix-Maria de), lord of the town of Arraya, and an inhabitant of Laguardia in the province of Alava. He composed some fables and lyric poems of great merit, and was one of the greatest Spanish literati, during the reign of Charles IV. The Inquisition of Logroño prosecuted him, on suspicion of having embraced the errors of the modern philosophers, and of having read prohibited books. He was on the point of being arrested, when discovering it by chance, he immediately set off for Madrid, where Don Eugene Llaguno, the minister of justice, and his friend and countrymen, privately arranged his affairs with the inquisitor-general.

Samaniego (Don Philip).   See following Chapter.

Santo Domingo (Fray antonio de), Dominican, rector of the college of St. Gregory at Valladolid, was prosecuted by the Inquisition of that city in 1559 and 1560.   The proceeding was founded on several accusations; in 1558, he had approved of some reprehensible propositions in the Catechism of Carranza: he was also accused of having said in 1559, *that the arrest of this prelate was as unjust as that of Jesus Christ;* that the prosecutions of the tribunal were of the same character; that Fray Melchior Cano ought to die first, because he was the most guilty; and that his death would be as agreeable to God as the sacrifice of mass.   The accused was imprisoned, and a penance was imposed on him.

Santa Maria (Fray Juan de), barefooted Franciscan, and confessor to the Infanta Maria-Anne of Austria, Empress of Germany, and daughter to Philip IV.   In 1616 he published a work called *Christian Republics and Politics*, which he dedicated to Philip III.   Having occasion to say in this work that the Pope Zachariah had deposed Childeric, King of France, and crowned Pepin in his place, he added; " *It is from this time that we date the right which the Popes have arrogated to themselves of deposing and establishing kings.*"
The Inquisition receiving information of it, reprimanded the author, and altered the sentence as follows: " *It is from this time that the Popes have made use of their right of deposing and establishing kings.*"

Sese (Don Joseph de.)   See following Chapter.

Siguenza (Fr. Joseph de), Jeronimite of the Convent of the Escurial; he was born in the town of that name.   He was one of the most learned men of the reigns of Philip II., and Philip III., and well versed in history and the oriental

languages. In 1595 he published the life of St. Jerome, and
in 1600, a history of his order. He experienced much persecution, because he was one of the best preachers of his
time, and the most esteemed by the king. The other monks
(whose sermons were not so well received) denounced him
to the Inquisition of Toledo, as suspected of Lutheranism.
He remained in seclusion for nearly a year, in the monastery
of *La Sisla*, belonging to his order, and he was obliged to
appear before the tribunal whenever he was summoned. He
justified himself, was acquitted, and died the superior of the
convent of the Escurial.

Sobanos. See Chapter 26.

Solorzano. See following Chapter.

Soto (Fray Dominic). See Chapter 29.

Soto (Fray Pedro). *Ibid.*

Sotomayor (Fray Pedro), Dominician; he was one of those
who, in 1558, approved the Catechism of Carranza. The
Inquisition of Valladolid tried him in 1559, on the suspicion
that he was tinctured with some heretical sentiments attributed to the archbishop ; he was confined in the Convent
of St. Paul, and afterwards severely reprimanded. He did
not suffer any other punishment, because he declared (like all
the others), that his confidence in the virtue and great learning of the author of the Catechism had induced him to act
without any bad intention.

Tabira (Don Antonio), bishop of Salamanca, knight of the
order of St. James, almoner and preacher to the king, and
the author of several unpublished works: his great virtue, his
literary talent and exquisite judgment, made him the ornament of the church during the reigns of Charles III. and
Charles IV. The government consulted him several times
on affairs of the greatest importance, and his opinions deserved the approbation of enlightened men: his sermons
passed in Spain for the best which the age had produced.
In 1809, I published the reply of this prelate to a consulta-

tion addressed to him in 1799, concerning the validity of
marriages contracted before the civil authority, as in France.
The piety and erudition of Tabira are displayed in this writing.   It was impossible that the ex-jesuits should not employ
the influence of their party to persecute a prelate who gave
the preference to a decision given by the church legally assembled in a general council, to a bull expedited by its chief.
Calvo, Guerrero, and other *Jesuits of the short robe*, attacked
Tabira as a Jansenist; they denounced him to the holy office,
but did not succeed in their attempt, since they could not
impute to him any fact tending to heresy.

Talavera (Don Ferdinand de), first archbishop of Grenada.
See Chapter 10.

Tobar (Bernardine de).   See Chapter 14.

Tordesillas (Fray Francis de), Dominican, member of the
college of St. Gregory of Valladolid, and pupil of Carranza :
he was a learned theologian.   Tordesillas was imprisoned a
short time after his master, on the suspicion that he entertained the same opinions.   He appears to have justified this
suspicion, by the care which he took to copy all his treatises
on theology, and other works.   He abjured *de levi*, submitted to a penance, and was obliged to relinquish giving
lessons on theology.

Tormo (Don Gabriel de), bishop of Orihuela.   See
Chapter 26.

Urquijo (Don Marianno Louis de), secretary of state
under Charles IV.   See Chapter 43.

Valdés (Juan de), author of some works which are mentioned by Nicolas Antonio ; one of them, the *Commentary
on the First Epistle of St. Paul to the Corinthians*, is prohibited in the Index.   He was tried on account of this
treatise and another, which was found among the papers of
Carranza, and which was at first supposed to be his composition; this work is called *Thoughts on the Interpretations of
the Holy Scriptures*.   Valdés also composed another called

Acharo; all these works were noted as being Lutheran, and the author was declared to be a *formal heretic.* Valdés left Spain, and thus escaped imprisonment. In 1559, Fray Louis de la Cruz, a prisoner in the Inquisition of Valladolid, declared that Valdés was living at Naples, that his *Thoughts,* &c. had been sent twenty years before to Carranza, in the form of a letter, but that it had its origin in the *Christian Institutions* of Thaulero. Fray Dominic de Roxas (another prisoner in the Inquisition), spoke of this Valdés as if he was the secretary of Charles V.; if that was the case, he he must be called *Juan Alonzo de Valdés.* Nicolas Antonio mentions him as a different person in his *Bibliothèque.*

Vergara (Juan de). See Chapter 14.

Vicente (Doctor Don Gregory de), priest and professor of philosophy at Valladolid. The tribunal of this city tried and imprisoned him in 1801, for some theses which had been maintained and printed in Spanish, on the manner of studying, examining, and defending true religion. He abjured *naturalism* publicly in a lesser *auto-da-fé,* and several penances were imposed on him. His theses appear to be orthodox, if they are understood literally. The masters of scholastic theology declared against Vicente, because he had attacked the manner of teaching and studying religion practised in his time; he was also accused of having preached against the pious exercises of devotion. The sermon which was the origin of this accusation was severely examined, and it was found that he had said, that true devotion consists in the actual practice of virtue, and not in exterior ceremonies; his theses were publicly condemned, and he was detained in prison for eight years. He was nephew to an inquisitor of Santiago, which induced those of Valladolid to pronouce him to be insane, in order to save him; but when he returned home he gave such unequivocal proofs of being in his senses, that the inquisitors thought the honour of the tribunal would not allow the affair to be left in this state, and again arrested him.   He had been in the prison more than a year when the *auto-da-fé* was celebrated.

Villagarcia (Fray Juan), Dominican, a pupil of Carranza, and his companion during his travels in Germany, England, and Flanders.   He was one of the greatest theologians of his age.   His arrest took place at Medemblick, in Flanders, at the same time as that of the Archbishop of Torrelaguna, in Spain.   He was imprisoned at Valladolid, on the 19th of September, 1559.   Several letters were found among his papers, and those of the archbishop, from Fray Louis de la Cruz, and Fray Francis de Tordesillas, in which they gave an account of all that they could learn concerning the trial of the archbishop.   The same errors were imputed to Villagarcia as to Carranza, principally because he had copied part of the prelate's MS. works.   Some person having told him that Carranza's Catechism would be better in Latin than in the vulgar tongue, he occupied himself in translating it, during his stay in England. This was the source of another accusation, and a consultation took place to decide if he ought not to receive the question *in caput alienum*, in order to make him confess certain facts brought against the archbishop, but without any proof concerning his having read the works of *Œcolampadius* and other prohibited books. The opinions were different, and the council decreed, that Villagarcia should first be formally examined on some other propositions,   His replies were so favourable to the archbishop, that he could not have answered more conclusively for himself. Villagarcia remained four years in prison ; he abjured, and was subjected to several penances, one of which was, never again to teach or write on theology.

Villalba (Fray Francis de).   See Chapter 29.

Villegas (Alphonso de).   See Chapter 13.

Virues (Don Alphonso de).   See Chapter 14.

Yeregui (Don Joseph de), secular priest, doctor of theology and canon law, born at Vergara de Guipuzcoa : he was preceptor to the infants Don Gabriel, and Don Antonio de Bourbon, and knight of the royal order of Charles III. He published a good catechism, and was denounced three times to the Inquisition of Madrid, on suspicion of being a Jansenist. In 1792, he was commanded not to go out of the city of Madrid. He lived in this kind of captivity for six months, and was then acquitted by the inquisitors of the court. Unfortunately he had enemies in the Supreme Council, who wished to order the trial to be suspended, and they would have succeeded if the inquisitor-general, Rubin de Cevallos, had not died at that time. His successor, Don Manuel Abad-la-Sierra, archbishop of Selimbria, professed the same opinions as Yeregui, who at last received a certificate of absolution, and regained his liberty; the king then appointed him to be an honorary inquisitor. Yeregui in his new office incurred other inconveniences, because he had spoken to his friends of the circumstances of his trial, which was interpreted as a sign of contempt for the holy office, which always enjoins secrecy to those who appear before it. Yeregui however apologized, and refuted all that had been published concerning his opinions of the Inquisition.

Zeballos (Jerome de), native of Escalona; he was a professor in the University of Salamanca, and a member of the municipality of Toledo. In 1609 he published at Rome a volume in folio, containing several treatises on jurisprudence; the first is a *Discourse on the principal Reasons of the King of Spain and his Council, for taking Cognizance of Ecclesiastical Trials, or Trials between Ecclesiastics, when a Writ of Error is brought in.* Among the questions which he discusses, is the following : " Is an ecclesiastical judge permitted to arrest and imprison laymen in a trial on canonical affairs, without the intervention of the royal judge ?" The same author published at Salamanca, in 1613, another volume in folio, entitled, *Of the Cognizance of Ecclesiastical Trials, between Ecclesiastics, when an Appeal is made*

by one of the Parties to the royal Authority. He wrote
some other works recorded by Nicolas Antonio. Some
priests, who thought it heresy to defend the privileges of
the king against the power of the clergy, denounced Zeballos to the Inquisition of Toledo. The members of this
tribunal did not arrest him, but sent him the heads of the
accusations against the two works already mentioned; he
justified himself completely, and they were permitted to be
in circulation. Some time after the Inquisition of Rome
placed them on its Index, and that of Spain suppressed
some passages, which are not found in the modern editions.

This list might have been augmented by the names of
many less distinguished men, and I did not think it necessary to include those Spaniards whose works have been
prohibited, but who were not personally attacked by the
holy office. Those already mentioned are sufficient to shew
the danger of attempting to introduce the taste for good
literature in Spain.

Charles III., wishing to be made acquainted with the
affairs of the Jesuits, and some other circumstances relating
to them, assembled a council in 1768, composed of five archbishops and bishops; they were occupied in consulting upon
the tribunal of the Inquisition, and particularly of the prohibition of books. Don Joseph Moñino, Count de Florida-
Blanca, and Don Pedro Rodriguez de Campomanes, Count
de Campomanes, the king's procurators in the Council of
Castile, made a report to the assembly. Some extracts from
it will be interesting in this part of the history.

Speaking of the clandestine introduction of a brief relating to the Jesuits on the 16th of April, 1767, and of
another concerning the affairs of the Duke of Parma, on the
30th of January, 1768, these ministers thus express themselves : " The council is not ignorant of the intrigues employed by the nuncios with the Inquisition, to gain their
ends by clandestine means. During the first fifteen cen-

turies there were no tribunals of the Inquisition in Spain.
The bishops alone were acquainted with points of doctrine,
and heretics and blasphemers were punished by civil law.
The abuse of the prohibitions of books commanded by the
Inquisition, is one cause of the ignorance which prevails
over the greatest part of this nation . . . . . According to the
bulls which created the holy office, the bishops are joint
judges with the inquisitors, and sometimes the principal
judges in the affairs which depend on the tribunal. This
power of the bishops was acquired by their rank and their
respectable office of pastors. Why then have these natural
judges of all discussions which may arise on matters of faith
and the morals of the faithful, no part or influence in the
prohibitions of books, and the choice of qualifiers? It is
from this circumstance that the subject has been treated with
a negligence which excites and perpetuates the complaints
of learned men . . . . . Supposing that the regulations of
Benedict XIV. were not sufficiently clear, the same cannot be
said of the brief of Innocent VIII., which commands the
Inquisition to follow the rules of justice in their proceedings : Can there be anything more just, than that the parties
should be heard ? Is it not contrary to the public interest,
that books which might be useful in instructing subjects
should be prohibited, from passion, or to gain some particular
end ? The fiscal would say too much if he dwelt upon this
subject, to prove how much the tribunal has always abused
its authority, in commanding the prohibition of doctrines
which even Rome has not dared to condemn, such as the
four propositions of the clergy of France, in supporting the
indirect power of the Court of Rome against that of kings ;
and lastly, in sanctioning opinions equally reprehensible. It
might be proved that the tribunal has constantly favoured
and encouraged the wickedness committed by certain ecclesiastics who remain unmolested, contrary to the respect due
to the king and his magistrates. *The regular priests of the*

Society of Jesus have had the greatest influence in the holy
office, since the minority of Charles II., when the Jesuit
Juan Everard Nitardo, confessor to the queen-mother, was
inquisitor-general..... The last general expurgatory index,
published in 1747, is still remembered. *Casani* and *Carrasco*
(both Jesuits) so falsified and confused it, that it was a disgrace to the tribunal: the fact is so well known, and had
such important consequences, that that circumstance alone
furnished sufficient motives to suppress the Inquisition entirely, or at least to reform it, since it only uses its authority
to injure the state, and the purity of morals and the Christian religion..... It may be said that the expurgatory
index drawn up in Spain is more injurious to the rights of
the sovereign and the instruction of his subjects, than that
of Rome. In that court the qualifiers are well chosen, the
prohibitions moderate, and the interests of individuals are
never considered .... We cannot forbear to mention the memoir presented by Monsignor Bossuet to Louis XIV., against
the inquisitor-general Rocaberti, on the subject of a decree
of the Inquisition of Toledo, in which the doctrine, refusing
to the Pope the direct or indirect power of depriving sovereigns of their kingdoms, is declared to be erroneous and
schismatic .... The procurators cannot conceal from themselves that the tribunals of the Inquisition compose the most
fanatical body in the state, and the most attached to the
Jesuits, who have been banished from the kingdom; that
the inquisitors profess the same doctrines and the same
maxims; lastly, that it is necessary to accomplish a reform
in the Inquisition."

In their conclusion, the procurators proposed, that in
consideration of the edict of 1762, and to ensure its execution, the holy office should be compelled to hear the defence
of the authors of the works before they are prohibited, according to the provision of the bull *Sollicita et Provida*, of
Benedict XIV.; that the tribunal should only condemn those

books which contain errors in doctrine, superstition, or relaxed moral opinions ; that it should particularly avoid prohibiting works written in the defence of the prerogatives of
the crown ; that it should not be allowed to seize or retain
any unprohibited book, on pretence of correcting or qualifying it, but should leave it to the proprietor ; that it should
be obliged to present to the king the minutes of the decrees
of prohibition before publication, and to the Council of
Castile all the briefs sent to it, in order that they may be
submitted to his majesty for his approbation.

The Council of Castile, with the extraordinary Council of
Archbishops and Bishops, approved of the opinion of the king's
procurators. They presented it to Charles III., who wished to
know the opinion of Don Manuel de Roda, Marquis de Roda,
minister of justice. This nobleman (one of the most distinguished scholars in Spain, during the last century) remitted
his opinion to his majesty on the 16th of March in the same
year : it entirely accorded with those of the fiscals ; he added,
" on the 5th of September, 1761, the King of Naples, being
informed of what was passing at Rome concerning the condemnation of Mazengui's work, commanded that the Inquisition of Sicily and the ecclesiastical superiors throughout his
states should not print or publish, in any way whatever, any
kind of proclamation without permission from his majesty
. . . . I was then at Rome, and I demanded in your majesty's
name some reparation from his Holiness, for the offence committed by his nuncio at Madrid, in inducing the inquisitor-general to publish the brief, for the prohibition of
Mazengui's work, without his knowledge . . . . His Holiness
approved of the nuncio's proceedings ; but was convinced of
the justice of our complaint, when I supported it by facts and
arguments. The Pope, however, did not dare to express his
opinion operly, as he was entirely governed by Cardinal
Torregiani, who had managed all the intrigues under the influence of the Jesuits . . . . . Torregiani knew that the brief

would not be received in any court either in Italy, France, or even at Venice. The Pope wrote to that Republic to prevent the work from being reprinted, but it was, nevertheless, published not only then against the Pope's command, but afterwards, with a dedicatory epistle to his Holiness.... I have seen, in the library of the Vatican, a printed proclamation of the Inquisition of Spain in 1693: this tribunal condemns two authors, called the *Barclayos*, because their books contained two propositions which the Romans consider heretical: one was, that *the Pope has no authority over the temporalities of kings, and can neither depose them, nor release their subjects from their oath of fidelity;* the other, that *the authority of the general council is greater than that of the Pope.*"

The same minister, in 1776, wrote a letter from Aranjuez to Don Philip Bertrand, inquisitor-general. Speaking with approbation of his intention to correct the Spanish expurgatory index, he says, " A thousand absurdities were committed in the last expurgatory (confided in 1747 by the Bishop of Teruel to two Jesuits), and it is necessary to correct them; the fact is proved by the denunciations and printed notes of Fray Martin Llobet. But the appendix, or catalogue of authors called *Jansenists*, is the most intolerable; the names are all taken from the *Bibliothèque Janseniste* of Father Colonia, a Jesuit, which was condemned by a brief of Benedict XIV. Instead of placing this work in the Index, as it ought to have been, the names are copied from it. You know the brief addressed by that Pope to the Bishop of Teruel, on the 31st of July, 1748, and in which he disapproves of the insertion of the works of Cardinal Noris in the Index. His Holiness also addressed five letters to Ferdinand VI. on the same subject, but neither the Popes nor the king could get the name of *Noris* erased from the Index for ten years: at that time the Bishop of Teruel (who had at last consented) died, and the king dismissed his confessor, the Jesuit Rabago, who had been the most averse to the measure. I took the necessary steps, and the king's order was sent to Monsignor Quintano, inquisitor-general, and his majesty's confessor, with whom I had a long conference on this subject: I at last obtained a decree, declaring *that the works of Noris had neither been condemned, censured, nor denounced to the holy office.*

CHAPTER XXVI.

OFFENCES COMMITTED BY THE INQUISITORS AGAINST THE ROYAL AUTHORITY AND MAGISTRATES.

In addition to the prevention of the progress of literature, the Inquisition was so much dreaded by the magistrates, that criminals were frequently left unpunished. Ferdinand and his successors had granted privileges to this tribunal, which the encroachments of the inquisitors soon rendered insupportable. They even endeavoured to humiliate three sovereigns: Clement VIII. at home; the Prince of Bearn, King of Navarre; and the Grand Master of the Order of St. John of Jerusalem, at Malta. They also attacked and qualified, as suspected of heresy, the whole Council of Castile; excited seditions in several cities by their arbitrary measures; and persecuted several members of their own *Supreme* Council.

This system of domination has never been repressed either by the general laws of Spain and America, the particular resolutions taken in each of the kingdoms of the crown of Arragon, the king's ordinations, or the circular letters of the Council of the Inquisition. The inquisitors have been punished (though rarely) by being deprived of their offices, this, however, had no effect. Lastly, the general conventions have not been less impotent in restraining the ambition which led them to endeavour to establish their dominion throughout the world by fear.

The Inquisition presents to our view a tribunal, whose judges have neither obeyed the laws of the kingdom in which it was established, the bulls of the Popes, the first constitutions of the tribunal, nor the particular orders of its chiefs; which has even dared to resist the power of the Pope, in whose name it acts, and has disowned the king's authority eleven different times; which has suffered books to circulate, favouring regicides and the authority of the Popes to dethrone kings, and at the same time condemned and prohibited works containing a contrary doctrine, and defending the rights of the sovereign; which acted in this manner in circumstances entirely foreign to the crime of heresy, which was the only one they were competent to judge. Some examples will be given of the contests for jurisdiction which have so much injured Spain.

In 1553, the inquisitors of Calahorra excommunicated and arrested the licentiate Izquierdo, *alcalde-major*. of Arnedo, for having attempted to prosecute Juan Escudero, a familiar of the holy office, who had assassinated a soldier. They also ordered divine service to cease at Arnedo. The Chancery of Valladolid demanded the writings of the trial, but the inquisitors eluded two of their ordinances. In the mean time the culprit was left at liberty in the town of Calahorra, and afterwards made his escape, so that the crime remained unpunished.

In 1567, the inquisitors of Murcia excommunicated the Chapter of the Cathedral, and the municipality of that city; their competence was contested, and the Supreme Council decided that some members of the chapter and municipality should make public reparation in the capital of the kingdom, and receive absolution; they received it in public, and in the character of penitents, before the altar.

In 1568, a royal ordinance prescribed the execution of the

Convention, known as that of *Cardinal Espinoza.* It was issued, on the inquisitors of Valencia claiming the right of judging in affairs concerning the police of the city and many others, such as contributions, smuggling, trade, &c. They asserted that this right belonged to them, particularly if one of the individuals concerned in the affair was in the service of the Inquisition. They would not allow any criminal to be arrested in the houses of the inquisitors either in the town or country, while even the churches were no longer a refuge for those they pursued.

In 1569, the tribunal of Barcelona excommunicated and imprisoned the military deputy and the civil vice-governor of the city, and several of their people. Their crime was, having exacted from an usher of the Inquisition a certain privilege called *la Merchandise.* The royal Council of Arragon contested the competence of the Council of the Inquisition ; but Philip II. put an end to the dispute, by liberating the prisoners : the inquisitors were not punished for disobeying the law, which forbids them to excommunicate a magistrate.

In 1574 the Inquisition of Saragossa excommunicated the members of the deputation which represented the kingdom of Arragon during the interval of the assembly of the Cortes. The deputies complained to Pius V., who paid no attention to them : after his death they applied to his successor, Gregory XIII. The Pope commissioned the inquisitor-general to arrange the affair; but, being influenced by the Supreme Council, he rejected the papal commission, and asserted that the cognizance of the complaint belonged to him by right. Philip II., that fanatical protector of the holy office, commanded his ambassador at R me to defend the Inquisition to the Pope; and he obtained what he required, while the deputies were still suffering under the excommunication, which lasted nearly two years. It must be remarked, that this deputation was composed of eight persons : two of them were ecclesiastics, generally bishops; two for the highest order of nobility, who were counts or grandees of Spain ; two gentlemen of illustrious birth to represent the second class of nobility; and two for the third class, selected from the most distinguished citizens.

In 1588, the inquisitors of Toledo excommunicated the licentiate Gudiel, alcalde of the king's house, and judge of the royal court of justice at Madrid : this magistrate had prosecuted Iñigo Ordoñez, secretary of the holy office, for having wounded Juan de Berrgos, who died in consequence, and for having wilfully fired a pistol at the Canon Don Francis Monsalve. The Council of the Inquisition pleaded the cause of the culprit before the king, and excused the use of censures, alleging that *such was the usual proceeding of the holy office.*

In 1591, violent contests took place between the Inquisition of Saragossa and the chief justice of Arragon. Two seditions were the result, and several grandees of Spain, many gentlemen, and a still greater number of private individuals, were condemned to death. An account of the intrigues of the inquisitors in this affair will be [given in the trial of Antonio Perez.

In 1598, the Inquisitors of Seville went to the metropolitan church, with the president and members of the royal court of justice, to attend the funeral of Philip II. ; they pretended that they ought to precede the judges, who resisted, and the inquisitors excommunicated them in the church. The king's attorney protested against this act, and the scandalous scene which ensued may be easily conceived. The judges repairing to the place where they held their sessions, declared that the inquisitors had used violence in proceeding against the law, and passed a decree commanding the inquisitors to take off the excommunication. The inquisitors did not obey the order, and the judges repeated it, with the threat of depriving them of all civil rights, and condemning them to banishment and confiscation. Philip III. disapproved of the conduct of the inquisitors, commanded them to take off the excommunication and repair to Madrid, where they were confined to the city. In the December following, the king issued a decree, importing that the inquisitors should only take precedence in the ceremony of the *auto-da-fé*. The inquisitor-general Portocarrero was deprived of his office, and banished to his bishopric of Cuença.

In 1622 the town of Lorca, which was within the jurisdiction of the Inquisition of Murcia, appointed a familiar of the holy office to be the collector of a tax upon the sale of goods called *Alcaballa*. The man refused the employment, but his representations were not admitted, upon which the inquisitors excommunicated the judge of Lorca, and required the assistance of Don Pedro Porres, the corregidor of Murcia, to take him to their prisons. On his refusal, they excommunicated him also, and decreed that divine service should cease in all the churches of Murcia. This measure threw the inhabitants into the greatest consternation, and they entreated their bishop, Don Antonio Trejo, to interpose his authority. This prelate remonstrated with the inquisitors, but not succeeding, in order to tranquillize the people, he published a mandate, announcing that he was not obliged to submit to the interdict, or to the order for the *cessation of divine service*. Don Andrea Pacheco, the inquisitor-general, condemned the mandate, and ordered this measure to be proclaimed in all the churches of Murcia. At the same time he imposed a penalty of eight thousand ducats on the bishop, and cited him to appear within twenty days at Madrid, to answer the complaint preferred against him, by the fiscal of the Supreme Council, on pain of another penalty of four thousand ducats. The bishop and the chapter of his cathedral sent the dean and a canon to Madrid as his deputies. The inquisitor-general excommunicated them, without hearing their defence, and threw them into separate prisons, and at the same time caused this excommunication to be announced in all the pulpits of Madrid. The inquisitors also excommunicated the Curé of St. Catherine, who refused to submit to this interdict without an order from his bishop. The king and the Pope were at last obliged to interfere, they re-established the bishop in his rights; but this act of justice did not destroy the cause of the evil which was complained of.

In the same year, the Inquisitors of Toledo excommunicated the sub prefect of that city, who had seized and sentenced a butcher as a thief, and convicted him of having sold bad meat with false weights : the inquisitors pretended that the culprit came under their jurisdiction, because he furnished the holy office with meat, and they accordingly required that the prisoner and the writings of the trial should be given up to them. Their demand was refused, because the offence was committed in the exercise of a public profession. The inquisitors then published the excommunication 'in all the churches of Toledo ; they imprisoned the usher and the porter of the sub-prefect for having obeyed their master, and they remained in prison several days; they were then subjected to the punishment of having their beards and hair shaven, which was at that time considered infamous, and to appear in the chamber of audience without their shoes and girdles ; they were examined on their genealogy, to discover if they were descended from the Moors or Jews ; they were made to repeat the catechism as if they were heretics, and were then condemned to perpetual banishment; the inquisitors even refused to give them a certificate, to shew that they had not been condemned for heresy. The compassion excited by the fate of these unfortunate men was so general, that the people rose against the Inquisition ; but some persons of high rank, and who were devoted to the public good, succeeded in appeasing the tumult. The king being informed of what had passed by the Council of Castile, appointed an extraordinary commission of eleven members selected from his councils; they passed several resolutions against the inquisitors, which had only the effect of correcting the present disorder, without entirely destroying the evil.

In the following year, the Inquisitors of Grenada excommunicated Don Louis Gudiel de Peralta, and Don Mathias Gonzalez ; the first a member of the royal civil court, and the other the king's procurator in the same court. They condemned as heretical two works of these excellent jurisconsults, in which they defended the rights of the royal jurisdiction in all cases of *competence*. The Council of Castile respectfully remonstrated with the king, and shewed that the inquisitors acted in opposition to *Instructions to the holy office of* 1485,which directed them to consult the king in affairs of this nature. In order to remedy this abuse, a committee was appointed in 1625, to decide upon all difficulties which might arise on this subject. This committee did not exist long, but it was re-established in 1657.

In 1530, the Inquisitors of Valladolid behaved with still greater insolence. The bishop of that city (who was at the same time president of the royal chancery) was to officiate pontifically in a solemn mass. The inquisitors chose that day to publish the edict of *denunciations;* and asserting that their power as inquisitors was superior to that of the bishop, they attempted to take away the canopy which was raised when the prelate officiated. The canons resisted, and the inquisitors sent some of their officers to the church, who arrested Don Alphonso Niño the chanter, and Don Francis Milan a canon; they carried them away in their canonical robes, and deposited them in that dress in the prisons of the holy office. The Council of Castile made a representation to the king on this event, which was the origin of the convention of the following year, known as that of *Cardinal Zapata*. Several resolutions were passed, and it was decided that censures should only be employed in cases of emergency; but this had little effect on the inquisitors. Much more would have been done, if the king had taken the advice of

the Council of Castile, which (after giving an account of
evils arising from the system of the inquisitors) recommended,
that he should allow the other tribunals to proceed against
them for abuse of power. This advice was addressed to the
king by his councils, in the consultations of the years 1634,
1669, 1682, 1696, 1761, and in several others, when the
Inquisition of Spain prohibited works in which the privileges
of the crown were defended, particularly that of Don Joseph
de Mur, president of the royal court at Majorca. It was
printed in that island in 1615, and called, *Allegations in
favour of the King, on the Conflicts for Jurisdiction which
have arisen between the Royal Court of Justice and the
Tribunal of the Inquisition of Majorca.*

In 1634, another contest took place on the subject of competency, concerning certain taxes which had been received
from an inhabitant of Vicalboro, near Madrid. The inquisitors of Toledo excommunicated a judge of the royal court,
and of the king's court, and committed the greatest excesses
against the authority of the Council of Castile, which, impressed with a sense of its dignity, as the Supreme Senate of
the nation, commanded the Dean-inquisitor of Toledo to
repair to Madrid, to answer in person the charges brought
against him, and threatened, in case he refused, to deprive
him of his property and temporal rights. It also condemned
a priest, the secretary of the holy office, to banishment and
confiscation, and ordered the Inquisitor of Madrid to give up
the prisoners and the writings of the trial to the chamber of
judges of the court. The council made an address to the
king, requesting him to forbid the inquisitors the use of censures, and to deliver his people from the oppression under
which they suffered. The king merely renewed the prohibition of employing excommunication without an absolute
necessity, and decreed that it should never be employed
against judges without a particular permission. This ordinance shews the neglect or contempt into which the Conven-

tion of Cardinal Zapata had fallen, only three years after it
had been established.

In 1640 the Inquisitors of Valladolid had another contest
with the bishop, who complained to the king, representing
that the permission granted by royal council to print or
publish, without suppressing what those authors who depend
on the Inquisition write on the privileges of that tribunal,
would have the most fatal consequences. This assertion
was proved in 1641. Some disputes arose on the subject of
competency, between the Inquisition and the Chancery of
Valladolid; the Council of Castile was obliged to consult the
king several times during the course of the affair, and in
one of its memorials stated, *that the jurisdiction which the in-*
quisitors exercise in the name of the king is temporal, secular,
and precarious, and cannot be defended by the use of cen-
sures. The members of the council of the Inquisition in
which Don Antonio de Sotomayor the inquisitor-general
presided, carried their presumption so far as to convoke an
assembly of ignorant scholastic theologians, all chosen from
the monks, to *qualify* the proposition advanced by the Council
of Castile. These qualifiers, eager to display their penetration, divided it into three parts.

" *First part.* The jurisdiction which the inquisitors exercise in the name of the king is temporal and secular.—QUA-
LIFICATION. *This proposition is probable, if considered on*
the fairest side."

" *Second part.* The said jurisdiction is precarious.—
QUALIFICATION. *This proposition is false, improbable, and*
contrary to the welfare of his majesty."

" *Third part.* Ecclesiastical censures cannot be employed
to defend the said jurisdiction.—QUALIFICATION. *This pro-*
position is audacious, and approaching to heresy."

After this measure, the fiscal of the Council of the Inquisition accused the Council of Castile; he demanded that the
tribunal should procure the copies and the minutes of the

consultation addressed to the king; that the condemnation of
it should be published, and the authors should be proceeded
against. The council of the holy office intending to act according to circumstances, represented all that had passed to
the king, referring to the judgment of the theologians. The
king, with the carelessness which was natural to him, merely
told the inquisitor-general that he had failed in his duty, in
approving a proceeding so contrary to the honour and dignity
of the senate of the nation. The effects of the obstinacy and
violence of the inquisitors was felt for some time after. In
1643, the king obliged Don Antonio de Sotomayor to give in
his resignation.

In America, the ordinances of the king, and other regulations, could not prevent violent quarrels from arising between the civil tribunals and those of the holy office. But
in all these affairs the viceroys shewed more firmness, and
repressed the arrogance of the inquisitors with more success
than was displayed in the Peninsula. This is not surprising,
because in distant countries the inquisitors are not supported
by an inquisitor-general, who, possessing the king's favour,
may influence him in private conversations. Besides this,
the viceroys, jealous of the power with which they are invested, are careful that it shall meet with no obstacles or
contradictions.

In 1686, a quarrel arose between the inquisitors of Carthagena in America, and the bishop. The inquisitor Don
Francis Barcia, after excommunicating the prelate, caused
his decree to be read in all the churches. The bishop replied,
and shewed by his manner to the inquisitor, his contempt for
the excommunication. Don Francis (in concurrence with his
consultors) arrested and threw into prison the bishop and
many respectable persons of the cathedral and the city, who
had spoken freely on the subject. The Pope being informed
of this affair on the 13th February, 1687, commanded the inquisitor-general, Don Diego Sarmiento de Valladares, to

cause the inquisitor Barcia and the consultors to be brought
to Madrid, and to deprive them of their offices. This order
not being obeyed, on the 15th of December he expedited a
second brief, which was comminatory. The inquisitor-general
then had recourse to the king, and gave so unfaithful an account of the transaction, that neither his majesty nor the
council of the Indies were ever informed of the truth. The
Pope persisted in his resolution, and wished to decide on the
affair himself. It was not finished when Clement XI. ascended
the pontifical throne; this Pope assembled the cardinals, and
taking their opinions, confirmed by a formal decree all that
the bishop had done, and annulled the extravagant measures
of the inquisitor. A bull, in 1706, commanded the restitution
of the penalties which had been imposed, and suppressed the
tribunal of Carthagena. This suppression was not executed,
because it was contrary to the king's policy.

In 1713, the Cardinal Francis Judice, inquisitor-general,
prohibited a work of Don Melchior Macanaz, procurator of
the king in the Council of Castile : the cardinal knew that
this work had been printed by the order of Philip V., who
had approved it after having read it. The king was at first
very much irritated at this proceeding; but the cardinal,
accustomed to the intrigues of Rome and Paris, succeeded
in eluding the orders of his sovereign; although he was not
in the kingdom, he continued to exercise his office, and sent
orders to his creatures which were extremely displeasing to
Philip. This prince could not obtain the dismission of Judice,
until Cardinal Alberoni had exerted his influence at Rome
and Paris, to second his master's views. Judice retired in
1716.

Don Melchior Macanaz continued to live in exile. His
trial became important, from the great number of denunciations which were made against different works which he had
written: in some of these he inveighed against the abuses
which were committed at the Court of Rome, against those of

the immunities of the clergy and of the ecclesiastical tribunals, and called the public attention to the fatal effects of
increasing the number of monks and other societies. The
qualifiers, in judging his works, clearly shewed the spirit of
hatred and revenge which actuated them. In the trial of
Macanaz, one of his works, called *A Critical Defence of the
Inquisition*, is mentioned; the inquisitors qualified it as *ironical*, because they found some things in it which were not
true. They were confirmed in their opinion some time after,
by another work of Macanaz, called, *An Apology for the Defence of Fray Nicolas Jesus de Belando, in Favour of the
Civil History of Spain, unjustly prohibited by the Inquisition*.

Although the inquisitors treated him with so much severity,
Ferdinand VI., and the inquisitor-general Don Emmanuel
Quintano Bonifaz, permitted Macanaz to return to Spain,
and the king sent him to Aix-la-Chapelle as his ambassador.

In 1768, the inquisitors endeavoured to obtain the right
of trying persons for polygamy: Charles III. ordered that
the cognizance of this offence should belong to the secular
judge, except when the criminals thought that it was permitted. It was his pleasure that the inquisitors " should only
punish heresy and apostasy, and, above all, that none of his
people should be subjected to the disgrace of an arrest, if
they had not been previously convicted of a crime."

In 1771, the Council of the Inquisition represented to the
king, that the simple fact of marrying another person, while
the first wife was alive, was sufficient to create a suspicion
that the persons guilty of it erred in faith on the article of
marriage. For this reason the inquisitors continued to receive the denunciations on this pretended crime, and to take
cognizance of it.

In 1781, the inquisitor-general commanded that the con-
fessionals in the convents of nuns should be placed within
sight of the persons in the churches. This was done by the
inquisitors, without consulting the archbishops and bishops

of the dioceses; they were extremely offended at this conduct, but dissembled their anger, that the public tranquillity
might not be disturbed.

In 1797, the Inquisitors of Grenada removed the confes-
sional of the convent of the nuns of St. Paul, which was
under the immediate direction of the archbishop: the ecclesiastical governor of the archbishopric complained to the
king. The minister of justice, Don Gaspard Melchior de
Jovellanos, resolved to take advantage of this event; he addressed himself to the Archbishop of Burgos, inquisitor-
general, to the Bishops of Huesca, Tuy, Placentia, Osma,
Avila, and to Don Joseph Espiga, the king's almoner, and
requested them to propose "whatever they thought most
proper to correct the abuses committed in the holy office,
and to destroy the false principles on which that tribunal
founded all its measures." The archbishop (as may be supposed) sent notes favourable to the tribunal; those of all
the others were of quite an opposite nature. This attempt,
however, did not lead to any satisfactory result: Jovellanos
quitted the ministry before Charles IV. had decided on the
subject; the minister who succeeded him had other views,
and Jovellanos was denounced on suspicion of heresy.

Of the Magistrates who were persecuted.

The examples which have been given of the quarrels between
the Inquisition and the civil tribunals, sufficiently prove the
constant attention of the inquisitors in endeavouring to extend their influence and privileges, even in defiance of the
sovereign power; yet a list of the persecuted magistrates
may be useful and interesting.

Almodovar (Don Christopher Ximenez Gongora, duke of).
He was ambassador to the Court of Vienna, and published
a work *on the Establishments of the European Nations beyond
Sea.* This book is only a free translation of that of the Abbé

Raynal. He concealed his name under that of *Eduardo Malo de Luque*, which is the anagram of El Duque de Almodovar. He presented some copies of his book to the king, but though he had taken this precaution, and had suppressed some articles, he was denounced to the Inquisition as being tinctured with the opinions of the incredulous philosophers. The inquisitors endeavoured to find out how the duke conversed in society with learned men ; but they did not learn enough to authorize an accusation, as it almost always happened, during the reigns of Charles III. and Charles IV., when they wished to attack the literati.

Aranda (Don Pedro-Paul Abarca de Bolea y Ximenez d'Urrea, Count d'), grandee of Spain. He rendered himself more illustrious by his talents and learning than he was by his birth and high offices. As a soldier he attained the rank of Captain-general, which is equivalent to that of Field-marshal : his diplomatic talents obtained the office of ambassador to Paris; his knowledge as a statesman, that of prime-minister, secretary of state, under Charles IV.; and for his talents as a politician he was made president of the Council of Castile. In these four branches of the art of governing he was always truly great. He was president in the royal council extraordinary, assembled by Charles III. to consider the affairs of the Jesuits. Although the members of this assembly deliberated in secret, the public were informed not only of its objects in general, but the particular opinions of each councillor. The Count d'Aranda was denounced to the holy office as being suspected of professing the sentiments of the philosophers of the eighteenth century, because his political opinions were extremely liberal. The ordinance signed by Charles III. in 1770 (forbidding the inquisitors to take cognizance of any crime but heresy) was thought to be the work of the Count d'Aranda, and the inquisitors hated him in consequence. The trial of Don Paul Olavide, which took place about this time, furnished some details which caused a suspicion that the opinions of the Count d'Aranda on the subject of mere exterior devotion were the same as those of the accused. However the inquisitors could not obtain a sufficient mass of evidence to authorize proceedings against him, and he died after having been denounced four times to the holy office, but without ever being put upon his trial.

Arroyo (Don Stephen d'), corregidor of Ecija, a town in Andalusia, and a member of the royal civil court of the district of Granada. He was excommunicated by the Inquisition of Cordova in 1664, because he opposed the attempts made by the inquisitors to extend their jurisdiction at the expense of the civil tribunals.

Avalos (Don Diego Lopez d'), corregidor of the city of Cordova, was threatened to be excommunicated and imprisoned in 1501, because he refused to give up two archers of the holy office, who had been taken to the royal prison, unless they were demanded with the proper forms.

Azara (Don Nicolas d'), born in Arragon, was successively director of the office of the minister for foreign affairs, minister plenipotentiary at Rome, and ambassador extraordinary to Paris. He published a translation of the *Life of Cicero*, with notes, illustrations, and plates. He was considered one of the most learned men in Spain during the reigns of Charles III. and his successor. Although he almost always resided in Italy or France, his name was in the registers of the holy office. He was denounced at Saragossa and Madrid as an incredulous philosopher; but there were no proofs, and the trial was suspended until fresh charges should be brought against him.

Arragon (the deputation of). See the preceding Article.

Arragon. The Chief Justice of Arragon was invested with supreme power, and placed between the king and the nation, to decide, without appeal, if the king's ministers infringed the laws established at the beginning of the mo-

narchy. Even the king was obliged to submit to the
decisions of this magistrate in all constitutional affairs. In
order to prevent disputes between the two powers, the
chief justice and his tribunal were independent of the king
in the criminal proceedings. The inquisitors of Saragossa, re-
gardless of these regulations, commenced proceedings against
the chief justice, and in 1591 threatened to excommunicate
him. Some account of this affair will be given in the trial of
Antonio Perez.

Bañuelos (Don Vincent), was excommunicated by the
Inquisition of Toledo, for endeavouring to defend the jurisdiction of the civil tribunal in a trial for homicide.

Barcelona. See the preceding Article.

Barrientos (the Commandant), knight of the military
order of St. James, and Corregidor and Sub-prefect of Logroño, was obliged, in 1516, to go to Madrid, and appear
before the inquisitor-general and the Supreme Council, to
ask pardon for having refused to lend assistance to the
archers of the holy office in arresting some monks. He was
subjected to the lesser *auto-da-fé*, attended mass, standing
with a torch in his hand, and received some slight strokes of
a whip from the inquisitor; this ceremony was concluded by
a solemn absolution from all censures.

Benalcazar (the Count de) was excommunicated and
menaced with an arrest by the inquisitors of Estremadura in
1500. The same threat was made to the governor of the
fortress of Benalcazar; their offence was having defended
their temporal power against the pretensions of the holy
office, in the case of a woman who was arrested for having
uttered some words against the faith.

Campomanes (Don Pedro Rodriguez de Campomanes,
Count de) was, perhaps, the most eminent literary man in
Spain, during the reign of Charles III. and Charles IV.
He is the author of several works mentioned in the *Spanish
Library of the time of Charles III.* published by Don Juan

de Sempere Guarinos. He first filled the office of procurator to the king in the Council of Castile, and in the
chamber of the king, of which he was afterwards the governor. In all his works he constantly maintained the independence of sovereigns with respect to the Court of Rome,
the obligation that all the citizens of the state should pay
their part of the public expenses, and the impossibility that
the contentious jurisdiction should form part of the ecclesiastical power, unless accorded by the special favour of the
sovereign. It is easy to suppose that Campomanes had a
great many enemies among the clergy; he was denounced to
the holy office as an anti-catholic philosopher. The charges
were numerous, but they did not prove that he had advanced
any heretical proposition; they only tended to create a
suspicion that his works were opposed to the spirit of Christianity. He was invited to attend the *auto-da-fé* of Don
Paul Olavide, in order to inform him of the punishment he
would incur by professing the same opinions; but though
the inquisitors knew him to be their enemy, they did not
dare to go any further.

Cardona (Don Pedro de), captain-general of Catalonia.
See Chapter 16.

Castile (Council of). See preceding Article.

Chaves (Don Gregorio Antonio de), corregidor and sub-
prefect of Cordova, was excommunicated and threatened with
imprisonment by the inquisitors of Cordova in 1660.

Chumacero (Don Juan), Count de Guaro, president of the
Council of Castile, ambassador at Rome, composed several
works which are mentioned by Nicolas Antonio, and some
discourses in defence of the temporal against the ecclesiastical power, and in favour of the independence of sovereigns
against the abuses of the Court of Rome. The inquisitors
of Spain, at the instigation of the Pope's nuncio, undertook
to condemn his doctrine, and to prohibit his works, with
those of some other authors who wrote in the same spirit, in

order to force them to retract, on pain of excommunication and imprisonment.

Cordova (Don Pedro Fernandez de), Marquis de Priego, member of the municipality of Cordova, was persecuted by the Inquisition in 1506. See Chapter 10.

Cordova (Don Diego Fernandez de), Count de Cabra, and also a member of the municipality of Cordova, was treated in the same manner. *Ibid.*

Godoy (Don Emanuel), Prince of Peace, Duke of Alcudia, secretary of state to Charles IV. See Chapter 43.

Gonzalez (Don Mathias). See the preceding Article.

Gudiel (the Licentiate). *Ibid.*

Gudiel de Peralta (Don Louis). *Ibid.*

Guzman (Don Gaspar de), Count-Duke d'Olivarez, prime minister to Philip IV. See Chapter 37.

Izquierdo (the Licentiate). See the preceding Article.

Jovellanos (Don Gaspard Melchior de), Secretary of State in the department of grace and justice under Charles IV., was one of the most learned men in Spain ; he wrote several pamphlets on politics and different branches of literature. In 1798 he resolved to reform the mode of proceeding in the holy office, and intended to take advantage of a memorial which I had composed in 1794, according to the orders of the inquisitor-general Abad-la-Sierra ; but from a secret court intrigue he was denounced to the Inquisition as a Jansenist and an enemy to the tribunal. Charles IV. was persuaded first to banish him to his native place Gijon, in the Asturias, and afterwards to confine him in the Chartreuse, in the island of Majorca, where he was informed that he was to study the Christian doctrine. This treatment was extremely unjust, for Jovellanos was not only a good Catholic, but a just and irreproachable man, whose memory will do honour to Spain.

Juan (D. Gabriel de), president of the royal Court of Appeal at Majorca, was excommunicated in 1531 ; he maintained the rights of the sovereign against the inquisitors.

Lara (Don Juan Perez de), procurator to the king, and fiscal of the royal Court of Appeal at Seville, was extremely ill-treated by the inquisitors in 1637, because he maintained the rights of the royal jurisdiction in a manifesto, which the inquisitors declared contained propositions offensive to the holy office.

Macanaz (Don Melchior de). See the preceding article.

Moñino (Don Joseph), Count de Florida-Blanca, first secretary of state under Charles III., and Charles IV. He had been successively an advocate at Madrid, procurator to the king and fiscal of the Council of Castile, and minister plenipotentiary at Rome. His celebrity as a lawyer was the origin of his elevation, and his subsequent conduct fully justified the favourable opinion which had been formed of him. In his quality of fiscal he wrote several works. Don Juan Sempere Guarinos, in his *Catalogue of the Authors of the Reign of Charles III.*, has inserted notices of those which had been printed and those which remained unpublished. Among the first are some of great merit : the *Advice of a Fiscal*, which he gave to the council on the memorial presented to Charles III. by Monseñor Carhajal, Bishop of Cuença, and on the *impartial judgment* of the brief issued by Clement XIII. against the sovereign Duke of Parma, induced some ignorant and prejudiced priests to denounce him to the Inquisition as an enemy to religion. The Count furnished them with additional arms against himself, when he gave his opinion as procurator-fiscal on the abuses committed by the inquisitors in the prohibition of books, and on the system which they had adopted of taking cognizance of crimes not relating to doctrine. However, the inquisitors, not finding in his writings any proposition which might be qualified as heretical, were afraid to continue the trial of a minister for whom the king shewed the greatest esteem.

Mur (Don Joseph de,) president of the royal Court of Appeal at Majorca, being obliged to maintain the rights of the tribunal against the holy office, composed, in 1615, a work on competency, in which he supported the royal jurisdiction against the ecclesiastical power in all contests not relating to spiritual concerns. The holy office made the author suffer much, and inserted his work in the *Index*. Philip IV. caused it to be erased in 1641, at the request of the Council of Castile.

Ossuna (the Duke of). See Chapter 37.

Olavide (Don Paul), born at Lima, in Peru, *Assistant*, that is, Prefect of Seville, and director of the towns and villages recently built in the *Sierra-Morena* and in Andalusia, was arrested in 1776, and taken to the secret prisons of the Inquisition of Madrid; on the suspicion that he possessed impious opinions, particularly those of Rousseau and Voltaire, with whom he maintained an intimate correspondence. It appeared from the trial, that Olavide had, in the new towns which he governed, uttered the opinions of these philosophers, on the exterior worship which is rendered to God in this country. The accused denied many of the words and actions imputed to him; he explained others which might not have been understood by the witnesses, but he confessed enough to induce the inquisitors to believe that he secretly held the same opinions as his two friends. Olavide asked pardon for his imprudence, but declared that he could not do so for the crime of heresy, as he had never lost his interior faith. On the 24th of November, 1778, an *auto-da-fé* was celebrated with closed doors, in the hall of the Inquisition of Madrid, in the presence of sixty persons of high rank: Don Paul Olavide appeared before them, in the habit of a penitent, and holding in his hand an extinguished torch. The sentence declared him to be convicted of *formal heresy ;* he ought to have appeared in the *San-benito,* with a cord round his neck, but this was dispensed with, as well as the obligation of wearing the *San-benito* afterwards. He was condemned to pass eight years in a convent, and to live according to the orders of a spiritual director chosen by the Inquisition ; to be banished from Madrid, Seville, Cordova, and the new towns in the Sierra Morena. His property was confiscated; he was forbidden to possess any office or honourable title ; to ride on horseback, or to wear any jewels or ornaments of gold, silver, pearls, diamonds, precious stones, or habits of silk, or fine wool, but only those of coarse serge or some other stuff of that kind. The reading of the *factum* of his trial, by the secretary, lasted four hours ; the fiscal accused him of having advanced seventy heretical propositions, and seventy-two witnesses were examined. Towards the conclusion, Olavide exclaimed, *Whatever the fiscal may say, I have never lost my faith.* No answer was made to him. When he heard his sentence he fainted, and fell off the bench on which he had been permitted to sit. When he had recovered, and the reading of the sentence was finished, he received absolution on his knees after having read and signed his profession of faith ; he was then taken back to the prison. The sixty individuals who were invited to this ceremony were dukes, counts, marquisses, generals, members of the councils, and knights of different military orders ; they were most of them his friends. These persons were, from some circumstances in the trial, suspected of partaking his opinions, and the invitation was intended to inform them of what they might expect, and to induce them to be more reserved in their conversation. Olavide went to the convent where he was to be confined, but made his escape some time after, and retired to France. He lived at Paris under the name of the *Count de Pilo*, a title which he had never borne in Spain. A few years after he published a work called, *The Gospel Triumphant ; or, the Converted Philosopher.* This composition obtained his pardon, and permission to return to Spain, where no penances were imposed on him.

Perez (Antonio). See Chapter 35.

Ramos del Manzano (Don Francis), Count de Francos,

tutor of Charles II. and president of the Sovereign Council of the Indies, composed some treatises on politics, which are mentioned by Nicolas Antonio. In these writings he maintains the prerogatives and independence of the sovereigns against the indirect powers of the Popes, the abuses of the Court of Rome, and the ecclesiastical judges in the holy office. The Count de Francos suffered much persecution, and his works were prohibited; if Philip IV. had not protected him, he would have been arrested, and his books burnt.

Ricla (the Count de), minister of war, and lieutenant-general in the army under Charles III., was denounced to the holy office as having adopted the opinions of the philosophers of the eighteenth century. There was not sufficient proof against him, and the trial was suspended.

Roda (Don Manuel de), Marquis de Roda, minister and secretary of state in the department of grace and justice, under Charles III. He had been a celebrated advocate at Madrid, and minister-plenipotentiary at Rome ; his talents and learning made him of the greatest use to Charles III. in the important affairs relative to the expulsion of the Jesuits. The imputation of Jansenism, incurred by the archbishops and bishops of the Council extraordinary, was also brought against this minister, who had made many enemies by advising Charles III. to reform the six great colleges established at Salamanca, Alcala, and Valladolid. This denunciation failed, because it contained no *particular proposition* which deserved to be censured.

Salcedo (Don Pedro Gonzalez de), procurator to the king in the Council of Castile, published a treatise *On Political Law,* and some other works, in which he attacked the abuses committed by the judges of the privileged tribunals, and the pretensions of the inquisitors and other ecclesiastics to the royal jurisdictions. He was persecuted, and his works were condemned, but Philip IV. revoked the prohibition; however some passages were afterwards retrenched, and they are not found in the later editions.

Salgado (Don Francis de), member of the Council of Castile, published some works in defence of the royal jurisdiction against the ecclesiastical authority; they are mentioned by Nicolas Antonio. The Court of Rome condemned them; the inquisitors of Spain persecuted the author, but when they were on the point of publishing the prohibition of his works, Philip IV. commanded them to suspend their proceedings.

Samaniego (Don Philip de), priest, archdeacon of Pampeluna, knight of the order of St. James, councillor to the king, and chief secretary and interpreter of foreign languages. He was invited to attend the *auto-da-fé* of Don Paul Olavide, and was so alarmed that he voluntarily denounced himself. He presented a declaration, in which he confessed that he had read prohibited books, such as those of Voltaire, Mirabeau, Rousseau, Hobbes, Spinosa, Montesquieu, Bayle, d'Alembert, Diderot, and others; that from this course of reading he had fallen into a religious pyrrhonism; that having thought seriously on the subject, he had resolved to remain firmly attached to the Catholic faith, and that in consequence he had resolved to demand to be absolved from the censures *ad cautelam*. The tribunal ordered that he should confirm his declaration by taking an oath. They then obliged him to confess by what means he had obtained the books, who he had received them from, and where they were at that time; with what persons he had conversed on the subject of religion, and revealed his opinions; what individuals had refuted or adopted them; who had appeared to be ignorant of the doctrine, or were acquainted with it; and lastly, how long he had known it himself: these declarations were the conditions on which he was to receive absolution. Samaniego wrote a declaration, in which almost all the learned men of the court were implicated. Some of these persons had been invited to the *auto-da-fé* of Don Paul Olavide.

Sardinia (the viceroy of) was excommunicated in 1498, and punished by the inquisitors for having lent assistance to the Archbishop of Cagliari in taking a criminal from the prisons of the holy office to those of the archbishopric.

Sesé (Don Joseph de), president of the royal Court of Appeal of the kingdom of Arragon. This magistrate wrote a work, in which he had collected many definitive sentences which had been pronounced in trials for competency; they were all favourable to the secular power. The author was the victim of his zeal; he was persecuted, and his work prohibited, but Philip IV. caused it to be revoked.

Solorzano (Don Juan de), member of the Sovereign Council of the Indies. He was the author of a work on *Indian Politics*, and several others of the same nature. They were written in the same spirit as those of Salgado; Solorzano and his works shared his fate.

Sotomayor (Don Guiterrez de), knight commander of the order of Alcantara, brother of the Count de Benalcazar, and governor of the fortress of that name. See *Benalcazar*.

Terranova (the Marquis de). See Chapter 16.

Toledo (the royal judge of) was excommunicated, imprisoned, and received much ill treatment from the inquisitors in 1622, in a contest for jurisdiction.

Valdés (Don Antonie), member of the royal Council of Castile. He was excommunicated by the inquisitors in 1639, because he refused to exempt the familiars of the holy office who possessed land, from paying a contribution.

Valencia (the viceroy of), captain-general, was obliged in 1488, to appear before the Supreme Council of the Inquisition, and ask pardon and absolution for having set at liberty a soldier who was detained in the prisons of the holy office. He had the mortification of being obliged to appear in a *lesser auto-da-fé*.

Vera (Don Juan-Antonio de). See Chapter 36.

Zarate (Diego Ruiz de), chief alcade of Cordova, was

punished by the Supreme Council in 1500, and suspended from his office for six months, because he refused to allow the inquisitors of Cordova to take cognizance of the trial of the chief alguazil of that city.

Many other instances might be quoted; but these are sufficient to shew that the nature of the tribunal of the holy office will be contrary to the independence of the sovereign, while the royal jurisdiction is confounded with that of the inquisitors, and while the members of the holy office are exempted from the civil and criminal jurisdiction of the royal tribunals.

CHAPTER XXVII.

OF THE TRIALS OF SEVERAL SOVEREIGNS AND PRINCES UNDERTAKEN BY THE INQUISITION.

It is not surprising that the Inquisition should persecute magistrates and learned men, when it has not scrupled to attack kings, princes, and grandees. Some writers (particularly the French and Flemish) have singularly exaggerated the accounts of these trials ; some of them having but a vague and slight foundation for what they have advanced, and others have filled their accounts with invectives and fictions. This history is derived from the archives and writings of the trials of the Inquisition, and I have attended more to these authentic documents than to the narratives of those who have not had the same advantages. This Chapter will contain *all that is certainly known* of the trials of the princes and other potentates by the Inquisition.

The *Holy Tribunal* was scarcely established in Arragon, when it attacked Don James de Navarre, sometimes called the *Infant of Tudela*, and the *Infant of Navarre*. His crime was an act of benevolence. The assassination of Pedro Arbues, the first inquisitor of Arragon, which took place in 1485, obliged many of the principal inhabitants of Saragossa to take flight. One of these persons went to Tudela de Navarre, where the Infant of Navarre resided, and asked and obtained an asylum in his house for several days, until he could make his escape into France. The inquisitors being informed of this humane action, arrested and took Don James to their prisons in 1487, as an enemy to the holy office. He was condemned to hear a solemn mass, standing in the presence of a great concourse of people, and of his cousin Don Alphonso of Arragon (a natural son of Ferdinand V. and Archbishop of Saragossa), and to receive absolution from the censures which he was supposed to have incurred, after submitting to be *scourged* by two priests, and having gone through all the ceremonies prescribed in such cases by the Roman ritual.

In 1488, the Inquisition tried John Pic de la Mirandola and de Concordia, a prince who was considered a prodigy of science, from the age of twenty-three years. Innocent VIII. instigated them to this measure by a brief addressed to Ferdinand and Isabella, dated the 16th of December, 1487, in which he said, that he had been informed that John Pic was going into Spain, with the intention of maintaining, in the universities and other schools of the kingdom, the erroneous doctrine of several theses which he had already published at Rome, and had abjured, which rendered him still more culpable. His Holiness added, that he was most afflicted in perceiving that the youth, the pleasing manners and agreeable conversation of the prince would gain him many partisans ; he said that these considerations had induced him to request the two sovereigns to arrest the prince when he arrived in Spain, as the fear of corporal punishment might have more effect than the anathemas of the Church. De la Mirandola doubtless received information of what awaited him in Spain, as he did not undertake the journey; at least nothing is to be found in the archives concerning it. The learned historian Fleury must have been ignorant of the existence of this bull, since he says that the affair of the Prince de la Mirandola terminated in the suppression of his theses at Rome, in 1486. This prince had published and defended nine hundred propositions on theology, mathematics, physics, cabala, and other sciences. Thirteen of these were examined and qualified as heretical; the author published an apology, shewing the ignorance of his judges. His adversaries, finding that they could not dispute with him, accused him of being a magician; and asserted, that so much knowledge in so young a person could only be acquired by a compact with the devil.

In 1507, the Inquisition, instigated by Ferdinand V., undertook to persuade and arrest Cæsar Borgia, Duke de Valentinois, and brother-in-law to John d'Albret, King of Navarre. It is most probable that this prince would have been taken, if he had not been killed in the same year before Viana, not far from Logroño, by the governor of the fortress, Juan Carces de los Fayos. Cæsar Borgia was the natural son of Don Rodrigo de Borgia (afterwards raised to the papal see, by the name of Alexander VI.), and the famous *Vanoci*. He had been a cardinal, but, in 1499, his father, in compliance with the request of Louis XII., King of France, who adopted him, granted him dispensations to marry the sister of the King of Navarre; he then obtained the titles and estates of the dukedom of Valentinois. A short time after the death of Cæsar Borgia's father, in 1503, he was arrested at Naples, by the order of Gonzalez de Cordova, viceroy of that monarchy, on the pretence that he disturbed the tranquillity of the kingdom. He was taken to Spain, and confined in the Castle of Medina del Campo, from whence he made his escape, and fled to Navarre. Ferdinand, finding that his niece, the Queen of Navarre, would not give up this prince to him, resolved to secure him by means of the Inquisition.

It has been already stated that the inquisitors did not prosecute the memory of Charles V.; but in 1565, they were concerned in the proceedings against Jane d'Albert, the hereditary Queen of Navarre, and against her son, Henry de Bourbon, afterwards Henry IV. of France, and his sister, Margaret de Bourbon Albret, who married the sovereign Duke of Bar. The holy office, however, did not take an active part in this affair. After Ferdinand V. had taken possession of the five districts of the kingdom of Navarre, called *Merindades*, he refused to recognise either Jane or Henry de Bourbon as sovereigns of Navarre. These princes were deprived of all their dominions, except the sixth *Merindade* of Navarre, by a papal bull in 1512; the Court of Rome also refused to grant them the title of Kings of Navarre until the year 1561. The first to whom it was given was Anthony de Bourbon.

Charles V. had ordered in his will that the right of his successors to the crown of Navarre should be examined, and that it should be restored to its rightful owners if it had been unjustly seized. In 1561, Philip II., who had not yet thought of executing the intentions of his father, perceiving that the king, Anthony de Bourbon, inclined towards Calvinism, entered into a negotiation with him on this subject. In order to attach him to the Catholic party, Philip promised to obtain a dissolution of his marriage with Jane, who was a heretic, to induce his Holiness to excommunicate her, and give her states to him, with the consent of the Kings of France and Spain; to restore Navarre, or to give the island of Sardinia in exchange for it, and to negotiate a marriage between him and Mary Stuart, Queen of Scotland. Anthony accepted this offer, but died before it could be executed. Philip then, through the intrigues of his agents at Rome, obtained the excommunication of Jane d'Albret, and that her states should be offered to the first Catholic prince who would take possession of them on the condition of expelling the heretics. Pius V. published a bull on the 28th September, 1563, excommunicating Queen Jane, for having adopted the heresy of Calvin, and promulgating his doctrines in her states ; and according to the requisition of the pro-curator-fiscal of the Inquisition, his Holiness summoned her to appear at Rome, within six months, to answer these charges.

Catherine de Medicis, regent of France, who was then reconciled to the Prince of Condé, the brother of the late King of Navarre, was displeased at the Inquisition of Rome; and in order to stop the proceedings, sent an ambassador extraordinary to the Pope, with a very learned memorial, which has been printed, with the bull, in the *Mémoires du Prince de Condé.*

Charles IX., and Catherine de Medicis, his mother, wrote to Philip II., (who was married to Elizabeth of France, the daughter of Catherine,) and informed him of what had passed, requesting that he would act in concert with them. Philip replied, that he not only disapproved of the conduct of the Court of Rome, but he offered to protect the Princess Jane against any one who should attempt to deprive her of her states. It has, however, been proved by the letters of the French king to the Cardinal d'Armagnac, that Philip at the same time offered assistance to the Catholic subjects of Jane, to induce them to rebel against her, and that he privately introduced Spanish troops into her territories. This event was the origin of a confederation, known by the name of the *Catholic League,* which forms part of the histories of M. de Varillas, and of the secret memoirs of M. de Villeroi.

The Spanish monarch endeavoured to obtain, by means of the Inquisition of Spain, what he had been refused by that of Rome. The inquisitor-general Cardinal Espinosa, in concert with the Cardinal de Lorraine, caused several witnesses to be examined, to prove that Jane d'Albret and her children were Huguenots, and that as they encouraged this heresy in their states, it might spread into Spain. Espinosa (who pretended that Philip was ignorant of his proceedings) informed the council that it was necessary to impart this circumstance to his majesty, and entreat him to do all in his power to prevent Jane from persecuting the Catholics.

Philip secretly directed the affairs of the *League* in France, by means of communications with the chiefs of the party; and according to his orders the inquisitor-general formed a plot to carry off the Queen of Navarre and her two children, and confine them in the dungeons of the Inquisition of Saragossa. He hoped to succeed in this enterprise, through the assistance afforded him by the Cardinal de Lorraine, and the other chiefs of the *League*.

Those French historians who wrote after this period (such as the Abbé St. Real, Mercier, and others) have endeavoured to throw all the odium of this plot on Philip II. and the Duke of Alva; but as truth is the first duty of historians, I am compelled to say, that the de Guises were the authors of it. Nicolas de Neuville, Lord of Villeroy, minister and first secretary of state during the reigns of Charles IX., Henry III., Henry IV., and Louis XIII., has left details of this affair, in a *Memoir* which was found after his death among his papers, and which has been printed with many others, under the title of *Secret Memoirs of M. de Villeroi*. This author, who was a contemporary, and acquainted with the secrets of the government, seems to be more deserving of confidence than any other.

Philip II. took advantage of the attempt, though it entirely failed; and wrote to represent to the Pope, that his subjects in the neighbourhood of France might imbibe the heresy, and demanded and obtained an order to separate from the bishopric of Bayonne the villages of the valley of Bastan, and those of the arch-priesthood of Fontarabia.

In 1563, the Inquisition of Murcia condemned another prince, called Don Philip of Arragon. See Chapter 23.

In 1589, the Prince Alexander Farnese, governor-general of the Low Countries and Flanders, and uncle to Philip II., was denounced to the Inquisition of Spain, as suspected of Lutheranism, and a favourer of heretics ; it was also said, that he intended to become the sovereign of Flanders, for which purpose he courted the Protestants. No proofs of heresy were produced, and the inquisitor-general suspended the proceedings. Although the enemies of Prince Farnese made every effort to ruin him, Philip did not deprive him of his office, and he remained Governor of the Low Countries till his death in 1592. It has been said that he was poisoned by Philip II.

The Cardinal Quiroga, and the Council of the Inquisition, treated the Sovereign Pontiff, Sextus Quintus, with little respect. This Pope published a translation of the Bible in Italian, and prefaced it by a bull, in which he recommended every one to read it, saying, that the faithful would derive the greatest advantages from it. This conduct of the Pope was contrary to all the regulations from the time of Leo X. All doctrinal works had been forbidden to be in the vulgar tongue for fifty years, by the expurgatory index of the council, and by the Inquisitions of Rome and Madrid. The Cardinals, Quiroga at Madrid, and Toledo at Rome, and others, represented to Philip II., that great evils would arise from it, if he did not employ his influence to induce the Pope to relinquish his design. Philip commissioned the Count d'Olivarez, to expostulate with the Pontiff; the Count obeyed, but at the peril of his life, for Sextus Quintus was on the point of depriving him of it, without respect for the rights of nations, or for the privileges of Olivarez as an ambassador.

This formidable Pope died in 1592, and Philip was suspected of having shortened his days by slow poison. After this event, the Inquisition of Spain having received witnesses to prove that the *infallible* oracle of the law was a favourer of heretics, condemned the Sextine Bible, as they had already condemned those of Cassiodorus de Reyna, and many others.

A preparatory instruction was commenced against Don John of Austria, a natural son of Philip IV., but the proceedings were suspended by the king. This event was caused by the intrigues of the inquisitor-general, John Everard Nitardo, who was the mortal enemy of Don John; and some persons were found base enough to accuse the king'sbrother of Lutheranism, in order to flatter him.

The Grandees of Spain may be numbered among the princes, since Charles V. declared them to possess that title, and that they were equal in rank to the sovereigns of the Circles of Germany; they had likewise the privileges of being seated and covered in the presence of the king, as, for example, when the emperor was crowned.

Among the princes humiliated by the Inquisition, the following persons must be included. The Marquis de Prugo, the grand-master of the military order of Montesa, the Duke de Gaudia, St. Francis de Borgia, the Blessed Juan de Ribera, the venerable Don Juan de Palafox, and many others, among whom were several ladies. None of these trials had any serious result; the denounced persons only received a severe remonstrance, except in the case of the Dowager Marchioness d'Alcagnices, who was imprisoned in the Convent of St. Catherine, at Valladolid. These persons were all innocent; the only foundation for the accusations was, their intimacy with the Doctors Pedro and Augustin Cazalla, Fray Dominic de Roxas, and Don Pedro Samiento de Roxas: they were also accused of having heard conversations on justification, and of not having denounced them.

CHAPTER XXVIII.

OF THE CONDUCT OF THE HOLY OFFICE TOWARDS THOSE PRIESTS WHO ABUSED THE SACRAMENT OF CONFESSION.

WHILE the Inquisition was occupied in persecuting the peaceable Lutherans, they were obliged to take measures to punish Catholic priests, who abused the ministry of confession, by seducing their penitents. The inquisitors were compelled to act with great reserve and caution in this affair, that they might not furnish the Lutherans with new arguments against auricular confession, and the Catholics with a motive for employing it less frequently.

On the 18th of January, 1556, Paul IV. addressed a brief to the Inquisitors of Granada, in which his holiness commanded them to prosecute those priests whom *the public voice* accused of seduction, and not to pardon *one* of them. He also recommended that they should ascertain if the doctrine of the priests on the sacrament of penitence was orthodox, and if it was necessary to pursue the course prescribed for the prosecution of heretics. The inquisitors communicated this brief to the Archbishop of Granada, and the Council of the Inquisition, which informed them in reply, that the publication of the brief in the usual form would produce great inconveniences, and that it was necessary to act with prudence and moderation.

For this reason the archbishop summoned the curés, and other ecclesiastics, while the inquisitors did the same with the prelates of the regular communities, to recommend to them to notify the brief of the Pope to all the confessors, that they might be more strict in their conduct for the future, and that the people might not be made acquainted with the order of his holiness. At the same time, informations were taken against those who were suspected, and some who were guilty were privately punished under other pretexts.

This measure convinced the Pope that the abuse was not confined to the kingdom of Granada, and, in 1561, he addressed a brief to the inquisitor-general Valdés, authorizing him to proceed against the confessors guilty of this crime in the domains of Philip, as if they were heretics. As this bull did not effect the inquisitors-general who succeeded Valdés, several others were afterwards expedited.

It was the custom to read the *Edict of Denunciations* in the churches every year, on some Sunday in Lent, and as the number of crimes increased, new articles were added to the Edict. The inquisitors of some provinces introduced that of the priests who corrupted their penitents, and Raynaldus Gonzalvius Montanus, speaking of the occurrences at Seville after the publication of this edict, declares that it was published in 1563, and that the denunciations were so numerous, that the notaries of the holy office refused to receive them, and that the inquisitors were obliged to relinquish the prosecution of the criminals.

The edict was not published till 1564, and the denunciations were much less numerous than he pretends. The denunciations ceased, because the obligation imposed on the penitents to inform against the criminals was annulled by the Supreme Council. Several other edicts were afterwards published on this subject, and they were framed to include a greater number of cases.

This crime is never punished in a public *auto-da-fé*, because it might prevent the faithful from confessing themselves. The *auto-da-fé* was held in the hall of the holy office ; the secular confessors were summoned to attend it, two from each of the establishments in the town, and four from that of the condemned person, if there were any. No laymen were permitted to be present, except the notaries. When the sentence, and the motives for it, had been read, the dean of the inquisitors exhorted the criminal to acknowledge his crime, and prepared him to make the abjuration of all heresies in general, and of that of which he was suspected in particular. He then placed himself on his knees, pronounced his confession of faith, and signed his abjuration: the inquisitor absolved him *ad cautelam* from all the censures he had incurred: this act terminated the *auto-da-fé,* the criminal was taken back to the prison, and the next day he was transferred to the convent in which he was to be imprisoned, according to his sentence. The confessors who attended this ceremony, were commanded to inform others of the affair, to deter them from committing the same crime.

CHAPTER XXIX.

OF THE TRIALS INSTITUTED BY THE INQUISITION AGAINST THE PRELATES AND SPANISH DOCTORS OF THE COUNCIL OF TRENT.

Prelates.

EIGHT venerable prelates and nine doctors of theology, who were sent by Spain to the Council of Trent, were attacked in secret by the Inquisition of their country. From particular circumstances, rather than from the will of the inquisitors, some of these trials were suspended, before any attempt had been made on the liberty of the doctors.

The trial of the Archbishop of Toledo ought to be introduced in this place, but its importance and interest renders it worthy of a separate chapter.

Don Pedro Guerrero, born at Leza-de-rio-Leza, in Rioxa, archbishop of Granada, was one of those prelates who, from their learning and virtue, had the greatest influence in the

Council of Trent. He was prosecuted by the Inquisition of
Valladolid, for the favourable opinion he expressed in 1558,
of the Catechism of Carranza, and for the letters he wrote
to him in the following year. It was also known that he
voted for the archbishop, in the commission employed by the
Council of Trent to examine his book, and likewise in the
particular congregation of that assembly, which approved
his conduct in 1563. Guerrero averted the danger by retracting his opinion in 1574, when he was informed of the
inclinations of Philip on this subject. He then gave a new
opinion, entirely different from the first, persuaded that it
would be sent to Rome, which in fact was done, in order to
strengthen the charges against Carranza: this is proved by
the letter of the Supreme Council to Philip II., in which it
announces that the censures which his majesty had demanded
of the Archbishop of Granada were prepared, and that it
was absolutely necessary to send them to Rome, because *it
was to be apprehended that the affair would be soon concluded, that the trial went on quickly*, and that it was necessary to send this document, on account of the high esteem
in which the opinion of the archbishop was held in Rome.*

It would be difficult to give a just idea of the intrigues
which were employed to obtain so contrary an opinion from
Guerrero. The Pope commanded, in a particular brief, that
those censors who had been favourable to the catechism should
examine and censure it again, and afterwards give their opinions
of the inedited works of Carranza. On the arrival of this brief,
the Cardinal Quiroga, who was in the king's confidence, despatched persons whom he could depend upon, to the Archbishop of Granada, to induce him to renew his censure,
*without saying that he had done it before, to conform to the
king's intentions, but as if he only did it in obedience to the
orders of his holiness.* This intrigue is proved by the private

* The trial began in 1558; it had already lasted more than fifteen
years, yet the council said that it went on quickly.!

instructions which Quiroga gave to his messengers. It must be confessed that the conduct of the archbishop of Granada does little honour to his memory, but it must also be remembered how formidable the policy of Philip II. rendered him, and that Guerrero was advanced in years.

Don Francisco Blanco, born at Capillas, in the bishopric of Leon, had been bishop of Orense and Malaga, when he was prosecuted on suspicion of Lutheranism, for the same reason as Guerrero.

The arrest of Carranza alarmed Blanco so much, that he wrote immediately to the inquisitor-general, and sent him several inedited works of the archbishop of Toledo. He received an order to repair to Valladolid, where he entered into the convent of Augustins: he made his declarations on the 14th of September, and on the 13th of October, 1559, acknowledged two of his approbations, but declared that he could not consent to ratify them, until he had re-examined the book, since he had given them without reflection, and was only influenced by the great reputation of Carranza. It is impossible to read his declarations, and the letters which he wrote to the inquisitor-general, without perceiving the extreme terror which had seized him. He had recourse to the same means as Guerrero, to extricate himself from his embarrassment. This prelate died in 1581, after having composed several works, which are mentioned by Nicolas Antonio.

Don Francisco Delgado, born at Villa de Peru, in Rioxa, founder of the eldership of the Counts de Berberana, bishop of Lugo, and afterwards of Jaen, and one of the fathers of the council of Trent, was suspected of heresy for the same reasons as the two preceding prelates. He avoided the sentence which threatened him, by retracting his opinions in 1574.

Don Andres Cuesta, bishop of Leon, was prosecuted for thesame cause. The inquisitor-general wrote to him before the arrest of Carranza, to know if he had given a favourable opinion of his catechism. The Bishop replied in the affirmative, and sent him a copy of his opinion. Valdés kept this paper, but could not make any use of it. As the Archbishop of Toledo had then been arrested, the trial of the Bishop of Leon was begun, and the inquisitor-general resolved to summon him to Valladolid. Valdés informed the king of this resolution, and he wrote to Cuesta, saying, that all that was to be done was in the cause of God, and the service of his majesty. The Bishop of Leon submitted without resistance, and on the 14th of October, 1559, he was examined in the Council of the Inquisition, and in the presence of all its members. The opinion which he had given of the catechism, in 1558, was shewn to him, and he acknowledged it to be his, but said that if he examined it again, he should be able to judge differently of Carranza's doctrine. He returned to his diocese, and sent another favourable opinion of the catechism to the inquisitor-general; it was founded on many doctrinal considerations and reflections, which he had not made in that which he sent to Carranza. His letters, declarations, and opinions, shew a bold and strong mind, which may induce one to believe that he was not provoked to retract in 1574, or that his trial recommenced at that period; for the inquisitor-general and the Supreme Council finding in 1560 that the trial of Carranza caused them much trouble and embarrassment, resolved to *suspend* the trials of the other bishops, until the result of the first was known.

Don Antonio Gorrionero, bishop of Almeria, was prosecuted for his favourable opinion of the catechism, and some letters which he wrote on the subject. He however attended the third convocation of the Council of Trent, which took place in 1560, and the following years.

Don Fray Melchior Cano, born in Tarracon, in the province of Cuença: he had resigned the bishopric of the Canaries, and attended the second session of the Council of

Trent, in 1552.   He was a member of the order of St. Dominic, as well as Carranza, and his rival in the government
and administration of the affairs of his order, particularly
after Carranza had obtained the preference, when they were
both candidates for the office of Provincial of Castile. When
the catechism was denounced to the Inquisition, Valdés appointed Cano to examine it, affecting to favour its author,
by choosing qualifiers from the monks of his order, but not
doubting, at the same time, that the opinion of Fray Melchior
would be unfavourable.

Fray Melchior examined the catechism, and some inedited
works of Carranza ; but it appears that he did not strictly
observe the secrecy recommended by the inquisitors, since
Carranza received information of what was passing, while he
was in Flanders, and wrote to Fray Melchior, who replied
to him from Valladolid, in 1559. About this time, Fray
Dominic de Roxas, and some other Lutherans confined in the
secret prisons of the holy office, deposed to certain facts,
which caused some suspicion of Fray Melchior.

However, the prosecution begun against him had no result; for at the time when Cano was about to be reproved by
the inquisitor-general, he offered him the dedication of his
Treatise *de Locis Theologicis*, which was accepted; and as he
had not time to publish it, he left it to the inquisitor-general
in his will, some time before his death, which happened in
1560.   His censure of the Catechism of Carranza, and some
propositions which he had maintained against the archbishop,
and which caused the faith of that prelate to be suspected,
contributed to preserve him from punishment.   His calum-
nious discourse concerning Carranza was no doubt the reason
why he was thought to be his denouncer.

Don Pedro del Frago, bishop of Jaca, was born in 1490,
in Uncastillo, in the diocese of Jaca.   Pedro studied at
Paris, and became a Doctor of the Sorbonne; he learnt Hebrew and Greek, and was considered one of the best Latin

poets of his age. He was appointed theologian to Charles
V., for the first convocation of the Council of Trent; he assisted at it in 1545, and when the second assembly took place
in 1551, he preached a Latin sermon to the fathers, on As-
sumption-day: this discourse forms part of the collection of
documents relating to the council. In 1561, Philip II.
created him Bishop of Alger in Sardinia, and he attended
the third convocation of the council in that quality. Don
Pedro was made, first, Bishop of Jaca, in 1572; and in the
following year, when he was sixty-four years of age, the
Council of the Inquisition commanded the inquisitors of Saragossa to take informations against this worthy prelate, as
suspected of heresy, because he had been denounced as not
being known to confess himself, and that he had no regular
confessor; he was likewise accused of not celebrating mass
with sufficient solemnity. It is surprising that the council
should admit these charges, since a bishop is not obliged to
have a regular confessor, and it is not necessary for any person to confess, so that the public may be informed of it. The
other charge brought against an old man of sixty-four, shews
that there was nothing more serious to accuse him of.
Philip II., to reward his services, gave Don Pedro the bishopric of Huesca, in 1577, where he founded an episcopal
seminary. He died in 1584. He held a synod at Huesca, in
which he established constitutions, which he had drawn up
and caused to be printed; he also composed a Journal of the
most remarkable events in the Council of Trent, from the
year 1542 to 1560, and much Latin poetry.

Among the doctors of theology of the Council of Trent,
who were persecuted or punished by the Inquisition, the
most celebrated is *Benedict Arias Montano*, perhaps the
most learned man of his age in the oriental tongues.

Several towns in Spain have disputed the honour of being
the place of his birth. Montano understood Hebrew,
Chaldee, Syriac, Arabic, Greek, Latin, French, Italian,

English, Dutch, and German: he was almoner to the king, a knight of the order of St. Jago, and doctor of theology in the university of Alcala.

As there were no more copies in the trade of the *Polyglott* Bible of the Cardinal Ximenez de Cisneros, the celebrated Plantin, a printer at Antwerp, represented to Philip II. the advantages which might arise from a new edition, with corrections and additions. The king approved of the scheme, and in 1568 appointed Arias Montano to be the director of the undertaking; he went to Flanders to fulfil the intentions of that monarch, and to compose the Expurgatory *Index*, known as that of the Duke of Alva's. In order to make the reimpression of the Polyglott Bible as perfect as possible, a great number of unpublished copies of the Bible, in all languages, were procured; this great work is in eight folio volumes. St. Pius V. and Gregory XIII. expressed their approbation of the execution of this undertaking, in particular briefs addressed to their nuncios in Flanders. Arias Montano went to Rome, and presented a copy to the Pope in person: he made a very eloquent speech in Latin on the occasion, which gave great pleasure to the Pope and cardinals. The king of Spain made presents of these Bibles to all the Princes of Christendom: it has been called the *Royal Bible*, because it was done by the king's command; the *Philippine*, from his name; of *Antwerp*, because it was printed in that place; *Plantinian*, from the name of the printer; *Polyglott*, from being in several tongues, and of *Montano*, because he had the direction of it, though he was assisted by many learned men of the universities of Paris, Louvain, and Alcala de Henares.

Arias returned to Spain, where the reputation he had acquired caused many persons to become his enemies, particularly among the Jesuits, because he had not consulted Diego Lainez, Alphonso Salmeron, or the other Jesuits of the Council of Trent: he made another enemy in Leon de

Castro, a secular priest, professor of the oriental languages at Salamanca, because he did not consult the university, and employ him in the work. The certainty that he should be protected by the Jesuits induced him to denounce Arias Montano to the Inquisition of Rome. This denunciation was in Latin; he addressed another in Spanish to the Supreme Council at Madrid. Leon de Castro accused him of having given the Hebrew text of the Bible according to the Jewish MSS., and of having made the version accord with the opinions of the Rabbis, without regarding those of the fathers of the church. He also qualified him as suspected of Judaism, because he affected to take the title of Rabbi, *master;* this, however, may be looked upon as a calumny, for in a copy of this Bible, which I have seen, his superscription is that of *Thalmud,* which means *disciple.* Other accusations were brought against him by the Jesuits. Leon de Castro, impatient to see Arias arrested, wrote on the 9th of November, 1576, to Don Fernando de la Vega Tonseca, a counsellor of the *supreme,* and renewed his denunciation, shewing by his letter that he was only actuated by resentment, at finding his pretended zeal so ill repaid. There is no doubt that Arias would have been arrested, if he had not been protected by the king, and if the Pope had not signified his approbation of his Bible by a special brief; he, however, thought it necessary to go to Rome to justify himself.

Leon de Castro circulated copies of his denunciation, and the Jesuits did the same. He was attacked by Fray Luis Estrada, in a discourse addressed to Montano, in 1574, and his denunciation was also refuted by Pedro Chacon, another learned Spaniard, who proved the injury that would accrue to the Christian religion, if it was admitted that the Hebrew MSS. were falsified. De Castro published a reply, which he called *Apologetic.*

Arias returned from Rome, and he could depend upon

the favour of the king ; he was not arrested, but confined to the city of Madrid. The council decreed that a copy of the denunciations should be given to him ; Arias replied to, and refuted the charges, insinuating that this attack was a plot of the Jesuits.

The inquisitor-general, in concert with the council, appointed different theologians as qualifiers in the trial of Arias, and remitted to them the denunciation of de Castro and his apology, the reply of the accused, and the two writings of Estrada and Chacon. The principal censor was Juan de Mariana, a Jesuit, who was considered very learned in the oriental languages, and in theology. This choice, in which the Jesuits had some influence, induced them to suppose that Arias would be condemned. They were, however, disappointed ; for though Mariana declared that the Polyglott Bible was full of errors and inaccuracies, he acknowledged that they were of no importance, and were not deserving of theological censure. This decision induced the council to pronounce in favour of Arias, who was soon after informed that he had gained his cause at Rome. Mariana was never forgiven by the Jesuits for his impartiality, and they afterwards made him a victim of the Inquisition.

Doctor Don Diego Sobaños, rector of the university of Alcala, a theologian of the third convocation of the Council of Trent, not only expressed a favourable opinion of the catechism of Carranza, but chiefly by his ascendency over the theologians of his university, induced them to approve the work. He was tried by the Inquisition of Valladolid, and condemned to a pecuniary penalty, and to be absolved *ad cautelam*, from the censures which he had incurred by approving the catechism.

Diego Lainez, born in Almazan, in the diocese of Siguenza, second general of the Society of Jesus, was denounced to the Inquisition as suspected of Lutheranism, and the heresy of the *illuminati*. The Jesuits did not pardon Valdés for having prosecuted their general, and they contributed to his dismission in 1566. Diego Lainez, who was at Rome, succeeded in evading the jurisdiction of the Inquisition of Spain.

Fray Juan de Regla, a Jeronimite, who had been confessor to Charles V., and provincial of his order in Spain, theologian of the Council of Trent at the second convocation, was arrested by the Inquisition of Saragossa, on the denunciation of the Jesuits, as suspected of Lutheranism : he abjured eighteen propositions, was absolved and subjected to a penánce.

Fray Francisco Villalba, a Jeronimite of Montamarta, born at Zamora, was one of the theologians at the second Council of Trent, and preacher to Charles V. and Philip II. He attended the emperor at his death, and pronounced his funeral oration. Philip II. had often consulted him. The Inquisition of Toledo began an action against him as a Lutheran, and being descended from the Jews. This arose from the envy of some monks of his order, who denounced him. The general of his order, and his coadjutors, made inquiries on the genealogy of Villalba, and discovered that he was not descended either from the Jews or any persons punished by the Inquisition. The protection of the king prevented the Inquisition from obtaining witnesses soon enough to substantiate the charges, and they did not dare to arrest him without further information. At this period, in 1575, Villalba died at the Escurial, leaving, among honest Spaniards, the reputation of being a good Catholic.

Fray Michel de Medina, a Franciscan, was a theologian of the third convocation of the Council of Trent. He was born at Benalcazar, and became a member of the college of St. Peter and St. Paul at the university of Alcala, and guardian of the convent of Franciscans at Toledo; he died in 1578, in the secret prisons of that city, after having been sentenced as suspected of professing the opinions of Luther.

This accusation was occasioned by his great esteem for the theological writings of Fray Juan de Fero, a monk of his order. He published some of his works, which were denounced to the Inquisition, and Medina wrote an apology for them, which was placed in the index by Cardinal Quiroga, in 1583. Nicolas Antonio has given notices of some works of Medina, and asserts that he justified himself on his doctrine. This statement is inaccurate, for Medina was declared to be suspected, and however innocent he may be supposed, his works were condemned, and he would have been obliged to abjure and receive absolution *ad cautelam*, if death had not arrested the progress of his trial.

Fray Pedro de Soto, a Dominican, confessor to Charles V. and first theologian of Pope Pius IV. in the third convocation of the Council of Trent. He was persecuted by the Inquisition of Valladolid in 1560, on suspicion of Lutheranism: this suspicion was founded on the declarations of some accomplices of Cazalla, of the favourable opinion given by Fray Pedro on the Catechism of Carranza, of his letters to the archbishop, his efforts to induce Fray Dominic de Soto to retract his first opinions of the work, and to approve it, and on what he said at the council. Pedro de Soto was not arrested, as he died at Trent in 1563, during the first forms of his trial. He was taken by Philip II. to England, to labour in the cause of religion. Nicolas Antonio mentions his works.

Fray Dominic de Soto, a Dominican, professor at Salamanca, attended the two first convocations of the Council of Trent; he had a great knowledge of theology, but he shewed himself full of deceit and without any resolution, when, wishing to favour two adverse parties at the same time, he lost the esteem of both. An account of his conduct towards the Doctor Egidius has been already given. He did not act with more sincerity in the affair of the companion of his studies, the Archbishop of Toledo. The inquisitors of Valladolid

commissioned him to examine and censure the Catechism of
Carranza : he noted two hundred propositions, as *heretical,
ill-sounding*, or *favouring the heretics*. The archbishop being
informed of his conduct, wrote to Pedro de Soto in September, 1558, to complain of Fray Dominic, and begged that he
would take his part and defend him. An epistolary correspondence was the result of this letter, and when Carranza
was arrested, the letters were found among his papers :
among them was one which deserves particular attention ; in
it Fray Dominic speaks of the trials he had been put to by
the inquisitors of Valladolid, and the violence which was
used to make him censure the Catechism as he had done,
although he had said that he thought it good and according
with sound doctrine. These words were the origin of his
trial, and it is certain that he would have been arrested and
taken to the secret prisons ; but he died on the 17th of December, 1560, when his trial began to assume a dangerous
aspect.

Fray Juan de Ludeña, Dominican, born at Madrid, prior
of the convent of St. Paul at Valladolid, and the author of
several controversial works against the Lutherans. He was
prosecuted by the Inquisition of Valladolid in 1559 for Lutheranism, because he gave a favourable opinion of the Catechism of Carranza. He was not taken to the prisons, but appeared at the *audiences of the charges* in the hall of the tribunal. He justified himself by declaring that he had only
read the work through rapidly, on account of his great confidence in the virtue of the author, and because he did not
discover any error in doctrine : he was condemned to a private
penance, which was not at all humiliating. This precaution,
which prevented his trial from becoming public, gave him
the liberty of attending the third convocation of the Council
of Trent in the quality of procurator to the Bishop of Siguenza, and of preaching before the fathers of that assembly
on the first Sunday in Advent, 1563. If Ludeña had had the

boldness to defend his censure, he would certainly have been punished severely.

To this account a list of other prelates prosecuted by the Inquisition is added, but those mentioned in the former chapters are omitted.

Abad la Sierra (Don Augustine), bishop of Barbastro. He was denounced at Madrid in 1796 as a Jansenist, because he corresponded with some of the French bishops who had taken the oaths. This denunciation had no result. He was attacked a second time at Saragossa in 1801. His accusers renewed the charge of correspondence with the French bishops, and his having granted matrimonial dispensations according to a royal order was imputed to him as a crime. This accusation failed as well as the former.

Abad la Sierra (Don Emmanuel), archbishop of Selimbria *in partibus infidelium*, inquisitor-general after Don Augustine Rubin de Cevallos. In 1794 Charles IV. commanded him to quit his office, and to retire to Sopetran, a Benedictine monastery near Madrid. Don Emmanuel was possessed of great talents and profound learning; his opinions were enlightened in the highest degree. In 1793 this prelate commanded me to make him a plan for an establishment of learned qualifiers to censure books and persons. After being informed of the principles of my system, he commissioned me to write a work to expose the vices of the procedure of the holy office, and to propose one more useful to religion and the state. When this prelate lost his office of inquisitor-general, he was denounced a Jansenist by a fanatical monk, but the information was neglected.

Arrellano (Don Joseph Xavier Rodriguez d'), archbishop of Burgos, and a member of the council extraordinary of Charles III. This prelate has composed a great number of works on the theological principles of the *Summary of St. Thomas*, which are taught by the Dominicans, and are in opposition to the moral of the Jesuits. The partisans of the

Jesuits and some friends of the Inquisition denounced Arellano as a Jansenist, because he expressed opinions favourable to temporal power, and defended the royal and civil authorities against the holy office. The inquisitors could not take any advantage of the denunciation, because it did not express any particular proposition.

Buruaga (Don Thomas Saenz de). He was archbishop of Saragossa, and incurred the same danger as Arellano.

Muzquiz (Don Raphaël de), born at Viana in Navarre. He was almoner and preacher to Charles III. and Charles IV., confessor of the Queen Louisa, successively bishop of Avila and archbishop of Pantiago. He was implicated in the affairs of Don Antonio de la Cuesta and his brother, and this was sufficient to induce the inquisitors to prosecute him. This prelate was one of the persecutors of the two brothers. Charles IV., having ordered the writings of the trial to be submitted to him, discovered the intrigue, and condemned the archbishop to pay a considerable fine, and receive a reprimand.

Acuña (Don Antonio), bishop of Zamora, commander of one of the armies of Castile, which were raised by the people for the war of the *Commons* against the oppression of the Flemings, who governed Spain in the name of Charles V. That prince wished that the bishop and the priests who engaged in the war, as soldiers, should be punished by the Inquisition as suspected of heresy, because they acted in opposition to the spirit of peace taught by Jesus Christ and his Apostles, and contrary to the spirit of the Catholic Church. Leo X., however, pretended that it would be a scandal if the bishop was punished by the holy office, and that it would be sufficient if he was judged at Rome, and the priests by their diocesan prelates.

La Plana-Castillon (Don Joseph de), bishop of Tarragona. He was a member of the council-extraordinary convoked by Charles III. The inquisitors noted him as a Jansenist for the same reasons as *Arellano*.

Mendoza (Don Alvarez de), bishop of Avila. He was noted in the registers of the Inquisition as suspected of heresy, from the declarations of some of the witnesses in the trial of Carranza.

CHAPTER XXX.

OF THE PROSECUTION OF SEVERAL SAINTS AND HOLY PERSONS BY THE INQUISITION.

An account has been already given of the persecutions of Don Ferdinand de Talavera, first Archbishop of Granada; of Juan Davila, surnamed the Apostle of Andalusia; and of St. John-de-Dieu, founder of the congregation of Hospitallars. The following is a list of other holy persons who have been prosecuted by the holy office :—

St. Ignacius de Loyola was denounced as an *illuminati* to the Inquisition of Valladolid, and when the inquisitors were about to arrest him, he went to France, afterwards to Italy, and arrived at Rome, where he was tried and acquitted; after having been so likewise in Spain by a juridical sentence of the vicar-general of the Bishop of Salamanca. His real name was Iñigo.

Melchior Cano says, in an unpublished work written during the life of Iñigo, " that he fled from Spain when the Inquisition intended to arrest him as a heretic of the sect of *Illuminati.* He went to Rome, and wished to be judged by the Pope. As no person appeared to accuse him, he was discharged."

It is certain that St. Ignacius was arrested at Salamanca in 1527, as a *fanatic* and *illuminati*, and that he recovered his liberty in about twenty-two days; he was enjoined in his preaching from qualifying mortal or venial sins, until he had studied theology four years. It is also true that when the inquisitors of Valladolid learnt that the saint was in prison,

they wrote to cause an inquest to be made of the words and
actions which caused a suspicion that he was one of the
Illuminati.

But it is not proved that Ignacius quitted Spain to escape
from punishment ; it appears that he only fulfilled his intention of studying theology at Paris. The humility of the
saint was so great, that when he was denounced a second
time in that city, to Matthew d'Ory, the apostolical inquisitor, he surrendered himself voluntarily, and had no difficulty in proving his orthodoxy.

It is not more certain that he went to Rome at that time,
since he was still at Paris in 1535, and he afterwards
returned to Spain, where he remained a year without being
molested, though he preached in several provinces. He then
embarked for Italy, went first to Bologna, and then to
Venice, where he was a third time denounced as an heretic,
but justified himself to the papal nuncio, and was admitted
into the priesthood in that city. Ignacius arrived in Rome
in 1538.

It cannot be proved that he was acquitted at Rome because he had no accuser, since any criminal may be prosecuted
by the minister of the public and punished. It is true that
there was not at that time a particular tribunal of the Inquisition at Rome; but the civil judges could punish heretics,
and the procurator-fiscal impeached the criminals. St.Ignacius
was again denounced by a Spaniard named Navarro. The
informer deposed that Ignacius had been accused and convicted of several heresies in Spain, France, and Venice, and
charged him with some other crimes. Fortunately his three
judges knew his innocence, and he was acquitted. His accuser was banished for life, and three Spaniards who had
supported his evidence were condemned to retract.

Thus it appears that Melchoir Cano was misinformed
when he wrote, ten years after, that Iñigo was acquitted because no accuser appeared.

St. Francis de Borgia, a disciple of Loyola, and third general of his order, succeeded Lainez, in 1565, and died 1572. He had been the Duke de Gandia, and was cousin to the king in the third degree, by his mother, Jane of Arragon.

In 1559, the Inquisition of Valladolid tried several Lutherans, who were condemned. Many of these heretics, who endeavoured to justify themselves by supporting their doctrine by the opinions of St. Francis de Borgia, whose virtue was well known, related some discourses and actions of this saint, to prove that they thought as he did, on the justification of souls by faith, on the passion and death of Jesus Christ; and added, to strengthen their defence, the authority of some mystic treatises. Among these involuntary persecutors, was Fray Dominic de Roxas, his near relation, and advantage was taken of a former denunciation of his *Treatise on Christian Works*, which he composed while he was known as the Duke of Gandia.

This book, the discourse of Melchior Cano, and the Dominicans, caused him to be accused as favouring the heresy of the Illuminati. Neither his merit, nor his near relationship to the king, would have saved him from the prisons of Valladolid, if he had not hastened to Rome the moment he was informed that his trial had commenced, and that his enemies would endeavour to secure his person. He escaped from the Inquisition, but he had the mortification of seeing his work twice placed in the Index, in 1559 and in 1583.

Juan de Ribera was a natural son of Don Pedro Afan de Ribera, Duke of Alcala, and Viceroy of Naples and Catalonia. In 1568, he passed from the bishopric of Badajoz to the archbishopric of Valencia; his life was irreproachable: but his great charity and ardent zeal, in endeavouring to reform the clergy, made him many enemies.

In 1570 Philip II. commanded him to visit the University of Valencia, and reform some of its rules. The archbishop began to fulfil his commission, but offended some of the doctors, who conspired against him. They circulated defamatory libels concerning him, during a whole year, and the affair was carried so far, that a monk prayed for his conversion publicly in the church of Valencia. Ribera was denounced to the Inquisition, as a heretic, fanatic, and one of the Illuminati.

St. Juan de Ribera would not demand the punishment of his slanderers; but the procurator-fiscal being informed that Onuphrius Gacet, a member of the college, was the principal author of the intrigue, denounced him to the provisor and vicar-general of the archbishop. Gacet being convicted, was imprisoned. The archbishop did not think it proper that a judge belonging to his own household should take cognizance of offences which concerned him personally, and in order to remove all suspicion of partiality, he wished that the trial should be transferred 'to the Inquisition of Valencia, as some of the libels and texts of Scripture were employed in so scandalous a manner, that they came under the jurisdiction of the tribunal.

St. Juan de Ribera communicated his design to the Cardinal Espinosa, inquisitor-general, who commanded the inquisitors of Valencia to continue the trial. The inquisitors had already begun the preparatory instruction against the archbishop according to the denunciations; witnesses were found to support them, which is not surprising, since every accuser caused the men devoted to his party to sign his deposition as witnesses. The trial, however, took a sudden turn; instead of proceeding in the usual forms, the inquisitor caused a decree to be read in all the churches of Valencia, enjoining every individual to denounce all those who employed passages of the Holy Scriptures in a scandalous manner, on pain of excommunication. The informations began, and the inquisitors arrested both priests and laymen. The affair was carried on as a matter of faith; some of the accused were already condemned, and others on the point of being so, when the procurator of the holy office declared that doubts existed of the competence of the inquisitors, and advised that the affair should be referred to the Pope, who would appease the scruples.

The tribunal approved of the proposition, and in 1572, Gregory XIII. expedited a brief, which contained all that has been here related, and authorized the inquisitor-general, and the provincial inquisitors, to decide-in similar cases, and at the same time sanctioned all that had been done. The inquisitors then condemned several persons, some to corporal punishments, others to pecuniary penalties, declaring that they should have been more severe, but from consideration for the archbishop, who had solicited the pardon of the criminals, that no person might suffer from an injury done to him.

St. Theresa de Jesus, one of the most celebrated women in Spain for her talents, was accused before the Inquisition of Seville. She was not imprisoned, because the trial was suspended after the preparatory instructions. She was born at Avila, in 1515.

St. Juan de la Croix, who united with St. Theresa, in reforming the Convents of Carmelites, was born at Ontiveros in the diocese of Avila, in 1542. He was prosecuted by the Inquisitions of Seville, Toledo, and Valladolid. He was denounced as a fanatic, and of the Illuminati: the proceedings did not go farther than the preparatory instruction. St. Juan de la Croix died at Ubeda, in 1591. He composed several works on mental orisons.

St. Joseph de Calasanz, founder of the institute of regular clerks of the Christian schools. He was imprisoned in the dungeons of the holy office as a fanatic, and of the *Illuminati*; but he justified himself and was acquitted. He died some time after, at the age of ninety-two. He was born in 1556.

Venerables.

The venerable Fray Louis de Grenada, born in 1504, was

the disciple of Juan d'Avila ; he was of the order of St. Dominic, and left several works on religion. He was implicated in the trial of the Lutherans at Valladolid; Fray Dominic de Roxas defended his opinions, by saying that they were the same as those of Fray Louis de Grenada, Carranza, and other good Catholics. The procurator-fiscal made Fray Dominic renew his declaration, with the intention of producing him as a witness in the trial of Fray Louis: Fray Dominic was burnt five days after. A sentence condemning some of his works was also brought against Fray Louis.

He was denounced a third time as one of the *Illuminati*, but was acquitted. Fray Louis died in 1588. His works are well known : it is singular that the Index in which his condemnation was published, was afterwards prohibited by the inquisitor-general Quiroga.

The venerable Don Juan de Palafox y Mendoza, the natural son of Don James Palafox, afterwards Marquis de Hariza and of Donna Maria de Mendoza, (who soon after became a Carmelite); he was born in 1600. He was made Bishop de la Puebla de los Angelos, in America, in 1639 ; afterwards Archbishop and Viceroy of Mexico, and lastly, Bishop of Osma, in Spain, in 1653. He died in 1659, leaving several works on history, devotion, and mysticity, and with so great a reputation of sanctity, that his canonization is pending at Rome.

Don Juan had great disputes with the Jesuits in America, on account of the privileges of his rank, of which the Fathers wished to deprive him. The most important of his writings, is his letter to Pope Innocent X., who terminated their disputes, to a certain degree, by a brief, in 1648. The Jesuits did not consider themselves vanquished; they denounced the archbishop as one of the *Illuminati* and a false devotee, at Rome, at Madrid, and at Mexico. The provincial inquisitors of the last city applied to the Supreme Council, and the venerable Palafox suffered everything from them which they could inflict, except imprisonment. They condemned and prohibited the writings which the archbishop had published in his defence, and circulated those of his adversaries, and some libels which they had framed to ruin Don Antonio Gabiola, procurator-fiscal to the Inquisition, who openly disapproved of the conduct of the Jesuits.

This officer wrote to Palafox in 1647, exhorting him to make every effort, that the trials before the Inquisition of Mexico should proceed in a regular manner, according to the spirit of the institution, and encouraging him to oppose his formidable enemies.

The Jesuits, by their intrigues, succeeded in causing some of the works of Palafox to be placed in the Index, but the congregation of cardinals having afterwards declared that they contained nothing reprehensible, or which could impede his beatification, the inquisitors were obliged to efface them from the catalogue.

CHAPTER XXXI.

OF THE CELEBRATED TRIAL OF DON CARLOS, PRINCE OF THE ASTURIAS.

ALL Europe has believed that Philip II. caused the Inquisition to proceed against Don Carlos his only son; that the inquisitors condemned the prince to death, and that they only differed on the manner in which the sentence was to be executed. Some writers have gone so far as to record the conversations which took place, on this occasion, between Philip and the inquisitor-general, Don Carlos and other persons, with as much confidence as if they had been present at them, and have even quoted part of the sentence as if they had read it.

As it has been my principal aim to ascertain the truth, I

have examined the archives of the Council of the Inquisition and others, and I, in consequence, affirm, that Don Carlos was never tried or condemned by the Inquisition; an opinion only was given against the prince by the councillors of state, whose president was the Cardinal Espinosa, who at that time was the king's favourite. The circumstance of the cardinal being inquisitor-general may have been the cause of the mistake; the deaths of the Count de Egmont and other noblemen, and the intention of establishing the Inquisition in the Low Countries, may have tended to confirm the general opinion.

Don Carlos lost his life in consequence of a verbal sentence approved by his father, and the holy office was not concerned in it. As I write only the history of the Inquisition, this fact renders it unnecessary to say more on the subject; but as almost all the historians of Europe have said that the inquisitors condemned Don Carlos, the best way of disproving it, is to relate the facts as they occurred.

Don Carlos was born at Valladolid, on the 8th of July in 1545, and lost his mother, Maria of Portugal, four days after his birth. Charles V. scarcely ever saw him until the year 1557, when he abdicated and retired to the monastery of St. Juste in Estremadura. He visited his grandson in passing through Valladolid. It is not true that Charles V. educated Don Carlos, and formed his mind; but during his various journeys he gave him good preceptors. The young prince was nine years old, and his father was on the point of embarking for England, when the emperor wrote a letter from Germany, dated the 3rd of July, 1554, in which he speaks (among other tutors intended for his grandson) of Don Honoré de Juan, one of the greatest humanists of his age, and afterwards Bishop of Osma*. It is evident that Don Carlos was not fond of learning, by a letter from his

---

* Father Kircher has inserted this letter in his work called *Principis Christiani Archetipon Politicum.*

father, dated Brussels, 15th of March, 1558, in which he thanks the preceptor for the trouble he took to give his pupil a taste for reading, and to inculcate moral principles ; he desires him to pursue the same plan, adding, that " though Don Carlos may not profit by it so much as he ought, it will not be entirely useless. I have also written to Don Garcia to pay particular attention in selecting those who see and visit the prince ; it will be better to put a taste for study into his head than many other things*." Philip had imbibed a very disadvantageous opinion of his son's character ; he had been informed that the prince amused himself with cutting the throats of the young rabbits which were brought to him, and that he appeared to take pleasure in seeing them expire. Fabian Estrada relates that the same thing was remarked by a Venetian ambassador †.

War had been declared between France and Spain, and the two powers were on the point of giving battle in August, 1558, but at the same time were negotiating a peace in the secret conference held at the Abbey of Corpans. One of the articles states that Don Carlos, when he arrived at a proper age, should marry Isabella, daughter to Henry II., King of France : the prince was thirteen years of age, and the princess twelve. This circumstance, and the custom observed at that period, of keeping the preliminaries of a peace secret till its conclusion, entirely disproves all that has been said of the love of the young princess, which is the more improbable, as she had never even seen the prince's picture, and very unfavourable accounts of his education had been received. Charles V., after his retirement, had been heard to say, that he thought his grandson shewed a very vicious disposition. This may be attributed to the education given him by his uncle and aunt, Maximilian, King of Bohemia, afterwards

---

* Kircher has inserted the whole of this letter in the work before mentioned.

† Estrada : Decades of the War of Flanders. Decade i. b. 7.

Emperor, and Jane of Austria. They paid the greatest attention to the health of Don Carlos, but neglected to repress his
violent inclinations, and confided the care of forming his character to his governor, his master, and his principal chaplain.

The secret preliminaries only preceded the definitive treaty
of peace, which was concluded at Cambray on the 8th of
April, 1559.   Mary, Queen of England, died during the interval, and Philip II., being then a widower, and only thirty-
two years of age, while Don Carlos was scarcely fourteen,
Henry II. thought it better to marry his daughter to the
king.   The marriage of Isabella to Philip was therefore
agreed upon in the twenty-seventh article, and the secret
article in the preliminiaries was not mentioned.

The marriage was celebrated at Toledo, on the 2nd of February, 1560.   The general Cortes of the kingdom was then
held: the members took the oaths of fidelity to Don Carlos,
and acknowledged him as the successor to the crown, on the
22nd of the same month.   The young queen could not attend this ceremony, as she was attacked by the small-pox a
few days after her marriage. Don Carlos had also fallen sick
of the quartan fever, some time before the arrival of the
queen in Spain. Although this disorder did not prevent him
from riding on horseback, and attending at the assembly of
the Cortes, it appears, from cotemporary writers, that it
rendered him thin, weak, and pale. This circumstance makes
it improbable that he was handsome, and renders the journey
which Mercier pretends that he made to meet the queen at
Alcala, extremely doubtful.

When she became convalescent, Isabella must certainly
have been made acquainted with the neglected education of
Don Carlos, his bad principles, and his insupportable pride.
She could not be ignorant how ill he treated his attendants ;
that when he was angry he broke anything he could seize ;
and she was probably informed of his behaviour to the Duke
of Alva, at the assembly of the Cortes.   The duke had the

entire regulation of everything relating to the ceremonies, and was so much occupied, that he forgot to attend Don Carlos, when he ought to have taken the oath of fidelity. He was sought for, and found, but the young prince was furious, and insulted him so grossly, that he almost made him forget the respect which was due to him. The king compelled Don Carlos to make an apology to the duke ; but it was too late, they hated each other mortally all their lives.

I have not found, in the MSS. I have examined, anything which might lead to the supposition that Don Carlos was in love with the queen; the opinion must have been founded on the article in the secret preliminaries, which, there is reason to suppose, the prince was never acquainted with. He had scarcely recovered, and the queen was still in a state of convalescence, when the king sent him to Alcala de Henares. He was accompanied by Don John of Austria, his uncle, and by Alexander Farnese, the hereditary Prince of Parma, his cousin; his governor, master, and almoner, also attended him, with other domestics. The king expected that this journey would restore the health of his son, and also wished that he should apply himself to his studies, for he did not yet understand Latin. Don Honoré de Juan perceived his dislike to learning foreign languages, and therefore gave him his lessons in Spanish.

On the 9th of May, 1552, Don Carlos, who was then seventeen years of age, fell down the staircase of his palace, and received several wounds, principally in the spine and head, some of which appeared to be mortal. As soon as the king was informed of the accident, he set off for the palace, that he might give him every assistance, and ordered all the archbishops, and other superior ecclesiastics of the kingdom, to offer up prayers for the recovery of his son. The king, supposing him to be already at the point of death, sent for the body of the blessed Diego, a lay Franciscan, by which it

was said that many miracles had been performed. This
body was laid on that of Don Carlos, and as he began to recover from that time, it was attributed to the protection of
St. Diego, who was canonized a short time after, at the request of Philip II. It must be observed, that the prince was
attended by the celebrated Don Andrea Basilio, the king's
physician, who opened his skull, freed it from a considerable
quantity of water which had accumulated, and thus saved
his life; but he never entirely recovered, and was subject to
pains and weakness in the head, which prevented him from
studying, and by producing a disorder in his ideas, rendered
his character still more insupportable.

Don Carlos returned to court in 1564, emancipated from
his masters: Philip recompensed Don Honoré de Juan, by
making him Bishop of Osma. The solid piety and amiable-
ness of this prelate had inspired Don Carlos with an affection, which their separation did not interrupt: this is proved
by his letters, which do not give a very advantageous idea
of his capacity or information. He often left sentences im-
perfect, and a different meaning might be inferred from them
from what he wished to express. The following is a letter
addressed to the prelate :—

" To my master the bishop.—My master : I have received
your letter in the wood : I am well. God knows how much
I should have been delighted to go to see you with the
queen* : let me know how you were, and if there was much
expense. I went from Alameda to Buitrago, which appeared
to me very well. I went to the wood in two days ; I returned here in two days, where I have been from Wednes-
day till to day. I am well ; I finish. From the country,
June 2d. My best friend in this world. I will do every
thing that you wish : I, the Prince." He finishes another
letter, dated on St. John's day, in the same terms.

---

* This refers to the queen's journey to Bayonne, to confer with her
mother on the political affairs of the League. It took place in 1565.

Don Carlos was so much attached to the bishop, that he obtained a brief from the Pope, granting him permission to reside half the year in Madrid, that he might enjoy his society; but the infirmities of Don Honoré prevented him from making use of the permission, and soon caused his death. This prelate availed himself of the attachment of Don Carlos to give him good advice : the prince appears to have received it as he ought, but his conduct was not improved by it. He gave himself up without restraint to the impetuosity of his passions. Some instances may undeceive those who approve the pompous eulogium bestowed on the talents and generosity of Don Carlos, by St. Real, Mercier, and others.

One day, when the prince was hunting in the wood of Aceca, he was in such a passion with his governor, Don Garcia de Toledo, that he rode after him to beat him. Don Garcia, fearing that he should be forced to forget the respect due to his prince, took flight, and did not stop till he reached Madrid, where Philip II. bestowed several favours on him to induce him to forget the insult he had received : he, however, requested to be dismissed, and the king appointed in his place Rug Gomez de Sylva, Prince of Evoli. This nobleman was also subjected to the most disagreeable scenes from the violent fits of rage to which Don Carlos gave way*.

Don Diego Espinosa (afterwards a Cardinal, and Bishop of Siguenza, Inquisitor-general and Counsellor of State) was the president of the Council of Castile, and banished from Madrid a comedian named *Cisneros*, at the time when he was about to perform in a comedy in the apartment of Don Carlos. The prince desired the president to suspend the sentence until after the representation ; but receiving an unfavourable answer, he ran after him in the palace with a poinard in his hand. In a transport of rage he insulted him publicly, saying to him, " What, is a little priest like that, who

* Cabrera : History of Philip II., chap. 28.

dares to oppose me, and prevent Cisneros from doing as I
wish? By the life of my father, I will kill you!" He would
have done so, if some grandees who were present had not interposed, and if the president had not retired *.

Don Alphonso de Cordova, brother of the Marquis de
Nava, and the prince's chamberlain, slept in his apartment.
It once happened that he did not wake soon enough to attend
the prince when he rung his bell; Don Carlos quitted his
bed in a fury, and attempted to throw him out at the window. Don Alphonso, fearing to fail in respect to the prince
in resisting him, cried out, and the servants immediately came
in; he then repaired to the king's apartment, who, on being
informed of what had passed, took him into his own service †.

He often struck his servants. His boot-maker having unfortunately brought him a pair of boots which were too small,
he had them cut to pieces and cooked, and forced the man to
eat them, which made him so ill that he nearly lost his life.
He persisted in going out of the palace at night contrary to
all advice, and in a short time his conduct became extremely
scandalous and irregular. It is scarcely possible that the
queen could be ignorant of all these occurrences; and if she
was acquainted with them, it cannot be reasonably supposed
that she could have any inclination for Don Carlos.

In 1565, Don Carlos attempted to go secretly to Flanders, contrary to the will of his father; he was assisted in
this enterprise by the Count de Gelbes and the Marquis de
Tabera, his chamberlain. The prince intended to take his
governor, the Prince d'Evoli, with him (not considering
that he was in the confidence of the king); he thought his
presence would make it supposed that he travelled with the
king's consent. His flatterers procured fifty thousand crowns
for him, and four habits to disguise themselves when they

---

* Wander-Hamer: History of Philip II., p. 115. Cabrera: Prudence
of Philip II., b. vii. chap. 22.

† Cabrera. Ibid. chap. 28.

left Madrid : they were persuaded that if the Prince d'Evoli began the journey, he would be obliged to go on, or that they might get rid of him; but that able politician baffled this scheme in the manner related by Cabrera in his Life of Philip II.

The Bishop of Osma being informed of the irregular conduct of Don Carlos, and having also received private orders from the king, wrote a long letter to him *, directing him how to behave to the king's ministers, and demonstrating the incalculable evils that would arise from a different line of conduct. He took particular pains to avoid an insinuation that the prince stood in need of these admonitions. Don Carlos received the letter with the respect he always shewed for the worthy prelate, but he did not follow his advice, and had given himself up to the greatest excesses, when he learnt that his father had bestowed the government of Flanders on the Duke of Alva. The duke went to take leave of the prince, who told him that the government was more suitable to the heir of the crown. The duke replied, that doubtless the king did not wish to expose him to the dangers which he would incur in the Low Countries from the quarrels which had arisen between the principal noblemen. This reply, instead of appeasing Don Carlos, irritated him still more ; he drew his dagger, and endeavoured to stab the duke, crying, *I will soon prevent you from going to Flanders, for I will stab you to the heart before you shall go.* The duke avoided the blow by stepping back ; the prince continued the attack, and the duke had no means of escaping but by seizing Don Carlos in his arms, and although their strength was very unequal, he succeeded in arresting the blows of this madman. As Don Carlos still struggled, the duke made a noise in the apartment, and the chamberlains entered ; the prince then made his escape, and retired to his cabinet to await the result

* Kircher: *Vide* the Work before mentioned, B. ii. Chap. 2.

of this scene, which could not but be disagreeable if the king was informed of it *.

The vices of Don Carlos could not destroy the affection of the Emperor of Germany, his uncle, or that of the Empress Maria, his aunt. These sovereigns wished to marry him to Anne of Austria, their daughter : this princess had been known to Don Carlos from her earliest years, as she was born at Cigales in Spain in 1549. Philip consented to this marriage ; but fearing, perhaps, to make his niece miserable if the character and morals of Don Carlos did not change, he proceeded in the affair with his usual tardiness. On the contrary, as soon as the prince was informed of what was in contemplation, he wished to marry his cousin immediately; and for that purpose resolved to go to Germany without the consent of his father, hoping that his presence at Vienna would induce the emperor to overcome all difficulties. Full of this idea, he employed himself in the execution of his design, and was assisted by the Prince of Orange, the Marquis de Berg, the Counts Horn and Egmont, and by the Baron de Montigny, the chiefs of the conspiracy in Flanders. Don Carlos must be also included among the victims of this conspiracy†.

The Marquis de Berg and the Baron de Montigny were sent to Madrid as the deputies of the provinces of Flanders, with the consent of Margaret of Austria, then governess of the Low Countries, to arrange some points relative to the establishment of the Inquisition, and other circumstances which had caused disturbances. These deputies discovered the prince's intention ; they endeavoured to confirm him in his resolution, and offered to assist him : it was necessary to make use of an intermediate person in this affair, and they had recourse to M. de Vendome, the king's chamberlain. They promised Don Carlos to declare him chief governor of

---

* Estrada: Wars of Flanders, Decade i. b. 7.

† Cabrera: Hist. Philip II. B. vii. Chap. 28.

the Low Countries, if be would allow liberty of opinion in religion. Gregorio Leti speaks of a letter from Don Carlos to the Count d'Egmont, which was found among the papers of the Duke of Alva, and was the cause of the execution of the Counts Egmont and Horn : the Prince of Orange made his escape. At the same time the government was preparing (though by indirect means) the punishment of the deputies in Spain.

The prince did not accept the money offered by these noblemen for his journey, and the steps he took to obtain it himself, occasioned the discovery of the conspiracy. He wrote to almost all the grandees of Spain, to request their assistance in an enterprise which he had planned. He received favourable answers; but most of them contained the condition, *that the enterprise should not be directed against the king.* The Admiral of Castile was not satisfied with this precaution. The mysterious silence in which this scheme was wrapped, and his knowledge of the small share of understanding possessed by Don Carlos, made him suspect that the enterprise was criminal.

In order to prevent the danger, the admiral remitted the prince's letter to the king, who had already been informed of the affair by Don John of Austria, to whom Don Carlos had communicated it. Some persons suspected that the assassination of the king formed part of the conspiracy, but the letters only prove the attempt to obtain money. Don Carlos had taken into his confidence Garcia Alvarez Osorio, his valet-de-chambre, and commissioned him to give explanations of the design alluded to in the letters which he carried. This confidant made several journeys to Valladolid, Burgos, and other cities in Castile, in pursuance of his master's plan.

The prince did not obtain as much money as he required, and on the 1st of December, 1567, wrote to Osorio from Madrid ; the letter was countersigned by his secretary,

Martin de Gaztelu. He says that he had only received six thousand ducats on all the promises and letters of change which had been negotiated in Castile, and that he wanted six hundred thousand for the plan in question. In order to procure this sum he sent him twelve blank letters, signed by himself, and with the same date, that he might fill them up with the names and surnames of the persons to whom they were remitted: he also ordered him to go to Seville, and make use of these letters*.

As the hopes of succeeding in his plan increased, Don Carlos gave way to more criminal thoughts, and before Christmas in the same year he had formed the design of murdering his father. He acted without any plan or discretion, and by the little pains he took to conceal his secret and secure himself from danger, proved that his resolution was that of a madman, rather than of a villain and a conspirator.

Philip II. was at the Escurial, and all the royal family at Madrid ; they were to confess and take the sacrament on Sunday the 28th of December, which was Innocents' Day. This was a custom established at the Court of Madrid, to obtain a jubilee granted to the kings of Spain by the Popes. Don Carlos confessed on the 27th to his confessor in ordinary, Fray Diego de Chaves (afterwards confessor to the king.) The prince soon after told several persons, that having declared his intention of killing a man of very high rank, his confessor had refused to give him absolution, because he would not promise to renounce his intention. Don Carlos sent for other priests, but received the same refusal from them all. He then endeavoured to exact a promise from Fray Juan de Tobar, prior of the Convent of the Dominicans of *Atocha*, to give him an unconsecrated wafer at the sacrament; he wished to make it appear that he could approach the altar as well as Don John of Austria, Alexander Farnese, and the rest of the royal family. The prior perceived that

Wander-Hamen: Life of Don John of Austria, Book i.

the prince was a madman, and in that persuasion he asked
who the person was that he wished to assassinate, adding, if
he was made acquainted with his rank it might induce him
not to require the renunciation of his design.   This was a
bold proposition, but the prior only wished to make Don
Carlos name the individual, and he succeeded.   The unfortunate Don Carlos did not hesitate to name the king, and
afterwards made the same declaration to his uncle, Don
John.   One of the prince's ushers, who witnessed all that
passed, has given a faithful relation of it.   As it is of great
importance, and has never been printed, a copy of it is inserted in the account of the arrest of Don Carlos, at which
he was also present.

Garcia Alvarez Osorio soon procured a sufficient sum of
money at Seville, and Don Carlos prepared to commence his
journey towards the middle of January, 1568.   He requested
his uncle, Don John, to accompany him according to a promise he had made when informed of his design.   Don Carlos
made many promises to his uncle, who replied that he was
ready to do whatever he thought proper, but that he feared
the journey could not take place, on account of the danger
they would incur.   Don John informed the king, who was
at the Escurial, of this circumstance ; Philip consulted several
theologians and jurisconsults to ascertain if he could consci-
entiously continue to feign ignorance, in order to cause his
son to perform his journey.   Martin d'Alpizcueta (so celebrated under the title of the Doctor de Navarro) was one
of the persons consulted ; he advised the king not to allow
Don Carlos to depart, urging that it was the duty of a sovereign to avoid civil wars, which were likely to be the
result of such a journey, as the loyal subjects of Flanders
might go to war with the rebels.   Cabrera says that Melchior
Cano was likewise consulted in this affair*, but Fray Melchior died in 1560.

* Cabrera: Hist. Philip II. Book vii. Chap. 22.

The prince communicated his intentions to Fray Piego de
Chaves, who endeavoured to dissuade him, but without
success. Don Carlos went to make a visit to the wife of
Don Louis de Cordova, the king's master of the horse. This
lady discovered, from some expressions which dropped from
Don Carlos, that he was prepared to depart, and immediately informed her husband, who was at the Escurial with
the king, and who gave the letter to his majesty. At last,
on the 17th January, 1568, Don Carlos sent an order to Don
Ramon de Tasis, director-general of the posts, to have eight
horses ready for him on the following night. Tasis, fearing
that this order covered some mystery, and knowing the
prince's character, replied that all the post-horses were engaged, and gained sufficient time to inform the king. Don
Carlos sent a more peremptory order, and Tasis, who dreaded
his violence, sent all the post-horses out of Madrid, and
repaired to the Escurial. The king went to the Pardo (a
castle about two leagues from Madrid), where Don John
joined him. Don Carlos, who was ignorant of his father's
removal, wished to have a conference with his uncle, and went
as far as *Retamar**, whence he sent for him to come to him.
The prince recounted all the arrangements for his journey.
Don John replied that he was ready to set out with him, but
as soon as he left him, he returned to the king to tell him
all that he had heard. The king immediately went to Madrid,
where he arrived a few minutes after Don Carlos †.

The arrival of the king altered the measures of Don Carlos,
and prevented him from insisting upon having horses that
night. Louis Cabrera has given some details of the circumstances of his arrest, but I prefer inserting the account of
the affair, which was written by the usher a few days after.

" The prince, my master," says he, " had been for some

* Retamar is a place situated half-way between Madrid and the Pardo.
† Cabrera, Book vii. Chap. 22.—Wander-Hamen: Life of Don John
f Austria, Book i.

days unable to take a moment's rest; he was continually
repeating that he wished to kill a man whom he hated.
He informed Don John of Austria of his design, but concealed the name of the person. The king went to the Escurial, and sent for Don John. The subject of their conversation is not known; it was supposed to be concerning the
prince's sinister designs. Don John, doubtless, revealed all
he knew. The king soon after sent post for the Doctor
Velasco; he spoke to him of his plans, and the works at the
Escurial, gave his orders, and added that he should not return immediately. At this time happened the day of jubilee,
which the court was in the habit of gaining at Christmas;
the prince went on the Saturday evening to the Convent of St.
Jerome*. I was in attendance about his person. His royal
highness confessed at the convent, but could not obtain absolution, on account of his evil intentions. He applied to
another confessor, who also refused. The prince said to him,
' *Decide more quickly.*' The monk replied, ' *Let your highness
cause this case to be discussed by learned men.*' It was eight
o'clock in the evening; the prince sent his carriage for the
theologians of the convent of *Atocha* †. Fourteen came, two
and two; he sent us to Madrid to fetch the monks Albarado,
one an Augustine, the other a Maturin; he disputed with
them all, and obstinately persisted in desiring to be absolved,
always repeating that he hated a man until he had killed him.
All these monks declaring that it was impossible to comply
with the prince's request, he then wished that they should
give him an unconsecrated wafer, that the court might believe that he had fulfilled the same duties as the rest of the
royal family. This proposal threw the monks into the greatest
consternation. Many other delicate points were discussed in
this conference, which I am not permitted to repeat. Every-

---

* St. Jerome is a monastery of the order of Jeronimites, founded by
Henry IV. Near this monastery is the old royal palace called *Buen
Retiro.*

† *Atocha* is a Convent of Dominicans near *Buen Retiro,* on the east side.

thing went wrong; the prior of the Convent of *Atocha* took the prince aside, and endeavoured to learn the quality of the person he wished to kill. He replied that he was a man of very high rank, and said no more. At last the prior deceived him, saying, ' *My Lord, tell me what man it is; it may, perhaps, be possible to give you absolution according to the degree of satisfaction your highness wishes to take.*' The prince then declared that it was the king, his father, whom he hated, and that he would have his life. The prior then said, calmly, ' *Does your highness intend to kill the king yourself, or to employ some person to do it?*' The prince persisted so firmly in his resolution, that he could not obtain absolution, and lost the jubilee. This scene lasted until two hours after midnight; all the monks retired overwhelmed with sorrow, particularly the prince's confessor. The next day I accompanied the prince on his return to the palace, and information was sent to the king of all that had passed.

" The monarch repaired to Madrid on Saturday[*]; the next day he went to hear mass in public, accompanied by his brother and the princes[+]. Don John, who was ill with vexation, went to visit Don Carlos on that day, who ordered the doors to be shut, and asked him what had been the subject of his conversation with the king. Don John replied that it was about the galleys[‡]. The prince asked him many questions to find out something more, and when he found that his uncle would not be more explicit, he drew his sword. Don John retreated to the door; finding it shut, he stood on his defence, and said, ' *Stop, your highness.*' Those who were outside having heard him, opened the doors, and Don John retired to his hotel. The prince feeling indis-

---

[*] This was not the Saturday following, which was the 3rd of January, 1568, but on the 17th of January, the day before Don Carlos was arrested.

[+] The princes of Bohemia and Hungary, then at Madrid, also Don John of Austria and Alexander Farnese.

[‡] Some galleys which were then being prepared under the command of Don John.

posed, went to bed, where he remained till six in the evening ; he then rose and put on a dressing-gown. As he was still fasting at eight o'clock, he sent for a boiled capon; at half-past nine he again retired to bed. I was on duty on that day also, and I supped in the palace.

" At eleven o'clock I saw the king descending the stairs; he was accompanied by the Duke de Feria, the grand prior*, the lieutenant-general of the guards, and twelve of his men : the king wore arms over his garments, and had a helmet on ; he walked towards the door where I was ; I was ordered to shut it, and not to open it to any person whatever. These persons were already in the prince's chamber, when he cried, *Who is there ?* The officers went to the head of his bed, and seized his sword and dagger. The Duke de Feria took an arquebuse loaded with two balls †. The prince having uttered cries and menaces, was told, " *The Council of State is present.*' He endeavoured to seize his arms, and to make use of them ; he had already jumped out of bed when the king entered. His son then said to him, *What does your majesty want with me ?*' ' *You will soon know,*' replied the king. The door and windows were fastened ; the king told Don Carlos to remain quietly in that apartment until he received further orders ; he then called the Duke de Feria, and said, ' *I give the prince into your care, that you may guard him and take care of him :*' then addressing Louis Quijada, the Count de Lerma, and Don Rodrigo de Mendoza ‡, he said to them, ' *I commission you to serve*

* Grand prior of the order of St. John of Jerusalem: his name was Don Antonio de Toledo, brother to the Duke of Alva, and a councillor of state.

† The Duke de Feria was captain-general of the king's guards, and a councillor of state.

‡ Louis Quijada was Lord of Villagarcia, son of him who was major-domo to Charles V. in his retirement. The Count de Lerma was afterwards first duke and favourite of Philip III. Don Rodrigo de Mendoza was the eldest son of the Prince d'Evoli.

and amuse the prince; do not do anything he commands you without first informing me. I order you all to guard him faithfully, on pain of being declared traitors.' At these words the prince began to utter loud cries, and said, ' *You had much better kill me, than keep me a prisoner; it is a great scandal to the kingdom : if you do not do it, I shall know how to kill myself.'* The king replied, ' *that he must take care not to do so, because such acts were only committed by madmen.'* The prince said, ' *Your majesty treats me so ill, that you will force me to come to that extremity, either from madness or desperation.'* Some other conversation passed between them, but nothing was decided on, because neither the time nor place permitted it.

" The king retired ; the duke took the keys of the doors, and sent away the valets and other servants of the prince He placed guards in the cabinet, four *Monteros d'Espinosa*, four Spanish Halberdiers, and four Germans with their lieutenant. He afterwards came to the door where I was, and placed there four *Monteros*, and four guards, and told me to retire. The keys of the prince's escrutoires and trunks were then taken to the king ; the beds of the valets were taken away. The Duke de Feria, the Count de Lerma, and Don Rodrigo, watched by his highness that night; he was afterwards watched by two chamberlains, who were relieved every six hours. The persons appointed by the king for this service, were the Duke de Feria, the Prince of Evoli, the prior, Don Antonio de Toledo, Louis Quijada, the Count de Lerma, Don Fadrique Enriquez, and Don Juan de Valesco* ; they did not wear arms for this service. The guards did not allow us to approach either night or day. Two chamberlains prepared the table; the major-domo came to fetch the dinner in the court. No knives were allowed, the meat was taken in already cut up. Mass was not said in

* Son of Don Gabriel, Count de Siruela.

the prince's apartment, and he has not heard it since he was imprisoned*.

" On Monday† the king assembled in his apartment all the councillors and their presidents; he made to each council a report of the arrest of his son; he said that it had taken place for things which concerned the service of God and the kingdom. Eye-witnesses have assured me that his majesty shed tears in making this recital. On Tuesday, his majesty convoked in his apartment the members of the Council of State; they remained there from one o'clock till nine in the evening. It is not known what they were occupied with. The king made an inquest; Hoyos was the secretary ‡. The king was present at the declarations of each witness; they were written down, and formed a pile six inches in height. He gave to the council the privileges of the *Majorats* §, as well as those of the king and prince of Castile, that they might take cognizance of them.

" The queen and the princess were in tears ‖. Don Juan went to the palace every evening; he went once plainly dressed and in mourning; the king reproached him, and told him to dress himself as usual. On the Monday above-mentioned his majesty gave orders that all the prince's valets-de-chambre should retire to their respective homes, promising to provide for them. He caused Don Fadrique, the admiral's brother, and the prince's major-domo, and Don Juan de Valesco to enter into the service of the queen." *Here finishes the relation of the usher.*

* Mass was afterwards said in the prince's apartment; this shews that the account was written before the 2nd of March, when the order was given to have it performed.

† The 19th of January, 1568.

‡ *Hoyos.* His name was Pedro del Hoyo.

§ That is of the eldest sons who have the right of succeeding to the crown, which is a *majorat*, or a perpetual substitution by the order of primogeniture.

‖ Jane, the king's sister, who had brought up Don Carlos before he had masters.

Philip II. saw very plainly that an event of this nature could not long remain concealed, and would not fail to excite the curiosity of the public.   He therefore thought it necessary to give notice of it to all the civil and ecclesiastical authorities, to the Pope, the Emperor of Germany, to several sovereigns of Europe, to Catherine of Austria, Queen of Portugal, widow of John III., sister of Charles V., aunt and mother-in-law of Philip II., grandmother of the unfortunate prisoner, and aunt and grandmother of Anne of Austria, to whom he was to have been married.   This relationship is the reason why Philip calls her in his letter *the mother and mistress of all the family*.   Louis Cabrera says, that this letter was addressed to the Empress of Germany, his sister, to whom he also wrote, but the Queen of Portugal was the only one to whom the title could be applied.

In the letter addressed to the Pope, and dated from Madrid on the 20th of January, the king says, that though he is afflicted, he has the consolation of knowing that he had done his utmost to procure a good education for his son, and had shut his eyes to all that might arise from his physical organization ; but that the service of God and his duty to his subjects would no longer permit him to tolerate his conduct. He finishes by promising to inform his holiness further of the affair, and asks his prayers for a happy result.   On the same day Philip wrote another letter to Queen Catherine, his aunt, in which he imparts all his paternal grief.   He reminds her that he had already informed her of some preceding circumstances which caused fears for the future, and tells her that the arrest would not be followed by any other punishment, but that it had been decided on to put a stop to his irregularities: the letter to the empress is in much the same terms.

In that which the king addressed to the cities, he said, that if he only had been a father, he should never have decided upon such a determination, but that as a king he could not do otherwise, and that it was only in acting thus that he could prevent the evils which his clemency would have occasioned. Diego de Colmenares has inserted, in his history of Segovia, the letter sent by the king to that city. All the other cities and the different authorities received similar letters, which were enclosed in others to the corregidors. In that to the Corregidor of Madrid, Philip commands him to prevent the municipality from making representations in favour of his son, since it was not necessary that a father should be solicited to grant a pardon. He also commands that, in the reply, no detail of the affair should be entered into. On the address from Murcia, the king (who had read them all) wrote the following note: " *This letter is written with prudence and reserve.*" As it has never been published, and will shew the style approved by Philip on this occasion, it is here inserted.

"Sacred, Catholic, and Royal Majesty:—The municipality of Murcia has received your majesty's letter, containing your determination relating to the imprisonment of our prince. The municipality kisses your majesty's feet a thousand times for the distinguished favour shewn them in informing them of this event; it is fully persuaded that the reasons and motives which have guided your majesty were so important, and so conducive to the public good, that you could not do otherwise. Your majesty has governed your kingdom so well, maintained your subjects in such a state of peace, and caused religion to prosper so much, that it is natural to conclude, that in an affair which concerns you so nearly, your majesty has only resolved on it for the service of God and the general welfare of your people. Nevertheless, this city cannot help experiencing unfeigned sorrow, for the important causes which have given fresh grief to your majesty; it cannot consider without emotion, that it possesses a sovereign sufficiently just and attached to the good of his kingdom, to prefer it before everything, and to make him forget his tender affection for his own son. So great a proof of love must compel your majesty's subjects to testify their gratitude by their submission and fidelity. This city, which has always been distinguished for its zeal, will, at this time, give a greater proof of it in immediately obeying your majesty's commands. God preserve the royal and Catholic person of your majesty! In the municipal council of Murcia, February 16th, 1568."

Pius V., and all the other persons to whom Philip had written, replied, by interceding for his son. They said it might be hoped that so striking an event would be a check to the prince, and induce him to alter his conduct. No one made more earnest intercessions than Maximilian II.; it is true that he was more interested on account of the marriage intended for his daughter. He was not satisfied with writing, but sent the Archduke Charles to Madrid, for the purpose of interfering. The journey which the archduke was obliged to make into Flanders and France, was the ostensible motive for that to Madrid. Philip was inflexible; he not only detained the prince as a prisoner, but proved, by the following ordinance, that he intended to keep him so. It was confirmed by the secretary Pedro del Hoyo, and the execution of it confided to the Prince of Evoli, who was appointed his lieutentant-general in everything relating to the prince. It was as follows :—

" The Prince of Evoli is the chief of all the persons employed in the service of the prince, in guarding, supplying him with food, and in his health, and other ways. He shall cause the door to be fastened by a latch, and not locked, either night or day, and he shall not allow the prince to come out. His majesty appoints to guard, serve, and keep the prince company, the Count de Lerma, Don Francis Manriquez, Don Rodrigo de Benavides, Don Juan de Borgia, Don Juan de Mendoza, and Don Gonzalez Chacon. No other individual (except the physician, the barber, and the *montero* *, who has the care of the prince's person) shall be allowed to enter the apartment, without the king's permission. The Count de Lerma shall sleep in the chamber of Don Carlos. If he cannot do this, one of his colleagues must take his place; one of them shall watch all night; this duty they may fulfil in turns. During the day they shall endeavour to be all together in the apartment, that Don Carlos may be diverted and enlivened by their company, and they shall not dispense with this duty, unless they are compelled by business. These noblemen shall converse on indifferent topics with the prince; they shall take care to avoid conversing on anything relating to his affair, and as much as possible all that concerns the government; they shall obey all the orders which he gives for his service or satisfaction, but they shall not take charge of any commission from him to people without. If Don Carlos happens to speak of his imprisonment, they shall not answer him; and they shall relate all that passes to the Prince d'Evoli. The king particularly recommends to them (if they would not fail in the fidelity and obedience they have sworn), never to report elsewhere anything that has been said or done in the interior, without first obtaining his consent; if any of them hear the affair spoken of, in the city, or in particular houses, he or they must report it to the king. Mass shall be said in the chapel, and the prince shall hear it from his chamber, in the presence of two of the noblemen who have the care of him. The breviary, hours, rosary, and any other books which he asks for, shall be given him, provided they treat of nothing but devotion. The six *monteros* who guard and serve the prince

---

* The *monteros* are the king's body-guard for the night. All the individuals of this guard are called *Monteros de Espinosa,* because they ought to have been born in the borough called *Espinosa de la Monteros :* this is a privilege which was granted to them, by the sovereign Count of Castile, Ferdinand Gonzalez, as a recompense for a distinguished act of fidelity.

shall take the food for his table into the first saloon, to be
served to his highness by the noblemen : a *montero* shall take
the dishes in the second chamber.   The *monteros* shall be
employed, and serve night and day, according to the regulations of Rui Gomez de Sylva.   Two halberdiers shall be
placed in the porch of the hall, leading to the court; they
shall not allow any person to enter, without the permission of
the Prince d'Evoli.   In his absence, they shall ask it of the
Count de Lerma, or of any one of the others, who is appointed
to act as chief in their absence.   Rui Gomez de Sylva is
commissioned to command, in the name of the king, the lieu-
tenant-captains of the Spanish and German guards, to place
eight or ten halberdiers outside the porch.   These men shall
also mount guard at the doors of the infantas; two shall be
placed in the apartment of Rui Gomez, from the time when
the great gate of the palace is opened, until midnight, when
the prince's chamber shall be closed, and the *monteros*
commence their service.   Each nobleman is permitted to
have a servant for his own use; he shall select from his people
the one he has most confidence in.   All these persons shall make
oath, before the Prince d'Evoli, to execute faithfully the
regulations contained in this ordinance.   Rui Gomez, and
the noblemen under his orders, shall inform the king of any
negligence in this respect.   The said Rui Gomez is com
manded to supply all that shall be considered necessary in the
service, and which has not been stated in this ordinance.   As
all the responsibility rests upon him, his orders must be executed by the people under him."

The secretary Hoyo read this ordinance to all the persons employed, and to each in particular; they all took the
oath required.

It has been shewn by the recital of the usher, that Philip
gave orders for the trial of his son.   The king having proceeded to the interrogation of the witnesses, by means of the
secretary Hoyo, created a special commission to examine

into the affair. It was composed of Cardinal Espinosa, the inquisitor-general, the Prince of Evoli, and Don Diego Bribiesca de Muñatones, a counsellor of Castile: the king presided. Muñatones was charged with the instruction of the process. Philip, who wished to give this affair the air of a proceeding for a crime of *lese-majesté*, caused to be brought from the royal archives of Barcelona, the writings of a trial instituted by his great-great grandfather, John II., King of Arragon and Navarre, against Charles, his eldest son, Prince of Biana and Girone, who had already been acknowledged as the successor to the throne.

The ordinance concerning the imprisonment of Don Carlos was so strictly observed, that the queen and the princess Jane, who wished to see and console him, were refused permission to do so by the king. Philip was so suspicious of every one, that he lived in a kind of captivity, and did not make his accustomed excursions to Aranquez, the Pardo, and the Escurial. He kept himself shut up in his apartment; the least noise in the street drew him to the window, such was his dread of some tumult. He had always suspected the Flemings, or other persons, of being the prince's partisans, or at least to affect it.

The unhappy Don Carlos, who was not accustomed to conquer his passions, could never make use of any means to palliate his misfortune. He gave himself up to the greatest impatience, and refused to confess, to enable himself to fulfil the duty always performed by the royal family on Palm Sunday. His old master, the Bishop of Osma, had died in 1566. The king commanded the Doctor Suarez de Toledo, his first almoner, to visit him, and try to persuade him : his efforts were unavailing, though Don Carlos always treated him with great respect. On Easter-day, Suarez wrote a long and touching letter to him, in which he proved by unanswerable arguments, that his highness did not take the proper means of terminating the affair favourably. He represented that his highness had no longer either friends or partisans, and reminded him of several scandalous scenes which had increased the number of his enemies; he finishes his letter in the following terms: "Your highness may easily imagine all that will be said when it is known that you do not confess, and when many other terrible things are discovered; some are so much so, that if it concerned any other person than your highnesss, *the holy office would be entitled to inquire if you are really a Christian.* I declare to your highness, with all truth and fidelity, that you only expose yourself to lose your rank, and (what is worse) your soul. I am obliged to say, in the grief and bitterness of my heart, that there is no remedy, and the only advice I can give you, is to return towards God and your father, who is his representative on earth. If your highness will follow my advice, you will apply to the president, and other virtuous persons, who will not fail to tell you the truth, and conduct you in the right way." This letter had no more success than any of the other attempts; the prince still refused to confess.

The despair which Don Carlos soon felt, made him neglect all regularity in taking food and rest. He became so heated by the rage which preyed on him, that iced water (which he used continually) had no effect on him. He caused a great quantity of ice to be put into his bed, to temper the dryness of his skin, which was become insupportable. He walked about naked, and without shoes or stockings, on the pavement, and remained whole nights in this state. In the month of June, he refused all nourishment but iced water, for eleven days, and became so weak that it was supposed he had not long to live. The king being informed, went to visit him, and addressed some words of consolation to him, the result of which was to induce the prince to eat more than was proper for him in his weak state, and this excess brought on a malignant fever, accompanied by a dangerous dysentery. The prince was attended by Doctor Olivarez, chief physician to the king; he went in alone to the patient, and when he returned, held a consultation with the other physicians of the king, in the presence of the Prince d'Evoli.

The preliminary case, drawn by Don Diego Bribiesca de Muñatones, was sufficiently advanced in the month of July, to allow of a final sentence, without examining the criminal, or to appoint a procurator for the king, who in quality of fiscal accused the prince of the crimes stated in the *preparatory instruction*. No judicial notice was sent to the prince; they had only the declarations of the witnesses, letters, and other papers.

These writings proved that, according to the laws of the kingdom, Don Carlos must be condemned to death, for high treason, on two counts: first, for having attempted parricide; and secondly, for having framed a plan to usurp the sovereignty of Flanders, by means of a civil war. Muñatones made a report of this, and the punishments established for such crimes, to the king; he added, that particular circumstances, and the rank of the criminal, might authorize his majesty to declare, that general laws could not affect the eldest sons of kings, because they were subject to laws of a higher nature, those which related to policy, and the welfare of the state; lastly, that the monarch might, for the good of his subjects, commute the punishment.

Cardinal Espinosa and the Prince of Evoli were of the opinion of Muñatones; Philip then said, that his heart inclined him to follow their advice, but that his conscience would not permit him to do so: that he thought it would be far from being a benefit to Spain; that, on the contrary, he thought it would be the greatest misfortune that could happen to his kingdom, to be governed by a king devoid of knowledge, talents, judgment, or virtue, full of vices and passions, and, above all, furious, ferocious and sanguinary; that these considerations compelled him, notwithstanding his attachment to his son, and his anguish at so terrible a sacrifice, to suffer the laws to take their course ; but considering that the health of Don Carlos was in such a state that there was no hope of prolonging his life, he thought it would be better to suffer him to satisfy himself in his inclinations in eating and drinking, since, from the disorder of his ideas, he would not fail to commit some excess, which would lead him to the tomb : that the only thing which concerned him, was the necessity of persuading his son that his death was inevitable, and that in consequence he must confess himself to ensure salvation; that this was the greatest proof of affection which he could shew to his son and the Spanish nation.

This decision of the king is not mentioned in the writings of the trial. There was no sentence written or signed; but the secretary Hoyo, in a note, says, *that at this period of the trial the prince died of his malady, and this was the reason why no sentence was pronounced.* The proof of the fact exists in other papers, in which the curious anecdotes of the time have been related. Although these documents are not authentic, they merit attention, as they were written by persons employed in the king's palace, and accord with what some writers have insinuated. It is true that they did think proper not to speak plainly on such delicate subjects, but they have said enough to lead to the truth.

Cardinal Espinosa and the Prince of Evoli thought that they should fulfil the intentions of Philip in hastening the death of Don Carlos; they agreed that the physician should inform the prince of his condition, without saying anything of the king's displeasure or of the trial, and that he should prepare him to receive the exhortations which would be made for the benefit of his soul: by these means they hoped to induce him to confess and prepare himself for death, which would put an end to his misfortunes.

The Prince of Evoli held a conference with the Doctor Olivares. He spoke to him in that mysterious and important manner which persons versed in the politics of courts know so well how to employ, when it is necessary to further the views of their sovereign, or their own designs. Rui Gomez de Sylva was perfect in this art, according to the opinion of his friend Antonio Perez, the first secretary of state, who was well acquainted with all that passed. In one of his letters he says, *that after the death of the Prince of Evoli, there would be no one but himself initiated in these mysteries.*

Olivares perfectly understood that he was expected to execute the sentence of death pronounced by the king ; and that it was to be done in such a manner, that the prince's honour should not be affected; in short, that his death was to appear natural. He therefore endeavoured to express himself, so as to inform the Prince of Evoli that he comprehended him, and considered it as an order from the king.

On the 20th of July, Olivares ordered a medicine which Don Carlos took. Louis Cabrera, who was employed in the palace at that time, and who often saw Rui Gomez, says in his history of Philip II., that "*this medicine did not produce any beneficial effect; and the malady appearing to be mortal,* the physician informed the patient, that he must prepare to die like a good Christian, and receive the sacraments."

The histories published by Cabrera, Wander-Hamen, Opmero and Estrada, all agree with the secret memoirs of the times which I have read. It is not surprising, then, that the Prince of Orange, in his manifesto against Philip II., should impute to him the death of his son [*]; that James Augustus de Thou, a French contemporary historian, has done the same, from the accounts given him by Louis de Foix, a French architect, employed in building the Escurial, and Pedro Justiniani, a Venetian nobleman, who resided some time in Spain ; although he was mistaken in making the holy office interfere in this affair ; in supposing that the prince died, in a few hours, from poison ; and in advancing some

[*] Watson: History of the Reign of Philip II., in English and French, Appendix.

other errors on the authority of his two informants*. It is
not more surprising that the authors cited by Gregorio Leti
have stated things which appear to be written by the pen of
a novelist or romance writer, because the death of the
prince being occasioned by a mysterious medicine, administered according to a private order, no one doubted that it
was caused by violence, and endeavoured to conjecture how
it was done.

But the truth is always discovered sooner or later, and
after a century and a half, we find so many isolated facts
and accounts of this event, that they produce conviction, and
shew that the death of Don Carlos had the external appear-
ances of a natural death, and that he himself considered it to
be so. The accounts of some foreign historians, of the result
of the medicine, have been refuted by authentic documents :
those of the writers, who have composed romances under the
names of histories, are equally disproved. I shall therefore
proceed to relate the facts as they occurred.

Don Carlos, on being informed by Olivares that death was
approaching, desired that Fray Diego de Chaves, his confessor, might be sent for : his orders were executed on the
21st of July. The prince commissioned the monk to ask
pardon of his father, in his name : the king sent to tell him,
that he granted it with all his heart, as well as his blessing,
and that he hoped his repentance would obtain pardon from
God. On the same day he received the sacraments of the
Eucharist and Extreme Unction with great devotion. He
also, with the king's consent, made a will, which was written
by Martin de Gatzelu, his secretary. On the 22nd and 23rd
he was in a dying state, and tranquilly listened to the exhortations of his confessor and Doctor Suarez de Toledo. The
ministers proposed to the king that he should see his son, and
give him his blessing in person, as it would be a consolation
to him on his death-bed. Philip asked the opinion of the

*De Thou : History of his Time, in Latin, vol. ii. b. 43.

two ecclesiastics above-mentioned. They said that Don Carlos was well-disposed, and it might be feared that the sight of his father would occasion some disturbance in his mind. This motive restrained him for the present ; but being informed, on the night of the 23rd, that his son was at the point of death, he went to his apartment, and extending his arms between the Prince of Evoli and the grand prior, he gave him his blessing a second time, without being perceived. He then retired weeping, and Don Carlos expired soon after, at four o'clock in the morning of the 24th of July, which was the day before the festival of St. James, the patron Saint of Spain.

The death of Don Carlos was not kept secret. He was interred, with all the pomp due to his rank, in the church of the Convent of the Nuns of St. Dominic *el Real*, at Madrid, but there was no funeral oration. Philip II. announced the death of Don Carlos to all the authorities who had been informed of his imprisonment. The city of Madrid also celebrated solemn obsequies on the 14th of August. The sermon was preached by Fray Juan de Tobar, the same monk who had deceived the prince, to make him confess who he wished to kill. In the same year a long account of the sickness, death, and funeral of Don Carlos was printed. The muncipality of Madrid had ordered it to be written by Juan Lopez del Hoyo, professor of Latin in that capital.

Spain regretted the death of Don Carlos, as the king had no other son. By his third wife, Elizabeth of France, he had only had two daughters, and that virtuous princess died of a miscarriage in the same year, 1568. This misfortune (and the bad opinion conceived by all Europe of Philip II., who was considered as a cruel and hypocritical prince) occasioned the imputation of having caused the queen's death. He was first accused of it by the Prince of Orange, and afterwards by many other persons. France had proofs of the contrary, since Charles IX. sent an ambassador extraordinary to Madrid, with compliments of condolence to the king, who was really inconsolable for the loss of his expected heir. Juan Lopez del Hoyo, in 1569, published a faithful account of the illness and death of the queen; and some circumstances which he mentions seem incompatible with the use of poison, which is said to have occasioned her death. It is evident that the Prince of Orange suffered himself to be misled by hatred and revenge. The reality of a crime cannot be believed when neither the end nor motives for it can be perceived, and Philip was certainly interested in the queen's life. Some writers, after having supposed that the crime was committed, have endeavoured to discover the cause, and some romance-writers have thought that they discovered it in the pretended intrigue with Don Carlos. Supposing it to be true, there are historical proofs that it could not have commenced till after his return from Alcala, and at that time he ardently wished to marry his cousin, Anne of Austria. This princess became the fourth wife of Philip, and the mother of his successor, Philip III.

Philip II., wishing to commemorate the justice of his conduct towards his son, ordered that the writings of the trial, with the original, and translation from the Catalonian tongue of that of Don Charles, Prince of Biana, should be collected and preserved. Don Francis de Mora, Marquis de Castel Rodrigo, who became the king's confidant after the death of Rui Gomez de Sylva, in 1592, deposited these writings in a green coffer, which the king afterwards sent shut, and without a key, to the royal archives of Simancas, where it is still, if it has not been carried away by the order of the French government, as it has been reported in Spain.

CHAPTER XXXII.

TRIAL OF THE ARCHBISHOP OF TOLEDO.

ONE of the most illustrious victims of the holy office was Don Bartholomew Carranza de Miranda, Archbishop of Toledo. The writings of the trial amount to twenty-four folio volumes, each containing one thousand or twelve hundred pages. This immense mass of writings must doubtless contain many facts, unknown to Don Pedro Salazar de Mendoza, the author of the life of Carranza. This respectable writer spared no expense to discover the truth, but could not penetrate the mystery which envelopes the proceedings of the Inquisition. I have read this trial, which enables me to fill up the omissions of Salazar de Mendoza, and correct his involuntary errors.

Bartholemew Carranza was born in 1503, at *Miranda de Arga*, a little borough in the kingdom of Navarre: he was the son of Pedro Carranza, and grandson of Bartholomew, both members of the nobility of Miranda. His true family name, consequently, was *Carranza*; but while he was a Dominican monk, he was only called Miranda. When he was made Archbishop of Toledo, he was named Carranza de Miranda, to prove the identity: he however only signed the name Fray Bartholomeus Toletanus, according to the custom of the times. The family of Carranza has been perpetuated to the eighteenth century, in the direct male line from Pedro, brother to the archbishop. At twelve years of age, Bartholomew, through the interest of his uncle Sancho de Carranza, a doctor in the University of Alcala de Henares, and the antagonist of Erasmus, was received into the College of St. Eugenius, which was dependant on the university. When he attained his fifteenth year, he passed into the College of St. Balbina, to study what was then called *philosophy and the arts*, which was confined to some general ideas of logic, metaphysics, and physics. In 1520 he took the habit of a Dominican, in the Convent of *Venalec*, in the *Alcarria*, which was afterwards transferred to the city of *Guadalaxara*. As soon as he had professed, he was sent to study theology in the College of St. Stephen of Salamanca; and in 1525 he was placed in that of St. Gregory of Valladolid.

A proof of the rapid progress of Bartholomew may be seen in his trial. Fray Michel de St. Martin, a Dominican monk, and a professor in the same college at Valladolid, denounced him to the holy office, in 1530, deposing that, two or three years before, he had had several conversations with Carranza, on subjects concerning his conscience; that he had remarked that he limited the power of the Pope, relating to the ecclesiastical ceremonies; and that he had reprimanded him for so erroneous an opinion. Carranza was also denounced in 1530, by Fray Juan de Villamartin, as having been the ardent defender of Erasmus, even on the subject of the sacrament of penance, and the frequent confession of persons who are only in a state of venial sin; that having opposed to him the example of St. Jerome, he maintained that it was impossible to support the fact by the authority of any respectable ecclesiastical historian; that Carranza also said Erasmus ought not to be contemned, for saying that the Apocalypse was not the work of St. John the Evangelist, but of another priest, who bore the same name.

These denunciations were not made use of until the instruction of the trial of the archbishop was far advanced, when every method was employed to find materials for accusations; the *denunciations* and *suspended trials* were then looked over, and those above-mentioned were found. They were noted as declarations of witnesses, under the numbers ninety-four, and ninety-five; while, according to the dates, they ought to have been the first.

As these denunciations were not known out of the holy

office, the rector and counsellors of the College of St. Gregory de Valladolid presented Carranza, in 1530, as a professor of philosophy; in 1534 he was appointed professor of theology, and soon after a qualifier to the holy office of Valladolid. In 1539 he was sent to Rome, to attend a general chapter of his order, where he was chosen to maintain the theses, which were only confided to persons capable of performing their duty well; the talents he displayed in these exercises obtained him the rank of Doctor and Master of Theology, and Paul III. permitted him to read prohibited books.

On his return to Spain, he professed theology, with the greatest success, in his College of St. Gregory. The harvest having entirely failed in the mountains of Leon and Santander in 1540, the inhabitants went to Valladolid in great numbers. Carranza not only maintained forty of these poor people in his college, but sold his books to assist others in the city, only retaining his Bible, and the *Summary* of St. Thomas. During this period he was continually occupied, either at the holy office as a qualifier, or at home in censuring books sent to him by the Supreme Council, or in preaching sermons at the *auto-da-fé*.

In the same year, 1540, Carranza was appointed Bishop of Cuzco, but he refused to go to South America, except as a preacher of the gospel. In 1545, Carranza was sent to the Council of Trent, as theologian to Charles V. He remained there three years, and it was there that Cardinal Pacheco (dean of the Spanish prelates who attended at the council) engaged him to preach on *Justification* before the Fathers. In 1546, he published at Rome one of his works, called *The Summary of Councils*, and another at Venice, of *Theological Controversies*. In 1547 he published a Treatise *On the Residence of Bishops*, which created him many enemies, and which was attacked by Fray Ambrose Caterino, and defended by Fray Dominic de Soto, both Dominicans.

On his return to Spain in 1548, he refused the appointment of confessor to Philip II., then prince of the Asturias, and in 1549 declined accepting the bishopric of the Canaries. He was elected in the same year prior of the Dominicans of Palencia, which he accepted. In 1550 he was made provincial of the Convents of Castile, and visited his province.

The Council of Trent being again convoked in 1651, Carranza was commanded by the emperor to attend it, and furnished with full powers by the Cardinal Archbishop of Toledo; he assisted at the different assemblies until 1552, when he was suspended the second time. Among the different commissions confided to him, was that of preparing an *Index.* On his return to Spain, the period of his provincialship had expired, and he re-entered his College of St. Gregory of Valladolid.

The alliance between Philip II. and Mary, Queen of England, being fixed, Fray Bartholomew, in 1554, went to England, in order to assist Cardinal Pole in preparing the kingdom to return to the Catholic faith. Carranza passed the greatest part of his time in preaching, and succeeded in converting a great number of heretics. When the king left England to go to Brussels, Carranza remained with the queen, to whom he was useful in supporting the Catholic doctrine in the universities, and arranging other affairs of the greatest importance. He revised, by the order of Cardinal Pole, the canons which had been decreed by a national council, and caused several obstinate heretics to be punished, particularly Thomas Cranmer, Archbishop of Canterbury, and Martin Bucer; his zeal often exposed him to great danger.

In 1557 he went to Flanders, where he caused all books infected with the heresy of Luther to be burnt. He did the same at Frankfort, and also informed the king that many of these books were introduced into Spain by way of Arragon. Philip, in consequence, gave the necessary orders to the inquisitor-general to intercept these works. In order to render this measure more effectual, Carranza drew up a list of suspected Spaniards who had fled to Germany and Flanders. The original copy of this list was found among his papers when he was arrested.

On the death of Cardinal Siliceo, Archbishop of Toledo, the king appointed Carranza to succeed him; he however refused to accept the dignity, and named Don Gaspard de Zuñiga y Avellanada, Bishop of Segovia, Don Francis de Navarre, Bishop of Badajoz, and Don Alphonso de Castro, a Franciscan, as more worthy of the king's choice than himself. He persisted in his refusal, until the king commanded him on his allegiance to accept the archbishopric : the original of this royal order was also found among the papers of Carranza. Paul IV. dispensed with the usual formalities ; he was *preconised* in a full consistory on the 16th December, 1557, and his bulls were expedited. Pedro de Merida, canon of Palencia, administrated until the arrival of the archbishop. The Inquisition of Valladolid afterwards prosecuted him for some letters which he had written to Carranza, and which were found among his papers ; he was also implicated by Fray Dominic de Roxas, and by other accomplices of Dr. Cazalla.

The Archbishop Carranza was consecrated at Brussels on the 27th of February in the same year, by the Cardinal de Granville, afterwards first archbishop of Malines. He published at Antwerp his Catechism in Spanish, under the title of *Commentaries of the very Reverend Fray Bartholomew Carranza de Miranda, Archbishop of Toledo, on the Christian Catechism, in four parts**.

* Comentarios del Reverendissimo señor Fray Barthome Carranza de Miranda, Arzobispo de Toledo, sobre el cathecismo christiano, divididos en quatro partes, las quales contienent odo lo que profesamos en el santo bautismo, como se vera en la plana siguiente, dirigida al serenisimo senor rey de Espana, &c., nuestro senor. En Anveres, en casa de Martin Nucio, Anno M. D. LVIII., con privilegio real.

He afterwards returned to Spain, and assisted several times at the Councils of Castile and the Inquisition. About the middle of September he went to the monastery of St. Juste, to make a report to Charles V. of some affairs confided to him by Philip II., and to pay his respects to the emperor, who was then ill, and died two days after. An account has been given in the eighteenth chapter of what passed at this visit. He then repaired to his archbishopric, where he remained six months, and then went to Alcala de Henares, with the intention of visiting his diocese. During the six months that he passed in the capital, his conduct was exemplary, passing his time in preaching, distributing alms, visiting the prisoners and the sick, and in causing prayers to be said for the dead. He employed himself in the same manner in all the places he passed through, until he arrived at Torrelaguna, where he was arrested by the Inquisition on the 22nd of August. He was taken back to Valladolid, and imprisoned in a house belonging to the eldest branch of the family of Don Pedro Gonzalez de Leon, where Don Diego Gonzalez, an inquisitor, was appointed to guard him.

Carranza had made enemies of several bishops, when he published his treatise *On the Residence of Bishops:* the reputation which he acquired for learning in the Council of Trent, at the expense of several individuals who considered themselves superior to him, rendered them also his enemies, or at least his rivals. Of this number were Melchior Cano, who has been already mentioned; their rivalry was changed into open jealousy on his part, and on that of Fray Juan de Regla, when Carranza was appointed Archbishop of Toledo. This hatred became common to others, when, after refusing the archbishopric, Fray Bartholomew recommended the three persons before-mentioned to the king: among them were Don Ferdinand Valdes, inquisitor-general; Don Pedro de Castro, Bishop of Cuença, a son of the Count de Lemos; and a man of much greater merit, and Don Antonio Augustine, Archbishop of Tarragona, who was the luminary of Spain in sacred literature. These persons endeavoured to conceal their sentiments, but their words and actions betrayed them.

Besides this principal motive for the conspiracy against the archbishop, we may be permitted to suppose another. Carranza had given a copy of his Catechism to the Marchioness d'Alcañices in several detached pieces; when it was printed, he distributed it as it came from the press.

The Marchioness d'Alcañices intrusted the work to several pupils or partisans of the archbishop, among whom were Fray Juan de la Peña, Fray Francis de Tordesillas, and Fray Louis de la Cruz; it was also read by Melchior Cano, who, in different conversations, plainly insinuated that it contained propositions tending to the Lutheran heresy. Don Ferdinand Valdés being informed of these circumstances, bought several copies of the Catechism, and sent them to persons with whose opinions he was well acquainted, desiring them to read it attentively, and to observe all that merited theological censure, but not to give their opinions in writing until they had again communicated with him. The persons he selected, were Fray Melchior Cano, Fray Dominic Soto, Fray Dominic Cuevas, the Master Charles, and Fray Pedro Ibarra, provincial of the Franciscans.

This work was also sent to Don Pedro de Castro, Bishop of Cuença, and it may be said that his reply, dated from Parega, April 28, 1558, was the foundation of the trial of Carranza. It appears from the letter to the inquisitor-general, that he had requested to know the opinion of de Castro on the Catechism, and he informs him that he thinks it a dangerous work, promises to give him his reasons for it, and adds that the article on *justification* tends towards Lutheranism. He says that having heard the author speak in the same manner at the Council of Trent, he had conceived a bad opinion of his doctrine, although he did not think that Car-

ranza really possessed such erroneous sentiments. Don Pedro
further says, that his present opinion is supported by facts,
which he had already communicated to Doctor Andrea Perez,
a member of the Supreme Council.

It appears, by a paper signed by the same bishop, on the
first of September, 1559, that his communications to the
counsellor were confined to the following articles: that being
present at a sermon preached by Carranza before the king in
London, he observed that he spoke of the *justification of men
by a lively faith in the passion and death of Jesus Christ*, in
terms approaching to Lutheranism; that Fray Juan de Villagarcia informed him that Don Bartholomew had preached
the sermon in the preceding year at Valladolid, and that he
then thought it reprehensible. The bishop adds, that he
spoke to Carranza on the subject, and attributed his silence
to humility; that at another time when he was preaching
before the king he said, that some sins were irremissible.
At first he thought he had not understood him, but Carranza afterwards repeated the same proposition several times.
The bishop concluded by stating, that in another sermon
preached before the king, Don Bartholomew spoke of the
indulgences granted by the bull of the Crusade, as if they
might be bought for two rials *(ten-pence)*; and that he
thought such language very dangerous to hold in England in
the midst of heretics. All this accords with the declaration
of Fray Angelo de Castillo, after the arrest of the archbishop,
who deposed that de Castro said that *Carranza had preached
like Philip Melancthon.*

It appears from this statement, that Don Pedro de Castro
did not feel any scruples until three years after his journey
to London, and did not think himself obliged to denounce
Carranza, until he had lost all hope of becoming Archbishop
of Toledo; if Don Bartholomew had remained a single month,
he would never have been accused. The inquisitor-general
gave up the letter he had received from de Castro, to begin

the proceedings, but he did not mention that which he had written himself, which shews that it was not official. The counsellor Don Andrea Perez neither deposed nor proved any of the facts related by the bishop, so that the declaration was not entered in the proceedings when the order for the arrest was issued; about a year and a half after, it was thought proper to supply the place of it, by the insertion of a writing signed by the bishop. The Court of Rome was astonished at the irregularity of the proceedings, when it received the writings of the trial.

Fray Juan de Villagarcia, being already imprisoned, in 1561, declared that he perfectly remembered hearing de Castro mention the sermon preached by Carranza in London, but not that he had been scandalized at it, or that he had said anything which could produce that effect. Villagarcia said, that as the confidant of the archbishop, and having been employed to transcribe his works, he was more capable of defending the purity of his faith than any other person; and endeavoured to prove that there were none but Catholic propositions in his works.

It is evident that the trial originated in the malice of the inquisitor-general, which induced him to give the catechism to the enemies of Carranza: when he was informed by Cano of the existence of the propositions which caused the denunciation, he sent the work officially to him, and to the other *qualifiers*, Soto and Cuevas; but this did not take place till after some circumstances occurred, during the trials of several Lutherans, which seem to have caused that of Carranza, although the fact was entirely false. The inquisitor-general being informed that Carranza was intimate with the Marquises d'Alcañices and de Poza, many of whose friends and relations were in the prisons of the Inquisition, ordered the inquisitors of Valladolid to obtain information of the prisoners concerning the faith of the archbishop. A report was also spread, that several persons had discovered a similarity between the opinions of Carranza and Cazalla ; which succeeded so well, that a partisan of Cano had the audacity to announce from the pulpit, when Cazella was arrested, that an order had been issued to arrest the Archbishop of Toledo.

On the 25th of April, 1558, Donna Antoinetta Mella deposed, that Christopher de Padilla had given her a MS. containing Lutheran doctrines, which he said was written by Carranza. This declaration was not communicated to the archbishop, because the work was composed by Fray Dominic de Roxas. On the 17th of the same month, Pedro de Sotelo made a similar declaration.

On the 29th of April, Donna Anne Henriquez d'Almanza deposed, that she asked Fray Dominic de Roxas if he should treat of points of doctrine with the archbishop, and that he said he should not, because Carranza had just written a book against the Lutherans. She added that she had heard Francis de Vibero say, that the archbishop would burn in hell, because knowing better than any person that the doctrine of Luther was orthodox, he had condemned several persons to the flames in England, for professing it. Francis de Vibero, on being interrogated, declared that he did not remember to have used these words, and that he thought it doubtful, because Carranza had always been a Roman Catholic.

Donna Catherine de Rios, prioress of the convent of St. Catherine, at Valladolid, deposed, on the 24th of April, that she heard Fray Dominic de Roxas say, that Don Bartholomew had declared that *he did not find any evidence of the existence of purgatory in the Holy Scriptures :* she added however, on the following day, that she was persuaded that Carranza did believe in purgatory, because he always exhorted his monks to perform masses for the dead; she deposed, that having asked Donna Anne Henriquez, if the archbishop held the same opinion, that she did, she replied, that on the contrary he had written a book in refutation of them; that Donna Bernardina de Roxas told her that she had learnt from Fray

Dominic, that the archbishop had advised him *not to suffer himself to be led away by his genius;* that Sabin Astele, canon of Zamora, assured her that he had heard Fray Dominic declare that he had the greatest compassion for Carranza, because he did not hold the same opinions as he did. This declaration was not communicated to the archbishop in the *publication of the depositions of the witnesses,* because it contained nothing against him. If these declarations had been made known to his defender, he might have derived great benefit from them.

Fray Dominic de Roxas being summoned on the proposition relating to purgatory, declared that Don Bartholomew had always spoken on that subject like a good Catholic.

Fray Juan Manuelez, a Dominican, deposed on the 18th October, 1560, that nine or ten years before, he conversed with Don Bartholomew concerning a Lutheran who was condemned to be burnt, but could not be certain whether the archbishop advanced the following proposition: *It is certain that the Holy Scriptures do not assure us that there is a purgatory.*—This witness makes his deposition a year after the arrest of the archbishop, and is not certain of the fact. Would he not have denounced him ten years before, if he had heard him speak in that manner?

On the 4th of May, 1559, Pedro de Cazalla deposed that in 1554 he heard Don Charles de Seso deny the existence of a purgatory, and repeat the proposition before Don Bartholomew Carranza, who appeared scandalized, but did not attempt to refute or denounce him. The deponent also said, that Fray Dominic de Roxas told him, that he had informed Carranza that he could not reconcile the doctrines of justification and purgatory, and he replied that *it would not be a great evil if there was no purgatory;* that having an swered from the decision of the Church, his master said to him, *You are not yet capable of understanding this matter.*

Don Charles de Seso being interrogated on this subject on

the 27th June, replied that Don Bartholomew had told him that he ought to believe in the existence of purgatory, and that if he was not obliged to depart, he would answer his arguments in a satisfactory manner; that Pedro Cazalla was the only person to whom he had communicated his conversation with Carranza; that he had reason to believe his present summons was occasioned by the declaration of Cazalla, who had not spoken the truth. On the 20th and 23rd, Fray Dominic declared that Carranza had always spoken of purgatory like a good Catholic. Thus it appears that the declarations of Cazalla were proved to be false, before the order for an arrest was issued.

On the 7th of May, 1559, the inquisitor, William, remitted a letter from Carranza, in which he mentions Don Charles de Seso, and says that he did not denounce him, because he thought he had only been led into error; which was proved by the reply of Seso, when reprimanded by him, that he would only believe that which was really commanded by the Catholic religion, and that he then told him he could not do better.

Garcia Barbor de Bexega, an alguazil of the Inquisition of Calahorra, deposed on the 12th of May, that he arrested Fray Dominic de Roxas, when he endeavoured to fly from Spain, and that when conversing with him on the increase of the number of Lutherans, he asked if his master Carranza was of that sect; Roxas replied in the negative; that he was not going to seek him in Flanders for that reason, but to obtain from the king the favour of not being degraded. This declaration was not communicated to the archbishop in the *publication of the depositions.*

On the 13th of May, Fray Dominic de Roxas declared that Fray Francis de Tordesillas had expressed pity for him, when he heard him speak of *justification*, and make use of phrases in his discourses tinctured with Lutheranism; that this also happened to Carranza. Fray Francis, on being examined, deposed, that having copied several works of the archbishop, and translated others into Latin, for the Marchioness d'Alcañices and different persons, he had introduced a *preface* into one MS., stating that the way to avoid falling into error in reading these works, was to understand in a Catholic sense some propositions on *justification*, which might be interpreted in a different manner; that all that Carranza had written was in the spirit of the Catholic religion; that he, deponent, knew his intentions to be pure, because he had seen him practise good works, and his sermons, conferences, and private life, perfectly accorded with the true principles of faith.

Donna Frances de Zuñiga, deposed on the 2d of June, that Carranza had told her, that provided she was not in a state of mortal sin, she might approach the holy table without confessing; that on the 13th of July she heard Fray Dominic de Roxas say that Carranza thought as he did on some of Luther's opinion, but not on all; that the nuns of the convent of Bethlehem did not believe in purgatory, because Pedro Cazalla had told them that such was the opinion of Carranza. Fray Dominic, being summoned, made the deposition relating to purgatory above mentioned: he added, on the 21st of March, that Don Bartholomew always explained his propositions in a Catholic sense, and detested the Lutheran doctrine; and that if he, deponent, had always profited by these explanations, he would not have fallen into error. Pedro Cazalla being interrogated concerning the nuns of Bethlehem, replied that he did not remember to have spoken in that manner, but that he had concluded that such were the opinions of Carranza, when he did not denounce Don Charles de Seso.

On the 13th of July the inquisitors seized all the books composed by Carranza in the house of the Marchioness d'Alcañices, who on the 28th deposed, that having read the *Commentaries on the Prophecies of Isaiah*, written by Carranza, she asked Fray Juan de Villagarcia from what book the author had taken so much erudition ? Fray Juan replied that it was contained in a work of Luther, and that the book could not be confided to every person, because the good was too often mixed with evil in those authors. Fray Juan de Villagarcia being interrogated on this subject, replied that it was a work of *Œcolampadius*, and that the archbishop always kept it concealed ; that it was true that he had taken from it materials for the treatise in which he explained the prophecies of Isaiah ; but he was accustomed to say that no confidence could be placed in the heretical authors; that the archbishop had been seduced by them, but always defended the Catholic religion. It has been already stated that Paul III. granted him permission to read prohibited works; the brief was found among his papers.

On the 3rd of July, Elizabeth Estrada deposed, that Fray Dominic de Roxas had told her, that it depended upon Don Bartholomew to make her sister the Marchioness d'Alcañices adopt the errors of Luther, and that he hoped to see that event take place, because then the king and all Spain would embrace that religion. The deponent also said that Fray Dominic told her that Don Bartholomew had read the works of Luther. Fray Dominic, being examined, replied that he often spoke in that manner to the nuns who were of his opinions, and to other individuals of his society of Lutherans, adding that Carranza thought as he did on *justification* and purgatory; that he (Roxas) composed an *Explanation of the articles of faith*, according to his own creed, and attributed it to Carranza, to give it more consequence ; that he always said the archbishop approved the doctrine of Luther to persuade those persons to persevere in the faith, but that he never said that Don Bartholomew had read the works of Luther, because he did not know that he had. The deponent declared that the changes in his situation induced him to confess the truth ; that the archbishop had never adopted such doctrines, and that he always gave a Catholic meaning to those phrases which would bear a contrary interpretation.

On the 23rd of August, Fray Bernardin de Montenegro, and Fray Juan de Meceta, (both monks of the convent of St. Francis, at Valladolid), voluntarily denounced a sermon, which was preached by the archbishop two days before, in the convent of St. Paul, and in which he used some expressions similar to those employed by the heretics. He also said, that converted heretics should be treated with clemency, and that persons were sometimes called heretics, illuminati, or quietists, merely because they were seen on their knees before a crucifix, and smiting their breasts with a stone : he invoked the authority of St. Bernard, to support his last proposition, which (according to the denouncers) did not agree with what he had advanced. The sermon being afterwards found among the papers of the archbishop, was examined by the qualifiers, and did not appear to contain any proposition deserving of censure. Yet the inquisitors presumed to demand officially of the princess Jane, governess of the kingdom, what she thought of the sermon ; the princess had the complaisance to reply, that she only remembered to have heard some propositions which appeared to her to be improper.

On the 25th of the same month, Ferdinand de Sotelo denounced Don Bartholomew, for having said in the presence of Pedro de Sotelo, his brother, and Christopher Padilla, that if he had a notary with him when he was dying, he would desire him to draw up an act of *renunciation of all his good works*. Pedro and Christopher declared that they did not remember that they had repeated this to Ferdinand de Sotelo. But Fray Dominic de Roxas deposed, during the torture, on the 10th of September, 1559, that he thought he remembered being once in the village of Alcañices, and hearing Don Bartholomew say, that at the point of death he should wish to have a notary, to draw up an act of renunciation of the merit of his good works, because he relied solely on those of Jesus Christ, and that he considered his sins as nothing, because Jesus had expiated them; Dominic added, that Don Louis de Roxas, his nephew, related the same thing, as having occurred at his return from Flanders in the king's suite, and that all these expressions did not make him consider the archbishop as a Lutheran, but as a good Catholic; because the heretics denied that the good works of the creature could expiate sin, and attributed the expiation to the merits of Jesus Christ, while Carranza only asserted, that the expiation by the good works of a sinner was so little when compared with the infinite merits of our Redeemer, that the sinner might regard them as nothing if he fervently prayed for the application of the merits of our Saviour dying on the cross. There seems to be no doubt that Fray Dominic was the author of the denounced proposition; he explained it to the advantage of the accused during the torture.

On the 8th of September, Fray Dominic declared that Don Bartholomew had said, that the expression, *say the mass*, was not exact, that it would be more correct to say *perform the mass*, from the Latin, *facere rem sacram*, and that he used this expression in the pulpit and in his writings. This accusation was certainly not sufficient to authorize a decree of arrest.

On the 23rd of September, Doctor Cazalla declared, that ten or twelve years before, he heard Fray Dominic de Roxas say, that Don Bartholomew held the doctrines of the Lutherans. Fray Dominic on being examined denied the fact, but afterwards, on being tortured, confessed, that he had often declared that Don Bartholomew believed in the doctrines of the Lutherans, to give weight to his own opinions, and acknowledged that he did not speak the truth.

The same Doctor Cazalla (being examined on the evidence of Donna Frances de Zuñiga, who said he had instructed her in the doctrine of Luther) declared, that Donna Frances, and her brother Juan, had told him, that they were instructed by Don Bartholomew. The brother and sister denied the fact, and Cazalla being tortured, retracted his declaration.

On the 9th of December, Fray Ambrose de Salazar, Dominican, being summoned to declare if it was true that he had said, that some persons held the same language as the heretics of Germany, replied that it was true, and that he alluded to Dominic de Roxas, Christopher Padilla, and Juan Sanchez. He was pressed to name all those to whom his allusion could be applied, and he said that he did not remember any others. He was then requested to consult his memory, and return the next day to the tribunal of the Inquisition. He obeyed, but did not add anything to his former declaration. He was then told that the inquisitors had been informed that he alluded to some other person, that he must endeavour to recollect him, and then return. The monk repaired to the Inquisition on the 14th of the same month, and said, that he had thought the questions put to him related to the archbishop, particularly after a report that his trial had commenced ; that until then he had been far from suspecting the most zealous defender of the Catholic religion of heresy; that his words agreed with his writings; that he had converted many heretics, and burnt some others ; that if he adopted certain phrases used by the heretics, he always explained them in an orthodox manner, and that in this case he only followed the example of several saints.

Don Francis Manrique de Lara, bishop of Salamanca, deposed, on the 10th of October, that, at Naxera, he heard it said, that the archbishop had been arrested on account of his catechism, and that Fray Ambrose remarked, *it may not be for that alone; it is possible that his belief in purgatory was suspected.*

When the *publication of the depositions* took place, the evidence of Salazar was not mentioned, and the defenders of the accused never knew that he had given it. It is thus that the inquisitors in their proceedings violate natural right, in concealing all that may be taken advantage of by a defender.

On the 9th of December, Fray Juan de Regla voluntarily denounced Carranza, for some expressions used by him to Charles V., on the forgiveness of sins. This affair has already been mentioned in the thirteenth chapter. On the 23rd Fray Juan again denounced Don Bartholomew, for having supported the arguments of the Lutherans, in the second session of the council of Trent, concerning the holy sacrifice of mass ; and for having dared to say *ego hæro certe,* which scandalized several fathers of the council ; he admitted that the accused afterwards explained his words, but said it was without energy. This monk was the only witness who deposed to this fact. Don Diego de Mendoza, ambassador of Spain to the council, who had been punctual in attending the sessions, declared that he did not remember the circumstance, which had not been denounced before by any of the numerous rivals of Carranza. Fray Juan was extremely mortified that he could not obtain a bishopric, and we may suppose that nothing but jealousy could inspire him with such scruples, sixteen years after the event. It must be observed that he had been condemned by the Inquisition of Saragossa, that he had abjured eighteen propositions, and had been pursued by the Jesuits, of whom he and Cano had shewn themselves the most violent adversaries, while Don Bartholomew was their friend. Cano and de Regla therefore endeavoured to mortify Carranza, and persecuted him as being secretly attached to the Jesuits.

The licentiate Hornuza, judge of appeals of the district of Santiago, states in a writing annexed by the fiscal to the trial six weeks after the arrest of the archbishop, that this prelate, having presented to the Council of Trent some arguments in favour of Luther, he acknowledged that they might be answered conclusively ; the witness added that Doctor Grados could confirm the truth of his testimony. The doctor was not examined. Who indeed can believe that Carranza would have spoken in that manner in the Council of Trent ? On the 14th December, Fray Dominic de Roxas presented a writing containing a confession of his errors and a prayer for pardon : he made the same declarations concerning the archbishop as before ; adding, that *he was obliged to confess that he thought* if the prelate and some *others had not been prepared by the syrup of the Lutheran phrases, the works of the heresiarch would not have made so much impression on their minds.* Fray Dominic said this to palliate his own crime, and in the hope of being reconciled ; but being informed, on the 7th October, 1559, that he must prepare to die the next day, he demanded an audience in order to make a declaration necessary to the repose of his soul ; and having obtained it, he said " that he had never heard Don Bartholomew utter any words contrary to the doctrine of the Holy Church, that he always spoke against the Lutherans, and explained those phrases which he (Fray Dominic) had seen in heretical books, and heard from the preachers in Valladolid, in an orthodox sense."

The above are all the declarations contained in the process of the Archbishop of Toledo when a brief was denounced for his arrest. It may even be supposed that there were not so many, since the brief was expedited on the 7th January, 1559, and therefore it must have been demanded, at the latest, in the beginning of December 1558. The censure of the works of Carranza and the opinion of the Bishop of Cuença were also made use of as a motive for the demand. The qualifiers were Melchior Cano, Dominic Cuevas, Dominic Soto, Pedro Ybarra, and the Master Charles. The following is a list of the MS. works of the archbishop which are mentioned with the printed Catechism in this part of the process.

1. Notes on the Explanation of the Book of Job, by another author.
2. Notes on the Explanation of the verse *Audi filia* of the 44th Psalm, by Juan d'Avila, 83.
3. Explanation of Psalm 83.
4. Explanation of Psalm 129.
5. Explanation of Psalm 142.
6. Explanation of the Prophet Isaiah.
7. Explanation of the Epistle of St. Paul to the Romans.
8. Ditto Galatians.
9. Ditto Ephesians.
10. Ditto Philippians.
11. Ditto Colossians.
12. Explanation of the Canonical Epistle of St. John.
13. Treatise on the Love of God to Man.
14. Ditto on the Sacrament of the Order, with notes on the same subject.
15. Ditto on the holy Sacrifice of Mass.
16. Ditto on the Celibacy of Priests.
17. Ditto on the Sacrament of Marriage.
18. Ditto on the Utility and Efficacy of Prayer.
19. Ditto on the Tribulation of the Just.
20. Ditto on the Christian Widow.
21. Ditto on Christian Liberty.
22. Remarks on the Commandments of God and the Sins of Mortals.
23. Apology for the *Commentaries on the Catechism.*
24. Proofs taken from Holy Writ for the defence of the publication of a Catechism in the Spanish language.
25. Abridgment of the *Commentaries on the Catechism.*
26. Sermons for all the Year.
27. Ditto on the Love of God.
28. Ditto, *Super flumina Babylonis.*
29. Ditto on the Manner of hearing Mass.
30. Ditto on Holy Thursday.

31. Sermons preached before the Prince at Valladolid.

32. Ditto on the Circumcision of Our Saviour.

33. Ditto, intituled *Pœnitentiam agite.*

34. Ditto, *Si revertamini et quiescatis salviti eritis.*

35. Ditto on Prayer.

36. Ditto, *Hora est jam nos de somno surgere.*

37. Ditto, *Dirigite viam Domine.*

38. Ditto, *Spiritus est Deus.*

39. Ditto on the Psalm *De profundis clamavi.*

40. Ditto, *Filius quidem hominis vadit.*

41. Abridgment of two Sermons sent to Flanders to the Licentiate Herrera.

Some MS. copies which had been given to the Marchioness d'Alcañices, and other persons, before the Catechism was printed, were also annexed to the process; the contents were the same, except some corrections afterwards made by the author. The Marchioness d'Alcañices gave them to Don Diego de Cordova, a member of the Supreme Council, who died soon after. The MSS. were then taken by St. Francis de Borgia, who informed Carranza, on his return from Flanders, that they were in his possession, but that he wanted them to assist him in composing a sermon. Don Bartholomew being arrested before the MSS. were returned to him, St. Francis de Borgia sent them to the grand inquisitor, in whose house they were lost; it is stated in the process that only one of them was found there some time after.

The holy office endeavoured to ascribe to Carranza some other works condemned on the trial: these were the

Explanation of the Articles of the Faith, by Fray Dominic de Roxas.

Opinions on the Interpretation of the Holy Scriptures, by Juan Valdés, secretary to Charles V., who became a Lutheran.

Treatise on Prayer and Meditation, which appears to have been written by some other Lutheran author.

Explanation of the Book of Job, of which Carranza only wrote the notes, which refute the text in several places.

Explanation of the verse *Audi filia*, explanatory notes only by Carranza.

Several papers which Fray Dominic de Roxas and Christopher de Padilla had distributed, maliciously attributing them to Don Bartholomew, although they belonged to Fray Dominic, and other Lutherans.

As to the *Exposition of the Canonical Epistle of St. John*, the archbishop declared that, in the state in which it was, he did not acknowledge it as his work; that he had only given it verbally to his pupils, and that, doubtless, one of them had written it from memory; that although the foundation of it was what he had taught, the errors which it contained could not be imputed to him.

The grand inquisitor was at first only acquainted with the Catechism of Carranza, the censure of which was confided to Cano and others. Cano, whose heart was full of hatred, wanted no incitements to condemn it; of the inclinations of the others we may judge by letters, in which Fray Dominic de Soto speaks of his embarrassment at being obliged to censure some propositions which he considered very orthodox. Of all the works of Carranza, those only were marked with the theological censure which are numbered 3, 4, 13, 27, 28, 29, and 30. The Master Charles, and afterwards Cano and Cuevas, were employed in this work.

As there were among the Lutherans many persons intimate with the archbishop, and even some who had been his pupils, he wished to be informed of the state of their affairs. Fray Juan de la Peña, Fray Francis de Tordesillas, and Fray Louis de la Cruz, sent the details to Flanders to Fray Juan de Villagarcia, the companion of the archbishop, and by this means he learnt that his Catechism was to be condemned for two reasons: first, on the pretext that it contained several heretical propositions; and secondly, because the principle which caused the Bible in the vulgar tongue to be prohibited in Spain in the present state of the kingdom, would not admit of the permission of a work on *justification*, and other points of controversy with the Lutherans, in the same language. The archbishop first commissioned Villagarcia, and afterwards the Jesuit Gil Gonzalez, to translate his Catechism into Latin, with notes on the obscure passages; they began, but never finished the work.

The archbishop, however, was far from suspecting that he would be attacked for his personal profession of faith, when he received a letter from Fray Louis de la Cruz, dated Valladolid, May 21, 1558, in which he informed him that the Lutherans declared he partook their opinions. Carranza replied that he was more grieved for their misfortune in having embraced heresy than for their false testimony against him. As he was perfectly convinced of the purity of his faith, and believed that he had given sufficient proofs of it in combating the opinions of the heretics, he persuaded himself that only the sense of his *Commentaries* was to be discussed. He therefore returned to Spain, expecting to arrange the affair on a few conferences with the grand inquisitor ; and in order to facilitate the attainment of his object, he obtained approbations of his work from some of the most famous theologians in Spain,—Don Pedro Guerren, archbishop of Granada ; Don Francis Blanco, archbishop of Santiago ; Don Francis Delgado, bishop of Lugo and Jaen ; Don Andrea Cuesta, bishop of Leon ; Don Antonio Gorrionero, bishop of Almeria ; Don Diego Sobaños, rector of the university of Alcala ; Fray Pedro de Soto, confessor to Charles V. ; Fray Dominic Soto, professor of Salamanca ; Don Ferdinand de Gorrionero, canon, magistrate, and professor of Toledo ; and

Fray Mancio del Corpus, professor of Alcala; besides many other Doctors of Salamanca, Valladolid, and Alcala.

While the archbishop was at Valladolid in 1558, he demanded that the theological censures of his works should be communicated to him, that he might reply to them, and give any satisfaction required of him. He thought he had a right to this concession, for several reasons: first, as he was the author; secondly, as the primate of Spain; and thirdly, as a man who might expect such an act of deference from the holy office, in consideration of his labours in its cause. But the grand-inquisitor Valdés (who was his enemy, though he pretended to be his friend) would not grant his request, alleging that it was not the custom to hear an author on the qualification of his works. Carranza then endeavoured to avail himself of the approbations he had obtained from the illustrious theologians already mentioned, who were almost all of them fathers of the council of Trent; but they were not received, and he experienced the same rejection from the Supreme Council. The mystery which shrouded all the proceedings of that body was impenetrable, and he departed from Valladolid in ignorance of the causes of his trial.

He however afterwards obtained information, that some witnesses had been examined on his personal faith, and that the censurers of his work noted it, as containing *heresies, propositions savouring of heresy, fomenting heresy, tending to heresy, and capable of causing it.* Some idea may be formed of the state of his mind from his application to the king and the pope, to whom he sent an account of all that had passed between him and the grand-inquisitor, and implored their protection; the minutes of this account, and the letters which accompanied it, were afterwards found among his papers.

On the 20th of September, he arrived at Yuste, in Estremadura. His misfortune, it may be presumed, rendered him prudent in his exhortations to Charles V.; it is not likely

that he would use the phrases attributed to him by Fray
Juan de Regla, without adding expressions to limit the absolute sense which the denouncer imputed to him.   On the
5th of October he again wrote to the king, on the occasion
of the death of the emperor, and also to Ruy Gomez de
Sylva, and to Don Antonio de Toledo, grand-prior of the
order of St. John, both high in favour with his majesty, and
with whom he was intimate, but more particularly with Don
Antonio, who always endeavoured to be useful to him.   His
letters and those of many others at Rome, who wished to
serve him, were found among his papers.   The papal nuncio
in Spain had already informed his court of what was passing at Madrid, and it was believed that the grand-inquisitor
acted in concert with the king ; this circumstance prevented
Paul IV. (though he esteemed Carranza) from interfering
in the affair, until he clearly perceived what was to be thought
of it.

Philip II., who then resided at Brussels, was far from being
capable of arresting the progress of a trial undertaken by
the inquisitors for a matter of faith; he contented himself
with promising to protect Carranza, as long as it was compatible with the Catholic religion.   The demand of being
heard in his defence, before the condemnation of his Catechism, might have been granted, if the depositions concerning
his personal faith had not presented an obstacle.   Don Ferdinand Valdés represented to the princess Jane, governess of
the kingdom, the declarations of the witnesses, which, read
by a person without discrimination, and with the intention of injuring, made the archbishop appear to be a real
heretic.   The princess communicated this to the king, her
brother, who being naturally suspicious, and knowing that
Valdés was inimical to Carranza, resolved to take the cow-
ardly part of remaining inactive, and waiting until the affair
should be elucidated.   It is not true that Philip repented of
having elevated Carranza to the see of Toledo ; the proof of

this exists in the procedure : he was favourably disposed towards the archbishop, till Valdés and the counsellors of the
Inquisition persuaded him that Carranza was an hypocritical
heretic.   The absolute inactivity of this prince's character,
and the formidable and continual activity of Valdés, were
the cause of the misfortunes of Carranza.

The archbishop now thought it would be better to submit
in order to avoid the infamy, and without waiting for replies
from Brussels and Rome, on the 21st of September, 1558, he
addressed a petition to Don Sanche Lopez de Otalora, counsellor of the Inquisition, in which he consented that his Catechism should be placed in the Index, provided his name
was not mentioned, and that the prohibition did not extend
beyond Spain, because the work was in the Spanish language.
He hoped by these means to preserve the reputation of being
a Catholic author, the only fame of which he was ambitious.
In November, he sent letters to the grand-inquisitor and
others, and remitted petitions to the Supreme Council, earnestly requesting, that in order to terminate all difficulties as
soon as possible, his Catechism might be printed in Spanish,
and given to him to be revised, corrected, and translated
into Latin.   His efforts were unsuccessful; the grand-inquisitor, far from wishing to serve him, obtained from the Pope
the brief which completed his disgrace.   He then perceived
that he ought to have followed the advice which had been
given to him in Flanders, to repair to Rome, instead of
Spain.   The Bishop of Orense gave him to understand that
there were in his case some things savouring of heresy, when
he made the following reply :—*Unless this crime entered by
the sleeve of my habit, I am, thank God, innocent of any
thing of the kind.   I shall therefore allow the affair to take
the common course.*

On the 7th of June, 1558, Paul IV. declared in full consistory, " that being informed that the heresies of Luther,
and some others, had been propagated in Spain, he had

reason to suspect that several prelates had adopted them; and in consequence he authorized the grand inquisitor, *for two years from that day,* to make inquests concerning all the bishops, archbishops, patriarchs, and primates, of that kingdom: to commence their trials, and, in case that an *attempt to escape* was suspected, to arrest them and lodge them in a place of security, and that the inquisitor should *immediately* report the same to the sovereign pontiff, and send the criminals to Rome as soon as possible, with their process sealed up." The archbishop received notice of the expedition of this brief, in a letter from Cardinal Theatire, on the 18th of January. Valdés also demanded of the king, his permission to put it in execution. A letter from Don Antonio de Toledo to Carranza, dated Brussels, 27th of February, informed him, that his majesty had commanded the grand-inquisitor to suspend the proceedings till he arrived in Spain; adding, that his majesty was quite convinced of the wickedness with which the archbishop was treated. Valdés renewed his demand in March, representing the inconveniences of delay, and at last obtained permission to execute the brief.

During this period, the inquisitors of Valladolid continued to receive every possible deposition unfavourable to the archbishop, to justify the proceedings against him.

On the 20th of February, 1559, Fray Gaspard Tamayo, a Franciscan, voluntarily denounced the Catechism: he said, he thought it wrong in the author, to exhort the faithful to read the Scriptures, and not to address to the saints the prayers beginning *Pater-Noster* and *Ave-Maria.*

On the 11th of April, Don Juan de Accuña, count de Buendia, deposed that the archbishop had recommended him to renounce that practice, and to pray to the saints in the manner he had taught in his book; that he and all his family, and Don Francis de Cordova, had followed his advice, until the Bishop of Ciudad Rodrigo had persuaded them to the contrary; the deponent added, that he knew that Carranza

had given the same advice to several other persons employed
in the palace. This deposition was followed by those of the
countess his wife, their chaplain, and seven of their servants.

On the same day, Fray Dominic de Roxas deposed, that
the Marquis de Boza, his father, asked Carranza if he should
cause a thousand masses to be said for his soul during his
life, or after his death, and that the archbishop replied, " *If
my lord the marquis will believe me, he will say the masses
during his life.*" The deponent further said, that the archbishop, in going to Trent to attend the second convocation
of the council, was in company with some Lutherans who
were with the King of Bohemia ; that he disputed with one
of them in the presence of the Bishop of Segovia, and though
he appeared to have the advantage in the argument, he afterwards said privately to the deponent: " *I was never so
much embarrassed as to-day ; although I am a master of
theology, yet I am not so learned in the Scriptures as this
Lutheran, who is only a layman.*" The witness also said,
that the archbishop had read and approved his *explanation
of the articles of the faith,* and that he had even inserted part
of it in his Catechism. It has been already stated, that Fray
Dominic recanted all his depositions before his death.

On the 5th of May, Donna Catherine de Castilla, who
was a prisoner of the holy office, declared that she believed
the archbishop to be a Lutheran ; but repenting, she retracted her declaration, and said that she knew that Carranza had maintained to Don Carlos de Seso, her husband,
that he committed a fatal error in denying the existence of
purgatory. She persisted in her recantation.

I appeal to my readers, if the state of the trial and the depositions of the witnesses were sufficient allegation: Canino the
fiscal, reserving to himself the right of accusing him with more
formality hereafter, demanded that the person of the archbishop should be seized, that he should be imprisoned, and
his goods and revenues sequestrated, to be at the disposal of

the grand-inquisitor. Valdés, after consulting the Supreme Council, commanded the fiscal to present the papers of which he had spoken in his requisition ; these were the Catechism with the qualifications of Cano, Cuevas, Soto, and Ybarra ; two MSS. bound, containing the articles of faith by Fray Dominic de Roxas, and the other works of Carranza mentioned under the numbers 3, 4, 13, 27, 28, 29, and 30, with their qualifications ; two sermons sent by Carranza to the licentiate Herrera, judge of the trials for smuggling, who was under arrest for Lutheranism ; the depositions of the witnesses, with a summary of them, and to cause the archbishop to be pronounced attainted of heresy.   Valdés, having drawn up, on the 8th of April, a verbal process of the reception of the powers granted by the Pope, the licentiate Canino, fiscal of the council of the Inquisition, on the 6th of May, presented to the grand-inquisitor a requisition, in which he demanded the execution of the brief, and declared that he would designate, in time and place, the person which it was to strike.   Valdés remitted a declaration, in which he announced that he was ready to do justice whenever he was required.   On the same day, the fiscal presented another requisition, in which he stated that Don Bartholomew Carranza, archbishop of Toledo, had preached, insinuated, written, and taught, in his conferences, his sermons, and his catechism, and in other books and writings, several heresies of Luther, according to the depositions of witnesses, and the books and writings which he presented to support his charges : the letters were those of the bishop of Cuenza, Don Pedro de Castro ; a letter from the archbishop to Doctor Cazalla, dated Brussels, 18th of February, 1558, in reply to compliments on his elevation to the see of Toledo ; (in this letter he begs Cazalla to "*pray that he may have the light necessary to govern his diocese well;*" adding, "*that it was more needful to ask it then than before, for those who formed part of the church of God*") ; two letters of Juan

Sanchez, a Lutheran, in which he says *that he was going to Flanders, because he hoped to be well received by Carranza.*

As these formalities were all fulfilled in one day, it is not to be doubted that it was a concerted scheme between the grand-inquisitor, some members of the council, and the fiscal : if this had not been the case, three days would have been necessary for these ceremonies. On the 13th of May, the grand-inquisitor and the council determined that Carranza should be cited to appear, and reply to the accusations of the fiscal.

When the king had given his consent that the archbishop should be prosecuted, he required that he should be treated *with the respect due to his dignity :* this he repeated in a letter to Cardinal Pacheco, who informed him that Carranza had demanded that his affair should be judged at Rome. The king also wrote two letters to Carranza on the 30th of March, and the 4th April, in which he promised to protect him. The letter to Cardinal Pacheco induced the grand-inquisitor to write to the king on the 19th of May, when he informed him of the measure which had been decreed, adding, that he thought a citation to appear more moderate, less humiliating, and more private than an arrest by alguazils. The king, however, had still some regard for Carranza, since he did not approve of what had been done. At this period Don Antonio de Toledo, who continued to correspond with Carranza, informed him, that though he did not think the affair had taken so favourable a turn as might be wished, yet he thought he still perceived some marks of attachment for him in the king, in spite of the evil report made of him.

At last, on the 26th of June, the king sent an answer to the inquisitor-general, in which he gives his consent to what had been resolved upon; adding, that he hoped the execution of this measure would be attended with *all the consideration due to the merit of Carranza, and the dignity with which he was invested.* The prelate was informed of this event, in a letter written by Don Antonio de Toledo, the next day. The approbation of the king was received on the 10th of July, and on the 15th the fiscal presented a second requisition, in which he insisted on the execution of the demand contained in the first, that Carranza should be arrested, and his goods seized. He represented that the instruction of the process furnished proofs which ought to have been considered sufficient on the 13th of May; that nevertheless he would add to them the deposition of Donna Louisa de Mendoza, wife of Don Juan Vasquez de Molina, secretary to the king. This lady deposed, that the Marchioness d'Alcañices told her, that, *according to the instructions of the archbishop, it was not meritorious in the sight of God to deprive ourselves of pleasures, and that it was not necessary to wear haircloth.* The marchioness, who was examined, declared that she had never said anything of the kind, but only that all these things were less meritorious; that she had been intimate with the archbishop for more than twenty years, and had been his penitent, but during all that time she had never heard him say any thing against the faith.

On the 1st of August, the grand-inquisitor, in concert with the Supreme Council, and several consultors, issued the order for the arrest of the archbishop. At this juncture, Philip II. wrote to his sister, the governess of the kingdom, saying, that in order to avoid the scandal and inconveniences arising from the measures decreed by the holy office, it would be proper to send for the archbishop to court upon some decent pretext. Don Antonio de Toledo having heard some hints of this, hastened to communicate it to Carranza, on the 19th of July; this was the last letter that faithful friend wrote to him. Among the papers of the archbishop, were found letters from persons, who afterwards, from want of courage, joined his enemies. There was also found the minutes of a representation in Latin, addressed to the Pope, in the name of the chapter of Toledo, entreating his holiness not to allow

the cause of Carranza to be judged by the holy office of
Spain, alleging that its members were swayed by human
motives, and not from zeal to religion : it is not certain if
this petition reached the Court of Rome, but the chapter
behaved to the prelate with great generosity.

The regent wrote a letter to the archbishop on the 3rd of
August, in which she says, that before the arrival of the king,
which would soon take place, she wished to communicate
some affairs to him, and therefore begged him to repair
immediately to Valladolid, adding, that as the least delay
might occasion very disagreeable consequences, she should
be pleased if he came as soon as possible, even if without
ceremony or equipage, and that she sent Don Rodrigo de
Castro that he might not lose time, and might inform her of
his arrival.

This Don Rodrigo de Castro was the nephew of the Bishop
of Cuença, the first denouncer of Carranza : he departed
from Valladolid on the 4th of August ; on the 6th he delivered the letter to the archbishop, who, on the next day,
replied to the princess that he would obey her orders.   He
immediately sent his equipages and part of his household to
Valladolid, but followed slowly, that he might visit the
towns and villages of his diocese, which he was to pass
through.

During this interval, Don Rodrigo wrote several letters to
Valdés, one dated the 4th of August, from Arevalo, and
four from Alcala de Henares, dated the 7th, 9th, 10th, and
14th, from which the inquisitor-general concluded that
the delay of eight days was too long, and concealed some
bad design : he pretended to think that Carranza intended to
make his escape to Rome, yet Don Rodrigo de Castro lodged
in the same house, and never lost sight of him.   This pretext, futile as it was, gave Valdés the opportunity of issuing
a mandate on the 17th, appointing Don Rodrigo and Don
Diego Ramirez de Sedeño inquisitors of the districts of Toledo

and Valladolid. He commissioned them and the chief alguazil of Valladolid to seize the person of the archbishop, to
sequestrate his goods, and draw up an inventory of them.

This order was executed at Torre-Laguna, on the 22nd,
before day, and while the archbishop was still in bed. When
he was told that he was under arrest, he demanded to know
by whose order he was made prisoner; that of the inquisitor-
general, and the brief of the Pope, were shewn to him. He
replied, that the brief was general, and that it ought to be a
special commission expedited with a knowledge of the cause,
which was out of the jurisdiction of the inquisitor-general:
that even supposing him to be competent, the conditions prescribed in the brief were not observed in his case, since
nothing but malice could inspire the fear that he should
attempt to eacape ; that from all these considerations, he
protested against the order of the grand inquisitor, and the
violence of his measures, and demanded satisfaction of the
Pope for the insult he had received. Not being able at that
moment to put his intentions into execution, the archbishop
desired Juan de Ledesma, the notary of the holy office, who
was present at his arrest, to write down his replies to the
inquisitors, and that he obeyed the order only to avoid ill-
treatment.

The archbishop requested that great care might be taken
of his papers, some of which belonged to trials concerning
the archiepiscopal see, and were of great importance. All
that he requested was complied with on this subject.

On the 23rd of August he left Torre-Laguna, and arrived
at Valladolid on the 28th ; he was imprisoned in the house
of Don Pedro Gonzalez de Leon: his portfolio, and a box
containing papers, were sent to the inquisitor-general, who
immediately caused them to be opened, and an inventory
taken of their contents. On the 6th of September he addressed a letter to the king, giving an account, in his manner,
of the arrest, and alleging his pretended fear of the flight of

Carranza, as the motive for it.   He added, that the archbishop appeared to be informed of his proceedings ; an insinuation which might have injured Don Antonio de Toledo,
whose correspondence he had read.

<hr>

CHAPTER XXXIII.

CONTINUATION OF THE TRIAL UNTIL THE ARCHBISHOP WENT TO ROME.

THE enemies of Carranza procured new witnesses, in order
to justify their conduct.   Valdés and his coadjutors feared
that public opinion would be against them, if, when they
pronounced the definitive sentence, the archbishop was not
proved, to all Europe, to be guilty of heresy.

To attain this end, the inquisitors examined ninety-six witnesses, who, most of them, unfortunately, added nothing to
what had been already deposed ; some of them attested the
purity of Carranza's faith, and the few who were against him,
deposed only what they had heard from other persons, who
either did not confirm, or denied the facts.   It is worthy of
remark, that the greatest number of the witnesses who spoke
in favour of the archbishop, were in the dungeons of the
Inquisition, and made their depositions during, or after the
torture, and when they were liable to have it renewed, and
to be subject to the cruel treatment of the judges, whose
schemes they frustrated.   While these miserable people
shewed so much courage, the bishops, archbishops, and theologians, who aspired to the episcopacy, basely retracted their
first and true opinion, and qualified as *violently suspected of
Lutheranism*, the man whom they had before considered
almost as an apostle, and that in the same trial and for the
same work.

On the 26th of August, the grand-inquisitor delegated his powers to the counsellors Valtodano and Simancas, reserving to himself the right of pronouncing the definitive sentence; at the same time he appointed Baca, Riego, and Gonzalez, inquisitors of Valladolid, to take the proper measures to guard the archbishop, and sequestrate his property.

When the prelate arrived at the house intended for his prison, he was asked what domestics he wished to have; he named six, but only two were permitted to attend him. He begged Valtodano and Simancas not to allow any person to see certain papers and letters from the Pope, Fray Ferdinand de St. Ambrose, and the licentiate Cespedes, because they related to a trial for the lordship of Cazorla; he asked the same favour for a bundle of letters from the king, on some affairs which it would be improper to make public. He demanded the originals of his consultations, and some approbations of his book, because he wished to present them to the Pope, who was the only competent judge of his trial; and lastly, some other writings relative to conferences which took place at the Council of Trent, in England, and in Flanders, and which were so many proofs of his efforts in the cause of the Catholic religion.

On the 1st of September, Valtodano and Simancas summoned the archbishop to take an oath to speak the truth. The prelate replied that he would do so when he received an order from the Pope or the king; that he protested against all that had been done, because they were not competent; that he did not acknowledge the grand-inquisitor as his judge, until he was furnished with special powers for that purpose; that supposing him to have sufficient authority, he did not believe that he could delegate it; that he should prove his assertions much better if he had the brief, of which he demanded a copy. His request was granted the next day; on the 3rd the grand-inquisitor, after a consultation with the Council, declared that he was a competent judge, and that he could

delegate his powers; he announced that he should attend
with the Council at the sessions of the tribunal: he attended
on the 4th, and required Carranza to take the oath to speak
the truth, either against himself or any other person, informing him that if he confessed all he knew, he would be treated
with clemency, but in the contrary case he would be used
with all the rigour of justice: he also told him that if he was
reluctant to reply in the presence of the Council, he would
be permitted to do so before two counsellors, or the inquisitors of Valladolid.   Carranza made the same reply as on
the preceding day, adding, that he was not certain that truth
had been spoken in soliciting the brief from the Pope, since
at that time there were no Spanish prelates suspected of heresy; that if they had him in view, he was not in Spain at
the time, but in Flanders, occupied in labouring for the
defence of the Catholic religion, and converting heretics;
that he exerted himself to destroy all the heresies, and for that
purpose informed the king that heretical books were sold
even at his palace-gates, and that the king, in consequence,
gave the necessary orders to prevent the evil, which would
be proved by the testimony of the king and the noblemen of
his court.

Not satisfied with these arguments, the archbishop challenged the grand inquisitor for reasons which he explained
at the same session, and in his presence: on the 5th and the
following days he continued to give the motives for his
challenge in writing; his charges against Valdés were numerous, and very serious.   He mentions persons, times,
subjects, and reasons, which authorized him to represent
Valdés as a perfidious, envious, vindictive man; to maintain
that he continually abused his authority in order to satisfy
his vengeance, which could be proved by some writings
which were registered: he particularly applied himself to
shew that Valdés concealed his hatred to him, under the
mask of an hypocritical zeal for religion; that this enmity

was caused by his spite and envy after he (Carranza) was elevated to the see of Toledo, and had published his work on the Residence of Bishops;—in short, he filled eight folio sheets in a small hand, with the motives which induced him to challenge Valdés, and added those concerning the counsellors Perez and Cobos, promising to establish the proofs.

The archbishop chose for his advocates those men whom he considered most able to defend him; but they were, by different intrigues, induced to refuse their assistance; this plan was pursued with all the others whom he chose in case of their default, so that he was obliged to apply to some advocates who defended in the chancery his right to the lordship of some villages, although they knew nothing of the affairs of the holy office. Don Juan Sarmiento de Mendoza, counsellor of the Indies, for Valdés, and the licentiate Isunza, judge of the civil court of Valladolid, for the fiscal, were appointed arbitrators, to decide on the validity of the challenge. On the 23rd of February, 1560, they pronounced that the allegations were just, reasonable, and well proved. The fiscal not being satisfied with the decision, intended to appeal to Rome, but soon renounced the measure; in fact, how could the inquisitor-general think of sending a trial to Rome, which if made public, would cover him and many others, who afterwards attained the highest dignities of the church, with eternal infamy? However, this appeal took place at a later period, after a thousand intrigues, but Valdés was not the inquisitor-general at that time.

The lodgings assigned to the archbishop were neither commodious, agreeable, nor airy; he was allowed only two rooms for himself, a monk, and his page. He complained of the inconvenience, but the fiscal presented a verbal process, stating that the house was large, convenient, and healthy: this was true, for he spoke of it in general, and did not mention the place where Carranza was confined. The rooms

were very remote from all communication; in 1561 there
was a great fire at Valladolid, which consumed four hundred houses in the quarter nearest to the prison of the
archbishop, yet he heard neither the cries of the people,
nor the noise which must have been occasioned by such an
event, and only learnt that it had happened a long time after,
when he was at Rome. This privation of air and exercise
produced in the archbishop a tertian fever, which weakened
him considerably, but the inquisitors had not sufficient humanity to remove him to a more suitable place. They
dreaded that he would appeal to the Pope, or the king, on
whom however it would not have had any effect, as Valdés
had contrived to persuade him, in some private conversations,
that Carranza was really an heretic, and that all that he
had done in England and Flanders was intended to conceal
his opinions.

Although Valdés persisted in maintaining that he had the
right of delegating his powers to prosecute the archbishop,
yet as several counsellors, and particularly Baco de Castro,
held a contrary opinion, he was obliged to appeal to the
Pope. Paul IV. was dead, and had been succeeded by
Pius IV., who, on the 23rd of February, confirmed to Valdés
the powers granted to him by his predecessor, and that of
delegating confidential persons to proceed in the trial of the
Archbishop of Toledo. This brief was of no use, because
the arbitrators had declared on the same day that the
motives for the challenge were just and valid; his holiness,
in consequence, expedited another special brief, confirming
all that had passed, provided that the proceedings had been
lawful, and authorizing Philip II. to choose judges in his
own name, to whom he gave from that moment the power of
continuing the trial until it was in a state to be terminated,
for the space of two years, beginning from the 7th of
January, 1561. This brief was interpreted at Madrid to be
a permission to pass a definitive sentence. The Pope being

informed of this circumstance, on the 3rd of July issued a fourth brief, in which he disapproved of the interpretation of that preceding it, and commanded that the trial should be remitted to him, *instructed* but not judged, within a certain time.

Philip II. appointed Don Gaspard de Zuñiga y Avellanada, archbishop of Santiago, to be the judge, with the power of delegating his authority. This choice was pleasing to Carranza, because that prelate was one of the persons he had proposed for the see of Toledo; in fact, he derived some advantage from the change of his guards, and other measures. But Zuñiga appointed Voltodano and Simancas, who had begun the trial, to be the judges. Carranza intended to challenge them, as having voted his arrest; but being told that the king had said that no person who had ordered the imprisonment of a criminal could afterwards be his judge, if this challenge was allowed, he abandoned his design. The right which the prelate had intended to make use of, is now recognised as a principle among civilized nations; to it we owe the establishment of *Juries*.

The trial having been commenced more than two years after the arrest of the archbishop, he was at last permitted, in consequence of an order from the king, to choose four advocates : these were Doctor Martin d'Alpizcueta, known by the name of *Doctor* Navarro; Don Antonio Delgado, canon of Toledo; Doctor Santander, archdeacon of Valladolid; and Doctor Morales, an advocate of the Chancery. The two first of these lawyers were allowed to see the archbishop, but the writings of the trial were not communicated to any of them, consequently it was impossible for them to demonstrate the insufficiency of the proofs of the charges brought against him by the witnesses. It is true that the answers of Carranza were decided and conclusive.

The unqualified works of Carranza, and even some of those which had been examined, were confided to Fray Diego de

Chabes, who had been the confessor of Don Carlos, and afterwards of the king; to Fray Juan d'Ybarra, and to Fray Rodrigo de Vadillo, and Fray Juan de Azoloros, who were afterwards the bishops of Cephalonia and the Canaries. These qualified as heretical some propositions contained in works not written by Carranza, but found among his papers; others were qualified as approaching to heresy, and likely to cause it; and the author was declared to be violently suspected of being an heretic. The edicts condemning the Catechism, and the Explanation of the Canonical Epistle of St. John, had been already published.

The Council of Trent having been convoked for the third time, Valdés feared that the Fathers might take notice of the affairs of Carranza, and he persuaded the king that it was important to the rights of the crown to prevent them from taking cognizance of the trial. Philip had appointed the Count de Luna to be the ambassador to the council, and on the 30th October, 1562, he sent him instructions, in which he says, that he has been informed that it was intended to form a *general index* of the prohibited books contained in the *index* of Paul IV., which had occasioned much expostulation. The king added, that he could not allow this measure to extend its influence into Spain, which had an *index*, and particular regulations; that this exception might also apply to other Christian countries, since books, which were dangerous in one, might not be so in others. The king commanded his ambassador to oppose such a resolution in the council, because he could not receive into Spain books approved by the council which had been prohibited in that kingdom, and *some persons suspected that this project concealed particular views;* that he had already commanded his ambassador at Rome, and the Marquis of Pescara, to use every effort, consistent with prudence, to baffle the scheme.

These instructions shew very plainly that the Court of Madrid were afraid that the council would approve the Catechism of Carranza, and the explanation of St. John, which had been prohibited in Spain. The fathers, who were displeased to see the proceedings so long in the hands of the inquisitors, addressed several remonstrances to the Pope against them and the King of Spain, and even refused to open the letters which that prince wrote to them, until he had atoned for the offence committed against the episcopal dignity, in the person of one of its members. At last the fathers declared that they would not assemble, unless his Holiness did not cause the proceedings, and the person of the archbishop to be sent to Rome. The Pope had just prolonged the period destined for the trial (which would otherwise have expired on the 7th of January, 1568), he however replied that he would write to Philip, to demand that the Archbishop of Toledo and the writings of his trial should be sent to him ; and to prove how much he wished to satisfy the fathers, he sent this letter by Odescalche, to whom he gave the title of nuncio extraordinary.

On the 15th of August following, Philip replied, with an energy unusual to him, that he was very much surprised that the Fathers of the council occupied themselves with particular affairs, instead of those which concerned religion in general ; that the imperative dispositions of the brief presented by the nuncio were contrary to the rights of his sovereignty and the honour of his person, and that he hoped his Holiness would not take it ill, if he did not order it to be published, and continued the trial. The Pope feared to irritate Philip, who was already offended that the ambassador of France had obtained precedence over his own, and therefore he granted the delay requested by that prince ; at the same time, he charged the cardinal-legate, president of the council, to pacify the fathers, promising to do what they desired when the process was *instructed*. His Holiness also commanded that the archbishop should be treated with as much gentleness as was consistent with the proceedings.

The resolution of the Pope appeased the fathers of the council for the present; but they soon began to discuss an affair equally displeasing to the King of Spain. The bishops and theologians commissioned to examine books, pronounced the doctrine of the Catechism of Carranza to be Catholic. They communicated their decision to the Archbishop of Prague, who was president of the congregation of the *Index*, who, together with the theologians composing it, approved the Catechism, and resolved to send an act of their approbation to Carranza, that he might make make use of it in his defence. The decree of approbation was to be confirmed by the general assembly, but violent measures were employed to prevent it. The Pope permitted the Catechism to be printed at Rome on the 26th of June.

The Spanish ambassador vehemently protested against this resolution; he said that as the Catechism was prohibited by the Inquisition of Spain, it was an insult to his master and the Supreme Council to declare it orthodox, and he demanded that the decree of the congregation should be revoked. Don Antonio d'Augustine, Bishop of Lerida, was a member of the congregation of the *Index*, and had not been present on the 2nd of June, when the members approved the Catechism. This circumstance induced him to support the Count de Luna. His enmity to Carranza, and his desire to please the king, made him go so far as to say that *the congregation approved heresies, since the Catechism contained them*. The Archbishop of Prague, anxious to defend his honour and that of his colleagues, addressed to the papal legates a formal complaint against the Bishop of Lerida, demanding in their names and his own a public reparation for the injury they had received, and protesting that if it was refused, they would not attend the assemblies. The cardinal succeeded in reconciling the two parties, by proposing to maintain the decree of approbation, but to forbid a literal copy to be given, and to commission the Count de Luna to obtain that which had been already remitted to the agent of Carranza, on the condition that the bishop made a public apology to the congregation, and one in private to the president. The bishop complied, and the Count de Luna, by his entreaties and promises, at last succeeded in obtaining the decree which the agent had received; but he had already sent an authenticated copy into Spain*.

Philip II., on the 3rd of August, wrote to the Count de Luna, complaining bitterly of all that had occurred, and charging him to represent to the Pope and the Council, that this resolution was the effect of an intrigue which tended to favour particular views, *as injurious to the Pope* as to himself, and to give the authors of the decree to understand that they could not expect to succeed in causing the trial to be transferred to Rome, as the king would never permit it.

On the 26th of October, the Count de Luna wrote to his master, informing him of all that he had done. He said that after he had received his instructions, he endeavoured to suppress the commission for the examination of books, or to render their decrees concerning books prohibited in Spain null and void; that the cardinal legates had assured him that it was impossible to grant his request, because the commission was the work of the council, and not of the Pope; that he must, therefore, apply to the general assembly, but that he must not expect to succeed, and the only thing that he could ask would be that the commission should not go beyond its powers.

The Count de Luna also said, that though the commission was formed to examine the book contained in the *Index* of Paul IV., a particular brief had been obtained from Pius IV. to extend the examination to the prohibited books of the other indexes of Christendom; that the affair concerning the Catechism of Carranza had been carried on unknown to the

* Reinaldo: Ecclesiastical Annals for 1563, No. 137. Paul Sarpi: History of the Council of Trent, b. viii. p. 32.

Bishop of Lerida, and to Doctor Pedro *Zumel*, canon of Malaga, commissary of the Inquisition ; that in consequence, the
Bishop of Lerida and the Bishop of Caba had appealed against
the decree of the congregation, and demanded that it should
be annulled ; that he could still make a remonstrance in full
synod, but that he found it necessary to renounce that intention, *as it might be the occasion of great inconveniences* * :
and that the only cause for this event was that the Cardinal
de Lorraine, the Archbishop of Braga, the Bishop of Modena,
and several others, defended Carranza to the Pope.

The fathers of the council could not succeed in their
attempt to cause the trial of Carranza to be transferred to
them. When the assembly was dissolved, the grand-inquisitor, who had now only the Pope to contend with, commissioned
the Council of the Inquisition to request the king to obtain a
brief to allow the trial to be terminated in Spain; representing to him that he might say that it would be useful in
alarming those Spaniards who had adopted heretical opinions; that the King of Spain merited such a favour, because
he was the only prince who had used every means to extirpate heresy ; that the ancient canons permitted that the
trial should take place where the crime was committed ; that
*if that of Carranza was transferred to Rome, the names
of the witnesses would be revealed,* which would occasion
serious consequences ; that the trial must be translated into
Latin or Italian, which would take much time, and that
none but Spaniards could understand the strength of the
expressions of the witnesses; that the procurator-fiscal would
be obliged to go to Rome, where he would have the mortification of not being heard or well received, because many
persons of high rank had been zealous in the cause of the archbishop ; that the crimes were committed before he was raised

---

* These expressions shew that the Count foresaw that the resolution of
the council would be favourable to the Catechism ; and in that case the
holy office of Spain would be dishonoured.

to the episcopal dignity ; that it would not be convenient to allow the archbishop to go to Rome, and that the trial could not be properly judged unless he did so ; that from all these considerations it would be better for the sovereign pontiff to appoint persons to finish the trial in Spain, in concert with the Supreme Council.

On the other side, Don Martin d'Alpizcueta represented to the king all the ill treatment which the archbishop had suffered, and demanded that he should be sent to Rome. He represented that the archbishop might have made his escape to Rome, but that he did not do so, because his majesty *had commanded him in a letter written with his own hand, not to apply to any one but himself, and to have confidence in his protection.* Alpizcueta, speaking of the injustice Carranza had suffered, says that his arrest was decreed before anything was proved against him, since all impartial persons would see that the propositions imputed to him were not heretical ; that his Catechism had been approved by the Council of Trent, and that it was read in every country but Spain, where his enemies resided.

The advocate states, that suspected judges had been appointed, and that nothing but the fear of displeasing his majesty could prevent his client from challenging them.

That his enemies, taking advantage of his captivity, always prevented him from informing the king and the Pope of the secret intrigues ;

That his act of accusation had been divided into fifteen or twenty parts, and the same charges multiplied into four hundred articles, while it might and ought to have been reduced to thirty points ;

That he had been accused of having advanced heretical propositions, when they were perfectly Catholic ;

That the accusations had been accumulated to embarrass his client, and cause him to contradict himself ;

That the copies of the requisitions of the fiscal were not

given to him until the period allowed for the reply had
nearly expired ; that the archbishop might render his detention longer by demanding fresh delays, or might reply
without reflection ;

That works had been imputed to him, of which he was
not the author ;

That consequently he did not expect to be tried fairly
unless the process was transferred to the throne ;

That the king ought not to listen to his flatterers; that
all Spain murmured at the treatment the archbishop had
received, and that it was spoken of still more severely than
in other countries.

He then goes on to accuse the judges of partiality, and
says that their boldness in preferring their judgment to that
of the Council of Trent, resembles that of the Lutherans who
were prosecuted by them.

The advocate continues, " These judges are so offended at
this decision, (concerning the Catechism,) that one of them
said to my two colleagues and myself: *All the council could
not defend two propositions contained in that book ;* he quoted
one, which I immediately proved to be Catholic, and told
him that if I had the authority of the grand inquisitors, I
should perhaps denounce him, for I thought there was as
much heresy in looking upon a Catholic proposition as heretical, as in thinking an heretical opinion Catholic; besidesi
is certain that it is heretical, to suppose that the council can
approve a doctrine as Catholic, which is not so."

That the Lutherans, when they found that the king had
more confidence in the Inquisition of Spain than in the sovereign Pontiff, would take advantage of the circumstance, to
persist in their opposition to the holy see, and would say
that his majesty's faith was subordinate to his interest;

That he had been informed in a *confession,* that the *real
design* of these men was to let the archbishop die in prison,
without concluding his trial ; that such proceedings lead to

the supposition, *that the authors of them dissipate the revenues of the archbishopric to their own profit, which they really do, without any person to call them to an account;* besides that such a plan is equivalent to a condemnation, since every one will suppose that his client is guilty, if the inquisitors do not judge him; that it even concerned the honour of his majesty, because it would be said, that he spared heretics of high rank, and punished those of no importance.

Alpizcueta concludes, by declaring that he believes the archbishop would be acquitted and received with the greatest honours, if he was sent to Rome, and conjures the king to grant permission that the trial should be transferred.

Martin d'Alpizcueta was doubtless a very learned man, and told the king many truths; but he did not understand the character of that prince, for the letter he wrote to the Pope, on the 15th of April, shews that he had become even more unjust than the judges. Persuaded that Carranza was an heretic, he resolved to shew the world that if he knew how to reward merit, he also knew how to punish his creatures.

He therefore resolved to demand permission of the Pope to conclude the trial in Spain. He selected for this commission Don Rodrigo de Castro, to whom were remitted on the 24th November, 1564, the instructions decreed by the council, and others from the king, which were private, and without a date; an alphabet of the cipher, in which he was to correspond with the king, and letters of credit to the Pope, and many cardinals.

The king, who foresaw the events which might arise from this journey, also sent letters to the King and Queen of France, to the constable of that kingdom, and his own ambassador there, to his ambassador at Genoa, to the Viceroy of Naples, the Governor of Milan, the Grand Duke of Tuscany, and Prince Marcantonio Colonna.

Among the instructions, the following may be remarked: " That although it is to be hoped that God will influence the decision of the Pontiff, yet the means of succeeding in so just an enterprise ought not to be neglected: therefore *the persons who have most influence in the affair must be gained over by any means which may appear most convenient.*"

Don Rodrigo de Castro succeeded in obtaining the required permission. On the 13th of July, 1565, Pius IV. appointed as judges, the Cardinal Buoncompagni (afterwards Pope Gregory XIII.) with the title of Legate; the Archbishop of Rosano (afterwards Pope Urban VII.), the auditor of the *Rota*, Aldobrandini, and the general of the Franciscans (afterwards Sextus Quintus). The Pope informed Philip of these nominations in a brief, dated the 21st of August following.

The papal envoys arrived in Spain in the month of November. Philip went to Alcala to meet the legate, and received him in the most flattering manner, to induce him to consent that the counsellors of the Inquisition should be associated with the papal judges: this, the legate, who was aware of the inexpedience of the measure, refused. Many powerful intrigues were by the king's order employed to obtain his wish, but they were in vain; and the Pope dying on the night of the 8th of December, Buoncompagni, who wished to assist at the conclave, immediately set off for Rome, without even informing the king of his intention, and leaving the archbishop and his trial in exactly the same state as in the year 1562.

On the 17th of January, 1566, Pius V. was elected. Buoncompagni was informed of this event while he was on the road, and stopped at Avignon. Philip sent a courier to the new Pontiff, to entreat him to confirm the arrangements of his predecessor, which was complied with; his Holiness at the same time commanded the cardinal to return to Spain; he replied that he thought it necessary to have a private conference with his Holiness, before he obeyed his orders, and therefore continued his journey. As soon as he arrived at Rome, he proved to the new Pontiff that the trial of Carranza could never be judged with impartiality in Spain, even by judges appointed by the holy see; Pius V. then determined that the Archbishop of Toledo, and the writings of his trial, should be transferred to Rome, and that Don Ferdinand Valdés should be deprived of the office of inquisitor-general: this he considered necessary, in case the proceedings required that fresh witnesses should be examined in Spain.

Salazar de Mendoza says, that Philip obeyed immediately, but he had not read the history of the trial: it is certain that a great contest ensued; that Pius V. was firm, and the pride of Philip was obliged to give way, when the Pope threatened to excommunicate him, and to put his kingdom under an interdict. The writings of the trial are still in existence; and *I refer to those documents.*

The king appointed Don Diego Espinosa, Bishop of Siguenza, to be inquisitor-general; and on the 9th of September, the Pope expedited a bull, in which he says, that on account of the great age and infirmities of Valdés, he had thought proper to appoint Don Diego Espinosa to be his coadjutor, authorizing him to act as inquisitor-general, without any dependance on Valdés. This bull was published, that Valdés might not be dishonoured; but his Holiness privately imparted his intentions to Espinosa, in a brief on the 1st of October, commanding him to avoid speaking of the trial of Carranza to Valdés.

The Pope sent Pedro Camayani, Bishop of Asculi, to Spain, with the title of nuncio-extraordinary, and with the most positive orders not to return to Rome without the archbishop, and the writings of his trial. On the 30th of July he addressed a brief to Camayani, which it is necessary to abridge, though of much importance. His Holiness says, that the delay of the trial, and the detention of Carranza, had scandalized all Christendom. He commands him, on pain of excommunication, to signify to the Archbishop of Seville, the Council of the Inquisition, and the other persons concerned in the trial of Carranza, with a menace of the same penalties, the absolute revocation of all the powers intrusted to them ; and a positive order, on pain of *excommunication in its full extent,* to set Carranza immediately at liberty without delay or protestation, and even without requiring any security from him ; to place all the papers of the trial in the hands of the nuncio, to be by him transferred to Rome ; to subject the detainers of the papers to the same censures, if they did not give them up immediately ; to inform the archbishop, when set at liberty, of the order to repair to Rome, and to permit him to appoint an administrator for his see.

Nothing, however, was done as the Pope had ordained. The archbishop was not liberated; the king sent a detachment of his guards to escort him to Carthagena, where he was to embark. He was detained at Valladolid so long by the preparations for his departure, that he only reached Rome on the 29th of May in the following year.

The nuncio was obliged to issue fresh menaces of excommunication, before he could obtain the papers, which detained the Archbishop at Carthagena for four months. The ignorance of the nuncio concerning the affair was taken advantage of, and only part of the proceedings were remitted to him, the rest being claimed when the deficiency was discovered at Rome, and thus the delay of a whole year occurred ; in short, it was evident that the inquisitors wished to defer the conclusion of the trial till after the death of Carranza. The members of the Chapter of Toledo were remarkable for their courageous devotion to their chief; they appointed two of their body to attend him during his detention, and to render him every service in their power, charging them never to leave him during his voyage and his residence at Rome.

Carranza left his prison on the 5th of December, 1566, after seven years, three months, and fourteen days' captivity, which he had passed in two rooms, from which he could see neither the country nor the street, and without conversing with any persons but his two domestics, and his two advocates. He was not permitted to name an administrator to his arch-bishopric according to the commands of the Pope : the reason given for this was, that his holiness did not know that an administrator had been already appointed by the king, and that Paul IV. had confirmed the nomination.

Carranza travelled in a litter, and was accompanied by Don Diego Gonzalez, Inquisitor of Valladolid, and Don Lope de Avellaneda, who had been appointed him gaoler in 1561. On his arrival at Carthagena, Gonzalez and the guard re-turned to Valladolid, as the captain-general of the province was then responsible for his person.

On the 27th of April, 1567, he embarked, and on the 25th of May he arrived at Civita Vecchia, where the Spanish ambassador, and Paul Vislersio, nephew to the Pope and captain of his guards, received him, and on the 29th he arrived at Rome. Besides his servants and Avellaneda, he was accompanied by two counsellors of the Inquisition, Don Diego de Simancas, and Don Antonio Pazos; by Don Pedro Fernandez de Temiño, inquisitor of Callahorra, Don Jerome Ramirez, fiscal to the Supreme Council, Sebastian de Lan-deta and Alphonso de Castellon, secretaries to the Inqui-sition of Valladolid, and several *familiars*, who all travelled at the archbishop's expense. He had also with him Don Martin d'Alpizcueta and Don Alphonso Delgado, his advo-cates.

CHAPTER XXXIV.

END OF THE TRIAL OF CARRANZA.—HIS DEATH.

On the arrival of Carranza at Rome, the Pope assigned to him the apartments occupied by the sovereign pontiffs in the Castle of St. Angelo ; the size of these rooms allowed him to

take exercise, and he enjoyed a view of the country. His
health became better, and his strength returned; he was also
allowed three more domestics. The Pope forbade any person to speak to him of his trial, and while it lasted he was
not permitted to take the sacrament, or to say mass. In
Spain he was not suffered to confess, but in Rome he was
allowed to do so four times in a year.

Pius V. appointed sixteen consultors for the trial; these
were Cardinals Reviva, Pacheco, Gambaya, and Chiesa; the
Archbishop of Tarragona ; the Bishop of Ciudad Rodrigo ;
the Bishop of Pati in Sicily; the Bishop of Chefalu; Don
Pedro Fernandez de Temiño, counsellor of the Spanish Inquisition; Fray Thomas Manriquez, a Dominican ; the Archbishop of St. Severin ; the Bishop of St. Agatha; the Bishop
of Arezzo; the Bishop of Fiesol, and Doctor Artimo, auditor
of the causes of the apostolical palace. The Pope also
appointed the fiscal of the Supreme Council to the same
office ; two Italian secretaries, and the two who came from
Spain. The rest of the year 1567, and part of the following,
were employed in translating the trial into Italian.

The Canons of Toledo presented a letter to the Pope, entreating him to take into consideration the merit of the archbishop and his high rank, as well as the honour and consolation of their church, which had been deprived of its pastor
for eight years, and soliciting him to shew him as much
favour as was compatible with religion and justice. This his
Holiness promised to do, and expressed great satisfaction at
the noble sentiments contained in the letter, and the tender
interest the chapter displayed in the welfare of their pastor.

The works and MSS. of the archbishop remained in Spain;
they were claimed and sent to Rome in 1570 : this circumstance caused fresh delays. When the translation was finished,
the fiscal required that no conferences of the consultors should
take place unless the Pope was present, which prolonged the
affair excessively, as his Holiness was often unable to attend.

The fiscal also challenged Fray Thomas Manriquez, because he was the friend of Carranza. The Pope then appointed Doctor Toledo, a Jesuit, but he was also challenged, because he was related to Don Antonio de Toledo, another friend of the archbishop.

Don Gomez Tellez Giron, governor of the archbishopric, dying at this time, the Chapter of Toledo wrote to the Pope a second time, expressing the utmost anxiety to see the trial terminated. His Holiness replied to this letter with peculiar graciousness, excusing himself on account of his numerous avocations, and the nature of the trial, and promising to hasten the conclusion, which he said he had already endeavoured to do.

When the writings were arranged, it was discovered that several sheets were missing ; Pius V. therefore considering that it would be difficult to express in writing what he thought on this subject, sent John de Bedoya, agent of the Council of the Inquisition, into Spain, with a brief addressed to the king, requesting him to listen to the commission of John de Bedoya with his usual benevolence and goodness.

It is not known what Bedoya said to the king, but the trial informs us that he caused the papers concerning the trial to be sought for, and that some of these were given by the inquisitor-general to the king, to be sent to Rome : among these were found some qualifications and depositions, which were favourable to the archbishop. The persons who had concealed these documents were so blinded by passion, that they did not consider that they were cited in the papers which were sent. Although his Holiness and Philip intended to transfer all the papers concerning Carranza, yet all the MS. copies of the Catechism, which were taken from the Marchioness d'Alcañices, and which had been used in the qualification of the work, and the duplicates and triplicates of the unprinted works, remitted by Alphonso de Castro, and Doctor Astate, were retained in Spain. This omission was not at first supposed to be occasioned by malevolence, since all the rest had been sent ; but it was afterwards discovered that the papers were retained to be made use of on some other opportunity, which in fact occurred ; and to give occasion for fresh delays if they were claimed by the Pope.

Pius V. prepared the definitive sentence ; but he did not pronounce it until he knew the inclinations of Philip, whom he did not wish to offend. In his judgment he declared that the accusation of the fiscal was not proved, and acquitted the prelate. He commanded that the *Catechism* should be restored to the author, to be translated into Latin, and that he should insert the necessary corrections, and explain the censured propositions in a Catholic sense ; secondly that the prohibition of that work should be held to be valid, until the explanations were furnished ; that that of the *explanation of St. John* should remain, and that none of the manuscript works of Carranza should be printed or published, until he had made the necessary corrections.

The Pope sent this sentence to the King of Spain, by Alexander Casali, his chamberlain. He was persuaded that Philip would be pleased to see that he had acknowledged the innocence of Carranza, and that he would be satisfied with the measures taken to prevent the books from being dangerous. The Pope did not understand the character of Philip II., who considered himself as much dishonoured as the holy office, by the exoneration of Carranza. He wrote to his Holiness, to prove that it was impossible that the works of the prelate could contain so many errors of Luther, if he was not an heretic. He therefore requested the Pope to defer the judgment until the return of his chamberlain, to whom he would give important documents proving the truth of his statement.

The king ordered a *Refutation of the Apology for the Catechism of Carranza, published by Alpizcueta and Delgado,* to be composed, and also another work by the

Abbé of Alcala de Henares, under the title of a *New Quali-fication of the Catechism of Carranza, and the Faith of its Author*. Philip sent these two writings to Rome, in 1572, by Casali. When he arrived, he found that his master, Pius V. was dead, and Gregory XIII. his successor, received the documents, and joined them to the trial.

The death of Pius has been attributed to the agents of the Inquisition. Such reports are not often worthy of credit, but there are letters on the subject in existence, which contain very bold expressions. One of them says: "The death of a man who shewed himself so much attached to a Dominican monk, and who compromised by his discourse the honour of the Spanish Inquisition, ought not to be considered of much im-portance. It (the Inquisition) would be benefited by the death of such a Pope."

Philip II. congratulated the new Pontiff on his accession, and at the same time requested him to suspend the judgment of the trial, until he had heard the opinions of four Spanish theologians, whom he intended to send to throw a new light on the affair: these doctors were, Don Francis Sancho, pro-fessor of theology at Salamanca; Fray Diego de Chabes, confessor to the king: Fray Juan Ochoa, and Fray Juan de la Fuente, masters of theology. Their censures were joined to the trial.

Philip II. perceiving the turn which the affair now took, made a last effort, and the counsellors of the Inquisition, in order to obtain a recantation of the favourable opinions emitted by respectable theologians before the arrest of Car-ranza, made use of terror and persuasion: the first, by mak-ing them dread that they would be arrested as being sus-pected of professing the errors which they had approved; and the second, by offering them an honourable pretext for reforming their first judgment, in the discovery of the in-edited works of Carranza, in which there were a greater number of propositions susceptible of an heretical inter-pretation.

The first who fell into the snare was a man truly respectable for his learning, his virtues, his birth, and many eminent qualities; but his great age, and his dread of the dungeons of the Inquisition may be considered as an excuse for his weakness, as well as for that of the venerable Osius.

On the 30th of March, 1574, the archbishop qualified as erroneous, seventy-five propositions of the same printed Catechism, which he had before pronounced to be orthodox; he however added, that the errors were owing to the Castilian language in which the work was written, and that if it was published in Latin, it would be necessary to suppress, correct, or explain thirty-one propositions. The prelate also declared, that there were two hundred and ninety-two errors in the MSS., numbered, 1, 2, 3, 4, 5, 6, and 7, and sixty-six in the explanations and sermons (of which a list has been given in a former part of this work), and from thence he concluded that the author was *violently suspected* of heresy.

Serrano, the reporter of the Supreme Council, who had taken these works to the Archbishop of Grenada, returned full of triumph to Madrid. The Supreme Council in a letter to the king, expresses great satisfaction on this account, and says, "It is absolutely necessary to send this qualification to Rome, because the activity with which the affair is proceeded in makes it likely that it will soon be concluded, and this measure is the more important as the opinion of the Archbishop of Grenada will have much influence." This letter was accompanied by a false estimate of the censures, plainly shewing the animosity of the council towards Carranza.

Serrano then repaired to Don Francis Blanco, then Bishop of Malaga. This prelate, on the 29th of April, retracted the opinion he had given in 1558. He censured sixty-eight propositions of the Catechism, although he had formerly praised the work. Serrano immediately informed the council of it, and that the bishop had pronounced Carranza to be *violently suspected* of heresy. The Archbishopric of Santiago being vacant at this time, the king bestowed it on this prelate.

Don Francis Delgado followed his example, and censured three hundred and fifteen propositions. Don Francis Delgado obtained the see of Santiago, on the death of Blanco, but he did not live long enough to take possession of it.

The king did not send the opinions of the prelates to Rome, but wrote to the Pope, and told him that he was informed that the archbishops of Santiago and Grenada had many important things to reveal concerning Carranza, and that he hoped his holiness would command all that was necessary to be done on this occasion.

On the 7th of August in the same year, Gregory XIII. expedited a brief, in which he commissioned Don Gaspard de Quiroga, inquisitor-general, to receive the declarations of the prelates in the presence of a notary, and of witnesses, and to send them signed and sealed to Rome. A similar brief was sent on the 17th of October, to the Bishop of Jaen, the magistral canon of Toledo, and Professor Mancio. The inquisitor-general appointed commissioners, to whom he gave written instructions. They were directed to exact an oath to speak the truth and observe secrecy, to induce the prelates to declare that the change in their opinion was founded on a more strict examination of the work, and a knowledge of the other writings of the author; lastly, to make them state in a separate paper what they now thought of the works and faith of Carranza, and not to allow them to say that they did so in obedience to the king, as they had stated at first, but to declare that they acted according to the brief.

These declarations were sent to Rome in December. Don Francis Blanco who had only censured sixty-eight propositions of the Catechism on the first examination, now censured two hundred and seventy-three in the Catechism and pamphlets together, sixty-three of which he pronounced to be heretical.

This extraordinary change was attributed by the prelates to a love of justice, to conscience, zeal for religion, and a wish to please God.

The declarations of five new witnesses of so much consequence, entirely changed the appearance of the trial. Gregory XIII. fell into the snare, which it was indeed difficult to avoid, since the intrigue which produced it was conducted by so powerful a sovereign as Philip, and so formidable and able a body as the Spanish Inquisition. Gregory had discovered the intrigues when at Madrid, and informed St. Pius V. that it would be impossible even for foreign judges to terminate the trial in an equitable manner in Spain ; but he was far from supposing that the animosity of Carranza's enemies would be still more active at Rome.

The Pope loved justice, and thought he was obeying its dictates, in commanding, on the 14th of April, 1576, that the Archbishop of Toledo should abjure all heresies in general, and particularly the sixteen Lutheran propositions which he was *violently* suspected of believing. He was suspended for five years from performing his archiepiscopal duties, and condemned to be confined during that time in the dominican convent of Orvietta in Tuscany, and for the present in that of the Minerva at Rome, where some penances were also imposed, one of which was to visit in one day the seven churches of St. Peter, St. Paul, St. John de Lateran, St. Croix of Jerusalem, St. Sebastian, St. Mary Major, and St. Laurence. The prohibition of the Catechism by the holy office was maintained.

The sixteen Lutheran propositions abjured by Carranza, were the following :—

1. Works performed without the spirit, of whatever nature, are sins, and offend God.

2. Faith is the first and principal means of obtaining justification.

3. Man is formally justified by the justice of Jesus Christ ; by that, Christ has merited for us.

4. No one can obtain the justice of Christ, except by firmly believing that he has obtained it.

5. Those who are in a state of mortal sin cannot comprehend the Holy Scriptures, or discern things relating to faith.

6. Natural reason is contrary to faith, in all that relates to religion.

7. The *germ* of sin exists in baptized persons with the quality of sin.

8. True faith does not exist in the sinner when he has lost grace by sin.

9. Repentance is equal to baptism, and is equal to a new life.

10. Our Lord Jesus Christ has atoned for our sins in so efficacious and entire a manner, that no other atonement is required of us.

11. Faith without works is sufficient for salvation.

12. Jesus Christ was not a legislator, and it did not enter into his plan to give laws.

13. The actions and works of Saints can only serve for an example, but they cannot aid us in any way.

14. The use of holy images, and the veneration for the relics of Saints, are customs purely human.

15. The Church of the present age has not the same light, or an authority equal to the primitive Church.

16. The condition of the apostles and a religious life, do not differ from the common state of Christians.

The declarations of the witnesses do not prove that Carranza ever uttered any of these propositions, and from the censures we may perceive that he only advanced in writing some which led the censurers to suppose that he professed those and many others, since he was not obliged to abjure several hundred propositions which had been censured, or the seventy-two which were qualified as heretical. As it could not be proved that he had ever spoken or expressed in writing any of the sixteen propositions considered as Lutheran, I do not hesitate to say that this sentence cannot be approved by upright men.

The archbishop heard his sentence with humility, and was absolved *ad cautelam ;* he performed mass on the four first days of the holy week, and on the 23rd of April he performed his penance of visiting the churches. He refused the letter which the Pope offered him, as a public testimony of his esteem and interest in his fate. He celebrated mass on another day in the church of St. John Lateran, for the last time in his life ; he expired at three o'clock in the morning of the 2nd of May, 1576, aged seventy-two years, eighteen of which he had passed in prison.

The Pope being informed of his illness, on the 30th of April, sent him a general absolution and exemption of the penance imposed on him ; the holy father did this for the consolation of Carranza, who in fact shewed great satisfaction, and received extreme unction with tranquillity, and even with some demonstrations of joy.

He made his will in the presence of one of the secretaries of his trial, and appointed as his executors his faithful friend Don Antonio de Toledo ; the doctors d'Alpizcueta and Delgado, who never forsook him ; Don Juan de Navarre y Mendoza, chanter, dignitary, and canon of the cathedral of Toledo, (he was the son of the Count de Lodoza, and descended in the direct male line from the kings of Navarre); Fray Ferdinand de San Ambrosio, his procurator, always faithful to his cause ; and Fray Antonio d'Utrilla, a model of fidelity and affection, who voluntarily shared his captivity for eighteen years. He had not obtained the permission which was necessary for bishops, to make a will; but as the Popes at that time disposed of the revenues of the stewardships, he approved and confirmed the pious arrangements of the archbishop.

On the 30th of April, after the prelate had received abso-

lution, and before he pronounced his act of faith, he made
the following declaration in Latin, in the presence of the
three secretaries, several Spaniards, and some Italians, speaking slowly and with a distinct utterance, that all present
might hear him.

. " Considering that I have been suspected of having fallen
into the errors imputed to me, I think it my duty to make
known my sentiments on this subject; it was for this purpose that I requested the attendance of the four secretaries
who have been employed in my trial. I call then to witness
the celestial court, and for my judge the sovereign Lord,
whose sacrament I am about to receive, the angels who
accompany him whom I have always chosen as my inter-
cessors; I swear by that Almighty God, by my approaching
death, by the account I shall soon render up to God, that
while I professed theology in my order, and afterwards when
I wrote, taught, preached, and argued in Spain and Germany, Italy and England, I always intended to make the
faith of our Lord Jesus Christ triumphant, and to combat
heretics. His divine Majesty came to my assistance, since in
England I converted several heretics to the Catholic faith;
with the king's permission I caused the bodies of the greatest
heretics of those times to be disinterred, and they were
burnt, to secure the power of the Inquisition. The Catholics, as well as the heretics, have always given me the title of
First Defender of the Faith. I can truly affirm that I have
always been one of the first to labour in this holy work, and
have done many things concerning it by the order of the
king my master. His majesty has been a witness of part of
what I have asserted. I have loved him, and I still love
him truly; no son could have a greater affection for him than
I have.

" I also declare, that in the whole course of my life I
have never taught, preached, or maintained any heresy, or
anything contrary to the true faith of the Roman Church;

that I never fell into any of the errors of which I have been suspected, from having different meanings attributed to my words to what I gave them myself; I swear by all that I have already said, by that God to whom I have appealed as my judge, that the errors I have mentioned or those reported in my trial never entered into my mind; that I never had the least doubt on any of these points of doctrine, but on the contrary I have professed, written, taught, and preached the holy faith, with the same firmness as I now believe and profess it at the hour of my death.

" Nevertheless I acknowledge my sentence to be just, because it was pronounced by the vicar of Christ; I have received and regarded it as such, because to the quality of vicar of Jesus Christ the person who pronounced it joins the character of an upright and prudent judge. I pardon, at the hour of my death, as I have always done, all offences, of whatever nature, which have been committed against me; I also pardon those who have shewn themselves against me in my trial; also those who have taken the smallest part in it. I have never felt any resentment against them; on the contrary I have always recommended them to God; I do so at this moment, loving them with all my heart, and I promise that if I go to that place where I hope to be by the mercy of our Lord, that I will not ask anything against them, but pray to God for all."

The corpse of the archbishop was deposited, on the 3rd of May, in the choir of the convent of *the Minerva*, between two cardinals of the family of Medicis. The Pope caused an inscription to be engraved on his tomb, in which he calls him a *man illustrious by his doctrine and his sermons*. From this it appears probable that he did not consider his works full of heresies; but, perhaps, it was occasioned by the protestation of Carranza before his death. Solemn obsequies were performed at Rome, and those celebrated at Toledo, some time after, were still more agnificent.

Although the holy office had obtained an unjust victory, the inquisitors were vexed that Carranza had not been degraded from his dignity. The suspension for five years appeared to them a singularly slight punishment, and they feared that the Pope would grant him a dispensation from it, which he, in fact, did, eight days after the sentence.

Their rage is displayed in several letters written from Rome on the three first days after the judgment, and which were found among the papers of the trial at Madrid. Among many things which are disgraceful to the writers, is the advice given to the king, not to permit Carranza to return to Spain, and, above all, not to suffer him to govern his see even after the lapse of the suspension: their envy and animosity making them suppose, that it would be a disgrace to the diocese of Toledo to be governed by a man who had been prosecuted by the Inquisition : they said that it would be better for the king to request the Pope to induce Carranza to give up his diocese and accept a pension, that some person might be placed in his see more worthy to occupy it ; but God in his infinite wisdom destroyed, by the death of the archbishop, the cause, the motive, and the matter for new intrigues. In the writings of the process I saw with sorrow, that far from relinquishing their pursuits, the inquisitors had prepared a fresh persecution for him.

CHAPTER XXXV.

TRIAL OF ANTONIO PEREZ, MINISTER AND FIRST SECRETARY OF STATE TO PHILIP II.

ANTONIO PEREZ was another illustrious victim to the Inquisition and the evil disposition of Philip II. The misfortunes of Perez commenced when Philip put to death Juan Escobedo, secretary to Don John of Austria ; he succeeded in making his escape to Arragon, where he hoped to live in tranquillity under a government which only allowed the sovereign to have an accusing fiscal in the tribunals. It is not necessary to relate all that Perez suffered at Madrid during twelve years before he made his escape ; these details may be found in a work published by this minister, under the title of *Relations*, in the recital which Antonio Valladares de Sotomayor inserted in the *Seminario erudito*, and in a volume in octavo which appeared in 1788, entitled *The Trial of Antonio Perez.*

Antonio Perez having retired to Arragon in 1590, Philip issued an order for his arrest, which took place at Calatayud. Perez having protested against this measure, and claimed the privilege of the *manifestados*, he was conducted to Saragossa, and confined in the prison of the *kingdom*, or of *liberty*. The prisoners were there free from the immediate authority of the king, and only depended on an intermediate judge called the chief justice of Arragon. It was also called the prison of the *Fuero* or *Constitutional*, because the constitution of the king alone was named the *Fuero d'Arragon ;* it was sometimes named the prison of the *manifestados ;* no persons were received into it, except those who presented themselves, or claimed the benefit of the constitution, in order to avoid the royal prison, and declared that they submitted to the laws of the kingdom, and invoked the support of its privileges : those of a prisoner in the case of Perez consisted in not being put to the torture; in being set at liberty, after taking an oath to present himself to reply to the charges, and being allowed, even if condemned to death by any other judge, to appeal to the tribunal of the chief justice of Arragon*, who examined if the execution of the sentence was

* The chief justice of Arragon was an intermediate judge between the king and his subjects, and independent of him as an officer of justice, before whom the king only was the pleading party. This magistracy had been established by the constitution of the kingdom ; the person invested with it was authorized to declare, at the demand of any inhabitant, that the

contrary to any *Fuero* of the kingdom. This tribunal resembles that in France called the *Court of Cassation*.

Philip II., after many earnest but useless endeavours to induce the permanent deputation of the kingdom to transfer Perez to Madrid, sent the commencement of the trial into Arragon, and gave the necessary powers to his fiscal at Saragossa, to accuse him of having made false reports to the king, which had induced him to put Juan Escobedo to death; of having forged letters from the cabinet, and revealed state secrets. After many incidents, Perez reduced the king to the necessity of renouncing the prosecution, by a public act on the 18th of August, in order to avoid the disgrace of seeing him acquitted.

His majesty, however, reserved to himself the right of making use of his privileges; and to prevent Perez from obtaining his liberty, he caused another trial to be commenced, under the form of an *inquest**, before the regent of the royal audience of Arragon. To give occasion for this trial, it was decided that the domestics of the king were exempted from the privileges of the *Fueros*, and that Antonio Perez was the king's servant, in the office of Secretary of State. Perez asserted that the Secretary of State was a servant of the public, and had never been confounded with the king's domestics; that supposing he had been of that class, the law could only extend to the Secretary of State for Arragon; that the constitution only alluded to those royal domestics who were natives of Arragon; that no one could be tried

---

king, his judges, or his magistrates, abused their power, and acted against the law in violating the constitution and privileges of the kingdom; in this case, the chief justice could defend the oppressed by force of arms against the king, and of course against his agents or lieutenants.

* This expression is ancient in the Arragonese dialect, and taken from the French, which derived it from the Latin *inquisitio*. It is the title given in the code of *Fueros* to the sentence pronounced against magistrates or other public officers guilty of infidelity, abuse of power, or other crimes.

twice for the same crime before two different tribunals ; that he had been tried at Madrid in 1582 ; that he then submitted to much ill-treatment, rather than justify himself by divulging the private letters of the king, which he had in his possession ; lastly, that though the papers useful in his defence had been obtained from his wife by fraudulent means, yet he had still documents enough to justify himself entirely.

Perez had, in fact, retained several notes in the king's own hand-writing, which were sufficient to exculpate him : he sent copies of them to the Marquis d'Almenara and other persons attached to the king, and told them that having been informed that his majesty was vexed that his letters had been exposed in the trial, he wished to spare him the pain of seeing other original documents presented, which contained very important secrets relating to different people ; but if the disposition to persecute him continued, he would produce them, because he was no longer capable of making useless sacrifices to the prejudice of his wife and seven children.

The *inquest* was then given up, and Perez demanded his liberty on his parole, or at least on giving security ; this was refused by the regent ; he then appealed to the privileges of the kingdom against force, before the tribunal of the chief justice, who did not shew him more favour.

It appears that Perez then, with his companion in misfortune, Juan Francis Mayorini, formed a plan to escape into Bearn. Their design was discovered at the moment they were about to execute it, but Perez conducted himself with so much address, that he reduced his part in the transaction to a simple suspicion.

The depositions of the witnesses before the regent, furnished the Inquisition with a pretext to prosecute Perez ; this event was very agreeable to the Court, because no means to prolong the *inquest* could be invented.

On the 19th of February, 1591, the regent wrote to the inquisitor, Molina, that Perez and Mayorini intended to escape from prison to go to Bearn, and to other places in France, where the heretics resorted, with intentions which would be proved by the declarations of witnesses.

The proof mentioned in this letter, is an attestation, without date, given by the notary, Juan Montagnes, into which had been copied the 8th chapter of the first additions and the 5th of the second, which had been made to the principal charges against Perez by the royal fiscal, and the depositions which had been obtained from Juan Louis de Luna, Anton de la Almunia and Diego Bustamente. In these chapters an attempt had been made to prove, " that Antonio Perez and Juan Francis Mayorini intended to escape from confinement, saying that they intended to go to Bearn, to Vendome and his sister*, and to other parts of France, where they would find many heretics inimical to his majesty; that they hoped to be well received, because Perez knew a great many state secrets which he could communicate to them ; that they had added to this discourse many expressions criminal and offensive to the majesty of the king, and that they were resolved to do him as much harm as they could." I should not have believed that such depositions would have been sufficient to denounce Perez to the Inquisition as guilty of heresy, if I had not seen the writings of the trial.

We may be permitted to suppose, from what passed at Madrid, and the commencement of the *inquest* which threatened Perez with capital punishment, that the accusation of heresy was a stroke of policy of the agents of the king. They did not dare to present the depositions they had obtained as being decisive, but they hoped that when the holy office began the trial of their victim, the charges would be multiplied.

The inquisitors of Saragossa were Don Alphonso Molina de Medrano, and Don Juan Hurtado de Mendoza : the one

* Henry IV. of France, then called the Duke of Vendome, and Catherine de Bourbon, afterwards Sovereign Duchess of Bar.

was the cousin of the Marquis d'Almenara, and the other an intriguing and immoral man, who wished to obtain a bishopric at any price. For this reason the marquis placed more confidence in him than in his cousin, who was less learned, and too good to become a persecutor. In fact, Don Juan avoided, as much as possible, taking any part in this transaction, and even obtained leave to remove to another tribunal. Molina received the letter of the regent, and the depositions which accompanied it; but instead of communicating them to the tribunal, he sent them by the first courier to Quiroga, the inquisitor-general. The Marquis d'Almenara gave information of the event to the Count de Chinchon, who communicated it to the king; after having consulted the cardinal, Philip commanded him to take proper measures to prove the heresy of Perez, and to punish him accordingly. On the 5th of March, Quiroga ordained that Molina alone should receive the depositions; that the inquisitors should examine them without the concurrence of the diocesan and consultors, and send them immediately to Madrid.

On the 20th of March ten witnesses were examined: Diego Bustamente, the servant of Perez, and Juan de Basante, a teacher of Latin, who often saw him in prison, quoted sentences which, in the original, did not prove anything against him, but which, on being separated from the others, had a meaning which gave an appearance of justice to the measure employed.

The tribunal remitted the information to Quiroga, who sent it to Fray Diego de Chabes, who qualified four propositions imputed to Perez, and one to Mayorini.

The latter was reduced to some indecent oaths, used by Italians, which had escaped Mayorini in losing at play, and were qualified as *heretical blasphemies;* this was sufficient to authorize his imprisonment.

First proposition, taken from the testimony of Diego de Bustamente.—Some one told Perez not to speak ill of Don

John of Austria : he replied, " After being accused by the king of having disguised the sense of my letters, and betraying the secrets of the council, it is just that I should vindicate myself without respect of persons : *If God the Father put any obstacle in the way of it, I would cut off his nose for having permitted the king to behave like a disloyal knight towards me.*"—QUALIFICATION. This proposition is blasphemous, scandalous, offensive to pious ears, and approaching to the heresy of the Vaudois, who suppose that God the Father has a body.

Second proposition, taken from the deposition of Juan de Basante.—Antonio Perez considering the bad state of his affairs, said to me one day, in a fit of grief and anger : " I shall perhaps no longer believe in God. *One would say that he sleeps during my trial ; if he does not perform a miracle in my favour, I shall lose all faith.*"—QUALIFICATION. This proposition is scandalous, offensive to pious ears, and suspected of heresy, because it supposes that God sleeps, and has an intimate relation with the preceding proposition. The two remaining accusations were very similar, with similar qualifications. It appears that the words he used were uttered in moments of grief and despair. It is remarkable that the Inquisition has provided for this case, for in one of their ordinances it is decreed, that no person shall be arrested for uttering a blasphemy, when excited by impatience or rage. To this may be added, that the proof was defective, since the second proposition rested solely on the testimony of Basante. With respect to the three others, I shall quote the third article of the instruction of Toledo, in 1498. " We also command the inquisitors to be prudent when a person is to be arrested, and not to issue the decree *until they* have obtained sufficient proof of the crime of heresy imputed to the accused."

However, as religion was only the ostensible motive for this trial, the Supreme Council, after having seen the censures, decreed on the 21st of May, that Perez and Mayorini should be arrested and confined in the secret prisons of the Inquisition, that they should be strictly watched, and arrested so promptly, that no one should have any suspicion of it.

On the 24th of May, the inquisitors sent an order to the grand alguazil of the holy office, to seize the persons of the accused. The gaoler of the prison of the kingdom declared, that he could not give them up without an order from the chief justice, or one of his lieutenants. The inquisitors wrote on the same day to the lieutenant, and commanded him on pain of excommunication, and a penalty of a thousand ducats, to give up the prisoners in the space of three hours, *without allowing the Fuero of the manifestation to be any obstacle, since it could not be applied to a trial for heresy; and for that reason the inquisitors revoked and annulled any such interpretation of the Fuero, as preventing the free exercise of the holy tribunal.*

The secretary presented these letters to the chief justice, Don Juan de la Nuza, in a public audience, in the presence of five judges who formed his council, and of all the persons employed in his tribunal. The chief justice submitted to the order of the inquisitors, and the prisoners were conducted to the Inquisition in separate carriages. It was afterwards known that the courier, who brought the order from Madrid, also brought letters from the Count de Chinchon to the Marquis d'Almenara, who, in a private conversation with the chief justice, persuaded him not to insist upon his privileges; and that the two letters of the inquisitors were written on the same night, though they were dated the 24th, because they were previously informed by the marquis of what would take place.

Perez, who foresaw his danger, had imparted his fears to the Count d'Aranda and other nobles, who resolved to oppose this measure as an infraction of the most valuable privilege of the kingdom. Don Diego Fernandez de Heredia, baron de Barboles, afterwards, declared, in the trial which brought him to the scaffold, that the Count and Perez agreed to assassinate the Marquis d'Almenara, because if they got rid of him, the king and the Count de Chinchon would renounce their plan of making a Castilian the viceroy of Arragon, who would not fail to destroy all their privileges in succession.

Perez, in his *Relations*, informs us that the father of the Count d'Aranda above mentioned, and several other persons, claimed and were allowed the privileges of the *Fuero de Manifestados*, when arrested by the Inquisition.

When Perez was transferred to the prison of the holy office, he told his servants to inform the Baron de Barboles and several other gentlemen of the circumstance. At this news the Arragonese excited the people of Saragossa to revolt, by cries of " Treason! Treason! Live the nation! Live our liberty! Live the Fueros! Death to the traitors!" In less than an hour, more than a thousand men, under arms, surrounded the house of the Marquis d'Almenara, and treated him with so much violence, that he would have been killed if he had not been immediately taken into the royal prison, where he died of his wounds fourteen days after. The insurgents insulted the archbishop, and threatened to kill him and burn his hotel if he did not make the inquisitors give up the prisoners: they menaced the viceroy Bishop of Teruel in the same manner, and assembling to the number of three thousand men, began to set fire to the Castle of Aljaferia, (an ancient palace of the Moorish kings, where the Inquisition was held,) crying that they would burn the inquisitors if they did not give up Perez and Mayorini. Many other events occurred in the city, because Molina de Medrano obstinately persisted in endeavouring to quell the insurrection, contrary to the entreaties twice repeated of the archbishop, the viceroy, of the Counts d'Aranda and Morata, and of

many of the first noblemen of Arragon. At last, finding that
the danger increased, he appeared to yield, and announced
that he would not set the prisoners at liberty, but would
give them for the prison of the holy office that of the kingdom, and they were removed thither on the same day.

The inquisitors were left in a critical situation, and did
not dare to arrest any one; they addressed several letters
to the commissioners of the holy office, some of them accompanied by the order to the lieutenants and their decree,
to shew that they had not violated the prison of the kingdom,
but had only received the persons given up to them by the
chief justice: the others were sent with the bull of Pius V.,
dated 1st of April, 1569, concerning those who opposed the
exercise of the holy office; they also proposed to publish an
edict, excommunicating several persons already noted in the
registers of the Inquisition as having opposed the execution
of the orders of the inquisitors, but they were persuaded to
relinquish the intention by the archbishop. At this period,
some persons who fled to Madrid when the revolt took place,
and who were known to be devoted to the king, were examined as witnesses; and it appeared from their depositions,
that the Counts d'Aranda and Morata, the Barons de Barboles, de Biescas, de Purray, de la Laguna, and many others
of the first noblemen of the country, had excited the people
to sedition, and increased the disturbance by persuading
them that the *Fuero* was attacked.

The members of the permanent deputation of the kingdom
thought, that being interested in the defence of the political
constitution, they might be accused of having failed in their
duty; they therefore endeavoured to justify themselves, by
declaring that as theirs was not an armed body or a judicial
authority, they could not prevent the revolt. They also
thought proper to pronounce by a commission of jurisconsults, that those who had given up the prisoners to the inquisitors, from the prison of the kingdom, had violated its privi-

leges. However the secret intrigues of the inquisitors, the archbishop, the viceroy, and the chief justice, were so adroitly conducted, that some members remarked, that four lawyers were not enough to discuss the rights of the king and the holy office. This observation caused nine other jurisconsults to be appointed, and it was decreed that they should decide, by a majority of three votes. They declared that the inquisitors had exceeded their powers, when they cancelled the *manifestation*, because no authority could do so, except that of the king, and the deputies assembled in Cortes; but that if the inquisitors required the prisoners to be given up to them, and the *privilege of manifestation was suspended* during their prosecution, it would not be contrary to the laws of the kingdom. Antonio Perez wrote to the deputation, to represent that his cause was that of all the Arragonese; several of his friends undertook to shew, that the *suspension* was equally contrary to the laws, since the prisoner might be tortured, was deprived of his right to his liberty on oath, and was exposed to the misery of an interminable trial; these efforts were all in vain. It was privately decided that the inquisitors should demand the prisoners a second time, without threats or orders, and resting only on the *suspension of the privileges*. The king was given to understand that it would be useful if he wrote to the Duke de Villahermosa, and the Counts d'Aranda, de Morata, and de Sastago, to engage them to lend assistance to the viceroy, with their relations and friends, and to aid the constituted authorities, if any event rendered it necessary. Philip followed the advice, and his letters to those noblemen were as gracious and flattering, as if he had been ignorant of the part they had taken in the late disturbances.

Perez now saw no safety except in flight, and had everything in readiness to force his prison, when he was betrayed some hours before, by the perfidious Juan de Basante, his false friend and accomplice.

The removal of Perez was to take place on the 24th of September; the Inquisition, the viceroy, the archbishop, the deputation of the kingdom, the municipality, and the civil and military governors, were all to assist. The inquisitors had summoned to Saragossa, from the neighbouring towns, a great number of the *familiars* of the holy office, and the military governor had in attendance three thousand men, well armed. This expedition was to have been made without the knowledge of the inhabitants; but the Barons de Barboles, de Biescas, and de Purray, and some other individuals, were informed of it. At the moment when the prisoners were coming out of the prison, in the presence of the principal magistrates of the city, and while the avenues and streets through which they were to pass were lined with soldiers, a furious troop of insurgents broke through the lines, killed a great number of men, dispersed the others, put the magistrates to flight, and seizing Perez and Mayorini, carried them off in triumph, shouting, *Live our liberty! Live the Fueros of Arragon!* Perez and Mayorini were received into the house of the Baron de Barboles; when they had reposed for a few minutes, they were taken out of the town, and taking different roads, hastened away from it.

Perez repaired to Tauste, with the intention of crossing the Pyrenees by the valley of Ronçal, but as the frontiers were strictly guarded, he returned to Saragossa. He entered it in disguise, on the 2nd of October, and remained concealed in the house of the Baron de Biescas until the 10th of November. He then thought it dangerous to remain there longer, because Don Alphonso de Vargas was advancing with an army to take the town, and punish the rebels. This event has been related very incorrectly in several histories.

The presence of Perez in Saragossa was suspected by means of some letters from Madrid, which Basante had seen, and of which he had given information. The inquisitors searched the houses of the Baron de Barboles and several other persons. Don Antonio Morejon, the second inquisitor *, suspected that de Biescas knew the place of his concealment, and pressed him to discover it, promising that Perez should be well treated if he presented himself voluntarily. Perez had several times declared that he would surrender to the holy office, if he was not almost certain that he should be given up to the government, which would immediately execute the sentence of death passed upon him in 1590, without allowing him to be heard. On the 11th of November, Perez went to Sallen, in the Pyrenees, on the estates of the Baron de Biescas.

On the 18th he wrote to the Princess of Bearn, to ask an asylum in the states of her brother, Henry IV., or to be permitted to pass through them to some other country. This letter was given to the princess by Gil de Messa, an Arragonese gentleman, and an old and faithful friend of Perez.

Catherine received Perez into her brother's states on the 24th of November when the Barons de Concas; and de la Pinilla arrived at Sallen, with three hundred men to take him, they had offered to betray him if they were pardoned: the first had been condemned by the Inquisition, for having sent horses to France, and the other was to be executed for having excited a revolt, in an attempt of the same nature.

Perez went to Pau, and while he was in that place the inquisitor Morejon again requested the Baron de Biescas to persuade him to submit to the Inquisition ; he replied that he would do so, if they would promise to try him at Saragossa instead of Madrid, and that he should require that his wife and children should be set at liberty, of which they had been deprived, although they were innocent. Perez made the same reply to another requisition.

* Molina was then at Madrid, where he had been rewarded by a place in the council of military orders. He was succeeded at Saragossa by Don Pedro de Zamora.

In order to satisfy the curiosity of the Princess Catherine and her subjects, Perez composed two little works, the first called : *Morceau Historique, sur ce qui est arrivée à Saragosse d'Arragon, le* 24th Septembre, 1591: and the other: *Précis du Récit des Avantures d'Antoine Perez, depuis le Commencement, de sa première Detention jusqu'à sa Sortie des Domaines du Roi Catholique.* These works were printed at Pau, without the name of the author; the inquisitors examined them, and derived from them some additional charges.

Philip II. and the inquisitors offered life, offices, money, and honours, to any condemned criminal who would kill Perez or bring him as a prisoner into Spain. I refer the reader for all that relates to this part of the history to the work entitled *Relations*, in which Perez takes the name of *Raphaël Peregrino.* Perez obtained leave from Henry IV. to go to London, where he was extremely well received by Queen Elizabeth and the Earl of Leicester : he afterwards went to Paris, where he passed the rest of his life, pining unceasingly for his wife and children.

On the 15th of February, 1592, the inquisitors declared Antonio Perez to be a fugitive; they affixed an edict on the metropolitian church of Saragossa, summoning him to appear within one month ; this measure was most revoltingly unjust, since they well knew that Perez was in a country then at war with Spain, and the laws of the holy office allowed even the space of a year, according to the distance the accused had to travel.

The declarations of the witnesses who were interrogated at Madrid, after the first revolt of Saragossa in 1591, deposed to facts to which no importance could have been attached, if they had related to other persons and events. But Antonio Perez was concerned in them, and that was sufficient to cause them to be censured as *audacious*, and *suspected of heresy.* I shall not stay to prove the insufficiency of this act, but shall give the third of the propositions as an example of the rest. " In speaking of Philip II., and of Vendome, Antonio Perez said that the king was a tyrant, but that Vendome would be a great monarch, for he was an excellent prince, and governed the state to the satisfaction of every one; that he therefore rejoiced on hearing of his victories, and *that it was not heresy to pay court to him and speak to him.*" QUALIFICATION. " The accused shews himself to be impious in respect to God and the holy Catholic faith, a favourer and violently suspected of heresy; and as he now lives in the midst of heretics, it proves that he is himself an heretic."

The inquisitors, who wished to favour the views of the court at any rate, took advantage of a vague report, communicated to them by one of their *familiars*, that Antonio Perez was descended from the Jews, because in the borough of Hariza, near Montreal, from whence his family came, there had lived a New Christian called Juan Perez, who was burnt by the Inquisition as a judaizing heretic. The registers of the holy office were immediately consulted, and it appeared that one Juan Perez de Fariza had been burnt, and that Antonio Perez de Fariza had died a heretic.

Pascal Gilbert, a priest and commissioner of the holy office, was appointed, on the 16th of April, 1592, to ascertain if there was any degree of relationship between the condemned heretics and the father of Antonio Perez. Many witnesses were examined, both in Montreal, and the neighbouring towns, but they all declared that the two families were perfectly distinct.

All that is known concerning the genealogy of Perez is, that he was the natural son of Gonzalez Perez, and Donna Jane d'Escobar, and that he was legitimatized by Charles V. That his paternal grandfather was Bartholomew Perez, secretary to the Inquisition of Calahorra, that his grandmother was Donna Louisa Perez del Hierro, of a noble family of Segovia ; that he was great grandson to Juan Perez, an inhabitant of Montreal, and of Mary Tirado his wife ; and that there was no relationship, direct or indirect, between his family and that of Juan and Antonio Perez de Fariza. This was afterwards fully proved by the wife and children of Antonio Perez. It must be observed, that if the inquisitors had wished to be truly informed, they might have had a copy of the contract of marriage between Perez and Donna Jane Coello, which states that his father was born at Segovia. In that city, at Calahorra, and even in the Supreme Council, they might have found his real genealogy.

However, the fiscal abused the privilege of secrecy, in the accusation he brought against Perez, on the 6th of July, by supposing that he was descended from the Jews, in order to strengthen the suspicion of heresy, according to the custom of the Inquisition. The accusation was composed of forty-three articles, each more vague than the others, and only founded on words uttered without reflection, during a fit of rage, or in extreme pain, which had no connexion with doctrine, and concerning which no two witnesses agreed in the time, place, or circumstances.

On the 14th of August the fiscal demanded that the depositions of the witnesses should be published; and on the 16th the qualifiers again assembled to censure the propositions already noted, and the works printed at Pau. They censured sixteen as *audacious* and *erroneous;* some others as *blasphemous* and *approaching to heresy*, and concluded that Antonio Perez was *suspected of heresy in the most violent degree**.

On the 18th the fiscal required that Perez should be declared contumacious, and that the definitive sentence should be pronounced. On the 7th of September, the diocesan, different consultors, and jurisconsults (among whom was the first informer, Don Urban Ximenez de Aragues, regent of the royal audience), were convoked, and voted the punishment of *relaxation* in effigy. The Supreme

* See *Relations* of Perez.

Council confirmed the sentence on the 13th of October, and on the 20th the judges pronounced the definitive sentence, condemning Perez as a *formal heretic*, *a convicted Huguenot*, and *an obstinate impenitent*, to be *relaxed* in person when he could be taken, and in the mean time to suffer that punishment in effigy, with the mitre and San-benito. His property was confiscated, and his children and grandchildren in the male line devoted to infamy, besides other penalties. Many other persons suffered in this *auto-da-fé*, of whom an account will be given in the next chapter.

Perez was in England when he was condemned to death. A conspiracy against his life by some Spaniards was discovered there: it was renewed at Paris by the Baron de la Pinilla, who declared that he had been sent to kill him by Don Juan Idiaquez, minister to Philip II.

The death of that prince, and the consequent change in the politics of the government, inspired Perez with the hope of arranging his affairs at Madrid; but the misfortune of having been prosecuted by the Inquisition rendered his efforts unavailing. The reader is referred to the *Relations* for all that concerns this part of the history.

Perez had, at Paris, been intimate with Fray Francis de Sosa, general of the Franciscans, then Bishop of the Canaries, and a counsellor of the Inquisition, who often advised him to give himself up to the holy office, as the only means of obtaining a reconciliation. Perez replied that he would do so, and even wished it, but was deterred by the fear of being arrested by the government, after being set at liberty by the Inquisition. Sosa then tried to persuade him that he would avoid that danger by obtaining a safe conduct from the inquisitor-general and the Supreme Council, promising that he should be set at liberty when his trial was terminated by the holy office. Sosa, at that time, was little acquainted with the Inquisition, of which he was afterwards a member.

Perez wrote again to Sosa in 1611 concerning this affair ; the bishop replied, and his letter determined Perez to inform him that he was ready to surrender to the Inquisition as soon as the safe conduct was sent to him ; he sent at the same time to his wife, a petition addressed to the Supreme Council, in which he renewed his promise.   His wife presented it, and added to it one from herself, to interest the judges in her husband's favour.   The attempt was fruitless, and Perez died at Paris on the 3rd of November, in the same year, after giving many proofs of his Catholicism, which were afterwards useful to his children in obtaining the revocation of the sentence given at Saragossa in 1592, and in *rehabilitating* his memory.

CHAPTER XXXVI.

OF SEVERAL TRIALS OCCASIONED BY THAT OF ANTONIO PEREZ.

THE trial of Antonio Perez was the cause of a great number of prosecutions against persons who had taken part in the tumults and the flight of Perez and his companion.   The censures and penalties of the bull of Pius V., destined to punish those who opposed the exercise of the ministry of the holy office, were applied to them.

On the 12th of November, 1591, Don Alphonso de Vargas entered Saragossa at the head of his army ; this expedition re-established the inquisitors, and they secretly informed against the instigators of the rebellion.

On the 8th of January, 1592, the fiscal of the holy office gave in a complaint against the rebels in general, as suspected in matters of faith ; and he composed a list of the authors of the sedition, and of those who were suspected of being implicated in it; it amounted to three hundred and seventy-two individuals, who had compromised themselves either by their words or actions.

The inquisitors imprisoned a hundred and seventy, and made arrangements for the arrest of others who were only suspected, as the charges were not proved against them. Of this number only an hundred and twenty-three individuals were taken, because the others had either been already taken to the royal prison by the command of Vargas, to be tried by Doctor Lanz, a senator of Milan, and the king's special commissioner on this occasion, or had made their escape; some who had only taken an indirect part in the event came under the jurisdiction of the commissioner, and obtained permission to remain as prisoners in their own houses. The following are some of the most remarkable trials, from the high rank of the individuals:—

Don Juan de la Nuza, Chief Justice of Arragon, not only had not opposed the exercise of the holy office, but might have been reproached for having given up more than the privileges of the kingdom allowed. He however suffered the fate of a rebel subject, because in the struggle which ensued he was unfortunately the weakest; the oath which the king had taken to observe the privileges of the kingdom, did not allow him to send into it more than five hundred soldiers. The permanent deputation, on being informed of the preparations for the entrance of the army of Vargas, remonstrated; Philip replied that they were destined for France; the deputies then represented the danger which might arise from their being permitted to pass through Saragossa; they were then informed that the army would only remain in their city for the period necessary to restore the authority of justice, which had been almost entirely destroyed in the late seditions.

The deputies, on receiving this last reply, consulted thirteen lawyers on the sense of the *Fueros;* they declared that

their rights were infringed by the entrance of the troops
into Arragon, and that every Arragonese was bound to resist
and prevent them.   Circulars were then sent to all the
towns, and to the permanent deputation of Catalonia and
Valencia, to demand the aid stipulated by the treaties, in
case either country was invaded.   The chief justice, whom
the laws of the kingdom called to the command, was ordered
to place himself immediately at the head of the troops.
When the Castilians came within six miles of Saragossa, the
chief justice found himself almost deserted, and consequently
retired and left the passage free to the troops, who entered
the town.

On the 28th of November, Don Francis de Borgia, Marquis de Pombay, arrived at Saragossa; he was commissioned
to treat with the permanent deputies and the principal
gentlemen of the kingdom concerning the points on which
it was asserted the privileges had been infringed.   Several
conferences took place without any result, because the deputies declared that the *Fueros* did not permit them while
the country was occupied by foreign troops.

Philip II. appointed the Count de Morata to be viceroy
in the place of the Bishop of Teruel, who had retired to his
see, alarmed at the danger he had incurred.   The viceroy
made his public entry into Saragossa, on the 6th of December,
to the great joy and satisfaction of the inhabitants; but their
joy was of short duration.   On the 18th of the same month,
Don Gomez Velasquez arrived with a commission to arrest
a great number of persons, and with a positive order to be-
head the chief justice of Arragon, as soon as he entered the
town; this order was obeyed with so much expedition, that
on the 28th Don Juan de la Nuza was no longer in existence.
All Arragon was filled with consternation at the news of this
execution.   It is impossible to express how much La Nuza
was respected by the people on account of his high office,
which had been filled by the illustrious members of his fa-

mily for more than an hundred and fifty years. On this event, many gentlemen fled to France and Geneva, and those who, from an ill-founded confidence, remained, soon had cause to repent.

Don Francis d'Arragon, Duke de Villahermosa, Count de Ribagorza, did not escape the persecution, although he had the advantage of being of royal blood, being descended from John II. King of Arragon and Navarre, by his son Don Alphonso d'Arragon. In his trial before the Inquisition he was not accused of having opposed the measures of the tribunal during the insurrections, or of taking any part in them: but Don Francis Torralba, lieutenant to the chief justice (who had been deprived of his office in consequence of some serious complaints of Perez), pretended that the duke was, by the nature of his blood, an enemy to the holy tribunal, since he descended from Jews, who had been burnt and subjected to penances, by Estengua Conejo, a Jewess, who, on her baptism, took the name of Mary Sanchez, and afterwards became the wife or concubine of Don Alphonso d'Arragon, first Duke of Villahermosa, and grandfather to the present duke, whom he denounced. Torralba minutely detailed the proofs of what he asserted.

When the inhabitants of Saragossa resolved to oppose the entrance of the Castilian army in their city, the duke, according to the laws of the kingdom, offered his services to the chief justice. The royal commissioner, not satisfied with his trial before the Inquisition, arrested him on the 19th of December, and sent him into Castile, in contempt of another law of the *Fuero.* The duke was beheaded at Burgos, as convicted of treason; his property was confiscated, and the king bestowed the duchy on the next in succession.

The Count d'Aranda, Don Louis Ximenez de Urrea, was also arrested on the 19th of December, but died in the prison of Alaejos, on the 4th of August, 1592. It appears from his trial by the Inquisition, that when Perez was sent to the

prison of the kingdom, he declared himself his protector, according to a promise he had given to the wife of Perez at
Madrid; that he was one of the principal instigators of the
popular commotions; that he had influenced the lawyers,
who declared the act, by which Perez was consigned a second
time to the Inquisition, to be illegal; and lastly, that he had
assisted in the military arrangements for the resistance of
the royal troops. It has been already stated, that Diego de
Heredia accused the Count d'Aranda and Antonio Perez of
having conspired against the life of the Marquis d'Almenara.
This deposition is not found in the trial, but Don Diego declared he had already informed the senator Lanz, while he
was imprisoned by that magistrate. But if the circumstances
independent of this conspiracy may be considered as crimes,
why did Philip after the first revolt write to request him to
lend assistance to the authorities, and afterwards to thank
him for having so well performed his mission? It must excite
indignation, to see a powerful monarch deceiving his subjects, and punishing them by surprise.

The Count de Morata, Don Michael Martinez de Luna,
Viceroy of Arragon, was denounced to the Inquisition, after
the insurrection of Saragossa. It appears that he blamed
the conduct of the tribunal and the civil authorities towards
Perez. Some witnesses supposed that he was one of the
principal instigators of the first insurrection; but that afterwards learning that Philip had said that Perez was an unfaithful minister, he ceased to defend him. This is certainly
an historical error, for the declaration of the king concerning
Perez was made in August, 1590, after the act by which the
king abandoned the prosecution relating to the death of Escobedo, and the insurrections at Saragossa took place in May,
1591. The change in the opinions of Martinez de Luna must
have had some other cause. Some circumstances in his trial
lead to the belief that he was acquainted with the proceedings of the council appointed at Madrid to consider the af-

fairs, and that he foresaw that the consequences would be serious, which induced him to change his system.

When he was made viceroy, the inquisitor suppressed the preparatory instruction of the trial, and the decree of arrest which had already been resolved upon. The tribunal had received another information against the Count in 1577, concerning some *ill-sounding* propositions, but they had not sufficient proof to proceed upon.

Although the inquisitors had been so indulgent to the count, he was not devoted to their party. His indifference induced the fiscal to bring a complaint against him in 1592, and to require that he should be arrested. He founded his requisition on the following allegation: the inquisitor-general Quiroga had published an edict of grace in favour of all the criminals who had not been arrested, that they might be absolved from all censures, and this edict having been communicated to the count before the publication, he declared that it was impertinent, useless, and ridiculous. The fiscal gave this as an instance of the contempt of the count for the censures under which he pretended that he had fallen, as the principal instigator of the first revolt. Some other expressions were construed into a sign of his hatred of the Inquisition.

It is certain that the count would not have escaped the vengeance of the inquisitors, in his quality of viceroy. When he quitted his office they were fully occupied with other trials, and his affair was too unimportant, and too old, to attract the attention of their successors. The opinion of the count on the edict of grace was very just. This *grace* was not accorded until the inquisitors had celebrated a solemn *auto-da-fé*, in which seventy-nine inhabitants of the town were *relaxed*, and a much greater number of honourable persons condemned to infamy, on pretence of publicly absolving them from censure; besides that, those already in prison were excluded from the pardon.

After the executions of the chief justice, the Duke de Villahermosa, and the Count d'Aranda, the king granted a general pardon on the 24th December, 1592, with the exception of many individuals who had excited and directed the sedition. This edict saved the lives of several thousand Arragonese; palliating circumstances afterwards caused the capital punishment to be remitted to all those who were excepted in the general pardon.

The Baron de Barboles, Don Diego Fernandez de Heredia, brother and presumptive heir to the Count de Fuentes, a grandee of Spain, was to have been arrested by the Inquisition; but he was taken by order of Vargas, claimed his privilege, and was taken to the prison of the *Manifestados*, and on the 9th of October, 1592, had his head struck off at the back of the neck, as guilty of treason. He had made several depositions before the Senator Lanz, and all that concerned Antonio Perez was communicated to the inquisitors; he had already been examined twice on that subject as a witness of the fiscal, and deposed to a great number of facts which proved that he had excited the people, and kept up the rebellion with the Count d'Aranda and others, and that he was engaged in the plan to assassinate the Marquis d'Almenara, but that he repented and revoked the orders he had given concerning it; nevertheless some witnesses deposed that they had seen him in the road encouraging the assassins. The Baron de Barboles also declared that he was the principal author of the complaint brought by Antonio Perez before the ordinary judge of Saragossa, against the secretary, major-domo, and squire of the Marquis d'Almenara and several other persons, whom he accused of having, by order of the marquis, suborned several witnesses in 1591 to depose against Perez several facts required by the inquisitors; that he had directed and instigated the efforts which were made to find witnesses to confirm by their declarations the articles of the complaint, and that he had deposed as from himself what he had only heard from the agent of Perez.

Another inquest against Don Diego existed in the Inquisition, in which he was accused of having made use of necromancy to discover treasures, and sending horses to France. The Judge Torralba also deposed that he had heard it said that Don Diego had been arrested by the Inquisition of Valencia for having concealed a Moresco from an alguazil; he added that it was not surprising that Don Diego was an enemy to the holy office, because, though the blood of his ancestors had not been sullied by that of the Jews, his children had not that advantage, since his wife, the Baroness d'Alcaraz, was of Jewish origin.

Philip II. wished to shew the Count de Fuentes that though he punished the guilty he knew how to reward a faithful subject, and made him governor of the Low Countries. The Count hated Perez, whom he considered as the cause of the misfortunes of de Barboles; it is not therefore surprising that he took an active part in the conspiracy formed in London against his life. This attempt did not succeed, and two of the conspirators were put to death at the requisition of the English fiscal, who had been commanded by Queen Elizabeth to prosecute the authors of the plot.

The Baron de Purray, Don Juan de Luna, a member for the nobility in the deputation of the kingdom, was executed on the same day with Barboles; the charges against him were very similar to the preceding. His offences against the Inquisition were, that he was the cause of the resolution taken in the committee of the deputation to defend the independence of the prison of the *Manifestados* against the pretensions of the inquisitors; to confine their jurisdiction to the crime of heresy, and to prevent them from taking cognizance of offences in the revolt and similar crimes, which they undertook, because they said that some of the persons concerned in it opposed the exercise of their office; lastly, Don Juan was implicated in the subornation of witnesses in the affair of Perez.

The Baron de Biescas, Don Martin de la Nuza, Lord of
Sallen and the towns of the valley of Tena, fled to France,
but afterwards returned to Spain ; he was arrested in Tudela of Navarre, and was beheaded. The trial before the
Inquisition states, that besides the crimes committed like the
other rebels, the Baron de Biescas was guilty of having received Antonio Perez into his house, and concealed him until
he could fly to France; and of entering into the Spanish territory at several points with a corps of Bearnese troops, and
declaring that he would not lay down his arms until he had
driven the Castilian army out of Arragon, and revenged the
death of his relation the chief justice.

The senator Lanz likewise condemned to death many
other noble gentlemen, besides labourers and artisans. Many
who fled to France or Geneva were condemned to death :
these individuals remained in exile till after the death of
Philip II. His successor, Philip III., permitted them to return to their country, and annulled all the articles in the sentences pronounced against those who had been executed,
which were contrary to the interests of their families; *the
king declaring that none of them were guilty towards the state ;
and that he acknowledged that each person had considered
himself bound to defend the rights of his country.*

The cruelty of the inquisitors was not satiated by these
executions. They represented to the Supreme Council that
they did not dare to demand the prisoners of the General
Vargas, although it would be much better if they were tried
by the Inquisition : but that nevertheless they thought it
would be useful if the Baron de Barboles was given up to
them, since his execution, in that case, would strike more
terror into the guilty. The council rejected the request of
the inquisitors; they, however, retained in their prisons
many illustrious persons, among whom were some women.

When the inquisitors published the edict of grace, more
than five hundred persons presented themselves to demand

absolution. Each person confessed the crime for which they were to be absolved; some of these are rather ludicrous.

Mary Ramirez declares, that on seeing Antonio Perez taken to prison, she exclaimed—*Poor wretch! after having left him in so many prisons, they have not yet found him an heretic.*

Christoval de Heredia *confesses that he has often wished that Perez might get out of his troubles.*

Donna Geronima d'Arteaga, *that she raised a little subscription for Antonio Perez, because he could not enjoy his own property.*

Louis de Anton, *that he was the procurator of Perez, and that he did several things to serve him.*

Martina de Alatucy, *that she prepared the food of Perez in her house, and that her son Antonio Añnoz, who was his servant, carried it to him in the prison.*

Don Louis de Gurrea *demands absolution only to reassure his conscience, for it does not reproach him!*

Don Michael de Sese also claims it, *to appease the same scruples!*

Doctor Murillo, *that he visited Perez in the prison when he was ill.*

The following are instances of a spirit quite contrary to the preceding examples:—

The Doctor Don Gregory de Andia, vicar of the parish of St. Paul, being informed that a priest had refused absolution to more than two hundred persons, because they had not been absolved from the censures incurred by the bull of St. Pius V., could not help saying, *That priest is an ignorant fellow. Let all those people come to me, and also all those who revolted: I would absolve them with pleasure of all their sins, and feel no fear for such an action.* The vicar was arrested for his boldness, and taken to the secret prisons. Many persons shared his fate, among whom were,—

Juan de Cerio, a familiar of the holy office, who on hearing

it remarked that the Arragonese ought not to endure the
Inquisition any longer, replied : " As for me, they may
burn the house, the papers, the prisons, and even the inquisitors : I shall have nothing to say against it."

A brother of the Trinity, who, on hearing that the
Castilians wished to reduce the Arragonese, and destroy
their privileges, said, " *If Jesus Christ was a Castilian, I
would not believe in him.*"

Michael Urgel, procuror of the royal audience, confessed
that after he had heard the declaration of the four counsellors, that it was an infringement of the *Fueros* to transfer
Perez to the Inquisition, he said: " We must treat the
letters of the inquisitors with contempt, and if the king
supports them, he is a tyrant : let us get rid of him and
elect a native king of Arragon, since we have a right to
do so."

These are a few instances of the pretended sins for which
absolution was demanded, and for which many persons were
arrested, but they are sufficient to shew the spirit of the
people and of the inquisitors.

Donna Jane de Coello, the wife of Perez, and her young
children, were also victims to the events at Saragossa.   They
had been detained in the Castle of Pinto, two leagues from
Madrid, since the month of April, 1590, where that heroine
had favoured the escape of her husband at the expense of
her own liberty.   After his second flight from Saragossa,
their imprisonment became still more rigorous.   It is proved
by the trial of Perez, that he often said when in prison,
that nothing should induce him to renounce the privileges
of the prison of the kingdom, except the assurance that his
wife and children enjoyed their liberty ; but that he was
certain if he gave himself up to the inquisitors he should be
sent to Madrid and executed.

This information induced the inquisitors at the end of
September, 1591, to request that Donna Jane and her chil-

dren might be more strictly imprisoned, since he would hear of it, and it might induce him to return to the prison of the kingdom. This idea was inspired by the perfidious Basante. In fact, Perez was informed that his wife and children were removed to a sort of bastion or tower of the castle, which was much more inconvenient than the former prison; however, Donna Jane requested her husband to think only of his own safety, since the news of his flight had been sufficient to keep her and her children in good health. Donna Jane remained in prison during the life of Philip II., who on his death advised his successor to set her and her family at liberty.

All the events above-mentioned, were occasioned by the trial of Antonio Perez, but the original cause was the extreme attachment of the Arragonese to a privilege which Philip II. wished to destroy, because it set bounds to his despotism ; they had not forgotten that this prince made use of the Inquisition, in his political schemes, of which they had experienced in some attempts made twenty years before.

The insurrection offered to Philip the opportunity he had so long desired, of making himself absolute monarch of Arragon, by the abolition of the intermediate office of the chief jus. tice, and of all the *Fueros* of the primitive constitution, which bounded the extent of his power. Another cause of the revolt was, the policy which disgraced, and kept in a perpetual state of uneasiness, all the first families of the kingdom, a great number of the second order, and even of the people. It was well known that these misfortunes were the consequence of the system of the inquisitors, who were always eager to disgrace and humiliate those who did not debase themselves before the lowest among them, and to sacrifice every man who did not acknowledge their tribunal to be the most holy of institutions, and the only bulwark of faith, which they still declare and publish through their partisans, though in their hearts they are convinced of the contrary.

CHAPTER XXXVII.

OF THE PRINCIPAL EVENTS IN THE INQUISITION DURING THE REIGN OF PHILIP III.

PHILIP II. died on the 13th of September, 1598, and left the crown to his son, Philip III., whose education had made him more worthy of wearing the habit of St. Dominic, than of governing a kingdom : the Inquisition was then as formidable and powerful as before the constitutions of 1561. As the new king wished to have an inquisitor-general of his own choice, he took advantage of a bull, commanding all bishops to reside in their dioceses, to invite Don Pedro Porto-Carrero, to retire to his see of Cuença, and appointed as his successor, in 1599, Don Ferdinard Niño de Guevara, cardinal of the Roman Church, and afterwards archbishop of Seville. This prelate retired to his diocese in 1602, in consequence of an order from the king; his successor was Don Juan de Zuñiga, bishop of Carthagena, who died in the same year. Juan Baptiste de Acebedo, bishop of Valladolid, took his place, and died in it in 1607, with the title of Patriarch of the Indies. He was succeeded by Don Bernard de Sandoval Roxas, cardinal archbishop of Toledo, brother to the Duke de Lerma. At his death Don Fray Louis Aliaga, a Dominican confessor to the king, was appointed inquisitor-general; Philip IV., on his accession, deprived him of his office.

Philip III., in 1607, assembled the Cortes of the kingdom at Madrid, where they remained for more than a year. The members represented to the king, that in 1579 and 1586, they had required a reform of the abuses committed in the tribunal of the Inquisition, to put an end to the right, which the inquisitors had usurped, of taking cognizance of crimes not relating to heresy; that Philip II. had promised to do

this, but died before he could perform it, and that in consequence they renewed the request.

Philip replied, that he would take proper measures to satisfy the Cortes. In 1611, when he convoked the new Cortes,
they made the same request and received the same answer,
but nothing was attempted, and the inquisitors daily became
more insolent, and filled their prisons with victims.

The archbishop of Valencia, Don Juan de Ribera, represented to Philip III., that it was impossible to convert the
Morescoes of Valencia, and that their skill in agriculture and
the arts gave just cause of apprehension, that they might some
day disturb the public tranquillity, with the assistance of the
Moors of Algiers, and the other African cities, with whom
they held constant intercourse; he therefore advised his
majesty to banish them from the kingdom.

The gentlemen whose vassals the Morescoes were, complained of the immense loss it would occasion, if their estates
were thus depopulated; they also declared that the statement
of the archbishop was shamefully exaggerated, since the holy
office had never failed to punish every Moresco who returned
to his heresy.

The king summoned his council, and after many discussions, it was resolved to send the Morescoes out of the kingdom of Valencia, on the 11th of September, 1609, and all
the others in the following year.

This emigration cost Spain a million of useful and industri-
ous inhabitants, who all went to Africa: they were invited by
Henry IV. to colonise the _Landes_ in Gascony, on condition
that they professed the catholic religion, but they feared
that they should be persecuted in the same manner, at some
future period. The inquisitors principally contributed to
induce Philip III. to take this resolution, and they noted all
who had condemned the measure, as suspected of heresy:
among these was the Duke of Ossuna, whose process they began. This trial had no particular result, because the charges

did not offer any heretical propositions, though some were qualified as audacious, scandalous, and offensive to pious ears. The duke was appointed Viceroy of Naples, but was deprived of the office some years after, and imprisoned by the king. The inquisitors seized this opportunity to renew their charges, but they were disappointed; the duke died in prison before the definitive sentence was pronounced.

On the 7th and 8th of November 1610, the Inquisition of Logroño celebrated an *auto-da-fé*, in which six persons were burnt, with five effigies, twenty-one individuals were reconciled, and twenty condemned to different penances; among these were eighteen sorcerers*.

A sufficient number of the trials of the Inquisition, during the reign of Philip III., have been already cited, therefore that of Don Antonio Manriquez, count de Marata, need only be mentioned; in 1603 he abjured some heretical propositions without being disgraced by an *auto-da-fé*.

CHAPTER XXXVIII.

OF THE TRIALS AND AUTOS-DA-FE DURING THE REIGN OF PHILIP IV.

PHILIP IV. ascended the throne on the 31st of March, 1621, and during the thirty-four years that he reigned, the following persons filled the office of inquisitor-general : Don Andrea Pacheco, in 1621 ; Cardinal Don Antonio de Zapyata Mendoza, in 1626 ; in 1632, Don Fray Antonio de Sotomayor; and in 1643, Don Diego de Arce y Reinoso. Don Diego died on the same day as the king.

Many circumstances had shewn the necessity of a reform in the Inquisition, but the indolence of Philip IV. prevented

* See Chapter 15.

him from attempting it ; on the contrary, he permitted the
inquisitors to take cognizance of the offence of exporting
copper money, and to dispose of a fourth of what fell into
their hands.

On the 21st of June, 1621, the Inquisition celebrated the
accession of Philip IV. by the *auto-da-fé* of Maria de la
Conception, a *Beata,* and famous hypocrite of the preceding
reign, who had deceived many persons by her feigned revelations and pretended sanctity. She appeared in the *auto-
da-fé* gagged, with the *san-benito,* and the mitre.

On the 30th of November, 1630, another *auto-da-fé* was
held at Seville, when six persons were burnt in effigy, and
eight in person; fifty were reconciled, and six absolved *ad
cautelam.*

On the 21st of December, 1627, a general *auto-da-fé* was
celebrated at Cordova, composed of eighty-one condemned
persons; fifty-eight were reconciled, among whom were
three sorcerers.

In 1532, a grand general *auto-da-fé* was held at Madrid,
at which the king and all the royal family attended. Seven
persons were burnt, with four effigies, and forty-two reconciled ; they were almost all Portuguese, or of Portuguese
parents. The following circumstance has rendered this
auto-da-fé very famous. Michel Rodriguez, and Isabella
Martinez Albarez, his wife, were the proprietors of a house
used by the condemned as a synagogue. They were accused
of having struck the image of Jesus Christ with a whip, and
of having crucified and insulted it in various ways, as if to
revenge themselves upon it for all the evils which the Christians made them suffer. The holy office caused this house
to be razed to the ground, and an inscription was placed on
the spot. A monastery for the Capuchins was afterwards
built on the site, and named the Convent of Patience, in
allusion to the outrages which our Saviour allowed them to
commit on his image: a report was then spread that the

image spoke to the Jews three times, and that they did not hesitate to burn it. Solemn masses were performed at Madrid and other cities in the kingdom, to expiate the sacrilege which had been committed.

On the 22nd of June, 1636, another general *auto-da-fé* was held at Valladolid, composed of twenty-eight persons. The punishment inflicted on the Jews seems entirely novel: one hand was nailed to a wooden cross, and in that state they were obliged to hear read the report of their trial, and the sentence which condemned them to perpetual imprisonment for having insulted our Saviour and the Virgin by their blasphemies. A *Beata* also appeared in this *auto-da-fé;* she was known by the name of *Lorenza:* her crimes were the same as those of the other women of her class ; she pretended that she had seen apparitions of the Devil, Jesus Christ, and the Virgin Mary, and an infinity of revelations, but she was, in fact, nothing but a libertine woman.

Another *Beata,* who was more celebrated, appeared before the tribunal of Valladolid, she was called *Louisa de l'Ascension.* M. Lavallée has spoken of the fragments of the cross which had belonged to this woman, in his history of the Inquisition, published at Paris in 1809. This author *(who has only added to the errors of the writers of the two last centuries)* says, that this cross was one of those which the inquisitors suspended round the necks of the condemned. This practice was never known in the Inquisition ; the cross belonged to the Beata. M. Lavallée has not explained the inscription correctly. I have seen a cross entire; on the upper part are the letters I. N. R. I., which are the initials of *Jesus Nazarenus Rex Judæorum ;* on the mounting and on the arm, and towards the foot, are these words—*Jesus. La Tres Sainte Marie, conçue sans péché originel. Sœur Louise de l'Ascension, esclave indigne de mon tres doux Jesus.* This Beata gave similar crosses to those who, deceived by her reputation for sanctity, came to demand her prayers. This cross being once given, the wish to possess them became so general, that they were engraved, and became the occasion and the subject of a trial: the Inquisition caused all that could be found to be remitted to them, and thus several were to be seen at Madrid and Valladolid.

Louisa de l'Ascension must not be confounded with the hypocrites and false devotees, such as Mary de la Conception, Lorenza de Simancas, Madeleine de la Croix, and some others, who were vicious women. The constant virtue of Louisa was acknowledged by the nuns of St. Clare de Carrion, and by the inhabitants of that place and of the country.

On the 23rd of January, 1639, there was a general *auto-da-fé* at Lima in Peru, in which seventy-two persons appeared. Eleven persons were burnt and one effigy. In this *auto-da-fé* were seen, on elevated seats, six persons who had been accused by false witnesses.

The cities of Toledo, Cuença, Grenada, and Seville, also celebrated *autos-da-fé* in 1661, 1654, and 1660, when many persons were burnt.

Besides the public *autos-da-fé* and trials mentioned in the Chapters 24, 25, and 26, several others worthy of notice took place in the reign of Philip IV. Don Rodrigo Calderona, Marquis de Siete Inglesias, secretary to Philip III., was prosecuted by the Inquisition, which had not time to condemn him, because he was beheaded at Madrid in 1621, according to the sentence of the royal judges. The inquisitors accused him of having bewitched the king, in order to gain his favour. This charge was also brought against him by the fiscal of the civil tribunal of Madrid, but the judges paid no attention to it. It is certain that Calderona was the victim of a court intrigue, and the Count Duke d'Olivares did an irreparable injury to his memory, in coldly witnessing the execution of a man, who, during his favour, had rendered him great services.

Don Fray Louis Aliaga, archimandrite of Sicily, confessor to Philip III., and inquisitor-general, resigned his place by the command of Philip IV.; and a short time after Cardinal Zapata had succeeded him, he was prosecuted by the Inquisition of Madrid, for some propositions suspected of Lutheranism and materialism. Aliaga died in 1626, when his trial had not advanced further than the preparatory instruction.

In the year 1645, the Inquisition of Madrid prosecuted Don Gaspard de Guzman, count duke d'Olivares, favourite and prime-minister to Philip IV. This took place under the ministry of the inquisitor-general, Don Diego de Arce, on whom he had bestowed the bishoprics of Tui, Avila, and Placencia. Don Diego did not forget his benefactor, and it was to his prudence that the duke owed the favourable issue of an affair, which, in other hands, might have had the most fatal result.

This minister was disgraced in 1643 : a short time after, memorials were presented to the king, accusing him of the most heinous crimes. The tribunal, where every false report was received, also seized this opportunity to prosecute him: he was denounced to the Inquisition as a believer in judicial astrology; and as a proof that he was an enemy to the church, it was asserted that he attempted to poison Urban VIII.; the apothecary at Florence, who prepared the poison, and the Italian monk, who was to administer it, were mentioned; in fact, proofs were offered of all the crimes he had committed. The inquisitors commenced the preparatory instruction, but their proceedings were so dilatory, that the Count Duke died before the order for his arrest could be issued.

The Jesuit, Count Juan Baptiste de Poza, occupied the Inquisitions of Spain and Rome for some time with his writings, during the reign of Philip IV., particularly from the year 1629 to 1636. I have spoken in Chapter 15 of the memorial presented by the university of Salamanca against the Jesuits, in order to prevent the imperial college of Madrid, which was under the direction of these fathers, from being made an university; Poza wrote several pamphlets in defence of the pretensions of his order, which were all condemned by the Inquisition of Rome in 1632. The enemies of the Jesuits hoped that the Spanish Inquisition would do the same, but the inquisitors were afraid of offending the Count Duke d'Olivares, whose confessor was a Jesuit. At this period, Francis Roates, doctor of the university of Salamanca, almoner and councillor of the king, professor of mathematics, and preceptor to the Cardinal-infant Don Ferdinand, published a work which created a great sensation. The author denounces the writings of Poza to the Catholic Church in general, and to each of its members in particular, as heretical and tainted with atheism, and also denounces all the Jesuits who defended his doctrine.

Urban VIII. would have pronounced Poza to be an heretic, if he had not feared to offend the Court of Madrid; he therefore contented himself with depriving him of his professorship, and commanding that he should be sent to a house of the Jesuits, in some small town in Castile, and forbade him to preach, teach, or write. Although the Jesuits in their fourth vow, promised to obey the Pope without restriction, and they were, generally speaking, the most zealous supporters of his authority, yet, in this instance, they refused to obey, because they were supported by the Court of Madrid At this time the work of Alphonso Vargas* was published out of Spain; Vargas exposes the stratagems, the perfidious politics, and the bad doctrine of the Jesuits. Their general alleged, as an excuse for their disobedience, that they were forbidden to execute the orders of his Holiness by the king of Spain: this was the state of the affair when Olivares was disgraced. The works of Poza were then prohibited in Spain, and he was condemned to abjure several heresies.

Juan Nicholas Diana, another Jesuit, known for the very

* See Chapter 15.

relaxed morals of his printed works, was prosecuted by the
Inquisition of Sardinia for some propositions contained in a
sermon, and was condemned to recant. The Jesuit published
his defence, and went to Spain, where he demanded to be
tried by the Supreme Council. The Council, after taking
the opinions of several qualifiers, annulled the sentence, and
not only acquitted the Jesuit, but made him a qualifier.

Ali Arraez Ferrarés, surnamed the *Renegado*, was tried
by the Inquisition of Sicily in this reign. He was a Moor
of Tunis, and high in the favour of the king of that country:
having been taken prisoner to Palermo, he was ransomed and
sent back to Tunis. Some Christian slaves, who were in that
city, expressed their surprise that an apostate had been ransomed instead of being sent to the dungeons of the Inquisition. The tribunal being informed of the opinion of these
slaves, published that they were ignorant that Ali Arraez
Ferrarés had been a Christian, and that he was surnamed the
Renegado. Ali was taken a second time in 1624, and though
no other proof of his guilt existed but the report above-
mentioned, he was taken to the prisons of the holy office .A
great number of Sicilians, Genoese, and others, who had
known him at Tunis, were examined ; they all declared that
he was called the *Renegado*, and some added that they had
heard him say that he had been a Christian. Ali denied the
fact, but the tribunal considered him as convicted, and condemned him to be burnt. The Supreme Council decided
that the proof was not complete, annulled the sentence, and
commanded that the prisoner should be tortured, in order to
obtain additional proofs, and that the sentence should then
be renewed. Ali still persisted in denying that he had been
a Christian, and found means to inform the king of Tunis of
his situation; the Moorish king received his letter at the
moment when Fray Bartholomew Ximenez, Fray Ferdinand
de Reina, Fray Diego de la Torre, and three other Carmelites were brought in captive; they had been taken in going

to Rome. The king commanded them to write to the inquisitors of Sicily to set Ali Arraez at liberty, and to accept his
ransom, and, in case they refused, to inform them that he
would imprison and torture all the Christian slaves in his
power. The monks excused themselves by alleging that they
did not know the inquisitors, and the affair was dropped.
At this period the Supreme Council commanded that Ali
should be confined in a dungeon and ironed. In 1628, Ali
found means to convey another letter to the Moorish king,
informing him that he was imprisoned in a dark and fetid
dungeon, with a Christian captain, and that they were almost
starved. When the king received the letter, the Spanish
monks were negotiating their ransom. He sent for them, and
said, " Why do they endeavour to make this renagado a
Christian by their tortures. If this Inquisition is not suppressed, or if the inquisitors do not send the renegado immediately to the galleys with the other slaves, I will burn all
the Christians who are in my power: write, and tell them
so." The monks obeyed, and added, that if justice and religion required the execution of the prisoner, they were ready
to suffer martyrdom. The king of Tunis afterwards accepted
the ransom of the monks. After detaining Ali for sixteen
years, the inquisitors had no greater proof of his crime, and
yet they refused to exchange him for a Christian priest, alleging that the relations of the priest ought to ransom him,
and that it would be taking an active part in the heresy and
damnation of the renegado to set him at liberty: it was represented that their refusal might have the most fatal consequences to the Christian slaves at Tunis; but this consideration did not affect them.

An affair, which created a great sensation, occupied the
Supreme Council at this time. A convent for Benedictine
nuns had been found in the parish of St. Martin. The
director and confessor Fray Francis Garcia was considered a learned and holy man. Donna Theresa de Sylva,

whose relations had founded the convent for her, was the abbess, though only twenty-six years of age. The community was composed of thirty nuns, who all appeared to be virtuous, and had voluntarily embraced the monastic life. While the new convent enjoyed the highest reputation, the gestures and words of one of the nuns indicated that she was in a supernatural state : Fray Garcia exorcised her, and on the 8th of September she was pronounced to be a demoniac. In a short time, the abbess and twenty-five nuns were attacked in the same manner. Many consultations took place on the condition of these women, between men of learning and virtue, who believed that they were really *possessed*,— their confessor repeated his exorcisms every day, and even spent days and nights in the convent to renew them. He at last brought the tabernacle of the holy sacrament into the room where the nuns worked, and they said the prayers of forty hours. This singular scene lasted for three years, when the Inquisition of Toledo put a stop to it in 1631, by arresting the confessor, the abbess, and some of the nuns. Fray Francis Garcia was denounced as an *illuminati*, and it was said that he had corrupted the nuns, who pretended to be possessed. The trial was terminated in 1633 ; the confessor and the nuns were declared to be suspected of having fallen into the heresy of the *Alumbrados*. They were condemned to several penances, and sent to different convents; the abbess was exiled, and deprived of the privilege of consulting for four, and of voting for eight, years : when this period had expired, she returned to her own convent, and was commanded by her superiors to demand a revision of her trial. The abbess obeyed, declaring at the same time, that she did it solely for the honour of her nuns and those of the other houses of St. Benedict. The enterprise was difficult, but the power of her relation, the prothonotary of Arragon, and of the Count Duke d'Olivares, overcame every obstacle. In 1642 the Supreme Council acknowledged the innocence of

the nuns, but not of Fray Francis, because he had been so
imprudent as to hold a correspondence with the demons to
satisfy his curiosity, before he drove them from the nuns.
Donna Theresa gives an account of her own feelings when
possessed, and says that she was in a state of delirium, and
did the most foolish things.

Don Jerome de Villanueva, prothonotary of Arragon, that
is, the royal secretary of state for that kingdom, had, in his
youth, been the secretary to the Inquisition. He was prosecuted by the tribunal on the disgrace of the Count Duke
d'Olivares, as his creature and principal confidant. Several
heretical propositions were imputed to him, and he was arrested in 1645, and condemned to abjure: this sentence was pronounced on the 18th of June, 1647. When he was set at liberty
to accomplish his penance, he appealed to Pope Innocent X.,
complaining of the injustice with which he had been treated
in depriving him of the means of defending himself, and protesting that he had only submitted to the sentence, that he
might bring his cause before an impartial tribunal; he therefore demanded that his trial should be revised by judges
appointed by his Holiness. Don Pedro Navarro, an opulent
gentleman, went to Rome to negotiate the affair, out of
friendship to Villanueva; and although Philip requested
through his ambassador that Navarro should be compelled
to leave Rome, his Holiness refused, and would not allow
him to be arrested. The Pope issued a brief of commission
to the bishops of Calahorra, Segovia, and Cuença, to revise
the trial, but Philip IV., in consequence of the insinuations
of the inquisitor-general, forbade them to accept the commission, because it was contrary to the prerogatives of the
crown. The Pope then commanded that the process should
be transferred to Rome; after some opposition he was
obeyed, and Villanueva was acquitted. The resistance and
the injustice witnessed by the Pope in this case induced him
to expedite a second brief in 1653, in which he declared that

he had discovered great irregularities in the trial of Villa-nueva, and charged the inquisitor-general to observe that the laws were more strictly followed, and the trials conducted with more justice, gravity, and circumspection.

New contests soon arose between the Courts of Madrid and Rome, and the Pope sent Francis Mancini as his nuncio to Madrid to settle the dispute, but he could not obtain an audience of the king, and in 1654 was obliged to apply in the name of his Holiness to the inquisitor-general, who told him that the Pope had offended the king in the affair above mentioned ; he asserted that the prosecution of Villanueva had been properly conducted, and that the Pope had approved it. If this assertion was true, the Pope must have expressed his approbation before he took cognizance of the trial, for when it was transferred to the tribunal of Rome, the injustice and defects were discovered.

CHAPTER XXXIX.

THE INQUISITION DURING THE REIGN OF CHARLES II.

Charles II. succeeded his father on the 17th of September, 1665, when he was only four years of age. The grand-inquisitors, during his reign, were, Cardinal Don Pascal d'Arragon, archbishop of Toledo ; Father John Everard de Nitardo, a German Jesuit ; Don Diego de Sarmiento de Valladarés, bishop of Oviedo and Placentia ; Don Juan Thomas Rocaberti, archbishop of Valencia ; Cardinal Don Alphonso Fernandez de Cordova y Aguilar ; and Don Balthazar de Mendoza-Sandoval, bishop of Segovia.

The infancy of Charles II., the ambition of his brother Don John of Austria, the imperious temper of the queen-mother, Maria Anne of Austria, and the machiavelism of the

Jesuit Nitardo, gave occasion for a number of scandalous events during this reign. The weakness of the government was the principal cause of the insolent conduct of the inquisitors.

When Charles II. married Maria Louisa de Bourbon in 1680, the taste of the nation was so depraved, that a grand *auto-da-fé*, composed of an hundred and eighteen victims was considered as a proper and flattering homage to the new queen ; nineteen persons were burnt, with thirty-four effigies. None of the cases were remarkable, and may therefore be passed over in silence, together with another *auto-da-fé* which was celebrated in the church of the convent of the nuns of St. Dominic. Some manuscript notes indicate that some of the condemned avoided the fate which awaited them by bribing the inferior officers of the tribunal ; I am persuaded that this assertion is incorrect, because the subalterns had very little influence after the criminals were arrested.

The most celebrated trial of the Inquisition in this reign is that of Fray Froilan Diaz, bishop elect of Avila, and confessor to the king. The habitual weakness of Charles II., and the failure of an heir, created a suspicion that he was *bewitched*. The Cardinal Portocarrero and the inquisitor-general Rocaberti believed in sorcery, and after persuading the king that he was bewitched, they entreated him to suffer himself to be exorcised according to the formulary of the church. Charles consented, and was exorcised by his confessor. The novelty of this proceeding occasioned many remarks, and Froilan was informed that another monk was at that time exorcising a nun at Cañgas de Tineo, in order to free her from the demons, which, she said, tormented her. Froilan and the inquisitor-general charged the exorcist of the *demoniac* to command the demon, by the formula of the ritual, to declare if Charles II. was bewitched or not, and if he replied in the affirmative, to make him reveal the nature of the sorcery; if it was permanent; if it was attached to anything that the king had eaten or drank, to images or other objects; in what place it might be found; and lastly, if there were any natural means of preventing its effects: the confessor added several other questions, and desired the exorcist to urge them with all the zeal which the interest of the king and the state required.

The monk at first refused to question the demon, because it is forbidden by the church; but on being assured by the inquisitor-general that it would not be sinful in the present circumstances, he faithfully performed all that had been requested of him. The demon declared by the mouth of the demoniac, that a spell had been put upon the king by a person who was named. According to the private notes of that time, the criminal was an agent of the Court of Vienna, but Cardinal Portocarrero and the confessor Diaz were the partisans of France for the succession of Spain.

Diaz was very much alarmed at this information, and redoubled his conjurations until he learnt some method of destroying the enchantment. Before this operation was concluded, Rocaberti died, and was succeeded by Don Balthazar de Mendoza, who was of the Austrian party; he signified to the king that all that had taken place had arisen from the imprudent zeal of his confessor, and that he must be removed. The king followed his advice, and made Froilan Bishop of Avila; but the new inquisitor-general, not contented with preventing the expedition of the bulls, prosecuted him for having made use of demons to discover hidden things.

Mendoza directed this attack in concert with Torres Palmosa, the king's confessor, who was as eager for the ruin of Froilan Diaz as himself; this man communicated to Mendoza the letters which Diaz had received from Cangas, which were found among his papers.

Mendoza examined witnesses, and after combining their

declarations with the contents of the letters, he gave them to five qualifiers who were devoted to him, and made Don Juan Arcemendi, a counsellor of the Inquisition, and Don Dominic de la Cantolla, official of the secretaryship of the Supreme Council, their president and secretary. However, the five qualifiers declared that the trial offered no fact or proposition worthy of theological censure.

This decision was very displeasing to Mendoza; but relying on his influence in the council, he proposed that Diaz should be arrested; the councillors refused, because the measure was unjust, and contrary to the laws of the holy office, according to the decision of the five qualifiers. This resistance irritated the inquisitor-general, who caused the decree to be drawn up, signed it, and sent it to the council, with an order to register it with the ordinary forms. The councillors replied that they could not perform a ceremony which they considered illegal, because the resolution had not been adopted by a majority of votes.

During these transactions, Diaz made his escape to Rome; Mendoza, who could depend upon the king's confessor, induced him to persuade the king that this was an offence against the rights of the crown, and obtained a letter from him to the Duke de Uzeda, his ambassador at Rome, commanding him to seize the person of Diaz, and send him under an escort to Carthagena.

The anonymous author of Anecdotes of the Court of Rome, says, that Diaz went thither to shew to the Pope the will of Charles II., by which Philip de Bourbon was called to the throne of Spain; and that his return as a prisoner was occasioned by a court intrigue; but there is no evidence to prove this assertion. The inquisitor-general sent Froilan Diaz to the prison of the Inquisition of Murcia, and commanded the inquisitors to begin his trial. They appointed as qualifiers nine of the most learned theologians of the diocese, who unanimously gave the same answer as those of the

Supreme Council: the inquisitors consequently declared that there was no cause for the arrest. The inquisitor-general then caused Diaz to be transferred to Madrid. Mendoza afterwards charged the fiscal of the Inquisition to accuse him as a dogmatizing arch-heretic, for having said that an intercourse with the demon might be permitted, in order to learn the art of curing the sick.

Charles II. died about this time, and Philip was at first too much engaged with the war against the Archduke Charles of Austria, to discover the intrigues and artifices of Mendoza. He at last submitted the affair to the Council of Castile, on the 24th December, 1703, which decided that the arrest of Diaz was contrary to the common laws, and those of the holy office. The Supreme Council then decreed that Diaz should be set at liberty and acquitted.

It must be observed, that the demon affirmed that God had permitted a spell to be put upon the king, and that it could not be taken off, because the holy sacrament was in the church without lamps or wax candles, the communities of monks dying of hunger, and other reasons of the same nature. Two other demons who were interrogated, only agreed in declaring the necessity of favouring the churches, convents, and communities of Dominican monks; perhaps because the inquisitor-generals Rocaberti and Diaz were of that order.

This prince convoked the *grand junta,* composed of two councillors of state, two members of each of the Councils of Castile, Arragon, Italy, the Indies, the military orders and the finances, and of one of the king's secretaries. The royal secretary informed the junta that the disputes between the inquisitors and the civil judges had caused so much disturbance, that the king had resolved to commission the assembly to propose a plain and fixed rule, to secure to the Inquisition the respect due to it, and to prevent the inquisitors from undertaking trials foreign to the jurisdiction of the holy office.

The king commanded the six councils to remit to the junta all the papers necessary for the examination of the affair.

On the 21st of May, 1696, the grand junta made a report, stating that it appeared from the papers which had been examined, that the greatest disorder had long existed in the different jurisdictions, because the inquisitors had arbitrarily extended their power, so that the common tribunals had scarcely anything to do; that they punished the slightest offence against themselves or their domestics with the greatest severity, as if it was a crime against religion; that not content with exempting their officers from taxes, they gave their houses the privileges of an asylum, so that a criminal could not be taken from them, even by a judicial order; and if the public authorities exercised their powers, they dared to complain of it as a sacrilegious violation of the church; that in their official letters, and in the conduct of their affairs, they shewed an intention of weakening the respect of the people towards the royal judges, and even to make the authority of superior magistrates contemptible; and that they affected a certain independent manner of thinking on the subjects of administration and public economy, which made them forgetful of the rights of the crown.

The junta then stated that these abuses had caused complaints from the subjects, division among the ministers, discouragement to the tribunals, and much trouble to his majesty in settling their differences. That this conduct had appeared so intolerable, even in the beginning, that the powers of the Inquisition had been suspended for ten years by Charles V., until it was restored by Philip II., in the absence of his father, with some restrictions, which had not been well observed; that the extreme moderation with which the inquisitors had been treated was the cause of their boldness.

The junta proposed for the reformation of the holy office; 1st. That the Inquisition should not make use of censures in civil affairs. 2nd. That in case they employed them, the royal tribunals should be charged to oppose them by the means in their power. 3rd. That the privileges of the inquisitorial jurisdiction should be limited, in respect to the ministers and familiars of the Inquisition, and the relations of the inquisitors. 4th. That measures should be adopted to ensure the immediate settlement of affairs relating to competence and mutual pretensions.

The Count de Frigiliana, councillor of state, added that the inquisitors ought to be compelled to give an account of the revenues of the holy office. These observations, and the propositions of the junta, had no effect ; for the inquisitor-general Rocaberti, and Froilan Diaz, succeeded in changing the favourable inclinations of the king.

CHAPTER XL.

OF THE INQUISITION IN THE REIGN OF PHILIP V.

PHILIP V. succeeded his uncle Charles II. on the 1st of November, 1700 ; he died on the 9th of July, 1746. The grand-inquisitors, during this period, were, Don Balthazar Mendoza-Sandoval ; Don Vidal Marin, Bishop of Ceuta ; Don Antonio Ibañez de la Riba-Herrera, Archbishop of Saragossa ; Cardinal Don Francis Judice ; Don Joseph de Molinos; Don Diego de Astorga Cespedes, Bishop of Barcelona ; Don Juan de Camargo, Bishop of Pampeluna ; Don Andrea de Orbe Larreategui, Archbishop of Valencia ; Don Manuel-Isidore Manriquez de Lara, Archbishop of Santiago ; and Don Francis Perez de Prado Cuesta, Bishop of Teruel, who was still in office at the death of Philip V.

The court had always been so favourable to the Inquisition, that the inquisitors thought that a solemn *auto-da-fé* in celebration of his accession would be agreeable to the king. It took place in 1701, but Philip refused to be present at this barbarous scene. He however protected the tribunal of the holy office, according to the advice of his grandfather, Louis XIV., who told him, that he must support the Inquisition as the surest means of maintaining the tranquillity of his kingdom. This system acquired fresh importance in his eyes when Don Vidal Marin, the inquisitor-general, published an edict excommunicating all those who did not denounce the persons who had been heard to say, that they thought themselves permitted to violate the oath of fidelity to Philip V. This edict gave occasion for several trials, but none of them were followed by a definitive sentence.

Judaism was nearly extirpated during the reign of Philip V.; it had been secretly propagated for the second time in a remarkable manner after the reunion of Portugal to Spain. A yearly *auto-da-fé* was celebrated by all the tribunals of the Inquisition, during the reign of this prince; some of them held two, and three were performed at Seville and Grenada. Thus, without including those of America, Sardinia and Sicily, seven hundred and eighty-two *autos-da-fé* took place at Madrid, Barcelona, the Canaries, Cordova, Cuença, Grenada, Jaen, Llerena, Logroño, Majorca, Murcia, Santiago, Seville, Toledo, Valencia, Valladolid and Saragossa.

In fifty-four of these ceremonies seventy-four persons were burnt, with sixty-three effigies, and eight hundred and eighty-one condemned to penances. From this statement we may calculate, that during the forty-six years of the reign of Philip V. fourteen thousand and sixty-six individuals were condemned by the Inquisition to different puuishments.

It has been a common opinion, that the inquisition began to be less severe towards heretics, when the princes of the house of Bourbon ascended the throne of Spain ; but other causes seem to have decreased the number of its victims, which will be considered in the following chapters.

Among the pretended sorcerers condemned by the Inquisition was Juan Perez de Espejo, who was punished at Madrid in 1743, as a blasphemous hypocrite and a sorcerer. This person, after taking the name of *Juan de St. Esprit*, is said to have been the founder of the *Congregation of Hospitaliers* or of the *Divine Shepherd*, which still exists. He was condemned to receive two hundred stripes, and to be imprisoned ten years in a fortress.

A number of the disciples of *Molinos* were also condemned. Don Joseph Fernandez de Toro, Bishop of Oviedo, was condemned for this doctrine in 1721. The Inquisition of Logroño burnt Don Juan de Causados, a prebend of Tudela, the most intimate friend and disciple of *Molinos*; he had promulgated his mystic doctrines with great zeal and enthusiasm. His nephew, Juan de Longas, maintained this doctrine after his death; he is still known in Navarre, Rioxa, Burgos, and Soria, by the name of *Brother John*. The inquisitors of Logroño condemned him, in 1729, to receive two hundred stripes, and sent him for ten years to the galleys: he was afterwards imprisoned for life. Unfortunately some monks of his order had adopted his sentiments, and had communicated them to several nuns of the Convents of Lerma and Corrella, which gave occasion to several *autos-da-fé*.

Donna Agueda was the principal of these: she was born of noble parents at Corella, in Navarre. In 1712 she entered the Carmelite Convent at Lerma, with so great a reputation for virtue, that she was looked upon as a saint. In 1713 she had already adopted the heresy of Molinos; she passed twenty years in the convent, and her fame was continually increased by the accounts of her ecstacies and miracles, which were promulgated by Juan de Longas, the Prior de Lerma, the provincial, and other monks of the first rank, who were all accomplices in the imposture of Agueda, and interested in her reputation for sanctity.

A convent was founded at the place of her birth, and she was made prioress; in this character she continued her iniquitous course of life without losing any of her reputation, which, on the contrary, became so great, that the inhabitants of all the neighbouring countries repaired to her to implore her intercession with God.

After having passed a life full of iniquity, concealed by an appearance of sanctity, Agueda was denounced to the Inquisition of Logroña: she was taken to the secret prison, where she died from the consequences of the torture, before her trial was terminated. She confessed during the question that her sanctity was an imposture; she appeared to repent in her last moments, and received absolution. It was said in the informations taken during the trial, that Agueda had made a compact with the demon, and had sold her soul to him. She was also accused of infanticide, and some bones were found in the spot where it was said that her children were murdered and buried.

Fray Juan de la Vega, provincial of the barefooted Carmelites, was also prosecuted as an accomplice of Agueda; he was her spiritual director, and according to the evidence in his trial, had participated in her crimes, and seduced several other nuns. Several persons declared that Fray Juan had likewise made a compact with the demon; but he denied the fact, and resisted the severity of the torture, although he was advanced in years. He only confessed that he had received the money for eleven thousand eight hundred masses which had not been said. He was declared to be suspected in the highest degree, and sent to the desert Convent of Duruelo, where he died a short time after.

The provincial, and the secretary, and the two monks who had held those offices in the three preceding years, were implicated in the charges, arrested, tortured, and denied the facts; they were confined in the convents of their order in Majorca, Bilboa, Valladolid, and Osma. The annalist of the order confessed his crime, and appeared in the *auto-da-fé* with the *San-benito*. The other nuns who were found guilty were dispersed in different convents.

The trial of Don Balthazar Mendoza-Sandoval, Bishop of Segovia and inquisitor-general, was equally famous, though from a different cause. The conduct of this bad prelate towards Froilan Diaz has been related in the preceding chapter. When the Supreme Council refused to sanction the enormous abuse of his powers which he meditated, Mendoza ordered the arrest of three of the councillors who had been the most remarkable in their opposition; he requested of the king, in a false representation, the dismissal of Don Antonio Zambraxa, Don Juan Arzemendi, and Don Juan Miguelez, whom he sent loaded with chains to Santiago de Grenada, and formed the bold design of depriving the council of the right of intervention in the trials submitted to them, and the members of the power of voting a definitive sentence.

This act of despotism roused the resolution of Philip V. On the 24th of December he submitted the affair to the Council of Castile. On the 21st of January, 1704, the council proposed that the Supreme Council should be re-established in the possession of the privileges it had enjoyed since the foundation of the Inquisition, and that the three members should be restored to their office. The king took this advice, and commanded Mendoza to give in his resignation and leave Madrid.

Mendoza complained to the Pope, who wrote to the king to remonstrate on the manner of treating one of his sub-delegates. The king, however, maintained his resolution with firmness, and Mendoza was obliged to obey.

The king gave another proof of his firmness in defending the privileges of the crown, in his conduct towards the Inquisitor-general Judice, in the affair of Don Melchior Macanaz *. Philip, however, endured an insult from the Inqui-

* See Chapter 26.

sition, which it is surprising that he did not avenge. He had complained of a decree which Cardinal Judice had signed at Marli in 1714, prohibiting the works of Macanaz. The members of the Supreme Council had the boldness to reply, that his majesty might *suppress* the holy office if he thought proper, but *that, according to the apostolic bulls, he could not prevent it from exercising its office while it continued in existence.*

The Council of Castile, on the 3rd of November, 1714, gave the king substantial reasons for the suppression of the holy office. The ordinance for that purpose was prepared, and the blow would have been struck, but for the intrigues of the Queen Isabella Farnese; the Jesuit Daubenton, her confessor, and Cardinal Alberoni, who made the faithful and zealous conduct of Macanaz appear in a criminal light. They reminded the king of the advice of Louis XIV., and obtained another decree annulling the first. In this ordinance the king acknowledges that he had paid too much attention to the evil advice of perfidious ministers, and approves the prohibition of the works of Macanaz as favourable to the rights of the crown, re-establishes the counsellors who had been dismissed, and praises the conduct of Cardinal Judice.

The Inquisition prohibited the works of *Barclay* and *Talon* in the same edict with those of Macanaz, because they defended the rights of the crown against the pretensions of the Court of Rome, and Philip had the weakness to sanction an act so prejudicial to his own authority. It was during this reign that the works of Nicolas Belando and Don Joseph Quiros were prohibited *.

Among the trials I examined at Saragossa, was one very similar to that of Corella, but the criminals had not committed the crime of infanticide, or made a compact with the demon.

* See Chapter 25.

CHAPTER XLI.

OF THE INQUISITION DURING THE REIGN OF FERDINAND VI.

PHILIP V. left his crown to Ferdinand VI., his eldest son by his first wife, Gabriella of Savoy. This prince reigned from the 9th of July, 1746, to the 10th of August, 1759 ; he died without children. He was succeeded by his brother, Charles III. of Naples, the son of Philip V. and Isabella Farnese, his second wife. Don Francis Perez del Prado, Bishop of Teruel, held the office of inquisitor-general at the accession of Ferdinand. He was succeeded by Don Manuel Quintano Bonifaz, Archbishop of Pharsala, who was still in office at the death of that prince.

The rise of good taste in literature in Spain, the restoration of which was prepared under Philip V., is dated from the reign of Ferdinand VI. On this circumstance is founded the opinion that the accession of the Bourbons caused a change in the system of the Inquisition ; yet these princes never gave any new laws to the institution, or suppressed any of the ancient code, and, consequently, did not prevent any of the numerous *autos-da-fé* which were celebrated in their reigns. But Philip established at Madrid two Royal Academies for History and the Spanish language, on the model of that of Paris, and favoured a friendly intercourse between the *literati* of the two nations.

The agreement made in 1737 with the Court of Rome, concerning the contributions to be imposed on the clergy, and some other points of discipline, had rendered appeals to the Pope more rare ; and many opinions were admitted to be reasonable, which had been long represented as unfavourable to religion and piety, by the ignorance and superstition of one side, and the malevolence of the other. The establishment of weekly papers made the people acquainted with works they had never before heard of, and informed them of resolutions of the Catholic princes, concerning the clergy, which a short time before they would have considered as an outrage against religion and its ministers. The *Diario de los Literatos* (Journal de Savans) also opened the eyes of many persons, who, till then, had not been able to judge of books.

These circumstances, and some other causes, during the reign of Philip V., prepared the way for the interesting revolution in Spanish literature under Ferdinand VI. This change was followed by a great benefit to mankind; the inquisitors, and even their inferior officers, began to perceive that zeal for the purity of the Catholic religion is exposed to the admission of erroneous opinions. The doctrine of Macanaz no longer shocked the people, who heard with tranquillity all that had been written on the appeal against violence *(fuerzas)*, and without dreading the anathemas fulminated every year by the Popes in the bull *in cœna dominum*.

The effect of this change in opinion was particularly conspicuous in the reduction of the number of trials for Judaism, and, consequently, in the victims in the *autos-da-fé*. During the reign of Ferdinand, no general, and not more than thirty-four private, *autos-da-fé* were celebrated; the persons who appeared in them were condemned for blasphemy, bigamy, and pretended sorcery. Ten persons only were relaxed, and one hundred and seventy subjected to penances: those who were burnt had relapsed into Judaism. The Jews had been so severely persecuted in the preceding reigns, that scarcely any remained.

Jansenism and Freemasonry particularly occupied the Inquisition under Ferdinand VI. The Jesuits called those persons Jansenists who did not adopt the opinions of Molina on grace and free-will : their adversaries designated them as Pelagians. These parties reciprocally accused each other of favouring heresy. But the faction of the Jesuits prevailed during the reigns of Philip V. and his successor, because their confessors were of that order.

Freemasonry was an object entirely new to the Inquisition. Clement XII. had expedited on the 28th of April, 1738, the bull *in Eminenti*, in which he excommunicates the freemasons. In 1740 Philip issued a royal ordinance against them, and many were arrested and sent to the galleys. The inquisitors took advantage of the example, and treated the members of a lodge discovered at Madrid with great severity. The punishment of death was decreed against freemasons, in 1739, by the Cardinal Vicar of Rome, in the name of the high-priest of the God of peace and mercy! Benedict XIV. renewed the bull of Clement, in 1751. Fray Joseph Torrubia, examiner of books for the holy office, denounced the existence of freemasons, and Ferdinand published an ordinance against them in the same year, in which it was said, that all who did not conform to the regulations contained in it, would be punished as state criminals guilty of *high treason*. Charles III., then King of Naples, prohibited the masonic assemblies on the same day. The following pages contain the notice of a trial of this nature, which took place at Madrid, in 1757.

M. Tournon, a Frenchman, had been invited into Spain, and pensioned by the government, in order to establish a manufactory of brass or copper buckles, and to instruct Spanish workmen. On the 30th of April, 1757, he was denounced to the holy office as suspected of heresy by one of his pupils, who acted in obedience to the commands of his confessor.

The charges were: 1st. That M. Tournon had asked his pupils to become freemasons, promising that the *Grand Orient* of Paris, should send a commission, to receive them into the order, if they should submit to the trials he should propose, to ascertain their courage and firmness; and that their titles of reception should be expedited from Paris. 2nd. That some of these young workmen appeared inclined to comply, if M. Tournon would inform them of the object of the institution. That in order to satisfy them, he told them several extraordinary things, and shewed them a sort of picture, on which were figured instruments of architecture and astronomy. They thought that these representations related to sorcery, and they were confirmed in the idea, on hearing the imprecations which, according to M. Tournon, were to accompany the oath of secrecy.

It appeared from the depositions of three witnesses, that M. Tournon was a freemason. He was arrested and imprisoned on the 20th of May. The following conversation, which took place in the first audience of *monition*, may be interesting to some readers. After asking his name, birthplace, and his reason for coming to Spain, and making him swear to speak the truth, the inquisitor proceeded:—

Question. Do you know or suppose why you have been arrested by the holy office.

Answer. I suppose it is for having said that I was a freemason.

Q. Why do you suppose so?

A. Because I have informed my pupils that I was of that order, and I fear that they have denounced me, for I have perceived lately that they speak to me with an air of mystery, and their questions lead me to believe that they think me an heretic.

Q. Did you tell them the truth?

A. Yes.

Q. You are then a freemason?

A. Yes.

Q. How long have you been so?

A. For twenty years.

Q. Have you attended the assemblies of freemasons?

A. Yes, at Paris.

Q. Have you attended them in Spain?

A. No; I do not know if there are any lodges in Spain.

Q. If there were, should you attend them?

A. Yes.

Q. Are you a Christian, a Roman Catholic?

A. Yes; I was baptized in the parish of St. Paul, at Paris.

Q. How, as a Christian, can you dare to attend masonic assemblies, when you know, or ought to know, that they are contrary to religion?

A. I did not know that; I am ignorant of it at present, because I never saw or heard anything there which was contrary to religion.

Q. How can you say that, when you know that freemasons profess *indifference* in matters of religion, which is contrary to the article of faith, which teaches us that no man can be saved who does not profess the Catholic, Apostolic, and Roman religion?

A. The freemasons do not profess that *indifference*. But it is *indifferent* if the person received into the order be a Catholic or not.

Q. Then the freemasons are an *anti-religious* body?

A. That cannot be, for the object of the institution is not to combat or deny the necessity or utility of any religion, but for the exercise of charity towards the unfortunate of any sect, particularly if he is a member of the society.

Q. One proof that *indifference* is the religious character of freemasons is, that they do not acknowledge the Holy Trinity, since they only confess one God, whom they call the *Great Architect of the Universe*, which agrees with the doctrine of the heretical philosophers, who say that there is no true religion but *natural religion*, in which the existence of God the Creator only is allowed, and the rest considered as a human invention. And as M. Tournon has professed himself to be of the Catholic religion, he is required by the respect he owes to our Saviour Jesus Christ, true God and man, and to his blessed mother, the Virgin Mary, our Lady, to declare the truth according to his oath ; because in that case, he will acquit his conscience, and it will be allowable to treat him with that mercy and compassion which the holy office always shewed towards sinners who confess : and if, on the contrary, he conceals anything, he will be punished with all the severity of justice, according to the holy canons and the laws of the kingdom ?

A. The mystery of the Holy Trinity is neither maintained nor combated in the masonic lodges: neither is the religious system of the natural philosophers approved or rejected ; God is designated as the Great Architect of the Universe, according to the allegories of the freemasons which relate to architecture. In order to fulfil my promise of speaking truth, I must repeat, that in the masonic lodges nothing takes place which concerns any religious system, and that the subjects treated of are foreign to religion, under the allegories of architectural works.

Q. Do you believe as a Catholic, that it is a sin of superstition to mingle holy and religious things with profane things ?

A. I am not sufficiently acquainted with the particular things which are prohibited as contrary to the purity of the Christian religion ; but I have believed till now, that those who confound the one with the other, either by mistake, or a vain belief, are guilty of the sin of superstition.

Q. Is it true that in the ceremonies which accompany the reception of a mason, the crucified image of our Saviour, the corpse of a man and a skull, and other objects of a profane nature, are made use of ?

A. The general statutes of freemasonry do not ordain these things; if they are made use of, it must have arisen from a particular custom, or from the arbitrary regulations of the members of the body, who are commissioned to prepare for the reception of candidates ; for each lodge has particular customs and ceremonies.

Q. That is not the question; say if it is true that these ceremonies are observed in masonic lodges?

A. Yes, or no, according to the regulations of those who are charged with the ceremonies of the initiation.

Q. Were they observed when you were initiated?

A. No.

Q. What oath is it necessary to take on being received a freemason?

A. We swear to observe secrecy.

Q. On what?

A. On things which it may be inconvenient to publish.

Q. Is this oath accompanied by execrations?

A. Yes.

Q. What are they?

A. We consent to suffer all the evils which can afflict the body and soul if we violate the oath.

Q. Of what importance is this oath, since it is believed that such formidable execrations may be used without indecency?

A. That of good order in the society.

Q. What passes in these lodges which it might be inconvenient to publish?

A. Nothing, if it is looked upon without prejudice; but as people are generally mistaken in this matter, it is necessary to avoid giving cause for malicious interpretations; and this would take place if what passes when the brothers assemble was made public.

Q. Of what use is the crucifix, if the reception of a freemason is not considered as a religious act?

A. It is presented to penetrate the soul with the most profound respect at the moment that the novice takes the oath. It is not used in every lodge, and only when particular grades are conferred.

Q. Why is the skull used?

A. That the idea of death may inspire a horror of perjury.

Q. Of what use is the corpse?

A. To complete the allegory of Hiram, architect of the temple of Jerusalem, who, it is said, was assassinated by traitors, and to induce a greater detestation of assassination and other offences against our neighbours, to whom we ought to be as benevolent brothers.

Q. Is it true that the festival of St. John is celebrated in the lodges, and that the masons have chosen him for their patron?

A. Yes.

Q. What worship is rendered him in celebrating his festival?

A. None; that it may not be mingled with profane things. This celebration is confined to a fraternal repast, after which a discourse is read, exhorting the guests to beneficence towards their fellow-creatures, in honour of God, the great architect, creator, and preserver of the universe.

Q. Is it true that the sun, moon, and stars, are honoured in the lodges?

A. No.

Q. Is it true that their images or symbols are exposed?

A. Yes.

Q. Why are they so?

A. In order to elucidate the allegories of the great, continual, and true light which the lodges receive from the great Architect of the world, and these representations belong to the brothers, and engage them to be charitable.

Q. M. Tournon will observe that all the explanations he has given of the facts and ceremonies which take place in the lodges, are false and different from those which he voluntarily communicated to other persons worthy of belief; he is therefore again invited, by the respect he owes to God and the Holy Virgin, to declare and confess the heresies of *indifferentism*, the errors of *superstition*, which mingle holy and profane things, and the errors of *idolatry*, which led

him to worship the stars : this confession is necessary for the
acquittal of his conscience and the good of his soul ; because
if he confesses with sorrow for having committed these
crimes, detesting them and humbly soliciting pardon (before
the fiscal accuses him of these heinous sins), the holy tribunal will be permitted to exercise towards him that compassion and mercy which it always displays to repentant
sinners ; and because if he is judicially accused, he must be
treated with all the severity prescribed against heretics by
the holy canons, apostolical bulls, and the laws of the
kingdom.

A. I have declared the truth, and if any witnesses have
deposed to the contrary, they have mistaken the meaning of
my words; for I have never spoken on this subject to any
but the workmen in my manufactory, and then only in the
same sense conveyed by my replies.

Q. Not content with being a freemason, you have persuaded other persons to be received into the order, and to
embrace the heretical superstitions and pagan errors into
which you have fallen.

A. It is true that I have requested these persons to become freemasons, because I thought it would be useful to
them if they travelled into foreign countries, where they
might meet brothers of their order, who could assist them in
any difficulty; but it is not true that I engaged them to
adopt any errors contrary to the Catholic faith, since no
such errors are to be found in freemasonry, which does not
concern any points of doctrine.

Q. It has been already proved that these errors are not
chimerical; therefore let M. Tournon consider that he has
been a dogmatizing heretic, and that it is necessary that he
should acknowledge it with humility, and ask pardon and
absolution for the censures which he has incurred; since, if
he persists in his obstinacy, he will destroy both his body
and soul; and as this is the first audience of *monition*, he is

advised to reflect on his condition, and prepare for the two other audiences which are granted by the compassion and mercy which the holy tribunal always feels for the accused.

M. Tournon was taken back to the prison; he persisted in giving the same answers in the first and second audiences. The fiscal presented his act of accusation, which, according to custom, was divided into the articles similar to the charges of the witnesses. The accused confessed the facts, but explained them as he had done before. He was desired to choose an advocate, but he declined this, alleging that the Spanish lawyers were not acquainted with the masonic lodges, and were as much prejudiced against them as the pub lic. He therefore thought it better for him to acknowledge that he was wrong, and might have been deceived from being ignorant of particular doctrines; he demanded absolution, and offered to perform any penance imposed on him, adding, that he hoped the punishment would be moderate, on account of the good faith which he had shewn, and which he had always preserved, seeing nothing but beneficence practised and recommended in the masonic lodges, without denying or combating any article of the Catholic faith.

The fiscal consented to this arrangement, and M. Tournon was condemned to be imprisoned for one year, after which he was to be conducted under an escort to the frontiers of France; he was banished from Spain for ever, unless he obtained permission to return from the king or the holy office. During the first month of his imprisonment, he was directed to perform spiritual exercises, and a general con fession ; to spend half an hour every morning in reading the meditations on the book of *spiritual exercises* of St. Ignatius de Loyola, and half an hour in the evening in reading the considerations of Father John Eusebius Nieremberg, in his work on the *difference between temporal and eternal;* to recite every day part of the Rosary of Our Lady, and often to repeat the acts of faith, hope, charity, and contrition ; to

learn by heart the catechism of Father Astete, and to prepare himself to receive absolution, at Christmas, Easter, and
Pentecost.

A private *auto-da-fé* was celebrated in the hall of the
tribunal, in which M. Tournon appeared without the *san-
benito*, and signed his abjuration, with a promise never again
to attend the assemblies of the freemasons.

M. Tournon went to France, and it does not appear that
he ever returned to Spain.

The society of freemasons has occupied the learned men,
since the middle of the seventeenth century, and the number
of fables which have been published concerning it have confused the subject, and done much injury to it. The mysterious initiations of this order first began to attract observation in England, during the reign of Charles I., who perished
on the scaffold in 1649. The enemies of Cromwell and the
republican system then established the dignity of *grand
master* of the English lodges, to prepare the minds of the
freemasons for the re-establishment of the monarchy. William
III. was a freemason, and though the dynasty was changed
by the accession of George I., it does not appear that freemasonry was suspected in England. It was introduced into
France in 1723, and Ramsay, a Scotchman, established a
lodge in London in 1728, giving out that the society had
been founded in 1099, by Godfrey de Bouïllon, King of
Jerusalem; preserved by the Knights Templars, and brought
to Edinburgh, where it was established by King Robert
Bruce in 1314. In 1729 the order was introduced into Ire-
land. Holland received it in 1731, and the first lodges were
opened in Russia in the same year: it appeared in Boston in
America in 1733, and in several other towns of the New
World, subject to England. It was also established in Italy
in that year, and two years after freemasons were found
at Lisbon.

I believe the first severe measure against the freemasons in

Europe, was that which was decreed on the 14th of December, 1732, by the Chamber of Police of the Chatelet at Paris ; it prohibited freemasons from assembling, and condemned M. Chapelot to a penalty of six thousand livres, for having suffered them to assemble in his house. Louis XV. commanded that those peers of France, and other gentlemen who had the privilege of the *entry*, should be deprived of that honour, if they were members of a masonic lodge. The grand-master of the Parisian lodges, being obliged to quit France, convoked an assembly of freemasons to appoint his successor. Louis XV., on being informed of it, declared that if a Frenchman was elected, he would send him to the Bastile. However, the Duke d'Antin was chosen, and after his death, Louis de Bourbon, prince of Conti, succeeded him. Louis de Bourbon, duke de Chartres, another prince of the blood, became grand-master.

In 1737, the Dutch prohibited the assemblies of freemasons as a precautionary measure, without charging them with any crimes ; the members of a lodge assembled, they were arrested and prosecuted, but they defended themselves with so much energy, that they were acquitted, and the prohibition revoked.

The Elector Palatine of the Rhine also prohibited the order in his states, and arrested several members at Manheim, in consequence of their disobedience.

John Gaston, grand duke of Tuscany, published a decree of proscription against the lodges in the same year. This prince died soon after, and the masons again assembled: they were denounced to Pope Clement XII. This pontiff sent an inquisitor to Florence, who imprisoned several members of the society, but Francis of Lorraine, when he became Grand Duke, set them at liberty. He declared himself the protector of the institution, and founded several lodges in Florence, and other towns in his states.

If I was a member of the society, I would do all in my

power to abolish those things which gave the inquisitors, and other ecclesiastics occasion to say, that sacred and profane things are mingled in the masonic ceremonies; particularly the following, which have already appeared in printed works.

In the sixth grade, or rank, which is that of *particular secretary*, *(secretaire intime,)* the history of Hiram, king of Tyre, is taken from the ninth chapter of the third book of Kings for the masonic allegories ; and *Jehovah*, the ineffable name of God, for the *sacred* word of freemasonry ; this custom is likewise observed with some slight differences in several other grades.

In the eighteenth, called the *Rosicrusian of Haradom* of Kilwiniug, is a representation of columns with inscriptions ; the highest is as follows : *In the name of the Holy and indivisible Trinity:* lower down, *May our salvation be eternal in God;* still lower, *We have the happiness of being in the pacific unity of the sacred numbers.* The history of the second chapter of the first, and the nineteenth of the second book of Esdras is made use of ; the word of order between two freemasons of the same rank is INRI, which some persons have supposed to be *Jesus Nazarenus, Rex Judæorum:* the word *passe* is added, which means Emmanuel, or *God is with us.*

The rank of Rosicrusiaci, in the Scotch lodges, is the perfection of the order ; the meaning is developed in fifteen sections. In the fifth, the allegories are the mounts of salvation, mounts *Moriah* and *Calvary,* the first for the sacrifices of Abraham, David, and Solomon, the second for that of Jesus of Nazareth: other allegories relate to the Holy Spirit, designated as the *Majesty of God* which descended on the tabernacle, and on the temple at the moment of its dedication. In the twelfth section a *holy mountain* is seen, on which is a large church in the form of a cross from east to west, in the neighbourhood of a city, which is the image of the *celestial Jerusalem;* in the thirteenth, three great lights, symbols of the natural law, the laws of Moses and of Jesus Christ, and the cabinet of wisdom, designated as the *stable for oxen*, in which is a faithful chevalier and his holy wife, and the sacred names of *Joseph, Mary, and Jesus;* the fourteenth is an allusion to the descent of our Saviour into the *Limbos* after his death, his resurrection and ascension; lastly, the fifteenth has the words *consummatum est*, which Jesus pronounced on the cross.

In the twenty-seventh grade of the *grand commander of the temple*, a cross is made on the forehead of the brother with the thumb of the right hand ; the sacred word INRI; the scarf has four crosses, the *disc* a triangle of gold, with the Hebrew characters of the ineffable name, *Jehovah*.

The seal of the order has between the devices of the shield of arms a cross, the arch of alliance, a lighted candle in a candlestick on each side, aud above the inscription, Glory to God. (Laus Deo).

All these things, and many others which allude to the sacred history of the temple of Jerusalem, built by Solomon, re-established by Esdras, restored by the Christians, and defended by the knights templars, present a mixture liable to an interpretation similar to that in the information of the witnesses at Florence, which was the first apostolical con-demnation ; it was renewed under Pius VII., in an edict of Cardinal Gonsalvi, in 1814.

There was not less inconvenience in the execratory oath of the famous masonic secret, for which no adequate object has been discovered, unless it was one which no longer exists.

John Mark Larmenio (who secretly succeeded the grand-master of the Templars, the unfortunate James de Molay, who requested him to accept the dignity) invented, in con-cert with some knights who had escaped the proscription, different signs of words and actions, in order to recognise and receive knights into the order secretly, and by means of a novitiate, during which they were to be kept in ignorance of the object of the association (which was to preserve the order, to re-establish it in its former glory, and to revenge the deaths of the grand-master, and the knights who perished with him); when the qualities of the new member were perfectly well known, the grand secret was to be confided to him, after a most formidable oath.

The secret signs were intended as a precaution against admitting into the order those Templars who had formed a schism during the persecution ; they retired into Scotland, and refused to acknowledge John Larmenio as grand-master, and pretended that they had re-established the order; this pretension was refuted by a chapter of legitimate knights : after this the new chief issued his diploma in 1324, and his successors have followed his example, on attaining the dignity of secret grand-master of the order of Templars in France. The list of grand-masters until the year 1776 has been published.   Philip de Bourbon, duke of Orleans, was appointed in 1705, Louis Augustus de Bourbon, duke de Maine, in 1724, Louis Henry de Bourbon Conde, in 1737, Louis Francis de Bourbon Conti, in 1745, Louis Henry Timoleon de Cossé Brissac, in 1776, and Bernard Raymond Fabre, in 1814.

The Knights Templars who retired to Scotland, founded an establishment in 1314, under the protection of Robert Bruce; their objects and their measures were the same, and they were concealed under the title of *architects;* this was the origin of *freemasonry*.   They soon, however, forgot the most criminal part of the execratory oath: since the deaths of Clement V. and Philip the Fair, the persecutors of the knights, deprived them of the power of revenging the executions of James de Molay and his companions, and had no other object but the re-establishment of the order; this intention shared the fate of the first, after the deaths of the authors of it, and their first disciples. From these facts it appears, that the execratory oath is without a motive or object in modern masonic lodges.

CHAPTER XLII.

OF THE INQUISITION UNDER CHARLES III.

CHARLES III. succeeded his brother Ferdinand on the 10th of August, 1759, and died on the 17th November, 1788. The inquisitors-general during this reign were Don Manuel Quintano Bonifaz, archbishop of Pharsala; Don Philip Bertran, bishop of Salamanca, and Don Augustin Rubin de Cevallos, bishop of Jaen. The characters of these persons were humane, compassionate, and inclined to benevolence; qualities which caused a remarkable decrease in the number of public *autos-da-fé*. If the reign of Charles III. is compared with that of Philip V. his father, they appear as if they had been separated by a period of several centuries. The pro gress of knowledge was very rapid under this prince; even the provincial inquisitors, though the laws of the Inquisition had not been altered, adopted principles of moderation, which were unknown under the Austrian princes. It is true, that from time to time great severity was shewn towards un-important offences, but among the trials of this reign, I have seen several which were suspended, though the proofs were much more conclusive than many which were sufficient to condemn the criminal to *relaxation*, under Philip II.

Yet, though the system was comparatively moderate, the number of trials was still immense, because all the denuncia-tions were received. The witnesses of the preparatory instruc-tion were examined immediately, in order to discover some charge, which the prejudices of the age rendered serious. If out of an hundred trials which were begun ten had been concluded, the number of persons subjected to *penances* would have been greater, than under Ferdinand V.; but the tribunal was no longer the same. Almost all the trials were suspended before the decree of arrest was issued. The denounced was sometimes induced to repair to the tribunal on the pretext of business, and then informed of the charges against him; he replied to them, and returned home, after having promised to return a second time when summoned. Sometimes the proceedings were abridged, and the criminal was only condemned to a private penance, which might be performed without the knowledge of any person but the commissary of the tribunal.

Several trials which were commenced against persons of rank, were not proceeded in after the preliminary instruction; such were those of the Marquis de Roda, minister secretary of state, of grace and justice; of the Count d'Aranda, president of the Council of Castile, and captain-general of New Castile, who was afterwards ambassador to Paris, and lastly, prime-minister; of the Count de Florida Blanca, then fiscal of the Council of Castile for civil affairs, afterwards successor to the Marquis de Roda, and prime-minister; of the Count de Campomanes, fiscal for criminal affairs, and afterwards governor of the same council; of those of the Archbishops of Burgos and Saragossa, and of the Bishops of Tarazona, Albarracin, and Orihuela, who had composed the council extraordinary, in 1767, for the expulsion of the Jesuits. The trials of all these distinguished men had the same origin.

The Bishop of Cuença, Don Isidore de Carbajal y Lancaster, highly respectable from his family, which was that of the Dukes of Abrantés, and from his dignity, his irreproachable conduct, and his charity to the poor, was less acquainted with the true principles of the canonic law than zealous for the maintenance of the ecclesiastical privileges. Influenced by this motive, he was so indiscreet as to represent to the king, that the *Church was persecuted in its rights, property, and ministers,* and drew a picture of the reign of Charles III., which would have been more applicable to that of the Emperor Julian. The king commissioned the Council of Castile to examine if the complaint was just, and to propose measures to repair the injury, if any had taken place. The two fiscals of the council both made learned replies, in which the ignorance of the bishop, and the consequences of his imprudent zeal, were exposed. These answers, and the other papers belonging to the proceedings, were printed by the king's order, and though they were generally approved, some priests and monks, who regretted the inordinate power once possessed by the Church, denounced several propositions contained in them, as Lutheran, Calvinistic, or defended by other parties inimical to the Roman Church.

The two archbishops, and the three bishops, already mentioned, who had voted for the requisition addressed to the Pope for the expulsion of the Jesuits, were also denounced, as suspected of professing the impious doctrines of philosophism, which, it was said, they had only adopted to please the court. They were commissioned to take cognizance of several affairs relating to the Jesuits, and only accidentally spoke of the Inquisition, and expressed opinions contrary to its system. The inquisitors were all creatures of the Jesuits, without even the exception of the inquisitor-general: it is not therefore surprising that they received so many denunciations. The exclusive right possessed by the Court of Rome to try bishops, never prevented the inquisitors from secretly examining witnesses against them, because it gave them a pretence to write to the Pope, and request permission to carry on the proceedings; and though it was the custom of the holy see to transfer the trials of bishops to Rome, the *Supreme Council* of Spain always put forward its fiscal, in order to justify its conduct in prosecuting bishops: this was the case in the affair of Carranza.

The denunciations had not the effect expected by the enemies of the prelates, because no *singular* and independent proposition, opposed to true doctrine, was proved to have been advanced. In a less enlightened age, these prelates would have been exposed to great mortification from this attack; but at this time the Inquisition found it dangerous to be too severe, because the court had adopted the system of vigorously opposing all the ancient doctrines which favoured the pretensions of the ecclesiastics at the expense of the royal prerogatives; and on the occasion of the publication of some conclusions on the canonical law, which were entirely favourable to the Pope and the ecclesiastical jurisdiction, a royal censor was appointed for each university, without whose approbation no conclusion could be published or maintained.

The perseverance of the government in the new system prevented the inquisitors from venturing to sentence the prelates of the extraordinary council; they however thought proper to endeavour to avert the storm, and applied to Don Fray Joachim de Eleta, the king's confessor. This man was an ignorant *Recollet*, and known for his blind attachment to the Court of Rome. The prelates declared that they condemned several propositions advanced by the two fiscals in their work called *An Impartial Judgment of the Monitory of Parma*, which was written by the king's order, because they thought they tended to the infringement of the privileges of the church. After this declaration, the prelates used every means to make the confessor persuade Charles III., that the printed copies ought not to be published, and that the work should be reprinted, after the suppression of several propositions. The inquisitor-general and the Supreme Council being informed of this circumstance, the affair took another turn, and the faction of the Jesuits became more calm.

These events exposed to great danger a person who had entered into them without being aware of it. M. Clement, a French priest treasurer of the cathedral of Auxerre, and afterwards bishop of Versailles, arrived at Madrid in 1768, at the time when the event above-mentioned occupied every mind. He held several conversations on this subject with

the Marquis de Roda, the fiscals of the council, and the
Bishops of Tarazona and Albarracin*. The zeal of this
theologian for the purity of doctrine on all points of discipline induced him to say, that the good dispositions of the
Court of Madrid ought to be taken advantage of, and proposed three measures. The first was to place the Inquisition
under each bishop, who should be the chief, with a delibera-
tive vote, with the addition of two inquisitors with a consul-
tive vote; the second, to oblige the monks and nuns to acknowledge the bishop as their chief, and to obey him as such
after renouncing all the privileges contrary to this arrangement; the third to abolish the distinct schools of theology,
under the titles of Thomists, Scotist, Suarists, or others, and
to have only one system of theology for the schools and
universities, founded on the principles of St. Augustin and
St. Thomas.

It is sufficient to be acquainted with Spain, and the state
of the monks at that period, to foresee the persecution which
the author of such a plan would incur. The confessor of
the king and the inquisitor-general were informed of it, by
their political spies, and several monks denounced M. Clement to the holy office, as a Lutheran, a Calvinistic heretic,
and an enemy of the regular orders.

M. Clement suspected the existence of this intrigue, from
some expressions made use of by a Dominican, with whom he
was intimate. The inquisitors, who saw that M. Clement
was received at court, did not dare to arrest him, but they
requested their chief to oblige him to quit the kingdom.
The treasurer of Auxerre imparted his fears to the Count
d'Aranda, and the Marquis de Roda; who being, from his
connexion at court, acquainted with all that had passed, advised him to depart, but without informing him of what
it was useless for him to know. M. Clement followed his

* A work, by M. Clement, was printed at Paris, in 1802, called *A Journal of Correspondences and Journeys for the Peace of the Church.*

advice, and though he had intended to go to Portugal, he returned immediately to France, to avoid the *Sbirri* of the holy office, who might have arrested him on his return from Lisbon, if the system of the court was changed. In fact a great number of charges were brought against him after his departure, but they were not made public, and he wrote his travels without knowing anything of the plots against him.

All that passed on the occasion of the apostolical prohibition of the catechism of Mesengui was made public: Charles III. had ordered that it should be made use of in the religious instruction of Charles IV.; and the inquisitor-general was openly and justly blamed, for having published the brief of prohibition, without waiting to obtain the consent of the king. This proceeding was the cause of the exile of the inquisitor-general. His disgrace might have rendered him more prudent, but in his reply to the king, in 1769, concerning some measures taken by the extraordinary council of five prelates, he advanced as certain, several propositions concerning the Inquisition, which might have been proved to be false, if the Marquis de Roda had consulted the registers of the Supreme Council. He said that the Inquisition had met with nothing but opposition from the beginning; that it was conspired against in the most cruel manner; that all the proceedings of the council were made public, except the trials for heresy, but that even those were always submitted to his Majesty; and that the charge against it of acting with *entire independence* was not just, he concluded with saying, that his Majesty might appoint an ecclesiastic as his secretary to attend the council, and inform him of all that passed.

It is impossible to find a reason for the necessity here imposed upon the king to have a *priest* for his secretary, since the inquisitors employed seculars in their offices, who were permitted to see the trial, though obliged to take an oath of secrecy, and two members of the Council of Castile also attend the Supreme Council. Yet neither an ecclesiastic nor a layman could prevent fraud: the same may be said of the members of the Council of Castile, because in case of any intrigues, for example, in a conflict for jurisdiction, the counsellors assembled at the house of the inquisitor-general, and their chief sealed their papers with his private seal.

The most decisive proof of the *entire* independence of the Inquisition, exists in two laws of Charles III., concerning bigamy and the prohibition of books; they were insufficient to restrain the inquisitors within their jurisdiction.

Yet though these abuses and many others were still continued, I do not hesitate to say that the inquisitors of the reigns of Charles III. and his successors were men possessed of extreme prudence and singular moderation in comparison with those of the time of Philip V. and the preceding reigns. This is confirmed by the very small number of *autos-da-fé* celebrated under the two kings, a period of twenty-nine years; only ten persons were condemned, four of whom were burnt, and fifty-six individuals subjected to penances. All the other trials were terminated by *individual autos-da-fé*; the condemned was taken into a church to hear his sentence read, when it was confirmed by the Supreme Council, without waiting for other prisoners to form a particular *auto-da-fé*. Other trials were concluded by a *lesser auto-da-fé* in the audience-hall of the tribunal; another mode, which was the least severe, was to celebrate the *auto-da-fé* in the presence of the secretaries of the Inquisition alone; no greater indulgence than this could be shewn.

The individual *auto-da-fé* was decreed in two famous trials of the reign of Charles III. Of the first, that of Olavide, an account has been given in Chapter 26. The second was that of Don Francis de Leon y Luna, a priest and knight of the military order of St. Jago. He was condemned as violently suspected of having fallen into the heresies of the *Illuminati* and of Molinos, for having seduced several women, for communicating several times with the

consecrated wafer from superstitious motives, and for preaching a false and presumptuous mysticity to several nuns and
other women who were the dupes of his error and their own
weakness.   Leon was imprisoned for three years in a convent; he was then banished for seven years from Madrid,
and forbidden to exercise the ministry of a confessor.   The
council of the orders requested the king to deprive Leon of
his cross and knighthood, according to the statutes which
ordain that measure towards all who commit a crime which
incurs an infamous punishment.   But the council ought to
have known that the *suspicion* of heresy was not sufficient,
since the tribunal always declares, if the condemned desire it,
that this sort of sentence does not prevent them from attaining offices and dignities.

At Saragossa the Marquis d'Aviles, intendant of Arragon,
was accused before the holy office of having read prohibited
books; but this denunciation, and that of the Bishop of
Barcelona for Jansenism at Madrid, and several others of the
same nature, were passed over without further notice.

CHAPTER XLIII.

OF THE SPANISH INQUISITION UNDER CHARLES IV.

CHARLES IV. ascended the throne on the 17th November,
1788; he abdicated on the 19th March, 1808, in consequence
of the popular commotions at Aranjuez.   The inquisitors-
general under Charles IV. were Don Augustin Rubin de
Cevallos, Bishop of Jaen; Don Manuel de Abad-y-la-Sierra,
Archbishop of Selimbria; the Cardinal Archbishop of Toledo, Don Francis Lorenzana; and Don Ramon Joseph de
Arce, Archbishop of Burgos.

The two obstacles which had principally contributed to
impede the progress of learning during the three preceding

reigns, were removed by the reform of the six grand colleges and the expulsion of the Jesuits. Before this revolution, all the canonical offices and magistracies were given to the members and fellows of the colleges; while the immense influence of the Jesuists prevented all who were not their disciples, or Jesuits of the *short-robe*, from obtaining any offices or honours. The Marquis de Roda was the author of this politic measure, which caused him to be hated by the disciples of St. Ignatius. But this minister has obtained an honourable place in history, because in granting to *all* classes the rewards due to merit, he excited a general emulation, which increased the influence of knowledge and a taste for the sciences. This has caused it to be said that the restoration of good Spanish literature was the work of de Roda, but the commencement of that change may be more correctly dated from the reign of Philip V.

During the twenty years preceding the accession of Charles IV. a multitude of distinguished men had arisen, who would doubtless have led Spain to rival France in the good taste and perfection of literary works, if one of the most terrible events recorded in history had not arrested the impulse these great men had given. The French revolution caused a great number of works to be written on the rights of man, of citizens, and of nations; the principles contained in them could not but alarm Charles IV. and his ministers. The Spaniards read these books with avidity; the minister dreaded the contagion of this political doctrine, but in attempting to arrest its progress, he caused the human mind to retrograde. He charged the inquisitor-general to prohibit and seize all the books, pamphlets, and French newspapers, relating to the revolution, and to recommend to his agents to use the greatest vigilance in preventing them from being clandestinely introduced into the kingdom. Another measure employed by the government was to suppress the office of teacher of the natural law in the universities and seminaries.

The Count de Florida-Blanca was then prime minister; this conduct entirely destroyed the good opinion entertained of him by the nation. He was said to be a novice in the art of government, because the prohibition would only excite greater curiosity. The commissioners of the holy office received an order to oppose the introduction of the works of the modern philosophers, as contrary to the sovereign authority, and commanded every person to denounce whom they knew to be attached to the principles of insurrection.

It would be difficult to calculate the number of denunciations which followed this order. The greatest number of the denounced were young students of the universities of Salamanca and Valladolid. Those who wished to read the French writings braved the prohibition, and employed every means to obtain them; so that the laws of nature and of persons were more studied than before the suppression of the office of teacher. The severity of the administration only caused the commencement of an immense number of trials, which were never finished, for want of proofs.

Many Spaniards, some of illustrious birth and others of great learning, were the objects of secret informations, as suspected of impiety and philosophism. The history of their trials, and those of many distinguished persons for Jansenism, have been given in the twenty-fifth and twenty-sixth chapters.

Don Bernard-Maria de Calzada, colonel of infantry, and brother-in-law to the Marquis de Manca, interested me much, when he had the misfortune to be arrested by the Duke de Medina-Celi, grand provost of the holy office : I accompanied him as secretary, the notary for the sequestrations being ill. Don Bernard was the father of a very large family, who were reduced to indigence by this event, and it gave me the greatest grief to witness the sad situation of their mother. I presume that that lady has not forgotten my conduct on that mournful night and on the following day, when I returned to visit her. The unfortunate Cal zada, whose appointment in the office of the minister of war was not sufficient to maintain his very numerous family, had undertaken the translation of some French books, and composed a satirical work, by which he made enemies of some fanatics and monks, who, affecting the most austere morals, were intolerant towards all who did not agree with their opinions. By their denunciations they ruined this family. Calzada, after passing some time in the prisons of the holy office, submitted to an abjuration *de levi*, which is almost equivalent to an absolution, and was banished from Madrid, after giving up his place and all hope of advancement.

The Inquisition of the *Court* was more indulgent towards the Marquis de Narros : although many witnesses deposed that they had heard him maintain some heretical propositions of Voltaire and Rousseau, whose works he boasted that he had read, as well as those of Mirabeau, Montesquieu, the Baron d'Holbac, and other philosophers of the same school, he was spared the disgrace of an imprisonment and a public censure. It was thought more decent to request the Count de Florida-Blanca to write to him by the ordinary courier to Guipuscoa, where he then resided, and inform him that the king commanded him to repair to Madrid on some affairs of the government. The Marquis hastened to court, flattering himself (as he informed his relation the Duke of Grenada) that he would be appointed sub-governor to the Prince of Asturias, now Ferdinand VII. On the next day he received an order not to quit Madrid, and to attend a summons to the Inquisition. Some time after, he confessed the truth of the charges, and added some other circumstances, protesting at the same time that he had always been a good Catholic, and that a desire of passing for the most learned man in his country induced him to advance the propositions. He abjured *de levi ;* some private penances were imposed on him, and the affair was only known to a few persons.

The inquisitors of Valencia prosecuted Fray Augustine

Cabades, commander of the convent of the nuns of the order
of Mercy, and professor of theology in that city : he abjured,
and was then released from prison. When he had obtained
his liberty, he demanded a revision of his judgment ; the
Supreme Council acknowledged the justice of his appeal, and
the sentence was declared null and void.

Don Marianno Louis de Urquijo, prime-minister and secretary of state under Charles IV., was also an object for the
persecutions of the holy office. His great strength of mind,
and a careful education, raised him above the errors of his
age. He made himself known in his early youth by a translation of the *Death of Cæsar*, a tragedy by Voltaire, which
he published with a preliminary *Essay on the Origin of the
Spanish Theatre, and its Influence on Morals*. This pro-
duction, which only displayed a generous wish to acquire
fame, and the ardent genius of its young author, attracted
the attention of the Inquisition. Private informations were
taken concerning the religious opinions of the Chevalier de
Urquijo, and the tribunal ascertained that he manifested
great independence in his opinions, with a decided taste for
philosophy, which the Inquisition called the doctrine of un-
believers. Everything consequently was prepared for his
arrest, when the Count d'Aranda, then prime-minister, who
discovered his merit (and had remarked his name in the list
of distinguished youths destined to serve the state, belonging to the Count de Florida-Blanca his predecessor), proposed
to the king that he should be initiated into public affairs.
Charles IV. appointed him to the office of first secretary of
state in 1792.

The inquisitors changed their manner of proceeding, when
they saw the elevation of their intended victim. Their
policy at this time led them to shew a deference towards the
ministry, which had not been observed in preceding ages.
They converted the decree of imprisonment into another
called the *audience of charges*, by which the Chevalier de

Urquijo was required to appear privately before the Inquisition of the court whenever he was summoned. The sentence pronounced him to be only *slightly suspected* of partaking the errors of the unbelieving philosophers. He was absolved *ad cautelam*, and some spiritual penances were imposed on him which he might perform in private. The tribunal exacted his consent to the prohibition of his preliminary essay and the tragedy; but as a remarkable testimony of consideration, his name was not mentioned in the edict, either as the author or translator. The inquisitors, even of modern times, have rarely shewn themselves so moderate; but the fear of offending the Count d'Aranda (who abhorred the tribunal) was the real motive of their conduct.

Urquijo, at the age of thirty, became prime-minister, and in that quality exerted himself to extirpate abuses, and to destroy the errors which opposed the prosperity of his party and the progress of knowledge. He encouraged industry and the arts, and the public owes to him the immortal work of the Baron de Humboldt. Contrary to the custom of Spain, he allowed him to travel in America, and supported him with the zeal of a person passionately attached to the arts and sciences. With the assistance of his friend Admiral Mazarredo he raised the navy. He was the first in Europe who meditated the abolition of slavery; and at that time concluded a treaty with the Emperor of Morocco for the exchange of prisoners of war, which is still in force. In the year 1800, when fortune seemed everywhere to attend the French arms, and the government persecuted the august house of Bourbon, he had the glory of establishing a throne in Etruria for a prince of that family, who had married a daughter of Charles IV., and signed the treaty to that effect at St. Ildephonso with General Berthier, afterwards Prince of Wagram.

The death of Pius VI. gave him an opportunity of freeing

Spain, to a certain degree, from its dependance on the Vatican. On the 5th September, 1799, he induced the king to sign a decree which restored to the bishops the powers which had been usurped by the Court of Rome, and delivered the people from an annual impost of several millions, produced by the sale of dispensations and other bulls and briefs.

The reform of the Inquisition ought to have followed this bold step. The minister wished to suppress the tribunal entirely, and apply its revenues to the establishment of useful and charitable institutions. He drew up the edict for that purpose, and presented it to Charles IV. for signature; though Urquijo did not succeed in this attempt, he convinced the king of the necessity of reforming the tribunal.

Among the many wise regulations suggested to the king by Urquijo, was that published in the form of an ordinance in 1799, on the liberty and independence of all the books, papers and effects of the foreign consuls established in the seaports, and in the trading towns belonging to Spain. It was occasioned by an inconsiderate disturbance made by the commissioners of the holy office at Alicant, in the house of Don Leonard Stuck, consul for Holland, and at Barcelona, at the residence of the French consul.

Those happy dispositions of the Court of Spain vanished at the fall of the minister who had inspired them. The victim of an intrigue, he shared the fate of those great men who do not succeed in destroying the prejudices and errors which they oppose. The chevalier de Urquijo was confined, and kept in the strictest solitude, in the humid dungeons of the citadel of Pampluna, where he was unable to obtain books, ink, paper, fire, or light.

Ferdinand VII. on his accession to the throne, declared his treatment to have been unjust and arbitrary, and forgetting the persecutions he had suffered for eight years, he blessed, in Ferdinand, the sovereign who would make the necessary reforms, and had voluntarily put a period to his sufferings. He repaired to Vittoria, when that prince stopped there on his way to Bayonne, and used every means to prevent him from making that fatal journey. The letters he wrote on this subject to his friend, General Cuesta, contain an exact prophecy of all the miseries which have since overwhelmed Spain*, and point out the means of avoiding them.

Urquijo refused to repair to Bayonne, although Napoleon sent him three orders to do so, until the renunciation and abdication of Charles IV., Ferdinand VII., and the princes of that house had been made known. After the royal family had left the place, he went there, and endeavoured to persuade Napoleon to give up his plans.

He accepted the appointment of Secretary to the Junta of Notables, which was then assembled at Bayonne, and soon after the office of Minister-Secretary of State. His generous intentions need no comments ; they are known to all. The eulogium of this great man has just been made by our energetic and sincere advocate ; the public will read it with pleasure and interest. During his ministry, he had the happiness of witnessing the decree which suppressed the formidable tribunal of the holy office, and declared it to be injurious to sovereignty.

Urquijo died at Paris, after an illness of six days, at the age of forty-nine. He died as he had lived—full of that courage, serenity, that philosophy, and love of virtue, which belong to the virtuous and wise alone. He was buried on the 4th of May, 1817, in the cemetery of Père la Chaise, where a magnificent monument of white Carrara marble has been erected to his memory.

In 1792 the inquisitors of Saragossa received a denuncia-

* These letters will be found in the second volume of the *Memoires pour servir à l'Histoire de la Révolution d'Espagne*, by Don Juan Nellerto, Nos. 34, 59, 67.

tion, and examined witnesses against Don Augustin Abad-la-Sierra, Bishop of Barbastro, who was accused of Jansenism, and of approving the principles which were the basis of the civil constitution of the French clergy under the constitutional assembly. During the progress of this affair, Don Manuel Abad-la-Sierra, the brother of Don Augustin, was made inquisitor-general, and the inquisitors were afraid to carry it on. When Don Manuel was dismissed from his office, he also was denounced as a Jansenist, but he was not prosecuted.

The bishop of Murcia and Carthagena, Victorin Lopez Gonzalo, was denounced in 1800 as suspected of Jansenism and other heresies, and for having permitted certain propositions on some points of doctrine to be maintained in his seminary. The trial of the bishop was not carried farther than the summary instruction ; because on being informed of the plots of some scholastic doctors who were partisans of the Jesuits, he defended himself so ably before the inquisitor-general, that the members of council did not proceed against him; but they continued the prosecution of the theses, when they perceived that they were favourable to some conclusions on miracles, which had been condemned by qualifiers.

The subject of Jansenism created a great sensation in Spain. The Jesuits, who had been permitted to return to that kingdom in 1798, soon acquired a numerous party, and accused all who did not adopt their opinions of Jansenism. Their conduct was so impolitic, that they were a second time banished from the kingdom. They were the authors of the denunciations against the Countess de Montijo, and many other distinguished persons, of whom an account has been given in a former chapter.

The accusation of Jansenism against Don Antonio and Don Jerome de la Cuesta was the cause of the trial of Don Raphaël Muzquiz, Archbishop of Santiago, who had been confessor to Queen Louisa, wife of Charles IV.

The energetic defence of Don Jerome de la Cuesta obliged Muzquiz to defend himself against the imputation of calumny : he made representations which injured his cause, for he vilified the inquisitors of Valladolid, and even the inquisitor-general, and accused them of partiality and collusion with Cuesta : his rank protected him from the danger of an arrest which he incurred by this temerity, but he was condemned to pay a penalty of eight thousand ducats, and the Bishop of Valladolid four thousand. Muzquiz would have been more severely punished, if he had not been protected by a person, who obtained from the Prince of Peace that the affair should not be carried farther.

The same pretence of Jansenism was the cause of the trial of Don Joseph Espiga, almoner to the king, and a member of the tribunal of the nunciature in 1799. His accusers represented him as the author of the royal decree of the 5th of September in that year, after the death of Pius VI., forbidding any person to apply to Rome for matrimonial dispensations. Espiga was then the most intimate friend of the minister Urquijo, but he never allowed any one to influence him in official affairs. The Nuncio Cassoni made many useless representations to the king on this subject; however he partly obtained his end by political intrigues, for though the bishops had promised to obey the ordinance, yet most of them avoided granting matrimonial dispensations, and those who did so were accused of Jansenism. The inquisitors, though they were all sold to the Nuncio and the Jesuits, were afraid to proceed, and the trial of Espiga was suspended. When his friend Urquijo was deprived of his office, he was obliged to retire to the cathedral of Lerida, of which he was a dignitary.

The year 1796 is remarkable for the prosecution commenced against the Prince of Peace, the king's cousin, by his marriage with Donna Maria Theresa de Bourbon, the daughter of the infant Don Louis. It may be easily supposed that much address was necessary in conducting an attack against a person so high in favour. Three denunciations were received at the holy office, accusing him of atheism, because he had not confessed himself or taken the pascal communion for eight years, and because he was married to two women at the same time, and the life he led with many others was a source of great scandal to the public. The three denouncers were monks, and there is some reason to suppose that they were directed by the authors of a court intrigue, to cause the prince to be disgraced.

The head of the Inquisition at that time was Cardinal Lorenzana, who was simple and easily deceived, but too timid not to be on his guard against anything which might displease the king and queen. Although the denunciations were presented to him, he did not dare to examine witnesses, or even the accusers. Don Antonio Despuig, Archbishop of Seville, and Don Raphaël Muzquiz, who were at the head of this intrigue, made every effort to induce Lorenzana to cause a private instruction to be taken, to arrest the prince in concert with the Supreme Council, and to obtain the approbation of the king, of which they thought themselves certain, if they could prove that his favourite was an atheist. This attempt was so repugnant to the disposition of Lorenzana, that the two conspirators agreed that Despuig should press his friend the Cardinal Vincenti, famous for his intrigues, to persuade Pius VI. to write to Lorenzana, and reproach him for the indifference with which he beheld a scandal so injurious to the purity of the religion professed by the Spanish nation. Vincenti obtained the letter from the Pope; Lorenzana promising, that if the Pope decided that the measure was necessary, he would do what they desired. Napoleon Bonaparte, who was then a general of the French Republic, intercepted a courier from Italy at Genoa. The letter of Cardinal Vincenti to Despuig, enclosing that of the Pope to Lorenzana, was found among his despatches : Bonaparte thought it necessary to the continuance of the good intelligence then established between France and Spain, to inform the Prince of Peace of the intrigue, and he commissioned General Pérignon, ambassador at Madrid, to remit the correspondence to Godoy. The favourite opposed another intrigue to his enemies, and succeeded in freeing himself from them by sending Lorenzana, Despuig, and Muzquiz to Rome, to carry the condolences of the king to the Pope on the occasion of the entrance of the French army into his states. Their commission was dated the 14th March, 1797.

At this period the Inquisition was in imminent danger of being deprived of the power of arresting individuals without the consent of the king. This circumstance arose from the trial of Don Ramon de Salas, which is related in the twenty-fifth chapter. The affair of Jovellanos also took place at this time.

In 1799 the inquisitors of Valladolid, with the approbation of the council, condemned Don Mariano and Don Raymond de Santander, booksellers of that city, to two months seclusion in a convent, to a suspension of their trade for two years, and to banishment ; they were also forbidden to approach Valladolid, Madrid, and other royal residences, within eight leagues. They were obliged to pay a penalty, and after having been a long time in the secret prisons, Don Mariano could not obtain permission to remove to another place, though he was subject to attacks of epilepsy. Their only offence was having received and sold prohibited books ; for though some fanatics had accused them of heresy, no proofs were obtained. On the 10th of November, Don Mariano solicited the inquisitor-general to allow them to reside in Valladolid, representing, that if this favour was refused, their families must die in poverty, and they offered to purchase the permission by paying another penalty.

The affair of a Beata at Cuença created a great sensation.

She was the wife of a labourer at Villar d'Aguilar. Among other fictions which she invented to make people suppose her a saint, she said that Jesus Christ revealed to her that he had changed her flesh and blood into the same substance as his own body. This imposture caused great theological discussion among the priests and monks. Some maintained that it was impossible, others that it was not impossible, if the infinite power of God was considered ; others believed all, and were astonished that any person could be so incredulous, for they thought that the Beata could have no interest in deceiving them ; lastly, there were some who were witnesses of the life of this *Beata*, and were her accomplices from the beginning of her imposture, or who were the dupes of their credulity, and who continued to believe, or appeared to do so, in her supernatural state. They carried their folly so far as to adore this woman ; they conducted her in procession in the streets and to the churches with lighted tapers ; they burnt incense before her as before the consecrated host ; lastly, they prostrated themselves before her, and committed many other sacrileges. The Inquisition could not but notice these scenes. The pretended saint and some of her accomplices were taken to the secret prisons, where the *Beata* ended her days. One of the articles of the sentence commanded that her effigy should be taken to the *auto-da-fé* on a traineau, and burnt ; the curate of Villar, and two monks, who were her accomplices, were condemned to follow the effigy barefooted, clothed in short tunics, and with a cord round their necks ; they were degraded and banished for life to the Philippine Isles. The Curate of Casasmarro was suspended for six years, and two men of the lowest class received two hundred stripes, and were imprisoned for life ; one of her servants was sent to the house of the *Recogidas* for ten years. I do not know any judgment of the Inquisition more just than this.

Another *Beata* at Madrid, called Clara, did not profit by

this example. She did not carry her phrensy so far as the other, but her miracles and her sanctity made a great noise; she pretended that she was paralytic, and could not leave her bed. On this report every one went to see her. The most distinguished ladies in Madrid repaired to her, and thought themselves happy in being admitted to see her; she was entreated to be the mediatrix with God for the cure of different maladies, to enlighten judges on the eve of an important judgment, and graces and assistance were implored against many other misfortunes. Clara replied to them all in an emphatic style, like an inspired person who saw into the future. She announced that, by an especial call from the Holy Spirit, she was destined to be a Capuchin nun, and she was extremely grieved that she had not the strength and health necessary for living in a community and a cloister. She imposed so well on the persons who surrounded her, that Pius VII. permitted her, in a special brief, to make her profession before Don Athanasius de Puyal, bishop coadjutor of the Archbishop of Toledo, at Madrid, and granted her a dispensation from the cloistered life, and the exercises of a community. From that moment nothing was spoken of in society but the miracles and heroic virtue of sister Clara. The bishop who had received her vows, obtained permission from the Pope and the Archbishop of Toledo to erect an altar in her chamber opposite her bed; several masses were performed there every day, and even the holy sacrament was placed there in a tabernacle. Clara communicated every day, and persuaded those who came to see her, that she took no sustenance but the bread of the eucharist. This delusion lasted for several years: but in 1802, Clara was taken to the prison of the holy office; her mother was likewise arrested, and a monk whom she had taken for her director. They were accused of having assisted the nun in her impostures, in order to obtain considerable sums of money, which the ladies of Madrid and other devout persons placed in her hands to be distributed as alms. When her deceit, her pretended sickness, and the other circumstances of her life were proved, Clara, her mother, and her director, were condemned to seclusion and other punishments, much less severe than they deserved.

Another *Beata* appeared after these, but the circumstances of her imposture are not so interesting.

The inquisitors no longer thought of condemning criminals to the flames. A proof of this laudable change in their system may be seen in the trial of Don Michel Solano, curate of Esco in Arragon*. It was proved by the depositions of the

* Don Michel Juan Antonio Solano was born at Veroline in Arragon. Nature had endued him with an inventive, penetrating genius, inclined to mathematical applications; he learned the trade of a joiner, for his own amusement. He invented a plough which would work without oxen or horses, and presented it to the government, but little notice was taken of it. Desiring to make himself useful to his parishioners, he undertook to fertilize the earth in a ravine situated between two mountains, and completely succeeded. He had brought into the ravine the waters of a fountain, which was about a quarter of a Spanish league from the spot. A long and severe illness had made him lame, and during his convalescence, he invented a chair in which he could go out into his garden. When his age inclined him to meditations of another nature, as he had not many books, he particularly applied himself to the study of the Bible, and from it he formed his religious system, which differed little from that of the reformed Protestants, who are most attached to the discipline of the first ages of the church; he was persuaded that all that is not expressed in the New Testament, or is opposed to the literal sense of the text, was invented by man. He put his sentiments in writing, and sent the work to his bishop, requesting him to instruct him and give his opinion. The bishop Lopez Gil promised to send him an answer; but as it did not arrive, Solano communicated his opinions to some professors of theology in the University of Saragossa, and to some curates in his neighbourhood : he was in consequence denounced to the Inquisition of Saragossa, who proceeded to take informations, and arrest the criminal. A curate, who called himself his friend, received the commission to arrest the unfortunate Solano, while entire liberty was allowed him to enable him to recover. Solano, however, found means to convey himself to Oleron, the nearest town on the French frontier, but soon after, depending on the goodness of his intentions, hoping that the inquisitors would respect his innocence, and shew him his errors, if he had fallen into any, he returned to Spain, and wrote to inform them that he would submit to anything, in order to be enlightened and convinced. His conduct proved that he was little acquainted with the tribunal of the Inquisition.

witnesses, that he had advanced several propositions condemned by the church.

He was conducted to the secret prisons of Saragossa, where he confessed all, alleging that having meditated for a long time with a sincere desire to discover the truth of the Christian religion, and that without the assistance of any book but the Bible, he had convinced himself that there was no truth in anything but which was contained in the Holy Scriptures; that all the rest might be erroneous, because though several fathers of the church maintained these opinions, they were but men, and, consequently, liable to err; that he considered all that had been established by the Roman Church, in opposition to the proper and literal meaning of the Scriptural text, as false, and that it was possible to fall into error, in admitting that which did not result either directly or indirectly from the text; that he considered it certain that the ideas of purgatory and the limbos were the invention of man, since Jesus spoke of only two receptacles for souls, paradise and hell; that it was a sin to receive money for performing mass, although it was called an alms, and for the support of the celebrator; and that the priests and other ministers of religion ought to receive their salaries from the government, like the judges and other officers. He thought, that the introduction and establishment of tithes was a fraud of the priests, and the manner of explaining the commandment of the church, which ordained that they should be paid without any deductions for seed, or the expenses of the harvest, was a shameful robbery; that no attention ought to be paid to the commands of the Pope, because no God but avarice is adored at Rome, and all the measures of that government only tend to take money from the people on religious pretences.

Solano had made a complete body of doctrine of these articles, and had composed a book on it, which he confided to his bishop and other theologians, as if he incurred no danger from such a proceeding.

The inquisitors of Saragossa undertook to persuade Solano to renounce his opinions, and employed for that purpose some respectable theologians; they exhorted him to acknowledge his errors and repent, and threatened him with *relaxation*. Don Michel replied that he was aware of his danger, but if he was induced to retract, he would be condemned before the tribunal of God, and that if he was in error, God would enlighten him or pardon him. The infallibility of the church, and the opinions of the saints and learned men who had decided on the meaning of the obscure texts, were represented to him; he replied, that in all their discussions the Court of Rome had interfered, and rendered their good intentions of no avail.

It was impossible to make Solano recant, and the inquisitors passed sentence of *relaxation;* it must be confessed that they could not do otherwise, according to the code of the Inquisition. But the Supreme Council, wishing to spare the Spanish nation the spectacle of an *auto-da-fé,* had recourse to the extraordinary measure of examining some persons who had been mentioned by the witnesses, but had been neglected, commanding the inquisitors, at the same time, to use every effort to make Solano retract. It was in vain, and the inquisitors, though they well knew the motives which led the council to vote against their sentence, did not dare to disobey the law. They pronounced sentence of *relaxation* a second time, and the council took advantage of a declaration made by one of the witnesses, to order an inquest to be taken among all the curates, priests, and physicians of Esco and the neighbourhood, in order to discover if Solano had ever suffered an illness which weakened or deranged his mind. The result of this inquest was to be communicated to the council, and in the mean time the trial was suspended. The physician, who suspected what they wished him to say, declared that Solano had had a severe illness for several years, before he was arrested, and that it was not surprising that it had weakened his mental powers; he said, that from that time he had spoken more frequently of his religious opinions, which were not those of the Catholics in Spain. On receiving this deposition, the council decreed, that without pronouncing definitively on the subject, every means should be used to convert the accused. At this juncture, Solano fell dangerously ill; the inquisitors charged the most able theologians of Saragossa to endeavour to make him return to the faith, and even entreated the bishop co-adjutor of the Archbishop of Saragossa, Don Fray Michel Suarez de Santander, to exhort him with that tenderness and goodness which were characteristics of that worthy prelate. The curate appeared to be sensibly affected at all that was done for him, but he said that he could not renounce his opinions, without fearing that he offended God, by betraying the truth. On the twentieth day of his illness, the doctor told him that he was dying, and desired him to take advantage of the few moments which were left him. "I am," said Solano, "in the hands of God; I have nothing more to do." Thus died the curate of Esco, in the year 1805: he was refused ecclesiastical sepulture, and was privately buried within the walls of the tribunal. The inquisitors reported all that had passed to the Supreme Council, which forbade them to continue the trial, that Solano might not be burnt in effigy.

Two years after the intrigue intended to ruin the Prince of Peace, another event which took place at Alicant ought to have been sufficient to cause the tribunal to be reformed, or even suppressed. On the death of Don Leonard Stuck, Consul for the Batavian Republic in that city, his executor, the Vice-Consul of France, put his seals upon the property of the deceased, until the formalities of the law had been fulfilled. The commissary of the Inquisition desired the governor of the town to take off the seals and give him the keys of the house, that he might register the books and prints, as some of them were prohibited. The governor demanded time, in order to consult his majesty's minister. The commissary, who was disconcerted at this delay, went in the night with his alguazils, broke the seals, opened the door, and made the inventory; and when he had done, replaced the seals as well as he could, and went away. The ambassador of the Batavian Republic complained to the government of this violation of the law of nations, and the king wrote to the inquisitor-general, through his minister Urquijo, informing him, that the Inquisition must avoid similar infringements for the future, and bounding its office to the care of observing that, on the death of foreign ministers, no prohibited books were sold to Spaniards or naturalized foreigners. Nearly the same thing happened to the French consul at Barcelona.

It may have been seen in the preceding chapters, that the Inquisition has been several times in danger of being suppressed, or subjected to the general forms of law. These occasions were more frequent during the reign of Charles IV.

The Counts d'Aranda, de Florida-Blanca, and Campomanes, and the extraordinary council, represented the continual abuses committed by the *holy office* to Charles III., but he contented himself with passing some ordinances, to curtail its power.

In 1794, Don Manuel Abad-la-Sierra, inquisitor-general under Charles IV., wished to reform the procedure of the tribunal, and commanded me to compose a work, entitled, *A Discourse on the Procedure of the Holy Office*, in which I represented the vices of the actual practice, and the means of obviating them, even though the proceedings for heresy should still continue to be secret. But, by various intrigues, an order was obtained from Charles IV., which forced the inquisitor-general to quit Madrid, and resign his office.

Another attempt was made, when the Prince of Peace discovered the plot against him; the royal decree for the suppression was drawn up, but never presented for the signature of the king, because Godoy was the dupe of counter-intrigue. In the following year, Jovellanos wished to make use of the work I had composed for Don Manuel Abad-la-Sierra, of which I had given him a copy, but he failed in his design, and Charles IV., who was ill-informed, and deceived by intriguers, commanded that minister to retire to his house at Gijon in the Asturias. The attempt of Urquijo has been already mentioned.

In 1808, Napoleon Buonaparte decreed the suppression of the Inquisition, at Chamastin, near Madrid; he alleged that the tribunal was an encroachment on the royal authority.

In 1813, the Cortes-general of the kingdom adopted the same measures, after declaring that the existence of the privileged tribunal of the holy office was incompatible with the political constitution which had been decreed, published, and received by the nation.

In spite of these two last suppressions, the tribunal still exists; because the greatest number of the men who surround the throne have been and will always be the partisans of ignorance, of the ultra-montane opinions, and of those which influenced the world before the invention of printing. These opinions are strenuously supported by the Jesuits, who have been recently recalled to Spain by Ferdinand VII.

CHAPTER XLIV.

OF THE INQUISITION DURING THE REIGN OF FERDINAND VII.

CHARLES IV. abdicated the crown in favour of his eldest son, Ferdinand, who began to reign on the same day, before any public act had proved the validity of the abdication. The royal and Supreme Council of Castile considered it necessary to observe the national custom on this occasion, and commissioned the royal fiscals to examine into the validity of the abdication, that the people might be informed that they were released from their oath of allegiance to Charles. But a strict order was immediately sent to the council to renounce the measure, to proclaim the validity of the abdication, and acknowledge Ferdinand as king. Charles protested against his abdication; he said that it was not voluntary, since he had only done it to save his own life and that of the queen, in the sedition at Aranjuez. Ferdinand paid no attention to this protestation; the emperor Napoleon took advantage of the event, and the Bourbons ceased to reign in Spain. While Charles IV. was at Marseilles, and Ferdinand at Valencé, Joseph Napoleon, King of Naples, was proclaimed King of Spain; Ferdinand wrote to Joseph to congratulate him, and request his friendship, and commanded all Spaniards to recognise him, to prevent the ruin and desolation of their country.

When Joseph was acknowledged King of Spain, the archives of the Supreme Council and of the Inquisition of the Court were confided to me, in consequence of an order from his majesty. With his approbation, I burnt all the criminal processes, except those which belonged to history, from their importance, and the rank of the accused ; but I preserved all the registers of the resolutions of the council, the royal ordinances, the papal bulls and briefs, the papers of the affairs of the tribunal, and all the informations taken concerning the genealogies of the persons employed in the holy office, on account of their utility in proving relationship in trials when it is necessary.

I have read in a work, intituled *Acta Latomorum*, that in the month of October, 1809, a grand national lodge of Spanish freemasons was founded even in the buildings of the Inquisition of Madrid. This assertion I consider entirely false, because at that time the keys of the building were in the possession of a subaltern under my orders, who would never have consented to give them up for such a purpose. I presume that the authors of this article wished to astonish, by the striking contrast between the different destinations of the same edifice.

My acquaintance with the archives already mentioned enabled me to compose for the Royal Academy of History (of which I have the honour to be a member), a dissertation, under the title of *A Memorial, in which the Opinion of the Spaniards concerning the Inquisition is examined.* The Academy published my work.

The above-mentioned materials, some others which I had collected since the year 1789, and some which were sent to me from Valladolid and other towns, enabled me to publish in 1812 and 1813, two volumes of the *Annals of the Inquisition,* which comprehend all the events which passed in the tribunal from 1477 to 1530. I was not able to finish that work, being obliged to repair to France in 1813.

On the 22d of February, in the same year, the Spanish assembly at Cadiz, which styled itself the *General Cortes,* suppressed the Inquisition, restoring to the bishops and secular judges their jurisdictions, that they might prosecute heretics in the same manner as before the existence of the Inquisition.

This measure was the cause of long discussions in the tribune, and many orators pronounced speeches of great eloquence. The liberty of the press which then existed allowed many works to be published both for and against the holy office. Its partisans neglected nothing in its defence; in short, all that could possibly be advanced in favour of such a tribunal as the Inquisition, was published at Cadiz during this celebrated discussion. But reason prevailed; not because the majority of the voters were irreligious persons, or Jacobins (as it has since been unjustly said), but because the Cortes found an irresistible strength in the reasoning which condemned a tribunal which had been so fatal to the prosperity of the nation for three centuries. The representatives of Spain received an infinite number of letters and addresses, returning thanks for the benefit bestowed on the nation : several of these letters were signed by persons employed in the Inquisition. I have the satisfaction to be able to declare, that this triumph of reason and humanity was principally owing to the documents which I furnished, and which became known to the public in 1812, by means of the *Memorial on the Opinion of the Spaniards concerning the Inquisition*, and the first volume of the *Annals of the Inquisition*. This is proved by the manifesto addressed by the Cortes to the Spanish people ; in which the representatives say, that they had seen the apostolical bulls addressed to the Inquisition, and the complaints and appeals of the prisoners : these details could only have been obtained from the works above mentioned, but they were not cited, because I was then a counsellor of state to King Joseph.

These measures of the Cortes were however useless. Buonaparte restored the crown of Spain to Ferdinand, by a treaty at Valencè, in 1813, and in March, 1814, the king re-entered Spain ; on his arrival at Valencia, he was immediately surrounded by persons imbued with the Gothic prejudices of the age of chivalry, and one of the first measures of his administration was the re-establishment of the holy ffce, on the 21st of July, 1814.

In the preamble to the royal decree, Ferdinand informed the people, that the object of the restoration of the Inquisition was to repair the evil caused to the religion of the state by the foreign troops, who were not Catholics ; to forestall that which might be caused hereafter by the heretical opinions imbibed by a great number of Spaniards, and to preserve the tranquillity of the kingdom ; that this measure was desired by learned and virtuous prelates, and by different bodies and corporations, who reminded him that, in the sixteenth century, Spain had preserved herself from the contagion of heresy, and the errors which desolated other countries ; while the arts and sciences flourished under many men, who were famed for their learning and sanctity ; that this happy influence of the Inquisition, was the reason why Buonaparte had destroyed the tribunal, and that the same resolution was afterwards adopted by the junta, falsely call-ing itself the *General Cortes* of the kingdom, on the pretence that the Inquisition was opposed to the constitution of Cadiz, and that it was only decreed in the midst of tumults, and against the wishes of the nation. The decree also declares, that as it had been found necessary to frame new laws, to cor-rect certain abuses and to limit privileges, it was his majesty's intention that they should be observed, and to appoint two members of the Council of Castile, and two of that of the *holy office*, to propose the necessary reforms and alterations in the mode of procedure concerning personal affairs, and the prohibition of books.

It appears that these commissioners were, Don Manuel de Lardizabal Uribe and Don Sebastian de Torres, of the Coun-cil of Castile ; Don Joseph Armarillas, and Don Antonio Galarza, counsellors of the Inquisition. These persons might have proposed a reform, which would have remedied several evils, or entirely destroyed them. I do not know what these commissioners have yet done to justify the confi-dence placed in them, but it is certain that hitherto no re-form has been made public.

On the 5th of May, 1815, Don Francis Xavier de Mier y Campillo, the inquisitor-general, published an edict, com-manding all those who felt themselves guilty, to denounce themselves before the end of the year, and announcing that *Spain was infected by the new and dangerous doctrines which had ruined the greatest part of Europe.* The inqui-sitor-general condemned the *new* and *dangerous doctrines* which followed the entrance of the French army, and did not mention the systems which were propagated and put in practice by the Spanish partisans for the war, though they really came under his jurisdiction, because they were formally opposed to the letter and spirit of the Gospel. This circumstance induces me to lay it before my readers, in order to prove that the *re-established* Inquisition differs little from that which was *suppressed*, since, if the latter allowed works inculcating regicide to be circulated, and condemned books which supported the royal authority, the former began by condemning the doctrine which taught us, that men were not slaves or animals to be bought and sold, and at the same time allowed such maxims as the following to be acted upon :—

1st. That it was allowable during the invasion, to assassinate any Frenchman in Spain, whether he was a soldier or not, without distinction of circumstances or means, because they were all enemies of the country, the defence of which ought to be the first consideration.

2nd. That according to the same principle it was lawful to kill any Spaniard, who was a partisan of the superior power, designated as a *francisé.*

3rd. That any Spaniards of the same party might be despoiled of their money, goods, or the produce of their estates, and that their houses, vineyards, olive-grounds, and other plantations might be burnt.

4th. That an oath of fidelity, taken on the sacrament, might be broken, even if no mental reservation was made, because the person was persuaded that it was the only means to avoid the danger threatened by the superior power, which could execute its threats, according to the general laws of war.

5th. The the priests and monks were authorized to abandon their tranquil life, and engage in a military career, provided it was against the French and the Francisés; this doctrine prevailed even when it was seen that the ecclesiastics and monks had become the chiefs of bands of robbers, and carried infamous concubines in their suites, and that they had imposed arbitrary contributions on different towns.

6th. That the war against France was a war of religion, and, consequently, that those who perished were to be condered as martyrs.

7th. That it was allowable, and even praiseworthy, to refuse sacramental absolution to a penitent who had submitted to the superior force, unless he promised to abandon it, and to contribute by every means to its destruction.

8th. That it was preferable to eat meat on Fridays and other fast-days without permission, than to receive it from the apostolical commissary-general of the Holy Crusade of Spain, resident at Madrid, who was charged by the Pope with this commission.

9th. That it was permitted to preserve an eternal hatred, and to excite others to an implacable war against the Spaniards who had submitted to the superior force.

It is not my intention to accuse the Bishop of Almeira, or the present inquisitors, of abusing their powers. The edict, on the whole, expresses an intention of pursuing mild measures, and hitherto it does not appear that they have been unfaithful to this maxim ; for I cannot credit certain reports circulated in Paris, or what was said in 1815, in *Acta Latomorum*. The author, after announcing the re-establishment of the Inquisition by Ferdinand VII., adds, that he had forbidden the masonic lodges, on pain of the punishments for high-treason. In another article of the same work, on the events of the year 1814, it is said:—

" On the 25th of September, twenty-five individuals were arrested, on suspicion that they were the members of a masonic lodge, and partisans of the Cortes: among them were the Marquis Tolosa, the Canon Marina, a learned and distinguished member of the academy, Doctor Luque, the court physician, and some French, and Italians, and Germans, who had settled in Spain. The brave General Alava, who was chosen by General Wellington for his aide-de-camp, on account of his merit, has been imprisoned by the holy office, as a freemason." I consider the latter assertion to be entirely false, because letters worthy of credit, and the gazettes of Spain, only stated that an order to leave Madrid had been sent to the general by the king, but it was revoked, as his majesty discovered that he had been deceived; it is certain that Ferdinand, some time after, sent him as his ambassador into the Low Countries.

The account given in the Madrid Gazette on the 14th May, 1816, of an *auto-da-fé* celebrated by the Inquisition of Mexico on the 27th December, 1815, is more worthy of belief. Don Joseph-Maria Morellos, a priest, had placed himself at the head of his countrymen, with the intention of freeing his country from the dominion of the King of Spain. The holy office prosecuted him for heresy, while the viceroy arrested him for rebellion. The prisons of the holy office were preferred to that of the government, and some witnesses were found who deposed to certain facts which the Mexican qualifiers thought sufficient to authorize them to pronounce Morellos suspected of atheism, materialism, and other errors. One proof of his guilt was, that he had two children. The accused abjured, and was absolved in an *auto-da-fé*, which was celebrated with as much parade as in the reign of Philip II. When the inquisitors treated Morellos with so much moderation, they knew that the viceroy would hang him ; before his execution he was degraded from the priesthood by the Bishop of Antequera in America.

I do not know if the Spanish Inquisition has celebrated an *auto-da-fé* since its re-establishment. I shall only say that if its members wish to follow the precepts of the Gospel more faithfully than their predecessors, they ought to follow the example of their chief, Pius VII. A letter from Rome, dated the 31st March, 1816, announces that his Holiness had abolished the use of torture in all the tribunals of the

holy office, and that the resolution had been communicated
to the ambassadors of Spain and Portugal*. A second
letter from the same city on the 17th of April following,
says that the procedure of the Inquisition was to be similar
to that of the other tribunals, and to be made public†.

A third letter on the 9th May, states that the Inquisition
of Rome had annulled the sentence which that of Ravenna
had pronounced against Solomon Moses Viviani, who had
relapsed into Judaism, after having abjured it to become a
Christian. In confirming the revocation, the Pope said:
" The divine law is not of the same nature as that of man,
but a law of persuasion and gentleness; persecution, exile,
and imprisonment, are only suitable to false prophets and
the apostles of false doctrines. Let us pity the man who
does not see the true light, or who even refuses to see it;
the cause of his blindness may tend to fulfil the profound
designs of providence, &c." His Holiness having since presided at a congregation of the holy office, has decreed that,
in all trials for heresy, the accuser shall be confronted with
the accused, in the presence of the judges, and has expressed
an intention that the trials shall be so conducted as to avoid
the punishment of death‡."

Another letter from Rome of the 17th January, 1817,
contains the following article: " It is reported that the
holy office will be reformed this year. It appears that it
will only be allowed to proceed in the same manner as the
other tribunals. The government considers it to be dangerous to allow a body to exist which is useless, and always
armed against the progress of reason. You may believe
that the Inquisition has already ceased to exist §."

In March, 1816, the Portuguese ambassador had sent

* See *Gazette de France*, for the 14th April, 1816, No. 103.
† *Gazette de France, Journal du Soir*, for the 1st May, 1816.
‡ *Gazette de France*, 22nd May, 1816, No. 41.
§ *Gazette de France*, January 31st, 1817, No. 31.

a diplomatic note to the cardinal-secretary of state to his Holiness, in which he informs him, in the name of his court, of the condemnation of a work printed by the Inquisitor Louis de Paramo, of the formal and judicial suppression of the holy office, and of the re-establishment of the bishops in their former privileges *.

These just and moderate measures ought to be the rule and guide of the Spanish inquisitors ; if they would make the proceedings public, and liberate the prisoners on bail, I confess that I should not be afraid to present myself to be tried by that tribunal.

Since this article was printed, I have been informed, that the inquisitor-general Mier-Campillo is dead, and that Ferdinand has appointed Monseigneur Jerome Castillon de Salas, Bishop of Taragona as his successor. God grant that he may understand the spirit of the Gospel, and the necessity of reforming the Inquisition better than his predecessor !

* *Gazette de France,* April 3rd, 1816, No. 94.

NUMBER OF THE VICTIMS

OF

THE INQUISITION.

IT is impossible to determine the exact number of persons who perished in the first years after the establishment of the holy office. Persons were burnt in the year 1481, and the Supreme Council was not created until 1483. The registers in its archives, and those of the inferior tribunals, are of a still later date; and as the inquisitor-general accompanied the court, which had no fixed residence until the reign of Philip II., many of the trials must have been lost during these journeys. These circumstances oblige me to found my calculations on the combination of certain data, which I found in the registers and writings of the holy office.

Mariana, in his History of Spain, informs us that, in 1481, the Inquisitors of Seville condemned two thousand persons to *relaxation*, that is, to be burnt, and that there were as many effigies; the number of persons reconciled was one thousand seven hundred. The latter were always subjected to severe penances.

The *autos-da-fé* of this period, which I examined at Saragossa and Toledo, lead me to suppose that each tribunal of the Inquisition celebrated at least four *autos-da-fé* every year. The provincial tribunals were successively organized. I do not speak of those of Mexico, Lima, Carthagena in America, Sicily or Sardinia, although they were subject to the inquisitors-general and the Supreme Council, because I am only enabled to establish my calculation for those of the Peninsula and the neighbouring isles.

Andrea Bernaldez, a contemporary historian, and very

much attached to the new institution, in which he held the office of almoner to the second inquisitor, states, in his in-edited History of the Catholic Kings, that from 1482 to 1489, more than seven hundred individuals were burnt, and more than five thousand subjected to penances, at Seville: he does not mention the effigies.

In 1481 the number equalled that of the persons burnt. I will, however, suppose that these were only half that num-ber, to avoid all exaggeration, though it was in general much more considerable; I may, therefore, say that in each year of this period 88 persons were burnt at Seville, 44 in effigy, and 600 condemned to different penances; total 757. The same mode of calculation may be applied to the other tribu-nals of the province which were then founded.

In the Castle of Triana, at Seville, where the inquisitorial tribunal was held, in an inscription placed there in 1524, im-porting that in the space of time from 1492 to that year, about 1000 persons had been burnt, and 20,000 condemned to penances;—I will suppose that 1000 individuals were burnt, and 500 effigies, which will give for each year 32 burnt, 16 effigies, and 625 subjected to penances. I might admit a similar result for all the tribunals of the kingdom, but I prefer taking the half, on the supposition that the commerce carried on in the kingdom of Seville drew thither many Jewish families.

With respect to the years 1490, 91, and 92, which elapsed between those mentioned by Bernaldez and the period of the inscription of Triana, I prefer calculating according to the thirty-two years after the inscription.

Such are the foundations of my calculations for the first eighteen years of the Inquisition. I shall consider it from that time as entirely belonging to the government of Tor-quemada, the first inquisitor-general; for, although his office was not created till 1483, the two preceding years may be united to his administration, because he was at that time one of the inquisitors appointed by the Pope. I shall, however, carefully distinguish the time when the inferior tribunals began to act, as a greater number of persons perished in the first year, because they were not sufficiently observant of their words and actions.

1481. Seville, the only tribunal. Burnt, 2000. Effigies, 2000. Penances, 1700. Total, 21,000.

I do not mention Arragon, where the old Inquisition was in full activity.

1482. Seville. Burnt, 88. Effigies, 44. Penances, 625. Total, 757.

The tribunals of Arragon, Catalonia, Valencia, and Majorca, belonged to the old Inquisition.

1483. Seville. Ditto.

Tribunals were established in this year at Cordova, Jaen, and Toledo; it is probable that as many persons were condemned at these places as in the first year at Seville, but I shall take the tenth part of that number.

Cordova. Burnt, 200. Effigies, 200. Penances, 17. Total, 2100. Jaen, ditto. Toledo, ditto. Total, 7057.

1484. Seville. Burnt, 88. Effigies, 44. Penances, 625. Total 757.

I calculate half that number for each of the three additional tribunals. Total 1892.

1485. Seville, ditto. Cordova, ditto. Jaen, ditto. Toledo, ditto.

Valladolid, Estremadura, Murcia, Calahorra, Saragossa, and Valencia; each, burnt, 200. Effigies, 200. Penances, 1700. Total, 2100.

For the ten tribunals. Total, 12,930.

1486. Seville, as before.

Cordova, Jaen, and Toledo, ditto.

Valladolid, Llerena, Murcia, Logroño, Saragossa, and Valencia; same number as Cordova.

For the ten tribunals. Total, 4149.

1487. Seville, and the other tribunals; the same number as the preceding year.

Barcelona and Majorca, burnt, 200. Effigies, 200. Penances, 1700.

Total for the twelve tribunals, 8359.

1488. Seville, ditto.

Eleven other tribunals, same number as before. Total, 4915.

1489. Same as the preceding year. Here finish the calculations founded on the statements of Mariana and Bernaldez.

1490. Seville. Burnt, 32. Effigies, 16. Penances, 625. Total 663. According to the calculation from the inscription of Triana.

The eleven other tribunals may be considered to have punished half that number. Total for the twelve, 4369.

1491 to 1498. According to my system of reduction, the total number of victims for the eight last years of Torquemada, was 34,952.

Total for the eighteen years of his administration, 105,294.

1499 to 1507. *Second inquisitor-general.* Don Fray Diego Deza. For the twelve tribunals during the eight years of his administration. Burnt, 1664. Effigies, 832. Penances, 32,456. Total 34,952.

1507 to 1518. *Third inquisitor-general.* Cardinal Ximenez de Cisneros. In 1513 he separated the tribunal of Cuença from that of Murcia.

Number of persons condemned during the eleven years of his administration. Burnt, 2536. Effigies, 1368. Penances, 47,263. Total 51,163.

1518 to 1524. *Fourth inquisitor-general.* Cardinal Adrian. Number of tribunals in the peninsula, the same as under his predecessor. Burnt, 1344. Effigies, 662. Penances, 26,214. Total, 28,230.

1524 to 1539. *Fifth inquisitor-general.* Cardinal Manriquez. For each year of this administration, I calculate that in each of the tribunals 10 were burnt, 5 in effigy, and 50 subjected to penances; total, 65. There were thirteen tribunals in the peninsula, and two in the adjacent isles. According to the preceding calculation, we find that during the fifteen years of the administration of Manriquez, there were, Burnt, 2250. Effigies, 1120. Penances, 11,250. Total, 14,625.

1539 to 1545. *Sixth inquisitor-general.* Cardinal Tabera. His administration may be considered as having lasted seven years. For the fifteen tribunals during that period, I calculate, Burnt, 840. Effigies, 420. Penances, 4200. Total, 5460.

Seventh inquisitor-general. Cardinal Loaisa was appointed in 1546, and died in the same year; the time of his administration may be said to be twelve months. In the fifteen tribunals, Burnt, 120. Effigies, 60. Penances, 600. Total, 780.

Eighth inquisitor-general. Don Ferdinand Valdés, Archbishop of Seville. Twenty years in the fifteen tribunals, Burnt, 2400. Effigies, 1200. Penances, 12,000. Total, 19,600.

Ninth inquisitor-general. Cardinal Espinosa, six years. Burnt, 720. Effigies, 360. Penances, 3600. Total, 4680.

Tenth inquisitor-general. Don Pedro de Cordova, Ponce de Leon, succeeded in 1572, and died in January, 1573, before he could enter on his office.

Eleventh inquisitor-general. Cardinal Quiroga, twenty-two years. Another tribunal was established in Galicia. In the sixteen tribunals were Burnt, 2816. Effigies, 1408. Penances, 14,080. Total, 18,304.

Twelfth inquisitor-general. Don Jerome Manriquez de Lara, Bishop of Carthagena and Avila, one year. Total for the sixteen Inquisitions, Burnt, 180. Effigies, 64. Penances, 640. Total, 832.

Thirteenth inquisitor-general. Don Pedro de Porto-

Carrero, Bishop of Cuença, three years. Burnt, 184. Effigies, 92. Penances, 1920. Total, 2196.

Fourteenth inquisitor-general. Cardinal Guevara, three years. Burnt, 240. Effigies, 96. Penances, 1728. Total, 2064.

Fifteenth inquisitor-general. Don Juan de Zuñiga, Bishop of Carthagena, one year. Burnt, 84. Effigies, 32. Penances, 576. Total, 688.

Sixteenth inquisitor-general. Don Juan Baptist d'Acebedo, Archbishop *in partibus infidelium,* five years. Burnt, 400. Effigies, 116. Penances, 2880. Total, 3440.

Seventeenth inquisitor-general. Cardinal Sandoval y Roxas, eleven years. Burnt, 880. Effigies, 352. Penances, 6336. Total, 7568.

Eighteenth inquisitor-general. Don Fray Louis de Aliaga, two years. Burnt, 240. Effigies, 96. Penances, 1728. Total, 2064.

Nineteenth inquisitor-general. Don Andrea Pacheco, four years. Burnt, 200. Effigies, 128. Penances, 1280. Total, 1664.

Twentieth inquisitor-general. Cardinal Mendoza, six years. Burnt, 384. Effigies, 192. Penances, 1920. Total, 2496.

Twenty-first inquisitor-general. Don Fray Antonio de Sotomayor, Archbishop *in partibus infidelium,* eleven years. Burnt, 704. Effigies, 352. Penances, 3520. Total, 4576.

Twenty-second inquisitor-general. Don Diego de Arce y Reynosa, Bishop of Placencia, twenty-three years. Burnt, 1472. Effigies, 736. Penances, 7360. Total, 9568.

Twenty-third inquisitor-general. Cardinal d'Arragon. Dismissed before he entered on his office.

Twenty-fourth inquisitor-general. Don Juan Everard Nitardo, three years. Burnt, 144. Effigies, 48. Penances, 576. Total, 768.

Twenty-fifth inquisitor-general. Don Diego Sarmiento de Valladares, twenty-six years. Burnt, 1248. Effigies, 416. Penances, 4992. Total, 6656.

Twenty-sixth inquisitor-general. Don Juan Thomas Rocaberti, Archbishop of Valencia, five years. Burnt, 240. Effigies, 80. Penances, 960. Total, 1280.

Twenty-seventh inquisitor-general. Cardinal Aguilar. Died before he entered on his office.

Twenty-eighth inquisitor-general. Don Balthazar Mendoza y Sandoval, Bishop of Segovia, five years. Burnt, 240. Effigies, 80. Penances, 960. Total, 1280.

Twenty-ninth inquisitor-general. Don Vidal Marin, Bishop of Ceuta, four years. Seventeen tribunals. Burnt, 136. Effigies, 68. Penances, 816. Total, 1020.

Thirtieth inquisitor-general. Don Antonio Ibañez de la Riva Herrera, Archbishop of Saragossa, two years. Burnt, 68. Effigies, 34. Penances, 408. Total, 510.

Thirty-first inquisitor-general. Cardinal Judice, six years. Burnt, 204. Effigies, 102. Penances, 1224. Total, 1530.

Thirty-second inquisitor-general. Don Joseph Molines, Auditor de Rote at Rome, two years. Burnt, 68. Effigies, 34. Penances, 408. Total, 510.

Thirty-third inquisitor-general. Don Juan de Arzamendi. Died before he entered on the office.

Thirty-fourth inquisitor-general. Don Diego d'Astorga y Cespedes, Bishop of Barcelona, two years. Burnt, 68. Effigies, 34. Penances, 408. Total, 510.

Thirty-fifth inquisitor-general. Don Juan de Camargo, Bishop of Pampluna, thirteen years. Burnt, 442. Effigies, 221. Penances, 2652. Total, 3315.

Thirty-sixth inquisitor-general. Don Andrea de Orbe y Larreategui, Archbishop of Valencia, seven years. Burnt, 238. Effigies, 119. Penances, 1428. Total, 1785.

Thirty-seventh inquisitor-general. Don Manuel Isidore
Manrique de Lara, Archbishop of Santiago, four years.
Burnt, 336. Effigies, 68. Penances, 816. Total, 1020.

Thirty-eighth inquisitor-general. Don Francis Perez de
Prado y Cuesta, Bishop of Teruel. He was confirmed by
the Pope in 1746; I do not know the exact term of his ad-
ministration, but I have fixed it in 1757, before the death of
Ferdinand VI., who appointed his successor. Burnt, 10.
Effigies, 5. Penances, 107. Total, 122.

Thirty-ninth inquisitor-general. Don Manuel Quintano
Bonifaz, Archbishop of Pharsala, seventeen years. Burnt, 2.
Penances, 10 in public, a greater number in private.

Fortieth inquisitor-general. Don Philip Bertrand,
Bishop of Salamanca, nine years. Two were burnt every
year of this administration, six condemned to public, and a
great number to private penances*.

Forty-first inquisitor-general. Don Augustin Rubin de
Cevallos, Bishop of Jaen, nine years. Fourteen condemned
to public penances, and a considerable number condemned
intra muros.

Forty-second inquisitor-general. Don Manuel Abad y
la Sierra, Archbishop of Selimbria, two years. Sixteen
individuals condemned to public, a greater number to private penances.

Forty-third inquisitor-general. Cardinal Lorenzana, three
years. Public penances, 14. A very great number condemned to private penances. One effigy was burnt at
Cuença.

Forty-fourth inquisitor-general. Don Ramon Joseph de
Arce, Archbishop of Saragossa, eleven years. Twenty individuals were condemned to public, and a very consider-

---

* The last person burnt by the Inquisition was a Beata, for having
made a compact with the devil. She suffered on the 7th November,
1781.

able number to private penances. The Curate of Esco was condemned to the flames, but the grand-inquisitor and the Supreme Council would not permit the sentence to be executed.

Number of persons who were condemned and perished in the flames - -	31,912
Effigies burnt - - - - -	17,659
Condemned to severe penances - -	291,450
	341,021

THE END.